PROGRAMMER'S GUIDE TO
PC® & PS/2™

VIDEO
SYSTEMS

Maximum Video

Performance from the

EGA™, VGA,

HGC, and MCGA.

PROGRAMMER'S GUIDE TO
PC® & PS/2™
VIDEO
SYSTEMS

Maximum Video

Performance from the

EGA™, VGA,

HGC, and MCGA.

RICHARD WILTON

PUBLISHED BY
Microsoft Press
A Division of Microsoft Corporation
16011 NE 36th Way, Box 97017, Redmond, Washington 98073-9717

Library of Congress Cataloging in Publication Data
Wilton, Richard, 1953–
The programmer's guide to PC and PS/2 video systems.
Includes index.
1. IBM Personal Computer—Programming.   2. Expansion boards (Microcomputers).
3. Computer graphics.   I. Title.
QA76.8.I2594W55   1987   005.265   87-20264
ISBN 1-55615-103-9

Printed and bound in the United States of America.

    3 4 5 6 7 8 9   FGFG   89098

Distributed to the book trade in the
United States by Harper & Row.

Distributed to the book trade in
Canada by General Publishing Company, Ltd.

Distributed to the book trade outside the
United States and Canada by Penguin Books Ltd.

Penguin Books Ltd., Harmondsworth, Middlesex, England
Penguin Books Australia Ltd., Ringwood, Victoria, Australia
Penguin Books N.Z. Ltd., 182-190 Wairau Road, Auckland 10, New Zealand

British Cataloging in Publication Data available

Acquisitions Editor: Claudette Moore
Technical Editor: Jeff Hinsch

Contents

Acknowledgments   vii

Introduction   ix

1   IBM Video Hardware and Firmware   1

2   Programming the Hardware   13

3   Alphanumeric Modes   45

4   Graphics Modes   85

5   Pixel Programming   111

6   Lines   161

7   Circles and Ellipses   221

8   Region Fill   243

9   Graphics Text   267

10   Alphanumeric Character Sets   297

11   Bit Blocks and Animation   343

12   Some Advanced Video Programming Techniques   373

13   Graphics Subroutines in High-Level Languages   407

Appendix A: Video BIOS Summary   433

Appendix B: Printing the Screen   493

Appendix C: Identifying Video Subsystems   511

Glossary   523

Index   527

Acknowledgments

The material in Chapters 6, 7, and 8 owes a great deal to the original efforts of several respected workers in the field of computer graphics. In each of these chapters I have included references to some of their best-known publications. If you are intrigued by the algorithms described in these chapters, by all means obtain the original publications and explore them yourself.

This book could not have been written without the encouragement of my family, friends, and colleagues, who deserve great thanks for their patience and support. My gratitude also to Andy Fischer and to Charles Petzold, both of whom graciously reviewed portions of this book and offered accurate criticism and suggestions.

And, of course, my special thanks to the enthusiastic people at Microsoft Press—Claudette Moore, Jeff Hinsch, and many others—who painstakingly transformed the raw material of this book into the finished product.

Introduction

I clearly remember the day I first plugged a new IBM Enhanced Graphics Adapter (EGA) into an IBM PC. It was good to have IBM's new "enhanced" video hardware, with its better resolution and control over colors, as well as features not found in any of IBM's earlier PC video hardware. Now I was ready to write some really sharp graphics applications.

Or so I thought. The problem was, I couldn't figure out how to program the contraption. I had no technical documentation at all. (It arrived in the mail six months and $125 later.) I tried disassembling the EGA's ROM BIOS, but studying 6000 uncommented machine instructions soon raised more questions than it answered. I desperately tried the shotgun approach—changing the contents of memory locations and machine registers just to see what would happen—but this was like chopping out random pieces of an automobile just to see what would stop working.

What I lacked was the details—conceptual descriptions of the hardware design, tables describing the programming interface, and, above all, source code examples for some typical programming techniques. A few well-chosen source code examples would have saved many hours of experimentation and frustration when I was trying to understand how to program that video adapter.

This book was inspired by the painful memory of that experience. It is filled with source code examples. Its text describes the source code, and vice versa. This book also has many tables and summary descriptions of the hardware programming interface. In short, this book is what I wish I'd had when I started to program PC video hardware.

What This Book Is About

The first chapter of this book is a general overview of the video display environment. It describes the commonly used PC and PS/2 video hardware the rest of the book deals with. It also introduces you (if you aren't already on speaking terms) to the well-known ROM BIOS video support routines.

The next 10 chapters contain the nuts and bolts of IBM video programming. The earlier chapters cover the fundamentals, including hardware architecture, video display modes, and the nature of the interface between your programs and the hardware. The later chapters build upon the fundamentals to demonstrate a number of techniques for producing text and graphics output.

The last two chapters of this book take you to the low and high levels of video graphics programming. Chapter 12 is the hardware tinkerer's chapter—if you want to work with vertical interrupts or play with bit planes, this one's for you. Finally, Chapter 13 tells how to link your video hardware drivers to high-level programs and introduces you to several commercial video output packages.

What You Need to Use This Book

This book is not really meant for beginners. That's not to say that a programmer who is just learning how to write working code will not benefit from this material. On the contrary, the many working examples of useful source code should be valuable to anyone who plans to do serious programming for PCs or PS/2s. Nevertheless, the broader your programming background, the more tools you will have for solving the diverse and exacting problems involved in video programming.

Languages

I use assembly language and C for most of the programming examples in this book, although I intentionally avoid some of C's more cryptic syntactic constructs. If you are comfortable with assembly language and with a high-level language such as C, Pascal, FORTRAN, PL/1, or structured BASIC, you should have no problem reading the source code examples.

Moreover, Chapter 13 discusses interfaces for several high-level languages using different memory models and subroutine-calling protocols. You can follow the guidelines there to convert any of the C-callable source code examples to the subroutine-calling protocol used by your favorite language translator.

You might want to use some other programming tools if you plan to experiment with the source code examples that follow. For example, a good assembly-language debugger can be extremely helpful. You will probably need an object linker if you plan to call the assembly-language routines in this book from high-level-language programs. Also, as source files and object modules proliferate, you might find a UNIX-like *make* utility quite useful in keeping things straight.

Operating System

Everything in this book is intended to run under MS-DOS, or PC-DOS, version 2.0 or later. However, there is nothing in any of the source code that verifies which operating system is in use, so be careful if you transport the code to earlier versions of MS-DOS or to another operating system.

Hardware

Having a PC or PS/2 with a video display attached is essential. Video programming is like swimming: It's one thing to read about it, but it's quite another experience to try it yourself. In fact, if you plan to do a great deal of video programming, you should consider installing two different video subsystems and displays in your PC. With two separate sets of video hardware in the same computer, you can run a debugger on one screen while a test program produces output on the other screen. This dual-display hardware configuration is a real timesaver, particularly when you're developing video graphics routines such as those described in Chapters 5 through 9.

Here is a list of the various computers and video adapters I used to develop the techniques discussed in this book:

Computers
    IBM PC/XT
    IBM PC/AT
    IBM PS/2 Model 30
    IBM PS/2 Model 60

Adapters
    IBM Monochrome Display Adapter
    IBM Color Graphics Adapter
    IBM Enhanced Graphics Adapter
    IBM PS/2 Display Adapter
    Hercules Graphics Card
    Hercules Graphics Card Plus
    Hercules Color Card
    Hercules InColor Card

If you are using one of these computers or adapters, or a hardware-compatible clone, then you should be able to run the source code examples.

Manuals

To program IBM PC video hardware effectively, you need to know what the hardware is designed to do and how software and the system BIOS are expected to interact with it. This basic information is found in IBM's Technical Reference manuals for the PC, PC/XT, PC/AT, and PS/2s and in its Options and Adapters Technical Reference manuals. Most second-source manufacturers of IBM PC video equipment also provide detailed technical information on their hardware.

The material in this book is intended to complement the discussions in the manufacturers' technical documentation. I tried to follow the manufacturers' terminology and hardware descriptions wherever possible. However, the manufacturers' documentation goes somewhat awry at times. If you find a discrepancy between the official documentation and this book, you can (I hope) rely on this book to contain the right information.

Still, in a book this size, I have certainly made some mistakes. I welcome your comments, criticisms, and suggestions.

I have found that writing good video software is challenging, but the rewards are particularly satisfying. I hope to share some of the challenges—and some of the satisfaction—with you in this book.

Special Offer

Companion Disk to
Programmer's Guide to PC & PS/2 Video Systems

Microsoft Press has created a valuable companion disk for PRO-GRAMMER'S GUIDE TO PC & PS/2 VIDEO SYSTEMS. The disk contains all 69 assembly-language programs and 25 C programs from the book — close to 6000 lines of code in all. The disk also contains a helpful demonstration program that uses several routines from the book. Save time, avoid those inevitable typing errors, and start using the source code in your programs right away.

If you have any questions about the files on the disk, you can send your written queries or comments to author Richard Wilton, c/o Microsoft Press, 16011 NE 36th Way, Box 97017, Redmond, WA 98073-9717.

The Companion Disk to PROGRAMMER'S GUIDE TO PC & PS/2 VIDEO SYSTEMS is available only from Microsoft Press. To order, use the special reply card bound in the back of the book. If the card has already been used, send $21.95, plus sales tax if applicable (CA residents 5% plus local option tax, CT 7.5%, FL 6%, MA 5%, MN 6%, MO 4.225%, NY 4% plus local option tax, WA State 7.8%) and $2.50 per disk for domestic postage and handling, $6.00 per disk for foreign orders, to: Microsoft Press, Attn: Companion Disk Offer, 21919 20th Ave S.E., Box 3011, Bothell, WA 98041-3011. Please specify 5.25-inch or 3.5-inch format. Payment must be in U.S. funds. You may pay by check or money order (payable to Microsoft Press) or by American Express, VISA, or MasterCard; please include both your credit card number and the expiration date. All orders are shipped 2nd day air upon receipt of order by Microsoft.

If this disk proves defective, please send the defective disk along with your packing slip to: Microsoft Press, Consumer Sales, 16011 NE 36th Way, Box 97017, Redmond, WA 98073-9717.

1

IBM Video Hardware and Firmware

IBM PC and PS/2 Video Hardware
IBM Monochrome Display Adapter and Color Graphics Adapter
Hercules Graphics Card ● Hercules Graphics Card Plus
IBM Enhanced Graphics Adapter ● Hercules InColor Card
Multi-Color Graphics Array ● Video Graphics Array

Introduction to the ROM BIOS Interface
Interrupt 10H ● Video Display Data Area
Accessing the Video BIOS from a High-Level Language

Microcomputer video systems keep getting better. Since the introduction of the IBM PC in 1981, engineering technology has improved, and the market for more powerful video hardware has widened. Both IBM and its competitors have responded by developing increasingly sophisticated video adapters and displays, as well as the software to accompany them.

This chapter provides an overview of the evolution of IBM PC and PS/2 video hardware. This overview is by no means comprehensive, but it covers the most widely used video equipment that IBM and Hercules offer. The chapter concludes with an introduction to IBM's video BIOS, a set of drivers built into ROM in all IBM PCs and PS/2s, which provides a basic programming interface for video applications.

IBM PC and PS/2 Video Hardware

A "plain vanilla" IBM PC/XT or PC/AT contains no built-in video hardware, so you must select and install the video hardware yourself. In a typical configuration, a video display (monitor) is attached with a 9-wire cable to a video adapter installed inside the PC. A typical video adapter is a printed circuit board with a 9-pin connector that attaches to the monitor's cable and a 2-by-31-connection card-edge tab that inserts into one of the slots on the PC's motherboard. Figure 1-1 shows these connectors, as well as some of the integrated circuits common to many IBM video adapters. The circuitry in the video adapter generates the signals that control what is displayed on the monitor's screen.

When you purchase an IBM PC, you must decide which video adapter and monitor to use. The most widely used video adapters with the most software written for them are IBM's Monochrome Display Adapter, Color Graphics Adapter, and Enhanced Graphics Adapter, and the monochrome Graphics Card made by Hercules.

In contrast, all IBM PS/2 series computers are equipped with a built-in video subsystem, so purchasing a separate video adapter is unnecessary. The video subsystem in the PS/2 Models 25 and 30 is called the Multi-Color Graphics Array. In Models 50, 60, and 80, the integrated video subsystem is commonly known as the Video Graphics Array. The Video Graphics Array subsystem also is available as an adapter for the PC/XT, PC/AT, and PS/2 Model 30. This adapter has essentially the same hardware features as the integrated PS/2 subsystem.

IBM Monochrome Display Adapter and Color Graphics Adapter

When the PC was introduced in 1981, IBM offered two video adapters: the Monochrome Display Adapter (MDA) and the Color Graphics Adapter (CGA). The MDA is designed for use with a monochrome monitor (the IBM Monochrome Display) that displays 80 columns and 25 rows of alphanumeric text. The CGA supports either an RGB display (a monitor with separate input signals for red, green, and blue) or a home television set (which uses a composite video signal). The CGA, of course, can display graphics information on a dot-by-dot basis as well as alphanumeric text.

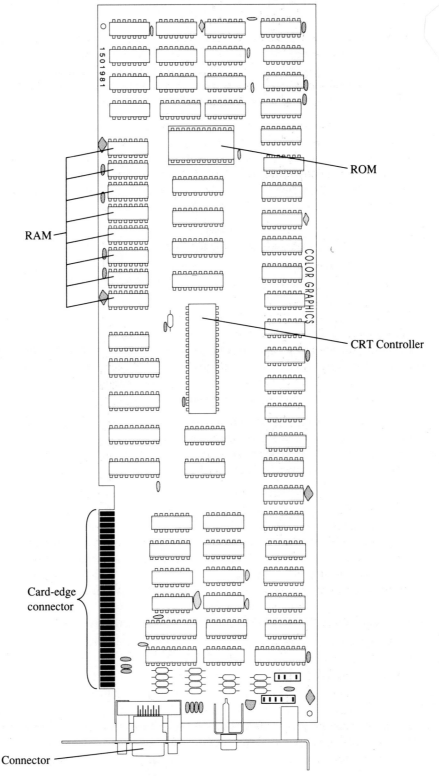

Figure 1-1. *A typical IBM PC video adapter.*

Even though both the MDA and the CGA can display 25 rows of 80-column text, most people find the MDA's green monochrome display easier on the eyes. This is because the monochrome display used with an MDA has significantly higher resolution than that of any monitor you can use with the CGA. Its resolution is 720 dots wide and 350 dots high; the maximum resolution of a CGA-driven display is 640 dots wide and 200 dots high.

Both adapters display characters in a rectangular matrix of dots. A simple calculation shows that each character is 9 dots wide and 14 dots high on a Monochrome Display but only 8-by-8 dots on a CGA display. The MDA's higher resolution produces more crisply defined characters that are easier to read. For this reason, most PC users who need to read text prefer an MDA to a CGA.

On the other hand, many computer users need to display charts, diagrams, and other graphics information in addition to alphanumeric text. Also, displaying colors on the screen is essential to many computer applications. Because the MDA can display only monochrome text, PC users who need graphics output can compromise by using the CGA, with its dot-by-dot color graphics capability but less-readable text.

Why not just attach the higher-resolution monochrome display to a Color Graphics Adapter and get the best of both worlds? Unfortunately, the video signals generated by an MDA are incompatible with those required to drive a CGA monitor, and vice versa. Mismatching the monitor and the adapter leads to a malfunctioning monitor instead of a higher-resolution display.

If you need sharp, readable text as well as color graphics, and you can afford the extra equipment, you can install both an MDA and a CGA in the same PC. You can then use the monochrome display (attached to the MDA) for text processing and an RGB color display (driven by the CGA) for color graphics.

Hercules Graphics Card

Hercules' solution to the problem of displaying readable text and dot-by-dot graphics on the same monitor was to add graphics capability to a monochrome display adapter. The monochrome Hercules Graphics Card (HGC), introduced in 1982, can display graphics and alphanumeric text on the same green monochrome display that is used with an IBM MDA. (In addition to its graphics capabilities, the HGC exactly duplicates the function of IBM's original MDA.) The ability to display a combination of readable text and monochrome graphics is sufficient for many applications, so many PC users find the HGC an economical option. Because it has received support from major software vendors, the HGC has become firmly established in the marketplace.

Hercules Graphics Card Plus

The HGC+ was released in June 1986. The big difference in this upgrade of the original HGC is that it can display customized, RAM-based alphanumeric character sets, whereas the MDA and HGC can display only one, predefined, ROM-based alphanumeric character set. Because alphanumeric characters can be displayed much more rapidly than dot-by-dot graphics characters, using the HGC+ can double or triple the speed of some text-oriented applications.

IBM Enhanced Graphics Adapter

A different response to the demand for better text and graphics resolution is IBM's Enhanced Graphics Adapter (EGA), released in early 1985. The EGA can be configured to emulate either an MDA or a CGA; what makes the EGA "enhanced" is that it can also do things its predecessors cannot. Unlike the MDA, the EGA can produce dot-by-dot graphics on a monochrome display. Furthermore, the EGA improves on the CGA with the ability to generate 16-color alphanumeric or graphics images with 640-by-350 resolution.

Although the resolution and color capabilities of the EGA are not that much greater than those of the CGA, both text and graphics appear much sharper on the EGA than on the CGA. The availability of low-priced EGA clones and of high-quality software applications that exploit the adapter's capabilities have made the EGA a de facto hardware standard in the marketplace.

Hercules InColor Card

The Hercules InColor Card, introduced in April 1987, is essentially a 16-color version of the HGC+. The InColor hardware fully emulates the HGC+, so programs that run properly on the HGC+ can run without change on the InColor Card. The InColor Card's resolution is the same as that of the HGC and HGC+: 720 horizontal by 348 vertical pixels. The adapter's color capabilities equal those of the EGA. It can display 16 colors at once from a palette of 64 colors. The adapter must be used with an EGA-compatible color display that has 350-line vertical resolution.

 Don't confuse the InColor Card with the Hercules Color Card, an augmented CGA clone designed for use in the same computer with an HGC or HGC+.

Multi-Color Graphics Array

The Multi-Color Graphics Array (MCGA) is the video subsystem integrated into the PS/2 Models 25 and 30. From a programmer's perspective, the MCGA resembles the CGA in many ways, yet the MCGA has much better resolution (a maximum of 640 horizontal by 480 vertical dots) and improved color-display capabilities.

A significant difference between the MCGA and the above video adapters is that the MCGA generates analog RGB video signals, whereas the others produce digital RGB signals. The difference between digital and analog RGB is something like the difference between an on-off wall switch and a dimmer switch. With digital RGB signals, the video display must recognize only whether the signal for a particular color (red, green, or blue) is on or off. On the other hand, a video display that uses analog RGB signals translates the voltage of each signal into a wide range of corresponding color intensities. Only an analog video display can be used with the MCGA.

 Some video monitors can be configured for either analog or digital video signals. If you use the right cable, these monitors can be connected to an MCGA if they are configured for analog video.

The justification for using analog video is that it can display a wider range of colors. The MCGA has a video Digital to Analog Converter (DAC) that enables the subsystem to display as many as 256 different colors at once from a palette of 262,144 (256 K or 2^{18}) colors. In addition to an analog color display, IBM supplies an analog monochrome display for use with the MCGA. With a monochrome monitor, the MCGA can display as many as 64 shades of gray.

Video Graphics Array

The term Video Graphics Array (VGA) refers specifically to part of the circuitry of the video subsystem in PS/2 Models 50, 60, and 80. The VGA is actually a single chip that integrates the same set of functions performed by several chips on the EGA. Nevertheless, people generally use the abbreviation VGA to describe the entire video subsystem.

The VGA's programming interface is similar to the EGA's, so many programs written for the EGA will run unchanged on the VGA. The VGA is capable of somewhat higher display resolution (as much as 720-by-400 in text modes, or 640-by-480 in graphics modes). Like the MCGA, however, the VGA contains a video DAC that can generate 256 colors at a time from a possible 262,144. Because the VGA generates the same analog RGB signals as the MCGA, it must be used with the same analog monochrome or color monitors.

Introduction to the ROM BIOS Interface

A set of BIOS (Basic Input/Output System) routines in ROM is built into every IBM PC and PS/2. The ROM BIOS routines provide an interface to standard hardware features, including the time-of-day clock, the keyboard, floppy and hard disks, and of course the video subsystem. The video BIOS routines comprise a set of simple tools for performing basic video programming tasks such as writing strings of characters to the screen, erasing the screen, changing colors, and so on.

Although the ROM BIOS video routines are sometimes slow and relatively unsophisticated, programs that use them are portable among different video subsystems in IBM PCs and PS/2s. Furthermore, most manufacturers of IBM PC clones have duplicated the functions of IBM's BIOS in their machines. Thus, a program that uses BIOS routines to access the video hardware is likely to be more portable than one that does not.

Interrupt 10H

The BIOS routines are written in assembly language, so accessing them is easiest when you program in assembly language. All BIOS video routines are accessed by executing 80x86 software interrupt 10H. (The term 80x86 refers to the microprocessors in the Intel 8086 family: 8086, 8088, 80286, and 80386.) For this reason, the ROM BIOS video interface is widely known as the INT 10H interface. The ROM BIOS supports a number of video input/output functions, each accessed by executing interrupt 10H. The functions are numbered; before executing interrupt 10H, you place the number of the desired function in 80x86 register AH.

At the time the interrupt is executed, the remaining 80x86 registers usually contain parameters to be passed to the BIOS routines. If the INT 10H function returns data to your program, it does so by leaving the data in one or more of the 80x86 registers. This register-based parameter-passing protocol is intended for use in assembly-language programs.

To see how the INT 10H interface is typically used, examine the assembly-language routine SetVmode() in Listing 1-1. This routine can be linked with a program written in Microsoft C. (The underscore preceding the procedure name, the *near* keyword in the PROC declaration, and the use of the stack to pass parameters all follow Microsoft C conventions.) The heart of the routine is its call to the ROM BIOS to configure the video hardware for a particular video mode. (The details of this operation are discussed in Chapter 2 and in Appendix A.)

```
                    TITLE    'Listing 1-1'
                    NAME     SetVmode
                    PAGE     55,132

;
; Name:             SetVmode
;
; Function:         Call IBM ROM BIOS to set a video display mode.
;
; Caller:           Microsoft C:
;
;                         void SetVmode(n);
;
;                         int n;                  /* video mode */
;

ARGn                EQU      byte ptr [bp+4] ; stack frame addressing

EQUIP_FLAG          EQU      byte ptr ds:[10h]

CGAbits             EQU      00100000b       ; bits for EQUIP_FLAG
MDAbits             EQU      00110000b

_TEXT               SEGMENT  byte public 'CODE'
                    ASSUME   cs:_TEXT

                    PUBLIC   _SetVmode
_SetVmode           PROC     near
```

Listing 1-1. *SetVmode().*   *(continued)*

Listing 1-1. *Continued.*

```
                push    bp                  ; preserve caller registers
                mov     bp,sp
                push    ds

                mov     ax,40h
                mov     ds,ax               ; DS -> Video Display Data Area

                mov     bl,CGAbits          ; BL := bits indicating presence of CGA

                mov     al,ARGn             ; AL := desired video mode number

                mov     ah,al               ; test if desired mode is monochrome
                and     ah,7
                cmp     ah,7
                jne     L01                 ; jump if desired mode not 7 or 0Fh

                mov     bl,MDAbits          ; BL := bits indicating presence of MDA

L01:            and     EQUIP_FLAG,11001111b
                or      EQUIP_FLAG,bl       ; set bits in EQUIP_FLAG

                xor     ah,ah               ; AH := 0 (INT 10h function number)

                push    bp
                int     10h                 ; call ROM BIOS to set the video mode
                pop     bp

                pop     ds                  ; restore caller registers and return
                mov     sp,bp
                pop     bp
                ret

_SetVmode       ENDP

_TEXT           ENDS

                END
```

The actual call to the video BIOS is simple. First, the desired function number is placed into register AH (XOR AH, AH). Then, after preserving the contents of register BP on the stack (PUSH BP), the routine invokes the ROM BIOS function by executing interrupt 10H (INT 10H).

In Listing 1-2, a complementary routine called GetVmode() interrogates the BIOS for the number of the current video mode. The routine obtains this number by executing interrupt 10H function 0FH. The ROM BIOS function leaves the mode number in register AL. GetVmode() then returns the number to the calling program.

```
                TITLE    'Listing 1-2'
                NAME     GetVmode
                PAGE     55,132

;
; Name:          GetVmode
;
; Function:      Call IBM ROM BIOS to set a video display mode.
;
; Caller:        Microsoft C:
;
;                        int      GetVmode();
;

_TEXT           SEGMENT byte public 'CODE'
                ASSUME  cs:_TEXT

                PUBLIC  _GetVmode
_GetVmode       PROC    near

                push    bp              ; preserve caller registers
                mov     bp,sp

                mov     ah,0Fh          ; AH := 0Fh (INT 10h function number)

                push    bp
                int     10h             ; call ROM BIOS to get video mode number
                pop     bp

                xor     ah,ah           ; AX := video mode number

                mov     sp,bp
                pop     bp
                ret

_GetVmode       ENDP

_TEXT           ENDS

                END
```

Listing 1-2. *GetVmode().*

Video Display Data Area

The code that precedes the actual call to the ROM BIOS in Listing 1-1 modifies one of several global variables that reflect the status of the PC's video subsystem. These variables are updated and referenced by all ROM BIOS video routines. They are collected in a block of RAM called, in IBM's technical documentation, the Video Display Data Area (or Video Control Data Area). The Video Display Data Area consists of two blocks of RAM. The first block is found between memory locations 0040:0049 and 0040:0066, the second between 0040:0084 and 0040:008A.

Some video BIOS routines also reference a 2-bit field in a global variable at 0040:0010 (called EQUIP_FLAG in IBM's technical documentation). Bits 4 and 5 of this variable indicate a default video mode to be used when the computer is first booted. The code in SetVmode() updates this bit field to conform with the video mode being selected. For example, if a Monochrome Display Adapter (MDA) is required for the desired video mode, the bit field in EQUIP_FLAG is updated accordingly. (Again, details on ROM BIOS video modes are found in Chapter 2 and in Appendix A.)

 Throughout this book are references to the INT 10H interface, the BIOS's Video Display Data Area, and the symbolic names of specific locations in the Video Display Data Area that are of particular interest. If you aren't already familiar with the available INT 10H functions and the contents of the Video Display Data Area, a perusal of Appendix A might be very helpful.

Accessing the Video BIOS from a High-Level Language

You can make ROM BIOS routines accessible in high-level language programs with an assembly-language routine such as SetVmode() or GetVmode(). Listings 1-3 and 1-4 are short C programs that can be executed as MS-DOS commands. The program in Listing 1-3 calls SetVmode() to select a video mode. This program may be executed interactively or from a batch file. The program in Listing 1-4 calls GetVmode() and returns the video mode number in a way that can be used in a batch file (that is, with IF ERRORLEVEL == commands).

```
/* Listing 1-3 */

main( argc, argv )
int      argc;
char     **argv;
{
        int      ModeNumber;
        void     SetVmode();


        if (argc != 2)                    /* verify command line syntax */
        {
          printf( "\nSyntax:  SETVMODE n\n" );
          exit( 1 );
        }

        sscanf( argv[1], "%x", &ModeNumber );   /* get desired mode number */

        SetVmode( ModeNumber );                  /* call ROM BIOS via INT 10h */
}
```

Listing 1-3. *A C program based on SetVmode().*

```
/* Listing 1-4 */

main()
{
        int     GetVmode();
        return( GetVmode() );
}
```

Listing 1-4. *A C program based on GetVmode( ).*

The overall process of generating an executable file for one of these programs consists of compiling the C code to produce an object module, assembling the assembly-language code to produce another object module, and linking the object modules to create the executable file. If the C source code in Listing 1-3 is contained in a file named *SM.C* and the assembly code in Listing 1-1 is saved in *SETVMODE.ASM*, you can build the executable file *SM.EXE* as follows:

```
msc     sm;           (compile the C code)
masm    setvmode;     (assemble the subroutine)
link    sm+setvmode;  (link the object modules)
```

 Some high-level language compilers can generate appropriate object code for loading the 80x86 registers, executing interrupt 10H, and copying the results from the registers to the calling program. If your compiler has this capability, you might prefer to access the INT 10H interface directly, instead of linking an assembly-language subroutine to your high-level program. For example, Listing 1-5 uses Microsoft C's int86() function to implement GetVmode().

```
/* Listing 1-5 */

#include        "dos.h"

main()
{
        struct  BYTEREGS regs;          /* BYTEREGS defined in dos.h */

        regs.ah = 0x0F;                 /* AH=0x0F (ROM BIOS function number) */

        int86( 0x10, &regs, &regs );    /* perform interrupt 10h */

        return( (int)regs.al );
}
```

Listing 1-5. *Microsoft C's int86() function.*

Many other INT 10H functions are available in the ROM BIOS. Your application program accesses them by loading the appropriate registers and executing interrupt 10H. Although the INT 10H support for video input/output admittedly is less than perfect, it is widely used in operating-system software (including MS-DOS) as well as in countless applications. If you want to write effective video and graphics programs, become familiar with the capabilities and the limitations of the INT 10H interface.

2

Programming the Hardware

**Functional Components of IBM PC and PS/2 Video
Subsystems**
Monitor ● Video Buffer
Color and Character Display Hardware
CRT Controller

The Display Refresh Cycle
Horizontal Timing ● Vertical Timing

Programming the CRT Controller
MDA ● CGA ● Hercules Adapters ● EGA ● MCGA ● VGA

Basic CRTC Computations
Dot Clock ● Horizontal Timing ● Vertical Timing

The CRT Status Register

Video Modes
Resolution ● Colors ● Video Buffer Organization

Hardware Video Mode Control
MDA ● CGA and MCGA ● HGC
HGC+ and InColor Card ● EGA and VGA
Video BIOS Support

Combinations of Video Subsystems
MDA ● Hercules ● CGA ● EGA ● MCGA ● VGA

This chapter describes IBM PC and PS/2 video hardware from a programmer's point of view. It covers the basics: which parts of the computer's video subsystem can be programmed, how a program interacts with the hardware, and how calculations for changing the video display format are performed. Many of the programming techniques in later chapters are based on the fundamental information discussed here.

The purpose of this chapter is to demystify the hardware programming interface. Because most programmers rely on the video BIOS to perform most, if not all, hardware-level programming in their applications, an aura of mystery surrounds the way software interacts with video hardware. Of course, after you learn about it, you may wish it had remained a mystery—but the more you know, the more your programs will be able to do with the video hardware.

Functional Components of IBM PC and PS/2 Video Subsystems

As you write programs that interact with IBM video hardware, it helps to visualize the relationships among the programmable components of IBM video subsystems (see Figure 2-1). You do not need a circuit designer's understanding of the hardware to write a good video interface. You do need to know where and how your program can interact with the hardware to produce video output efficiently.

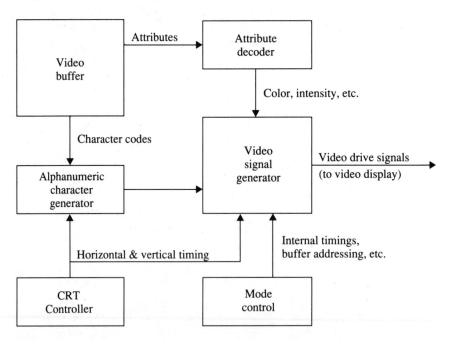

Figure 2-1. *Programmable components (video buffer, attribute controller, and so on) of the IBM PC and PS/2 video subsystems. Some or all of these components are under software control in each of the video subsystems described in this book.*

Monitor

The most tangible part of a computer's video hardware is the monitor, or video display. However, there's nothing you can directly program in the monitor's hardware. It is the computer's video subsystem that contains programmable hardware. The signals generated by the video subsystem control what appears on the screen.

The monitor differs from a home television receiver in that a group of separate timing and color signals drives it. In contrast, a home TV decodes a single "composite" signal that contains timing, color, and audio information. Although some IBM PC video adapters can generate such composite video output signals, as well as the direct drive signals that computer monitors use, most people avoid using a home television with their computers. Both text and colors appear sharper on a computer monitor than they do on a composite television screen.

All the video monitors discussed in this book are raster-scan devices. The image on the screen of a monitor is made up of a group of closely spaced horizontal lines called the raster. An electron beam scans each successive line from left to right, starting at the upper left corner of the display. As the beam sweeps each line, the color and brightness of each of several hundred points (pixels) in the line are varied, and the entire raster appears as a coherent image.

Conceptually, you can regard the electron beam as having "color" and "intensity," but in color video monitors the beam actually comprises three separate electron beams. Each beam controls the display of one of the three primary video colors (red, green, and blue) on the screen. Each pixel on a color display is physically represented by a small, closely spaced triad of red, green, and blue luminescent dots or stripes of phosphor. The three electron beams are masked in such a way that each illuminates dots of only one primary color. Thus, the relative intensity of the beams as they sweep over each triad determines the color and brightness of the pixels. Of course, unless you use a magnifying glass or look closely at the display, you do not perceive the red, green, and blue dots individually, but rather as blended colors.

Video Buffer

The video buffer is a block of RAM in the video subsystem where displayable data is stored. This RAM lies within the address space of the computer's CPU, so a program may read from and write to the video buffer in the same way it accesses any other portion of RAM.

The video subsystem's display circuitry updates, or refreshes, the screen by continually and repeatedly reading the data in the video buffer. Each bit or group of bits in the video buffer specifies the color and brightness of a particular location on the screen. The screen is refreshed between 50 and 70 times a second, depending on which video subsystem is in use. Obviously, when a program changes the displayed contents of the video buffer, the screen changes almost immediately.

The actual amount of RAM available as a video buffer varies with the video subsystem. Most IBM video subsystems incorporate video buffers large enough to hold more than one screen of displayable data, so only part of the buffer is visible on the screen at any time. (Chapter 3 discusses how to make full use of available video RAM.)

Color and Character Display Hardware

All IBM video subsystems incorporate hardware that reads and decodes the data in the video buffer. For example, an alphanumeric character generator translates ASCII codes from the video buffer into the dot patterns that make up characters on the screen. An attribute decoder translates other data in the video buffer into the signals that produce colors, underlining, and so forth. Software can control these and other specialized components of the video subsystem; later chapters describe such programming in detail.

CRT Controller

The CRT Controller (or CRTC for short) generates horizontal and vertical timing signals. It also increments a video buffer address counter at a rate that is synchronized with the timing signals. The video display circuitry reads data from the video buffer using the CRTC's address value, decodes the data, and sends the resulting color and brightness signals to the monitor along with the CRTC's timing signals. In this way the CRTC synchronizes the display of data from the video buffer with the timing signals that drive the video display.

The CRTC performs several other miscellaneous functions. Among them are determining the size and displayed position of the hardware cursor, selecting the portion of the video buffer to be displayed, locating the hardware underline, and detecting light pen signals. (Chapter 3 contains examples of CRTC programming for some of these functions.)

On the MDA, CGA, and Hercules cards, the CRTC is a single chip, the Motorola 6845. On the EGA, the CRTC is a custom LSI (large-scale integration) chip designed by IBM. On the MCGA, the CRTC is part of its Memory Controller Gate Array. The VGA's CRTC is one component of the single-chip Video Graphics Array. Regardless of the hardware implementation, the CRTC can be programmed to generate a variety of timing parameters in all these subsystems. Before delving into the techniques of CRTC programming, however, it is worthwhile to review how the CRTC's timing signals control the monitor's display of a raster-scan video image.

The Display Refresh Cycle

The video image is refreshed in a cyclic manner between 50 and 70 times a second, depending on the configuration of the video subsystem. During each refresh cycle, the electron beam sweeps across the screen in a zigzag fashion, starting at the left side of the topmost horizontal line in the raster (see Figure 2-2). After scanning a line from left to right, the beam is deflected down to the start of the next line until the entire raster is scanned. Then the beam returns to the upper left corner of the display, and the cycle repeats.

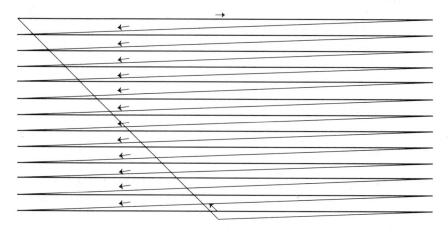

Figure 2-2. *The path followed by the electron beam in a raster scan.*

Horizontal Timing

A number of carefully timed events occur as the beam moves across the display. At the beginning of each line, the electron beam is turned on in response to a Display Enable signal that the CRTC generates. As the beam sweeps left to right across the line, the video display circuitry uses the CRTC's address counter to read a sequence of bytes from the video buffer. The data is decoded and used to control the color and brightness signals sent to the monitor. As the beam sweeps across the screen, its color and brightness vary in response to these signals.

Near the screen's right edge, the CRTC turns off the Display Enable signal and no further data is displayed from the video buffer. The CRTC then generates a horizontal sync signal, which causes the monitor to deflect the electron beam leftward and downward to the start of the next horizontal line in the raster. Then the CRTC turns the Display Enable signal back on to display the next line of data.

The short period of time between the end of one line of video data and the beginning of the next is called the horizontal blanking interval. Because the horizontal retrace interval (the amount of time required to deflect the beam to the start of the next line) is shorter than the horizontal blanking interval, a certain amount of horizontal overscan is generated on both ends of each line (see Figure 2-3).

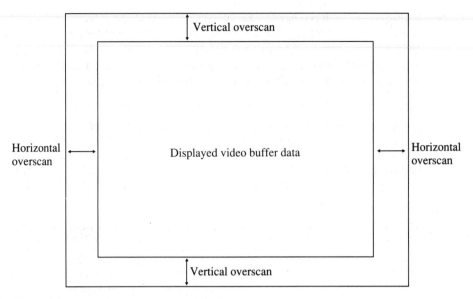

Figure 2-3. *Overscan.*

During periods of horizontal overscan, the electron beam can be left on, display-ing an overscan, or border, color. However, the primary reason horizontal over-scan is designed into a video subsystem is to provide a margin of error in centering the raster, so that no data is lost at the edges of the screen.

Vertical Timing

Once the electron beam has scanned all horizontal lines in the raster, the Display Enable signal is turned off. The CRTC then generates a vertical sync signal, which tells the monitor to deflect the electron beam from the bottom of the screen back to the upper left corner. The vertical retrace interval (during which the beam travels from the bottom to the top of the screen) is shorter than the vertical blank-ing interval (during which no data from the video buffer is displayed), so there are areas of vertical overscan at the top and bottom of the raster (see Figure 2-3). Like horizontal overscan, vertical overscan provides a border as well as a safety margin so that the raster can be centered on the screen.

Programming the CRT Controller

The CRTC programming interface is well defined and easy to use. The same gen-eral programming approach applies to all IBM PC and PS/2 video subsystems.

MDA

The Monochrome Display Adapter's CRTC, the Motorola 6845, has nineteen 8-bit internal data registers. The contents of each register control various characteris-tics of the timing signals generated by the 6845 (see Figure 2-4). One of these registers is an address register; its contents indicate which of the other 18 can be accessed. Most of the registers are write-only, but registers 0EH and 0FH, which control the position of the hardware cursor, may be read as well as written. On the MDA, the 6845's Address register is mapped to an I/O port at 3B4H, and the remaining 18 registers are all mapped to the next I/O port at 3B5H.

To access the 6845's data registers, you first write the register number to the 6845's Address register (I/O port 3B4H). Then you access the specified data register with an I/O write or read at port 3B5H. For example, Listing 2-1 shows how to determine the current cursor location by reading the contents of registers 0EH and 0FH on the 6845. These two registers (Cursor Location High and Cursor Location Low) contain the high-order and low-order bytes of the cursor location relative to the start of the video buffer.

Register	Name	Read/Write Access
00H	Horizontal Total	Write only
01H	Horizontal Displayed	Write only
02H	Horizontal Sync Position	Write only
03H	Horizontal Sync Pulse Width	Write only
04H	Vertical Total	Write only
05H	Vertical Total Adjust	Write only
06H	Vertical Displayed	Write only
07H	Vertical Sync Position	Write only
08H	Interlace Mode	Write only
09H	Maximum Scan Line	Write only
0AH	Cursor Start	Write only
0BH	Cursor End	Write only
0CH	Start Address High	Write only
0DH	Start Address Low	Write only
0EH	Cursor Location High	Read/Write
0FH	Cursor Location Low	Read/Write
10H	Light Pen High	Read only
11H	Light Pen Low	Read only

Figure 2-4. *Motorola 6845 CRTC data registers (for the MDA, CGA, and Hercules video adapters).*

```
        mov     ax,40h
        mov     es,ax           ; ES := video BIOS data segment
        mov     dx,es:[63h]     ; DX := 3x4h (3B4h or 3D4h)

        mov     al,0Eh
        out     dx,al           ; select 6845 Cursor Location
                                ;   High register
        inc     dx
        in      al,dx           ; read selected register at 3x5h
        mov     ah,al           ; AH := high byte of cursor
                                ;   location
        dec     dx
        mov     al,0Fh
        out     dx,al           ; select Cursor Location Low register
```

Listing 2-1. *Reading the 6845 Cursor Location registers.*   *(continued)*

Listing 2-1. *Continued.*

```
        inc     dx
        in      al,dx                ; AX := offset of cursor relative
                                     ;  to start of video buffer

; convert to character row and column

        mov     dx,es:[4Eh]          ; DX := CRT_START (buffer start offset
                                     ;  in bytes)
        shr     dx,1                 ; convert to words
        sub     ax,dx                ; subtract from cursor offset
        div     byte ptr es:[4Ah]    ; divide by CRT_COLS
        xchg    ah,al                ; AH := row, AL := column
```

With the MDA, there is rarely any reason to change the values in any of the 6845 registers except 0AH and 0BH (Cursor Start and Cursor End) and 0EH and 0FH (Cursor Location High and Low). Registers 00H through 09H control the horizontal and vertical timing signals, which should not be changed. Registers 0CH and 0DH (Start Address High and Start Address Low), which indicate what part of the MDA's video buffer is displayed, should always be set to 0.

CGA

The Color Graphics Adapter's CRTC is a Motorola 6845, as is the MDA's. The same programming technique used to access the CRTC on the MDA also works on the CGA. On the CGA, however, the CRTC Address register is mapped to I/O port 3D4H and the data registers are accessed at 3D5H. If you write a program that can run on either an MDA or a CGA, you can take advantage of the fact that the video BIOS routines in both the PC and PS/2 families maintain the value of the CRTC's Address register I/O port in a variable. Many of the programming examples in this book reference this variable, ADDR_6845, which is located at 0040:0063 in the BIOS Video Display Data Area.

Hercules Adapters

Like the MDA and CGA, the Hercules Graphics Card, Graphics Card Plus, and In-Color Card all use a Motorola 6845 as a CRTC. The CRTC registers are mapped at I/O ports 3B4H and 3B5H on all Hercules adapters. Although it is a color adapter, the InColor Card uses the MDA's I/O port and video buffer addresses in order to preserve compatibility with the MDA and with Hercules monochrome adapters.

 On all Hercules video adapters (as well as the EGA, MCGA, and VGA), you can set both the address and data registers of the CRTC with one 16-bit port write (OUT DX, AX) instead of two 8-bit port writes (OUT DX, AL). For example, the two sequences of code that follow do the same thing to the CRTC.

```
mov     dx,3B4h         ; CRTC address register
mov     al,0Ch          ; CRTC register number
cli                     ; disable interrupts
out     dx,al           ; select this register
inc     dx              ; DX := 3B5h (CRTC data register)
mov     al,8            ; data
out     dx,al           ; store data in register
sti                     ; restore interrupts
dec     dx
```

and

```
mov     dx,3B4h         ; CRTC address register
mov     ax,080Ch        ; AL := reg number, AH := data
out     dx,ax           ; store data in register
```

EGA

The Enhanced Graphics Adapter's CRTC is a proprietary LSI chip with a set of registers different from those in the 6845 (see Figure 2-5). The programming interface is similar to the 6845's, but the register assignments and formats are different enough that programs that write directly to CRTC registers on the MDA or CGA will probably crash on an EGA.

The EGA's CRTC supports a wider set of control functions than does the 6845. For example, the CRTC can cause a hardware interrupt at the start of a vertical blanking interval. The CRTC also supports the simultaneous display of two noncontiguous portions of the video buffer. (Chapter 12 describes these CRTC capabilities.)

A curious feature of the EGA's CRTC is its Overflow register (07H). Because the EGA can display a raster of more than 256 lines, the CRTC registers that contain a number of scan lines must be 9 bits wide instead of 8. The high-order bit in each of these registers is stored in the Overflow register.

Register	Name	EGA Read/Write Access
00H	Horizontal Total	Write only
01H	Horizontal Display Enable End	Write only
02H	Start Horizontal Blanking	Write only
03H	End Horizontal Blanking	Write only
04H	Start Horizontal Retrace	Write only
05H	End Horizontal Retrace	Write only
06H	Vertical Total	Write only
07H	Overflow	Write only
08H	Preset Row Scan	Write only
09H	Maximum Scan Line Address	Write only
0AH	Cursor Start	Write only
0BH	Cursor End	Write only
0CH	Start Address High	Read/Write
0DH	Start Address Low	Read/Write
0EH	Cursor Location High	Read/Write
0FH	Cursor Location Low	Read/Write

Figure 2-5. *EGA and VGA CRT Controller data registers.*   *(continued)*

Figure 2-5. *Continued.*

Register	Name	EGA Read/Write Access
10H	Vertical Retrace Start	Write only
10H	Light Pen High	Read only
11H	Vertical Retrace End	Write only
11H	Light Pen Low	Read only
12H	Vertical Display Enable End	Write only
13H	Offset (Logical Line Width)	Write only
14H	Underline Location	Write only
15H	Start Vertical Blanking	Write only
16H	End Vertical Blanking	Write only
17H	Mode Control	Write only
18H	Line Compare	Write only

MCGA

In the MCGA, the functions of a CRTC are integrated into a circuit component called the Memory Controller Gate Array. The first 16 Memory Controller registers are analogous to those in the 6845 (see Figure 2-6). As on the CGA, all MCGA Memory Controller registers, including the CRTC registers, are indexed through an address register at I/O port 3D4H. The data registers themselves may be accessed at port 3D5H.

Several features of the MCGA's CRTC distinguish it from the CGA's 6845. All of the Memory Controller registers can be read as well as written. Moreover, registers 00H through 07H may be designated read-only so that horizontal and vertical timing parameters are not inadvertently disrupted. Setting bit 7 of the Memory Controller Mode Control register (10H) to 1 protects registers 00H through 07H.

Another feature of the MCGA CRTC is that the hardware can compute the horizontal timing parameters for each of the available video modes. When bit 3 of the Mode Control register is set to 1, and when the values in registers 00H through 03H represent appropriate horizontal timing values for 40-by-25 alphanumeric mode (video BIOS mode 0), the Memory Controller generates proper horizontal timing signals in all available video modes.

If you compare the MCGA CRTC and the Motorola 6845 register by register, you will note several discrepancies in the interpretation of the values stored in some CRTC registers. In particular, the values expected in registers 09H, 0AH, and 0BH are specified in units of two scan lines on the MCGA, instead of one scan line on the 6845. Because the default alphanumeric character matrix on the MCGA is 16 scan lines high, this feature provides a certain amount of low-level compatibility, letting you use the same values for these registers as you would on a CGA.

Register	Name	Read/Write Access
00H	Horizontal Total	Read/Write
01H	Horizontal Displayed	Read/Write
02H	Start Horizontal Sync	Read/Write
03H	Sync Pulse Width	Read/Write
04H	Vertical Total	Read/Write
05H	Vertical Total Adjust	Read/Write
06H	Vertical Displayed	Read/Write
07H	Start Vertical Sync	Read/Write
08H	(reserved)	
09H	Scan Lines per Character	Read/Write
0AH	Cursor Start	Read/Write
0BH	Cursor End	Read/Write
0CH	Start Address High	Read/Write
0DH	Start Address Low	Read/Write
0EH	Cursor Location High	Read/Write
0FH	Cursor Location Low	Read/Write
10H	Mode Control	Read/Write
11H	Interrupt Control	Read/Write
12H	Character Generator, Sync Polarity	Read/Write
13H	Character Generator Pointer	Read/Write
14H	Character Generator Count	Read/Write
20–3FH	(reserved)	

Figure 2-6. *MCGA Memory Controller data registers. Registers 00H through 0FH are comparable to those in the CGA's CRT Controller.*

VGA

Functionally, the VGA's CRTC registers (see Figure 2-5) comprise a superset of those in the EGA's CRTC. The VGA's CRTC register set is addressable at the same I/O ports as the EGA's. A few more bit fields have been added to the register set, primarily so that the CRTC can handle 400-line and 480-line rasters. However, unlike the EGA's CRTC, the VGA's CRTC does not support the use of a light pen.

More important, however, all the EGA's CRTC register specifications have been carried over to the VGA. Thus, programs that write to the EGA's CRTC registers can be run unchanged on VGA-based hardware.

As on the MCGA, the VGA's CRTC data registers can all be read as well as written. Also, the VGA horizontal and vertical timing registers (CRTC registers 00H through 07H) can be write-protected by setting bit 7 of the Vertical Retrace End register (11H) to 1.

As on Hercules adapters, you can program the CRTC on the EGA, MCGA, and VGA using a 16-bit port write (OUT DX, AX). Moreover, you will find by experimenting that 16-bit port writes work on many non-IBM video adapters. But stay away from this technique on MDAs, CGAs, and clones if portability is important.

Basic CRTC Computations

To use the CRTC effectively, you must be able to perform the basic computations necessary to specify the CRTC's timings correctly. These computations are based on three constraints: the bandwidth of the video signal sent to the monitor and the monitor's horizontal and vertical synchronization rates.

Dot Clock

IBM PC video subsystems display pixels at a rate determined by the hardware. This rate is variously known as the video bandwidth, the dot rate, or the pixel rate; the oscillator that generates this rate is called the dot clock. The MDA, CGA, and Hercules adapter use only one dot clock; on the EGA and VGA, more than one dot clock is available (see Figure 2-7). The higher the dot clock frequency, the better the displayed pixel resolution.

Given the dot rate, the CRTC must be programmed so that the horizontal and vertical scan frequencies sent to the video display are limited to frequencies the display can handle. Older displays, such as the IBM Monochrome Display, are designed to handle only one horizontal and one vertical scan rate. Newer displays, such as the NEC MultiSync, can synchronize with a range of horizontal and/or vertical scan rates.

IBM Subsystem	Video Bandwidth (Dot Rate) in MHz	Horizontal Scan Rate in KHz	Vertical Scan Rate in Hz
MDA, HGC			
720x350 mono	16.257	18.43	50
CGA			
640x200 color	14.318	15.75	60
EGA			
640x350 color	16.257	21.85	60
640x200 color	14.318	15.75	60
720x350 mono	16.257	18.43	50
InColor			
720x350 color	19.000	21.80	60
MCGA			
640x400 mono/color	25.175	31.50	70
640x480 mono/color	25.175	31.50	60
VGA			
640x400 mono/color	25.175	31.50	70
720x400 mono/color	28.322	31.50	70
640x480 mono/color	25.175	31.50	60
640x350 mono/color	25.175	31.50	70

Figure 2-7. *Basic timings for IBM video subsystems.*

Horizontal Timing

Consider how you would calculate the typical CRTC register values shown in Figure 2-8 for an MDA with an IBM Monochrome Display. The MDA's video bandwidth (dot rate) is 16.257 MHz; that is, 16,257,000 dots per second. The monochrome display's horizontal scan rate is 18.432 KHz (18,432 lines per second). Dividing the dot rate by the horizontal scan rate gives 882 dots per line. Each character displayed by the MDA is 9 dots wide, so the total number of characters in each line is 882 ÷ 9, or 98.

This value is used to program the CRTC's Horizontal Total register. For the MDA's CRTC, a Motorola 6845, the value you store in the Horizontal Total register must be 1 less than the computed total, or 97 (61H).

Register	Name	Parameter	Description
00H	Horizontal Total	97 (61H)	(total characters per scan line) − 1
01H	Horizontal Displayed	80 (50H)	Characters displayed in each scan line
02H	Horizontal Sync Position	82 (52H)	Position in scan line where horizontal retrace starts
03H	Horizontal Sync Width	15 (0FH)	Duration of horizontal retrace interval (character clocks)
04H	Vertical Total	25 (19H)	Total character rows in one frame
05H	Vertical Total Adjust	2	Remaining scan lines in one frame
06H	Vertical Displayed	25 (19H)	Character rows displayed in each frame
07H	Vertical Sync Position	25 (19H)	Position in frame where vertical retrace starts
08H	Interlace Mode	2	Always set to 2
09H	Maximum Scan Line	13 (0DH)	(height of one character in scan lines) − 1

Figure 2-8. *Typical CRTC parameters for the Monochrome Display Adapter.*

In terms of CRTC timings, the Horizontal Total value describes the amount of time, in "character clocks," required to complete one horizontal scan. During this period, 80 characters are actually displayed. (This is the value used for the Horizontal Displayed register.) The other 18 character clocks are spent in horizontal overscan and in horizontal retrace.

The duration of the horizontal retrace interval is about 10 to 15 percent of the Horizontal Total value. The exact value depends on the video subsystem. On the MDA, the horizontal retrace interval is set at 15 character clocks by storing this value in the CRTC Horizontal Sync Width register. This leaves 3 character clocks of horizontal overscan. The horizontal retrace signal is programmed to start 2 character clocks after the rightmost displayed character by storing the value 82 (52H) in the CRTC Horizontal Sync Position register. Thus, there are 2 character clocks of right horizontal overscan and 1 character clock of left overscan.

Changing the value in the Horizontal Sync Position register changes the size of the right and left overscan areas and thus the horizontal position of the displayed raster. For example, to shift the displayed raster to the left, increase the size of the right overscan interval by increasing the value in the CRTC Horizontal Sync Position register.

Vertical Timing

Similar considerations apply in programming the CRTC to generate appropriate vertical timings. The nominal horizontal scan rate in the MDA's monochrome display is 18.432 KHz (18,432 lines per second) with a vertical scan rate of 50 Hz (50 frames per second), so the number of lines in one frame is 18,432 ÷ 50, or 368. Since each character displayed is 14 lines high, 25 rows of characters account for 350 lines. The MDA's CRTC always uses 16 lines for vertical retrace; this leaves 368 − (350 + 16), or 2 lines of vertical overscan.

The CRTC programming follows these calculations. The height of each displayed character is specified by the value in the CRTC Maximum Scan Line register. Since characters are 14 scan lines high, the maximum scan line value is 13 (0DH). Taken together, the values for Vertical Total (25 character rows) and Vertical Total Adjust (2 scan lines) indicate the total number of scan lines in one frame. The number of character rows displayed (25) is indicated in the Vertical Displayed register. The position in the frame where vertical retrace starts (25) is specified by the value in the Vertical Sync Position register.

The CRTCs on the MCGA, EGA, and VGA are more complex than the Motorola 6845 CRTC on the MDA and CGA. Nevertheless, the registers that control horizontal and vertical timings in the newer video subsystems are similar in nomenclature and functionality to the 6845's registers. The computations for the MCGA, EGA, and VGA CRTCs are derived from the dot rate, the character size, and the horizontal and vertical capabilities of the video display, just as they are for the MDA and CGA.

The CRT Status Register

All IBM video subsystems have a read-only CRT Status register. This register is located at I/O port 3BAH on the MDA and Hercules adapters and at 3DAH on the CGA and MCGA; on the EGA and VGA, this register is at 3BAH in monochrome configurations and at 3DAH in color configurations. Generally, two of the eight bits in this register reflect the current status of the horizontal and vertical timing signals generated by the CRTC. These status bits can be used to synchronize video buffer updates with the screen refresh cycle to minimize interference with the displayed image. (Chapter 3 contains examples of this type of programming.)

Unfortunately, the exact interpretation of the status bits in the CRT Status register varies among the different IBM video subsystems (see Figure 2-9). Therefore, programs should be designed to determine which hardware they are running on (Appendix C) before they attempt to use the status information in this register.

Listing 2-2 shows how the status bits in the CRTC Status register are used to synchronize program operation with the video refresh cycle. This subroutine can be used on the CGA to time the horizontal blanking interval. The subroutine uses bit 3 of the CRT Status register, which indicates when the CRTC's vertical sync signal is active, to synchronize with the start of a refresh cycle. The loops at L01 and L02 show how this is done.

The loops at L03 and L04 then synchronize with the Display Enable signal, using bit 0 of the CRT Status value. When the Display Enable signal goes off, the loop at L05 decrements the value in CX during the horizontal blanking interval, that is, while the Display Enable signal is off. The number of iterations counted in CX can then be used as a timeout value to determine when the last horizontal line in the frame has been scanned. (See Chapter 3.)

```
                    TITLE    'Listing 2-2'
                    NAME     HRTimeout
                    PAGE     55,132

;
; Name:             HRTimeout
;
; Function:         Determine a timeout value for the horizontal blanking interval
;
; Caller:           Microsoft C:
;
;                            int HRTimeout();
;


_TEXT               SEGMENT byte public 'CODE'
                    ASSUME  cs:_TEXT

                    PUBLIC  _HRTimeout
_HRTimeout          PROC    near

                    push    bp               ; usual C prologue to establish
                    mov     bp,sp            ;   stack frame

                    mov     ax,40h
                    mov     es,ax            ; ES := video BIOS data segment

                    mov     dx,es:[63h]      ; DX := port for CRTC Address register
                    add     dl,6             ; DX := port for CRTC Status register

; synchronize with start of refresh cycle

L01:                in      al,dx            ; AL := CRTC status
                    test    al,8             ; test bit 3
                    jz      L01              ; loop while NOT in vertical retrace

L02:                in      al,dx
                    test    al,8
                    jnz     L02              ; loop during vertical retrace
```

Listing 2-2. *Timing the horizontal blanking interval on the CGA.*   *(continued)*

Listing 2-2. *Continued.*

```
; synchronize with a horizontal scan and time the horizontal blanking interval

                mov     cx,0FFFFh       ; CX := loop counter

                cli                     ; disable interrupts

L03:            in      al,dx
                test    al,1
                jnz     L03             ; loop while Display Enable is inactive

L04:            in      al,dx
                test    al,1
                jz      L04             ; loop while Display Enable is active

L05:            in      al,dx
                test    al,1
                loopnz  L05             ; decrement CX and loop while Display
                                        ;  Enable is inactive

                sti                     ; enable interrupts again

                mov     ax,cx           ; AX := loop counter
                neg     ax
                shl     ax,1            ; AX := timeout value

                mov     sp,bp           ; discard stack frame and return to C
                pop     bp
                ret

_HRTimeout      ENDP

_TEXT           ENDS

                END
```

Video Modes

Despite the timing constraints imposed by the dot clock and the rated horizontal and vertical scan rates of available monitors, all IBM video subsystems except the MDA can be programmed with a variety of different CRTC parameters. This makes a number of video modes available. Each video mode is characterized by its resolution (the number of characters or pixels displayed horizontally and vertically), by the number of different colors that can be displayed simultaneously, and by the format of the displayable data in the video buffer.

Resolution

The horizontal and vertical resolution in a video mode is a function of the dot rate as well as the monitor's horizontal and vertical scan rates. The number of pixels displayed in each frame corresponds to the dot rate divided by the vertical scan rate. The actual horizontal and vertical resolution then depends on the horizontal scan rate.

	Register	Bit 7	Bit 3	Bit 2	Bit 1	Bit 0
MDA	3BA		Video drive			1 = horizontal sync
HGC, HGC+, InColor	3BA	0 = vertical sync	Video drive		1 = light pen trigger	1 = horizontal sync
CGA	3DA		1 = vertical sync	1 = light pen switch closed	1 = light pen trigger	0 = display enable
EGA	3BA or 3DA		1 = vertical sync	1 = light pen switch closed	1 = light pen trigger	0 = display enable
VGA	3BA or 3DA		1 = vertical sync			0 = display enable
MCGA	3DA		1 = vertical sync*			0 = display enable

*0 = vertical sync in 640-by-480 2-color mode

Figure 2-9. *CRTC Status register bit assignments.*

Colors

The number and variety of colors that can be displayed in a video mode depend on the design of the video subsystem's attribute decoding and video signal generator components. The attribute decoder uses data stored in the video buffer to control the color and brightness signals produced by the video signal generator. Establishing a particular video mode always involves programming a video subsystem's attribute decoder in addition to updating its CRTC parameters.

Video Buffer Organization

The format of the data in video RAM also characterizes a video mode. In all PC and PS/2 subsystems, video modes can be classified as alphanumeric or graphics modes, depending on the video buffer data format. In alphanumeric modes, the data in the video buffer is formatted as a sequence of ASCII code and attribute byte pairs; the alphanumeric character generator translates the ASCII codes into displayed characters while the attribute bytes specify the colors used to display them (see Chapter 3). In graphics modes, the video buffer is organized as a sequence of bit fields; the bits in each field designate the color of a particular pixel on the screen.

Hardware Video Mode Control

Establishing a video mode on an IBM PC or PS/2 video subsystem generally requires specific mode control programming apart from specifying CRTC parameters. For example, the alphanumeric character generator must be enabled in alphanumeric modes and disabled in graphics modes. Also, the subsystem's internal character clock, which determines the number of pixels generated for each alphanumeric character code read from the video buffer, may run at different rates in different video modes. These and other internal functions are controlled by loading one or more specialized mode control registers with values appropriate for each video mode.

MDA

The MDA's Mode Control register is a write-only register mapped to port 3B8H (see Figure 2-10). Only three of the eight bits in this register have meaning. Bit 0 is set to 1 at powerup and must always remain set to 1. Bit 3, when set to 1, enables video refresh; clearing this bit blanks the screen. Bit 5 is the Enable Blink bit; it controls whether characters can blink. On the MDA, most programs leave bit 3 set at all times. Chapter 3 explains how to use bit 5 (the Enable Blink bit).

Bit	Settings
0	1 = adapter enabled (should always = 1)
1	(unused, should always = 0)
2	(unused, should always = 0)
3	1 = video enabled
	0 = video disabled (screen blank)
4	(unused, should always = 0)
5	1 = blinking attribute enabled
	0 = blinking attribute disabled
6	(unused, should always = 0)
7	(unused, should always = 0)

Figure 2-10. *Bit settings for the MDA Mode Control register (3B8H).*

CGA and MCGA

The Mode Control register on the CGA and MCGA is found at 3D8H (see Figure 2-11a). The five low-order bits control internal timings appropriate for the video modes they select, while bit 5 is an Enable Blink bit just as it is on the MDA. The useful bit patterns for the CGA's Mode Control register are listed in Figure 2-11b. These values correspond to the available BIOS video modes on the CGA.

The Mode Control registers on the CGA and the MCGA have two differences. One is that the MCGA Mode Control register may be read as well as written; the CGA register is write-only. The other difference relates to the function of bit 2. On the CGA, setting bit 2 to 1 disables the color burst component of the composite video output signal. This can improve the quality of the display if you are using a composite green or amber monitor with a CGA. On the MCGA, which does not support

Bit	Settings
0	1 = 80-character alphanumeric modes
	0 = 40-character alphanumeric modes
1	1 = 320-wide graphics mode
	0 = (all other modes)
2	1 = color burst disabled (CGA only)
	1 = foreground color from video DAC register 7 (MCGA only)
	0 = color burst enabled (CGA only)
	0 = foreground color from the video DAC register specified in bits 0–3 of the Palette register (3D9H) (MCGA only)
3	1 = video enabled
	0 = video disabled (screen blank)
4	1 = 640-wide graphics modes
	0 = (all other modes)
5	1 = blinking attribute enabled
	0 = blinking attribute disabled
6	(unused, should always = 0)
7	(unused, should always = 0)

Figure 2-11a. *Bit settings for the CGA and MCGA Mode Control register (3D8H).*

BIOS Mode Number	Description	Value for Mode Control Register
0	40x25 alpha (color burst disabled)	00101100b (2CH)
1	40x25 alpha	00101000b (28H)
2	80x25 alpha (color burst disabled)	00101101b (2DH)
3	80x25 alpha	00101001b (29H)
4	320x200 graphics	00101010b (2AH)
5	320x200 graphics (color burst disabled)	00101110b (2EH)
6	640x200 graphics	00011100b (1CH)
7	80x25 alpha (MDA only)	00101001b (29H)
11H	640x480 graphics (MCGA only)	00011000b (18H)

Figure 2-11b. *MDA, CGA, and MCGA Mode Control register options.*

a composite monitor, the function of bit 2 of the Mode Control register is to select between two sources for the foreground color in 2-color graphics modes.

The MCGA has two additional mode control registers, which are not implemented on the CGA. The MCGA Memory Controller Mode Control register (10H) at port 3D4H/3D5H selects 640-by-480 2-color and 320-by-200 256-color graphics modes (see Figure 2-12). An Extended Mode Control register is mapped to I/O port 3DDH. This register is used only during machine coldstart; it has no practical use in applications programs.

Bit	Settings
0	1 = select 320x200 256-color mode
	0 = (all other modes)
1	1 = select 640x480 2-color mode
	0 = (all other modes)
2	(reserved)
3	1 = horizontal timing parameters computed for video mode
	0 = horizontal timing parameters as specified in registers 00–03H
4	1 = enable dot clock (should always be 1)
5	(reserved)
6	Inverse of bit 8 of Vertical Displayed register (06H)
7	1 = write-protect registers 00–07H
	0 = allow updating of registers 00–07H

Figure 2-12. *Bit settings for the MCGA Memory Controller Mode Control register.*

HGC

The Hercules Graphics Card has two control registers whose contents affect the video mode configuration. The Mode Control register at 3B8H is functionally compatible with the MDA's Mode Control register, but it maps additional mode configuration functions to bits 1 and 7 (see Figure 2-13). Bit 1, when set to 1, establishes internal timings for a 720-by-348 graphics mode. Setting bit 7 to 1 while the adapter is in graphics mode displays the second half of the adapter's 64 KB video buffer at B800:0000. These bits have no function, however, unless the appropriate bits in the adapter's Configuration Switch register are set properly.

The Configuration Switch register (3BFH) determines the function of the Mode Control register at 3B8H (see Figure 2-14). When bit 0 of the Configuration Switch register is 0, the HGC cannot be placed in its graphics mode, so bit 1 of the Mode Control register must also be 0. Bit 1 of the Configuration Switch register controls video buffer addressing when the adapter is used in combination with a CGA or compatible (see below).

Bit	Settings
0	(unused)
1	1 = 720x348 graphics mode
	0 = 80x25 alphanumeric mode
2	(unused, should always = 0)
3	1 = video enabled
	0 = video disabled (screen blank)
4	(unused, should always = 0)
5	1 = blinking attribute enabled
	0 = blinking attribute disabled
6	(unused, should always = 0)
7	1 = graphics mode buffer displayed from B800:0000 (video page 1)
	0 = graphics mode buffer displayed from B000:0000 (video page 0)

Figure 2-13. *Bit settings for the Hercules Mode Control register (3B8H). This register is the same on the HGC, HGC+, and InColor Card.*

Bit	Settings
0	1 = allows graphics mode
	0 = prevents graphics mode
1	1 = enables upper 32 KB of graphics mode video buffer at B800:0000
	0 = disables upper 32 KB of graphics mode buffer
2-7	(unused)

Figure 2-14. *Bit settings for the Hercules Configuration Switch register (3BFH). This register is the same on the HGC, HGC+, and InColor Card.*

HGC+ and InColor Card

The HGC+ and InColor Card implement an extended mode control register (called the xMode register) in addition to the Mode Control and Configuration Switch registers found on the HGC. The xMode register is a write-only register addressable as register 14H at port 3B4H/3B5H. (The register is addressed exactly as if it were a CRTC register.) The xMode register controls the alphanumeric character generator; Chapter 10 explains this in detail.

EGA and VGA

When you establish a video mode on the EGA and the VGA, you can control the internal timing and addressing of several different components of the video subsystem. These include the Sequencer, the Graphics Controller, and the Attribute Controller, each of which has several control registers. There is also a Miscellaneous Output register, which controls I/O port and video buffer addressing and selects the dot clock frequency.

All Sequencer, Graphics Controller, and Attribute Controller registers on the EGA are write-only registers, but on the VGA they can be read as well as written.

Sequencer

The Sequencer generates internal timings for video RAM addressing. It has five programmable data registers (see Figure 2-15) mapped to ports 3C4H and 3C5H in a manner analogous to CRTC register mapping. The Sequencer's Address register is located at 3C4H; its five data registers are selected by storing an index value between 0 and 4 in the Address register and then accessing the corresponding data register at 3C5H.

Register	Name
0	Reset
1	Clocking Mode
2	Map Mask
3	Character Map Select
4	Memory Mode

Figure 2-15. *EGA and VGA Sequencer registers.*

Graphics Controller

The Graphics Controller mediates data flow between the video buffer and the CPU, as well as from the video buffer to the Attribute Controller. The Graphics Controller has nine data registers, plus an Address register (see Figure 2-16). The Address register maps to port 3CEH, and the data registers map to port 3CFH.

Register	Name
0	Set/Reset
1	Enable Set/Reset
2	Color Compare
3	Data Rotate/Function Select
4	Read Map Select
5	Graphics Mode
6	Miscellaneous
7	Color Don't Care
8	Bit Mask

Figure 2-16. *EGA and VGA Graphics Controller registers.*

Attribute Controller

The Attribute Controller supports a 16-color palette on the EGA and VGA. It also controls the color displayed during overscan intervals. The Attribute Controller's Address register and 21 data registers all map to I/O port 3C0H (see Figure 2-17). A value written to port 3C0H will be stored in either the Address register or a data register, depending on the state of a flip-flop internal to the Attribute Controller.

Register(s)	Function
0–0FH	Palette
10H	Attribute Mode Control
11H	Overscan Color
12H	Color Plane Enable
13H	Horizontal Pixel Panning
14H	Color Select (VGA only)

Figure 2-17. *EGA and VGA Attribute Controller registers.*

To set the flip-flop, perform an I/O read (IN AL, DX) of the CRT Status register (port 3BAH in monochrome modes, 3DAH in color modes). Listing 2-3 illustrates how this is done in updating an Attribute Controller register. On the VGA, Attribute Controller data registers may be read as well as written. Do this by writing the register number to port 3C0H and then reading the value from port 3C1H.

```
; program the Attribute Controller directly

        mov     ax,40h
        mov     es,ax           ; ES := video BIOS data segment
        mov     dx,es:[63h]     ; DX := 3x4h (3B4h or 3D4h)
        add     dl,6            ; DX := 3xAh (CRT Status Register)

        cli                     ; clear the interrupts
        in      al,dx           ; reset Attribute Controller flip-flop
        push    dx              ; preserve Status Reg port
```

Listing 2-3. *Updating the EGA or VGA Attribute Controller register.*   *(continued)*

Listing 2-3. *Continued.*

```
        mov     dl,0C0h              ; DX := 3C0h
        mov     al,RegNumber
        out     dx,al                ; write to Address Register
        jmp     $+2                  ; waste a few cycles so that Attribute
                                     ;  Controller can respond
        mov     al,DataValue
        out     dx,al                ; write to data register

        pop     dx                   ; DX := 3xAh
        in      al,dx                ; reset that flip-flop
        mov     dl,0C0h
        mov     al,20h               ; restore palette
        out     dx,al
        sti                          ; enable interrupts


; using the video BIOS

        mov     ax,1000h             ; AH := 10h (INT 10h function number)
                                     ; AL := 0 (Set individual Attribute
                                     ;  Controller register)
        mov     bl,RegNumber
        mov     bh,DataValue
        int     10h
```

You can use 16-bit port writes (OUT DX,AX) to store data in EGA and VGA Sequencer and Graphics Controller registers. On the EGA, you can use the same technique to program the Attribute Controller, which recognizes I/O port writes at 3C1H as well as 3C0H. However, the VGA Attribute Controller does not emulate the EGA in this regard, so this technique should be used carefully when VGA compatibility is important.

Video BIOS Support

The video BIOS supports a number of different video modes on IBM PC and PS/2 video subsystems (see Figure 2-18). The video BIOS routines, which can be called with INT 10H, let you establish a video mode simply by specifying its number.

Not all of the BIOS video modes are available on all IBM PC video subsystems. Furthermore, the video BIOS does not support video mode configurations on non-IBM hardware unless it exactly emulates the corresponding IBM hardware.

For example, all Hercules video adapters emulate IBM's MDA exactly. Thus, the video BIOS can be used to select the monochrome alphanumeric mode (BIOS mode 7) on all Hercules products. However, the Hercules hardware also supports a 720-by-348 graphics mode which is not recognized by IBM's video BIOS. Consequently, to set up the Hercules graphics mode, a program must configure the hardware directly (see Listing 2-4).

Mode Number (hex)	Resolution	Colors	Mode Type	Buffer Segment	MDA	CGA	EGA	MCGA	VGA
0	40x25 chars (320x200 pixels)*†	16	Alpha	B800		X	X	X	X
0	40x25 chars (320x350 pixels)†	16	Alpha	B800			X		X
0	40x25 chars (320x400 pixels)	16	Alpha	B800				X	
0	40x25 chars (360x400 pixels)†	16	Alpha	B800					X
1	40x25 chars (320x200 pixels)†	16	Alpha	B800		X	X	X	X
1	40x25 chars (320x350 pixels)†	16	Alpha	B800			X		X
1	40x25 chars (320x400 pixels)	16	Alpha	B800				X	
1	40x25 chars (360x400 pixels)†	16	Alpha	B800					X
2	80x25 chars (640x200 pixels)*†	16	Alpha	B800		X	X	X	X
2	80x25 chars (640x350 pixels)†	16	Alpha	B800			X		X
2	80x25 chars (640x400 pixels)	16	Alpha	B800				X	
2	80x25 chars (720x400 pixels)†	16	Alpha	B800					X
3	80x25 chars (640x200 pixels)†	16	Alpha	B800		X	X	X	X
3	80x25 chars (640x350 pixels)†	16	Alpha	B800			X		X
3	80x25 chars (640x400 pixels)	16	Alpha	B800				X	
3	80x25 chars (720x400 pixels)†	16	Alpha	B800					X
4	320x200 pixels	4	Graphics	B800		X	X	X	X
5	320x200 pixels‡	4	Graphics	B800		X	X	X	X
6	640x200 pixels	2	Graphics	B800		X	X	X	X
7	80x25 chars (720x350 pixels)†	2	Alpha	B000	X		X		X
7	80x25 chars (720x400 pixels)†	2	Alpha	B000					X
8	(PCjr only)								
9	(PCjr only)								
0A	(PCjr only)								
0B	(used by EGA video BIOS)								
0C	(used by EGA video BIOS)								
0D	320x200 pixels	16	Graphics	A000			X		X
0E	640x200 pixels	16	Graphics	A000			X		X
0F	640x350 pixels	2	Graphics	A000			X		X

*On the CGA, the color burst component of the composite video signal is disabled. This improves the appearance of a monochromatic green or amber display. On the EGA, MCGA, and VGA, mode 0 is the same as mode 1, and mode 2 is the same as mode 3.

†On the VGA, the vertical pixel resolution in this mode is selected using INT 10H function 12H (see Appendix A).

‡On the CGA, color burst is disabled and the four-color palette contains black, cyan, red, and white (for details, see Chapter 4). On the EGA, MCGA, and VGA, mode 5 is the same as mode 4.

§Only four colors can be displayed on an EGA with only 64 KB of video RAM.

Figure 2-18. *ROM BIOS video modes.*   *(continued)*

Figure 2-18. *Continued.*

Mode Number (hex)	Resolution	Colors	Mode Type	Buffer Segment	MDA	CGA	EGA	MCGA	VGA
10	640x350 pixels§	4	Graphics	A000			x		
10	640x350 pixels	16	Graphics	A000			x		x
11	640x480 pixels	2	Graphics	A000				x	x
12	640x480 pixels	16	Graphics	A000					x
13	320x200 pixels	256	Graphics	A000				x	x

```
            TITLE    'Listing 2-4'
            NAME     HercGraphMode
            PAGE     55,132

;
; Name:          HercGraphMode
;
; Function:      Establish Hercules 720x348 graphics mode on HGC, HGC+, InColor
;
; Caller:        Microsoft C:
;
;                          void HercGraphMode();
;

DGROUP          GROUP    _DATA

_TEXT           SEGMENT byte public 'CODE'
                ASSUME  cs:_TEXT,ds:DGROUP

                PUBLIC   _HercGraphMode
_HercGraphMode  PROC     near

                push     bp                     ; preserve caller registers
                mov      bp,sp
                push     si
                push     di

; Update Video BIOS Data Area with reasonable values

                mov      ax,40h
                mov      es,ax
                mov      di,49h                 ; ES:DI := 0040:0049 (BIOS data area)

                mov      si,offset DGROUP:BIOSData
                mov      cx,BIOSDataLen
                rep      movsb                  ; update BIOS data area

; Set Configuration Switch

                mov      dx,3BFh                ; DX := Configuration Switch port
                mov      al,1                   ; AL bit 1 := 0 (exclude 2nd 32K of
                                                ;            video buffer)
```

Listing 2-4. *Configuring a Hercules adapter for 720-by-348 graphics mode.*   *(continued)*

Listing 2-4. *Continued.*

```
                                        ; AL bit 0 := 1 (allow graphics mode
              out       dx,al           ;                  setting via 3B8h)

; Blank the screen to avoid interference during CRTC programming

              mov       dx,3B8h         ; DX := CRTC Mode Control register port
              xor       al,al           ; AL bit 3 := 0 (disable video signal)
              out       dx,al           ; blank the screen

; Program the CRTC

              sub       dl,4            ; DX := CRTC Address reg port 3B4h

              mov       si,offset DGROUP:CRTCParms
              mov       cx,CRTCParmsLen

L01:          lodsw                     ; AL := CRTC register number
                                        ; AH := data for this register
              out       dx,ax
              loop      L01

; Set graphics mode

              add       dl,4            ; DX := 3B8h (CRTC Mode Control reg)
              mov       al,CRTMode      ; AL bit 1 = 1 (enable graphics mode)
                                        ;    bit 3 = 1 (enable video)
              out       dx,al

              pop       di              ; restore registers and exit
              pop       si
              mov       sp,bp
              pop       bp
              ret

_HercGraphMode  ENDP

_TEXT           ENDS


_DATA           SEGMENT word public 'DATA'

                          ; These are the parameters recommended by Hercules.
                          ; They are based on 16 pixels/character and
                          ; 4 scan lines per character.

CRTCParms       DB        00h,35h ; Horizontal Total:  54 characters
                DB        01h,2Dh ; Horizontal Displayed:  45 characters
                DB        02h,2Eh ; Horizontal Sync Position:  at 46th character
                DB        03h,07h ; Horizontal Sync Width:  7 character clocks

                DB        04h,5Bh ; Vertical Total:  92 characters (368 lines)
                DB        05h,02h ; Vertical Adjust:  2 scan lines
                DB        06h,57h ; Vertical Displayed:  87 character rows (348 lines)
                DB        07h,57h ; Vertical Sync Position:  after 87th char row

                DB        09h,03h ; Max Scan Line:  4 scan lines per char

CRTCParmsLen    EQU       ($-CRTCParms)/2
```

(continued)

Listing 2-4. *Continued.*

```
BIOSData        DB      7           ; CRT_MODE
                DW      80          ; CRT_COLS
                DW      8000h       ; CRT_LEN
                DW      0           ; CRT_START
                DW      8 dup(0)    ; CURSOR_POSN
                DW      0           ; CURSOR_MODE
                DB      0           ; ACTIVE_PAGE
CRTCAddr        DW      3B4h        ; ADDR_6845
CRTMode         DB      0Ah         ; CRT_MODE_SET (value for port 3B8h)
                DB      0           ; CRT_PALETTE (unused)

BIOSDataLen     EQU     $-BIOSData

_DATA           ENDS

                END
```

Combinations of Video Subsystems

IBM designed the original MDA and CGA such that both adapters can be used in the same PC. This is possible because the CRTC registers and other control and status registers are assigned to a different range of I/O ports on the MDA than on the CGA. The MDA's port addresses range from 3B0H through 3BFH, while the CGA's range from 3D0H through 3DFH. Also, the video buffers on the MDA and the CGA occupy different portions of the 80x86 address space: The MDA's 4 KB video buffer is at B000:0000, while the CGA's 16 KB buffer starts at B800:0000.

This separation was carried forward in the design of the EGA. The EGA's I/O port and video buffer addressing are programmable. When the EGA is attached to a monochrome monitor, the MDA-compatible addresses are used. When the EGA is used with a color monitor, the CGA-compatible addresses are used. Thus, an EGA can coexist with either an MDA or a CGA.

Figure 2-19 shows which PC and PS/2 video subsystems can coexist in the same computer. The table reflects the dichotomy between MDA-compatible and CGA-compatible I/O port and video buffer addressing. As a rule of thumb, you can usually combine one MDA-compatible adapter and one CGA-compatible adapter in the same system.

NOTE: The Hercules InColor Card should be regarded as an MDA-compatible adapter, even though it is ostensibly a color card. In fact, if you use the InColor Card in a PS/2 Model 30 with a monochrome monitor attached to the Model 30's MCGA, you end up with the strange combination of an MDA-compatible color subsystem and a CGA-compatible monochrome subsystem in the same computer.

The BIOS video mode routines generally support dual-display configurations. The video BIOS routines use bits 4 and 5 of the variable EQUIP_FLAG at 0040:0010 in the BIOS video data area to choose between two video subsystems. If there are addressing conflicts between two subsystems, the BIOS in the MCGA and VGA provides a "display switch" interface that lets you independently disable and enable each subsystem (see Appendix A).

	MDA	CGA	EGA	MCGA	VGA Adapter	HGC	HGC+	InColor
MDA		x	x	x	x			
CGA	x		x			x	x	x
EGA	x	x		x		x	x	x
MCGA	x		x		x	x	x	x
VGA Adapter	x			x		x	x	x
HGC		x	x	x	x			
HGC+		x	x	x	x			
InColor		x	x	x	x			

Figure 2-19. *Allowable combinations of IBM PC and PS/2 video subsystems.*

With some combinations of video adapters, the address space the two subsystems' video buffers occupy may overlap even if their I/O port address assignments do not. In this situation you must selectively exclude part or all of one subsystem's video buffer from the CPU memory map so that the CPU can access the other subsystem's buffer without addressing conflicts. The technique for doing this varies with the hardware.

MDA

The MDA's video buffer is mapped to the addresses between B000:0000 and B000:FFFF. The same buffer is also mapped to the 4 KB blocks of RAM starting at segments B100H, B200H, and so on through B700H, although there is no real reason for software to use these alternate address maps. The MDA's video buffer address mapping cannot be disabled.

Hercules

On the HGC, the HGC+, and the InColor Card, the video buffer occupies the 64 KB of RAM starting at B000:0000. The second 32 KB of the video buffer overlaps the address space of a CGA's video buffer (starting at B800:0000). For this reason these Hercules adapters are designed so that the second 32 KB can be selectively excluded from the CPU memory map. The extent of the video buffer address space depends upon the value you store in the Configuration Switch register (3BFH). When bit 1 of this register is 0 (the power-on default), video RAM occupies addresses from B000:0000 through B000:7FFF, which excludes the second 32 KB portion from the CPU memory map and allows the card to be used with a CGA. To make the second half of the video buffer addressable, set bit 1 to 1.

CGA

The CGA's video buffer maps to the addresses between B800:0000 and B800:3FFF. The same buffer is also mapped between BC00:0000 and BC00:3FFF, although few programs use this alternate address map. As with the MDA, the CGA's video buffer mapping cannot be altered.

This is not the case, however, for all CGA clones. The Hercules Color Card (not to be confused with the InColor Card) is a CGA work-alike whose video buffer can be excluded from the CPU's address space. This is achieved by setting bit 1 of the card's Configuration Switch register (3BFH) to 1. This register maps to the same I/O port as the equivalent register on an HGC, HGC+, or InColor Card, but the polarity of the control bit is opposite that on the other Hercules cards. Thus, by toggling this bit, software can address the video buffers on both a Hercules Color Card and another Hercules adapter without addressing conflicts.

EGA

The EGA's video buffer can be mapped to any of four locations, depending on the values of bits 2 and 3 in the Graphics Controller Miscellaneous register (see Figure 2-20). The default values for these bits depend on the video mode. When the video BIOS sets up a video mode, it sets these bits to appropriate values.

Bit 3	Bit 2	Video Buffer Address Range
0	0	A000:0000 – B000:FFFF
0	1	A000:0000 – A000:FFFF
1	0	B000:0000 – B000:7FFF
1	1	B800:0000 – B800:7FFF

Figure 2-20. *Control of EGA and VGA video buffer addressing with the Graphics Controller Miscellaneous register.*

The EGA also provides another level of control over the video buffer address map. When set to 0, bit 1 of the EGA's Miscellaneous Output register (3C2H) excludes the entire video buffer from the CPU memory address space.

MCGA

The MCGA's 64 KB video buffer occupies the addresses between A000:0000 and A000:FFFF, but the second 32 KB of the buffer, starting at A000:8000 (A800:0000), also maps to the CGA video buffer address range (B800:0000 through B800:7FFF). CPU addressing of the MCGA's video buffer and I/O ports can be disabled by setting bit 2 of the system board control port at 65H to 0. Listing 2-5 shows how INT 10H function 12H can be called to set or reset this bit.

```
        mov     ah,12h          ; AH := 12h (INT 10h function number)
        mov     al,1            ; AL := 1 (disable addressing)
                                ; (use AL = 0 to enable addressing)
        mov     bl,32h          ; INT 10H subfunction number
        int     10h

        cmp     al,12h
        jne     ErrorExit       ; jump if BIOS does not support this
                                ; function
```

Listing 2-5. *Enable or disable video I/O port and buffer addressing on an MCGA or VGA.*

VGA

Control over the VGA's video buffer address map is the same as on the EGA. However, there are two different methods of disabling CPU addressing of the video subsystem, depending on whether you are using an integrated VGA (in a PS/2 Model 50, 60, or 80) or the VGA Adapter. In the integrated subsystem, the Video Subsystem Enable Register (3C3H) controls both video buffer addressing and I/O port addressing; setting bit 0 of this register to 0 disables addressing, and setting bit 0 to 1 enables addressing.

On the VGA Adapter, the Video Subsystem Enable register does not exist. Instead, bit 3 of the control register at I/O port 46E8H enables and disables addressing: Writing a default value of 0EH to this port enables addressing; writing a value of 6 disables addressing.

In all VGA subsystems, however, INT 10H function 12H provides the same interface as it does on the MCGA (see Listing 2-5). Because of the hardware differences between the MCGA, the integrated VGA and the VGA Adapter, it is easier to use INT 10H function 12H to enable or disable addressing in the PS/2 video subsystems (see Listing 2-5).

3

Alphanumeric Modes

Using Alphanumeric Modes
BIOS and Operating-System Support
Speed ● Compatibility

Representation of Alphanumeric Data

Attributes
MDA ● HGC ● CGA ● EGA
InColor Card ● MCGA ● VGA

Gray-Scale Summing

Border Color
CGA ● EGA and VGA

Avoiding CGA Snow
Blanking the Display
Using the Vertical Blanking Interval
Using the Horizontal Blanking Interval

Using All the Video Buffer
CGA Video Pages
EGA, MCGA, and VGA Video Pages

Cursor Control
Cursor Size on the MDA and CGA
Cursor Location on the MDA and CGA
MCGA Cursor Control ● EGA and VGA Cursor Control
ROM BIOS Cursor Emulation
An Invisible Cursor

All IBM PC and PS/2 video subsystems except the MDA can be programmed to display characters in either alphanumeric or graphics modes. This chapter discusses what you need to know to use alphanumeric modes—the advantages and disadvantages of programming in alphanumeric modes; the basics of colors, blinking, and other character display attributes; and special techniques that exploit the capabilities of the hardware to improve the on-screen appearance and performance of your programs.

Using Alphanumeric Modes

The video BIOS on all IBM PCs and PS/2s always selects an alphanumeric video display mode when you boot the computer. In the IBM PC family, switches on the motherboard, the video adapter, or both determine whether a 40-column or 80-column mode is selected and whether a color or monochrome display is used. In the PS/2 series, the initial video mode is always an 80-column alphanumeric mode. Furthermore, the video mode set by the ROM BIOS is the one the operating system initially uses. Until you run a program that changes the video mode, all video output appears in the default mode—which is alphanumeric.

For this reason, the simplest way to write a program is to assume that it runs in an alphanumeric mode and to program the video interface accordingly. This assumption minimizes the coding required to send output to the screen. Not only are alphanumeric video output routines simpler than equivalent routines for graphics modes, but in most cases the ROM BIOS or the operating system provides character output routines that can be used in any alphanumeric mode.

BIOS and Operating-System Support

In the IBM PC, operating-system output routines are usually based on the set of primitive routines in the ROM BIOS that are called with software interrupt 10H. You can send characters to the video display either by using operating-system calls or by calling the INT 10H routines directly. In either case, use of these routines obviates the need for writing your own character output routines.

An additional advantage to using BIOS or operating-system character output functions is that programs using only such functions are more likely to run on different video hardware. For example, a program using only MS-DOS function calls for video output will run in almost any MS-DOS environment, regardless of the video hardware, including (but not limited to) the entire IBM PC and PS/2 family.

Of course, routing video output through an operating system is relatively slow compared with writing directly to the hardware. The use of operating-system character output routines introduces a certain amount of unavoidable overhead, particularly when such features as input/output redirection and multiprocessing are supported. Nevertheless, this overhead may be acceptable in many applications. You should always consider whether the extra programming and decreased portability required to improve video output performance are worthwhile in your application.

Speed

This is not to say that alphanumeric video output is inherently slow. When compared with character output in graphics modes, alphanumeric output is significantly faster, simply because much less data must be stored in the video buffer to display characters. In alphanumeric modes, each character is represented by a single 16-bit word; the video hardware takes care of displaying the pixels that make up the character. In graphics modes, every pixel in every character is represented explicitly in a bit field in the video buffer. For this reason, graphics-mode output is much more costly than equivalent character output in alphanumeric modes, both in terms of display memory used and processing required.

For example, in a 16-color graphics mode, each character drawn on the screen in an 8-by-8 dot matrix is represented by 32 bytes of data in the video buffer ($8 \times 8 \times 4$ bits per pixel). The memory overhead increases rapidly, in direct relationship to increasing resolution and the addition of more colors, as does the amount of time the CPU spends in manipulating data in the video buffer. On newer video adapters, dedicated graphics coprocessors such as the Intel 82786 or the TI 34010 may assume much of the computational burden of graphics-mode text display, thereby improving the speed of graphics-mode text output. Without a coprocessor, however, output in graphics modes is much slower than in alphanumeric modes.

Compatibility

Writing a program that is compatible with different IBM video subsystems is easier if you use only alphanumeric video display modes. The reason is simple: All commonly used IBM video subsystems support an 80-column by 25-row alphanumeric mode with the same video buffer format. If you design your video interface with an 80-by-25 alphanumeric display in mind, your program will run on a majority of PCs and compatibles with little or no modification.

Unfortunately, high compatibility is generally achieved only by sacrificing speed. Fast video output routines usually take advantage of hardware idiosyncrasies, so they are less likely to be portable to different video hardware than routines that rely on slower but more universal BIOS or operating-system calls. This trade-off will be implicit in almost every video output routine you write.

Representation of Alphanumeric Data

All IBM PC and PS/2 video subsystems use the same format for storing alphanumeric data in the video buffer. Each character is represented by a simple 2-byte data structure (see Figure 3-1). Characters are stored in the buffer in a linear sequence that maps across and down the screen (see Figure 3-2).

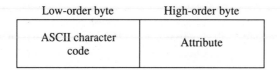

Figure 3-1. *Alphanumeric character and attribute mapping in a 16-bit word.*

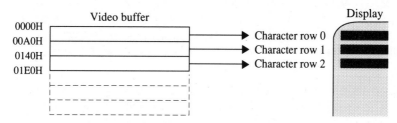

Figure 3-2. *Video buffer map in 80-by-25 alphanumeric modes.*

A hardware character generator converts each character code into the proper dot pattern on the display. At the same time, attribute decoder circuitry generates the appropriate attribute—color, intensity (brightness), blinking, and so on—for each character. Since each character code in the video buffer is accompanied by an attribute byte, you can independently control the displayed attributes of each character on the screen.

The hardware character generator displays each alphanumeric character within a rectangular matrix of pixels. Within this character matrix, the character itself is composed of a set of foreground pixels. The colors of the character's foreground and background pixels are specified by the low and high nibbles of the corresponding attribute byte.

To display a character, you store its ASCII code and attribute in the proper location in the video buffer. Because of the linear mapping scheme, you can easily calculate the buffer address of a particular screen location. The general formula is

```
offset = ((row × width) + column) × 2
```

In this formula, *width* is the number of characters in each row. The factor of 2 is included because each character requires 2 bytes (one 16-bit word) of storage in the video buffer. The values for *row* and *column* are zero-based, starting in the upper left corner of the screen. (The character in the upper left corner is located at row 0, column 0.)

If you examine the contents of the video buffer, you can see how this data corresponds to characters on the screen (see Figure 3-3). Note how each character code is followed by its attribute byte. (All of the attribute bytes in the portion of the video buffer shown in Figure 3-3 have the value 07H.)

```
                0  1  2  3  4  5  6  7  8  9  A  B  C  D  E  F   0123456789ABCDEF
B000:0000      43 07 68 07 61 07 72 07 61 07 63 07 74 07 65 07   C.h.a.r.a.c.t.e.
B000:0010      72 07 20 07 72 07 6F 07 77 07 20 07 30 07 30 07   r. .r.o.w. .0.0.
B000:0020      00 07 00 07 00 07 00 07 00 07 00 07 00 07 00 07   ................
B000:0030      00 07 00 07 00 07 00 07 00 07 00 07 00 07 00 07   ................
B000:0040      00 07 00 07 00 07 00 07 00 07 00 07 00 07 00 07   ................
B000:0050      00 07 00 07 00 07 00 07 00 07 00 07 00 07 00 07   ................
B000:0060      00 07 00 07 00 07 00 07 00 07 00 07 00 07 00 07   ................
B000:0070      00 07 00 07 00 07 00 07 00 07 00 07 00 07 00 07   ................
B000:0080      00 07 00 07 00 07 00 07 00 07 00 07 00 07 00 07   ................
B000:0090      00 07 00 07 00 07 00 07 00 07 00 07 00 07 00 07   ................
B000:00A0      43 07 68 07 61 07 72 07 61 07 63 07 74 07 65 07   C.h.a.r.a.c.t.e.
B000:00B0      72 07 20 07 72 07 6F 07 77 07 20 07 30 07 31 07   r. .r.o.w. .0.1.
B000:00C0      00 07 00 07 00 07 00 07 00 07 00 07 00 07 00 07   ................
B000:00D0      00 07 00 07 00 07 00 07 00 07 00 07 00 07 00 07   ................
B000:00E0      00 07 00 07 00 07 00 07 00 07 00 07 00 07 00 07   ................
B000:00F0      00 07 00 07 00 07 00 07 00 07 00 07 00 07 00 07   ................
B000:0100      00 07 00 07 00 07 00 07 00 07 00 07 00 07 00 07   ................
B000:0110      00 07 00 07 00 07 00 07 00 07 00 07 00 07 00 07   ................
B000:0120      00 07 00 07 00 07 00 07 00 07 00 07 00 07 00 07   ................
B000:0130      00 07 00 07 00 07 00 07 00 07 00 07 00 07 00 07   ................
```

Figure 3-3. *Hexadecimal dump of an alphanumeric video buffer.*

Attributes

Although all IBM PC and PS/2 video subsystems use the same pattern of alternating character codes and attribute bytes to represent alphanumeric data, the way the attribute byte is interpreted varies. In general, the attribute byte is formatted as two 4-bit nibbles. The low-order nibble (bits 0 through 3) determines the character's foreground attribute; that is, the color and intensity of the character itself. The high-order nibble (bits 4 through 7) indicates the character's background attribute, although bit 7 may also control blinking in some situations.

The 4-bit foreground and background attributes are ultimately decoded into a set of signals that drive the video monitor. In the simplest case, on the CGA, the four bits correspond directly to the three color signals and the intensity signal. The decoding scheme on other video subsystems can be complex, as on the EGA, MCGA, VGA, and InColor Card, or comparatively simple, as on the MDA.

MDA

Although you may specify any of 16 (2^4) attributes for both foreground and background attributes, the MDA only recognizes certain combinations (see Figure 3-4). Nevertheless, you can generate a useful variety of character attributes by creatively combining intensity, blinking, and underlining. You can also exchange the usual foreground and background attributes to obtain "reverse video"—black characters on a normal-intensity background.

		Foreground		
	Black	Dim*	Normal Intensity	High Intensity
Background				
Black	00	**	07	0F
Dim*	**	88	87	8F
Normal	70	78	**	**
High	F0	F8	**	**

* = not displayed by all monitors
** = not available

Underlined

	Foreground	
	Normal Intensity	High Intensity
Background		
Black	01	09
Dim*	81	89

* = not displayed by all monitors

Figure 3-4. *MDA foreground-background attribute combinations (values in hex). Attribute values not in this table always map to one of the combinations shown.*

On the MDA, as well as on all other IBM video hardware, bit 7 of each character's attribute byte can serve two purposes. By default, this bit controls whether a character blinks when displayed; setting the bit to 1 causes the associated character to blink. Bit 7 controls blinking because bit 5 (the Enable Blink bit) of the MDA's CRT Mode Control register (3B8H) is set to 1 by the video BIOS when the computer is powered up.

If the Enable Blink bit is 0, however, bit 7 of the attribute byte no longer controls blinking (see Listing 3-1). Instead, bit 7 is interpreted as an intensity bit for the background attribute. When bit 7 is set in a character's attribute byte, the character's background attribute is intensified; that is, normal green becomes intense green and black becomes dim green. Thus, to obtain all possible combinations of monochrome attributes listed in Figure 3-4, you must zero the Enable Blink bit.

```
        mov     ax,40h
        mov     es,ax               ; ES := video BIOS data segment
        mov     dx,es:[63h]         ; DX := 3B4h (MDA) or
                                    ;   3D4h (CGA) from ADDR_6845
        add     dl,4                ; DX := 3x8h (CRT Mode Control reg)
        mov     al,es:[65h]         ; AL := current value of reg (CRT_MODE_SET)
        and     al,11011111b        ; zero bit 5
        out     dx,al               ; update the register
        mov     es:[65h],al         ; update the BIOS data area
```

Listing 3-1. *Resetting the Enable Blink bit on the MDA or CGA.*

The value of the Mode Control register's Enable Blink bit affects the interpretation of bit 7 of all attribute bytes, so you can't display both blinking characters and characters with intensified background at the same time. You must decide which attribute is more useful in your program and set the Enable Blink bit accordingly.

All IBM PC and PS/2 video subsystems, including the MDA, blink alphanumeric characters by substituting the background attribute for the foreground attribute about twice a second. The effect is that each blinking character alternates with a blank character.

If you fill the display with blinking characters, the overall effect can be disconcerting, because the screen is blanked and restored twice each second. But if your purpose is to attract attention to the display, using the blink attribute can be very effective.

 If you use the underline attribute (foreground attribute 1 or 9) on a Compaq portable, you won't see underlined characters. This is because the Compaq portable decodes attribute values into 16 progressively brighter shades of green; the underline attribute values of 1 and 9 therefore appear as shades of green.

 Surprisingly, a few IBM MDAs generate color as well as monochrome output. Of course, the MDA's green monochrome display uses only two signals to control attributes (video on/off and intensity on/off); it ignores any color video signals. However, a color display that can use the MDA's 16.257 MHz horizontal sync and 50 Hz vertical sync signals will display eight colors (with and without intensity) when attached to some (but not all) MDAs. Unfortunately, you can never be certain which MDA will turn out to be a color adapter in disguise.

HGC

The HGC and HGC+ exactly emulate the MDA's monochrome alphanumeric mode. Programs written for the MDA run unchanged on either of these adapters.

CGA

The CGA uses the same foreground-background attribute scheme as does the MDA. However, the CGA's attribute decoder circuitry recognizes all 16 possible combinations of the four bits in each nibble of the attribute byte. For each character on the screen, you can independently specify any of 16 colors for foreground and background.

The available colors are simple combinations of the primary colors red, green, and blue. Each bit in each nibble of the attribute byte corresponds to a signal that the CGA supplies to the video monitor (see Figure 3-5). The low-order three bits

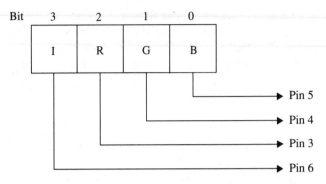

Figure 3-5. *CGA attributes and monitor color drive signals. Pin numbers refer to the CGA's 9-pin connector.*

of each nibble correspond to the red (R), green (G), and blue (B) signals. The eight possible combinations produce a gamut of red, green, blue, and their intermediate colors (see Figure 3-6).

Color	Binary (IRGB)	Hexadecimal
Black	0000	00
Blue	0001	01
Green	0010	02
Cyan	0011	03
Red	0100	04
Violet	0101	05
Yellow (brown)	0110	06
White	0111	07
Black (gray)	1000	08
Intense blue	1001	09
Intense green	1010	0A
Intense cyan	1011	0B
Intense red	1100	0C
Intense violet	1101	0D
Intense yellow	1110	0E
Intense white	1111	0F

Figure 3-6. *CGA display attributes.*

Setting bit 3 of the attribute byte (the intensity bit in the foreground nibble) displays the color designated in the R, G, and B bits (bits 0 through 2) with higher intensity. However, as on the MDA, the high-order bit (bit 7) of each attribute byte controls either background intensity or blinking. Again, the attribute displayed depends upon the state of a bit in a control register.

Bit 5 of the CGA's Mode Control register (I/O port 3D8H) is an Enable Blink bit analogous to bit 5 of the MDA's CRT Control register. When you set the Enable Blink bit to 0, bit 7 of a character's attribute byte signifies that the background color specified in bits 4 through 6 should be intensified. When you set the Enable Blink bit to 1, only nonintensified background colors are displayed, but characters whose attribute bytes have bit 7 set to 1 will blink.

The Enable Blink bit is set to 1 whenever you call the ROM BIOS to select an alphanumeric video mode. By default, therefore, bit 7 of each character's attribute byte controls blinking rather than background intensity. You must reset the Enable Blink bit to display characters with intensified background colors.

Many CGA-compatible displays squeeze a bit more out of the 16 available colors (8 nonintensified, 8 intensified) by displaying low-intensity yellow as brown and high-intensity black as gray. Unfortunately, a program cannot determine whether a particular display can do this. Be careful about displaying, for example, gray characters on a black background with a CGA, because such color combinations are invisible on some color displays.

EGA

In 16-color alphanumeric modes, the EGA uses the same attribute byte format as the CGA. However, the 4-bit foreground and background values do not correspond directly to the colors displayed. Instead, each 4-bit value is masked with the four low-order bits of the Attribute Controller's Color Plane Enable register (12H); the resulting 4-bit value designates one of the EGA's 16 palette registers (see Figure 3-7). Each bit of the 6-bit color value contained in the designated palette register corresponds to one of the six RGB signals that drive the monitor (see Figure 3-8).

An EGA-compatible color monitor is driven by six color signals—three primary (higher intensity) and three secondary (lower intensity). All 64 combinations of these six signals appear as different colors and/or intensities. With a 200-line color monitor—or in 200-line modes on an EGA-compatible monitor—bits 0, 1, and 2 control the color signals, while bit 4 controls the intensity signal.

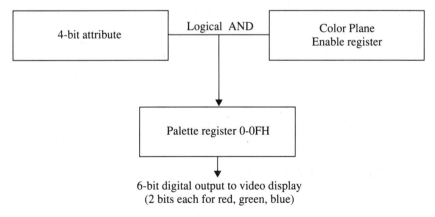

Figure 3-7. *Attributes and colors on the EGA.*

200-line monitors (CGA-compatible):

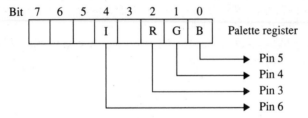

350-line color monitors (EGA-compatible):

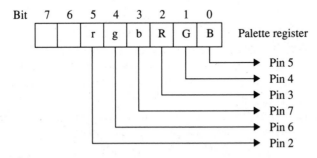

350-line monochrome monitors (MDA-compatible):

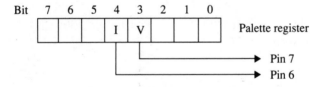

R,G,B = primary red, green, blue (higher intensity)
r,g,b = secondary red, green, blue (lower intensity)
I = intensity
V = monochrome video

Figure 3-8. *EGA palette register values and corresponding monitor color drive signals. Pin numbers refer to the EGA's 9-pin connector.*

The EGA's method of generating colors indirectly through palette registers is more complex than the CGA's direct scheme, but the EGA is more flexible. You can select the foreground and background colors for each character individually, yet you can produce global color changes by updating the value in a particular palette register.

The high-order bit of each character's attribute byte can control either blinking or background intensity, just as on the MDA and the CGA. Bit 3 of the EGA's Attribute Controller Mode Control register (register 10H at I/O port 3C0H) is the Enable Blink bit. Setting it to 1 enables blinking, so only the low-order 3 bits of the background nibble (bits 4 through 6 of the attribute byte) designate palette registers. Thus, when blinking is enabled, you can reference only the first eight palette registers to select the background color for a character. Setting the Enable Blink bit to 0 disables blinking, making all 16 palette registers available for background colors (see Listing 3-2).

```
mov     bl,0              ; BL := value for Enable Blink bit
mov     ax,1003h          ; AH := INT 10H function number
                          ; AL := subfunction number
int     10h
```

Listing 3-2. *Setting and resetting the Enable Blink bit on the MCGA, EGA, or VGA.*

When you select an alphanumeric video mode using the EGA BIOS, the palette registers are loaded with default values that correspond to the colors available on the CGA. The color values in the second eight palette registers are intensified versions of those in the first eight. Thus, if you simply treat bit 7 of the attribute byte as a "background intensity or blink" bit, your program will run on both an EGA and a CGA.

You can update the contents of any palette register either directly or with INT 10H function 10H (see Listing 3-3). Using the BIOS routine is more convenient and avoids the need to write hardware-dependent code. Moreover, the BIOS routine

```
; updating a palette register directly:

        mov     ax,40h
        mov     es,ax             ; ES := video BIOS data segment
        mov     dx,es:[63h]       ; DX := CRTC address reg (3x4h)
        add     dl,6              ; DX := Status reg (3xAh)
        push    dx                ; preserve this value
        cli
        in      al,dx             ; reset Attribute Controller address
                                  ;   flip-flop
        mov     dl,0C0h           ; DX := 3C0h
        mov     al,PaletteRegNumber
        out     dx,al             ; update one palette register
        mov     al,PaletteRegValue
        out     dx,al
        pop     dx                ; DX := Status register port
        in      al,dx             ; reset the flip-flop
        mov     dl,0C0h
        mov     al,20h
        out     dx,al             ; set bit 5 of
                                  ;   Attribute Controller address reg
        sti


; updating a palette register using the video BIOS

        mov     bl,PaletteRegNumber
        mov     bh,PaletteRegValue
        mov     ax,1000h          ; AH := INT 10H function number
                                  ; AL := subfunction number
        int     10h
```

Listing 3-3. *Palette register programming on the EGA or VGA.*

can also load all 16 palette registers at once, given a table of color values (see Appendix A). Nevertheless, you may still need to program the palette registers directly to produce very rapid color changes such as might be required in some types of animation.

In monochrome alphanumeric mode, the EGA emulates the MDA monochrome display attributes. The video BIOS initializes the palette registers with values that correspond to MDA attributes (see Figure 3-9). Bit 3 determines whether pixels are on or off, and bit 4 (if set in addition to bit 3) causes a higher-intensity display. The underline attribute is generated whenever a character's foreground attribute is 1 or 9, regardless of the value in the corresponding palette register.

Value	Attribute
0	Black
8	Normal intensity
10H	Dim
18H	High intensity

Figure 3-9. *Monochrome alphanumeric attribute values for the EGA palette registers.*

 The EGA also generates an underline attribute in 16-color alphanumeric modes when the foreground attribute is 1 or 9 and the background attribute is 0 or 8. However, you do not normally see an underline in 16-color modes because the video BIOS default value for the CRTC Underline Location register (14H) is 1FH. This value is greater than the number of scan lines normally displayed for alphanumeric characters, so the underline does not appear.

You can generate underlined characters in 16-color modes by storing a displayable value in the Underline Location register. Of course, only characters with attributes of 1, 9, 81H, or 89H will appear underlined, but you can change the values in the corresponding palette registers to produce underlined characters of any desired color.

InColor Card

The InColor Card can decode alphanumeric attributes in several different ways. The card has a set of 16 palette registers whose function is analogous to the EGA's Attribute Controller palette registers, but the InColor Card can be configured by your program to bypass the palette registers and decode each character's 4-bit foreground and background attributes in an MDA- or CGA-compatible manner. Bits 4 and 5 of the Exception register (17H) control how the InColor Card interprets alphanumeric attributes (see Figure 3-10). Bit 5 determines whether the InColor Card displays monochrome attributes (as on the MDA) or color attributes (as on the CGA or EGA). Bit 4 enables attribute mapping through the palette registers.

When the InColor Card is powered up, Exception register bit 5 has the value 1 and bit 4 has the value 0. Thus, by default, the card interprets attributes as an MDA would. However, if you set both bits 5 and 4 to 0 (see Listing 3-4), alphanumeric attributes specify the same set of 16 colors as on a CGA (refer to Figure 3-6).

```
mov     ax,0017h                ; AH bit 5 := 0 (disable
                                ;  monochrome attributes)
                                ; AH bit 4 := 0 (disable palette)
                                ; AH bits 0-3 := 0 (default cursor color)
                                ; AL := 17h (Exception Register number)
mov     dx,3B4h                 ; DX := I/O port
out     dx,ax
```

Listing 3-4. *InColor Exception register programming.*

Bit 5	Bit 4	Attribute Emulation
0	0	CGA
0	1	EGA
1	0	MDA
1	1	MDA mapped through palette registers.

Figure 3-10. *Exception register control of attributes on the Hercules InColor Card.*

Setting bit 4 to 1 causes attributes to map to the card's palette registers, regardless of the value of bit 5. Thus, if bit 4 is 1 and bit 5 is 0, the InColor Card interprets attributes as does the EGA. If bit 4 is 1 and bit 5 is 1, however, the card maps each character's foreground and background attributes only to the palette registers that correspond to valid monochrome attribute values. In this case, the "black," "dim," "normal intensity," and "high intensity" attributes select palette registers 00H, 08H, 07H, and 0FH respectively.

Bit 5 of the CRT Mode Control register at 3B8H is the Enable Blink bit. This bit controls background intensity regardless of the values of Exception register bits 4 and 5. However, characters are blinked only when Exception register bit 5 is 1 (MDA-compatible attributes); characters do not blink when bit 5 of the Exception register is 0 (CGA-compatible attributes), regardless of the Enable Blink bit's setting.

No video BIOS support is provided for the InColor Card's palette registers. Your program must therefore update the palette by directly storing values in the palette registers. Listing 3-5 is an example of how you might do this. The initial I/O read (IN AL,DX) of the Palette register (1CH) resets an internal index which points to the first of the 16 internal palette registers. Each subsequent I/O write (OUT DX,AL) updates one internal palette register and increments the internal index to point to the next palette register, so all 16 registers can be loaded by executing a simple loop.

TIP Because monochrome attributes can be mapped through palette registers, you can assign as many as four different colors to monochrome programs that run on the InColor Card. Do this by setting Exception register bits 4 and 5 to 1 and updating palette registers 00H, 08H, 07H, and 0FH with the desired colors.

```
        mov     dx,3B4h                 ; DX := CRTC address register
        mov     al,1Ch                  ; AL := 1Ch (Palette Register number)
        out     dx,al
        inc     dx                      ; DX := 3B5h
        in      al,dx                   ; reset palette register index

        mov     si,offset PaletteTable  ; DS:SI -> PaletteTable
        mov     cx,16                   ; CX := number of palette registers
L01:    lodsb                           ; AL := next byte from table
        out     dx,al                   ; update next palette reg
        loop    L01
        .
        .
        .

PaletteTable  db    00h,01h,02h,03h,04h,05h,06h,07h ; palette regs 0-7
              db    38h,39h,3Ah,3Bh,3Ch,3Dh,3Eh,3Fh ; palette regs 8-0Fh
```

Listing 3-5. *InColor palette register programming.*

On the InColor Card, the colors of both the cursor and the underscore are independent of the foreground colors of the characters in the video buffer. The cursor color is specified in bits 0 through 3 of the Exception register, and the underscore color value is specified in bits 4 through 7 of the Underscore register (CRTC register 15H). When the InColor Card is displaying MDA attributes (that is, when bit 5 of the Exception register is set to 1), you can specify only the three low-order bits of the cursor and underscore colors; the high-order bit of these color values is derived from the foreground attribute of the character where the cursor or underscore is displayed.

When palette mapping is enabled (Exception register bit 4 is set to 1), both the cursor and underscore color values select palette registers. When palette mapping is disabled, the cursor and underscore color values are displayed using the usual CGA colors. Also, if you specify a value of 0 for either the underscore color or the cursor color, the InColor Card uses the value 7 instead.

MCGA

The components of the PS/2 Model 30's video subsystem that transform attribute data into color video signals are the Video Formatter and the video Digital-to-Analog Converter (DAC). The Video Formatter gate array decodes attributes and generates an 8-bit digital output which is passed to the video DAC; from this, the DAC generates analog red, green, and blue signals for the video display. The DAC converts the 8-bit output from the Video Formatter to the three analog color signals by using the 8 bits to select one of the DAC's 256 color registers. Each DAC color register is 18 bits wide, comprising three 6-bit values for red, green, and blue (see Figure 3-12). The DAC converts each 6-bit value into an analog signal with the highest value (3FH) corresponding to the highest-intensity signal.

In alphanumeric modes, the four low-order bits of the Video Formatter's 8-bit digital output are derived from attribute bytes, while the four high-order bits are always 0 (see Figure 3-11). Thus, only the first 16 of the video DAC's color registers are used in MCGA alphanumeric modes. The remaining 240 registers can be accessed only in 320-by-200 256-color graphics mode (see Chapter 4). When an MCGA is attached to a color display, the video BIOS initializes the first 16 video DAC color registers with the same colors found on the CGA.

 The value in the video DAC Mask register (I/O port 3C6H) masks the 8-bit value passed to the video DAC. The Mask register value is set to 0FFH by the video BIOS initialization routines so that all 256 video DAC color registers can be accessed. IBM technical documentation recommends that this value not be modified.

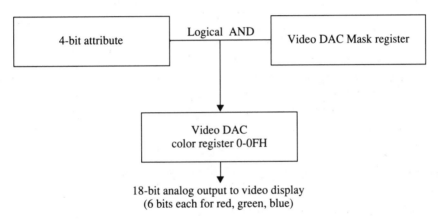

Figure 3-11. *Attributes and colors on the MCGA. (The value in the video DAC Mask register should normally be 0FFH.)*

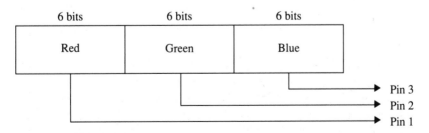

Figure 3-12. *Video DAC color register values and monitor color drive signals. Pin numbers refer to the MCGA's 15-pin connector.*

Unlike the EGA, an MCGA with a monochrome display does not emulate the
MDA's attributes. Instead, the 16 default video DAC color register values consist of
four groups of four shades of gray. Each group is displayed with higher intensity
than the preceding group. Within each group, the intensity increases from lower
to higher attribute values. Thus, attribute values 0 through 3 make up a range of
four shades of gray, values 4 through 7 a second range of somewhat higher intensity, and values 8 through 0BH and 0CH through 0FH a third and fourth range of
still higher intensity.

 Instead of this default MCGA monochrome gray-scale configuration,
you might prefer to use gray-scale values that increase uniformly with
increasing attribute values. The code in Listing 3-6 loads the video
DAC registers with appropriate values for this gray-scale gamut.

```
          mov     bx,0Fh                  ; BX := first video DAC
                                          ;   Color register number
          mov     di,offset VDACTable     ; DS:DI ->table

L01:      mov     dh,[bx+di]              ; DH := red value
          mov     ch,dh
          mov     cl,dh                   ; green and blue values are the same
          mov     ax,1010h                ; AH := INT 10h function number
                                          ; AL := subfunction number
          int     10h
          dec     bx
          jns     L01                     ; loop from register 0FH through register 0
            .
            .
            .
VDACTable  db      00h,05h,08h,0Bh,0Eh,11h,14h,18h
           db      1Ch,20h,24h,28h,2Dh,32h,38h,3Fh
```

Listing 3-6. *Loading an alternative MCGA monochrome gray-scale palette.*

VGA

In general, the VGA exactly emulates EGA alphanumeric attribute decoding. However, the VGA has both a video DAC and a set of 16 Attribute Controller palette
registers. Each palette register value selects one of 256 video DAC color registers.
The value in the selected video DAC color register determines the color displayed.

Depending on the value of bit 7 in the Attribute Controller's Mode Control register, you can use the palette register value to select a video DAC color register in
one of two ways. When bit 7 is set to 0, the Attribute Controller combines the 6-bit
palette-register value with bits 2 and 3 of its Color Select register (14H) to produce
an 8-bit value that selects a video DAC color register (see Figure 3-13). Alternatively, when bit 7 is set to 1, only the four low-order bits of each palette register
are meaningful. The Attribute Controller derives the other four bits of the 8-bit
value from bits 0 through 3 of the Color Select register (see Figure 3-14).

In the first case (when bit 7 of the Mode Control register is set to 0), the 6-bit palette registers are used to select one of four groups of 64 video DAC color registers, and bits 2 and 3 of the Color Select register determine which group of color registers is used. In the second case (when bit 7 of the Mode Control register is set to 1), each palette register value selects one of 16 groups of 16 video DAC color registers, and bits 0 through 3 of the Color Select register specify one of the 16 groups of DAC color registers.

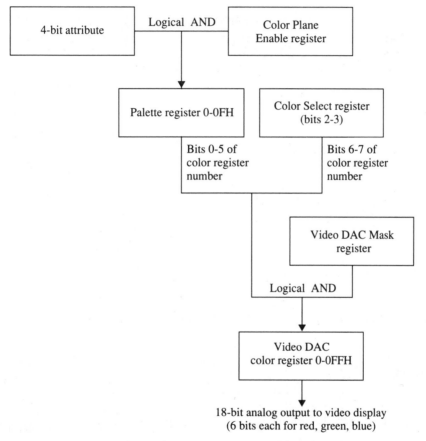

Figure 3-13. *Attributes and colors on the VGA (when bit 7 of the Attribute Controller's Mode Control register is set to 0).*

This added level of indirection, afforded by the combined use of palette registers and video DAC color registers, makes switching between palettes easy, since you can select any of 16 different 16-color palettes just by changing the value in the Attribute Controller's Color Select register. If you store 16 palettes of gradually increasing intensity in the DAC color registers, you can accentuate characters on the screen by cyclically increasing and decreasing their intensity. This effect is more subtle than simply blinking the characters on and off, particularly when applied to a large area of the display.

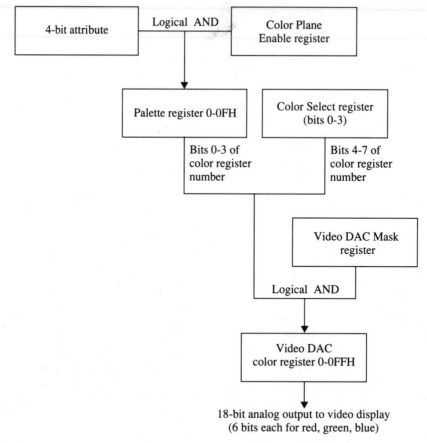

Figure 3-14. *Attributes and colors on the VGA (when bit 7 of the Attribute Controller's Mode Control register is set to 1).*

When the VGA emulates 80-by-25 16-color alphanumeric mode on a monochrome display, the palette consists of the same four groups of four gray-scaled values as does the corresponding palette on the MCGA. As on the MCGA, you can create a gray-scale palette with gradually increasing intensities. Listing 3-7 illustrates how you might do this. Note how the appropriate video DAC registers are selected by examining the values in the Attribute Controller's palette registers.

```
        mov     bx,0Fh                  ; BX := first Palette register number
        mov     di,offset VDACTable     ; DS:DI -> table

L01:    mov     dh,[bx+di]              ; DH := red value
        mov     ch,dh
        mov     cl,dh                   ; green and blue values are the same
```

Listing 3-7. *Loading an alternative VGA monochrome gray-scale palette.*   *(continued)*

Listing 3-7. *Continued.*

```
        push    bx                          ; preserve Palette register number
        mov     ax,1007h                    ; AH := INT 10h function number
                                            ; AL := subfunction number
                                            ;  (read Palette register)
        int     10h                         ; BH := Palette register value
        mov     bl,bh
        xor     bh,bh                       ; BX := desired video DAC
                                            ; Color register number

        mov     ax,1010h                    ; AH := INT 10h function number
                                            ; AL := subfunction number
        int     10h
        pop     bx
        dec     bx                          ; BX := next Palette register number
        jns     L01                         ; loop from Palette registers
                                            ;  0FH through 0
        .
        .
        .
VDACTable       db      00h,05h,08h,0Bh,0Eh,11h,14h,18h
                db      1Ch,20h,24h,28h,2Dh,32h,38h,3Fh
```

The VGA emulates the MDA's monochrome alphanumeric mode (video BIOS mode 7) on either a color or a monochrome display. The Attribute Controller palette register values and the control of blinking and underlining are the same as on the EGA. In this mode, the video DAC registers corresponding to the palette values 00H, 07H, 08H, and 18H are initialized with the appropriate gray-scale values. The palette and video DAC register values are the same in this mode regardless of whether a color or monochrome display is attached.

Gray-Scale Summing

Both the MCGA and the VGA BIOS contain logic which can transform the red-green-blue values in the video DAC registers into corresponding gray-scale values. This transformation is performed by taking a weighted average of the red, green, and blue components. To compute the gray-scaled equivalent value, the BIOS sums 30 percent of the red value, 59 percent of the green, and 11 percent of the blue. (These percentages approximate the displayed intensities of pure red, green, and blue.) For example, the default color for video DAC Color Register 02H (cyan) is made up of three 6-bit components. The value of the red component is 0, the green component 2AH, and the blue component 2AH. The gray-scale value is therefore 1DH, the sum of

```
(.30 × 0) + (.59 × 2AH) + (.11 × 2AH)
```

INT 10H function 10H includes a subfunction (AL = 1BH) that reads a set of video DAC color registers and updates them with equivalent gray-scale values. Appendix A contains an example of the use of this video BIOS function.

On both the MCGA and the VGA, INT 10H function 0 uses gray-scale summing by default when a monochrome display is attached. With a color display, gray-scale summing is disabled by default. You can selectively enable or disable default gray-scale summing by executing INT 10H function 12H with BL = 33H.

Border Color

On the CGA, EGA, MCGA, and VGA, you can specify a color to be displayed during the vertical and horizontal overscan intervals. This overscan or border color is not represented by any data in the video buffer. Instead, a special control register contains the value of the color displayed.

CGA

On the CGA, you select the border color with the four low-order bits of the Color Select register at I/O port 3D9H (see Listing 3-8). The color values parallel those available for character attributes: bits 0, 1, and 2 select the blue, green, and red primaries, and bit 3 is interpreted as an intensity bit.

```
; updating the CRT Color Register directly (CGA only)

        mov     ax,40h
        mov     es,ax                   ; ES := video BIOS data segment
        mov     dx,es:[63h]             ; DX := 3D4H (ADDR_6845)
        add     dl,5                    ; DX := 3D9H (CRT Color Select reg)
        mov     al,es:[66h]             ; AL := current value of reg (CRT_PALETTE)
        and     al,11110000b            ; zero bits 0-3
        or      al,BorderValue          ; update bits 0-3
        out     dx,al                   ; update the register
        mov     es:[66h],al             ; update the BIOS data area


; using the video BIOS interface (CGA, EGA, VGA)

        mov     bl,BorderValue
        mov     bh,0                    ; BH := subfunction number
        mov     ah,0Bh                  ; AH := INT 10h function number
        int     10h
```

Listing 3-8. *Setting a border color.*

Using INT 10H function 0BH to update the border color is probably more convenient than programming the Color Select register directly. The code is more portable, and the BIOS routine saves the most recently written value of the Color Select register in its Video Display Data Area in the byte at 0040:0066 (CRT_PALETTE). If you do write directly to the Color Select register, you should update CRT_PALETTE as in the example in Listing 3-8.

The MCGA does not generate a colored border, regardless of the value in its Color Select register.

EGA and VGA

On the EGA and VGA, the overscan color is specified by the contents of register 11H of the Attribute Controller (I/O port 3C0H). You could write directly to the I/O port, but doing the job with an INT 10H call is usually easier. You can use the EGA BIOS to update the overscan color in two ways. You can use function 0BH of INT 10H or you can include the border color as the 17th and last entry in the table of palette register colors you pass to INT 10H function 10H (see Appendix A).

On the VGA with a monochrome display, the only useful border attributes are 0 (black), 8 (normal), and 18H (intense).

The 350-line video modes on the EGA have relatively short vertical and horizontal overscan intervals. The displayed border may be only 1 or 2 mm wide, or it may bleed across the screen during the horizontal retrace interval. For this reason you should avoid setting the border color in any 350-line mode on the EGA.

You can increase the EGA's horizontal and vertical overscan intervals in 350-line modes by modifying the CRTC horizontal and vertical timing parameters. A reasonable border, about as wide as that displayed with the VGA, can be achieved by adding one or two characters to the Horizontal Total value and eight or ten scan lines to the Vertical Total value. The corresponding timing values for the Horizontal and Vertical Retrace and Blanking registers must be adjusted accordingly (see Figure 3-15).

The problem with reprogramming the CRTC in this way is that the horizontal and vertical frequencies that drive the video display are somewhat lower than nominal. For example, with the CRTC values shown in Figure 3-15, the horizontal scan rate becomes 16.257 MHz ÷ (94 chars/line × 8/char), or 21.62 KHz, which is about 1 percent lower than the nominal horizontal scan frequency of 21.85 KHz. Similarly, the vertical scan rate becomes 21.62 KHz ÷ 374 lines, or 58 Hz, almost 4 percent lower than the usual 60 Hz frame rate. Still, these scan rates are usually within the tolerances of an EGA-compatible video display.

80-by-25 16-Color Alphanumeric Mode:

CRTC register	Function	Setting (default)
0	Horizontal Total	5CH (5BH)
2	Horizontal Blanking Start	54H (53H)
3	Horizontal Blanking End	3CH (37H)
4	Horizontal Retrace Start	52H (51H)
5	Horizontal Retrace End	5CH (5BH)
6	Vertical Total	76H (6CH)
10H	Vertical Retrace Start	64H (5EH)
11H	Vertical Retrace End	25H (2BH)
15H	Vertical Blank Start	64H (5EH)
16H	Vertical Blank End	11H (0AH)

640-by-350 16-Color Graphics Mode:

CRTC register	Function	Setting (default)
0	Horizontal Total	5CH (5BH)
2	Horizontal Blanking Start	53H (53H)
3	Horizontal Blanking End	3CH (37H)
4	Horizontal Retrace Start	53H (52H)
5	Horizontal Retrace End	00H (00H)
6	Vertical Total	76H (6CH)
10H	Vertical Retrace Start	64H (5EH)
11H	Vertical Retrace End	25H (2BH)
15H	Vertical Blank Start	64H (5EH)
16H	Vertical Blank End	11H (0AH)

Figure 3-15. *CRTC parameters for increased border width in 350-line EGA video modes. (Default register values are listed in parentheses.)*

Avoiding CGA Snow

On the CGA, alphanumeric video display modes present a particular programming challenge whenever you are concerned about the speed of video display output. You must program carefully in alphanumeric modes to prevent interference with the display when you read or write data in the CGA's video buffer.

Directly accessing the contents of the CGA's video buffer from your program has its pros and cons. On the positive side, it enables your program to completely control the buffer's contents, and thus what is displayed. The negative side is that when both the CPU and the display-refresh circuitry access the buffer at the same time, interference, or ''snow,'' can appear on the display. The snow can be barely noticeable or greatly distracting, depending on the amount of data transferred to or from the video buffer.

In general, to avoid snow you must limit CPU accesses to the video buffer to intervals when data is not being fetched from the buffer to refresh the screen. In practice, this means that your program must transfer data to and from the video buffer only when the electron beam in the video display is moving through an overscan or retrace interval.

This synchronization can be achieved in several ways, but, unfortunately, all of them introduce a certain amount of hardware dependency into your program. As a general rule, the more hardware-dependent tricks you play, the faster your program runs on a CGA but the less likely it is to run on another video adapter.

Blanking the Display

One technique for preventing display interference on the CGA is to turn off the electron beam whenever you access the display buffer. You then leave the beam off while data is transferred to or from the video buffer. This method is used in the ROM BIOS routines which scroll the display.

The best time to blank the display is when it's blank anyway, at the start of a vertical blanking interval. If you do not take care to turn the electron beam off during the vertical blanking interval, you will instead blank the screen while it is being refreshed. This can produce an annoying flicker or interference stripes.

The technique is straightforward (see Listing 3-9). The trick is to synchronize buffer access with the start of a vertical blanking interval. Do this by detecting an interval when vertical blanking is not occurring. Then wait for the next subsequent vertical blanking interval to begin.

```
                        TITLE    'Listing 3-9'
                        NAME     DisplayText
                        PAGE     55,132

;
; Name:         DisplayText
;
; Function:     Display an alphanumeric string without interference on the CGA
;
; Caller:       Microsoft C:
;
;                       int DisplayText1(buf,n,offset);
;
;                       char *buf;               /* buffer containing text in
;                                                   CGA alphanumeric format
;                                                   (alternating character codes
;                                                   and attribute bytes) */
;
;                       int n;                   /* buffer length in bytes */
;
;                       unsigned int offset;     /* offset into video buffer */
;

Set80X25        EQU     (1 SHL 0)        ; bit masks for Mode Control Register
Set320X200      EQU     (1 SHL 1)
BlackAndWhite   EQU     (1 SHL 2)
EnableVideo     EQU     (1 SHL 3)
Set640X200      EQU     (1 SHL 4)
EnableBlink     EQU     (1 SHL 5)
```

Listing 3-9. *Display alphanumeric text on the CGA by blanking the display.* (continued)

Listing 3-9. *Continued.*

```
ARGbuf          EQU     word ptr [bp+4] ; stack frame addressing
ARGn            EQU     word ptr [bp+6]
ARGoffset       EQU     word ptr [bp+8]
TIMEOUT         EQU     6               ; Horizontal timeout loop limit

_TEXT           SEGMENT byte public 'CODE'
                ASSUME  cs:_TEXT

                PUBLIC  _DisplayText
_DisplayText    PROC    near

                push    bp              ; usual C prologue to establish
                mov     bp,sp           ;  stack frame and preserve registers
                push    di
                push    si

                mov     ax,0B800h
                mov     es,ax
                mov     di,ARGoffset    ; ES:DI -> destination in video buffer
                mov     si,ARGbuf       ; DS:SI -> source buffer
                mov     bx,ARGn
                shr     bx,1            ; BX := buffer length in words

                mov     dx,3DAh         ; DX := CGA Status Port

; wait for start of vertical blanking interval

L01:            mov     cx,TIMEOUT      ; CX := loop counter (timeout value)

L02:            in      al,dx           ; AL := video status
                test    al,8
                jnz     L02             ; loop if vertical sync active
                test    al,1
                jz      L02             ; loop if Display Enable active

                cli                     ; disable interrupts

L03:            in      al,dx
                test    al,1
                loopnz  L03             ; loop until end of horizontal
                                        ;  blanking or timeout

                sti                     ; reenable interrupts

                jz      L01             ; loop if no timeout

; blank the display

                mov     dl,0D8h         ; DX := 3D8h (Mode Control register)
                mov     al,(Set80X25 OR EnableBlink)
                out     dx,al           ; turn video off

; copy the data to the video buffer

                mov     cx,bx           ; CX := buffer length in words
                rep     movsw
```

(continued)

Listing 3-9. *Continued.*

```
; reenable the display

                or      al,EnableVideo
                out     dx,al

                pop     si          ; usual C epilogue to restore registers
                pop     di          ;   and discard stack frame
                mov     sp,bp
                pop     bp
                ret

_DisplayText    ENDP

_TEXT           ENDS

                END
```

The procedure for detecting the start of a vertical blanking interval requires you to first determine a timeout value for the horizontal retrace interval (see Listing 2-2). This value is then used to wait for the last horizontal scan in the current frame. When the last horizontal blanking interval times out, the vertical blanking interval has begun.

At this point, your program should explicitly disable the electron beam by resetting bit 3 of the CGA's Mode Control register (port 3D8H). When this bit is zeroed, the electron beam is disabled and the display remains dark. While the display is dark, you can move data to or from the video buffer without causing snow. When the data transfer is complete, restore the display by setting bit 3 of the Mode Control register to 1.

It is not necessarily desirable to wait for another vertical blanking interval before reenabling the electron beam. If the period during which you transferred data left the screen dark long enough to cause noticeable flicker, waiting until the next vertical retrace will only prolong the duration of the flicker. If you reenable the display somewhere in the middle of a refresh cycle, the flicker will be worse in the top part of the screen but better in the bottom part. Neither situation is ideal; it's up to you to decide which alternative is preferable.

The amount of time it takes to access the video buffer determines how long your program must keep the screen dark. Obviously, the longer the screen is dark, the more flicker you perceive. If your program is executed on one of the slower members of the IBM PC family (PC or PC/XT), the flicker effect can become annoying.

Consider what might happen whenever you scroll an entire 80-by-25 screen up one line. Within the video buffer, 4000 bytes of data must be moved. On a vintage IBM PC, with its 4.77 MHz 8088, this data transfer takes about 21 milliseconds. Since each video frame lasts about 16.7 milliseconds ($\frac{1}{60}$ second), the screen remains dark for about $1\frac{1}{3}$ frames. The resulting flicker is very noticeable, particularly if the background color is not black. On the other hand, on a PC with a faster CPU, the data transfer takes less time, so the flicker is less apparent.

Using the Vertical Blanking Interval

A technique that avoids the flicker problem is to access the video buffer only for the duration of the vertical blanking interval. However, this slows data transfer, because you can move only a limited number of bytes of data during a single vertical blanking interval.

The limitations here are the duration of the vertical blanking interval (about 4 milliseconds) and the rate at which the CPU can move data in the video buffer. A 4.77 MHz 8088 in a PC or PC/XT can move about 450 words (900 bytes) of data before the vertical blanking interval ends and snow becomes visible. Obviously, a PC with a higher clock speed or with an 80286 or 80386 can move more data during a single vertical blanking interval.

Using the Horizontal Blanking Interval

If your video output routine synchronizes with the start of horizontal blanking intervals, you have about 7 microseconds in which to access the video buffer at the end of each raster scan line without causing snow (see Listing 3-10). Although 7 microseconds may not seem like much time, it is long enough to move 2 bytes into or out of the video buffer without causing display interference. Since each frame contains 200 horizontal blanking intervals, you can significantly increase performance by taking advantage of them.

```
                TITLE   'Listing 3-10'
                NAME    DisplayText
                PAGE    55,132

;
; Name:          DisplayText
;
; Function:      Display an alphanumeric string without interference on the CGA
;
; Caller:        Microsoft C:
;
;                       int DisplayText(buf,n,offset);
;
;                       char *buf;               /* buffer containing text in
;                                                   CGA alphanumeric format
;                                                   (alternating character codes
;                                                   and attribute bytes) */
;
;                       int n;                   /* buffer length in bytes */
;
;                       unsigned int offset;     /* offset into video buffer */
;
ARGbuf          EQU     word ptr [bp+4]
ARGn            EQU     word ptr [bp+6]
```

(continued)

Listing 3-10. *Display alphanumeric text on the CGA during horizontal and vertical blanking intervals.*

Listing 3-10. *Continued.*

```
ARGoffset       EQU     word ptr [bp+8]
TIMEOUT         EQU     6                 ; horizontal timeout loop limit
VBcount         EQU     250               ; number of words to write during
                                          ;  vertical blanking interval


_TEXT           SEGMENT byte public 'CODE'
                ASSUME  cs:_TEXT

                PUBLIC  _DisplayText
_DisplayText    PROC    near

                push    bp                ; usual C prologue to establish
                mov     bp,sp             ;  stack frame and preserve registers
                push    di
                push    si

                mov     ax,0B800h
                mov     es,ax
                mov     di,ARGoffset      ; ES:DI -> destination in video buffer
                mov     si,ARGbuf         ; DS:SI -> source buffer
                mov     cx,ARGn
                shr     cx,1              ; CX := buffer length in words

                mov     dx,3DAh           ; DX := CGA Status Port

; write during remaining vertical blanking interval

L01:            mov     bx,cx             ; preserve buffer length in BX
                mov     cx,TIMEOUT        ; CX := horizontal timeout
                cli                       ; disable interrupts during loop

L02:            in      al,dx             ; AL := video status
                test    al,1
                loopnz  L02               ; loop while Display Enable inactive
                jz      L03               ; jump if loop did not time out

                movsw                     ; copy one word
                sti
                mov     cx,bx             ; CX := buffer length
                loop    L01

                jmp     short L10         ; exit (entire string copied)

; write during horizontal blanking intervals

L03:            sti
                mov     cx,bx             ; restore CX

L04:            lodsw                     ; AL := character code
                                          ; AH := attribute
                mov     bx,ax             ; BX := character and attribute

                push    cx                ; preserve word loop counter
                mov     cx,TIMEOUT        ; CX := timeout loop limit

                cli                       ; clear interrupts during one scan line
```

(continued)

Listing 3-10. *Continued.*

```
L05:            in        al,dx
                test      al,1
                loopnz    L05             ; loop during horizontal blanking
                                          ;  until timeout occurs
                jnz       L07             ; jump if timed out (vertical
                                          ;  blanking has started)
L06:            in        al,dx
                test      al,1
                jz        L06             ; loop while Display Enable is active

                xchg      ax,bx           ; AX := character & attribute
                stosw                     ; copy 2 bytes to display buffer

                sti                       ; restore interrupts
                pop       cx              ; CX := word loop counter
                loop      L04

                jmp       short L10       ; exit (entire string copied)

; write during entire vertical blanking interval

L07:            pop       bx              ; BX := word loop counter
                dec       si
                dec       si              ; DS:SI -> word to copy from buffer

                mov       cx,VBcount      ; CX := # of words to copy
                cmp       bx,cx
                jnb       L08             ; jump if more than VBcount words remain
                                          ;  in buffer
                mov       cx,bx           ; CX := # of remaining words in buffer
                xor       bx,bx           ; BX := 0
                jmp       short L09

L08:            sub       bx,cx           ; BX := (# of remaining words) - VBcount

L09:            rep       movsw           ; copy to video buffer

                mov       cx,bx           ; CX := # of remaining words
                test      cx,cx
                jnz       L01             ; loop until buffer is displayed

L10:            pop       si              ; usual C epilogue to restore registers
                pop       di              ;  and discard stack frame
                mov       sp,bp
                pop       bp
                ret

_DisplayText    ENDP

_TEXT           ENDS

                END
```

Because the horizontal blanking interval is so short, synchronization is critical.
The technique is parallel to that used for synchronizing with the vertical retrace
interval. In this case, you determine the status of the Display Enable signal by
testing bit 0 of the CRT Status register (3DAH). When this bit has a value of 1, the
Display Enable signal is off and a horizontal blanking interval is in progress.

Keep in mind two considerations if you take the trouble to use the horizontal blanking intervals. First, you might as well use the vertical blanking intervals as well, since they're there. Second, you should use MOVS or STOS instructions to do the actual data transfers. The slower MOV mem/reg instruction can take longer than the horizontal blanking interval lasts, so snow isn't eliminated.

The IBM ROM BIOS routines that write to the video buffer during horizontal retrace use the sequence

```
mov     ax,bx
stosw
```

to move a character and attribute into the buffer without snow. Nevertheless, if you use the same two instructions in a RAM-based program, you see snow on a CGA running on a 4.77 MHz PC. The reason is that, at the point where these instructions are executed, the 4-byte instruction prefetch queue in the 8088 has room for only two more bytes. This means that the STOSW opcode cannot be prefetched. Instead, the 8088 must fetch the opcode from memory before it can be executed.

That last memory access to fetch the STOSW instruction makes the difference. Because accesses to ROM are faster than accesses to RAM, the instruction fetch is slightly faster out of ROM, so no snow is visible because the STOSW can run before the horizontal blanking interval ends. The routine in Listing 3-10 sidesteps the problem by using XCHG AX,BX (a 1-byte opcode) instead of MOV AX,BX (a 2-byte opcode). This avoids the extra instruction fetch, so the code executes fast enough to prevent display interference.

Note how the interrupts are disabled in the loop that waits for the start of the horizontal blanking interval. Had an interrupt occurred between the JNZ L06 and the following XCHG AX,BX instructions, the horizontal blanking interval would have ended long before control returned from the interrupt handler. Disabling interrupts while each word is transferred into the video buffer avoids this possible loss of synchronization.

The routine in Listing 3-10 never explicitly detects the end of the vertical blanking interval, nor does it count the 200 horizontal scans in each display refresh cycle. Instead, the number of bytes that can be transferred during each vertical blanking interval (VBcount) is determined empirically for a "worst case" situation (for example, for a 4.77 MHz IBM PC).

The most important reason for this imprecision about the number of bytes to transfer during vertical blanking intervals is that interrupts can occur anywhere in a video output routine except where they are explicitly disabled. For example, clock-tick interrupts and keyboard interrupts can occur at any time. Because you can't simply disable all interrupts for the duration, you must design video output routines to accommodate the unpredictable time spent in interrupt handlers.

The problem of snow is avoided in the hardware design of every other IBM PC and PS/2 video subsystem, including the MDA, EGA, MCGA, and VGA (and even the PCjr). Also, many second-source manufacturers of CGA-compatible adapters design their hardware to eliminate the problem. This means that retrace synchronization loops may not be needed in many applications.

If you run a program either on a CGA (with snow) or on a CGA-compatible (without snow), the program should try to determine what type of hardware it is running on (see Appendix C). If the program is running on a machine without snow, it can skip over any vertical and horizontal synchronization loops. The slight extra overhead of detecting the presence of a CGA is repaid in greatly improved performance on video subsystems that have no snow problem.

Using All the Video Buffer

In alphanumeric video modes, the CGA, EGA, MCGA, and VGA have much more RAM available in their video buffers than is required to display one screen of text. In other words, you can display only a portion of the data in the video buffer at a time. In effect, what you see on the screen is a "window" on the video buffer.

For example, in 80-by-25-character alphanumeric modes, only 4000 bytes (80 × 25 × 2 bytes per character) are displayed at any one time. However, the CGA has 16 KB of video RAM, so you can actually store four 80-by-25 screens of data in the buffer. You can then program the CGA's CRT Controller to display any 2000 consecutive characters (4000 bytes) in the buffer.

CGA Video Pages

To program the CGA to display different portions of the buffer, you update two CRT Controller registers. When you call the ROM BIOS to select a video display mode, the BIOS initializes the CRTC to display the first 4000 bytes of the video buffer. It does this by storing 0, the offset of the first character to be displayed, in the CRTC Start Address registers (0CH and 0DH).

You can display any arbitrary portion of the CGA's video buffer by storing a video buffer offset in words (not bytes) in the CRTC Start Address registers. The high-order byte of the offset belongs in register 0CH, the low-order byte in register 0DH. For example, loading the Start Address registers with the word offset of the second row (50H) causes the display to begin there (see Listing 3-11).

Loading the Start Address registers is a much faster operation than transferring characters into the video buffer. Thus, you might regard the 16 KB video buffer as a 102-line "virtual" screen of which only 25 lines can be displayed at a time. When the video buffer is filled with text, you can rapidly display any 25 consecutive lines simply by changing the value in the CRTC Start Address registers.

```
        mov     ax,40h
        mov     es,ax                   ; ES := video BIOS data segment
        mov     dx,es:[63h]             ; DX := ADDR_6845

        mov     al,0Ch                  ; AL := reg number (Start Address High)
        out     dx,al
        inc     dx                      ; DX := 3x5h
        mov     al,HiByte               ; AL := high-order byte of start offset
        out     dx,al
        dec     dx                      ; DX := 3x4h

        mov     al,0Dh                  ; AL := reg number (Start Address Low)
        out     dx,al
        inc     dx                      ; DX := 3x5h
        mov     al,LoByte               ; AL := low-order byte of start offset
        out     dx,al
        mov     ah,HiByte               ; AX := start offset in words

        shl     ax,1                    ; AX := offset in bytes
        mov     es:[4Eh],ax             ; update CRT_START
```

Listing 3-11. *Setting the CRTC Start Address registers.*

Whenever you update the Start Address registers, also update the BIOS Video Display Data Area word at 0040:004E (CRT_START). This helps to maintain functionality across video BIOS calls and with MS-DOS.

Instead of deciding for yourself which portions of the video buffer to display, you might find it more convenient to adopt the conceptual model of the ROM BIOS, which supports four 80-by-25 (or eight 40-by-25) virtual "pages" in the CGA's video buffer. To simplify addressing, each page starts on a 1 KB (1024-byte) boundary. The four 80-by-25 pages thus start at B800:0000, B800:1000, B800:2000, and B800:3000. You can selectively display any video page by calling INT 10H function 05H (see Listing 3-12).

```
        mov     al,Vpage                ; AL := video page number
        mov     ah,5                    ; AH := INT 10h function number
        int     10h
```

Listing 3-12. *Video page selection using the ROM BIOS.*

A technique that can improve CGA performance is to display one video page while you fill another (nondisplayed) video page with data. Then you display the newly filled video page and make the previous page available for more data transfers. Design your user interface so that while the user reads the display, a nondisplayed video page is filled with the next screen of information. Careful use of the video pages can make screen updates appear "instantaneous."

You must still avoid display interference by using one of the techniques for synchronizing the update with vertical or horizontal blanking intervals, even if you write to a nondisplayed portion of the buffer.

EGA, MCGA, and VGA Video Pages

With the EGA, MCGA, and VGA, the techniques for using video RAM are similar to those used on the CGA. The Start Address registers in the CRT Controller are mapped to the same I/O port addresses as they are on the CGA's CRTC. Furthermore, the video BIOS supports video pages with the same interface used for the CGA. This simplifies writing a program to run on all of these video subsystems.

 One handy feature of the CRTC on the EGA, the MCGA, the VGA, and some but not all CGA look-alikes is that the Start Address registers can be read as well as written. This feature can be useful in programming these registers directly, because you can determine their contents at any time simply by inspecting them.

Cursor Control

The CRT Controller also controls the size and screen location of the hardware cursor in alphanumeric modes. You specify the cursor's size by loading a CRTC register with values that indicate its top and bottom lines. The top line is 0; the value for the bottom line depends on the size of the displayed character matrix—7 for an 8-by-8 matrix and 0DH for a 9-by-14 matrix. The cursor's location is specified with a word offset into the video buffer, exactly as you specify the CRT Controller's start address.

Cursor Size on the MDA and CGA

CRTC registers 0AH and 0BH control the cursor size on all IBM PC and PS/2 video subsystems. On the MDA and the CGA, the low-order five bits of register 0AH (Cursor Start) indicate the top line of the displayed cursor. The low-order five bits of register 0BH (Cursor End) specify the bottom line.

Changing the size of the hardware cursor is a matter of programming these two registers. For example, to display a "block" cursor, which is a rectangle filling an entire character space, set the Cursor Start register to 0 and the Cursor End register to one less than the height of the character matrix. To display the ROM BIOS's default cursor, set the Cursor Start and Cursor End registers to the values for the last two lines of the character matrix, as is done in Listing 3-13.

In most applications, however, you can use INT 10H function 1 (Set Cursor Type) to change the cursor's size. Using this function ensures compatibility with the video BIOS on all IBM PC and PS/2 video subsystems. Although performing the software interrupt and executing the BIOS routine is slower than programming the CRTC directly, in general you modify the cursor size so infrequently that you'll never notice the slight slowing of your program.

Also, the BIOS routine maintains the current cursor size in two bytes in the Video Display Data Area at 0040:0060 (CURSOR_MODE). On the MDA and CGA, the CRTC's Cursor Start and Cursor End registers are read-only registers, so you might as well use the BIOS to keep track of the current state of the cursor. The byte at 0040:0060 represents the value in 6845 register 0AH (Cursor Start), and the following byte, at 0040:0061, represents register 0BH (Cursor End). If you do bypass the BIOS routine and program the 6845 directly, keep the values in CURSOR_MODE up to date.

```
; updating the CRTC registers directly

        mov     ax,40h
        mov     es,ax               ; ES := video BIOS data segment
        mov     dx,es:[63h]         ; DX := ADDR_6845

        mov     al,0Ah              ; AL := reg number (Cursor Start)
        out     dx,al
        inc     dx                  ; DX := 3x5h
        mov     al,TopLine          ; AL := top scan line for cursor
        out     dx,al
        dec     dx                  ; DX := 3x4h

        mov     al,0Bh              ; AL := reg number (Cursor End)
        out     dx,al
        inc     dx                  ; DX := 3x5h
        mov     al,BottomLine       ; AL := bottom scan line for cursor
        out     dx,al

        mov     ah,TopLine          ; AX := top and bottom lines
        mov     es:[60h],ax         ; update CURSOR_MODE


; using the video BIOS interface

        mov     ch,TopLine
        mov     cl,BottomLine
        mov     ah,1                ; AH := INT 10h function number
        int     10h
```

Listing 3-13. *Setting the cursor size.*

Cursor Location on the MDA and CGA

To control the cursor's location, load a buffer offset into the CRTC's Cursor Location High (0EH) and Cursor Location Low (0FH) registers (see Listing 3-14). The Cursor Location offset is relative to the start of the video buffer. If you have changed the CRTC Start Address registers, you must adjust for the new Start Address offset in calculating the Cursor Location offset.

```
; updating the CRTC registers directly

        mov     ax,40h
        mov     es,ax               ; ES := video BIOS data segment
        mov     dx,es:[63h]         ; DX := ADDR_6845

        mov     al,0Eh              ; AL := reg number (Cursor Location High)
        out     dx,al
        inc     dx                  ; DX := 3x5h
        mov     al,HiByte           ; AL := high-order byte of cursor offset
        out     dx,al
        dec     dx                  ; DX := 3x4h

        mov     al,0Fh              ; AL := reg number (Cursor Location Low)
        out     dx,al
        inc     dx                  ; DX := 3x5h
        mov     al,LoByte           ; AL := low-order byte of cursor offset
        out     dx,al


; using the video BIOS interface

        mov     dh,CursorRow
        mov     dl,CursorColumn
        mov     bh,VideoPage
        mov     ah,2                ; AH := INT 10h function number
        int     10h
```

Listing 3-14. *Setting the cursor location.*

MCGA Cursor Control

The MCGA's CRTC doubles the values you store in the Cursor Start and Cursor End registers and doubles the number of scan lines in the displayed cursor. Thus, the size of the MCGA's alphanumeric cursor is a multiple of two scan lines.

This doubling of the Cursor Start and Cursor End values allows you to specify default alphanumeric cursor sizes with the same values you would use on a CGA. For example, in the MCGA's default alphanumeric modes, the character matrix is 16 lines high. If you set Cursor Start to 6 and Cursor End to 7, as you would in a CGA alphanumeric mode, you see the MCGA's cursor at the bottom of the character matrix in lines 0CH through 0FH. In this way the MCGA's Cursor Start and End registers emulate the CGA's despite the MCGA's taller character matrix.

However, there are several differences in the way the MCGA interprets the Cursor Start and Cursor End values (see Figure 3-16). On the MCGA, only the four low-order bits of the Cursor Start and Cursor End values are significant. Furthermore, since the character matrix can be at most 16 scan lines high, Cursor Start and Cursor End values are usually limited to the range 0 through 7. Values greater than 7 can produce a cursor that wraps around to the top of the character matrix (see Figure 3-16e).

EGA and VGA Cursor Control

On the EGA and the VGA, the Cursor Start, Cursor End, Cursor Location High, and Cursor Location Low registers are mapped to the same CRTC register numbers as on the MDA and CGA. This can lead to trouble if you're concerned about portability and need to write to the CRTC registers directly. This is because the EGA and VGA Cursor Start and Cursor End registers do not function exactly as do those on the MDA, CGA, or MCGA.

On the EGA, the value you specify for the Cursor End register must be 1 greater than the bottom line of the cursor (see Figure 3-17). The EGA's CRT Controller displays the alphanumeric cursor from the character scan line specified in the Cursor Start register to the line specified by the Cursor End register minus 1.

If the Cursor End value is less than the Cursor Start value, the cursor wraps around the character matrix. If the low-order four bits of the Cursor Start and Cursor End values are equal, the cursor appears only on the single line specified in the Cursor Start register. Finally, the Cursor End value must be less than the number of scan lines in the character matrix. Otherwise, the CRT Controller displays a full-height cursor regardless of the Cursor Start register's value.

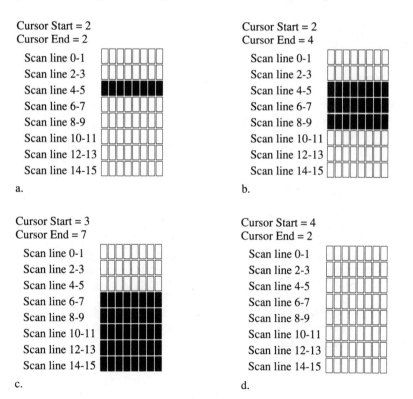

a.

b.

c.

d.

(continued)

Figure 3-16. *Sample MCGA alphanumeric cursor settings for an 8-by-16 character matrix.*

Figure 3-16. *Continued.*

Cursor Start = 3
Cursor End = 8

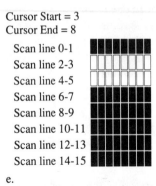

Scan line 0-1
Scan line 2-3
Scan line 4-5
Scan line 6-7
Scan line 8-9
Scan line 10-11
Scan line 12-13
Scan line 14-15

e.

The VGA's Cursor Start and Cursor End values (see Figure 3-18) work slightly differently than do the EGA's. The VGA's Cursor End value indicates the last line of the displayed cursor (not the last line plus 1), and the displayed cursor does not wrap around to the top of the character matrix if the Cursor End value is less than the Cursor Start value. (Compare Figures 3-17 and 3-18.)

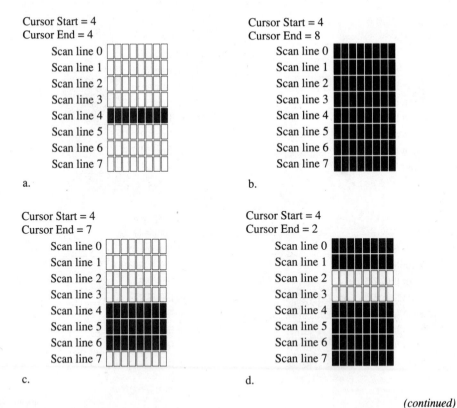

Cursor Start = 4
Cursor End = 4

Scan line 0
Scan line 1
Scan line 2
Scan line 3
Scan line 4
Scan line 5
Scan line 6
Scan line 7

a.

Cursor Start = 4
Cursor End = 8

Scan line 0
Scan line 1
Scan line 2
Scan line 3
Scan line 4
Scan line 5
Scan line 6
Scan line 7

b.

Cursor Start = 4
Cursor End = 7

Scan line 0
Scan line 1
Scan line 2
Scan line 3
Scan line 4
Scan line 5
Scan line 6
Scan line 7

c.

Cursor Start = 4
Cursor End = 2

Scan line 0
Scan line 1
Scan line 2
Scan line 3
Scan line 4
Scan line 5
Scan line 6
Scan line 7

d.

(continued)

Figure 3-17. *Sample EGA alphanumeric cursor settings for an 8-by-8 character matrix.*

Figure 3-17. *Continued.*

Cursor Start = 4
Cursor End = 0

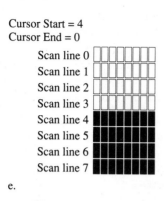

Scan line 0
Scan line 1
Scan line 2
Scan line 3
Scan line 4
Scan line 5
Scan line 6
Scan line 7

e.

> **TIP**
>
> Bits 5 and 6 of the Cursor End register (0BH) on the EGA and VGA control the rightward skew of the cursor. If bits 5 and 6 are not 0, the cursor appears one, two, or three characters to the right of the location that the Cursor Location registers specify. For most applications, the cursor skew should be 0.

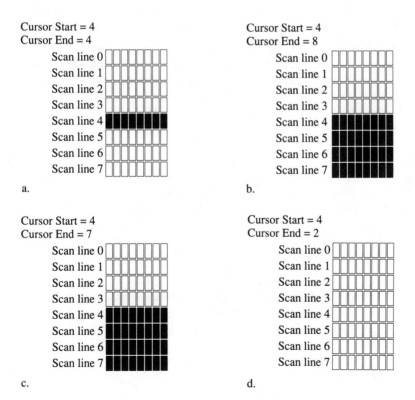

Cursor Start = 4
Cursor End = 4

Scan line 0
Scan line 1
Scan line 2
Scan line 3
Scan line 4
Scan line 5
Scan line 6
Scan line 7

a.

Cursor Start = 4
Cursor End = 8

Scan line 0
Scan line 1
Scan line 2
Scan line 3
Scan line 4
Scan line 5
Scan line 6
Scan line 7

b.

Cursor Start = 4
Cursor End = 7

Scan line 0
Scan line 1
Scan line 2
Scan line 3
Scan line 4
Scan line 5
Scan line 6
Scan line 7

c.

Cursor Start = 4
Cursor End = 2

Scan line 0
Scan line 1
Scan line 2
Scan line 3
Scan line 4
Scan line 5
Scan line 6
Scan line 7

d.

Figure 3-18. *Sample VGA alphanumeric cursor settings for an 8-by-8 character matrix.*

ROM BIOS Cursor Emulation

The ROM BIOS routine for INT 10H function 01H uses the values in 80x86 registers CH and CL to program the CRTC Cursor Start and Cursor End registers (see Listing 3-13). On an MDA or CGA, these values are simply copied into the CRTC registers. On an EGA or VGA, however, the BIOS can scale these values relative to an 8-line character matrix and program the CRTC with the scaled results. This scaling is called ''cursor emulation'' in IBM's technical manuals.

When ROM BIOS cursor emulation is in effect, the values you specify to INT 10H function 01H represent the position of the start and end of the displayed cursor relative to an 8-line character matrix. When the actual character matrix is larger than 8 lines, the BIOS routine adjusts the Cursor Start and Cursor End values to maintain the cursor's relative location in the matrix.

Consider what happens, for example, when you call INT 10H function 01H with CH = 6 and CL = 7. If the character matrix is 8 lines high, the cursor appears on the bottom two lines. (This is the usual cursor in 200-line video modes.) If the character matrix is 14 lines high, however, the BIOS routine adjusts the Cursor Start and Cursor End values so that the cursor appears near the bottom of the matrix; that is, on lines 0BH and 0CH. Thus, cursor emulation allows programs that change the cursor size with INT 10H function 01H to run unchanged regardless of the size of the character matrix.

The BIOS carries out cursor emulation in INT 10H functions whenever bit 0 of the Video Display Data Area INFO byte (0040:0087) is set to 0. (This is the power-on default for both the EGA and the VGA.) You can disable cursor emulation by setting this bit to 1 before calling INT 10H function 01H. On the EGA, you must set and reset the bit directly, but on the VGA, you should use INT 10H function 12H to set the bit's value.

 On the EGA, cursor emulation is implemented by adding 5 to any Cursor Start or Cursor End value greater than 4. This works well when the character matrix is the default 14 lines high. For character matrices of other heights, however, this simple algorithm breaks down and computes the Cursor Start and Cursor End values incorrectly. You should therefore disable cursor emulation when you program the EGA's character generator to change the size of its character matrix (see Chapter 10).

On the VGA, the cursor-emulation computation takes into account the height of the character matrix, so the emulated cursor is displayed correctly regardless of character matrix dimensions.

An Invisible Cursor

You can make the cursor "invisible" by programming the CRT Controller to display it at an offscreen location. Do this by setting the Cursor High and Cursor Low registers to a non-displayed buffer offset. Another way to make the cursor vanish is to load the Cursor Start and Cursor End registers with values below the displayed character matrix. On the MDA, CGA, and VGA, load the Cursor Start register with the value 20H to make the cursor disappear. On the EGA, set Cursor Start to a value greater than or equal to the number of lines in the character matrix and set Cursor End to 0 (see Listing 3-15).

```
        mov     cx,2000h                ; CH := top scan line for cursor
                                        ; CL := bottom scan line for cursor
        mov     ah,1                    ; AH := INT 10h function number
        int     10h
```

Listing 3-15. *An invisible alphanumeric cursor for IBM video subsystems.*

4

Graphics Modes

Using Graphics Modes

Mapping Pixels to the Screen
CGA ● HGC ● EGA
Hercules InColor Card ● MCGA and VGA

Pixel Coordinates
Pixel Coordinate Scaling
Aspect Ratio

Pixel Display Attributes
CGA ● HGC ● EGA
Hercules InColor Card ● MCGA ● VGA

This chapter covers the basics of graphics-mode programming on the CGA, EGA, MCGA, VGA, and Hercules cards. First the chapter describes how pixels are represented in the video buffer and how they are mapped to the screen. Then it focuses on pixel display attributes; that is, on how to determine a pixel's color, intensity, and blinking.

Using Graphics Modes

In graphics modes, your program can manipulate the color of every pixel on the display. For this reason, graphics modes are sometimes called All Points Addressable (APA) modes. Because you have control over each pixel in the displayed image, you can construct complex geometric images, fill arbitrary areas of the screen with solid colors or blends of colors, and display animated images that move smoothly across the screen.

Most programmers, however, use graphics modes only when pixel-by-pixel control over the screen is essential to an application. The reason: The price you pay for total control over the screen is increased source code complexity and decreased performance. A simple comparison of the amount of data required to display a full screen of information in alphanumeric and in graphics modes shows why.

For example, to display 25 rows of 16-color, 80-column text in alphanumeric mode on an EGA, you need to store 4000 bytes (80 × 25 × 2) in the video buffer. With a 350-line monitor, the text is displayed with 640-by-350-pixel resolution. Obtaining the same resolution in a 16-color graphics mode requires 112,000 bytes (640 × 350 × 4 bits per pixel ÷ 8 bits per byte). Obviously, a program that must manipulate 112,000 bytes of data is more complex and slower than a program that manipulates only 4000 bytes.

Of course, the performance penalty for using graphics-mode video output is less apparent when you use a faster computer, such as an 80286-based or 80386-based machine whose CPU runs at a high clock speed. Still, before you leap into graphics-mode programming, you should carefully consider the alternatives. Alphanumeric modes are sufficient for displaying text and simple block graphics and, hence, for the majority of real-world applications.

 An alternative in some applications is to use a video subsystem that has an alphanumeric character generator capable of displaying RAM-based character sets. (The EGA, MCGA, VGA, HGC+, and InColor Card all have this capability.) With these subsystems, you can design ''characters'' that are actually subunits of a larger graphics image and then assemble the subunits into a complete image in an alphanumeric mode. (Chapter 10 explains the technique in detail.)

Mapping Pixels to the Screen

PC and PS/2 video subsystems store pixel data as groups of bits that represent pixel values. The color of each pixel on the display is determined, directly or indirectly, by its pixel value. Furthermore, no pixel value is ever represented by more than eight bits, so one or more pixels are mapped into every byte in the video buffer.

The format of the pixel map or bit map in the video buffer depends on the number of bits required to represent each pixel, as well as on the architecture of the video RAM. Obviously, the number of colors that a given graphics mode can display at one time is determined by the number of bits used to represent each pixel.

When pixel values are smaller than eight bits, pixels are mapped in bit fields from left to right across each byte. The leftmost pixel represented in a given byte is always found in that byte's high-order bit(s). This is true on all PC and PS/2 video subsystems.

Color Graphics Adapter

On the CGA, each pixel is represented either by two bits, as in 320-by-200 4-color mode (see Figure 4-1a) or by one bit, as in 640-by-200 2-color mode (see Figure 4-1b). Because two bits are used to represent pixels in 320-by-200 mode, a pixel

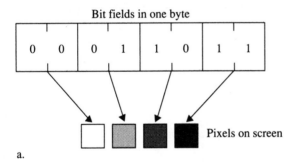

a.

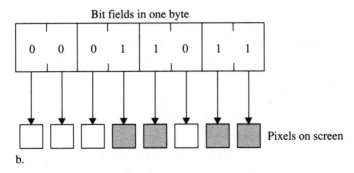

b.

Figure 4-1. *Pixel mapping in CGA graphics modes.*

can have any of four different pixel values, so this mode can display four different colors at a time. Only one bit is used to represent pixel values in 640-by-200 mode, so that mode can display only two colors at a time.

The pixel data is mapped in two interleaved halves of the CGA's 16 KB video buffer. Data for the 100 even-numbered scan lines starts at B800:0000, and data for the odd-numbered scan lines starts at B800:2000 (see Figure 4-2). If the scan lines are numbered consecutively from 0, the half of the video buffer in which the *n*th scan line is represented can be determined by calculating *n* MOD 2.

T I P This two-way buffer interleave lets the CGA's CRT Controller display 200 lines of graphics data without overflowing the 7-bit CRTC vertical timing registers. In CGA graphics modes, the CRTC is set up to display 100 rows of "characters," each two scan lines high. The top (even) line of each character is derived from the first half of the video buffer, and the bottom (odd) line is read from the second half of the buffer.

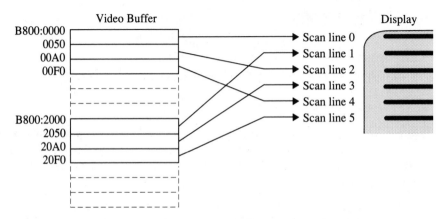

Figure 4-2. *Video buffer interleave in CGA graphics modes.*

Hercules Graphics Card

In 720-by-348 graphics mode on the HGC and HGC+, pixel representation is similar to that in the CGA's 640-by-200 2-color graphics mode. One bit represents each pixel, so only two "colors" (pixel on or pixel off) are available.

However, the HGC's 348 90-byte lines of pixel data are interleaved using four separate areas of the video buffer (see Figure 4-3), each containing 87 (348 ÷ 4) lines of data. With this buffer organization, the area in the buffer in which the *n*th scan line is represented can be determined by *n* MOD 4.

On Hercules video adapters, the four-way interleave allows the CRTC to be programmed to display 87 rows of characters which are four scan lines high. (See Listing 2-4 in Chapter 2.) Each of the four scan lines in a "character" is read from the corresponding location in one of the four interleaved portions of the video buffer.

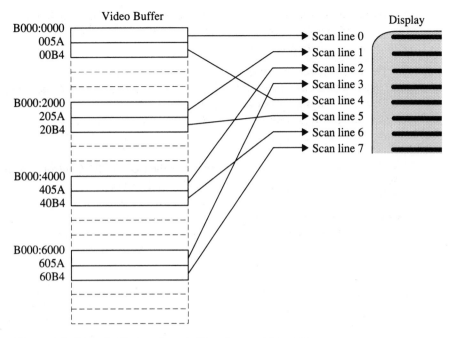

Figure 4-3. *Video buffer interleave in Hercules graphics mode.*

Enhanced Graphics Adapter

When the EGA is configured to emulate a CGA graphics mode, pixels are mapped in the video buffer just as they would be on the CGA. However, in the EGA's native graphics modes (200-line 16-color modes and all 350-line modes), pixels are always mapped eight to a byte.

This mapping is dictated by the architecture of the EGA's video buffer. The 256 KB video buffer consists of four 64 KB maps, or parallel banks of RAM. The maps are parallel in the sense that they occupy the same range of addresses in the CPU's address space; the EGA's Sequencer and Graphics Controller allow the maps to be accessed either individually or in parallel (more about this in Chapter 5).

A pixel's value is determined by the values of the corresponding bits at the same byte offset and bit offset in each map (see Figure 4-4). For this reason, in graphics modes, the four maps are called bit planes. You might imagine each pixel's value as the result of concatenating one bit from the same location in each bit plane.

 The relationship of memory maps to bit planes is altered in 350-line graphics modes on an IBM EGA equipped with only 64 KB of video RAM. (To bring IBM's original EGA up to 256 KB, you must install a piggyback board, called the Graphics Memory Expansion Card.) When you use INT 10H function 00H to select 640-by-350 graphics modes (mode 0FH or 10H) on an EGA with a 64 KB video buffer, video buffer address decoding is altered so that even-numbered addresses in the buffer reference the even-numbered maps and odd-numbered addresses refer to odd-numbered maps (see Figure 4-5).

In this way the four video buffer maps are chained together, with maps 0 and 1 forming bit plane 0 and maps 2 and 3 forming bit plane 2. Routines that access pixels in the video buffer must accommodate this relationship between the bit planes and buffer addresses.

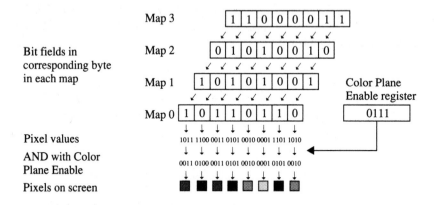

Figure 4-4. *Pixel mapping in native EGA graphics modes.*

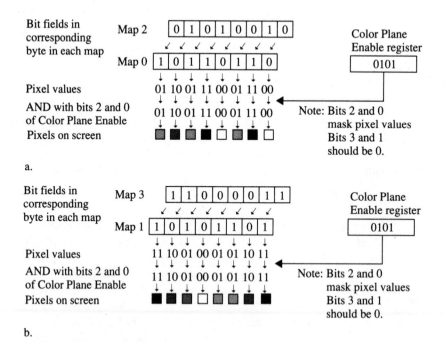

a.

b.

Figure 4-5. *Video buffer maps in 350-line graphics modes (EGA with 64 KB video RAM). Pixel values at even addresses are stored in maps 0 and 2 (Figure 4-5a); pixels at odd addresses are stored in maps 1 and 3 (Figure 4-5b).*

In native EGA graphics modes, there is no line-by-line interleaving of the pixel data in the video buffer, as in CGA and HGC graphics modes. Instead, rows of pixels are mapped linearly, just as rows of characters are mapped linearly in alphanumeric video modes.

Hercules InColor Card

In its 720-by-348 graphics mode, the InColor Card's video buffer has four parallel maps organized as four parallel bit planes. As on the EGA, a pixel's value is determined by concatenating the corresponding bits in each of the bit planes. However, video buffer addressing is not linear, as it is on the EGA.

Pixels are stored in the InColor Card's video buffer using the same four-way interleave that the HGC and HGC+ use. In the buffer, 348 lines of 90 bytes (720 pixels) are mapped in a four-way interleave starting at B000:0000. The buffer also contains two video pages (as on the monochrome HGC), at B000:0000 and B000:8000. This aspect of the InColor Card's design preserves its symmetry with Hercules monochrome graphics cards but differentiates it from the EGA.

MCGA and VGA

The PS/2 video subsystems support three graphics modes not found on earlier PC video adapters. The 640-by-480 2-color mode (MCGA and VGA) and 640-by-480 16-color mode (VGA only) resemble the native EGA graphics modes: Both use a linear bit map starting at A000:0000. A similar linear pixel map also is used in 320-by-200 (MCGA and VGA) 256-color mode, with one important difference: Each byte in the video buffer represents one pixel (see Figure 4-6). Since there are eight bits to a byte, each pixel can have any of 256 (2^8) different colors.

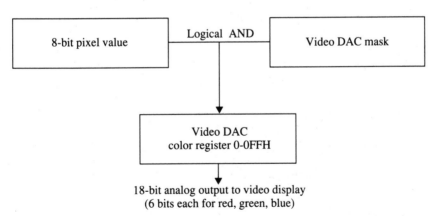

Figure 4-6. *Color selection in MCGA and VGA 320-by-200 256-color mode.*

On the VGA, 640-by-480 2-color mode is nearly identical to 640-by-480 16-color mode. All four bit planes remain active in the 2-color mode even though one bit plane is sufficient to store a full screen of pixels. The only difference between the two modes is that the video BIOS makes only two palette colors available in the 2-color mode, whereas it sets up 16 palette colors in the 16-color mode.

Pixel Coordinates

In graphics modes, the video buffer can be thought of as a flat, two-dimensional array of pixels with its origin at the upper left corner. What is visible on the screen is a subset of the pixels represented in the buffer. On the CGA, the video buffer can contain only one screenful of pixels, so the first byte in the buffer represents the pixels in the screen's upper left corner. On the EGA, MCGA, and VGA, however, the video buffer can store several screenfuls of pixels. You can thus select which portion of the video buffer appears on the screen.

Every pixel on the screen can be identified by a unique pair of (x,y) coordinates relative to the screen's upper left corner. Each (x,y) pair also corresponds to a particular byte offset in the video buffer and a bit offset in that byte. Thus, given a pixel's (x,y) coordinates on the screen, you can compute where in the video buffer the pixel is represented.

Converting from pixel coordinates to the corresponding byte and bit offsets is one of the most frequent operations in IBM video graphics programming. The program examples in Listings 4-1 through 4-5 demonstrate how to do this efficiently and in a uniform manner.

```
                TITLE   'Listing 4-1'
                NAME    PixelAddr04
                PAGE    55,132

;
; Name:         PixelAddr04
;
; Function:     Determine buffer address of pixel in 320x200 4-color mode
;
; Caller:       AX = y-coordinate (0-199)
;               BX = x-coordinate (0-319)
;
; Returns:      AH = bit mask
;               BX = byte offset in buffer
;               CL = number of bits to shift left
;               ES = video buffer segment
;


OriginOffset    EQU     0                       ; byte offset of (0,0)
VideoBufferSeg  EQU     0B800h
```

Listing 4-1. *Computing a pixel's address in 320-by-200 4-color mode.*   *(continued)*

Listing 4-1. *Continued.*

```
_TEXT           SEGMENT byte public 'CODE'
                ASSUME   cs:_TEXT
                PUBLIC   PixelAddr04
PixelAddr04     PROC     near

                mov     cl,bl           ; CL := low-order byte of x

                xchg    ah,al           ; AX := 100h * y
                shr     ax,1            ; AL := 80h * (y&1)
                add     bh,al           ; BX := x + 8000h*(y&1)
                xor     al,al           ; AX := 100h*(y/2)
                add     bx,ax           ; BX := x + 8000h*(y&1) + 100h*(y/2)
                shr     ax,1
                shr     ax,1            ; AX := 40h*(y/2)
                add     bx,ax           ; BX := x + 8000h*(y&1) + 140h*(y/2)
                shr     bx,1
                shr     bx,1            ; BX := x/4 + 2000h*(y&1) + 50h*(y/2)
                add     bx,OriginOffset ; BX := byte offset in video buffer

                mov     ax,VideoBufferSeg
                mov     es,ax           ; ES:BX := byte address of pixel

                mov     ah,3            ; AH := unshifted bit mask
                and     cl,ah           ; CL := x & 3
                xor     cl,ah           ; CL := 3 - (x & 3)
                shl     cl,1            ; CL := # bits to shift left

                ret

PixelAddr04     ENDP

_TEXT           ENDS

                END
```

```
                TITLE   'Listing 4-2'
                NAME    PixelAddr06
                PAGE    55,132

;
; Name:         PixelAddr06
;
; Function:     Determine buffer address of pixel in 640x200 2-color mode
;
; Caller:       AX = y-coordinate (0-199)
;               BX = x-coordinate (0-639)
;
; Returns:      AH = bit mask
;               BX = byte offset in buffer
;               CL = number of bits to shift left
;               ES = video buffer segment
;

OriginOffset    EQU     0               ; byte offset of (0,0)
VideoBufferSeg  EQU     0B800h
```

Listing 4-2. *Computing a pixel's address in 640-by-200 2-color mode.*   *(continued)*

Listing 4-2. *Continued.*

```
_TEXT           SEGMENT byte public 'CODE'
                ASSUME  cs:_TEXT

                PUBLIC  PixelAddr06
PixelAddr06     PROC    near

                mov     cl,bl          ; CL := low-order byte of x

                xchg    ah,al          ; AX := 100h * y
                shr     bx,1           ; BX := x/2
                shr     ax,1           ; AL := 80h*(y&1)
                add     bh,al          ; BX := x/2 + 8000h*(y&1)
                xor     al,al          ; AX := 100h*(y/2)
                add     bx,ax          ; BX := x/2 + 8000h*(y&1) + 100h*(y/2)
                shr     ax,1
                shr     ax,1           ; AX := 40h*(y/2)
                add     bx,ax          ; BX := x/2 + 8000h*(y&1) + 140h*(y/2)
                shr     bx,1
                shr     bx,1           ; BX := x/8 + 2000h*(y&1) + 50h*(y/2)
                add     bx,OriginOffset ; BX := byte offset in video buffer

                mov     ax,VideoBufferSeg
                mov     es,ax          ; ES:BX := byte address of pixel

                and     cl,7           ; CL := x & 7
                xor     cl,7           ; CL := number of bits to shift left
                mov     ah,1           ; AH := unshifted bit mask

                ret

PixelAddr06     ENDP

_TEXT           ENDS

                END
```

Transforming pixel coordinates to a buffer offset involves simple logic. Begin by calculating the offset of the start of pixel row *y*. (For CGA and Hercules graphics modes, this calculation accounts for the interleaving of the video buffer.) To this value, add the byte offset of the *x*th pixel in the row. Finally, add the byte offset of the start of the displayed portion of the video buffer to obtain the final byte offset of the pixel.

```
PixelByteOffset = RowOffset(y) + ByteOffset(x) + OriginOffset
```

The bit offset of the pixel within the byte that contains its value depends only on the number of pixels represented in each byte of the video buffer. You could express the relationship this way:

```
PixelBitOffset = PixelsPerByte - (x MOD PixelsPerByte) - 1
```

However, it is more practical to represent a pixel's bit offset as a bit mask rather than as an ordinal bit number. This can be done easily with a table lookup (for example, an assembler XLAT instruction) or with a logical shift instruction. (This is why Listings 4-1 through 4-4 return the bit offset as a number of bits to shift.)

```
              TITLE    'Listing 4-3'
              NAME     PixelAddrHGC
              PAGE     55,132

;
; Name:        PixelAddrHGC
;
; Function:    Determine buffer address of pixel in 720x348 Hercules graphics
;
; Caller:      AX = y-coordinate (0-347)
;              BX = x-coordinate (0-719)
;
; Returns:     AH = bit mask
;              BX = byte offset in buffer
;              CL = number of bits to shift left
;              ES = video buffer segment
;

BytesPerLine    EQU    90
OriginOffset    EQU    0                  ; byte offset of (0,0)
VideoBufferSeg  EQU    0B000h

_TEXT           SEGMENT byte public 'CODE'
                ASSUME  cs:_TEXT

                PUBLIC  PixelAddrHGC
PixelAddrHGC    PROC    near

                mov     cl,bl            ; CL := low-order byte of x

                shr     ax,1             ; AX := y/2
                rcr     bx,1             ; BX := 8000h*(y&1) + x/2
                shr     ax,1             ; AX := y/4
                rcr     bx,1             ; BX := 4000h*(y&3) + x/4
                shr     bx,1             ; BX := 2000h*(y&3) + x/8
                mov     ah,BytesPerLine
                mul     ah               ; AX := BytesPerLine*(y/4)
                add     bx,ax            ; BX := 2000h*(y&3) + x/8 +
                                         ; BytesPerLine*(y/4)
                add     bx,OriginOffset  ; BX := byte offset in video buffer

                mov     ax,VideoBufferSeg
                mov     es,ax            ; ES:BX := byte address of pixel

                and     cl,7             ; CL := x & 7
                xor     cl,7             ; CL := number of bits to shift left
                mov     ah,1             ; AH := unshifted bit mask

                ret

PixelAddrHGC    ENDP

_TEXT           ENDS

                END
```

Listing 4-3. *Computing a pixel's address in Hercules graphics mode.*

```
                       TITLE    'Listing 4-4'
                       NAME     PixelAddr10
                       PAGE     55,132              .

;
; Name:             PixelAddr10
;
; Function:         Determine buffer address of pixel in native EGA and VGA modes:
;                                 320x200 16-color
;                                 640x200 16-color
;                                 640x350 16-color
;                                 640x350 monochrome (4-color)
;                                 640x480 2-color
;                                 640x480 16-color
;
; Caller:           AX = y-coordinate
;                   BX = x-coordinate
;
; Returns:          AH = bit mask
;                   BX = byte offset in buffer
;                   CL = number of bits to shift left
;                   ES = video buffer segment
;

BytesPerLine       EQU      80               ; bytes in one horizontal line
OriginOffset       EQU      0                ; byte offset of (0,0)
VideoBufferSeg     EQU      0A000h

_TEXT              SEGMENT byte public 'CODE'
                   ASSUME  cs:_TEXT

                   PUBLIC  PixelAddr10
PixelAddr10        PROC    near

                   mov      cl,bl            ; CL := low-order byte of x
                   push     dx               ; preserve DX

                   mov      dx,BytesPerLine ; AX := y * BytesPerLine
                   mul      dx

                   pop      dx
                   shr      bx,1
                   shr      bx,1
                   shr      bx,1             ; BX := x/8
                   add      bx,ax            ; BX := y*BytesPerLine + x/8
                   add      bx,OriginOffset ; BX := byte offset in video buffer

                   mov      ax,VideoBufferSeg
                   mov      es,ax            ; ES:BX := byte address of pixel

                   and      cl,7             ; CL := x & 7
                   xor      cl,7             ; CL := number of bits to shift left
                   mov      ah,1             ; AH := unshifted bit mask
                   ret

PixelAddr10        ENDP

_TEXT              ENDS
                   END
```

Listing 4-4. *Computing a pixel's address in CGA and VGA graphics modes.*

Here is a high-level example of a pixel coordinate transformation for the CGA's 320-by-200 4-color graphics mode. As Figure 4-1a shows, each byte in the video buffer contains four pixels. At four pixels per byte, 80 bytes of data represent one row of 320 pixels. The origin of the screen—that is, the byte offset of the displayed portion of the buffer—is 0, since the CGA video buffer contains only one screenful of pixels.

```
int PixelsPerByte = 4;
int BytesPerRow = 80;
int OriginOffset = 0;
static int Masks[] = { 0xC0, 0x30, 0x0C, 0x03 };

unsigned int x,y;
unsigned int ByteOffset,BitMask;

/* buffer interleave (0 or 0x2000) */
ByteOffset = (y & 1) << 13;

/* offset of start of row */
ByteOffset += BytesPerRow * (y/2);

/* byte offset in screen */
ByteOffset += (x / PixelsPerByte) % BytesPerRow;

/* byte offset in video buffer */
ByteOffset += OriginOffset;

BitMask = Masks[x % PixelsPerByte];
```

The same routine in assembly language is much more efficient, because all arithmetic can be done in registers and register halves (refer to Listing 4-1). Also, if you know that the number of bytes per row of pixels is a constant, you can further increase performance by performing multiplication and division as a sequence of bit shifts.

For example, in Listing 4-5, the *y*-coordinate is multiplied by 320 through a series of logical shift operations instead of a single MUL instruction. The resulting routine runs about 40 percent faster on the 8086-based PS/2 Model 30 and about 10 percent faster on the 80286-based PS/2 Model 60. This optimization complicates the assembly code somewhat, but the speed gained is worth the effort—low-level routines such as those in Listings 4-1 through 4-5 may execute many thousands of times in a graphics-oriented application.

```
                    TITLE    'Listing 4-5'
                    NAME     PixelAddr13
                    PAGE     55,132

;
; Name:              PixelAddr13
;
; Function:          Determine buffer address of pixel in 320x200 256-color mode
;
; Caller:            AX = y-coordinate (0-199)
;                    BX = x-coordinate (0-319)
;
; Returns:           BX = byte offset in buffer
;                    ES = video buffer segment
;

OriginOffset     EQU     0                ; byte offset of (0,0)
VideoBufferSeg   EQU     0A000h

_TEXT            SEGMENT byte public 'CODE'
                 ASSUME  cs:_TEXT

                 PUBLIC  PixelAddr13
PixelAddr13      PROC    near

                 xchg    ah,al            ; AX := 256*y
                 add     bx,ax            ; BX := 256*y + x
                 shr     ax,1
                 shr     ax,1             ; AX := 64*y
                 add     bx,ax            ; BX := 320*y + x

                 add     bx,OriginOffset  ; BX := byte offset in video buffer

                 mov     ax,VideoBufferSeg
                 mov     es,ax            ; ES:BX := byte address of pixel
                 ret

PixelAddr13      ENDP

_TEXT            ENDS

                 END
```

Listing 4-5. *Computing a pixel's address in 320-by-200 256-color mode.*

Pixel Coordinate Scaling

One characteristic of most IBM graphics modes is that horizontal pixel resolution differs from vertical pixel resolution. For example, in a 640-by-200 mode, a typical 200-line color monitor displays about 70 pixels per horizontal inch, but only about 30 pixels per vertical inch.

This discrepancy complicates the mapping of pixels in the display buffer to screen locations, as is shown in Figure 4-7. For example, in a 640-by-200 mode, a line drawn between the pixel at (0,0) in the screen's upper left corner and the pixel at (100,100) has a mathematical slope of 1, so you would expect it to be displayed at a 45-degree angle from the display's top and left edges. However, the displayed line (line *a*, Figure 4-7) is "compressed" in the horizontal direction.

Displaying a line at a 45-degree angle requires scaling the pixel coordinates to account for the discrepancy in vertical and horizontal resolution. In a 640-by-200 mode, the horizontal scaling factor is about 2.4 (horizontal resolution ÷ vertical resolution). In the example, you would scale the x-coordinates of the endpoints to 0 (0 × 2.4) and 240 (100 × 2.4). The scaled line (line b, Figure 4-7), with endpoints at (0,0) and (240,100), appears at a 45-degree angle on the screen.

You must scale the (x,y) coordinates of all pixels in all geometric figures in all graphics modes—unless, of course, the scaling factor happens to be 1. Otherwise, squares appear as rectangles and circles as ellipses. Furthermore, you must adjust the scaling factor for the horizontal and vertical resolutions of each graphics mode. Figure 4-8 is a table of the horizontal-to-vertical scaling ratios for graphics modes on IBM video subsystems with typical monitors.

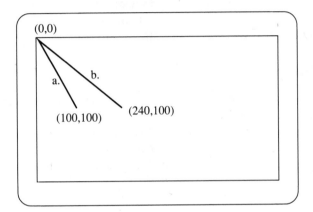

Figure 4-7. *Pixel coordinate scaling in 640-by-200 graphics.*

BIOS Mode Number	Mode Description	Scaling Factor (horizontal/vertical)
4,5	320-by-200 4-color	1.20
6	640-by-200 2-color	2.40
0DH	320-by-200 16-color	1.20
0EH	640-by-200 16-color	2.40
0FH	640-by-350 monochrome	1.26 (monochrome monitor)
10H	640-by-350 16-color	1.37
11H	640-by-480 2-color	1.00
12H	640-by-480 16-color	1.00
13H	320-by-200 256-color	2.40
	720-by-348 (Hercules)	1.43 (monochrome monitor)

Figure 4-8. *Pixel scaling values for PC and PS/2 graphics modes. An aspect ratio of 1.33 (4:3) for color monitors, 1.45 for monochrome monitors, is assumed.*

Aspect Ratio

A related programming concern is the screen's aspect ratio—the ratio of a screen's width to its height. The color monitors commonly used with IBM video subsystems have aspect ratios of about 1.33 (4:3); for the typical green monochrome monitor, the aspect ratio is about 1.45. Because the screen is rectangular instead of square, the maximum potential width of a screen image exceeds its maximum potential height. This limitation must always be considered in scaling pixel coordinates.

 One attractive feature of the MCGA, the VGA, and other video subsystems that offer 640-by-480 resolution is that horizontal resolution and vertical resolution are the same on a display with an aspect ratio of 4:3. You can think of the pixels in this situation as being "square." With "square" pixels, mapping the video buffer to the screen is simpler because the pixel coordinate scaling factor is 1.

Pixel Display Attributes

In general, pixel values determine video attributes—in other words, the bits that represent a pixel in the video buffer determine how the pixel looks on the screen. The way that pixel values are decoded in graphics modes is similar to the way that alphanumeric attributes are decoded. But in graphics modes, pixel values may range from one through eight bits, while alphanumeric attributes are four bits wide.

Color Graphics Adapter

In 640-by-200 2-color mode, one bit represents each pixel. If the bit is 0, the pixel is displayed as black. If the bit is 1, the pixel is displayed with the color specified in bits 0 through 3 of the CGA's Color Select register (port 3D9H). This is the same register that specifies the overscan color in alphanumeric modes. If you change video modes by directly programming the CGA's CRTC and Mode Control registers, you should avoid spurious border colors or pixel colors by programming the Color Select register as well.

You can use INT 10H function 0BH to select the displayed color of nonzero pixels in 640-by-200 2-color mode (see Listing 4-6). This BIOS function stores a color value in the Color Select register and updates the variable CRT_PALETTE in the Video Display Data Area at 0040:0066. If you bypass the video BIOS and program the Color Select register directly, you should also update CRT_PALETTE.

```
mov     ah,0Bh          ; AH := 0BH (INT 10H function number)
mov     bh,0            ; BH := subfunction number
mov     bl,ColorValue   ; BL := desired color (0-0FH)
int     10h
```

Listing 4-6. *Foreground color in CGA 640-by-200 2-color graphics.*

In 320-by-200 4-color modes, two bits represent each pixel, so pixel values can range from 0 through 3. Pixels with the value 0 are displayed with the color value stored in the Color Select register at port 3D9H. A quirk of the CGA is that the Color Select register value determines both the overscan (border) color and the color for pixel value 0. This means you cannot specify a border color independently of the background color on the CGA in this video mode.

The colors displayed for pixels with nonzero values are taken from one of three hardware palettes (see Figure 4-9). The palette is selected by the values of bit 5 of the Color Select register (port 3D9H) and of bit 2 of the Mode Control register at port 3D8H (Listing 4-7). If bit 2 of the Mode Control register is 1, the palette comprises cyan, red, and white. If this bit is 0, bit 5 of the Color Select register selects either green, red, and yellow (if bit 2 in the Color Select register is 0), or cyan, violet, and white (if bit 2 in the Color Select register is 1). In effect, setting bit 2 in the Color Select register adds blue to the palette; that is, green plus blue produces cyan, red plus blue produces violet, and yellow plus blue produces white.

 Setting bit 2 of the CGA's Mode Control register to 1 disables the color burst component of the adapter's composite video output signal. If you use a black-and-white display, appropriate shades of gray are generated for the four possible pixel values when bit 2 is set to 1.

Bit 2 of Mode Control register = 0
Bit 5 of Color Select register = 0

Pixel Value	Color Displayed
1	Green
2	Red
3	Yellow

Bit 5 of Color Select register = 1

Pixel Value	Color Displayed
1	Cyan
2	Violet
3	White

Bit 2 of Mode Control register = 1

Pixel Value	Color Displayed
1	Cyan
2	Red
3	White

Figure 4-9. *Palettes available in CGA 320-by-200 4-color mode.*

```
; cyan-red-white

mov     ax,40h
mov     es,ax          ; ES := Video BIOS data segment
mov     al,es:[65h]    ; AL := CRT_MODE_SET
or      al,00000100b   ; AL bit 2 := 1
mov     dx,3D8h        ; DX := Mode Control I/O port
out     dx,al          ; update Mode Control register
mov     es:[65h],al    ; update CRT_MODE_SET

; green-red-yellow or cyan-violet-white

mov     ax,40h
mov     es,ax          ; ES := Video BIOS data segment
mov     al,es:[65h]    ; AL := CRT_MODE_SET
and     al,11111011b   ; AL bit 2 := 0
mov     dx,3D8h        ; DX := Mode Control I/O port
out     dx,al          ; update Mode Control register
mov     es:[65h],al    ; update CRT_MODE_SET

mov     al,es:[66h]    ; AL := CRT_PALETTE
and     al,11011111b   ; AL bit 5 := 0
or      al,PaletteSelect; 00000000b for green-red-yellow
                        ; 00100000b for cyan-violet-white
inc     dx             ; DX := Color Select I/O port
out     dx,al          ; update Color Select register
mov     es:[66h],al    ; update CRT_PALETTE
```

Listing 4-7. *Four-color palettes in CGA 320-by-200 4-color mode.*

You can use INT 10H functions to select among the three 4-color palettes. The video BIOS assigns two video mode numbers to 320-by-200 4-color graphics mode: In BIOS mode 4, bit 2 of the Mode Control register is 0, and in mode 5, bit 2 is set to 1. Thus, to select the cyan-red-white palette, use INT 10H function 0 to set mode 5. To select the other two palettes, use INT 10H function 0 to set mode 4, and then call INT 10H function 0BH to choose either green-red-yellow or cyan-violet-white, as shown in Listing 4-8.

```
; cyan-red-white

        mov     ax,0005        ; AH := 0 (INT 10H function number)
                               ; AL := 5 (320x200 4-color mode, color burst
                               ;   disabled)
        int     10h

; green-red-yellow or cyan-violet-white

        mov     ax,0004        ; AH := 0 (INT 10H function number)
                               ; AL := 4 (320x200 4-color mode, color burst
                               ;   enabled)
        int     10h

        mov     ah,0Bh         ; AH := INT 10H function number
        mov     bh,1
        mov     bl,PaletteID   ; 0 for green-red-yellow
                               ; 1 for cyan-violet-white
        int     10h
```

Listing 4-8. *Four-color palettes in CGA 320-by-200 4-color mode using video BIOS.*

You can select high-intensity colors in the 320-by-200 4-color palette by setting bit 4 of the Color Select register to 1. When this bit is 0, the same four colors are displayed with normal intensity.

Hercules Graphics Card

Life is easy with an HGC as far as graphics attributes are concerned. In the 720-by-348 monochrome graphics mode on the HGC and HGC+, one bit represents each pixel. If the bit is set to 1, the pixel is displayed. If the bit is set to 0, the pixel is not displayed.

Enhanced Graphics Adapter

Although the EGA supports a number of graphics modes with pixel values ranging from 1 to 4 bits, it decodes pixel values in a straightforward manner. As in alphanumeric modes, each pixel's value is masked by the value in the Attribute Controller's Color Plane Enable register; the resulting 4-bit value selects one of the Attribute Controller's 16 palette registers. Thus, a pixel's displayed attribute is derived from the palette register that corresponds to the pixel value.

When you use INT 10H function 0 to select an EGA video mode, the BIOS routine loads a default set of color values into the palette registers (see Figure 4-10). The actual values depend on the video mode, but each set maps the palette registers so that the color displayed for a given pixel value is the same as a CGA would display. Using this function improves the portability of programs between the CGA and the EGA, since a program that never touches the palette registers can run with the same set of colors on both adapters.

 The BIOS default palette register values for 320-by-200 and 640-by-200 16-color modes are correct for 200-line monitors but incorrect for some EGA-compatible monitors. IBM's Enhanced Color Display converts the 4-bit default color values in 200-line graphics modes (see Figure 4-10) to 6-bit color values that emulate the 16 CGA colors. Unfortunately, not all EGA-compatible monitors do this. Thus, if you use INT 10H function 0 to invoke these modes (mode numbers 0DH and 0EH), you generally should program the palette registers with an appropriate set of values, such as the default set used in 640-by-350 16-color mode.

CGA Emulation Modes

In 640-by-200 2-color mode, when bit 3 of the Attribute Controller Mode Control register (10H) is 0, a pixel value of 0 designates palette register 0, and a pixel value of 1 designates palette register 1. When Mode Control bit 3 is 1, palette registers 8 and 9 are used. With a CGA-compatible display, these four palette registers can contain any of the 16 displayable color values. With an EGA-compatible 350-line monitor, these registers can contain any four of the 64 displayable color values.

350-Line 16-Color Modes

Palette Register	Color Value	Attribute
00H	00H	Black
01H	01H	Mid-intensity blue
02H	02H	Mid-intensity green
03H	03H	Mid-intensity cyan
04H	04H	Mid-intensity red
05H	05H	Mid-intensity violet
06H	14H	Brown
07H	07H	Mid-intensity white
08H	38H	Low-intensity white (gray)
09H	39H	High-intensity blue
0AH	3AH	High-intensity green
0BH	3BH	High-intensity cyan
0CH	3CH	High-intensity red
0DH	3DH	High-intensity violet
0EH	3EH	High-intensity yellow
0FH	3FH	High-intensity white

200-Line 16-Color Modes

Palette Register	Color Value	Attribute
00H	00H	Black
01H	01H	Blue
02H	02H	Green
03H	03H	Cyan
04H	04H	Red
05H	05H	Violet
06H	06H	Yellow (brown)
07H	07H	White
08H	10H	Black (gray)
09H	11H	High-intensity blue
0AH	12H	High-intensity green
0BH	13H	High-intensity cyan
0CH	14H	High-intensity red
0DH	15H	High-intensity violet
0EH	16H	High-intensity yellow
0FH	17H	High-intensity white

640-by-350 Monochrome Graphics

Palette Register	Color Value	Attribute
00H	00H	Not displayed
01H	08H	Normal intensity
04H	18H	High intensity
05H	18H	High intensity
08H	00H	Not displayed
09H	08H	Normal
0CH	00H	Not displayed
0DH	18H	High intensity

Figure 4-10. *Default EGA and VGA palette register values.*

In 320-by-200 4-color mode, each of the four possible pixel values (0 through 3) designates a corresponding palette register. When bit 3 in the Attribute Controller Mode Control register is 0, palette registers 0–3 are used; when bit 3 is 1, palette registers 8–0BH are used. With a CGA-compatible monitor, you can store any eight of the 16 displayable color values in these palette registers. With an EGA-compatible monitor, you can use any eight of the 64 displayable color values in these registers.

In both CGA emulation modes, the video BIOS initializes the palette registers with default color values that match the colors in the CGA hardware palettes. In 640-by-200 2-color mode, the default colors are black, white, and intense white. In 320-by-200 4-color modes, the BIOS supports the green-red-yellow and cyan-violet-white palettes in normal and high intensities.

16-Color Modes

In 320-by-200, 640-by-200, and 640-by-350 16-color modes, each 4-bit pixel value designates one of the 16 palette registers. For a CGA-compatible monitor, the palette registers can contain the usual 16 colors, but with an EGA-compatible monitor, you can specify any of the 64 displayable colors in each palette register.

Monochrome Graphics

There are two bits per pixel in the EGA's 640-by-350 monochrome graphics mode, so pixel values can range from 0 through 3. However, this graphics mode uses only even-numbered bit planes, so the EGA's Attribute Controller interprets only the even-numbered bits of the usual 4-bit pixel value. Thus, bits 0 and 1 of a 2-bit monochrome pixel value designate bits 0 and 2 of the corresponding 4-bit palette register number. (Bits 1 and 3 of the palette register number are always 0.) Thus, the four possible pixel values—0, 1, 2, and 3—actually reference palette registers 0, 1, 4, and 5 respectively (see Figure 4-11).

Pixel Value	Corresponding Palette Register
0 (00B)	0 (0000B)
1 (01B)	1 (0001B)
2 (10B)	4 (0100B)
3 (11B)	5 (0101B)

Figure 4-11. *Pixel values and palette registers in 640-by-350 monochrome graphics.*

 On EGAs with only 64 KB of video RAM, the odd bit planes represent pixels at odd buffer addresses, and the even bit planes represent pixels at even buffer addresses (see Figure 4-5). In this situation, pixel values in 640-by-350 monochrome and 640-by-350 4-color graphics modes are two bits in size, but bits 0 and 2 are used for pixels at even byte addresses, while bits 1 and 3 are used for pixels at odd byte addresses.

Monochrome pixels can be undisplayed (palette register value 0), can be displayed with normal intensity (08H), or can be displayed with high intensity (18H). INT 10H function 00H loads the palette registers with a default set of monochrome values whenever you select video mode 0FH (see Figure 4-11).

Blinking

In native graphics modes on the EGA (as well as on the VGA), pixels can have a blinking attribute. As in alphanumeric modes, you select blinking by setting the Enable Blink bit of the Attribute Controller's Mode Control register (bit 3 of register 10H at port 3C0H) to 1. In 16-color modes, this causes the adapter to interpret the high-order bit (bit 3) of each 4-bit pixel value as a blink attribute, in the same way the high-order bit of a character's attribute byte is used in alphanumeric modes. Thus, when the Enable Blink bit is set, pixels with values 8 through 0FH blink, and pixels with values 0 through 7 do not. In monochrome graphics mode, all pixels blink regardless of their value.

However, the EGA blinks pixels differently in graphics modes than it blinks characters in alphanumeric modes. In graphics modes, pixels are blinked by alternately selecting two different palette registers for each pixel's value. The two registers are designated by turning bit 3 of the pixel value on and off at the blink rate (about twice per second). Thus, pixels are blinked by alternating the values in the first eight palette registers (registers 00H through 07H) with the values in the second eight (08H through 0FH).

For example, a pixel with a value of 0AH is blinked by repeatedly changing the value of bit 3 whenever the Enable Blink bit is set. Thus, the pixel's color alternates between that designated by palette register 0AH (1010B) and that in palette register 02H (0010B). If you use the set of BIOS default palette registers, this pixel blinks between green and high-intensity green.

A peculiarity of the EGA's blinking attribute in color graphics modes is what happens to pixels with values from 0 through 7; that is, where bit 3 of the pixel value is 0. These pixels do not blink, but they are displayed as if bit 3 were 1. For example, if you use the BIOS default palette values, pixels displayed at lower intensity (pixel values 0 through 7) become nonblinking pixels displayed at high intensity using palette registers 08H through 0FH.

Thus, in using the blinking attribute in graphics modes, you should reprogram the palette registers each time you change the Enable Blink bit, to maintain a consistent set of colors. For example, the palette register values shown in Figure 4-12 might be useful in this context. This palette is designed for use as an alternative to the default BIOS palette (see Figure 4-10) when blinking is enabled. If this palette is used with the Enable Blink bit set to 1, all high-intensity pixels (pixel values 08H through 0FH) blink, but all normal-intensity pixels do not.

Border Color

As in alphanumeric modes, you can set the overscan (border) color by storing a color value in the Attribute Controller's Overscan Color register (register 11H, port 3C0H). Techniques for setting the border color are covered in Chapter 3.

Palette Register	Color Value	Attribute
00H	00H	Black (background)
01H	39H	
02H	3AH	
03H	3BH	
04H	3CH	(high-intensity colors)
05H	3DH	
06H	3EH	
07H	3FH	
08H	00H	Black (background)
09H	01H	
0AH	02H	
0BH	03H	
0CH	04H	(mid-intensity colors)
0DH	05H	
0EH	14H	
0FH	07H	

Figure 4-12. *Palette register values for blinking in 640-by-350 16-color mode.*

Hercules InColor Card

On the InColor Card, the value of bit 4 of the Exception register (17H) determines whether the palette registers are used to decode pixel values, just as it does in alphanumeric modes. When this bit is set to 1, each 4-bit pixel value specifies a palette register, and the 6-bit color value in the palette register determines the displayed color of the pixel.

Setting Exception register bit 4 to 0 bypasses the palette registers. Each 4-bit pixel value is extended to 6 bits by replicating the high-order bit, and the new value determines the color. This procedure, called sign extension, in effect causes the high-order bit of a pixel value to act as an ''intensity'' bit, similar to the way alphanumeric attributes are decoded.

MCGA

The MCGA emulates both of the CGA's graphics modes and adds two of its own, a 640-by-480 2-color mode and a 320-by-200 256-color mode. The 256-color mode is the only MCGA video mode that uses the video Digital to Analog Converter (DAC) to full advantage.

2-Color Graphics Modes

Pixel attributes in 640-by-200 and 640-by-480 2-color modes are directed through the video DAC registers. Pixels with the value 0 are always mapped through video DAC color register 0. Nonzero pixels also select a predesignated video DAC color register, but this is done in one of two ways, depending on the value of bit 2 of the Mode Control register at 3D8H. If bit 2 is 1, video DAC color register 7 is selected. If bit 2 is 0, bits 0 through 3 of the Color Select register (port 3D9H) designate a video DAC register.

On the MCGA, the background color in 2-color graphics modes is not necessarily black as it is on the CGA. Instead, both background and foreground can be any of the 256 K colors or the 64 gray-scale values that the MCGA can display. Use INT 10H function 10H to set the appropriate video DAC color registers.

When the video BIOS sets up 2-color graphics modes, it sets bit 2 of the Mode Control register to 0 and bits 0 through 3 of the Color Select register to 1111B (0FH). Since the first 16 video DAC color registers contain the 16 colors available on a CGA, this configuration emulates the default color configuration on a CGA in 640-by-200 2-color mode: Background pixels are displayed as black (the value in video DAC color register 0) and foreground pixels appear intense white (the value in video DAC color register 0FH).

4-Color Graphics Mode

The MCGA faithfully emulates this CGA graphics mode. The major difference is that the MCGA maps the four available colors through the video DAC color registers just as it does in 2-color graphics modes. Thus, all four colors can be selected from the 256 K possibilities that the video DAC offers.

The MCGA combines bits 4 and 5 of the Color Select register (port 3D9H) with each pixel's 2-bit value to create a 4-bit value that designates one of the first 16 video DAC color registers (see Figure 4-13). The video BIOS initializes the video DAC color registers with CGA-compatible palettes. The colors are chosen so that

3D9H Bit 4 (intensity)	Pixel Value		3D9H Bit 5 (palette)	Video DAC Color Register Number	Default Color
	Bit 1	Bit 0			
x	0	0	x	00H	Black
0	0	1	0	02H	Green
0	1	0	0	04H	Red
0	1	1	0	06H	Brown
1	0	1	0	0AH	High-intensity green
1	1	0	0	0CH	High-intensity red
1	1	1	0	0EH	High-intensity yellow
0	0	1	1	03H	Cyan
0	1	0	1	05H	Violet
0	1	1	1	07H	White
1	0	1	1	0BH	High-intensity cyan
1	1	0	1	0DH	High-intensity violet
1	1	1	1	0FH	High-intensity white

x = don't care

Figure 4-13. *Pixel values and palettes in MCGA 320-by-200 4-color mode.*

bit 5 of the Color Select register selects the green-red-yellow and cyan-violet-white palettes, and bit 4 toggles between normal- and high-intensity palettes, as they do on the CGA. Of course, you can establish completely arbitrary 4-color palettes by loading different color values into the video DAC color registers.

256-Color Graphics Mode

In 256-color mode, each pixel's value designates one of the 256 video DAC color registers. To select a video DAC color register, a pixel's value is combined (using

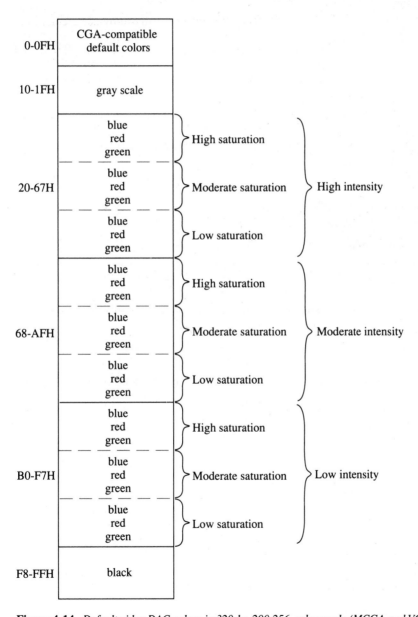

Figure 4-14. *Default video DAC colors in 320-by-200 256-color mode (MCGA and VGA).*

a logical AND) with the value in the video DAC Mask register (3C6H). The resulting value selects a DAC color register (see Figure 4-6). Since you can store any of 256 K color values in each video DAC color register, you can display a wide range of tones and intensities and create quite realistic video images.

Normally, the video BIOS programs the video DAC registers with a default spectrum of color values (see Figure 4-14) when 320-by-200 256-color mode is selected. Registers 0 through 0FH contain the default gamut of CGA-compatible colors. Registers 10H through 1FH contain a gray scale of gradually increasing intensity. The next 216 registers (20H through F7H) contain three groups of 72 colors, with the first group (registers 20H through 67H) at high intensity, the second (registers 68H through AFH) at an intermediate intensity, and the third (registers B0H through F7H) at low intensity. Each 72-color group is made up of three ranges of colors of decreasing saturation (increasing whiteness); each range varies smoothly in hue from blue to red to green.

 To disable or enable default video BIOS programming of the video DAC color registers, use INT 10H function 12H (see Appendix A).

VGA

As on the EGA, VGA pixel values are decoded by the Attribute Controller, using the palette registers, and then passed to the video DAC, following the same logic as in alphanumeric modes (see Chapter 3). Thus, a pixel value selects the corresponding palette register; the value in the palette register, along with the bit fields in the Attribute Controller's Color Select register, selects one of the 256 video DAC color registers. The video DAC converts the 18-bit RGB value in its color registers to the corresponding analog RGB signals, which drive the monitor.

The only exception to this scheme of attribute decoding occurs in 320-by-200 256-color mode. In this mode, as on the MCGA, each 8-bit pixel value specifies one of the video DAC's 256 color registers directly, without the Attribute Controller's mediation.

5

Pixel Programming

Bit-Plane Programming
EGA and VGA ● InColor Card

Reading a Pixel's Value
CGA ● HGC and HGC+ ● EGA
InColor Card ● MCGA ● VGA

Setting a Pixel's Value
CGA ● HGC and HGC+ ● EGA
InColor Card ● MCGA ● VGA

Filling the Video Buffer
CGA ● HGC and HGC+ ● EGA and VGA
InColor Card ● MCGA

Many graphics programming techniques are based on routines that manipulate individual pixels in the video buffer. This chapter presents the fundamentals of pixel programming: reading a pixel's value, setting the value of a pixel in the video buffer, and initializing an area of the video buffer with a pattern of pixels.

Bit-Plane Programming

There is a fundamental difference between graphics-mode programming using video subsystems whose video RAM is organized as parallel bit planes (the EGA, the VGA, and the InColor Card) and graphics-mode programming for the other IBM video subsystems. On the CGA, the MCGA, or the Hercules monochrome adapter, your program accesses pixels by directly reading and writing bytes in video RAM. In contrast, in native graphics modes on the EGA, VGA, or InColor Card, your program cannot access video RAM directly. Instead, special hardware logic in the video subsystem mediates accesses to pixels in the bit planes.

The graphics-mode bit planes on the EGA, VGA, and InColor Cards are addressed in parallel; that is, when you execute a CPU read or write at a particular address in the video buffer, the address refers not to one byte, but to four bytes, one in each of the bit planes.

When you execute an 80x86 instruction that attempts to read data from an address in the video buffer, four bytes of data are actually moved out of the buffer. The data does not go directly to the CPU, however. Instead, it is copied into a set of four 8-bit latches. Each latch is assigned to one of the four bit planes. Executing an 8-bit CPU read from an address in the video buffer thus has the effect of transferring four bytes (32 bits) of data from the video buffer into the latches (see Figure 5-1a). Instructions such as MOV reg,mem, LODS, and CMP reg,mem require a CPU read, and thus cause the latches to be updated.

Similarly, instructions such as MOV mem,reg, STOS, and XOR mem,reg cause a CPU write; in this case, all four bit planes can be updated in parallel using a combination of the data in the latches, the data byte that the CPU writes, and a predefined pixel value stored in a graphics control register (see Figure 5-1b).

Some CPU instructions require both a CPU read and a CPU write. (The CPU reads a value from memory, performs an operation on it, and then writes the result back to memory.) MOVS is an obvious example, but OR mem,reg, AND mem,reg, and XOR mem,reg also generate a CPU read and write. When such an instruction refers to an address in video RAM, the latches are updated during the CPU read, and then the bit planes are updated during the CPU write.

The use of latches to process bit-plane data in parallel lets you write deceptively simple code. For example, consider the following fragment, which copies the second byte of pixels in the video buffer to the first byte.

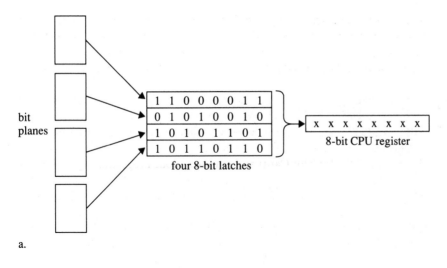

a.

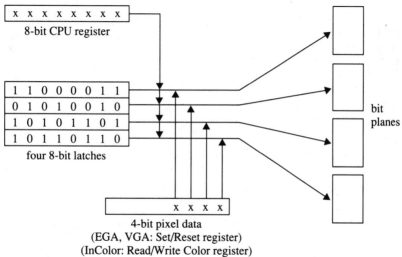

b.

Figure 5-1. *Graphics mode data flow on the EGA, the VGA, and the InColor Card during CPU (a.) read and (b.) write.*

```
mov      ax,VideoBufferSegment
mov      ds,ax
mov      es,ax
mov      si,1      ; DS:SI -> second byte
mov      di,0      ; ES:DI -> first byte
movsb
```

This code looks straightforward. The MOVSB instruction apparently copies one byte from the memory location at DS:SI to the location at ES:DI—but this is not really what takes place in graphics modes that use bit planes in the EGA, VGA, or InColor video buffer.

What actually happens is this: The MOVSB instruction causes a CPU read, followed by a CPU write. Because the CPU read references an address in the video buffer, a byte from each bit plane at that address is loaded into the latches. Then, because the CPU write references an address in the video buffer, the contents of the latches are copied into the bit planes at the specified address. Thus, the MOVSB actually causes four bytes of data to be moved instead of one.

 There is more to this example than meets the eye. Consider what would happen if you substituted a MOVSW instruction for the MOVSB. Without bit planes and latches, this would result in two bytes of data being copied instead of one byte. However, half of the pixel data would be lost on the EGA, the VGA, or the InColor Card. The reason is that the MOVSW executes as a sequence of two 8-bit CPU reads, followed by two 8-bit CPU writes, so the second CPU read updates the latches before the bytes latched by the first CPU read can be written.

For this reason, you should use 16-bit 80x86 instructions cautiously when accessing the video buffer on the EGA, the VGA, and the InColor Card. Instructions such as OR mem,reg, AND mem,reg, and XOR mem,reg do not work properly with 16-bit data.

The latches clearly improve efficiency in moving data to and from the video buffer, but the real fun begins in transferring data between the latches and the CPU. Since the latches contain 32 bits of data and a CPU byte register contains only eight bits, some sort of data compression must take place during CPU reads. Conversely, in transferring data from the CPU to the bit planes, you can combine the 8-bit CPU data byte with the contents of all four latches in a number of ways. The key to graphics-mode programming on the EGA, the VGA, and the InColor Card is to exploit the data transformations involving the CPU and the latches.

EGA and VGA

On the EGA and VGA, the Graphics Controller manages all transfers of data among the CPU, the latches, and the video buffer. The EGA's Graphics Controller consists of two LSI chips; the VGA's is part of the Video Graphics Array chip. The Graphics Controller has nine registers addressable at port 3CFH via an address register at port 3CEH. The values you store in the registers control the way the Graphics Controller processes latched data during CPU reads and writes.

In a sense, the Graphics Controller lets you manipulate the latched pixel data two-dimensionally. Some of the operations you can perform on the latched data are byte-oriented; they affect each latch separately. Other operations are pixel-oriented in that they regard the latched data as a set of eight pixel values; these operations affect each pixel value separately.

The Graphics Controller can perform three different byte-oriented operations on latched data. It can copy the contents of the latches to and from the video buffer; this action occurs implicitly when a CPU write or read is executed. It can return the contents of one of the latches to a CPU register during a CPU read. It can also combine a data byte from a CPU register with the bytes in any or all of the latches during a single CPU write.

The Graphics Controller also processes latched data pixel by pixel. During a CPU read, the Graphics Controller can compare each latched pixel value with a pre-defined value and return the result of the comparison to the CPU. During CPU writes, it can combine a 4-bit CPU value with any or all pixel values in the latches; it can use an 8-bit CPU value as a mask that indicates which of the eight latched pixels are copied back to the bit planes; and it can combine the latched pixel values with a predefined 4-bit value.

Both byte-oriented and pixel-oriented operations are programmed by selecting a write mode and a read mode. Each write mode sets up a predefined sequence of byte-oriented and pixel-oriented operations which occur when a CPU write is executed. Similarly, each read mode defines a set of actions performed during CPU reads. The EGA has three write modes and two read modes; the VGA has these five modes and one additional write mode.

Until you become familiar with each of the Graphics Controller's read and write modes, their *raison d'etre* may seem a bit obscure. However, each mode has practical advantages in certain programming situations, as the examples in this and subsequent chapters demonstrate.

The Graphics Controller's Mode register (05H) contains two bit fields whose values specify the graphics read and write mode. For example, to establish read mode 1 you would set bit 3 of the Mode register to 1; to set up write mode 2, you would store the value 2 (10B) in bits 0 and 1 of the Mode register (Listing 5-1).

```
        mov     ax,0105h        ; AH := 1 (reg 5 value)
                                ;  bit 3 := 0 (read mode 0)
                                ;  bits 0-1 := 1 (write mode 1)
                                ; AL := register number
        mov     dx,3CEh         ; DX := Graphics Controller port
        out     dx,ax
```

Listing 5-1. *How to set Graphics Controller read and write modes. This example sets read mode 0 and write mode 1 in in 640-by-350 16-color mode.*

The video BIOS default values for the Graphics Controller's Mode register and its other registers are listed in Figure 5-2. It is good practice to restore the Graphics Controller registers to their default values after you modify them in your program.

Register	Function	Value
0	Set/Reset	0
1	Enable Set/Reset	0
2	Color Compare	0
3	Data Rotate	0
4	Read Map Select	0
5	Mode	Bits 0–3 always 0
6	Miscellaneous	(depends on video mode)
7	Color Don't Care	0FH (16-color modes)
		01H (640-by-480 2-color mode)
8	Bit Mask	FFH

Figure 5-2. *Default ROM BIOS values for EGA and VGA Graphics Controller registers.*

Read mode 0

In graphics read mode 0, the Graphics Controller returns the contents of one of the four latches to the CPU each time a CPU read loads the latches (see Figure 5-3). The value in the Read Map Select register (04H) indicates which latch to read. Read mode 0 thus lets you read bytes from each individual bit plane; this is useful in transferring data between the bit planes and system RAM or a disk file.

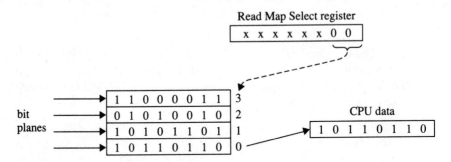

Figure 5-3. *EGA and VGA graphics read mode 0.*

Read Mode 1

In graphics read mode 1, each of the eight pixel values latched during a CPU read is compared with the value in the Color Compare register (02H). The result of the comparison is returned to the CPU as a single byte (see Figure 5-4). Where a pixel value matches the Color Compare value, a bit in the CPU data byte is set to 1; where the values are different, the corresponding bit in the data byte is 0.

Note how the value in the Color Don't Care register (07H) interacts with the pixel value and Color Compare value. In effect, setting a bit to 0 in the Color Don't Care value excludes a latch from the comparison. For example, a Color Don't Care value of 0111B causes only the three low-order bits of each pixel value to participate in the comparison. Another example: If you store a 0 in the Color Don't Care register, all four bits in the comparison become "don't care" bits, so all pixel values match the Color Compare value, and the CPU always reads the value 11111111B in read mode 1.

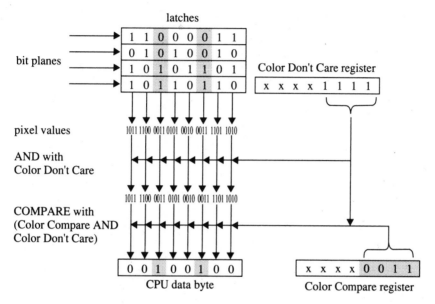

Figure 5-4. *EGA and VGA graphics read mode 1.*

Write mode 0

Graphics write mode 0 sets up a combination of byte-oriented and pixel-oriented operations that occur when a CPU write is executed. The data byte written by the CPU can be used to update any or all of the bit planes; at the same time, a pre-defined pixel value can be used to update any or all of the eight pixels involved. This two-dimensional update of the latches is controlled in several different ways using the values in the Enable Set/Reset, Data Rotate/Function Select, and Bit Mask registers (see Figure 5-5).

The Bit Mask register (08H) specifies how the new value of each of the eight pixels in the video buffer is derived. Where a bit in the Bit Mask register equals 0, the corresponding pixel value is copied directly from the latches into the video buffer. For each 1 bit in the Bit Mask value, the corresponding pixel is updated with the latched pixel value combined with either the CPU data or the pixel value in the Set/Reset register. Thus, if a CPU write immediately follows a CPU read at the same address, the only pixels updated are those for which the corresponding bit in the Bit Mask register is set to 1.

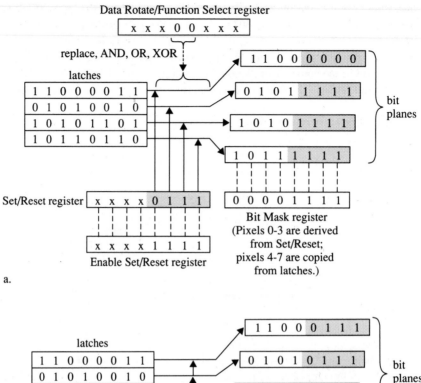

a.

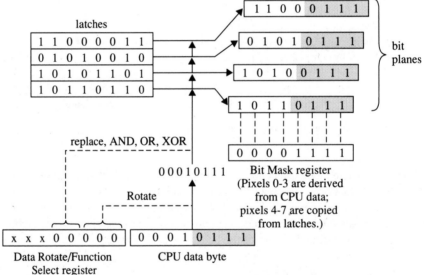

b.

Figure 5-5. *EGA and VGA graphics write mode 0: (a.) Enable Set/Reset Value = 1111B, (b.) Enable Set/Reset value = 0000B.*

The Data Rotate/Function Select register (03H) contains two bit fields whose contents affect the way the latched pixels are updated. Bits 3 through 4 are important because their value specifies which bitwise logical operation (AND, OR, XOR, or replace) is used to update the pixels (see Figure 5-6). Bits 0 through 2 specify the number of bits by which to right-rotate the CPU data byte before combining it with latched data.

Bit Value		Function
Bit 4	**Bit 3**	
0	0	Replace
0	1	AND
1	0	OR
1	1	XOR

Figure 5-6. *Functions available for updating pixels in EGA and VGA write modes 0, 2, and 3. Bits 3 and 4 of the Data Rotate/Function Select register specify which is used.*

This data-rotate capability is not particularly useful. In practice, it is generally easier to let the CPU rotate and shift data before writing it to the bit planes than it is to program the Graphics Controller to do this.

The value in the Enable Set/Reset register (register 01H) determines whether the bit planes are updated byte by byte or pixel by pixel. When the Enable Set/Reset value is 0FH (1111B), each pixel is updated by combining the latched pixel value with the value in the Set/Reset register (register 00H) using the logical operation that the Data Rotate/Function Select register specifies (refer to Figure 5-5a). When the Enable Set/Reset value is 0, the rotated CPU data byte is combined with the bytes in each of the latches, again using the function that the Data Rotate/Function Select register specifies (see Figure 5-5b). In either case, only the pixels masked by the Bit Mask register are updated.

Of course, you can set the Enable Set/Reset register to any value from 0 through 0FH. Each bit in each pixel is then updated by combining it either with the corresponding bit in the Set/Reset register or with the corresponding bit in the CPU data byte—depending on the value of the corresponding bit in the Enable Set/Reset register. Needless to say, this kind of programming is tricky and infrequently used.

Write mode 1
In write mode 1, the latches are copied directly to the bit planes when a CPU write occurs (see Figure 5-7). Neither the value of the CPU data byte nor those of the Data Rotate/Function Select, the Bit Mask, the Set/Reset, and the Enable Set/Reset registers affect this process. Clearly, for a write mode 1 operation to make sense, you must first perform a CPU read to initialize the latches.

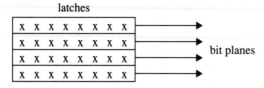

Figure 5-7. *EGA and VGA graphics write mode 1.*

Write mode 2

In write mode 2, the low-order bits of the byte written by the CPU play the same role as the Set/Reset register value in write mode 0. That is, the bit planes are updated by combining the pixel values in the latches with the CPU data, using the logical operation specified in the Data Rotate/Function Select register (see Figure 5-8). As in write mode 0, the Bit Mask register specifies which pixels are updated using the combined pixel values and which pixels are updated directly from the latches.

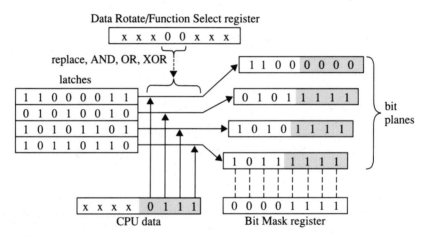

Figure 5-8. *EGA and VGA graphics write mode 2.*

Write mode 3

In write mode 3 (supported on the VGA only), the pixels are updated by combining the pixel values in the latches with the value in the Set/Reset register. Again, the Data Rotate/Function Select register specifies the logical operation used to combine the values. The CPU data byte is rotated by the number of bits indicated in the Data Rotate/Function Select register and combined with the value in the Bit Mask register using a logical AND. The resulting bit mask then plays the same role as the Bit Mask register value in write modes 0 and 2; that is, it determines which pixels in the bit planes are updated by combining the latched pixel values with the Set/Reset value, and which are updated directly from the latches (see Figure 5-9).

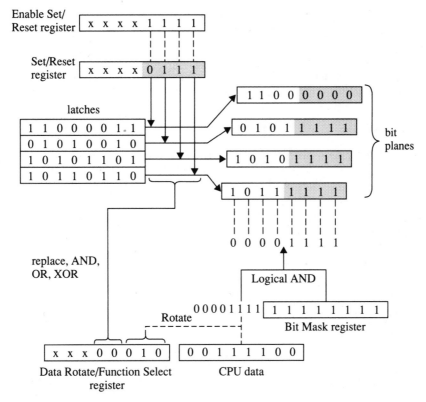

Figure 5-9. *VGA graphics write mode 3.*

Sequencer Map Mask

One additional level of control is available in all of the EGA's and the VGA's Graphics Controller write modes. You can use the Sequencer Map Mask register (Sequencer register 02H) to selectively enable or disable data transfers to the bit planes. In 16-color graphics modes, bits 0 through 3 of this register are normally set to 1 to allow graphics writes to access all four maps. However, by zeroing one or more of these bits, you can write-protect the corresponding memory maps.

The Sequencer Map Mask register is not often used, because the Graphics Controller provides better control for pixel-oriented operations. Use of this register is better suited to techniques such as bit-plane layering (see Chapter 12).

InColor Card

The InColor Card has two gate arrays, the Encoder and the Decoder, which mediate CPU accesses to video RAM. The Encoder gate array participates in CPU writes to video RAM. The Decoder gate array manages the transfer of data from video RAM to the CPU, as well as to the card's attribute-decoding circuitry.

The programming interface to the InColor Card's graphics-mode hardware, including the Encoder and Decoder chips, is unified through the card's control register set at I/O ports 3B4H and 3B5H (see Figure 5-10). There is no distinction between the Encoder, the Decoder, and their associated circuitry from a software point of view. The InColor Card's graphics-mode control registers are similar to control registers on the EGA and the VGA (see Figure 5-11).

Register Number	Register Function	Read/Write Status
18H	Plane Mask register	Write only
19H	Read/Write Control register	Write only
1AH	Read/Write Color register	Write only
1BH	Latch Protect register	Write only

Figure 5-10. *Graphics control registers on the Hercules InColor Card.*

InColor	EGA and VGA
Plane Mask register	Sequencer Map Mask register
	Attribute Controller Color Plane Enable register
Read/Write Control register	Graphics Controller Mode register
	Graphics Controller Color Don't Care register
Read/Write Color register	Graphics Controller Set/Reset register
Palette register	Attribute Controller Palette registers

Figure 5-11. *Functionally similar control registers on the EGA, VGA, and InColor Card.*

As on the EGA and VGA, video RAM accesses in graphics mode are performed using a set of four 8-bit latches. CPU reads and writes cause bytes to be transferred in parallel between the latches and the corresponding bit planes. When a CPU read is executed, the Decoder latches a byte from each bit plane and returns a single byte of data to the CPU. When a CPU write is executed, the Encoder combines the latched data with the pixel values stored in the Read/Write Color register and updates the bit planes with the result.

Like the EGA and VGA, the InColor Card can process CPU data and latched data in several ways. The card supports four graphics write modes (see Figure 5-12),

Write Mode	CPU Data Bit = 0	CPU Data Bit = 1
0	Background value	Foreground value
1	Latch	Foreground value
2	Background value	Latch
3	NOT latch	Latch

Figure 5-12. *Source of pixel data in InColor graphics write modes.*

selected by bits 4 and 5 of the Read/Write Control register (19H). There is only one graphics read mode, which is similar to read mode 1 on the EGA and VGA.

Write modes 0–3

In all four InColor graphics write modes, the CPU data functions as an 8-bit mask. The Encoder uses the value of each bit in the mask to determine how to update the corresponding pixel value in the latches. That is, the source of the pixel value at a particular bit position is determined by the value of the corresponding bit in the CPU data byte.

For example, in graphics write mode 1, when a bit in the CPU data byte is 1, the corresponding pixel in the video buffer is replaced with the foreground value in the Read/Write Control register; when a bit in the CPU data byte is 0, the corresponding pixel value is copied from the latches. For example, in Figure 5-13, the pixels corresponding to bits 0 through 3 are replaced with the Read/Write Control register foreground value, while the remaining pixels are updated from the pixel values in the latches.

Similarly, in the other three graphics write modes, the value of each bit in the CPU data byte controls how the corresponding pixel is updated. The write modes differ only in how the pixel values are derived (see Figure 5-12). In write mode 0, either the foreground or the background value in the Read/Write Control register replaces the pixels in the bit planes. In write mode 2, for each 0 bit in the CPU data byte, the Read/Write Control register background value is used to update the corresponding pixel in the bit planes. In write mode 3, each 0 bit in the CPU data byte causes the corresponding pixel in the video buffer to be replaced with the bit-wise NOT of the pixel value in the latches.

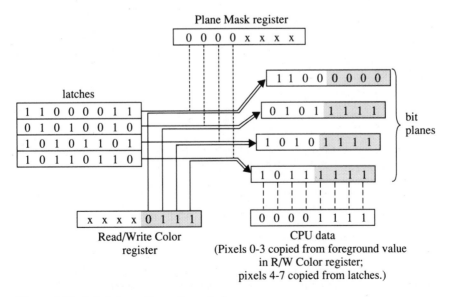

Figure 5-13. *InColor graphics write mode 1.*

CPU writes affect only those bit planes specified in the Plane Mask register (18H). This register's function is thus analogous to that of the EGA's Sequencer Map Mask register. Bits 4 through 7 of this register control which of the four bit planes are writable; setting any of these bits to 1 prevents updating of the corresponding bit planes during CPU writes.

Read mode

The InColor Card has only one graphics read mode (see Figure 5-14). It resembles read mode 1 on the EGA and the VGA. When a CPU read is executed, the latches are loaded with data from the bit planes. Unlike the EGA and the VGA, however, the InColor Card lets you control which individual pixel values are latched during a CPU read. The bit mask value in the Latch Protect register (1BH) indicates which pixel values are latched. Where a bit in the Latch Protect register is 0, the corresponding pixel value is latched; where a bit is 1, the corresponding pixel value in the latch remains unchanged.

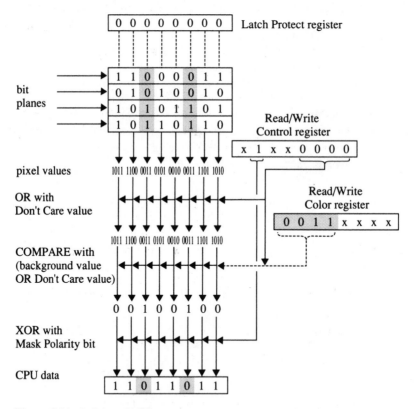

Figure 5-14. *InColor graphics read.*

After the specified pixel values in the latches have been updated from the bit planes, the Decoder compares each pixel value in the latches with the background value in the Read/Write Color register. The 8-bit result of the comparison is returned to the CPU. This is similar to read mode 1 on the EGA and the VGA.

Bits 0 through 3 of the Read/Write Control register are ''don't care'' bits analogous to the Color Don't Care value on the EGA and the VGA. Setting a Read/Write Control ''don't care'' bit to 1 has the effect of excluding a latch from the background value compare operation. If you set all four ''don't care'' bits to 1, all pixel values match the background value no matter what it is.

The polarity of the bits in the result returned to the CPU depends upon the value of the Mask Polarity bit (bit 6 of the Read/Write Control register). When this bit is 0, bits in the result are 1 where a pixel value in the latches matches the background value. Setting the Mask Polarity bit to 1 inverts the result; that is, bits are 1 where a pixel value in the latches does not match the background value.

Reading a Pixel's Value

Now it is time to turn to some specific programming techniques for manipulating pixels on the various PC and PS/2 video subsystems. Once you calculate the byte and bit offsets of a particular pixel in the video buffer, determining the pixel's value is a matter of isolating the bits that represent it in the buffer. This is as true on the CGA and HGC, with their simpler video RAM architecture, as it is on more complicated video subsystems that use bit planes.

CGA

In 640-by-200 2-color mode, the value of a pixel is determined simply by reading the byte that contains the pixel from the video buffer and testing the value of the bit that represents the pixel (see Listing 5-2).

```
                   TITLE   'Listing 5-2'
                   NAME    ReadPixel06
                   PAGE    55,132

;
; Name:          ReadPixel06
;
; Function:      Read the value of a pixel in 640x200 2-color mode
;
; Caller:        Microsoft C:
;
;                       int ReadPixel06(x,y);
;
;                       int x,y;                /* pixel coordinates */
;

ARGx               EQU     word ptr [bp+4] ; stack frame addressing
ARGy               EQU     word ptr [bp+6]


_TEXT              SEGMENT byte public 'CODE'
                   ASSUME  cs:_TEXT

                   EXTRN   PixelAddr06:near
```

Listing 5-2. *Determining a pixel value in CGA 640-by-200 2-color mode.*   *(continued)*

Listing 5-2. *Continued.*

```
                PUBLIC  _ReadPixel06
_ReadPixel06    PROC    near

                push    bp                      ; preserve caller registers
                mov     bp,sp

                mov     ax,ARGy                 ; AX := y
                mov     bx,ARGx                 ; BX := x
                call    PixelAddr06             ; AH := bit mask
                                                ; ES:BX -> buffer
                                                ; CL := # bits to shift

                mov     al,es:[bx]              ; AL := byte containing pixel
                shr     al,cl                   ; shift pixel value to low-order bits
                and     al,ah                   ; AL := pixel value
                xor     ah,ah                   ; AX := pixel value

                mov     sp,bp                   ; restore caller registers and return
                pop     bp
                ret

_ReadPixel06    ENDP

_TEXT           ENDS
                END
```

The technique for determining the value of a pixel in 320-by-200 4-color graphics mode, as shown in Listing 5-3, is similar. After isolating the bits that represent the pixel, however, your program must shift them rightward so that the value returned represents the actual pixel value.

```
                TITLE   'Listing 5-3'
                NAME    ReadPixel04
                PAGE    55,132

;
; Name:          ReadPixel04
;
; Function:      Read the value of a pixel in 320x200 4-color mode
;
; Caller:        Microsoft C:
;
;                       int ReadPixel04(x,y);
;
;                       int x,y;                /* pixel coordinates */
;

ARGx            EQU     word ptr [bp+4] ; stack frame addressing
ARGy            EQU     word ptr [bp+6]


_TEXT           SEGMENT byte public 'CODE'
                ASSUME  cs:_TEXT

                EXTRN   PixelAddr04:near
```

Listing 5-3. *Determining a pixel value in CGA 320-by-200 4-color mode.*   *(continued)*

Listing 5-3. *Continued.*

```
                PUBLIC    _ReadPixel04
_ReadPixel04    PROC      near

                push      bp              ; preserve caller registers
                mov       bp,sp

                mov       ax,ARGy         ; AX := y
                mov       bx,ARGx         ; BX := x
                call      PixelAddr04     ; AH := bit mask
                                          ; ES:BX -> buffer
                                          ; CL := # bits to shift

                mov       al,es:[bx]      ; AL := byte containing pixel
                shr       al,cl           ; shift pixel value to low-order bits
                and       al,ah           ; AL := pixel value
                xor       ah,ah           ; AX := pixel value

                mov       sp,bp           ; restore caller registers and return
                pop       bp
                ret

_ReadPixel04    ENDP

_TEXT           ENDS
                END
```

HGC and HGC+

The only difference between the pixel-read routines for the Hercules mono-chrome adapters and the ones used in the CGA's 640-by-200 2-color mode lies in how the pixel's address is computed. For example, you can adapt the CGA routine shown in Listing 5-2 for the HGC simply by substituting `PixelAddrHGC` for `PixelAddr06`.

EGA

In CGA-emulation modes, the routines used for the CGA work unchanged. However, in 16-color 200-line modes and in 350-line modes, you must program the Graphics Controller to isolate the bits that represent a pixel in the video buffer's bit planes, as the routine in Listing 5-4 does.

```
                TITLE     'Listing 5-4'
                NAME      ReadPixel10
                PAGE      55,132

;
; Name:         ReadPixel10
;
; Function:     Read the value of a pixel in native EGA graphics modes
;
; Caller:       Microsoft C:
;
;                         int ReadPixel10(x,y);
```

Listing 5-4. *Determining a pixel value in native EGA graphics modes.*   *(continued)*

Listing 5-4. *Continued.*

```
;
;                              int x,y;                    /* pixel coordinates */
;

ARGx            EQU        word ptr [bp+4] ; stack frame addressing
ARGy            EQU        word ptr [bp+6]


_TEXT           SEGMENT byte public 'CODE'
                ASSUME  cs:_TEXT

                EXTRN    PixelAddr10:near

                PUBLIC   _ReadPixel10
_ReadPixel10    PROC     near

                push     bp                   ; preserve caller registers
                mov      bp,sp
                push     si

                mov      ax,ARGy              ; AX := y
                mov      bx,ARGx              ; BX := x
                call     PixelAddr10          ; AH := bit mask
                                              ; ES:BX -> buffer
                                              ; CL := # bits to shift

                mov      ch,ah
                shl      ch,cl                ; CH := bit mask in proper position

                mov      si,bx                ; ES:SI -> regen buffer byte
                xor      bl,bl                ; BL is used to accumulate the pixel value

                mov      dx,3CEh              ; DX := Graphics Controller port
                mov      ax,304h              ; AH := initial bit plane number
                                              ; AL := Read Map Select register number

L01:            out      dx,ax                ; select bit plane
                mov      bh,es:[si]           ; BH := byte from current bit plane
                and      bh,ch                ; mask one bit
                neg      bh                   ; bit 7 of BH := 1 (if masked bit = 1)
                                              ; bit 7 of BH := 0 (if masked bit = 0)
                rol      bx,1                 ; bit 0 of BL := next bit from pixel value
                dec      ah                   ; AH := next bit plane number
                jge      L01

                mov      al,bl                ; AL := pixel value
                xor      ah,ah                ; AX := pixel value

                pop      si                   ; restore caller registers and return
                mov      sp,bp
                pop      bp
                ret

_ReadPixel10    ENDP

_TEXT           ENDS
                END
```

This routine uses the Graphics Controller's read mode 0 to read a single byte from each of the EGA's planes. As the bytes are read, the desired pixel's bits are masked and concatenated to form the pixel's value.

In 640-by-350 monochrome graphics mode, only bit planes 0 and 2 are used to represent pixel values. In these modes, only bits from these two planes are concatenated to form a pixel value (see Listing 5-5).

As described in Chapter 4, 640-by-350 graphics modes are mapped differently on an EGA with only 64 KB of video RAM than on an EGA with more memory. Memory maps 0 through 1 and 2 through 3 are chained to form two bit planes. Pixels at even byte addresses are represented in maps 0 and 2, while pixels at odd byte addresses are represented in maps 1 and 3. A routine to read pixel values in these modes must use the pixel's byte address to determine which maps to read (see Listing 5-6).

```
                TITLE    'Listing 5-5'
                NAME     ReadPixel0F
                PAGE     55,132

;
; Name:         ReadPixel0F
;
; Function:     Read the value of a pixel in 640x350 monochrome mode
;
; Caller:       Microsoft C:
;
;                       int     ReadPixel0F(x,y);
;
;                       int x,y;                /* pixel coordinates */
;

ARGx            EQU      word ptr [bp+4] ; stack frame addressing
ARGy            EQU      word ptr [bp+6]


_TEXT           SEGMENT byte public 'CODE'
                ASSUME  cs:_TEXT

                EXTRN    PixelAddr10:near

                PUBLIC   _ReadPixel0F
_ReadPixel0F    PROC     near

                push     bp              ; preserve caller registers
                mov      bp,sp
                push     si

                mov      ax,ARGy         ; AX := y
                mov      bx,ARGx         ; BX := x
                call     PixelAddr10     ; AH := bit mask
                                         ; ES:BX -> buffer
                                         ; CL := # bits to shift
```

Listing 5-5. *Determining a pixel value in EGA monochrome graphics mode.*   *(continued)*

Listing 5-5. *Continued.*

```
; concatenate bits from bit planes 2 and 0

                mov     ch,ah
                shl     ch,cl           ; CH := bit mask in proper position
                mov     si,bx           ; ES:SI -> regen buffer byte

                mov     dx,3CEh         ; DX := Graphics Controller port
                mov     ax,204h         ; AH := initial bit plane number
                                        ; AL := Read Map Select register number

                xor     bl,bl           ; BL is used to accumulate the pixel value

L01:            out     dx,ax           ; (same as before)
                mov     bh,es:[si]
                and     bh,ch
                neg     bh

                rol     bx,1
                sub     ah,2            ; decrement map number by 2
                jge     L01

                mov     al,bl
                xor     ah,ah

                pop     si
                mov     sp,bp
                pop     bp
                ret

_ReadPixel0F    ENDP

_TEXT           ENDS

                END
```

```
                TITLE   'Listing 5-6'
                NAME    ReadPixel10
                PAGE    55,132

;
; Name:         ReadPixel10
;
; Function:     Read the value of a pixel in 640x350 modes on 64K EGA
;
; Caller:       Microsoft C:
;
;                       int     ReadPixel10(x,y);
;
;                       int x,y;                /* pixel coordinates */
;

ARGx            EQU     word ptr [bp+4] ; stack frame addressing
ARGy            EQU     word ptr [bp+6]
```

(continued)

Listing 5-6. *Determining a pixel value in 640-by-350 modes on an EGA with 64 KB.*

Listing 5-6. *Continued.*

```
_TEXT           SEGMENT byte public 'CODE'
                ASSUME  cs:_TEXT

                EXTRN   PixelAddr10:near

                PUBLIC  _ReadPixel10
_ReadPixel10    PROC    near

                push    bp              ; preserve caller registers
                mov     bp,sp
                push    si

                mov     ax,ARGy         ; AX := y
                mov     bx,ARGx         ; BX := x
                call    PixelAddr10     ; AH := bit mask
                                        ; ES:BX -> buffer
                                        ; CL := # bits to shift

; concatenate bits from bit planes 2 and 0 (even byte address)
;   or 3 and 1 (odd byte address)

                mov     ch,ah
                shl     ch,cl           ; CH := bit mask in proper position

                mov     si,bx           ; ES:SI -> regen buffer byte

                mov     ah,bl           ; AH := low-order byte of address
                and     ax,100h         ; AH := low-order bit of address
                                        ; AL := 0
                add     ax,204h         ; AH := initial bit plane number (2 or 3)
                                        ; AL := Read Map Select register number

                mov     dx,3CEh         ; DX := Graphics Controller port
                xor     bl,bl           ; BL is used to accumulate the pixel value

L01:            out     dx,ax           ; (same as before)
                mov     bh,es:[si]
                and     bh,ch
                neg     bh

                rol     bx,1
                sub     ah,2
                jge     L01

                mov     al,bl
                xor     ah,ah

                pop     si
                mov     sp,bp
                pop     bp
                ret

_ReadPixel10    ENDP

_TEXT           ENDS

                END
```

InColor Card

As with the EGA, to read a pixel's value on the InColor Card requires reading each bit plane separately. To do this, you must use the "don't care" bits in the Read/Write Control register along with the background value in the Read/Write Color register to isolate the contents of each latch.

The routine in Listing 5-7 accumulates a pixel's 4-bit value by concatenating one bit from each of the InColor card's four bit planes. The routine determines the contents of each of the bit planes by setting the background value in the Read/Write Color register to 0FH (1111B) and by individually zeroing each Read/Write Control register "don't care" bit. When each CPU read is executed (with the AND CH, ES:[SI] instruction), the value returned to the CPU is thus the 8-bit value in one of the four latches. This value is ANDed with the bit mask in CH, and the isolated bits are accumulated in BL.

```
                    TITLE    'Listing 5-7'
                    NAME     ReadPixelInC
                    PAGE     55,132

;
; Name:         ReadPixelInC
;
; Function:     Read the value of a pixel in InColor 720x348 16-color mode
;
; Caller:       Microsoft C:
;
;                       int      ReadPixelInC(x,y);
;
;                       int x,y;
;

ARGx            EQU      word ptr [bp+4]  ; stack frame addressing
ARGy            EQU      word ptr [bp+6]

DefaultRWColor  EQU      0Fh                  ; default value for R/W Color Register


_TEXT           SEGMENT byte public 'CODE'
                ASSUME  cs:_TEXT

                EXTRN    PixelAddrHGC:near

                PUBLIC   _ReadPixelInC
_ReadPixelInC   PROC     near

                push     bp                   ; preserve caller registers
                mov      bp,sp
                push     si

                mov      ax,ARGy              ; AX := y
                mov      bx,ARGx              ; BX := x
                call     PixelAddrHGC         ; AH := bit mask
                                              ; ES:BX -> buffer
                                              ; CL := # bits to shift
```

Listing 5-7. *Determining a pixel value in InColor graphics mode.*   *(continued)*

Listing 5-7. *Continued.*

```
; set up to examine each bit plane separately

                mov     si,bx           ; ES:SI -> buffer

                shl     ah,cl
                mov     cl,ah           ; CL := bit mask in proper position

                mov     dx,3B4h         ; DX := graphics control port

                mov     ax,0F01Ah       ; AH bits 4-7 := 1111b (background value)
                                        ; AL := 1Ah (R/W Color Register)
                out     dx,ax           ; set background value

                mov     bx,800h         ; BH := 1000b (initial "don't care" bits)
                                        ; BL := 0 (initial value for result)

                dec     ax              ; AL := 19h (R/W Control Register number)

; loop across bit planes by updating "don't care" bits

L01:            mov     ah,bh           ; AH bits 0-3 := next "don't care" bits
                                        ; AH bit 6 := 0 (Mask Polarity bit)
                xor     ah,1111b        ; invert "don't care" bits
                out     dx,ax           ; set R/W Control Register

                mov     ch,cl           ; CH := bit mask
                and     ch,es:[si]      ; latch bit planes
                                        ; CH <> 0 if bit in latch is set

                neg     ch              ; cf set if CH <> 0
                rcl     bl,1            ; accumulate result in BL

                shr     bh,1            ; BH := shifted "don't care" bits
                jnz     L01             ; loop until shifted out of BH,
                                        ;  at which point BX = pixel value
; restore default state

                mov     ah,40h          ; AH := default R/W Control Register value
                out     dx,ax

                inc     ax              ; AL := 1Ah (R/W Color Register number)
                mov     ah,DefaultRWColor
                out     dx,ax

                mov     ax,bx           ; AX := pixel value

                pop     si              ; restore caller registers and return
                mov     sp,bp
                pop     bp
                ret

_ReadPixelInC   ENDP

_TEXT           ENDS

                END
```

As usual in bit-plane programming, the tricky part of this process is in setting up the control register values to produce the desired result. For example, here is what happens when the AND CH,ES:[SI] instruction executes:

1. One byte from each bit plane is copied into the latches.

2. Each of the eight pixels in the latches is compared with the background value (1111B), and the eight bits that reflect the result of the eight comparisons are returned to the CPU. Because only one of the four "don't care" bits in the Read/Write Control register is 0, only one of the four bits in each pixel value participates in each comparison. If this bit is 1, the comparison is true, and the Decoder returns a 1 in the bit position corresponding to this pixel value.

3. The eight bits returned to the CPU are ANDed with the bit mask in CH to give the desired result.

That's a lot of action for a single AND instruction.

MCGA

In 640-by-200 2-color and 320-by-200 4-color modes, the routines written for the CGA (shown in Listings 5-2 and 5-3) also work on the MCGA. The two other MCGA graphics modes pose no additional problems (see Listings 5-8 and 5-9), because they use no buffer interleave as do CGA-compatible modes, and because there are no bit planes to worry about.

```
                    TITLE    'Listing 5-8'
                    NAME     ReadPixel11
                    PAGE     55,132

;
; Name:          ReadPixel11
;
; Function:      Read the value of a pixel in 640x480 2-color mode (MCGA or VGA)
;
; Caller:        Microsoft C:
;
;                        int ReadPixel11(x,y);
;
;                        int x,y;                /* pixel coordinates */
;

ARGx            EQU      word ptr [bp+4] ; stack frame addressing
ARGy            EQU      word ptr [bp+6]


_TEXT           SEGMENT byte public 'CODE'
                ASSUME  cs:_TEXT

                EXTRN    PixelAddr10:near
```

(continued)

Listing 5-8. *Determining a pixel value in MCGA and VGA 640-by-480 2-color mode.*

Listing 5-8. *Continued.*

```
                PUBLIC   _ReadPixel11
_ReadPixel11    PROC     near

                push     bp                  ; preserve caller registers
                mov      bp,sp

                mov      ax,ARGy             ; AX := y
                mov      bx,ARGx             ; BX := x
                call     PixelAddr10         ; AH := bit mask
                                             ; ES:BX -> buffer
                                             ; CL := # bits to shift

                mov      al,es:[bx]          ; AL := byte containing pixel
                shr      al,cl               ; shift pixel value to low-order bits
                and      al,ah               ; AL := pixel value
                xor      ah,ah               ; AX := pixel value

                mov      sp,bp               ; restore caller registers and return
                pop      bp
                ret

_ReadPixel11    ENDP

_TEXT           ENDS

                END
```

```
                TITLE    'Listing 5-9'
                NAME     ReadPixel13
                PAGE     55,132

;
; Name:          ReadPixel13
;
; Function:      Read the value of a pixel in 320x200 256-color mode
;                 (MCGA and VGA)
;
; Caller:        Microsoft C:
;
;                     int ReadPixel13(x,y);
;
;                     int x,y;                  /* pixel coordinates */
;

ARGx            EQU      word ptr [bp+4] ; stack frame addressing
ARGy            EQU      word ptr [bp+6]


_TEXT           SEGMENT byte public 'CODE'
                ASSUME   cs:_TEXT

                EXTRN    PixelAddr13:near
```

(continued)

Listing 5-9. *Determining a pixel value in MCGA and VGA 320-by-200 256-color mode.*

Listing 5-9. *Continued.*

```
            PUBLIC   _ReadPixel13
_ReadPixel13  PROC   near

            push     bp                  ; preserve caller registers
            mov      bp,sp

            mov      ax,ARGy             ; AX := y
            mov      bx,ARGx             ; BX := x
            call     PixelAddr13         ; ES:BX -> buffer

            mov      al,es:[bx]          ; AL := pixel value
            xor      ah,ah               ; AX := pixel value

            mov      sp,bp
            pop      bp
            ret

_ReadPixel13  ENDP

_TEXT       ENDS

            END
```

VGA

Once you write pixel-read routines for the CGA, the EGA, and the MCGA, you have covered all the bases as far as the VGA is concerned. The only VGA graphics mode not available on the other subsystems is 640-by-480 16-color mode. However, pixel representation and addressing are the same in this mode as in the EGA's 640-by-350 16-color mode, so you can use the routine in Listing 5-4 for both.

Setting a Pixel's Value

In some ways, setting a pixel's value is the converse of determining its value. Once the byte and bit offsets of a particular pixel have been calculated, setting its value is a simple matter of putting the right bits in the right places in the video buffer.

What complicates pixel-setting routines is that you may not always wish simply to replace a pixel's old value with a new value. It is sometimes desirable to derive a pixel's new value by performing a bitwise logical operation on its old value. This is why the EGA and the VGA Graphics Controllers directly support logical AND, OR, and XOR operations on pixel values, as well as direct replacement of old values with new ones.

 Since the bulk of the overhead in a pixel-setting routine is in calculating the pixel's location in the video buffer, you can keep your code small and modular by integrating different pixel-value manipulations into a single routine rather than writing separate routines to replace pixels and to perform bitwise logical operations on them. The examples in this chapter combine these different pixel-value operations into unified routines.

Where each bitwise operation requires a different subroutine, the subroutine's address is stored in a variable (SetPixelOp). This technique is more flexible than coding a jump to the desired pixel operation (replace, AND, OR, or XOR), because you can change the address in the variable with another independent subroutine.

The examples in this chapter do not include code for updating a pixel's value by performing a bitwise NOT operation. You can use the XOR operation to obtain the same result as NOT without decreasing performance and without writing additional code.

CGA

To set a pixel in 640-by-200 2-color mode, mask the appropriate bit in a byte in the video buffer and then set the bit's value. The routine in Listing 5-10 implements four different ways of setting the value—by replacing the old pixel value with a new value and by using the logical operations OR, AND, and XOR.

```
                 TITLE    'Listing 5-10'
                 NAME     SetPixel06
                 PAGE     55,132

;
; Name:          SetPixel06
;
; Function:      Set the value of a pixel in 640x200 2-color mode
;
; Caller:        Microsoft C:
;
;                      void SetPixel(x,y,n);
;
;                      int x,y;                  /* pixel coordinates */
;
;                      int n;                    /* pixel-value */
;

ARGx             EQU      word ptr [bp+4] ; stack frame addressing
ARGy             EQU      word ptr [bp+6]
ARGn             EQU      byte ptr [bp+8]


DGROUP           GROUP    _DATA

_TEXT            SEGMENT  byte public 'CODE'
                 ASSUME   cs:_TEXT,ds:DGROUP

                 EXTRN    PixelAddr06:near

                 PUBLIC   _SetPixel06
```

Listing 5-10. *Setting a pixel value in CGA 640-by-200 2-color mode.*   *(continued)*

Listing 5-10. *Continued.*

```
_SetPixel06      PROC     near

                 push     bp                       ; preserve caller registers
                 mov      bp,sp

                 mov      ax,ARGy                  ; AX := y
                 mov      bx,ARGx                  ; BX := x
                 call     PixelAddr06              ; AH := bit mask
                                                   ; ES:BX -> buffer
                                                   ; CL := # bits to shift left

                 mov      al,ARGn                  ; AL := unshifted pixel value
                 shl      ax,cl                    ; AH := bit mask in proper position
                                                   ; AL := pixel value in proper position

                 jmp      word ptr SetPixelOp06    ; jump to Replace, AND,
                                                   ;   OR or XOR routine


                                                   ; routine to Replace pixel value

ReplacePixel06:  not      ah                       ; AH := inverse bit mask
                 and      es:[bx],ah               ; zero the pixel value
                 or       es:[bx],al               ; set the pixel value
                 jmp      short L02


                                                   ; routine to AND pixel value

ANDPixel06:      test     al,al
                 jnz      L02                      ; do nothing if pixel value = 1

L01:             not      ah                       ; AH := inverse of bit mask
                 and      es:[bx],ah               ; set bit in video buffer to 0
                 jmp      short L02


                                                   ; routine to OR pixel value

ORPixel06:       test     al,al
                 jz       L02                      ; do nothing if pixel value = 0

                 or       es:[bx],al               ; set bit in video buffer
                 jmp      short L02


                                                   ; routine to XOR pixel value

XORPixel06:      test     al,al
                 jz       L02                      ; do nothing if pixel value = 0

                 xor      es:[bx],al               ; XOR bit in video buffer

L02:             mov      sp,bp                    ; restore caller registers and return
                 pop      bp
                 ret

_SetPixel06      ENDP
```

(continued)

Listing 5-10. *Continued.*

```
_TEXT               ENDS

_DATA               SEGMENT word public 'DATA'

SetPixelOp06   DW        ReplacePixel06  ; contains addr of pixel operation

_DATA               ENDS

                    END
```

The routine for 320-by-200 4-color mode is similar. This routine, shown in
Listing 5-11, differs from the routine for 640-by-200 2-color mode (see Listing
5-10) only in its technique for computing pixel addresses and in its representation
of pixels in bit fields that are two bits wide.

```
                    TITLE   'Listing 5-11'
                    NAME    SetPixel04
                    PAGE    55,132

;
; Name:         SetPixel04
;
; Function:     Set the value of a pixel in 320x200 4-color mode
;
; Caller:       Microsoft C:
;
;                       void SetPixel(x,y,n);
;
;                       int x,y;                /* pixel coordinates */
;
;                       int n;                  /* pixel value */
;

ARGx            EQU     word ptr [bp+4] ; stack frame addressing
ARGy            EQU     word ptr [bp+6]
ARGn            EQU     byte ptr [bp+8]


DGROUP          GROUP   _DATA

_TEXT           SEGMENT byte public 'CODE'
                ASSUME  cs:_TEXT,ds:DGROUP

                EXTRN   PixelAddr04:near

                PUBLIC  _SetPixel04
_SetPixel04     PROC    near

                push    bp                      ; preserve caller registers
                mov     bp,sp

                mov     ax,ARGy         ; AX := y
                mov     bx,ARGx         ; BX := x
```

Listing 5-11. *Setting a pixel value in CGA 320-by-200 2-color mode.*   *(continued)*

Listing 5-11. *Continued.*

```
                        call    PixelAddr04     ; AH := bit mask
                                                ; ES:BX -> buffer
                                                ; CL := # bits to shift left

                        mov     al,ARGn
                        shl     ax,cl           ; AH := bit mask in proper position
                                                ; AL := pixel value in proper position

                        jmp     word ptr SetPixelOp04   ; jump to Replace, AND,
                                                        ;   OR or XOR routine


                                                ; routine to Replace pixel value

ReplacePixel04: not     ah              ; AH := inverse bit mask
                and     es:[bx],ah      ; zero the pixel value
                or      es:[bx],al      ; set the pixel value
                jmp     short L02

                                                ; routine to AND pixel value

ANDPixel04:     not     ah              ; AH := inverse bit mask
                or      al,ah           ; AL := all 1's except pixel value
                and     es:[bx],al
                jmp     short L02


ORPixel04:      or      es:[bx],al      ; routine to OR pixel value
                jmp     short L02


XORPixel04:     xor     es:[bx],al      ; routine to XOR pixel value


L02:            mov     sp,bp           ; restore caller registers and return
                pop     bp
                ret

_SetPixel04     ENDP

_TEXT           ENDS

_DATA           SEGMENT word public 'DATA'

SetPixelOp04    DW      ReplacePixel04  ; contains addr of pixel operation

_DATA           ENDS

                END
```

HGC and HGC+

As you might expect, a routine for writing a pixel in the HGC's 720-by-348 monochrome graphics mode can be derived from the equivalent routine for the CGA's
640-by-200 2-color mode in Listing 5-10 by substituting the HGC's pixel-address
computation routine (PixelAddrHGC) for the CGA's.

EGA

You don't need to worry about CGA-emulation modes (640-by-200 2-color and 320-by-200 4-color), because the routines that work on the CGA work equally well on the EGA. However, things become considerably more complicated in the EGA's native graphics modes. In these modes, there are several different ways you can program the Graphics Controller to set the value of an individual pixel. Also, the pixel-setting routine must properly handle the video memory maps in monochrome and 640-by-350 4-color graphics modes (on an EGA with 64 KB).

Write mode 0

The method for setting a pixel's value in write mode 0 is shown in Listing 5-12. First, as usual, you calculate the byte offset and bit mask, which identify the pixel's location in the video buffer. Then you program the Graphics Controller: Set up write mode 0, store the bit mask value in the Bit Mask register, and configure the Set/Reset and Enable Set/Reset registers for the pixel value. Then you can perform a CPU read to latch the bit planes, followed by a CPU write to copy the contents of the latches and the new pixel value into the bit planes.

```
                TITLE    'Listing 5-12'
                NAME     SetPixel10
                PAGE     55,132

;
; Name:         SetPixel10
;
; Function:     Set the value of a pixel in native EGA graphics modes.
;
;               *** Write Mode 0, Set/Reset ***
;
; Caller:       Microsoft C:
;
;                       void SetPixel(x,y,n);
;
;                       int x,y;                /* pixel coordinates */
;
;                       int n;                  /* pixel value */
;

ARGx            EQU      word ptr [bp+4] ; stack frame addressing
ARGy            EQU      word ptr [bp+6]
ARGn            EQU      byte ptr [bp+8]

RMWbits         EQU      18h             ; read-modify-write bits


_TEXT           SEGMENT byte public 'CODE'
                ASSUME   cs:_TEXT

                EXTRN    PixelAddr10:near
                PUBLIC   _SetPixel10
```

(continued)

Listing 5-12. *Setting a pixel value in native EGA graphics modes using write mode 0.*

Listing 5-12. *Continued.*

```
_SetPixel10      PROC     near

                 push     bp                 ; preserve caller registers
                 mov      bp,sp

                 mov      ax,ARGy            ; AX := y
                 mov      bx,ARGx            ; BX := x
                 call     PixelAddr10        ; AH := bit mask
                                             ; ES:BX -> buffer
                                             ; CL := # bits to shift left

; set Graphics Controller Bit Mask register

                 shl      ah,cl              ; AH := bit mask in proper position
                 mov      dx,3CEh            ; GC address register port
                 mov      al,8               ; AL := Bit Mask register number
                 out      dx,ax

; set Graphics Controller Mode register

                 mov      ax,0005h           ; AL :=  Mode register number
                                             ; AH :=  Write Mode 0 (bits 0,1)
                                             ;        Read Mode 0 (bit 3)
                 out      dx,ax

; set Data Rotate/Function Select register

                 mov      ah,RMWbits         ; AH := Read-Modify-Write bits
                 mov      al,3               ; AL := Data Rotate/Function Select reg
                 out      dx,ax

; set Set/Reset and Enable Set/Reset registers

                 mov      ah,ARGn            ; AH := pixel value
                 mov      al,0               ; AL := Set/Reset reg number
                 out      dx,ax

                 mov      ax,0F01h           ; AH := value for Enable Set/Reset (all
                                             ;  bit planes enabled)
                                             ; AL := Enable Set/Reset reg number
                 out      dx,ax

; set the pixel value

                 or       es:[bx],al         ; load latches during CPU read
                                             ; update latches and bit planes during
                                             ;  CPU write

; restore default Graphics Controller registers

                 mov      ax,0FF08h          ; default Bit Mask
                 out      dx,ax

                 mov      ax,0005            ; default Mode register
                 out      dx,ax

                 mov      ax,0003            ; default Function Select
                 out      dx,ax
```

(continued)

Listing 5-12. *Continued.*

```
                mov     ax,0001         ; default Enable Set/Reset
                out     dx,ax

                mov     sp,bp           ; restore caller registers and return
                pop     bp
                ret

_SetPixel10     ENDP

_TEXT           ENDS
                END
```

Note how the contents of the Graphics Controller registers determine how the bit planes are updated during the CPU write in the OR instruction. The value in the Bit Mask register has only one nonzero bit, so only one pixel is updated. This pixel takes its value from the Set/Reset register. (The other seven pixels are updated from the latches; since the CPU read loaded the latches with these same pixels, the CPU write doesn't change them.) The Enable Set/Reset value is 1111B, so the CPU data byte in AL plays no part in the operation.

 IBM's EGA BIOS uses write mode 0 to set the values of individual pixels in INT 10H function 0CH, but the BIOS routine does not use the Set/Reset register to specify the pixel value. Instead, it first zeroes the pixel by using the Bit Mask register to isolate it and by writing a CPU data byte of 0. Then the BIOS programs the Sequencer Map Mask register to select only those bit planes in which the desired pixel value contains a nonzero bit. The routine then performs a second CPU write to set the nonzero bits, as shown in Listing 5-13.

This technique has two weaknesses: There are easier ways to do the same job, and the routine requires extra coding if you want to AND, OR, or XOR the pixel value in the video buffer. For both reasons, video BIOS INT 10H function 0CH is limited in both speed and flexibility.

```
                TITLE   'Listing 5-13'
                NAME    SetPixel10
                PAGE    55,132
;
; Name:          SetPixel10
;
; Function:      Set the value of a pixel in native EGA graphics modes.
;
;                *** Write Mode 0, Sequencer Map Mask ***
```

(continued)

Listing 5-13. *Setting a pixel value in native EGA graphics modes using the Sequencer Map Mask.*

Listing 5-13. *Continued.*

```
;
; Caller:        Microsoft C:
;
;                       void SetPixel(x,y,n);
;
;                       int x,y;                /* pixel coordinates */
;                       int n;                  /* pixel value */

ARGx            EQU     word ptr [bp+4] ; stack frame addressing
ARGy            EQU     word ptr [bp+6]
ARGn            EQU     byte ptr [bp+8]

_TEXT           SEGMENT byte public 'CODE'
                ASSUME  cs:_TEXT

                EXTRN   PixelAddr10:near

                PUBLIC  _SetPixel10
_SetPixel10     PROC    near

                push    bp                      ; preserve caller registers
                mov     bp,sp

                mov     ax,ARGy         ; AX := y
                mov     bx,ARGx         ; BX := x
                call    PixelAddr10     ; AH := bit mask
                                        ; ES:BX -> buffer
                                        ; CL := # bits to shift left

; set Graphics Controller Bit Mask register

                shl     ah,cl           ; AH := bit mask in
                                        ;  proper position
                mov     dx,3CEh         ; Graphics Controller address
                                        ;  reg port
                mov     al,8            ; AL := Bit Mask register number
                out     dx,ax

; zero the pixel value

                mov     al,es:[bx]      ; latch one byte from each
                                        ;  bit plane
                mov     byte ptr es:[bx],0  ; zero masked bits in
                                        ;  all planes

; set Sequencer Map Mask register

                mov     dl,0C4h         ; DX := 3C4h (Sequencer addr
                                        ;  reg port)
                mov     ah,ARGn         ; AH := value for Map Mask
                                        ;  register
                                        ;  (nonzero bits in pixel
                                        ;  value select
                                        ;  enabled bit planes for
                                        ;  Sequencer)
```

(continued)

Listing 5-13. *Continued.*

```
                mov     al,2            ; AL := Map Mask register number
                out     dx,ax

; set the nonzero bits in the pixel value
                mov     byte ptr es:[bx],0FFh ; set bits in enabled
                                              ;   bit planes

; restore default Sequencer registers
                mov     ah,0Fh          ; AH := value for Map Mask reg
                                        ;   (all bit
                                        ;    planes enabled)
                out     dx,ax

; restore default Graphics Controller registers
                mov     dl,0CEh         ; DX := 3CEh (Graphics
                                        ;   Controller port)
                mov     ax,0FF08h       ; default Bit Mask
                out     dx,ax

                mov     sp,bp           ; restore caller registers
                                        ;   and return
                pop     bp
                ret

_SetPixel10     ENDP

_TEXT           ENDS

                END
```

Write mode 2

A somewhat simpler way to set the value of an individual pixel is to use write
mode 2. The routine in Listing 5-14 demonstrates this technique. As in write mode
0, the Bit Mask register determines how each of the eight pixels is updated. In
write mode 2, however, new pixel values are derived by combining the CPU data
byte with the latched pixel values; this avoids the need to program the Set/Reset
and Enable Set/Reset registers and leads to shorter, faster code.

```
                TITLE   'Listing 5-14'
                NAME    SetPixel10
                PAGE    55,132

;
; Name:          SetPixel10
;
; Function:      Set the value of a pixel in native EGA graphics modes.
;
;                *** Write Mode 2 ***
```

(continued)

Listing 5-14. *Setting a pixel value in native EGA graphics modes using write mode 2.*

Listing 5-14. *Continued.*

```
;
; Caller:        Microsoft C:
;
;                       void SetPixel(x,y,n);
;
;                       int x,y;                /* pixel coordinates */
;                       int n;                  /* pixel value */
;

ARGx            EQU     word ptr [bp+4] ; stack frame addressing
ARGy            EQU     word ptr [bp+6]
ARGn            EQU     byte ptr [bp+8]

RMWbits         EQU     18h                     ; read-modify-write bits


_TEXT           SEGMENT byte public 'CODE'
                ASSUME  cs:_TEXT

                EXTRN   PixelAddr10:near

                PUBLIC  _SetPixel10
_SetPixel10     PROC    near

                push    bp              ; preserve stack frame
                mov     bp,sp

                mov     ax,ARGy         ; AX := y
                mov     bx,ARGx         ; BX := x
                call    PixelAddr10     ; AH := bit mask
                                        ; ES:BX -> buffer
                                        ; CL := # bits to shift left

; set Graphics Controller Bit Mask register

                shl     ah,cl           ; AH := bit mask in proper position
                mov     dx,3CEh         ; GC address register port
                mov     al,8            ; AL := Bit Mask register number
                out     dx,ax

; set Graphics Controller Mode register

                mov     ax,205h         ; AL :=  Mode register number
                                        ; AH :=  Write Mode 2 (bits 0,1)
                                        ;        Read Mode 0 (bit 3)
                out     dx,ax

; set Data Rotate/Function Select register

                mov     ah,RMWbits      ; AH := Read-Modify-Write bits
                mov     al,3            ; AL := Data Rotate/Function Select reg
                out     dx,ax

; set the pixel value

                mov     al,es:[bx]      ; latch one byte from each bit plane
                mov     al,ARGn         ; AL := pixel value
                mov     es:[bx],al      ; update all bit planes
```

(continued)

Listing 5-14. *Continued.*

```
; restore default Graphics Controller registers

                mov     ax,0FF08h       ; default Bit Mask
                out     dx,ax

                mov     ax,0005         ; default Mode register
                out     dx,ax

                mov     ax,0003         ; default Function Select
                out     dx,ax

                mov     sp,bp           ; restore stack frame and return
                pop     bp
                ret

_SetPixel10     ENDP

_TEXT           ENDS

                END
```

The routines in Listings 5-12 and 5-14 are designed to work correctly when the
Function Select register specifies the AND, OR, or XOR function. Thus, you need
write no extra code to perform these alternative pixel manipulations in the EGA's
native graphics modes.

Furthermore, if you are careful to use the proper pixel values, the routines in Listings 5-12 and 5-14 can be used in any native EGA graphics mode. To ensure that
the appropriate bits in the memory maps are updated in 640-by-350 monochrome
mode, use pixel values of 0, 1, 4, and 5 only. On an EGA with 64 KB of RAM, use
pixel values 0, 3, 0CH, and 0FH.

InColor Card

The routine in Listing 5-15 updates a single pixel in the InColor Card's 720-by-348
16-color mode. The InColor Card lacks a functional equivalent of the EGA's Function Select register, so this routine contains four separate subroutines which perform AND, OR, or XOR operations on pixel values.

```
                TITLE   'Listing 5-15'
                NAME    SetPixelInC
                PAGE    55,132

;
; Name:         SetPixelInC
;
; Function:     Set the value of a pixel in 720x348 16-color mode
;
; Caller:       Microsoft C:
;
;                       void SetPixel(x,y,n);
;
```

Listing 5-15. *Setting a pixel value in InColor graphics mode.*   *(continued)*

Listing 5-15. *Continued.*

```
;                      int x,y;              /* pixel coordinates */
;
;                      int n;                /* pixel value */
;

ARGx            EQU    word ptr [bp+4] ; stack frame addressing
ARGy            EQU    word ptr [bp+6]
ARGn            EQU    byte ptr [bp+8]

DefaultRWColor  EQU    0Fh                   ; default value for R/W Color Register


DGROUP          GROUP  _DATA

_TEXT           SEGMENT byte public 'CODE'
                ASSUME  cs:_TEXT,ds:DGROUP

                EXTRN   PixelAddrHGC:near

                PUBLIC  _SetPixelInC
_SetPixelInC    PROC    near

                push   bp                ; preserve caller registers
                mov    bp,sp

                mov    ax,ARGy       ; AX := y
                mov    bx,ARGx       ; BX := x
                call   PixelAddrHGC  ; AH := bit mask
                                     ; ES:BX -> buffer
                                     ; CL := # bits to shift left

                shl    ah,cl         ; AH := bit mask in proper position

                mov    dx,3B4h       ; DX := CRTC port

                jmp    word ptr SetPixelOpInC  ; jump to Replace, AND,
                                               ;   OR or XOR routine


ReplacePixelInC:                            ; routine to Replace pixel value

                mov    ch,ah         ; CH := bit mask for pixel
                mov    ax,1F19h      ; AH bit 6 := 0 (Mask Polarity)
                                     ; AH bits 5-4 := 1 (Write Mode)
                                     ; AH bits 3-0 := "don't care" bits
                                     ; AL := R/W Control Register number
                out    dx,ax         ; set R/W Control Register

                inc    ax            ; AL := 1Ah (R/W Color Reg number)
                mov    ah,ARGn       ; AH := foreground value
                out    dx,ax         ; set R/W color register

                and    es:[bx],ch    ; update bit planes
                jmp    short L01
```

(continued)

Listing 5-15. *Continued.*

```
ANDPixelInC:                            ; routine to AND pixel value

          mov    ch,ah               ; CH := bit mask for pixel
          mov    ax,1F19h            ; AH bit 6 := 0 (Mask Polarity)
                                     ; AH bits 5-4 := 1 (Write Mode)
                                     ; AH bits 3-0 := "don't care" bits
                                     ; AL := R/W Control Register number
          out    dx,ax               ; set R/W Control Register

          dec    ax                  ; AL := 18h (Plane Mask Register number)
          mov    ah,ARGn             ; AH := pixel value
          mov    cl,4
          shl    ah,cl               ; AH bits 7-4 := writeable plane mask
          or     ah,0Fh              ; AH bits 3-0 := visible plane mask
          out    dx,ax               ; set Plane Mask Register

          mov    ax,001Ah            ; AH := 0 (foreground value)
                                     ; AL := 1Ah (R/W Color reg)
          out    dx,ax               ; set R/W Color Register

          and    es:[bx],ch          ; update bit planes
          jmp    short L01

                                     ; routine to OR pixel value
ORPixelInC:

          mov    ch,ah               ; CH := bit mask for pixel
          mov    ax,1F19h            ; AH bit 6 := 0 (Mask Polarity)
                                     ; AH bits 5-4 := 1 (Write Mode)
                                     ; AH bits 3-0 := "don't care" bits
                                     ; AL := R/W Control Register number
          out    dx,ax               ; set R/W Control Register

          dec    ax                  ; AL := 18h (Plane Mask Register number)
          mov    ah,ARGn             ; AH := pixel value
          not    ah                  ; AH := complement of pixel value
          mov    cl,4
          shl    ah,cl               ; AH bits 7-4 := writeable plane mask
          or     ah,0Fh              ; AH bits 3-0 := visible plane mask
          out    dx,ax               ; set Plane Mask Register

          mov    ax,0F1Ah            ; AH := 0 (foreground value)
                                     ; AL := 1Ah (R/W Color reg)
          out    dx,ax               ; set R/W Color Register

          and    es:[bx],ch          ; update bit planes
          jmp    short L01

XORPixelInC:                            ; routine to XOR pixel value
          mov    ch,ah               ; CH := bit mask for pixel
          mov    ax,3F19h            ; AH bit 6 := 0 (Mask Polarity)
                                     ; AH bits 5-4 := 3 (Write Mode)
                                     ; AH bits 3-0 := "don't care" bits
                                     ; AL := R/W Control Register number
          out    dx,ax               ; set R/W Control Register
```

(continued)

Listing 5-15. *Continued.*

```
                    dec     ax              ; AL := 18h (Plane Mask Register number)
                    mov     ah,ARGn         ; AH := pixel value
                    not     ah              ; AH := complement of pixel value
                    mov     cl,4
                    shl     ah,cl           ; AH bits 7-4 := writeable plane mask
                    or      ah,0Fh          ; AH bits 3-0 := visible plane mask
                    out     dx,ax           ; set Plane Mask Register

                    xor     es:[bx],ch      ; update bit planes
                    jmp     short L01

L01:                mov     ax,0F18h
                    out     dx,ax           ; restore default Plane Mask value

                    mov     ax,4019h        ; restore default R/W Control value
                    out     dx,ax

                    inc     ax              ; restore default R/W Color value
                    mov     ah,DefaultRWColor
                    out     dx,ax

                    mov     sp,bp           ; restore caller registers and return
                    pop     bp
                    ret

_SetPixelInC        ENDP

_TEXT               ENDS


_DATA               SEGMENT word public 'DATA'

SetPixelOpInC       DW      ReplacePixelInc ; contains addr of pixel operation

_DATA               ENDS

                    END
```

Each one of these subroutines begins by programming the Read/Write Control, Read/Write Color, and Plane Mask registers. Then a CPU read loads the latches, and a subsequent CPU write updates the bit planes.

Each subroutine starts by programming the Read/Write Control register for one of the four graphics write modes. At the same time, the ''don't care'' bits are all set to 1 and the Mask Polarity bit is zeroed so that the Decoder always returns 11111111B as the result of a CPU read. Then the Plane Mask and Read/Write Color foreground values are set up; these values depend upon whether the pixel value is to be replaced or manipulated by an AND, OR, or XOR operation.

The instruction AND ES: [BX] , CH (or XOR ES: [BX] , CH for the pixel XOR operation) causes the CPU read and write. During the CPU read, the latches are loaded and the value 11111111B is returned to the CPU; the CPU ANDs (or XORs) this value with the bit mask in CH and writes the result back to the same address in the video buffer. In this way, the bit mask in CH selects which pixel value is updated during the CPU write.

Except for the pixel that the bit mask specifies, the contents of the latches are copied back into the bit planes from which they were just read; the value of the pixel being updated derives from the foreground value in the Read/Write Color register. Only the bit planes that the Plane Mask register specifies are modified, so the only bits in the bit planes that are updated are those that the replace, AND, OR, or XOR operation modifies.

 It is instructive to compare the interaction of the write mode, foreground color, and Plane Mask values within each of the subroutines. The logical operation that takes place (replace, AND, OR, or XOR) is not programmed explicitly with an 80x86 instruction. It is implicit in the contents of the graphics control registers, which are programmed to emulate the logical operation by modifying the individual bits in the updated pixel.

MCGA

In CGA-compatible graphics modes, the same routines for setting pixel values run unchanged on both the CGA and the MCGA. The two non-CGA modes (640-by-480 2-color and 320-by-200 256-color) can be handled easily with simple modifications to the routine for 640-by-200 2-color mode. Listings 5-16 and 5-17 show the necessary changes.

```
                TITLE    'Listing 5-16'
                NAME     SetPixel11
                PAGE     55,132

;
; Name:          SetPixel11
;
; Function:      Set the value of a pixel in 640x480 2-color mode (MCGA or VGA)
;
; Caller:        Microsoft C:
;
;                       void SetPixel(x,y,n);
;
;                       int x,y;                 /* pixel coordinates */
;
;                       int n;                   /* pixel value */
;

ARGx            EQU      word ptr [bp+4] ; stack frame addressing
ARGy            EQU      word ptr [bp+6]
ARGn            EQU      byte ptr [bp+8]


DGROUP          GROUP    _DATA

_TEXT           SEGMENT  byte public 'CODE'
                ASSUME   cs:_TEXT,ds:DGROUP
```

(continued)

Listing 5-16. *Setting a pixel value in MCGA or VGA 640-by-480 2-color mode.*

Listing 5-16. *Continued.*

```
                EXTRN    PixelAddr10:near

                PUBLIC   _SetPixel11
_SetPixel11     PROC     near

                push     bp                  ; preserve caller registers
                mov      bp,sp

                mov      ax,ARGy             ; AX := y
                mov      bx,ARGx             ; BX := x
                call     PixelAddr10         ; AH := bit mask
                                             ; ES:BX -> buffer
                                             ; CL := # bits to shift left

                mov      al,ARGn             ; AL := unshifted pixel value
                shl      ax,cl               ; AH := bit mask in proper position
                                             ; AL := pixel value in proper position

                jmp      word ptr SetPixelOp11    ; jump to Replace, AND,
                                                  ;   OR or XOR routine


                                             ; routine to Replace pixel value

ReplacePixel11: not      ah                  ; AH := inverse bit mask
                and      es:[bx],ah          ; zero the pixel value
                or       es:[bx],al          ; set the pixel value
                jmp      short L02


                                             ; routine to AND pixel value

ANDpixel11:     test     al,al
                jnz      L02                 ; do nothing if pixel value = 1

L01:            not      ah                  ; AH := inverse of bit mask
                and      es:[bx],ah          ; set bit in video buffer to 0
                jmp      short L02


                                             ; routine to OR pixel value

ORPixel11:      test     al,al
                jz       L02                 ; do nothing if pixel value = 0

                or       es:[bx],al          ; set bit in video buffer
                jmp      short L02


                                             ; routine to XOR pixel value

XORPixel11:     test     al,al
                jz       L02                 ; do nothing if pixel value = 0

                xor      es:[bx],al          ; XOR bit in video buffer


L02:            mov      sp,bp               ; restore caller registers and return
                pop      bp
                ret
```

(continued)

Listing 5-16. *Continued.*

```
_SetPixel11      ENDP

_TEXT            ENDS


_DATA            SEGMENT word public 'DATA'

SetPixelOp11     DW      ReplacePixel11 ; contains addr of pixel operation

_DATA            ENDS

                 END
```

```
                 TITLE   'Listing 5-17'
                 NAME    SetPixel13
                 PAGE    55,132

;
; Name:          SetPixel13
;
; Function:      Set the value of a pixel in 320x200 256-color mode (MCGA or VGA)
;
; Caller:        Microsoft C:
;
;                        void SetPixel(x,y,n);
;
;                        int x,y;               /* pixel coordinates */
;
;                        int n;                 /* pixel value */
;

ARGx             EQU     word ptr [bp+4] ; stack frame addressing
ARGy             EQU     word ptr [bp+6]
ARGn             EQU     byte ptr [bp+8]

DGROUP           GROUP   _DATA

_TEXT            SEGMENT byte public 'CODE'
                 ASSUME  cs:_TEXT,ds:DGROUP

                 EXTRN   PixelAddr13:near

                 PUBLIC  _SetPixel13
_SetPixel13      PROC    near

                 push    bp              ; preserve caller registers
                 mov     bp,sp

                 mov     ax,ARGy         ; AX := y
                 mov     bx,ARGx         ; BX := x
                 call    PixelAddr13     ; ES:BX -> buffer

                 mov     al,ARGn         ; AL := pixel value
```

(continued)

Listing 5-17. *Setting a pixel value in MCGA or VGA 320-by-200 256-color mode.*

Listing 5-17. *Continued.*

```
                    jmp      word ptr SetPixelOp13   ; jump to Replace, AND,
                                                     ;   OR or XOR routine

ReplacePixel13: mov      es:[bx],al
                jmp      short L01

ANDPixel13:     and      es:[bx],al
                jmp      short L01

ORPixel13:      or       es:[bx],al
                jmp      short L01

XORPixel13:     xor      es:[bx],al


L01:            mov      sp,bp               ; restore caller registers and return
                pop      bp
                ret

_SetPixel13     ENDP

_TEXT           ENDS


_DATA           SEGMENT word public 'DATA'

SetPixelOp13    DW       ReplacePixel13

_DATA           ENDS

                END
```

VGA

Once you create routines to update pixels on the MCGA and EGA, doing the same for the VGA is easy. The only VGA video mode that does not exist on the other subsystems is 640-by-480 16-color mode. Pixel addressing in this mode is the same as in the EGA's 640-by-350 16-color mode, so the routines in Listings 5-12 through 5-14 may be used.

Filling the Video Buffer

Usually the first thing you do after selecting a new video mode is clear the video buffer by filling it with a uniform background of repetitive data. In alphanumeric modes, it is easy and efficient to fill the buffer with blanks or nulls by using the 80x86 STOSW instruction.

Filling the video buffer in graphics modes is more of a challenge. Zeroing the entire buffer is relatively easy, but filling the screen with a solid color or pixel pattern is more difficult, particularly on the EGA, the VGA, and the InColor Card.

CGA

On the CGA, you can set the entire buffer to a single pixel value or a pattern of vertical stripes with a REP STOSW operation, as the routine in Listing 5-18 does. Because of the two-way interleave in the video buffer map, this technique fills all even-numbered scan lines before filling the odd-numbered lines. You might prefer to clear the buffer from the top down by filling it a line at a time. This technique, used in Listing 5-19, achieves a slightly smoother appearance, but requires slower and bulkier code.

```
        mov     di,0B800h
        mov     es,di
        xor     di,di           ; ES:DI -> start of video buffer
        mov     al,11110000b    ; AL := pixel pattern
        mov     ah,al           ; AX := replicated pixel pattern
        mov     cx,2000h        ; CX := number of words in video buffer
        rep     stosw           ; fill buffer with pixel pattern

; this may also be accomplished using the video BIOS

        mov     ah,0Fh          ; AH := 0Fh (INT 10H function number)
        int     10h             ; get current video state; AH = number of
                                ;  character columns
        mov     dl,ah           ; DL := number of character columns

        mov     ax,600h         ; AH := 6 (INT 10H function number)
                                ; AL := 0 (number of rows to scroll)
        mov     bh,11110000b    ; BH := pixel pattern
        mov     cx,0            ; CH := 0 (upper left character column)
                                ; CL := 0 (upper left character row)
        mov     dh,18h          ; DH := 18h (lower right character row)
        dec     dl              ; DL := lower right character column
        int     10h
```

Listing 5-18. *Simple CGA graphics buffer fill.*

```
        mov     di,0B800h
        mov     es,di
        xor     di,di           ; ES:DI -> start of video buffer

        mov     al,11001100b    ; AL pixel pattern
        mov     ah,al           ; AX := replicated pixel pattern

        mov     bx,100          ; BX := number of pairs of rows

L01:    mov     cx,40           ; CX := number of words in each row
        rep     stosw           ; fill even row

        add     di,2000h-80     ; ES:DI -> odd row
        mov     cx,40
        rep     stosw           ; fill odd row

        sub     di,2000h        ; ES:DI -> next even row
        dec     bx
        jnz     L01
```

Listing 5-19. *CGA graphics buffer fill using two-way interleave.*

You can exploit the two-way interleave in the video buffer map to create a color blend or a simple pattern (see Listing 5-20). In this case, the pixel pattern in the even-numbered scan lines is shifted in position from the pattern in the odd-numbered scan lines. This creates a dithered or halftone pattern on the screen. Because the pixels are so close together, the eye blends them, perceiving the dithered pattern as gray in 640-by-200 2-color mode or as an intermediate color blend in 320-by-200 4-color mode.

```
        mov     di,0B800h
        mov     es,di
        xor     di,di           ; ES:DI -> start of pixel row 0

        mov     al,10101010b    ; AL := pixel pattern for even rows
        mov     ah,al           ; AX := replicated pixel pattern
        mov     cx,1000h        ; CX := number of words in video buffer
        rep     stosw           ; fill even pixel rows

        mov     di,2000h        ; ES:DI -> start of pixel row 1
        mov     al,01010101b    ; AL := pixel pattern for odd rows
        mov     ah,al
        mov     cx,1000h
        rep     stosw           ; fill odd pixel rows
```

Listing 5-20. *CGA graphics buffer fill with different pixel pattern in odd and even rows.*

HGC and HGC+

You can use the same basic techniques for clearing the video buffer in the HGC's 720-by-348 monochrome graphics mode as in the CGA's 640-by-200 2-color mode. However, your routine must be able to clear either of the two displayable portions of the HGC's video buffer. Listing 5-21 demonstrates how you can do this. Again, you can take advantage of the interleaved video memory map to create a dithered pattern as you clear the buffer.

```
        mov     es,BufferSeg    ; ES := 0B000h for first video page
                                ;    or 0B800h for second video page
        xor     di,di           ; ES:DI -> first byte to fill

        mov     al,10101010b    ; AL pixel pattern
        mov     ah,al           ; AX := replicated pixel pattern

L01:    mov     cx,1000h        ; CX := number of words in
                                ;   each 8 KB buffer interleave
        rep     stosw           ; fill interleave; increment DI by 2000h

        ror     ax,1            ; shift pixel pattern between rows
        or      di,di
        jns     L01             ; jump if DI < 8000h
```

Listing 5-21. *HGC graphics buffer fill using four-way interleave.*

EGA and VGA

The Graphics Controller can provide a certain amount of hardware assistance in filling the EGA and VGA video buffer. Also, because the buffer holds more data than can be displayed on the screen, you can choose to clear only the displayed portion, an undisplayed portion, or the entire buffer.

In 640-by-200 2-color and 320-by-200 4-color modes you can use the routines for the CGA (see Listings 5-18 through 5-20). Remember, however, that the EGA and the VGA have enough video RAM to support two screens of data in 320-by-200 4-color mode. Your routine should therefore be capable of clearing any designated area of the buffer. Filling the video buffer in 640-by-480 2-color mode (see Listing 5-22) and 320-by-200 256-color mode (see Listing 5-23) is also a relatively easy task, because pixel addressing in these modes is simple.

```
mov     di,0A000h
mov     es,di
xor     di,di           ; ES:DI -> start of video buffer
mov     al,01010101b    ; AL := pixel pattern
mov     ah,al           ; AX := replicated pixel pattern
mov     cx,480*40       ; CX := (pixel rows) * (words per row)
rep     stosw           ; fill buffer with pixel pattern


; this may also be accomplished using the video BIOS

mov     ax,1130h        ; AH := 11h (INT 10H function number)
                        ; AL := 30h (character generator info)
int     10h             ; get info; DL = number of
                        ;  character rows - 1

mov     ax,600h         ; AH := 6 (INT 10H function number)
                        ; AL := 0 (number of rows to scroll)
mov     bh,01010101b    ; BH := pixel pattern
mov     cx,0            ; CH := 0 (upper left character column)
                        ; CL := 0 (upper left character row)
mov     dh,dl           ; DH := lower right character row
mov     dl,4Fh          ; DL := 4Fh (lower right character column)
int     10h
```

Listing 5-22. *MCGA and VGA 640-by-480 2-color graphics buffer fill.*

```
mov     di,0A000h
mov     es,di
xor     di,di           ; ES:DI -> start of video buffer
mov     ah,PixelValue1  ; AX := 2-pixel pattern
mov     al,PixelValue2
mov     bx,100          ; BX := number of pairs of rows
```

(continued)

Listing 5-23. *MCGA and VGA 320-by-200 256-color graphics buffer fill. This routine fills alternate pixel rows separately to allow dithered pixel patterns.*

Listing 5-23. *Continued.*

```
L01:    mov     cx,160          ; CX := number of words per row
        rep     stosw           ; fill even-numbered row
        xchg    ah,al           ; exchange pixels in pattern

        mov     cx,160
        rep     stosw           ; fill odd-numbered row
        xchg    ah,al           ; exchange pixels in pattern

        dec     bx
        jnz     L01
```

In 16-color 200-line graphics modes and all 350-line graphics modes, your routines should program the Graphics Controller to exploit its parallel processing capabilities. The most efficient way to fill the video buffer with a solid color is to use write mode 0 to repeatedly copy the Set/Reset value into the video buffer. Because no CPU read is required for this operation, you can set the entire video buffer to a solid color with a single REP STOSW instruction as shown in Listing 5-24.

```
        mov     di,0A000h
        mov     es,di
        xor     di,di           ; ES:DI -> start of video buffer

        mov     dx,3CEh         ; DX := Graphics Controller I/O port

        mov     ah,PixelValue   ; AH := pixel value for fill
        mov     al,0            ; AL := 0 (Set/Reset register number)
        out     dx,ax           ; load Set/Reset register

        mov     ax,0F01         ; AH := 1111b (mask for Enable Set/Reset)
                                ; AL := 1 (Enable Set/Reset reg number)
        out     dx,ax           ; load Enable Set/Reset register

        mov     cx,PixelRows*40 ; CX := (pixel rows) * (words per row)
        rep     stosw           ; fill the buffer

        mov     ax,0001         ; AH := 0 (default Enable Set/Reset value)
                                ; AL := 1 (Enable Set/Reset reg number)
        out     dx,ax           ; restore default Enable Set/Reset
```

Listing 5-24. *Solid buffer fill for EGA and VGA native graphics modes. The code assumes that the Graphics Controller is already in write mode 0 (the BIOS default).*

Filling the video buffer with an arbitrary pixel pattern is more difficult. Although the basic technique is the same, each component of the pattern must be written separately to the bit planes. The example in Listing 5-25 fills the video buffer with an 8-by-2 pattern of pixels in the VGA's 640-by-480 16-color mode. You can adapt the routine to 200-line and 350-line 16-color modes on both the EGA and VGA.

```
        mov     di,0A000h
        mov     es,di
        xor     di,di           ; ES:DI -> start of video buffer

        mov     dx,3CEh         ; DX := Graphics Controller I/O port

        mov     ax,105h         ; AH bits 0-1 := 01b (write mode 1)
                                ; AL := 5 (Graphics Mode register)
        out     dx,ax           ; establish write mode 1

        mov     ax,PixelRows/2  ; AX := number of pairs of rows to fill

L01:    mov     cl,es:[0]       ; latch pixel pattern for even rows
        mov     cx,40           ; CX := words per row of pixels
        rep     stosw           ; copy latches across even-numbered row

        mov     cl,es:[50h]     ; latch pixel pattern for odd rows
        mov     cx,40
        rep     stosw           ; fill odd-numbered row

        dec     ax
        jnz     L01             ; loop down the buffer

        mov     ax,0005
        out     dx,ax           ; restore write mode 0 (default)
```

Listing 5-25. *Patterned buffer fill for EGA and VGA native graphics modes. The code assumes that the desired pixel pattern is already stored in the first eight pixels of the first two rows of the video buffer (that is, at A000:0000 and A000:0050).*

InColor Card

As with the EGA and the VGA, you should use the InColor Card's graphics data latches to update the four bit planes in parallel. Filling the video buffer with a solid color is straightforward, as shown in Listing 5-26. Filling it with a pixel pattern demands the same sort of logic used in the equivalent routine for the EGA and VGA (shown in Listing 5-27).

```
        mov     es,BufferSeg    ; ES := 0B000h for first video page
                                ;     or 0B800h for second video page
        xor     di,di           ; ES:DI -> first byte to fill

        mov     dx,3B4h         ; DX := control register I/O port

        mov     ah,PixelValue   ; AH := pixel value for fill
        mov     al,1Ah          ; AL := 1AH (Read/Write Color register number)
        out     dx,ax           ; load Read/Write Color register

        mov     ax,4019h        ; AH bits 5-6 := 00b (write mode 0)
                                ; AL := 19H (Read/Write Control register)
        out     dx,ax           ; load Read/Write Control reg

        mov     ax,0FFFFh       ; AX := pixel bit mask
        mov     cx,4000h        ; CX := number of words in buffer (32K / 2)
        rep     stosw           ; fill the buffer
```

Listing 5-26. *Solid buffer fill for Hercules InColor graphics mode.*

```
            mov     es,BufferSeg      ; ES := 0B000h for first video page
                                      ;    or 0B800h for second video page
            xor     di,di             ; ES:DI -> first byte to fill

            mov     dx,3B4h           ; DX := control register I/O port

            mov     ax,6019h          ; AH bits 5-6 := 10b (write mode 2)
                                      ; AL := 19H (Read/Write Control register)
            out     dx,ax             ; load Read/Write Control reg

            mov     ax,0FFFFh         ; AX := pixel bit mask

L01:        mov     cl,es:[0]         ; latch pixel pattern for even rows
            mov     cx,1000h          ; CX := number of words in
                                      ;   each 8 KB buffer interleave
            rep     stosw             ; fill even-numbered interleave;
                                      ;   increment DI by 2000h

            mov     cl,es:[2000h]     ; latch pixel pattern for odd rows
            mov     cx,1000h
            rep     stosw             ; fill odd-numbered interleave

            or      di,di
            jns     L01               ; loop while DI < 8000H

            mov     ax,4019h          ; restore default value of
            out     dx,ax             ;   Read/Write Control register
```

Listing 5-27. *Patterned buffer fill for InColor Card. The code assumes that the desired pixel pattern is already stored in the first eight pixels of the first two rows of the video buffer (that is, at offsets 0 and 2000H in BufferSeg).*

MCGA

You can use the routines written for the CGA and the VGA to fill the video buffer in equivalent graphics modes on the MCGA.

6

Lines

An Efficient Line-drawing Algorithm
Scan-converting a Straight Line ● Bresenham's Algorithm

Optimization
Efficient Pixel Addressing
Performance Comparisons ● Special Cases

PC and PS/2 Implementations
Modular Routines
Minimizing Video Buffer Accesses
Efficient Address Calculations
CGA ● HGC ● EGA
MCGA ● VGA
InColor Card

Line Attributes

Clipping
Pixel-by-Pixel Clipping ● A Brute-Force Approach
A Better Algorithm

Most video graphics applications rely on routines that draw straight lines on the screen. Straight lines are components of many graphics images, including polygons, filled areas (made up of groups of contiguous lines), and curves (made up of a series of short line segments joined end to end). Because lines are used frequently in video graphics, you need fast line-drawing subroutines to obtain high-performance video graphics. This chapter describes how to construct efficient and flexible line-drawing routines for IBM video subsystems.

An Efficient Line-drawing Algorithm

Imagine what would happen if you tried to draw a straight line on a piece of paper by painting through the square holes in a sieve (see Figure 6-1). The result would not really be a line, but a group of square dots that approximates a line.

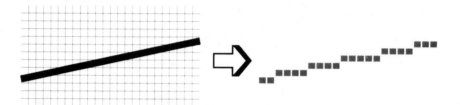

Figure 6-1. *Line painted through a sieve.*

A raster video display's rectangular grid of pixels resembles an electronic "sieve" when it comes to drawing straight lines and geometric curves. The best you can do is to represent each line or curve with a group of pixels that closely approximates it. The process of determining which set of pixels in the video buffer best approximate a particular geometric figure is called scan-conversion.

The visual consequence of scan-conversion is that mathematically smooth lines and curves appear jagged on the screen. Consider the nearly horizontal line in Figure 6-2a. The only way to represent such a line within a grid of pixels is as a series of connected horizontal line segments. The more nearly horizontal or vertical the line, the more jagged it appears. Although sophisticated software techniques can minimize the jagged appearance of a scan-converted line, the easiest way to smooth out a line is to "use a finer sieve"; that is, to use a higher-resolution video mode or higher-resolution video display hardware (see Figure 6-2b).

a.

b.

Figure 6-2. *A nearly horizontal line displayed with (a) low resolution and (b) higher resolution.*

Scan-converting a Straight Line

The simplest way to draw a line is to use the equation of the line

```
y = mx + b
```

where *m* is the slope of the line and *b* is the *y*-intercept (the value of *y* at the point where the line crosses the *y*-axis). You can use this equation to calculate the corresponding *y*-coordinate for each pixel *x*-coordinate between the line's endpoints as shown in Listing 6-1. This technique is slow, but it is easy to implement.

```
/* Listing 6-1 */

Line( x1, y1, x2, y2, n )
int     x1,y1;                    /* endpoint */
int     x2,y2;                    /* endpoint */
int     n;                        /* pixel value */
{
        int     x,y;
        float   m;                /* slope */
        float   b;                /* y-intercept */


        if (x2 == x1)                             /* vertical line */
        {
          if (y1 > y2)
            Swap( &y1, &y2 );                     /* force y1 < y2 */

          for (y=y1; y<=y2; y++)                  /* draw from y1 to y2 */
            SetPixel( x1, y, n );

          return;
        }

        if (x1 > x2)                              /* force x1 < x2 */
        {
          Swap( &x1, &x2 );
          Swap( &y1, &y2 );
        }
```

Listing 6-1. *Drawing a line using the equation of the line.*   *(continued)*

Listing 6-1. *Continued.*

```
        m = (float)(y2-y1) / (float)(x2-x1);    /* compute m and b */
        b = y1 - (m*x1);

        for (x=x1; x<=x2; x++)                   /* draw from x1 to x2 */
        {
          y = m*x + b;
          SetPixel( x, y, n );
        }
}

Swap( a, b )                                     /* exchange values of a and b */
int     *a,*b;
{
        int     t;

        t = *a;
        *a = *b;
        *b = t;
}
```

The problem is that the computational overhead in performing the multiplication, addition, and rounding necessary to generate *y* for each *x* in the line is considerable. Furthermore, the slope *m* must be maintained as a floating-point number, and using floating-point arithmetic in the calculations slows them down.

Bresenham's Algorithm

Incrementally calculating the appropriate *y*-coordinates is much more efficient. Given the *x*- and *y*-coordinates of the first pixel in the line, you can calculate the location of each subsequent pixel by incrementing the *x*- and *y*-coordinates in proportion to the line's slope. The arithmetic is simpler and faster than that involved in directly using the equation of the line.

The algorithm presented by J. E. Bresenham in 1965 (IBM Systems Journal 4 (1) 1965, pp. 25-30) plots the set of pixels that lie closest to the line between two given pixels—(*x1,y1*) and (*x2,y2*)—assuming that *x1* is less than *x2* and that the slope of the line is between 0 and 1. To simplify the equation of the line, the algorithm assumes the location of the first endpoint (*x1,y1*) is (0,0). The equation of the resulting line is

$$y = (dy/dx) * x$$

where

$$dy = y2 - y1$$

and

$$dx = x2 - x1$$

To visualize how Bresenham's algorithm works, consider the portion of a line shown in Figure 6-3. The algorithm proceeds by iteratively determining the corresponding *y*-coordinate for each value of *x* from *x1* to *x2*. After plotting the pixel at

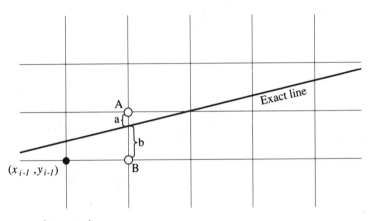

Given $(x_{i\text{-}1}, y_{i\text{-}1})$:
    if $(a < b)$, $(x_i, y_i) = $ pixel A
    else $(x_i, y_i) = $ pixel B

Figure 6-3. *Bresenham's incremental line-drawing algorithm. Given the pixel at (x_{i-1}, y_{i-1}), the algorithm selects either pixel A or B depending on the values of a and b.*

(x_{i-1}, y_{i-1}), for example, the algorithm determines whether pixel A or pixel B is closer to the exact line and plots the closer pixel.

The difference between pixel A's y-coordinate and the y-coordinate on the exact line at x_i is

```
a = (y_i+1) - (dy/dx)*x_i
```

where (*dy/dx*) represents the line's slope. Similarly, the distance *b* from pixel B to the line is

```
b = (dy/dx)*x_i - y_i
```

If distance *b* is smaller than distance *a*, pixel B lies closer to the exact line. If *a* is smaller than *b*, pixel A is closer. In other words, the sign of the difference $(b - a)$ determines whether pixel A or pixel B is closer to the line.

Now, this may seem like much more work than simply using the equation for the line. However, the values of *a* and *b* can be compared implicitly for each x_i by iteratively computing the value of $(b - a)$ for each succeeding x_i in terms of simpler quantities like *dy* and *dx*. The resulting computation is simple, although deriving it requires a bit of algebra.

To derive the computation, combine the equations for *a* and *b*:

```
(b-a) = 2*(dy/dx)*x_i - 2*y_i - 1
```

Since *x1* is less than *x2*, *dx* is always positive, so *dx* $*(b - a)$ can be used instead of $(b - a)$ to decide whether to plot pixel A or pixel B:

```
dx*(b-a) = 2*dy*x_i - 2*y_i*dx - dx

         = 2*(dy*x_i - dx*y_i) - dx
```

Let d_i represent the quantity $dx*(b-a)$. To calculate d_i iteratively, you need to know how to compute it from d_{i-1}:

```
(d_i-d_{i-1}) = (2*(dy*x_i - dx*y_i)) - (2*(dy*x_{i-1} - dx*y_{i-1}))

            = 2*(dy*(x_i-x_{i-1}) - dx*(y_i-y_{i-1}))
```

$x_i - x_{i-1}$ is always 1, and $y_i - y_{i-1}$ is either 1 (if pixel A at $(x_i, y_i + 1)$ is plotted) or 0 (if pixel B at (x_i, y_i) is plotted). Thus, computing the difference between d_i and d_{i-1} is easy, and d_i can be calculated simply by incrementing d_{i-1} with one of two constants:

If $d_{i-1} >= 0$, plot pixel A at $(x_i, y_i + 1)$. The increment for d_{i-1} is then

```
(d_i-d_{i-1}) = 2*(dy-dx)
```

If $d_{i-1} < 0$, plot pixel B at (x_i, y_i). The increment for d_{i-1} is then

```
(d_i-d_{i-1}) = 2*dy
```

To calculate d_i's initial value, remember that the first pixel in the line is assumed to be at (0,0). Substituting $x_i = 1$ and $y_i = 0$ into the equation for d_i gives

```
d_i = 2*dy - dx
```

The resulting algorithm is efficient, because the most complicated calculations are performed only once, outside the loop that plots the pixels (see Listing 6-2). Within the loop, incrementally determining which pixels lie closest to the desired line (using the decision variable d_i) eliminates the need for time-consuming floating-point arithmetic. The result is a faster line-drawing algorithm.

Optimization

Nevertheless, there is still room for improvement. The slowest part of the line-drawing primitive in Listing 6-2 is the call to SetPixel(), which calculates the pixel's address in the video buffer and then sets the pixel's value. The pixel address calculation is clearly the slowest part of the procedure.

```
/* Listing 6-2 */

Line( x1, y1, x2, y2, n )          /* for lines with slope between -1 and 1 */
int      x1,y1;
int      x2,y2;                    /* endpoints */
int      n;                        /* pixel value */
{
        int     d,dx,dy;
        int     Aincr,Bincr,yincr;
        int     x,y;

        if (x1 > x2)                               /* force x1 < x2 */
        {
          Swap( &x1, &x2 );
          Swap( &y1, &y2 );
        }
```

Listing 6-2. *A high-level implementation of Bresenham's algorithm.*   *(continued)*

Listing 6-2. *Continued.*

```
                if (y2 > y1)                          /* determine increment for y */
                    yincr = 1;
                else
                    yincr = -1;  .

                dx = x2 - x1;                         /* initialize constants */
                dy = abs( y2-y1 );
                d = 2 * dy - dx;

                Aincr = 2 * (dy - dx);
                Bincr = 2 * dy;

                x = x1;                               /* initial x and y */
                y = y1;

                SetPixel( x, y, n );                  /* set pixel at (x1,y1) */

                for (x=x1+1; x<=x2; x++)              /* do from x1+1 to x2 */
                {
                    if (d >= 0)
                    {
                        y += yincr;                   /* set pixel A */
                        d += Aincr;
                    }
                    else                              /* set pixel B */
                        d += Bincr;

                    SetPixel( x, y, n );
                }
        }


Swap( pa, pb )
int     *pa,*pb;
{
        int     t;

        t = *pa;
        *pa = *pb;
        *pb = t;
}
```

Efficient Pixel Addressing

Fortunately, you can optimize the pixel address calculation significantly: The
pixel addresses themselves can be calculated incrementally, in the same way you
increment the decision variable d_i. After calculating the address of the first pixel
in the line, you can find its neighbors in the video buffer either by incrementing
the pixel's byte offset or by rotating the bit mask that represents its bit offset. Calculating pixel addresses incrementally is significantly faster than performing the
computation from scratch for each (x,y) coordinate pair in the line.

For example, you can identify the pixel immediately to the right of a given pixel
by rotating the given pixel's bit mask one pixel position to the right. (If the given
pixel is the rightmost pixel in its byte, increment the byte offset as well.) To find

the pixel immediately above a given pixel, decrement the byte offset by the number of bytes per row of pixels, but keep the bit mask the same. This calculation is slightly more complicated in video modes with an interleaved video buffer map, but the principle is the same.

Performance Comparisons

When you compare the techniques for scan-converting lines, the performance gains from using an incremental line-drawing algorithm and incremental address calculations are remarkable (see Figure 6-4). Writing your line-drawing routines in assembly language also helps. Coding and optimizing bit mask manipulation and address computations is much easier in assembly language than in a high-level language.

Algorithm	Language	Pixels per Second
Algorithm based on the equation of a line	C	4,800
Bresenham's algorithm	C	16,000
Bresenham's algorithm	Assembler	26,000
Bresenham's algorithm with incremental pixel address calculation	Assembler	70,000

Figure 6-4. *Performance of line-drawing algorithms in C and in assembly language. Timings were obtained on a 6 MHz IBM PC/AT with a Hercules Graphics Card.*

Special Cases

To further improve the overall performance of your video graphics drivers, use special routines for drawing horizontal and vertical lines. In many applications, these special cases account for a surprising percentage of the calls to the line-drawing primitive. This is especially true if you use lines to fill regions.

```
/* Listing 6-3 */

FilledRectangle( x1, y1, x2, y2, n )
int     x1,y1;                     /* upper left corner */
int     x2,y2;                     /* lower right corner */
int     n;                         /* pixel value */
{
        int     y;

        for (y=y1; y<=y2; y++)             /* draw rectangle as a set of */
           Line( x1, y, x2, y, n );        /*  adjacent horizontal lines */
}
```

Listing 6-3. *A routine that draws horizontal lines.*

For example, the routine FilledRectangle() in Listing 6-3 calls on the line-drawing function to draw horizontal lines exclusively. If you fill a rectangle that is 100 pixels high, the line-drawing function is called 100 times to draw a horizontal line. When the line-drawing function recognizes the special case of horizontal lines, functions such as `FilledRectangle()` run significantly faster.

A special-purpose routine can draw horizontal lines 10 times faster than a general-purpose line-drawing routine. For vertical lines, a special-purpose routine is about 25 percent faster. Horizontal lines are represented in the video buffer by contiguous sequences of bytes you can fill with an 80x86 `REP STOSB` instruction, which runs much faster than the iterative loop the general line-drawing primitive requires. In drawing vertical lines, no logic is required to determine pixel locations. You simply increment the pixel address. Again, the resulting code is simpler and faster.

PC and PS/2 Implementations

Implementations of Bresenham's line-drawing algorithm on IBM video hardware are strongly influenced by the CPU's capabilities and by the idiosyncrasies of pixel mapping in the video buffer in various graphics modes. Nevertheless, once you write a line-drawing routine for one graphics mode, you can adapt the source code to other graphics modes or to other video hardware with little difficulty.

Modular Routines

You should build your line-drawing routines with a modular structure. One practical way to break your code into modules is to write separate routines for horizontal lines, vertical lines, lines with slope less than 1, and lines with slope greater than 1. Each module itself comprises a set of modules for performing each of the necessary pixel manipulations—XOR, AND, OR, and pixel replacement.

 Bresenham's algorithm as derived in this chapter is applicable only to lines whose slope lies between 0 and 1. However, it is easy to use the same algorithm for lines with other slopes. For lines with slopes between -1 and 0, simply change the sign of the y-increment (see Listing 6-2). For lines with slopes less than -1 or greater than 1 (that is, $|(dy/dx)| > 1$), use the same algorithm but exchange the x- and y-coordinates.

For example, each of the assembly-language line-drawing routines in this chapter contains two similar subroutines, one for $|(dy/dx)| <= 1$ and another for $|(dy/dx)| > 1$. Each routine contains a prologue that detects the special cases of horizontal and vertical lines, initializes the appropriate increment values, and selects the proper subroutine for the slope.

Breaking your routines into modules helps when you customize your code for an application. It also simplifies the task of writing code to run symmetrically in different graphics modes. For example, a routine that draws a vertical line in 640-by-200 2-color mode on a CGA requires little modification to run properly in 320-by-200 4-color mode.

Minimizing Video Buffer Accesses

In the 8086 family of microprocessors, data transfer instructions of the form `MOV mem,reg` are among the slowest. Try to minimize use of this CPU instruction within your line-drawing primitives. Neighboring pixels in a line frequently are grouped in the same byte in the video buffer. (Obviously, such groups occur more frequently in more nearly horizontal lines.) You can speed your line-drawing routines by updating all neighboring pixels in each byte you store in the video buffer.

Efficient Address Calculations

To maximize performance, use CPU registers carefully to hold the values most frequently updated in the inner loops of your routines: the pixel bit mask, the buffer offset, and the decision variable. In Listing 6-4, for example, registers DH and DL hold bit masks, register BX holds the buffer offset, and the decision variable d is maintained in register DI. These values are the ones most frequently updated in these routines, so they are the ones you should try to keep in registers rather than in memory variables.

If you neglect to use the CPU registers effectively, your routines may run much slower than necessary. Consider what would happen if you rewrote the routine in Listing 6-4 to store the decision variable in a memory variable instead of in register DI. Just this minor change would cause the routine to run about 20 percent slower. (Not only does this emphasize why you must make the best possible use of the CPU registers, but it also suggests why writing highly optimized video graphics primitives in a high-level language is very difficult.)

CGA

Listing 6-4 contains code for drawing lines in the CGA's 640-by-200 2-color graphics mode. The routine consists of a prologue and four line-drawing modules. The prologue puts the endpoints in ascending order by their x-coordinates, sets up appropriate vertical increments for computing the pixel address within the inner loop, and selects an appropriate line-drawing module according to the slope of the line. The line-drawing modules (`VertLine06`, `HorizLine06`, `LoSlopeLine06`, and `HiSlopeLine06`) contain the inner loops that actually update pixels and increment addresses.

```
                TITLE    'Listing 6-4'
                NAME     Line06
                PAGE     55,132

;
; Name:          Line06
;
; Function:      Draw a line in 640x200 2-color mode
;
; Caller:        Microsoft C:
```

Listing 6-4. *A line-drawing routine for CGA 640-by-200 2-color mode.*   *(continued)*

Listing 6-4. *Continued.*

```
;
;                      void Line06(x1,y1,x2,y2,n);
;
;              int x1,y1,x2,y2;        /* pixel coordinates */
;
;              int n;                  /* pixel value */
;

ARGx1          EQU    word ptr [bp+4] ; stack frame addressing
ARGy1          EQU    word ptr [bp+6]
ARGx2          EQU    word ptr [bp+8]
ARGy2          EQU    word ptr [bp+10]
ARGn           EQU    byte ptr [bp+12]
VARleafincr    EQU    word ptr [bp-6]
VARincr1       EQU    word ptr [bp-8]
VARincr2       EQU    word ptr [bp-10]
VARroutine     EQU    word ptr [bp-12]

ByteOffsetShift EQU   3                    ; used to convert pixels to byte offset

DGROUP         GROUP  _DATA

_TEXT          SEGMENT byte public 'CODE'
               ASSUME  cs:_TEXT,ds:DGROUP

               EXTRN   PixelAddr06:near

               PUBLIC  _Line06
_Line06        PROC    near

               push   bp               ; preserve caller registers
               mov    bp,sp
               sub    sp,8             ; stack space for local variables
               push   si
               push   di

               mov    si,2000h         ; increment for video buffer interleave
               mov    di,80-2000h      ; increment from last to first interleave

               mov    cx,ARGx2
               sub    cx,ARGx1         ; CX := x2 - x1
               jz     VertLine06       ; jump if vertical line

; force x1 < x2

               jns    L01              ; jump if x2 > x1

               neg    cx               ; CX := x1 - x2

               mov    bx,ARGx2         ; exchange x1 and x2
               xchg   bx,ARGx1
               mov    ARGx2,bx

               mov    bx,ARGy2         ; exchange y1 and y2
               xchg   bx,ARGy1
               mov    ARGy2,bx
```

(continued)

Listing 6-4. *Continued.*

```
; calculate dy = ABS(y2-y1)

L01:            mov     bx,ARGy2
                sub     bx,ARGy1        ; BX := y2 - y1
                jnz     L02

                jmp     HorizLine06     ; jump if horizontal line

L02:            jns     L03

                neg     bx              ; BX := y1 - y2
                neg     si              ; negate increments for buffer interleave
                neg     di
                xchg    si,di           ; exchange increments

; select appropriate routine for slope of line

L03:            mov     VARleafincr,di  ; save increment for buffer interleave

                mov     VARroutine,offset LoSlopeLine06
                cmp     bx,cx
                jle     L04             ; jump if dy <= dx (slope <= 1)
                mov     VARroutine,offset HiSlopeLine06
                xchg    bx,cx           ; exchange dy and dx

; calculate initial decision variable and increments

L04:            shl     bx,1            ; BX := 2 * dy
                mov     VARincr1,bx     ; incr1 := 2 * dy
                sub     bx,cx
                mov     di,bx           ; DI := d = 2 * dy - dx
                sub     bx,cx
                mov     VARincr2,bx     ; incr2 := 2 * (dy - dx)

; calculate first pixel address

                push    cx              ; preserve this register
                mov     ax,ARGy1        ; AX := y
                mov     bx,ARGx1        ; BX := x
                call    PixelAddr06     ; AH := bit mask
                                        ; ES:BX -> buffer
                                        ; CL := # bits to shift left

                mov     al,ARGn         ; AL := unshifted pixel value
                shl     ax,cl           ; AH := bit mask in proper position
                                        ; AL := pixel value in proper position

                mov     dx,ax           ; DH := bit mask
                                        ; DL := pixel value
                not     dh              ; DH := inverse bit mask

                pop     cx              ; restore this register
                inc     cx              ; CX := # of pixels to draw

                test    bx,2000h        ; set zero flag if BX in 1st interleave
                jz      L05
                xchg    si,VARleafincr  ; exchange increment values if 1st pixel
                                        ;   lies in 1st interleave
```

(continued)

Listing 6-4. *Continued.*

```
L05:            jmp     VARroutine      ; jump to appropriate routine for slope


; routine for vertical lines

VertLine06:     mov     ax,ARGy1        ; AX := y1
                mov     bx,ARGy2        ; BX := y2
                mov     cx,bx
                sub     cx,ax           ; CX := dy
                jge     L31             ; jump if dy >= 0

                neg     cx              ; force dy >= 0
                mov     ax,bx           ; AX := y2

L31:            inc     cx              ; CX := # of pixels to draw
                mov     bx,ARGx1        ; BX := x
                push    cx              ; preserve this register
                call    PixelAddr06     ; AH := bit mask
                                        ; ES:BX -> video buffer
                                        ; CL := # bits to shift left
                mov     al,ARGn         ; AL := pixel value
                shl     ax,cl           ; AH := bit mask in proper position
                                        ; AL := pixel value in proper position
                not     ah              ; AH := inverse bit mask
                pop     cx              ; restore this register

                test    bx,si           ; set zero flag if BX in 1st interleave
                jz      L32

                xchg    si,di           ; exchange increment values if 1st pixel
                                        ;   lies in 1st interleave

L32:            test    al,al
                jz      L34             ; jump if pixel value = 0

L33:            or      es:[bx],al      ; set pixel values in buffer
                add     bx,si           ; increment to next portion of interleave
                xchg    si,di           ; toggle between increment values
                loop    L33             ; loop down the line
                jmp     short L35

L34:            and     es:[bx],ah      ; reset pixel values in buffer
                add     bx,si           ; increment to next portion of interleave
                xchg    si,di           ; toggle between increment values
                loop    L34

L35:            jmp     Lexit


; routine for horizontal lines (slope = 0)

HorizLine06:    mov     ax,ARGy1
                mov     bx,ARGx1
                call    PixelAddr06     ; AH := bit mask
                                        ; ES:BX -> video buffer
                                        ; CL := # bits to shift left
                mov     di,bx           ; ES:DI -> buffer
```

(continued)

Listing 6-4. *Continued.*

```
              mov     dh,ah
              not     dh                ; DH := unshifted bit mask for leftmost
                                        ;       byte
              mov     dl,0FFh           ; DL := unshifted bit mask for
                                        ;       rightmost byte

              shl     dh,cl             ; DH := reverse bit mask for first byte
              not     dh                ; DH := bit mask for first byte

              mov     cx,ARGx2
              and     cl,7
              xor     cl,7              ; CL := number of bits to shift left
              shl     dl,cl             ; DL := bit mask for last byte

; determine byte offset of first and last pixel in the line

              mov     ax,ARGx2          ; AX := x2
              mov     bx,ARGx1          ; BX := x1

              mov     cl,ByteOffsetShift    ; number of bits to shift to
                                            ;   convert pixels to bytes

              shr     ax,cl             ; AX := byte offset of x2
              shr     bx,cl             ; BX := byte offset of x1
              mov     cx,ax
              sub     cx,bx             ; CX := (# bytes in line) - 1

; propagate pixel value throughout one byte

              mov     bx,offset DGROUP:PropagatedPixel
              mov     al,ARGn           ; AL := pixel value
              xlat

; set pixels in leftmost byte of the line

              or      dh,dh
              js      L43               ; jump if byte-aligned (x1 is leftmost
                                        ;   pixel in byte)
              or      cx,cx
              jnz     L42               ; jump if more than one byte in the line

              and     dl,dh             ; bit mask for the line
              jmp     short L44

L42:          mov     ah,al
              and     ah,dh             ; AH := masked pixel bits
              not     dh                ; DH := reverse bit mask for 1st byte
              and     es:[di],dh        ; zero masked pixels in buffer
              or      es:[di],ah        ; update masked pixels in buffer
              inc     di
              dec     cx

; use a fast 8086 machine instruction to draw the remainder of the line

L43:          rep     stosb             ; update all pixels in the line

; set pixels in the rightmost byte of the line
```

(continued)

Listing 6-4. *Continued.*

```
L44:            and     al,dl           ; AL := masked pixels for last byte
                not     dl
                and     es:[di],dl      ; zero masked pixels in buffer
                or      es:[di],al      ; update masked pixels in buffer

                jmp     Lexit


; routine for dy <= dx (slope <= 1)    ; ES:BX -> video buffer
                                        ; CX = # pixels to draw
                                        ; DH = inverse bit mask
                                        ; DL = pixel value in proper position
                                        ; SI = buffer interleave increment
                                        ; DI = decision variable

LoSlopeLine06:

L10:            mov     ah,es:[bx]      ; AH := byte from video buffer

L11:            and     ah,dh           ; zero pixel value at current bit offset
                or      ah,dl           ; set pixel value in byte

                ror     dl,1            ; rotate pixel value
                ror     dh,1            ; rotate bit mask
                jnc     L14             ; jump if bit mask rotated to
                                        ;   leftmost pixel position


; bit mask not shifted out

                or      di,di           ; test sign of d
                jns     L12             ; jump if d >= 0

                add     di,VARincr1     ; d := d + incr1
                loop    L11

                mov     es:[bx],ah      ; store remaining pixels in buffer
                jmp     short Lexit

L12:            add     di,VARincr2     ; d := d + incr2
                mov     es:[bx],ah      ; update buffer

                add     bx,si           ; increment y
                xchg    si,VARleafincr  ; exchange interleave increment values
                loop    L10
                jmp     short Lexit


; bit mask shifted out

L14:            mov     es:[bx],ah      ; update buffer
                inc     bx              ; BX := offset of next byte

                or      di,di           ; test sign of d
                jns     L15             ; jump if non-negative

                add     di,VARincr1     ; d := d + incr1
                loop    L10
                jmp     short Lexit
```

(continued)

Listing 6-4. *Continued.*

```
L15:            add     di,VARincr2         ; d := d + incr2

                add     bx,si               ; increment y
                xchg    si,VARleafincr

                loop    L10
                jmp     short Lexit


; routine for dy > dx (slope > 1)       ; ES:BX -> video buffer
                                        ; CX = # pixels to draw
                                        ; DH = inverse bit mask
                                        ; DL = pixel value in proper position
                                        ; SI = buffer interleave increment
                                        ; DI = decision variable
HiSlopeLine06:

L21:            and     es:[bx],dh          ; zero pixel value in video buffer
                or      es:[bx],dl          ; set pixel value in byte

                add     bx,si               ; increment y
                xchg    si,VARleafincr      ; exchange interleave increment values

L22:            or      di,di               ; test sign of d
                jns     L23                 ; jump if d >= 0

                add     di,VARincr1         ; d := d + incr1
                loop    L21

                jmp     short Lexit


L23:            add     di,VARincr2         ; d := d + incr2

                ror     dl,1                ; rotate pixel value
                ror     dh,1                ; rotate bit mask
                cmc                         ; cf set if bit mask not rotated to
                                            ;   leftmost pixel position

                adc     bx,0                ; BX := offset of next byte

                loop    L21


Lexit:          pop     di                  ; restore registers and return
                pop     si
                mov     sp,bp
                pop     bp
                ret

_Line06         ENDP

_TEXT           ENDS


_DATA           SEGMENT word public 'DATA'
```

(continued)

Listing 6-4. *Continued.*

```
PropagatedPixel DB      00000000b       ; 0
                DB      11111111b       ; 1

_DATA           ENDS

                END
```

Most of the execution time in this routine is spent in the inner loops of the four line-drawing modules. To optimize the speed of the inner loops, as much computation as possible is performed outside of them. In particular, the inner loop of `HorizLine06` (at label `L43`) is very fast because it consists only of a single 80x86 machine instruction.

The routines `LoSlopeLine06` and `HiSlopeLine06` implement Bresenham's algorithm. The inner loop of `HiSlopeLine06` (at `L21`) is simpler than the inner loop of `LoSlopeLine06` (at `L11`). This is because `HiSlopeLine06` increments the pixel *y*-coordinate, and thus the buffer offset, on every iteration, so the only other code needed in the loop is the code to increment the decision variable and update the pixel bit mask. In `LoSlopeLine06`, the *x*-coordinate is incremented on each iteration by rotating the pixel bit mask. This necessitates some extra code to update the bit mask and buffer offset in accordance with the decision variable's value.

The routine for 320-by-200 4-color mode, shown in Listing 6-5, is similar to the one for 640-by-200 2-color mode. In fact, you could write a single routine that works in either mode without undue sacrifice in performance. The differences lie in how the address of the first pixel in the line is calculated (that is, a call to `PixelAddr04` versus one to `PixelAddr06`) and in how many bits are masked and updated for each pixel in the buffer. The bit mask is 1 bit wide in 640-by-200 2-color mode and 2 bits wide in 320-by-200 4-color mode.

```
                TITLE   'Listing 6-5'
                NAME    Line04
                PAGE    55,132

;
; Name:         Line04
;
; Function:     Draw a line in 320x200 4-color mode
;
; Caller:       Microsoft C:
;
;                       void Line04(x1,y1,x2,y2,n);
;
;                       int x1,y1,x2,y2;        /* pixel coordinates */
;
;                       int n;                  /* pixel value */
;
```

Listing 6-5. *A line-drawing routine for CGA 320-by-200 4-color mode.*   *(continued)*

Listing 6-5. *Continued.*

```
ARGx1             EQU      word ptr [bp+4] ; stack frame addressing
ARGy1             EQU      word ptr [bp+6]
ARGx2             EQU      word ptr [bp+8]
ARGy2             EQU      word ptr [bp+10]
ARGn              EQU      byte ptr [bp+12]
VARleafincr       EQU      word ptr [bp-6]
VARincr1          EQU      word ptr [bp-8]
VARincr2          EQU      word ptr [bp-10]
VARroutine        EQU      word ptr [bp-12]

ByteOffsetShift EQU        2                ; used to convert pixels to byte offset

DGROUP            GROUP    _DATA

_TEXT             SEGMENT byte public 'CODE'
                  ASSUME  cs:_TEXT,ds:DGROUP

                  EXTRN    PixelAddr04:near

                  PUBLIC   _Line04
_Line04           PROC     near

                  push     bp               ; preserve caller registers
                  mov      bp,sp
                  sub      sp,8             ; stack space for local variables
                  push     si
                  push     di

                  mov      si,2000h         ; increment for video buffer interleave
                  mov      di,80-2000h      ; increment from last to first interleave

                  mov      cx,ARGx2
                  sub      cx,ARGx1         ; CX := x2 - x1
                  jz       VertLine04       ; jump if vertical line

; force x1 < x2

                  jns      L01              ; jump if x2 > x1

                  neg      cx               ; CX := x1 - x2

                  mov      bx,ARGx2         ; exchange x1 and x2
                  xchg     bx,ARGx1
                  mov      ARGx2,bx

                  mov      bx,ARGy2         ; exchange y1 and y2
                  xchg     bx,ARGy1
                  mov      ARGy2,bx

; calculate dy = ABS(y2-y1)

L01:              mov      bx,ARGy2
                  sub      bx,ARGy1         ; BX := y2 - y1
                  jnz      L02

                  jmp      HorizLine04      ; jump if horizontal line
```

(continued)

Listing 6-5. *Continued.*

```
L02:            jns     L03

                neg     bx              ; BX := y1 - y2
                neg     si              ; negate increments for buffer interleave
                neg     di
                xchg    si,di           ; exchange increments

; select appropriate routine for slope of line

L03:            mov     VARleafincr,di  ; save increment for buffer interleave

                mov     VARroutine,offset LoSlopeLine04
                cmp     bx,cx
                jle     L04             ; jump if dy <= dx (slope <= 1)
                mov     VARroutine,offset HiSlopeLine04
                xchg    bx,cx           ; exchange dy and dx

; calculate initial decision variable and increments

L04:            shl     bx,1            ; BX := 2 * dy
                mov     VARincr1,bx     ; incr1 := 2 * dy
                sub     bx,cx
                mov     di,bx           ; DI := d = 2 * dy - dx
                sub     bx,cx
                mov     VARincr2,bx     ; incr2 := 2 * (dy - dx)

; calculate first pixel address

                push    cx              ; preserve this register
                mov     ax,ARGy1        ; AX := y
                mov     bx,ARGx1        ; BX := x
                call    PixelAddr04     ; AH := bit mask
                                        ; ES:BX -> buffer
                                        ; CL := # bits to shift left

                mov     al,ARGn         ; AL := unshifted pixel value
                shl     ax,cl           ; AH := bit mask in proper position
                                        ; AL := pixel value in proper position

                mov     dx,ax           ; DH := bit mask

                                        ; DL := pixel value
                not     dh              ; DH := inverse bit mask

                pop     cx              ; restore this register
                inc     cx              ; CX := # of pixels to draw

                test    bx,2000h        ; set zero flag if BX in 1st interleave
                jz      L05

                xchg    si,VARleafincr  ; exchange increment values if 1st pixel
                                        ;  lies in 1st interleave

L05:            jmp     VARroutine      ; jump to appropriate routine for slope
```

(continued)

Listing 6-5. *Continued.*

```
; routine for vertical lines

VertLine04:     mov     ax,ARGy1        ; AX := y1
                mov     bx,ARGy2        ; BX := y2
                mov     cx,bx
                sub     cx,ax           ; CX := dy
                jge     L31             ; jump if dy >= 0

                neg     cx              ; force dy >= 0
                mov     ax,bx           ; AX := y2

L31:            inc     cx              ; CX := # of pixels to draw
                mov     bx,ARGx1        ; BX := x
                push    cx              ; preserve this register
                call    PixelAddr04     ; AH := bit mask
                                        ; ES:BX -> video buffer
                                        ; CL := # bits to shift left
                mov     al,ARGn         ; AL := pixel value
                shl     ax,cl           ; AH := bit mask in proper position
                                        ; AL := pixel value in proper position
                not     ah              ; AH := inverse bit mask
                pop     cx              ; restore this register

                test    bx,si           ; set zero flag if BX in 1st interleave
                jz      L32

                xchg    si,di           ; exchange increment values if 1st pixel
                                        ;   lies in 1st interleave

L32:            and     es:[bx],ah      ; zero pixel in buffer
                or      es:[bx],al      ; set pixel value in buffer

                add     bx,si           ; increment to next portion of interleave
                xchg    si,di           ; toggle between increment values

                loop    L32

                jmp     Lexit



; routine for horizontal lines (slope = 0)

HorizLine04:    mov     ax,ARGy1
                mov     bx,ARGx1
                call    PixelAddr04     ; AH := bit mask
                                        ; ES:BX -> video buffer
                                        ; CL := # bits to shift left
                mov     di,bx           ; ES:DI -> buffer

                mov     dh,ah
                not     dh              ; DH := unshifted bit mask for leftmost
                                        ;       byte
                mov     dl,0FFh         ; DL := unshifted bit mask for
                                        ;        rightmost byte

                shl     dh,cl           ; DH := reverse bit mask for first byte
                not     dh              ; DH := bit mask for first byte
```

(continued)

Listing 6-5. *Continued.*

```
                mov     cx,ARGx2
                and     cl,3
                xor     cl,3
                shl     cl,1            ; CL := number of bits to shift left
                shl     dl,cl           ; DL := bit mask for last byte

; determine byte offset of first and last pixel in the line

                mov     ax,ARGx2        ; AX := x2
                mov     bx,ARGx1        ; BX := x1

                mov     cl,ByteOffsetShift      ; number of bits to shift to
                                                ;   convert pixels to bytes

                shr     ax,cl           ; AX := byte offset of x2
                shr     bx,cl           ; BX := byte offset of x1
                mov     cx,ax
                sub     cx,bx           ; CX := (# bytes in line) - 1

; propagate pixel value throughout one byte

                mov     bx,offset DGROUP:PropagatedPixel
                mov     al,ARGn         ; AL := pixel value
                xlat                    ; AL := propagated pixel value

; set pixels in leftmost byte of the line

                or      dh,dh
                js      L43             ; jump if byte-aligned (x1 is leftmost
                                        ;   pixel in byte)
                or      cx,cx
                jnz     L42             ; jump if more than one byte in the line

                and     dl,dh           ; bit mask for the line
                jmp     short L44

L42:            mov     ah,al
                and     ah,dh           ; AH := masked pixel bits
                not     dh              ; DH := reverse bit mask for 1st byte
                and     es:[di],dh      ; zero masked pixels in buffer
                or      es:[di],ah      ; update masked pixels in buffer
                inc     di
                dec     cx

; use a fast 8086 machine instruction to draw the remainder of the line

L43:            rep     stosb           ; update all pixels in the line

; set pixels in the rightmost byte of the line

L44:            and     al,dl           ; AL := masked pixels for last byte
                not     dl
                and     es:[di],dl      ; zero masked pixels in buffer
                or      es:[di],al      ; update masked pixels in buffer

                jmp     Lexit
```

(continued)

Listing 6-5. *Continued.*

```
; routine for dy <= dx (slope <= 1)    ; ES:BX -> video buffer
                                       ; CX = # pixels to draw
                                       ; DH = inverse bit mask
                                       ; DL = pixel value in proper position
                                       ; SI = buffer interleave increment
                                       ; DI = decision variable
LoSlopeLine04:

L10:           mov    ah,es:[bx]       ; AH := byte from video buffer

L11:           and    ah,dh            ; zero pixel value at current bit offset
               or     ah,dl            ; set pixel value in byte

               ror    dl,1             ; rotate pixel value
               ror    dl,1
               ror    dh,1             ; rotate bit mask
               ror    dh,1
               jnc    L14              ; jump if bit mask rotated to
                                       ;   leftmost pixel position

; bit mask not shifted out

               or     di,di            ; test sign of d
               jns    L12              ; jump if d >= 0

               add    di,VARincr1      ; d := d + incr1
               loop   L11

               mov    es:[bx],ah       ; store remaining pixels in buffer
               jmp    short Lexit

L12:           add    di,VARincr2      ; d := d + incr2
               mov    es:[bx],ah       ; update buffer

               add    bx,si            ; increment y
               xchg   si,VARleafincr   ; exchange interleave increment values

               loop   L10
               jmp    short Lexit

; bit mask shifted out

L14:           mov    es:[bx],ah       ; update buffer
               inc    bx               ; BX := offset of next byte

               or     di,di            ; test sign of d
               jns    L15              ; jump if non-negative

               add    di,VARincr1      ; d := d + incr1
               loop   L10
               jmp    short Lexit


L15:           add    di,VARincr2      ; d := d + incr2

               add    bx,si            ; increment y
               xchg   si,VARleafincr
```

(continued)

Listing 6-5. *Continued.*

```
                loop    L10
                jmp     short Lexit


; routine for dy > dx (slope > 1)        ; ES:BX -> video buffer
                                         ; CX = # pixels to draw
                                         ; DH = inverse bit mask
                                         ; DL = pixel value in proper position
                                         ; SI = buffer interleave increment
                                         ; DI = decision variable
HiSlopeLine04:

L21:            and     es:[bx],dh       ; zero pixel value in video buffer
                or      es:[bx],dl       ; set pixel value in byte

                add     bx,si            ; increment y
                xchg    si,VARleafincr   ; exchange interleave increment values

L22:            or      di,di            ; test sign of d
                jns     L23              ; jump if d >= 0

                add     di,VARincr1      ; d := d + incr1
                loop    L21

                jmp     short Lexit


L23:            add     di,VARincr2      ; d := d + incr2

                ror     dl,1             ; rotate pixel value
                ror     dl,1
                ror     dh,1             ; rotate bit mask
                ror     dh,1
                cmc                      ; cf set if bit mask not rotated to
                                         ;   leftmost pixel position

                adc     bx,0             ; BX := offset of next byte

                loop    L21


Lexit:          pop     di               ; restore registers and return
                pop     si
                mov     sp,bp
                pop     bp
                ret

_Line04         ENDP

_TEXT           ENDS


_DATA           SEGMENT word public 'DATA'
```

(continued)

Listing 6-5. *Continued.*

```
PropagatedPixel  DB        00000000b        ; 0
                 DB        01010101b        ; 1
                 DB        10101010b        ; 2
                 DB        11111111b        ; 3

_DATA            ENDS

                 END
```

On the CGA, the code that handles vertical increments is complicated by the need to step across the interleaves in the video buffer. The pixel address is incremented by 2000H to move from the first interleave (even *y*-coordinates) to the second interleave (odd *y*-coordinates). To increment from a pixel at an odd *y*-coordinate to the pixel just below it, you add −2000H (to increment from the second to the first interleave) plus 80 (the number of bytes in each pixel row in the buffer). The increment is thus 0E050H (80 − 2000H).

The routines for the CGA presented in Listings 6-4 and 6-5 can only copy the specified pixel value into the video buffer. To perform a XOR, an OR, or an AND operation on the preexisting values in the buffer using the specified pixel value, change the inner loops of each of the four line-drawing modules.

In selecting among pixel operations (XOR, AND, and so on), you face the usual trade-off between speed and code size. To maximize speed, write a separate line-drawing module for each pixel operation (AND, OR, XOR, and replace). To minimize redundant code, call a short subroutine, or add some branching logic to perform one of the pixel operations.

HGC

The routine for the HGC, contained in Listing 6-6, is similar to the one for the CGA's 640-by-200 2-color mode. The important difference is in how the HGC's video buffer is mapped. Because of the Hercules video buffer's four-way interleave, the pixel address is incremented by adding the buffer interleave value (2000H or −2000H) until the result exceeds the limit of valid buffer offsets. Because valid buffer offsets lie in the range 0 through 7FFFH, the routine detects the overflow condition by examining the high-order bit of the result. When the result overflows, it adds another value (90 − 8000H or 8000H − 90) to it, so that the new result is the proper offset in the next buffer interleave.

```
         TITLE   'Listing 6-6'
         NAME    LineHGC
         PAGE    55,132
```

(continued)

Listing 6-6. *A line-drawing routine for Hercules monochrome graphics mode.*

Listing 6-6. *Continued.*

```
;
; Name:          LineHGC
;
; Function:      Draw a line in HGC or HGC+ 720x348 graphics
;
; Caller:        Microsoft C:
;
;                       void LineHGC(x1,y1,x2,y2,n);
;
;                       int x1,y1,x2,y2;        /* pixel coordinates */
;
;                       int n;                  /* pixel value */
;

ARGx1           EQU     word ptr [bp+4] ; stack frame addressing
ARGy1           EQU     word ptr [bp+6]
ARGx2           EQU     word ptr [bp+8]
ARGy2           EQU     word ptr [bp+10]
ARGn            EQU     byte ptr [bp+12]
VARleafincr     EQU     word ptr [bp-6]
VARincr1        EQU     word ptr [bp-8]
VARincr2        EQU     word ptr [bp-10]
VARroutine      EQU     word ptr [bp-12]

ByteOffsetShift EQU     3                       ; used to convert pixels to byte offset

DGROUP          GROUP   _DATA

_TEXT           SEGMENT byte public 'CODE'
                ASSUME  cs:_TEXT,ds:DGROUP

                EXTRN   PixelAddrHGC:near

                PUBLIC  _LineHGC
_LineHGC        PROC    near

                push    bp                      ; preserve caller registers
                mov     bp,sp
                sub     sp,8                    ; stack space for local variables
                push    si
                push    di

                mov     si,2000h                ; increment for video buffer interleave
                mov     di,90-8000h             ; increment from last to first interleave

                mov     cx,ARGx2
                sub     cx,ARGx1                ; CX := x2 - x1
                jz      VertLineHGC             ; jump if vertical line

; force x1 < x2

                jns     L01                     ; jump if x2 > x1

                neg     cx                      ; CX := x1 - x2

                mov     bx,ARGx2                ; exchange x1 and x2
                xchg    bx,ARGx1
                mov     ARGx2,bx
```

(continued)

Listing 6-6. *Continued.*

```
                mov     bx,ARGy2            ; exchange y1 and y2
                xchg    bx,ARGy1
                mov     ARGy2,bx

; calculate dy = ABS(y2-y1)

L01:            mov     bx,ARGy2
                sub     bx,ARGy1            ; BX := y2 - y1
                jz      HorizLineHGC        ; jump if horizontal line

                jns     L03

                neg     bx                  ; BX := y1 - y2
                neg     si                  ; negate increments for buffer interleave
                neg     di

; select appropriate routine for slope of line

L03:            mov     VARleafincr,di      ; save increment for buffer interleave

                mov     VARroutine,offset LoSlopeLineHGC
                cmp     bx,cx
                jle     L04                 ; jump if dy <= dx (slope <= 1)
                mov     VARroutine,offset HiSlopeLineHGC
                xchg    bx,cx               ; exchange dy and dx

; calculate initial decision variable and increments

L04:            shl     bx,1                ; BX := 2 * dy
                mov     VARincr1,bx         ; incr1 := 2 * dy
                sub     bx,cx
                mov     di,bx               ; DI := d = 2 * dy - dx
                sub     bx,cx
                mov     VARincr2,bx         ; incr2 := 2 * (dy - dx)

; calculate first pixel address

                push    cx                  ; preserve this register
                mov     ax,ARGy1            ; AX := y
                mov     bx,ARGx1            ; BX := x
                call    PixelAddrHGC        ; AH := bit mask
                                            ; ES:BX -> buffer
                                            ; CL := # bits to shift left

                mov     al,ARGn             ; AL := unshifted pixel value
                shl     ax,cl               ; AH := bit mask in proper position
                                            ; AL := pixel value in proper position

                mov     dx,ax               ; DH := bit mask
                                            ; DL := pixel value
                not     dh                  ; DH := inverse bit mask

                pop     cx                  ; restore this register
                inc     cx                  ; CX := # of pixels to draw

                jmp     VARroutine          ; jump to appropriate routine for slope
```

(continued)

Listing 6-6. *Continued.*

```
; routine for vertical lines

VertLineHGC:    mov     ax,ARGy1        ; AX := y1
                mov     bx,ARGy2        ; BX := y2
                mov     cx,bx
                sub     cx,ax           ; CX := dy
                jge     L31             ; jump if dy >= 0

                neg     cx              ; force dy >= 0
                mov     ax,bx           ; AX := y2

L31:            inc     cx              ; CX := # of pixels to draw
                mov     bx,ARGx1        ; BX := x
                push    cx              ; preserve this register
                call    PixelAddrHGC    ; AH := bit mask
                                        ; ES:BX -> video buffer
                                        ; CL := # bits to shift left
                mov     al,ARGn         ; AL := pixel value
                shl     ax,cl           ; AH := bit mask in proper position
                                        ; AL := pixel value in proper position
                not     ah              ; AH := inverse bit mask
                pop     cx              ; restore this register

; draw the line
                test    al,al
                jz      L34             ; jump if pixel value is zero

L32:            or      es:[bx],al      ; set pixel values in buffer

                add     bx,si           ; increment to next portion of interleave
                jns     L33
                add     bx,di           ; increment to first portion of interleave
L33:            loop    L32
                jmp     short L36

L34:            and     es:[bx],ah      ; reset pixel values in buffer

                add     bx,si           ; increment to next portion of interleave
                jns     L35
                add     bx,di           ; increment to first portion of interleave
L35:            loop    L34

L36:            jmp     Lexit


; routine for horizontal lines (slope = 0)

HorizLineHGC:   mov     ax,ARGy1
                mov     bx,ARGx1
                call    PixelAddrHGC    ; AH := bit mask
                                        ; ES:BX -> video buffer
                                        ; CL := # bits to shift left
                mov     di,bx           ; ES:DI -> buffer
                mov     dh,ah
                not     dh              ; DH := unshifted bit mask for leftmost
                                        ;       byte
                mov     dl,0FFh         ; DL := unshifted bit mask for
                                        ;       rightmost byte
```

(continued)

Listing 6-6. *Continued.*

```
                    shl     dh,cl               ; DH := reverse bit mask for first byte
                    not     dh                  ; DH := bit mask for first byte

                    mov     cx,ARGx2
                    and     cl,7
                    xor     cl,7                ; CL := number of bits to shift left
                    shl     dl,cl               ; DL := bit mask for last byte

; determine byte offset of first and last pixel in the line

                    mov     ax,ARGx2            ; AX := x2
                    mov     bx,ARGx1            ; BX := x1

                    mov     cl,ByteOffsetShift      ; number of bits to shift to
                                                    ;   convert pixels to bytes

                    shr     ax,cl               ; AX := byte offset of x2
                    shr     bx,cl               ; BX := byte offset of x1
                    mov     cx,ax
                    sub     cx,bx               ; CX := (# bytes in line) - 1

; propagate pixel value throughout one byte

                    mov     bx,offset DGROUP:PropagatedPixel
                    mov     al,ARGn             ; AL := pixel value
                    xlat                        ; AL := propagated pixel value

; set pixels in leftmost byte of the line

                    or      dh,dh
                    js      L43                 ; jump if byte-aligned (x1 is leftmost
                                                ;   pixel in byte)
                    or      cx,cx
                    jnz     L42                 ; jump if more than one byte in the line

                    and     dl,dh               ; bit mask for the line
                    jmp     short L44

L42:                mov     ah,al
                    and     ah,dh               ; AH := masked pixel bits
                    not     dh                  ; DH := reverse bit mask for 1st byte
                    and     es:[di],dh          ; zero masked pixels in buffer
                    or      es:[di],ah          ; update masked pixels in buffer
                    inc     di
                    dec     cx

; use a fast 8086 machine instruction to draw the remainder of the line

L43:                rep     stosb               ; update all pixels in the line

; set pixels in the rightmost byte of the line

L44:                and     al,dl               ; AL := masked pixels for last byte
                    not     dl
                    and     es:[di],dl          ; zero masked pixels in buffer
                    or      es:[di],al          ; update masked pixels in buffer

                    jmp     Lexit
```

(continued)

Listing 6-6. *Continued.*

```
; routine for dy <= dx (slope <= 1)    ; ES:BX -> video buffer
                                       ; CX = # pixels to draw
                                       ; DH = inverse bit mask
                                       ; DL = pixel value in proper position
                                       ; SI = buffer interleave increment
                                       ; DI = decision variable

LoSlopeLineHGC:

L10:            mov     ah,es:[bx]      ; AH := byte from video buffer

L11:            and     ah,dh           ; zero pixel value at current bit offset
                or      ah,dl           ; set pixel value in byte

                ror     dl,1            ; rotate pixel value
                ror     dh,1            ; rotate bit mask
                jnc     L14             ; jump if bit mask rotated to
                                        ;   leftmost pixel position

; bit mask not shifted out

                or      di,di           ; test sign of d
                jns     L12             ; jump if d >= 0

                add     di,VARincr1     ; d := d + incr1
                loop    L11

                mov     es:[bx],ah      ; store remaining pixels in buffer
                jmp     short Lexit

L12:            add     di,VARincr2     ; d := d + incr2
                mov     es:[bx],ah      ; update buffer

                add     bx,si           ; increment y
                jns     L13             ; jump if not in last interleave

                add     bx,VARleafincr  ; increment into next interleave

L13:            loop    L10
                jmp     short Lexit

; bit mask shifted out

L14:            mov     es:[bx],ah      ; update buffer
                inc     bx              ; BX := offset of next byte

                or      di,di           ; test sign of d
                jns     L15             ; jump if non-negative

                add     di,VARincr1     ; d := d + incr1
                loop    L10
                jmp     short Lexit

L15:            add     di,VARincr2     ; d := d + incr2

                add     bx,si           ; increment y
                jns     L16             ; jump if not in last interleave

                add     bx,VARleafincr  ; increment into next interleave
```

(continued)

Listing 6-6. *Continued.*

```
L16:            loop    L10             ; loop until all pixels are set
                jmp     short Lexit


; routine for dy > dx (slope > 1)     ; ES:BX -> video buffer
                                       ; CX = # pixels to draw
                                       ; DH = inverse bit mask
                                       ; DL = pixel value in proper position
                                       ; SI = buffer interleave increment
                                       ; DI = decision variable
HiSlopeLineHGC:

L21:            and     es:[bx],dh      ; zero pixel value in video buffer
                or      es:[bx],dl      ; set pixel value in byte

                add     bx,si           ; increment y
                jns     L22             ; jump if not in last interleave

                add     bx,VARleafincr  ; increment into next interleave

L22:            or      di,di
                jns     L23             ; jump if d >= 0

                add     di,VARincr1     ; d := d + incr1
                loop    L21
                jmp     short Lexit


L23:            add     di,VARincr2     ; d := d + incr2

                ror     dl,1            ; rotate pixel value
                ror     dh,1            ; rotate bit mask
                cmc                     ; cf set if bit mask not rotated to
                                        ;  leftmost pixel position
                adc     bx,0            ; BX := offset of next byte

                loop    L21


Lexit:          pop     di              ; restore registers and return
                pop     si
                mov     sp,bp
                pop     bp
                ret

_LineHGC        ENDP

_TEXT           ENDS

_DATA           SEGMENT word public 'DATA'

PropagatedPixel DB      00000000b       ; 0
                DB      11111111b       ; 1

_DATA           ENDS

                END
```

The routines for the HGC never access the video buffer with 16-bit read/write operations such as MOVSW or AND [BX],DX. Avoiding these 16-bit operations ensures that the routines will run on the InColor Card as well as on the HGC and HGC+.

 You can use the same line-drawing routines on either of the HGC's video pages by setting the appropriate value for VideoBufferSeg in PixelAddrHGC. For video page 0, set VideoBufferSeg to B000H. For video page 1, use B800H.

EGA

For the EGA, three line-drawing routines can cover all available graphics modes. The routines for the CGA's 640-by-200 2-color and 320-by-200 4-color modes work equally well in equivalent modes on the EGA. The routine for the remaining graphics modes (200-line 16-color modes and all 350-line modes) is complicated by the need to program the Graphics Controller, but simplified in that the Graphics Controller hardware handles some pixel manipulations that must be performed in software on the CGA.

The routine in Listing 6-7 uses Graphics Controller write mode 0 to update the video buffer. The routine stores the pixel value for the line in the Set/Reset register. For each pixel updated in the buffer, the routine writes the appropriate bit mask to the Bit Mask register. Thus, a single 80x86 instruction can read, update, and rewrite up to 8 pixels at a time.

```
                        TITLE   'Listing 6-7'
                        NAME    Line10
                        PAGE    55,132


;
; Name:          Line10
;
; Function:      Draw a line in the following EGA and VGA graphics modes:
;                        200-line 16-color modes
;                        350-line modes
;                        640x480 16-color
;
; Caller:        Microsoft C:
;
;                        void Line10(x1,y1,x2,y2,n);
;
;                        int x1,y1,x2,y2;          /* pixel coordinates */
;
;                        int n;                    /* pixel value */
;


ARGx1           EQU     word ptr [bp+4] ; stack frame addressing
ARGy1           EQU     word ptr [bp+6]
ARGx2           EQU     word ptr [bp+8]
ARGy2           EQU     word ptr [bp+10]
ARGn            EQU     byte ptr [bp+12]
```

Listing 6-7. *A line-drawing routine for native EGA graphics modes.* (continued)

Listing 6-7. *Continued.*

```
VARvertincr      EQU      word ptr [bp-6]
VARincr1         EQU      word ptr [bp-8]
VARincr2         EQU      word ptr [bp-10]
VARroutine       EQU      word ptr [bp-12]

ByteOffsetShift EQU      3                        ; used to convert pixels to byte offset
BytesPerLine     EQU      80
RMWbits          EQU      0                        ; value for Data Rotate/Func Select reg


_TEXT            SEGMENT byte public 'CODE'
                 ASSUME  cs:_TEXT

                 EXTRN   PixelAddr10:near

                 PUBLIC  _Line10
_Line10          PROC    near

                 push    bp               ; preserve caller registers
                 mov     bp,sp
                 sub     sp,8             ; stack space for local variables
                 push    si
                 push    di

; configure the Graphics Controller

                 mov     dx,3CEh          ; DX := Graphics Controller port addr

                 mov     ah,ARGn          ; AH := pixel value
                 xor     al,al            ; AL := Set/Reset Register number
                 out     dx,ax

                 mov     ax,0F01h         ; AH := 1111b (bit plane mask for
                                          ;   Enable Set/Reset)
                 out     dx,ax            ; AL := Enable Set/Reset Register #

                 mov     ah,RMWbits       ; bits 3 and 4 of AH := function
                 mov     al,3             ; AL := Data Rotate/Func Select reg #
                 out     dx,ax

; check for vertical line

                 mov     si,BytesPerLine ; increment for video buffer

                 mov     cx,ARGx2
                 sub     cx,ARGx1         ; CX := x2 - x1
                 jz      VertLine10       ; jump if vertical line

; force x1 < x2

                 jns     L01              ; jump if x2 > x1

                 neg     cx               ; CX := x1 - x2

                 mov     bx,ARGx2         ; exchange x1 and x2
                 xchg    bx,ARGx1
                 mov     ARGx2,bx
```

(continued)

Listing 6-7. *Continued.*

```
              mov     bx,ARGy2      ; exchange y1 and y2
              xchg    bx,ARGy1
              mov     ARGy2,bx

; calculate dy = ABS(y2-y1)

L01:          mov     bx,ARGy2
              sub     bx,ARGy1      ; BX := y2 - y1
              jz      HorizLine10   ; jump if horizontal line

              jns     L03           ; jump if slope is positive

              neg     bx            ; BX := y1 - y2
              neg     si            ; negate increment for buffer interleave

; select appropriate routine for slope of line

L03:          mov     VARvertincr,si  ; save vertical increment

              mov     VARroutine,offset LoSlopeLine10
              cmp     bx,cx
              jle     L04           ; jump if dy <= dx (slope <= 1)
              mov     VARroutine,offset HiSlopeLine10
              xchg    bx,cx         ; exchange dy and dx

; calculate initial decision variable and increments

L04:          shl     bx,1          ; BX := 2 * dy
              mov     VARincr1,bx   ; incr1 := 2 * dy
              sub     bx,cx
              mov     si,bx         ; SI := d = 2 * dy - dx
              sub     bx,cx
              mov     VARincr2,bx   ; incr2 := 2 * (dy - dx)

; calculate first pixel address

              push    cx            ; preserve this register
              mov     ax,ARGy1      ; AX := y
              mov     bx,ARGx1      ; BX := x
              call    PixelAddr10   ; AH := bit mask
                                    ; ES:BX -> buffer
                                    ; CL := # bits to shift left

              mov     di,bx         ; ES:DI -> buffer
              shl     ah,cl         ; AH := bit mask in proper position
              mov     bl,ah         ; AH,BL := bit mask
              mov     al,8          ; AL := Bit Mask Register number

              pop     cx            ; restore this register
              inc     cx            ; CX := # of pixels to draw

              jmp     VARroutine    ; jump to appropriate routine for slope
```

(continued)

Listing 6-7. *Continued.*

```
; routine for vertical lines

VertLine10:     mov     ax,ARGy1         ; AX := y1
                mov     bx,ARGy2         ; BX := y2
                mov     cx,bx
                sub     cx,ax            ; CX := dy
                jge     L31              ; jump if dy >= 0

                neg     cx               ; force dy >= 0
                mov     ax,bx            ; AX := y2

L31:            inc     cx               ; CX := # of pixels to draw
                mov     bx,ARGx1         ; BX := x
                push    cx               ; preserve this register
                call    PixelAddr10      ; AH := bit mask
                                         ; ES:BX -> video buffer
                                         ; CL := # bits to shift left
; set up Graphics Controller

                shl     ah,cl            ; AH := bit mask in proper position
                mov     al,8             ; AL := Bit Mask reg number
                out     dx,ax

                pop     cx               ; restore this register

; draw the line

L32:            or      es:[bx],al       ; set pixel
                add     bx,si            ; increment to next line
                loop    L32

                jmp     Lexit



; routine for horizontal lines (slope = 0)

HorizLine10:
                push    ds               ; preserve DS

                mov     ax,ARGy1
                mov     bx,ARGx1
                call    PixelAddr10      ; AH := bit mask
                                         ; ES:BX -> video buffer
                                         ; CL := # bits to shift left
                mov     di,bx            ; ES:DI -> buffer
                mov     dh,ah            ; DH := unshifted bit mask for leftmost
                                         ;       byte
                not     dh
                shl     dh,cl            ; DH := reverse bit mask for first byte
                not     dh               ; DH := bit mask for first byte

                mov     cx,ARGx2
                and     cl,7
                xor     cl,7             ; CL := number of bits to shift left
                mov     dl,0FFh          ; DL := unshifted bit mask for
                                         ;       rightmost byte
                shl     dl,cl            ; DL := bit mask for last byte
```

(continued)

Listing 6-7. *Continued.*

```
; determine byte offset of first and last pixel in the line

            mov     ax,ARGx2        ; AX := x2
            mov     bx,ARGx1        ; BX := x1

            mov     cl,ByteOffsetShift      ; number of bits to shift to
                                            ;   convert pixels to bytes

            shr     ax,cl           ; AX := byte offset of x2
            shr     bx,cl           ; BX := byte offset of x1
            mov     cx,ax
            sub     cx,bx           ; CX := (# bytes in line) - 1

; get Graphics Controller port address into DX

            mov     bx,dx           ; BH := bit mask for first byte
                                    ;-BL := bit mask for last byte
            mov     dx,3CEh         ; DX := Graphics Controller port
            mov     al,8            ; AL := Bit Mask Register number

; make video buffer addressable through DS:SI

            push    es
            pop     ds
            mov     si,di           ; DS:SI -> video buffer

; set pixels in leftmost byte of the line

            or      bh,bh
            js      L43             ; jump if byte-aligned (x1 is leftmost
                                    ;   pixel in byte)
            or      cx,cx
            jnz     L42             ; jump if more than one byte in the line

            and     bl,bh           ; BL := bit mask for the line
            jmp     short L44

L42:        mov     ah,bh           ; AH := bit mask for 1st byte
            out     dx,ax           ; update Graphics Controller

            movsb                   ; update bit planes
            dec     cx

; use a fast 8086 machine instruction to draw the remainder of the line

L43:        mov     ah,11111111b    ; AH := bit mask
            out     dx,ax           ; update Bit Mask Register
            rep     movsb           ; update all pixels in the line

; set pixels in the rightmost byte of the line

L44:        mov     ah,bl           ; AH := bit mask for last byte
            out     dx,ax           ; update Graphics Controller

            movsb                   ; update bit planes

            pop     ds              ; restore DS
            jmp     short Lexit
```

(continued)

Listing 6-7. *Continued.*

```
; routine for dy >= dx (slope <= 1)      ; ES:DI -> video buffer
                                         ; AL = Bit Mask Register number
                                         ; BL = bit mask for 1st pixel
                                         ; CX = # pixels to draw
                                         ; DX = Graphics Controller port addr
                                         ; SI = decision variable
LoSlopeLine10:

L10:            mov     ah,bl            ; AH := bit mask for next pixel

L11:            or      ah,bl            ; mask current pixel position
                ror     bl,1             ; rotate pixel value
                jc      L14              ; jump if bit mask rotated to
                                         ;   leftmost pixel position

; bit mask not shifted out

                or      si,si            ; test sign of d
                jns     L12              ; jump if d >= 0

                add     si,VARincr1      ; d := d + incr1
                loop    L11

                out     dx,ax            ; update Bit Mask Register
                or      es:[di],al       ; set remaining pixel(s)
                jmp     short Lexit

L12:            add     si,VARincr2      ; d := d + incr2
                out     dx,ax            ; update Bit Mask Register

                or      es:[di],al       ; update bit planes

                add     di,VARvertincr   ; increment y
                loop    L10
                jmp     short Lexit

; bit mask shifted out

L14:            out     dx,ax            ; update Bit Mask Register ...

                or      es:[di],al       ; update bit planes
                inc     di               ; increment x

                or      si,si            ; test sign of d
                jns     L15              ; jump if non-negative

                add     si,VARincr1      ; d := d + incr1
                loop    L10
                jmp     short Lexit

L15:            add     si,VARincr2      ; d := d + incr2
                add     di,VARvertincr   ; vertical increment
                loop    L10
                jmp     short Lexit
```

(continued)

Listing 6-7. *Continued.*

```
; routine for dy > dx (slope > 1)        ; ES:DI -> video buffer
                                         ; AH = bit mask for 1st pixel
                                         ; AL = Bit Mask Register number
                                         ; CX = # pixels to draw
                                         ; DX = Graphics Controller port addr
                                         ; SI = decision variable
HiSlopeLine10:
                mov    bx,VARvertincr    ; BX := y-increment

L21:            out    dx,ax             ; update Bit Mask Register
                or     es:[di],al        ; update bit planes

                add    di,bx             ; increment y

L22:            or     si,si             ; test sign of d
                jns    L23               ; jump if d >= 0

                add    si,VARincr1       ; d := d + incr1
                loop   L21
                jmp    short Lexit


L23:            add    si,VARincr2       ; d := d + incr2

                ror    ah,1              ; rotate bit mask
                adc    di,0              ; increment DI if when mask rotated to
                                         ;   leftmost pixel position

                loop   L21


; restore default Graphics Controller state and return to caller

Lexit:          xor    ax,ax             ; AH := 0, AL := 0
                out    dx,ax             ; restore Set/Reset Register

                inc    ax                ; AH := 0, AL := 1
                out    dx,ax             ; restore Enable Set/Reset Register

                mov    al,3              ; AH := 0, AL := 3
                out    dx,ax             ; AL := Data Rotate/Func Select reg #

                mov    ax,0FF08h         ; AH := 11111111b, AL := 8
                out    dx,ax             ; restore Bit Mask Register

                pop    di                ; restore registers and return
                pop    si
                mov    sp,bp
                pop    bp
                ret

_Line10         ENDP

_TEXT           ENDS

                END
```

Within the line-drawing modules, the value 3CEH (the port for the Graphics Controller Address register) is maintained in DX, the value 8 (the Bit Mask register number) is kept in AL, and the current pixel bit mask is kept in AH. This lets you update the bit planes with only two machine instructions: OUT DX,AX to update the Bit Mask register and a MOVSB or OR ES:[DI],AL instruction that causes a CPU read and CPU write to occur.

This routine makes careful use of the 80x86 registers and the Graphics Controller. The Graphics Controller's parallel processing helps the routine run at about the same speed as do CGA and HGC line-drawing routines.

Native EGA graphics modes use no video buffer interleave, so locating a pixel's vertical neighbors in the video buffer is easy. If each line contains *n* bytes of pixels, the next pixel up from a given pixel is –*n* bytes away, and the next pixel down is *n* bytes away. The code for incrementing pixel addresses vertically is thus simpler than the corresponding code for the CGA or the HGC. (Compare, for example, the code in the loop at label L32 in Listings 6-4 and 6-7.)

The Graphics Controller handles any of four pixel operations for you (XOR, AND, OR, and replace), so the only extra code required to support these functions consists of a few instructions to load the Data Rotate/Function Select register (03H). This task is part of the ''configure the Graphics Controller'' code near the beginning of the routine in Listing 6-7.

 You can use this line-drawing routine in 640-by-350 4-color and monochrome modes. Be sure to specify the proper pixel value in these modes so that the routine sets bits in the proper bit planes (see Chapter 4).

MCGA

In CGA-compatible modes, you can use the CGA line-drawing routines on the MCGA. The non-CGA modes (640-by-480 2-color and 320-by-200 256-color) require their own routines, as shown in Listings 6-8 and 6-9, but these are easily derived from the code for 640-by-200 2-color mode.

```
                TITLE    'Listing 6-8'
                NAME     Line11
                PAGE     55,132

;
; Name:          Line11
;
; Function:      Draw a line in 640x480 2-color mode (MCGA, VGA)
;
; Caller:        Microsoft C:
;
;                        void Line11(x1,y1,x2,y2,n);
;
```

(continued)

Listing 6-8. *A line-drawing routine for MCGA and VGA 640-by-480 2-color mode.*

Listing 6-8. *Continued.*

```
;                       int x1,y1,x2,y2;        /* pixel coordinates */
;
;                       int n;                  /* pixel value */
;

ARGx1           EQU     word ptr [bp+4] ; stack frame addressing
ARGy1           EQU     word ptr [bp+6]
ARGx2           EQU     word ptr [bp+8]
ARGy2           EQU     word ptr [bp+10]
ARGn            EQU     byte ptr [bp+12]
VARincr1        EQU     word ptr [bp-6]
VARincr2        EQU     word ptr [bp-8]
VARroutine      EQU     word ptr [bp-10]

BytesPerLine    EQU     80                      ; bytes in one row of pixels
ByteOffsetShift EQU     3                       ; used to convert pixels to byte offset

DGROUP          GROUP   _DATA

_TEXT           SEGMENT byte public 'CODE'
                ASSUME  cs:_TEXT,ds:DGROUP

                EXTRN   PixelAddr10:near

                PUBLIC  _Line11
_Line11         PROC    near

                push    bp                      ; preserve caller registers
                mov     bp,sp
                sub     sp,6                    ; stack space for local variables
                push    si
                push    di

; check for vertical line

                mov     si,BytesPerLine ; SI := initial y-increment

                mov     cx,ARGx2
                sub     cx,ARGx1                ; CX := x2 - x1
                jz      VertLine11              ; jump if vertical line

; force x1 < x2

                jns     L01                     ; jump if x2 > x1

                neg     cx                      ; CX := x1 - x2

                mov     bx,ARGx2                ; exchange x1 and x2
                xchg    bx,ARGx1
                mov     ARGx2,bx

                mov     bx,ARGy2                ; exchange y1 and y2
                xchg    bx,ARGy1
                mov     ARGy2,bx
```

(continued)

Listing 6-8. *Continued.*

```
; calculate dy = ABS(y2-y1)

L01:            mov     bx,ARGy2
                sub     bx,ARGy1        ; BX := y2 - y1
                jnz     L02

                jmp     HorizLine11     ; jump if horizontal line

L02:            jns     L03
                neg     bx              ; BX := y1 - y2
                neg     si              ; negate y-increment

; select appropriate routine for slope of line

L03:            mov     VARroutine,offset LoSlopeLine11
                cmp     bx,cx
                jle     L04             ; jump if dy <= dx (slope <= 1)
                mov     VARroutine,offset HiSlopeLine11
                xchg    bx,cx           ; exchange dy and dx

; calculate initial decision variable and increments

L04:            shl     bx,1            ; BX := 2 * dy
                mov     VARincr1,bx     ; incr1 := 2 * dy
                sub     bx,cx
                mov     di,bx           ; DI := d = 2 * dy - dx
                sub     bx,cx
                mov     VARincr2,bx     ; incr2 := 2 * (dy - dx)

; calculate first pixel address

                push    cx              ; preserve this register
                mov     ax,ARGy1        ; AX := y
                mov     bx,ARGx1        ; BX := x
                call    PixelAddr10     ; AH := bit mask
                                        ; ES:BX -> buffer
                                        ; CL := # bits to shift left

                mov     al,ARGn         ; AL := unshifted pixel value
                shl     ax,cl           ; AH := bit mask in proper position
                                        ; AL := pixel value in proper position

                mov     dx,ax           ; DH := bit mask
                                        ; DL := pixel value
                not     dh              ; DH := inverse bit mask

                pop     cx              ; restore this register
                inc     cx              ; CX := # of pixels to draw

                jmp     VARroutine      ; jump to appropriate routine for slope

; routine for vertical lines

VertLine11:     mov     ax,ARGy1        ; AX := y1
                mov     bx,ARGy2        ; BX := y2
                mov     cx,bx
                sub     cx,ax           ; CX := dy
                jge     L31             ; jump if dy >= 0
```

(continued)

Listing 6-8. *Continued.*

```
                neg     cx                  ; force dy >= 0
                mov     ax,bx               ; AX := y2

L31:            inc     cx                  ; CX := # of pixels to draw
                mov     bx,ARGx1            ; BX := x
                push    cx                  ; preserve this register
                call    PixelAddr10         ; AH := bit mask
                                            ; ES:BX -> video buffer
                                            ; CL := # bits to shift left
                mov     al,ARGn             ; AL := pixel value
                shl     ax,cl               ; AH := bit mask in proper position
                                            ; AL := pixel value in proper position
                not     ah                  ; AH := inverse bit mask
                pop     cx                  ; restore this register

; draw the line

                test    al,al
                jz      L33                 ; jump if pixel value = 0

L32:            or      es:[bx],al          ; set pixel values in buffer
                add     bx,si
                loop    L32
                jmp     short L34

L33:            and     es:[bx],ah          ; reset pixel values in buffer
                add     bx,si
                loop    L33

L34:            jmp     Lexit


; routine for horizontal lines (slope = 0)

HorizLine11:    mov     ax,ARGy1
                mov     bx,ARGx1
                call    PixelAddr10         ; AH := bit mask
                                            ; ES:BX -> video buffer
                                            ; CL := # bits to shift left
                mov     di,bx               ; ES:DI -> buffer

                mov     dh,ah
                not     dh                  ; DH := unshifted bit mask for leftmost
                                            ;        byte
                mov     dl,0FFh             ; DL := unshifted bit mask for
                                            ;        rightmost byte

                shl     dh,cl               ; DH := reverse bit mask for first byte
                not     dh                  ; DH := bit mask for first byte

                mov     cx,ARGx2
                and     cl,7
                xor     cl,7                ; CL := number of bits to shift left
                shl     dl,cl               ; DL := bit mask for last byte
```

(continued)

Listing 6-8. *Continued.*

```
; determine byte offset of first and last pixel in the line

                mov     ax,ARGx2            ; AX := x2
                mov     bx,ARGx1            ; BX := x1

                mov     cl,ByteOffsetShift      ; number of bits to shift to
                                                ;   convert pixels to bytes

                shr     ax,cl               ; AX := byte offset of x2
                shr     bx,cl               ; BX := byte offset of x1
                mov     cx,ax
                sub     cx,bx               ; CX := (# bytes in line) - 1

; propagate pixel value throughout one byte

                mov     bx,offset DGROUP:PropagatedPixel
                mov     al,ARGn             ; AL := pixel value
                xlat

; set pixels in leftmost byte of the line

                or      dh,dh
                js      L43                 ; jump if byte-aligned (x1 is leftmost
                                            ;   pixel in byte)
                or      cx,cx
                jnz     L42                 ; jump if more than one byte in the line

                and     dl,dh               ; bit mask for the line
                jmp     short L44

L42:            mov     ah,al
                and     ah,dh               ; AH := masked pixel bits
                not     dh                  ; DH := reverse bit mask for 1st byte
                and     es:[di],dh          ; zero masked pixels in buffer
                or      es:[di],ah          ; update masked pixels in buffer
                inc     di
                dec     cx

; use a fast 8086 machine instruction to draw the remainder of the line

L43:            rep     stosb               ; update all pixels in the line

; set pixels in the rightmost byte of the line

L44:            and     al,dl               ; AL := masked pixels for last byte
                not     dl
                and     es:[di],dl          ; zero masked pixels in buffer
                or      es:[di],al          ; update masked pixels in buffer

                jmp     Lexit


; routine for dy <= dx (slope <= 1)     ; ES:BX -> video buffer
                                        ; CX = # pixels to draw
                                        ; DH = inverse bit mask
                                        ; DL = pixel value in proper position
                                        ; SI = bytes per pixel row
                                        ; DI = decision variable
```

(continued)

Listing 6-8. *Continued.*

```
LoSlopeLine11:

L10:            mov     ah,es:[bx]      ; AH := byte from video buffer

L11:            and     ah,dh           ; zero pixel value at current bit offset
                or      ah,dl           ; set pixel value in byte

                ror     dl,1            ; rotate pixel value
                ror     dh,1            ; rotate bit mask
                jnc     L14             ; jump if bit mask rotated to
                                        ;   leftmost pixel position

; bit mask not shifted out

                or      di,di           ; test sign of d
                jns     L12             ; jump if d >= 0

                add     di,VARincr1     ; d := d + incr1
                loop    L11

                mov     es:[bx],ah      ; store remaining pixels in buffer
                jmp     short Lexit

L12:            add     di,VARincr2     ; d := d + incr2
                mov     es:[bx],ah      ; update buffer

                add     bx,si           ; increment y
                loop    L10
                jmp     short Lexit

; bit mask shifted out

L14:            mov     es:[bx],ah      ; update buffer
                inc     bx              ; BX := offset of next byte

                or      di,di           ; test sign of d
                jns     L15             ; jump if non-negative

                add     di,VARincr1     ; d := d + incr1
                loop    L10
                jmp     short Lexit

L15:            add     di,VARincr2     ; d := d + incr2

                add     bx,si           ; increment y
                loop    L10
                jmp     short Lexit

; routine for dy > dx (slope > 1)    ; ES:BX -> video buffer
                                     ; CX = # pixels to draw
                                     ; DH = inverse bit mask
                                     ; DL = pixel value in proper position
                                     ; SI = bytes per pixel row
                                     ; DI = decision variable

HiSlopeLine11:

L21:            and     es:[bx],dh      ; zero pixel value in video buffer
                or      es:[bx],dl      ; set pixel value in byte
```

(continued)

Listing 6-8. *Continued.*

```
                add     bx,si           ; increment y

L22:            or      di,di           ; test sign of d
                jns     L23             ; jump if d >= 0

                add     di,VARincr1     ; d := d + incr1
                loop    L21

                jmp     short Lexit


L23:            add     di,VARincr2     ; d := d + incr2

                ror     dl,1            ; rotate pixel value
                ror     dh,1            ; rotate bit mask
                cmc                     ; cf set if bit mask not rotated to
                                        ;  leftmost pixel position

                adc     bx,0            ; BX := offset of next byte

                loop    L21


Lexit:          pop     di              ; restore caller registers and return
                pop     si
                mov     sp,bp
                pop     bp
                ret

_Line11         ENDP

_TEXT           ENDS


_DATA           SEGMENT word public 'DATA'

PropagatedPixel DB      00000000b       ; 0
                DB      11111111b       ; 1

_DATA           ENDS

                END
```

```
                TITLE   'Listing 6-9'
                NAME    Line13
                PAGE    55,132

;
; Name:         Line13
;
; Function:     Draw a line in MCGA/VGA 320x200 256-color mode
;
```

(continued)

Listing 6-9. *A line-drawing routine for MCGA and VGA 320-by-200 256-color mode.*

Listing 6-9. *Continued.*

```
; Caller:        Microsoft C:
;
;                        void Line13(x1,y1,x2,y2,n);
;
;                        int x1,y1,x2,y2;        /* pixel coordinates */
;
;                        int n;                  /* pixel value */
;

ARGx1           EQU     word ptr [bp+4] ; stack frame addressing
ARGy1           EQU     word ptr [bp+6]
ARGx2           EQU     word ptr [bp+8]
ARGy2           EQU     word ptr [bp+10]
ARGn            EQU     byte ptr [bp+12]
VARincr1        EQU     word ptr [bp-6]
VARincr2        EQU     word ptr [bp-8]
VARroutine      EQU     word ptr [bp-10]


BytesPerLine    EQU     320


_TEXT           SEGMENT byte public 'CODE'
                ASSUME  cs:_TEXT

                EXTRN   PixelAddr13:near

                PUBLIC  _Line13
_Line13         PROC    near

                push    bp                  ; preserve caller registers
                mov     bp,sp
                sub     sp,6                ; stack space for local variables
                push    si
                push    di

; check for vertical line

                mov     si,BytesPerLine ; initial y-increment

                mov     cx,ARGx2
                sub     cx,ARGx1            ; CX := x2 - x1
                jz      VertLine13          ; jump if vertical line

; force x1 < x2

                jns     L01                 ; jump if x2 > x1

                neg     cx                  ; CX := x1 - x2

                mov     bx,ARGx2            ; exchange x1 and x2
                xchg    bx,ARGx1
                mov     ARGx2,bx

                mov     bx,ARGy2            ; exchange y1 and y2

                xchg    bx,ARGy1
                mov     ARGy2,bx
```

(continued)

Listing 6-9. *Continued.*

```
; calculate dy = ABS(y2-y1)

L01:            mov     bx,ARGy2
                sub     bx,ARGy1        ; BX := y2 - y1
                jz      HorizLine13     ; jump if horizontal line

                jns     L03             ; jump if slope is positive

                neg     bx              ; BX := y1 - y2
                neg     si              ; negate y-increment

; select appropriate routine for slope of line

L03:            push    si              ; preserve y-increment

                mov     VARroutine,offset LoSlopeLine13
                cmp     bx,cx
                jle     L04             ; jump if dy <= dx (slope <= 1)
                mov     VARroutine,offset HiSlopeLine13
                xchg    bx,cx           ; exchange dy and dx

; calculate initial decision variable and increments

L04:            shl     bx,1            ; BX := 2 * dy
                mov     VARincr1,bx     ; incr1 := 2 * dy
                sub     bx,cx
                mov     si,bx           ; SI := d = 2 * dy - dx

                sub     bx,cx
                mov     VARincr2,bx     ; incr2 := 2 * (dy - dx)

; calculate first pixel address

                push    cx              ; preserve this register
                mov     ax,ARGy1        ; AX := y
                mov     bx,ARGx1        ; BX := x
                call    PixelAddr13     ; ES:BX -> buffer

                mov     di,bx           ; ES:DI -> buffer

                pop     cx              ; restore this register
                inc     cx              ; CX := # of pixels to draw

                pop     bx              ; BX := y-increment
                jmp     VARroutine      ; jump to appropriate routine for slope

; routine for vertical lines

VertLine13:     mov     ax,ARGy1        ; AX := y1
                mov     bx,ARGy2        ; BX := y2
                mov     cx,bx
                sub     cx,ax           ; CX := dy
                jge     L31             ; jump if dy >= 0

                neg     cx              ; force dy >= 0
                mov     ax,bx           ; AX := y2
```

(continued)

Listing 6-9. *Continued.*

```
L31:            inc     cx              ; CX := # of pixels to draw
                mov     bx,ARGx1        ; BX := x
                push    cx              ; preserve this register
                call    PixelAddr13     ; ES:BX -> video buffer
                pop     cx

                mov     di,bx           ; ES:DI -> video buffer
                dec     si              ; SI := bytes/line - 1

                mov     al,ARGn         ; AL := pixel value

L32:            stosb                   ; set pixel value in buffer
                add     di,si           ; increment to next line
                loop    L32

                jmp     Lexit


; routine for horizontal lines (slope = 0)

HorizLine13:
                push    cx              ; preserve CX
                mov     ax,ARGy1
                mov     bx,ARGx1
                call    PixelAddr13     ; ES:BX -> video buffer
                mov     di,bx           ; ES:DI -> buffer

                pop     cx
                inc     cx              ; CX := number of pixels to draw

                mov     al,ARGn         ; AL := pixel value

                rep     stosb           ; update the video buffer

                jmp     short Lexit


; routine for dy <= dx (slope <= 1)    ; ES:DI -> video buffer
                                        ; BX = y-increment
                                        ; CX = # pixels to draw
                                        ; SI = decision variable

LoSlopeLine13:

                mov     al,ARGn         ; AL := pixel value

L11:            stosb                   ; store pixel, increment x

                or      si,si           ; test sign of d
                jns     L12             ; jump if d >= 0

                add     si,VARincr1     ; d := d + incr1
                loop    L11
                jmp     short Lexit
```

(continued)

Listing 6-9. *Continued.*

```
L12:              add     si,VARincr2     ; d := d + incr2
                  add     di,bx           ; increment y
                  loop    L11
                  jmp     short Lexit


; routine for dy > dx (slope > 1)     ; ES:DI -> video buffer
                                      ; BX = y-increment
                                      ; CX = # pixels to draw
                                      ; SI = decision variable
HiSlopeLine13:
                  mov     al,ARGn         ; AL := pixel value

L21:              stosb                   ; update next pixel, increment x

                  add     di,bx           ; increment y

L22:              or      si,si           ; test sign of d
                  jns     L23             ; jump if d >= 0

                  add     si,VARincr1     ; d := d + incr1
                  dec     di              ; decrement x (already incremented
                                          ;   by stosb)
                  loop    L21
                  jmp     short Lexit


L23:              add     si,VARincr2     ; d := d + incr2
                  loop    L21


Lexit:            pop     di              ; restore registers and return
                  pop     si
                  mov     sp,bp
                  pop     bp
                  ret

_Line13           ENDP

_TEXT             ENDS

                  END
```

VGA

Once you implement routines for the EGA and the MCGA, you can draw lines in any of the VGA's graphics modes. To draw lines in 640-by-480 16-color mode, use the 640-by-350 16-color routine.

InColor Card

Because pixel addressing in the video buffer is the same on the InColor Card as on Hercules monochrome cards, the only significant difference in the line-drawing routines for the InColor Card, as you'll see in Listing 6-10, is some extra code to select the specified pixel value. Note how the InColor Card's write mode 1 is used along with an appropriate foreground value in the Read/Write Color register to set the values of neighboring pixels in each byte of the buffer. This technique parallels the use of write mode 0 and the Set/Reset register on the EGA.

```
                    TITLE   'Listing 6-10'
                    NAME    LineInC
                    PAGE    55,132

;
; Name:          LineInC
;
; Function:      Draw a line in Hercules InColor 720x348 16-color mode
;
; Caller:        Microsoft C:
;
;                       void LineInC(x1,y1,x2,y2,n);
;
;                       int x1,y1,x2,y2;        /* pixel coordinates */
;
;                       int n;                  /* pixel value */
;

ARGx1           EQU     word ptr [bp+4] ; stack frame addressing
ARGy1           EQU     word ptr [bp+6]
ARGx2           EQU     word ptr [bp+8]
ARGy2           EQU     word ptr [bp+10]
ARGn            EQU     byte ptr [bp+12]
VARleafincr     EQU     word ptr [bp-6]
VARincr1        EQU     word ptr [bp-8]
VARincr2        EQU     word ptr [bp-10]
VARroutine      EQU     word ptr [bp-12]

ByteOffsetShift EQU     3               ; used to convert pixels to byte offset
DefaultRWColor  EQU     0Fh             ; default value for R/W Color register


_TEXT           SEGMENT byte public 'CODE'
                ASSUME  cs:_TEXT

                EXTRN   PixelAddrHGC:near

                PUBLIC  _LineInC
_LineInC        PROC    near

                push    bp              ; preserve caller registers
                mov     bp,sp
                sub     sp,8            ; stack space for local variables
                push    si
                push    di
```

(continued)

Listing 6-10. *A line-drawing routine for the InColor Card's 720-by-348 16-color mode.*

Listing 6-10. *Continued.*

```
                mov     si,2000h        ; increment for video buffer interleave
                mov     di,90-8000h     ; increment from last to first interleave

; set up InColor control registers

                mov     dx,3B4h         ; DX := CRTC I/O port
                mov     ax,5F19h        ; AH bit 6 := 1 (Mask Polarity)
                                        ; AH bits 5-4 := 1 (Write Mode)
                                        ; AH bits 3-0 := "don't care" bits
                                        ; AL := R/W Control Register number
                out     dx,ax           ; set R/W Control Register

                inc     ax              ; AL := 1Ah (R/W Color Reg number)
                mov     ah,ARGn         ; AH := foreground value
                out     dx,ax           ; set R/W color register


                mov     cx,ARGx2
                sub     cx,ARGx1        ; CX := x2 - x1
                jz      VertLineInC     ; jump if vertical line

; force x1 < x2

                jns     L01             ; jump if x2 > x1

                neg     cx              ; CX := x1 - x2

                mov     bx,ARGx2        ; exchange x1 and x2
                xchg    bx,ARGx1
                mov     ARGx2,bx

                mov     bx,ARGy2        ; exchange y1 and y2
                xchg    bx,ARGy1
                mov     ARGy2,bx

; calculate dy = ABS(y2-y1)

L01:            mov     bx,ARGy2
                sub     bx,ARGy1        ; BX := y2 - y1
                jz      HorizLineInC    ; jump if horizontal line

                jns     L03

                neg     bx              ; BX := y1 - y2
                neg     si              ; negate increments for buffer interleave
                neg     di

; select appropriate routine for slope of line

L03:            mov     VARleafincr,di  ; save increment for buffer interleave

                mov     VARroutine,offset LoSlopeLineInC
                cmp     bx,cx
                jle     L04             ; jump if dy <= dx (slope <= 1)
                mov     VARroutine,offset HiSlopeLineInC
                xchg    bx,cx           ; exchange dy and dx
```

(continued)

Listing 6-10. *Continued.*

```
; calculate initial decision variable and increments

L04:            shl     bx,1            ; BX := 2 * dy
                mov     VARincr1,bx     ; incr1 := 2 * dy
                sub     bx,cx
                mov     di,bx           ; DI := d = 2 * dy - dx
                sub     bx,cx
                mov     VARincr2,bx     ; incr2 := 2 * (dy - dx)

; calculate first pixel address

                push    cx              ; preserve this register
                mov     ax,ARGy1        ; AX := y
                mov     bx,ARGx1        ; BX := x
                call    PixelAddrHGC    ; AH := bit mask
                                        ; ES:BX -> buffer
                                        ; CL := # bits to shift left

                shl     ah,cl
                mov     dh,ah           ; DH := bit mask in proper position

                pop     cx              ; restore this register
                inc     cx              ; CX := # of pixels to draw

                jmp     VARroutine      ; jump to appropriate routine for slope


; routine for vertical lines

VertLineInC:    mov     ax,ARGy1        ; AX := y1
                mov     bx,ARGy2        ; BX := y2
                mov     cx,bx
                sub     cx,ax           ; CX := dy
                jge     L31             ; jump if dy >= 0

                neg     cx              ; force dy >= 0
                mov     ax,bx           ; AX := y2

L31:            inc     cx              ; CX := # of pixels to draw
                mov     bx,ARGx1        ; BX := x
                push    cx              ; preserve this register
                call    PixelAddrHGC    ; AH := bit mask
                                        ; ES:BX -> video buffer
                                        ; CL := # bits to shift left
                shl     ah,cl           ; AH := bit mask in proper position
                pop     cx              ; restore this register

L32:            or      es:[bx],ah      ; update pixel in buffer

                add     bx,si           ; increment to next portion of interleave
                jns     L33

                add     bx,di           ; increment to first portion of interleave

L33:            loop    L32

                jmp     Lexit
```

(continued)

Listing 6-10. *Continued.*

```
; routine for horizontal lines (slope = 0)

HorizLineInC:   mov     ax,ARGy1
                mov     bx,ARGx1
                call    PixelAddrHGC    ; AH := bit mask
                                        ; ES:BX -> video buffer
                                        ; CL := # bits to shift left
                mov     di,bx           ; ES:DI -> buffer
                mov     dh,ah
                not     dh              ; DH := unshifted bit mask for leftmost
                                        ;        byte
                mov     dl,0FFh         ; DL := unshifted bit mask for
                                        ;        rightmost byte

                shl     dh,cl           ; DH := reverse bit mask for first byte
                not     dh              ; DH := bit mask for first byte
                mov     cx,ARGx2
                and     cl,7
                xor     cl,7            ; CL := number of bits to shift left
                shl     dl,cl           ; DL := bit mask for last byte

; determine byte offset of first and last pixel in the line

                mov     ax,ARGx2        ; AX := x2
                mov     bx,ARGx1        ; BX := x1

                mov     cl,ByteOffsetShift      ; number of bits to shift to
                                                ;   convert pixels to bytes

                shr     ax,cl           ; AX := byte offset of x2
                shr     bx,cl           ; BX := byte offset of x1
                mov     cx,ax
                sub     cx,bx           ; CX := (# bytes in line) - 1

; set pixels in leftmost byte of the line

                or      dh,dh
                js      L43             ; jump if byte-aligned (x1 is leftmost
                                        ;   pixel in byte)
                or      cx,cx
                jnz     L42             ; jump if more than one byte in the line

                and     dl,dh           ; bit mask for the line
                jmp     short L44

L42:            or      es:[di],dh      ; update masked pixels in buffer
                inc     di
                dec     cx

; use a fast 8086 machine instruction to draw the remainder of the line

L43:            mov     al,0FFh         ; 8-pixel bit mask
                rep     stosb           ; update all pixels in the line

; set pixels in the rightmost byte of the line

L44:            or      es:[di],dl      ; update masked pixels in buffer
                jmp     Lexit
```

(continued)

Listing 6-10. *Continued.*

```
; routine for dy <= dx (slope <= 1)      ; ES:BX -> video buffer
                                         ; CX = # pixels to draw
                                         ; DH = bit mask
                                         ; SI = buffer interleave increment
                                         ; DI = decision variable

LoSlopeLineInC:

L10:            mov     ah,es:[bx]       ; latch bit planes
                                         ; AH := 0 because all planes
                                         ;   are "don't care"

L11:            or      ah,dh            ; set pixel value in byte

                ror     dh,1             ; rotate bit mask
                jc      L14              ; jump if bit mask rotated to
                                         ;   leftmost pixel position

; bit mask not shifted out

                or      di,di            ; test sign of d
                jns     L12              ; jump if d >= 0

                add     di,VARincr1      ; d := d + incr1
                loop    L11

                mov     es:[bx],ah       ; store remaining pixels in buffer
                jmp     short Lexit

L12:            add     di,VARincr2      ; d := d + incr2
                mov     es:[bx],ah       ; update buffer

                add     bx,si            ; increment y
                jns     L13              ; jump if not in last interleave

                add     bx,VARleafincr   ; increment into next interleave

L13:            loop    L10
                jmp     short Lexit

; bit mask shifted out

L14:            mov     es:[bx],ah       ; update buffer
                inc     bx               ; BX := offset of next byte

                or      di,di            ; test sign of d
                jns     L15              ; jump if non-negative

                add     di,VARincr1      ; d := d + incr1
                loop    L10
                jmp     short Lexit

L15:            add     di,VARincr2      ; d := d + incr2

                add     bx,si            ; increment y
                jns     L16              ; jump if not in last interleave

                add     bx,VARleafincr   ; increment into next interleave
```

(continued)

Listing 6-10. *Continued.*

```
L16:            loop    L10             ; loop until all pixels are set
                jmp     short Lexit


; routine for dy > dx (slope > 1)      ; ES:BX -> video buffer
                                       ; CX = # pixels to draw
                                       ; DH = bit mask
                                       ; SI = buffer interleave increment
                                       ; DI = decision variable
HiSlopeLineInC:

L21:            or      es:[bx],dh      ; set pixel value in video buffer

                add     bx,si           ; increment y
                jns     L22             ; jump if not in last interleave

                add     bx,VARleafincr  ; increment into next interleave

L22:            or      di,di
                jns     L23             ; jump if d >= 0

                add     di,VARincr1     ; d := d + incr1
                loop    L21
                jmp     short Lexit


L23:            add     di,VARincr2     ; d := d + incr2

                ror     dh,1            ; rotate bit mask
                adc     bx,0            ; BX := offset of next byte (incremented
                                        ;   if bit mask rotated to
                                        ;   leftmost pixel position)

                loop    L21
                jmp     short Lexit


Lexit:          mov     dx,3B4h         ; DX := CRTC I/O port
                mov     ax,0F18h
                out     dx,ax           ; restore default Plane Mask value

                mov     ax,4019h        ; restore default R/W Control value
                out     dx,ax

                inc     ax              ; restore default R/W Color value
                mov     ah,DefaultRWColor
                out     dx,ax

                pop     di              ; restore registers and return
                pop     si
                mov     sp,bp
                pop     bp
                ret

_LineInC        ENDP

_TEXT           ENDS

                END
```

Line Attributes

The line-drawing algorithm in this chapter draws lines that are exactly one pixel wide. Consequently, diagonal lines appear less bright than horizontal or vertical lines. You can fatten diagonal lines by modifying the pixel-setting inner loop of a Bresenham line-drawing routine so that it always sets pixel *B* before selecting the next pixel in the line. The resulting lines are fatter, but the modified routine runs more slowly because it must update more pixels, particularly in lines with slopes near 1 or −1.

To draw wider lines, simply draw contiguous, neighboring parallel lines. If you are using a pointing device to draw a wide line interactively, use a series of neighboring horizontal or vertical lines. After implementing a fast routine for drawing horizontal lines, you can write a high-level routine that paints wide lines by calling the horizontal line primitive.

In some applications, you may wish to draw dashed lines or multicolored lines that incorporate a pattern of pixel values. To do this, modify the inner loop of your line-drawing routine to select pixel values from a circular list of possible values. Rotate the list each time you set a pixel.

Clipping

Not one of the assembly-language routines in this chapter validates the pixel coordinates you supply as endpoints. For example, if you call the 640-by-200 2-color routine to draw a line from (0,0) to (1000,1000), the routine blithely updates about 800 pixels at memory locations that don't exist in the available video RAM, all the way from (200,200) through (1000,1000). To avoid this sort of error, you must determine which part of any arbitrary line lies within a given area of the video buffer. This process is known as clipping.

In the case of 640-by-200 2-color mode, the area into which lines must be clipped is the rectangular region defined by (0,0) in the upper left corner and (639,199) in the lower right corner. You would therefore clip a line with endpoints at (0,0) and (1000,1000) so that only the portion from (0,0) to (199,199) is drawn. In avoiding the error of updating nonexistent RAM, you might also improve your program's performance, since the line-drawing primitive will not attempt to update those nonexistent pixels.

Pixel-by-Pixel Clipping

A simplistic approach to clipping is to include a clipping test in the inner loop of your line-drawing routines. Just before setting the value of each pixel, your routine could compare the current pixel bit mask and buffer address with a set of precalculated limits. If the address, the bit mask, or both exceeded the limits, the routine would not update the video buffer. However, the overhead involved in clipping in this manner can be considerably greater than the work required to calculate and draw the pixels in the line.

In general, avoid integrating code for line clipping into low-level line-drawing routines, regardless of how efficient the code might be. Keeping the functions separate can improve performance, because an application can invoke the line-drawing routines directly, bypassing the clipping code altogether when it's not needed.

A Brute-Force Approach

Another way to clip a line is to use its equation to calculate where, if anywhere, the line segment to be drawn intersects the edges of the rectangular display region. For example, in Figure 6-5, the slope *m* of the line is

```
m = dy/dx = (y2-y1)/(x2-x1) = (100-40)/(750-150) = 0.1
```

The *y*-intercept can be calculated by substituting *x1* and *y1* into the equation of the line:

```
b = y1 - m*x1 = 40 - (0.1*150) = 25
```

The equation of the line is thus

```
y = 0.1*x + 25
```

To calculate the coordinates of the intersections of the line and the edges of the window, substitute the *x*-coordinates of the window's vertical edges and the *y*-coordinates of its horizontal edges into the equation. Each time you solve the equation for one side of the rectangle, check the result to see whether the intersection point actually lies within the line segment to be drawn as well as within the rectangle.

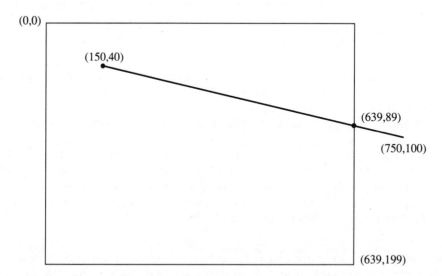

Figure 6-5. *Line segment (150,40)–(750,100) clipped at (639,89) in 640-by-200 2-color mode.*

This approach to line clipping involves a lot of computation, primarily because the equation of the line must be solved four times for every line segment you clip. You must also check the results against the limits of the line segment to determine whether the intersection points fall between the endpoints. Furthermore, you must still handle special cases such as horizontal and vertical lines or degenerate "lines" consisting of a single pixel. This computational burden makes brute-force clipping impractical.

A Better Algorithm

A more efficient algorithm for line clipping compares the endpoints of the line segment with the boundaries of the rectangular region before computing intersection points. Thus, little computation is performed for lines that need not be clipped. The Sutherland-Cohen algorithm, which uses this approach, is widely known because of its simplicity and computational efficiency. (See Sproull and Sutherland, "A Clipping Divider," *Conference Proceedings, Fall Joint Computer Conference*, volume 33, pp. 765–776. AFIPS Press, 1968.)

Conceptually, the algorithm extends the edges of the rectangular clipping region, dividing the plane into nine regions (see Figure 6-6). Each endpoint of the line segment to be clipped falls into one of these regions. Identifying the region that corresponds to each endpoint makes it easy to determine the location of the line segment relative to the rectangular clipping area.

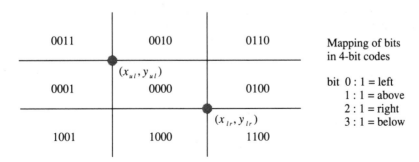

Figure 6-6. *Rectangular clipping using the Sutherland-Cohen algorithm.*

The algorithm uses a computational shortcut to determine the relative location of the line segment. Each of the nine regions is represented by a 4-bit code; each bit corresponds to whether the region is above, below, left, or right of the clipping rectangle. The relationship of the endpoints to the rectangle is then quickly determined by bitwise combination of the 4-bit codes.

If the logical OR of the two codes is 0 (that is, the 4-bit code for both endpoints is 0), both endpoints lie within the rectangle, and no clipping is needed. If the logical AND of the two 4-bit codes is nonzero, both endpoints lie on the same side of the rectangle, and the entire line is clipped out. These tests can be performed rapidly, because both the bitwise AND and OR operations can be implemented in single 80x86 machine instructions.

If the logical OR of the endpoints' 4-bit codes is nonzero but the logical AND is 0, then the line segment is clipped against one of the rectangle's edges. The values of the 4-bit codes then determine which edge is used. The resulting intersection point becomes a new endpoint for the line segment.

This process is repeated for the new line segment. The 4-bit codes are recalculated, the bitwise comparison is again performed, and, if necessary, a new endpoint is calculated. Since a rectangle has four sides, the algorithm requires at most four iterations.

The routine Clip() in Listing 6-11 is a C illustration of the Sutherland-Cohen algorithm. The while block repeats while neither of the two termination conditions (Inside or Outside) is true. The 4-bit codes are used to determine which of the four sides of the rectangle the clipping calculation uses. The intersection point between the line segment and the side of the rectangle becomes a new endpoint. At the bottom of the while block, the 4-bit code for the new endpoint is calculated, and the loop repeats.

```
/* Listing 6-11 */

struct  EndpointStruct           /* endpoints for clipped line */
{
  int   x1,y1;
  int   x2,y2;
};

struct  RegionStruct             /* rectangular clipping region */
{
  int   Xul;
  int   Yul;
  int   Xlr;
  int   Ylr;
};


union OutcodeUnion       /* outcodes are represented as bit fields */
{
  struct
  {
    unsigned code0 : 1;          /* x < Xul */
    unsigned code1 : 1;          /* y < Yul */
    unsigned code2 : 1;          /* x > Xlr */
    unsigned code3 : 1;          /* y > Ylr */
  }
        ocs;

  int   outcodes;
};


#define X1      ep->x1
#define Y1      ep->y1
#define X2      ep->x2
```

Listing 6-11. *An implementation of the Sutherland-Cohen clipping algorithm.*

Listing 6-11. *Continued.*

```
#define Y2        ep->y2
#define XUL       r->Xul
#define YUL       r->Yul
#define XLR       r->Xlr
#define YLR       r->Ylr


Clip(ep,r)
struct   EndpointStruct   *ep;
struct   RegionStruct     *r;
{
        union OutcodeUnion        ocu1,ocu2;
        int      Inside;
        int      Outside;


        /* initialize 4-bit codes */

        SetOutcodes( &ocu1, r, X1, Y1 );          /* initial 4-bit codes */
        SetOutcodes( &ocu2, r, X2, Y2 );

        Inside  = ((ocu1.outcodes | ocu2.outcodes) == 0);
        Outside = ((ocu1.outcodes & ocu2.outcodes) != 0);

        while (!Outside && !Inside)
        {
          if (ocu1.outcodes==0)            /* swap endpoints if necessary so */
          {                                /*  that (x1,y1) needs to be clipped */
            Swap( &X1, &X2 );
            Swap( &Y1, &Y2 );
            Swap( &ocu1, &ocu2 );
          }


          if (ocu1.ocs.code0)                    /* clip left */
          {
            Y1 += (long)(Y2-Y1)*(XUL-X1)/(X2-X1);
            X1 = XUL;
          }

          else if (ocu1.ocs.code1)               /* clip above */
          {
            X1 += (long)(X2-X1)*(YUL-Y1)/(Y2-Y1);
            Y1 = YUL;
          }

          else if (ocu1.ocs.code2)               /* clip right */
          {
            Y1 += (long)(Y2-Y1)*(XLR-X1)/(X2-X1);
            X1 = XLR;
          }

          else if (ocu1.ocs.code3)               /* clip below */
          {
            X1 += (long)(X2-X1)*(YLR-Y1)/(Y2-Y1);
            Y1 = YLR;
          }
```

(continued)

Listing 6-11. *Continued.*

```
        SetOutcodes( &ocu1, r, X1, Y1 );                    /* update for (x1,y1) */

        Inside  = ((ocu1.outcodes | ocu2.outcodes) == 0); /* update      */
        Outside = ((ocu1.outcodes & ocu2.outcodes) != 0); /*  4-bit codes */
        }

        return( Inside );
}


SetOutcodes( u, r, x, y )
union OutcodeUnion      *u;
struct RegionStruct     *r;
int     x,y;
{
        u->outcodes = 0;
        u->ocs.code0 = (x < XUL);
        u->ocs.code1 = (y < YUL);
        u->ocs.code2 = (x > XLR);
        u->ocs.code3 = (y > YLR);
}


Swap( pa, pb )
int     *pa,*pb;
{
        int     t;

        t = *pa;
        *pa = *pb;
        *pb = t;
}
```

A program could call Clip() before drawing a line with a fast primitive such as
Line(). If you are careful to define the values XUL, YUL, XLR, and YLR as
variables rather than constants, you can use Clip() in any video mode. Furthermore, line clipping need not be limited to clipping lines to the limits of available
RAM in the video buffer. You may instead want to define an arbitrary rectangular
region in the video buffer and clip lines against it. A good high-level video
graphics interface supports clipping into such arbitrary regions.

7

Circles and Ellipses

Circles and Pixel Scaling

An Ellipse-drawing Algorithm
Scan-converting an Ellipse
An Incremental Algorithm
A Typical Implementation
Problems and Pitfalls
Accuracy

Optimization

Clipping

True Circles

Circles and ellipses are probably the most common graphics elements other than straight lines. This chapter describes techniques for displaying circles, ellipses, and arcs with IBM video hardware. These techniques are similar to the algorithms and programming examples for displaying straight lines (described in Chapter 6). Although an ellipse-drawing routine is somewhat more complicated than a routine for drawing straight lines, the algorithmic design and programming techniques are similar.

Circles and Pixel Scaling

The only way to draw a circle on the IBM video subsystems discussed in this book is to calculate and draw an ellipse. The reason is that the horizontal scale in which pixels are displayed differs from the vertical scale in most graphics modes (Chapter 4). If you display a "circle" whose pixels are computed without scaling, what you see on the screen is an ellipse. For example, Figure 7-1a shows a "circle" with a radius of 100 pixels in both horizontal and vertical directions as displayed in a 640-by-200 graphics mode.

Because of this problem of pixel scaling, drawing a circle on the screen requires that you compute the pixels that correspond to a mathematical ellipse. In other

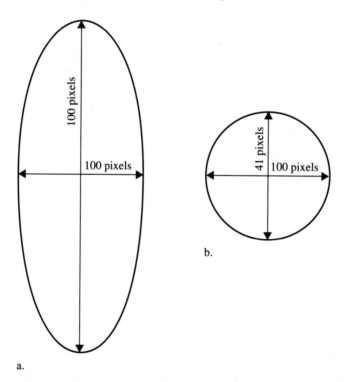

a.

b.

Figure 7-1. *In Figure 7-1a, a mathematical circle with a 100-pixel radius appears elliptical in 640-by-200 2-color mode. In Figure 7-1b, an ellipse whose axes have been properly scaled appears circular when displayed in this mode.*

words, to draw a circle that really looks like a circle, you must compute an ellipse whose major and minor axes are in the same ratio as the pixel coordinate scaling factor. On the screen, such an ellipse appears circular (see Figure 7-1b). For this reason, this chapter concentrates on a practical algorithm for drawing ellipses.

An Ellipse-drawing Algorithm

Scan-converting an Ellipse

You can use the algebraic formula for an ellipse to compute *x*- and *y*-coordinates for all of the pixels that represent a given ellipse. As in the case of scan-converting a straight line, many of these pixel coordinates will necessarily approximate the actual values, and the resulting figure will be jagged. This effect is especially noticeable when displaying a very thin ellipse (see Figure 7-2), but in most cases this side effect is acceptable.

Figure 7-2. *A thin ellipse can appear jagged when it is scan-converted.*

You can use the equation of the ellipse

$$\frac{(x - xc)^2}{a^2} + \frac{(y - yc)^2}{b^2} = 1$$

to scan-convert and display an ellipse. This equation describes an ellipse centered at (*xc,yc*) with major and minor axes *a* and *b* parallel to the *x*- and *y*-axes. However, the computational overhead of drawing ellipses by solving this equation, as in Listing 7-1, is very large. The multiplication, division, and square-root operations to determine each pixel's coordinates are very time-consuming. A better approach is to compute pixel coordinates incrementally in a manner similar to that used in the line-drawing algorithm in Chapter 6.

```
/* Listing 7-1 */

Ellipse( xc, yc, a0, b0 )        /* using equation of ellipse */
int     xc,yc;                   /* center of ellipse */
int     a0,b0;                   /* major and minor axes */
{
        double  x = 0;
        double  y = b0;
        double  Bsquared = (double)b0 * (double)b0;
        double  Asquared = (double)a0 * (double)a0;
        double  sqrt();
```

Listing 7-1. *Drawing an ellipse using the equation of the ellipse.*   *(continued)*

Listing 7-1. *Continued.*

```
        do                          /* do while dy/dx >= -1 */
        {
          y = sqrt( Bsquared - ((Bsquared/Asquared) * x * x) );
          Set4Pixels( (int)x, (int)y, xc, yc, PixelValue );
          ++x;
        }
        while ( (x <= a0) && (Bsquared*x > Asquared*y) );

        while (y >= 0)              /* do while dy/dx < -1 */
        {
          x = sqrt( Asquared - ((Asquared/Bsquared) * y*y) );
          Set4Pixels( (int)x, (int)y, xc, yc, PixelValue );
          --y;
        }
}

Set4Pixels( x, y, xc, yc, n )    /* set pixels in 4 quadrants by symmetry */
int      x,y;
int      xc,yc;
int      n;
{
        SPFunc(xc+x, yc+y, n);
        SPFunc(xc-x, yc+y, n);
        SPFunc(xc+x, yc-y, n);
        SPFunc(xc-x, yc-y, n);
}
```

An Incremental Algorithm

The derivation of an incremental algorithm for drawing ellipses resembles the derivation of Bresenham's line algorithm. The ellipse-drawing algorithm draws an ellipse pixel by pixel. After drawing each pixel, the algorithm selects the next pixel by determining which of the current pixel's two neighbors is closer to the actual ellipse.

Creating an ellipse-drawing algorithm is easiest for an ellipse centered at the origin of the coordinate system, with major and minor axes congruent with the *x*- and *y*-axes (see Figure 7-3). The equation of such an ellipse is

$$b^2x^2 + a^2y^2 - a^2b^2 = 0$$

Because the ellipse is symmetric in relation to both the *x*- and *y*-axes, you only need derive an algorithm to draw one of its quadrants. Your routine can then determine the pixel coordinates in the other three quadrants by symmetry.

 If you need an algorithm to draw ellipses with axes that are not parallel to the video buffer's *x*- and *y*-axes, refer to M. L. V. Pitteway, "Algorithm for Drawing Ellipses or Hyperbolae with a Digital Plotter," *Computer Journal* vol. 11 no. 3 (November 1967), p. 282.

The algorithm presented here is known as the "midpoint algorithm." It draws an ellipse iteratively, pixel by pixel. For each pixel it draws, the algorithm selects

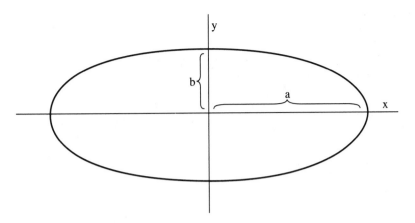

Figure 7-3. *An ellipse centered at the origin of the coordinate system.*

which of the pixel's neighbors is closer to the ellipse by computing whether the point halfway between the pixels lies inside or outside the ellipse (see Figure 7-4). (This algorithm was described by J. R. Van Aken in "An Efficient Ellipse-Drawing Algorithm," *IEEE Computer Graphics and Applications*, September 1984, p. 24, and improved by M. R. Kappel in "An Ellipse-Drawing Algorithm for Raster Displays," *Fundamental Algorithms for Computer Graphics*, R. A. Earnshaw [editor], Springer-Verlag 1985, p. 257.)

To determine which pixel lies closer to the ellipse, the algorithm uses the value of the equation of the ellipse at the midpoint between the pixels. If the value is 0, the midpoint lies on the ellipse. If the value is negative, then the midpoint lies inside the ellipse; if the value is positive, the midpoint is outside the ellipse. Thus, the algorithm can choose which of the two pixels lies closer to the ellipse by examining the value's sign.

One complication lies in determining which pair of neighboring pixels to investigate at each step in the iteration. This depends on *dy/dx*, the slope of the tangent to the ellipse (see Figure 7-5). When *dy/dx* is greater than −1, the algorithm chooses between two vertically oriented pixels (see Figure 7-6a). When *dy/dx* is less than −1, the choice is between two horizontally oriented pixels (see Figure 7-6b).

While *dy/dx* is greater than −1, the algorithm iteratively determines, for each pixel it draws, whether neighboring pixel *A* or *B* is closer to the ellipse. This is done by deciding whether the midpoint between *A* and *B* lies inside or outside the exact ellipse. In Figure 7-6a, the pixel selected in the previous iteration is at (x_{i-1}, y_{i-1}). The midpoint between *A* and *B* is therefore $(x_{i-1}+1, y_{i-1}-\frac{1}{2})$.

The algorithm chooses between pixel *A* and pixel *B* by examining the sign of the value of the ellipse equation evaluated at the midpoint:

```
d = b² (x_{i-1}+1)² + a² (y_{i-1}-1/2)² - a²b²
```

The variable *d*, the value of the function at the midpoint, is the algorithm's decision variable. As in Bresenham's line algorithm, the key to this algorithm's speed

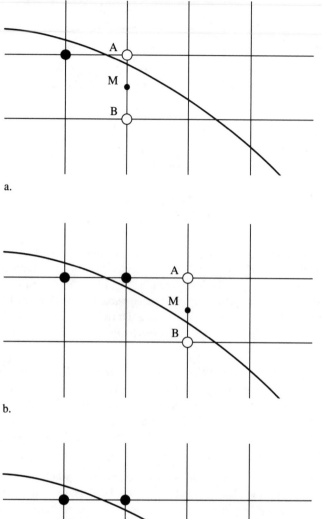

a.

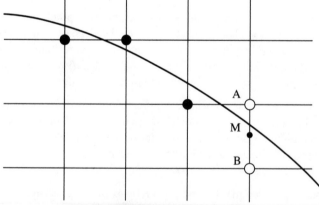

b.

c.

Figure 7-4. *Three iterations of the midpoint algorithm. After drawing the black pixel in illustration 7-4a, the algorithm chooses to draw either pixel A or pixel B by comparing the midpoint M to the actual ellipse. Because M is inside the ellipse, it chooses pixel A. Illustrations 7-4b and 7-4c represent the next two iterations.*

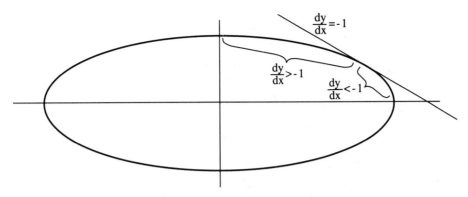

Figure 7-5. *The slope of the tangent to the ellipse within the first quadrant.*

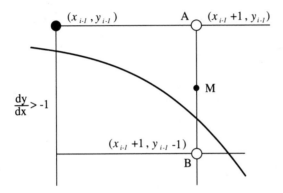

a.

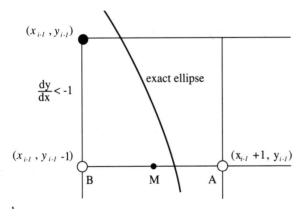

b.

Figure 7-6. *The midpoint algorithm chooses between A and B by substituting x and y at the midpoint M into the formula for the ellipse and testing the sign of the result. If the result is positive, pixel B is chosen; if the result is negative, pixel A is chosen.*

is that it can compute d iteratively on the basis of its value at each previous step in the iteration. The difference between the current value of d and its previous value is

$$
\begin{aligned}
d_i - d_{i-1} &= [b^2(x_{i-1}+1)^2 + a^2(y_{i-1}-1/2)^2 - a^2b^2] - \\
&\qquad [b^2(x_{i-1})^2 + a^2(y_{i-1}-1/2)^2 - a^2b^2] \\
&= b^2(2x_{i-1}+1) \\
&= 2b^2x_{i-1} + b^2
\end{aligned}
$$

Now, finding the difference between d_i and d_{i-1} (that is, dx) still involves multiplying the previous value of x by a constant. You can avoid this multiplication, however, by computing dx, as well as d, incrementally; that is, by adding $2b^2$ to dx at each step of the iteration.

If pixel A is nearer to the ellipse (that is, $d_i > 0$), the newly calculated value of d_i can be used as d_{i-1} in the next iteration. If pixel B is nearer, however, d_i must be adjusted for the downward step in the y direction. In this case, the value of the equation of the ellipse for the midpoint below pixel B must be computed. If $(x_{i-1}, y_{i-1}+\frac{1}{2})$ is the midpoint between pixels A and B, then $(x_{i-1}, y_{i-1}-\frac{1}{2})$ is the midpoint below pixel B, and dy is then

$$
\begin{aligned}
d_i - d_{i-1} &= [b^2(x_{i-1})^2 + a^2(y_{i-1}-\frac{1}{2})^2 - a^2b^2] - \\
&\qquad [b^2(x_{i-1})^2 + a^2(y_{i-1}+\frac{1}{2})^2 - a^2b^2] \\
&= -2a^2y_{i-1}
\end{aligned}
$$

When dy/dx is less than -1, pixels A and B are horizontal rather than vertical neighbors (see Figure 7-6b). The values of dy and dx are therefore computed somewhat differently. When pixel B is chosen, the midpoint at $(x_{i-1}+\frac{1}{2}, y_{i-1}-1)$ is used, so the increment for d is

$$
\begin{aligned}
d_i - d_{i-1} &= [b^2(x_{i-1}+1/2)^2 + a^2(y_{i-1}-1)^2 - a^2b^2] - \\
&\qquad [b^2(x_{i-1}+1/2)^2 + a^2(y_{i-1})^2 - a^2b^2] \\
&= a^2(-2y_{i-1}+1) \\
&= -2a^2y_{i-1} + a^2
\end{aligned}
$$

Also, when pixel A is chosen, d must be adjusted for the step in the rightward direction:

$$
\begin{aligned}
d_i - d_{i-1} &= [b^2(x_{i-1}+1/2)^2 + a^2(y_{i-1})^2 - a^2b^2] - \\
&\qquad [b^2(x_{i-1}-1/2)^2 + a^2(y_{i-1})^2 - a^2b^2] \\
&= 2b^2x_{i-1}
\end{aligned}
$$

These derivations provide a way to draw an ellipse iteratively, with only simple addition and subtraction required within the iterative loops. The analysis distinguishes between the case where dy/dx is greater than -1 and the case where dy/dx is less than -1. You determine when dy/dx has reached -1 by differentiating the equation of the ellipse and setting dy/dx to -1.

$$\frac{d}{dx}(b^2x^2 + a^2y^2 - a^2b^2) = 0$$

$$2b^2x + 2a^2y\frac{dy}{dx} = 0$$

$$\frac{dy}{dx} = \frac{-2b^2x}{2a^2y}$$

Thus, at the point where $dy/dx = -1$,

$$2b^2x = 2a^2y$$

Because the algorithm already keeps track of the quantities $2b^2x$ and $2a^2y$ to compute the differentials dx and dy, these quantities can be used to detect where dy/dx reaches -1. The algorithm can then start at the point $(0,b)$ on the y-axis and proceed clockwise around the ellipse until it reaches $(a,0)$.

Initially, the quantity dy/dx is greater than -1, and the choice is made iteratively between vertically oriented pixels (see Figure 7-6a). When dy/dx reaches -1, the algorithm chooses between horizontally oriented pixels (see Figure 7-6b) and continues to do so until it reaches the x-axis.

The only remaining computation occurs when the algorithm reaches the pixel for which $dy/dx = -1$. At this point, a new value for d will already have been computed (M_{old} in Figure 7-7) under the assumption that the next midpoint would have been between two vertically oriented pixels. Therefore, the value of d must be adjusted to reflect the value of the ellipse function at the midpoint between two horizontally oriented pixels (M_{new} in Figure 7-7). The increment for d (from M_{old} to M_{new}) in this case is

$$
\begin{aligned}
d_i - d_{i-1} &= [b^2(x_{i-1}+1/2)^2 + a^2(y_{i-1}-1)^2 - a^2b^2] - \\
&\quad\quad [b^2(x_{i-1}+1)^2 + a^2(y_{i-1}-1/2)^2 - a^2b^2] \\
&= b^2(-x_{i-1}-3/4) + a^2(-y_{i-1}+3/4) \\
&= 3(a^2-b^2)/4 - (b^2x_{i-1} + a^2y_{i-1})
\end{aligned}
$$

Again, since the algorithm already uses the quantities $2b^2x$ and $2a^2y$, the increment for d at this point can be computed by

$$d_i - d_{i-1} = 3(a^2-b^2)/4 - (2b^2x_{i-i}+2a^2y_{i-1})/2$$

Adding this value to d at the point where $dy/dx = -1$ gives the new value for d.

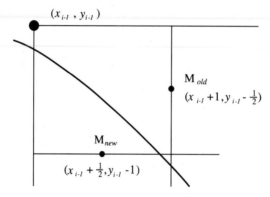

(x_{i-1}, y_{i-1})

M_{old}

$(x_{i-1}+1, y_{i-1}-\frac{1}{2})$

M_{new}

$(x_{i-1}+\frac{1}{2}, y_{i-1}-1)$

Figure 7-7. *When the value of* dy/dx *reaches −1, a new midpoint (M$_{new}$) is selected, and* d, *which has already been computed for M$_{old}$, is adjusted to reflect the value of the equation of the ellipse at M$_{new}$.*

A Typical Implementation

The C routine in Listing 7-2 is fast and efficient because all decision-variable computation within the inner iterative loops has been reduced to addition and subtraction. The routine eliminates multiplication within the inner loops by pre-calculating the values of a^2, b^2, $2a^2$, and $2b^2$. The initial values for the decision variables are computed assuming that the first pixel to be drawn is at $(0,b)$. Thus, the initial value of d is calculated for the midpoint between the pixels at $(1,b)$ and $(1,b−1)$; that is, at $(1,b−\frac{1}{2})$:

```
d = b² (1) ² + a² (b-1/2) ² - a²b²

  = b² - a²b + a²/4
```

The initial values for *dx* and *dy* are

```
dx = 2b² (x₀) = 0
```

and

```
dy = 2a² (y₀) = 2a²b
```

The routine `Ellipse()` follows the algorithm closely. It first draws all the pixels between $(0,b)$ and the point where *dy/dx* becomes −1. Then it updates *d* as in Figure 7-7. Iterative pixel selection continues until the routine reaches the *x*-axis. The routine calls the function `Set4Pixels()` to replicate each pixel in each of the four quadrants of the ellipse. `Set4Pixels()` also translates each pixel's coordinates relative to the actual center of the ellipse.

```
/* Listing 7-2 */

Ellipse( xc, yc, a0, b0 )
int     xc,yc;                   /* center of ellipse */
int     a0,b0;                   /* semiaxes */
```

Listing 7-2. *A high-level implementation of the midpoint algorithm.*   *(continued)*

Listing 7-2. *Continued.*

```
{
        int     x = 0;
        int     y = b0;

        long    a = a0;                         /* use 32-bit precision */
        long    b = b0;

        long    Asquared = a * a;               /* initialize values outside */
        long    TwoAsquared = 2 * Asquared;     /*  of loops */
        long    Bsquared = b * b;
        long    TwoBsquared = 2 * Bsquared;

        long    d;
        long    dx,dy;


        d = Bsquared - Asquared*b + Asquared/4L;
        dx = 0;
        dy = TwoAsquared * b;

        while (dx<dy)
        {
          Set4Pixels( x, y, xc, yc, PixelValue );

          if (d > 0L)
          {
            --y;
            dy -= TwoAsquared;
            d -= dy;
          }

          ++x;
          dx += TwoBsquared;
          d += Bsquared + dx;
        }


        d += (3L*(Asquared-Bsquared)/2L - (dx+dy)) / 2L;

        while (y>=0)
        {
          Set4Pixels( x, y, xc, yc, PixelValue );

          if (d < 0L)
          {
            ++x;
            dx += TwoBsquared;
            d += dx;
          }

          --y;
          dy -= TwoAsquared;
          d += Asquared - dy;
        }
}
```

(continued)

Listing 7-2. *Continued.*

```
Set4Pixels( x, y, xc, yc, n )          /* set pixels by symmetry in 4 quadrants */
int     x,y;
int     xc,yc;
int     n;
{
        SetPixel( xc+x, yc+y, n );
        SetPixel( xc-x, yc+y, n );
        SetPixel( xc+x, yc-y, n );
        SetPixel( xc-x, yc-y, n );

}
```

Problems and Pitfalls

One difficult problem you'll encounter is that tiny ellipses appear somewhat angular rather than elliptical when they are scan-converted. When an ellipse is small and comparatively few pixels are used to display it, the best approximation generated by the algorithm can appear polygonal.

Although it is possible to redesign the ellipse-drawing algorithm to draw "fatter" or "thinner" ellipses in this situation, a better solution is to display the ellipses with higher resolution. Tiny ellipses look much better with 640-by-480 resolution than they do with 320-by-200 resolution.

A related problem is that very eccentric ellipses may be drawn inaccurately at the points where they curve most sharply. This happens when the point where $dy/dx = -1$ lies nearly adjacent to either the *x*-axis or the *y*-axis. Again, you can modify the algorithm to accommodate this situation, but if your application requires accurate representations of very thin ellipses, a better solution is to display them at higher resolution.

A further consideration involves "degenerate" ellipses for which the length of either the major or minor axis is 0 (that is, $a = 0$ or $b = 0$). Because either *dy* or *dx* is 0 in this situation, the iterative routines do not terminate correctly. In these cases, either test for the special condition before executing the loops (and draw the appropriate straight line) or modify the termination conditions of the loops.

Accuracy

As does Bresenham's line algorithm, the midpoint algorithm attempts to minimize the vertical or horizontal distance to the ellipse from the pixels it selects. This is faster than minimizing the distance between each pixel and the nearest point to it on the ellipse, but if you examine its performance closely, you may find rare occasions when the pixel that the midpoint algorithm selects is not the one closest to the ellipse. Nevertheless, the accuracy of the midpoint algorithm in selecting the best pixels to represent the ellipse is sufficient for nearly all applications. (For more discussion of this topic, see Van Aken and Novak, "Curve-Drawing Algorithms for Raster Displays," *ACM Transactions on Graphics*, April 1985, p. 147, or Kappel, "An Ellipse-Drawing Algorithm for Raster Displays," *Fundamental Algorithms for Computer Graphics*, p. 257.)

Although the source code in Listing 7-2 is a straightforward implementation of the algorithm, you need to remember a few details if you plan to modify the code or translate it into another language. It is important to compute all decision variables as 32-bit integers. Because these values involve the squaring of pixel coordinates, 16 bits are inadequate to maintain precision.

Another detail to remember is that this routine can draw the same pixels twice. This is an artifact of the ellipse's four-way symmetry. For example, the pixels at $(\pm a, 0)$ and $(0, \pm b)$ are updated twice by Set4Pixels() in Listing 7-2. This becomes a problem when you use the routine to XOR pixels into the video buffer. If you perform a XOR on these pixels twice, they disappear. To avoid this, either test for these special cases in Set4Pixels() (Listing 7-3) or modify Ellipse() to draw these pixels separately.

```
/* Listing 7-3 */

Set4Pixels( x, y, xc, yc, n )    /* avoids setting the same pixel twice */
int     x,y;
int     xc,yc;
int     n;
{
        if (x!=0)
        {
          SetPixel( xc+x, yc+y, n );
          SetPixel( xc-x, yc+y, n );
          if (y!=0)
          {
            SetPixel( xc+x, yc-y, n );
            SetPixel( xc-x, yc-y, n );
          }
        }
        else
        {
          SetPixel( xc, yc+y, n );
          if (y!=0)
            SetPixel( xc, yc-y, n );
        }
}
```

Listing 7-3. *A modified version of Set4Pixels that avoids updating the same pixel twice.*

Optimization

For many applications, a high-level language implementation such as the one in Listing 7-2 is fast enough. The slowest part of the high-level version of Ellipse() is its repeated calls to the pixel-setting routine, which recomputes pixel addresses with every iteration. By writing Ellipse() in assembly language, you can calculate the pixel addresses much more efficiently. The resulting assembly-language routine is about three times faster than the equivalent high-level version.

Listing 7-4 is a typical assembly-language implementation, in this case for the EGA. Note how the routine Set4Pixels maintains a set of four buffer offsets and bit masks instead of (x,y) coordinates for the four pixels it updates. When

`Set4Pixels` increments a pixel *x*-coordinate, it rotates a bit mask in the proper direction. The *y*-coordinates are incremented by adding the number of bytes in each line of pixels to the buffer offset. (This is the same technique used in the line routines in Chapter 6.) This method of video buffer addressing is much faster than making a call to a `SetPixel()` function for every pixel in the ellipse.

```
                    TITLE    'Listing 7-4'
                    NAME     Ellipse10
                    PAGE     55,132

;
; Name:          Ellipse10
;
; Function:      Draw an ellipse in native EGA/VGA graphics modes.
;
; Caller:        Microsoft C:
;
;                       void Ellipse10(xc,yc,a,b,n);
;
;                       int xc,yc;              /* center of ellipse */
;
;                       int a,b;                /* major and minor axes */
;
;                       int n;                  /* pixel value */
;

ARGxc           EQU     word ptr [bp+4] ; stack frame addressing
ARGyc           EQU     word ptr [bp+6]
ARGa            EQU     word ptr [bp+8]
ARGb            EQU     word ptr [bp+10]
ARGn            EQU     byte ptr [bp+12]

ULAddr          EQU     word ptr [bp-6]
URAddr          EQU     word ptr [bp-8]
LLAddr          EQU     word ptr [bp-10]
LRAddr          EQU     word ptr [bp-12]
LMask           EQU     byte ptr [bp-14]
RMask           EQU     byte ptr [bp-16]

VARd            EQU     word ptr [bp-20]
VARdx           EQU     word ptr [bp-24]
VARdy           EQU     word ptr [bp-28]
Asquared        EQU     word ptr [bp-32]
Bsquared        EQU     word ptr [bp-36]
TwoAsquared     EQU     word ptr [bp-40]
TwoBsquared     EQU     word ptr [bp-44]

RMWbits         EQU     00h                  ; read-modify-write bits
BytesPerLine    EQU     80


_TEXT           SEGMENT byte public 'CODE'
                ASSUME  cs:_TEXT

                EXTRN   PixelAddr10:near
```

(continued)

Listing 7-4. *An assembly-language implementation of the midpoint algorithm.*

Listing 7-4. *Continued.*

```
                PUBLIC    _Ellipse10
_Ellipse10      PROC      near

                push      bp                    ; preserve caller registers
                mov       bp,sp
                sub       sp,40                 ; reserve local stack space
                push      si
                push      di

; set Graphics Controller Mode register

                mov       dx,3CEh               ; DX := Graphics Controller I/O port
                mov       ax,0005h              ; AL := Mode register number
                                                ; AH := Write Mode 0 (bits 0,1)
                out       dx,ax                 ;         Read Mode 0 (bit 4)

; set Data Rotate/Function Select register

                mov       ah,RMWbits            ; AH := Read-Modify-Write bits
                mov       al,3                  ; AL := Data Rotate/Function Select reg
                out       dx,ax

; set Set/Reset and Enable Set/Reset registers

                mov       ah,ARGn               ; AH := pixel value
                mov       al,0                  ; AL := Set/Reset reg number
                out       dx,ax

                mov       ax,0F01h              ; AH := value for Enable Set/Reset (all
                                                ;   bit planes enabled)
                out       dx,ax                 ; AL := Enable Set/Reset reg number

; initial constants

                mov       ax,ARGa
                mul       ax
                mov       Asquared,ax
                mov       Asquared+2,dx    ; a^2
                shl       ax,1
                rcl       dx,1
                mov       TwoAsquared,ax
                mov       TwoAsquared+2,dx ; 2 * a^2

                mov       ax,ARGb
                mul       ax
                mov       Bsquared,ax
                mov       Bsquared+2,dx    ; b^2
                shl       ax,1
                rcl       dx,1
                mov       TwoBsquared,ax
                mov       TwoBsquared+2,dx ; 2 * b^2
;
; plot pixels from (0,b) until dy/dx = -1
;

; initial buffer address and bit mask
```

(continued)

Listing 7-4. *Continued.*

```
                mov     ax,BytesPerLine ; AX := video buffer line length
                mul     ARGb            ; AX := relative byte offset of b
                mov     si,ax
                mov     di,ax

                mov     ax,ARGyc        ; AX := yc
                mov     bx,ARGxc        ; BX := xc
                call    PixelAddr10     ; AH := bit mask
                                        ; ES:BX -> buffer
                                        ; CL := # bits to shift left
                mov     ah,1
                shl     ah,cl           ; AH := bit mask for first pixel
                mov     LMask,ah
                mov     RMask,ah

                add     si,bx           ; SI := offset of (0,b)
                mov     ULAddr,si
                mov     URAddr,si
                sub     bx,di           ; AX := offset of (0,-b)
                mov     LLAddr,bx
                mov     LRAddr,bx

; initial decision variables

                xor     ax,ax
                mov     VARdx,ax
                mov     VARdx+2,ax      ; dx = 0

                mov     ax,TwoAsquared
                mov     dx,TwoAsquared+2
                mov     cx,ARGb
                call    LongMultiply    ; perform 32-bit by 16-bit multiply
                mov     VARdy,ax
                mov     VARdy+2,dx      ; dy = TwoAsquared * b

                mov     ax,Asquared
                mov     dx,Asquared+2   ; DX:AX = Asquared
                sar     dx,1
                rcr     ax,1
                sar     dx,1
                rcr     ax,1            ; DX:AX = Asquared/4

                add     ax,Bsquared
                adc     dx,Bsquared+2   ; DX:AX = Bsquared + Asquared/4
                mov     VARd,ax
                mov     VARd+2,dx

                mov     ax,Asquared
                mov     dx,Asquared+2
                mov     cx,ARGb
                call    LongMultiply    ; DX:AX = Asquared*b
                sub     VARd,ax
                sbb     VARd+2,dx       ; d = Bsquared - Asquared*b + Asquared/4

; loop until dy/dx >= -1

                mov     bx,ARGb         ; BX := initial y-coordinate
```

(continued)

Listing 7-4. *Continued.*

```
                        xor     cx,cx           ; CH := 0 (initial y-increment)
                                                ; CL := 0 (initial x-increment)
        L10:            mov     ax,VARdx
                        mov     dx,VARdx+2
                        sub     ax,VARdy
                        sbb     dx,VARdy+2
                        jns     L20             ; jump if dx>=dy

                        call    Set4Pixels

                        mov     cx,1            ; CH := 0 (y-increment)
                                                ; CL := 1 (x-increment)
                        cmp     VARd+2,0
                        js      L11             ; jump if d < 0

                        mov     ch,1            ; increment in y direction
                        dec     bx              ; decrement current y-coordinate

                        mov     ax,VARdy
                        mov     dx,VARdy+2
                        sub     ax,TwoAsquared
                        sbb     dx,TwoAsquared+2 ; DX:AX := dy - TwoAsquared
                        mov     VARdy,ax
                        mov     VARdy+2,dx      ; dy -= TwoAsquared

                        sub     VARd,ax
                        sbb     VARd+2,dx       ; d -= dy

        L11:            mov     ax,VARdx
                        mov     dx,VARdx+2
                        add     ax,TwoBsquared
                        adc     dx,TwoBsquared+2 ; DX:AX := dx + TwoBsquared
                        mov     VARdx,ax
                        mov     VARdx+2,dx      ; dx += TwoBsquared

                        add     ax,Bsquared
                        adc     dx,Bsquared+2   ; DX:AX := dx + Bsquared
                        add     VARd,ax
                        adc     VARd+2,dx       ; d += dx + Bsquared

                        jmp     L10
        ;
        ; plot pixels from current (x,y) until y < 0
        ;

        ; initial buffer address and bit mask

        L20:            push    bx              ; preserve current y-coordinate
                        push    cx              ; preserve x- and y-increments

                        mov     ax,Asquared
                        mov     dx,Asquared+2
                        sub     ax,Bsquared
                        sbb     dx,Bsquared+2   ; DX:AX := Asquared-Bsquared
```

(continued)

Listing 7-4. *Continued.*

```
          mov     bx,ax
          mov     cx,dx           ; CX:BX := (Asquared-Bsquared)

          sar     dx,1
          rcr     ax,1            ; DX:AX := (Asquared-Bsquared)/2
          add     ax,bx
          adc     dx,cx           ; DX:AX := 3*(Asquared-Bsquared)/2

          sub     ax,VARdx
          sbb     dx,VARdx+2
          sub     ax,VARdy
          sbb     dx,VARdy+2      ; DX:AX := 3*(Asquared-Bsquared)/2 - (dx+dy)

          sar     dx,1
          rcr     ax,1            ; DX:AX :=
                                  ; ( 3*(Asquared-Bsquared)/2 - (dx+dy) )/2
          add     VARd,ax
          adc     VARd+2,dx       ; update d

; loop until y < 0

          pop     cx              ; CH,CL := y- and x-increments
          pop     bx              ; BX := y

L21:      call    Set4Pixels

          mov     cx,100h         ; CH := 1 (y-increment)
                                  ; CL := 0 (x-increment)

          cmp     VARd+2,0
          jns     L22             ; jump if d >= 0

          mov     cl,1            ; increment in x direction

          mov     ax,VARdx
          mov     dx,VARdx+2
          add     ax,TwoBsquared
          adc     dx,TwoBsquared+2 ; DX:AX := dx + TwoBsquared
          mov     VARdx,ax
          mov     VARdx+2,dx      ; dx += TwoBsquared

          add     VARd,ax
          adc     VARd+2,dx       ; d += dx

L22:      mov     ax,VARdy
          mov     dx,VARdy+2
          sub     ax,TwoAsquared
          sbb     dx,TwoAsquared+2 ; DX:AX := dy - TwoAsquared
          mov     VARdy,ax
          mov     VARdy+2,dx      ; dy -= TwoAsquared

          sub     ax,Asquared
          sbb     dx,Asquared+2   ; DX:AX := dy - Asquared
          sub     VARd,ax
          sbb     VARd+2,dx       ; d += Asquared - dy

          dec     bx              ; decrement y
          jns     L21             ; loop if y >= 0
```

(continued)

Listing 7-4. *Continued.*

```
; restore default Graphics Controller registers

Lexit:          mov     ax,0FF08h       ; default Bit Mask
                mov     dx,3CEh
                out     dx,ax

                mov     ax,0003         ; default Function Select
                out     dx,ax

                mov     ax,0001         ; default Enable Set/Reset
                out     dx,ax

                pop     di
                pop     si
                mov     sp,bp
                pop     bp
                ret

_Ellipse10      ENDP


Set4Pixels      PROC    near            ; Call with:   CH := y-increment (0, -1)
                                        ;              CL := x-increment (0, 1)

                push    ax              ; preserve these regs
                push    bx
                push    dx

                mov     dx,3CEh         ; DX := Graphics Controller port

                xor     bx,bx           ; BX := 0
                test    ch,ch
                jz      L30             ; jump if y-increment = 0

                mov     bx,BytesPerLine ; BX := positive increment
                neg     bx              ; BX := negative increment

L30:            mov     al,8            ; AL := Bit Mask reg number

; pixels at (xc-x,yc+y) and (xc-x,yc-y)

                xor     si,si           ; SI := 0
                mov     ah,LMask

                rol     ah,cl           ; AH := bit mask rotated horizontally
                rcl     si,1            ; SI := 1 if bit mask rotated around
                neg     si              ; SI := 0 or -1

                mov     di,si           ; SI,DI := left horizontal increment

                add     si,ULAddr       ; SI := upper left addr + horiz incr
                add     si,bx           ; SI := new upper left addr
                add     di,LLAddr
                sub     di,bx           ; DI := new lower left addr

                mov     LMask,ah        ; update these variables
                mov     ULAddr,si
                mov     LLAddr,di
```

(continued)

Listing 7-4. *Continued.*

```
            out     dx,ax               ; update Bit Mask register

            mov     ch,es:[si]          ; update upper left pixel
            mov     es:[si],ch
            mov     ch,es:[di]          ; update lower left pixel
            mov     es:[di],ch


; pixels at (xc+x,yc+y) and (xc+x,yc-y)

            xor     si,si               ; SI := 0
            mov     ah,RMask

            ror     ah,cl               ; AH := bit mask rotated horizontally
            rcl     si,1                ; SI := 1 if bit mask rotated around

            mov     di,si               ; SI,DI := right horizontal increment

            add     si,URAddr           ; SI := upper right addr + horiz incr
            add     si,bx               ; SI := new upper right addr
            add     di,LRAddr
            sub     di,bx               ; DI := new lower right addr

            mov     RMask,ah            ; update these variables
            mov     URAddr,si
            mov     LRAddr,di

            out     dx,ax               ; update Bit Mask register

            mov     ch,es:[si]          ; update upper right pixel
            mov     es:[si],ch
            mov     ch,es:[di]          ; update lower right pixel
            mov     es:[di],ch

            pop     dx                  ; restore these regs
            pop     bx
            pop     ax
            ret

Set4Pixels  ENDP


LongMultiply PROC   near                ; Caller:       DX = u1 (hi-order word
                                        ;                     of 32-bit number)
                                        ;               AX = u2 (lo-order word)
                                        ;               CX = v1 (16-bit number)
                                        ; Returns:      DX:AX = 32-bit result)

            push    ax                  ; preserve u2
            mov     ax,dx               ; AX := u1
            mul     cx                  ; AX := hi-order word of result
            xchg    ax,cx               ; AX := v1, CX := hi-order word
            pop     dx                  ; DX := u2
            mul     dx                  ; AX := lo-order word of result
                                        ; DX := carry
            add     dx,cx               ; CX := hi-order word of result
            ret
```

(continued)

Listing 7-4. *Continued.*

```
LongMultiply    ENDP

_TEXT           ENDS

                END
```

One optimization technique used in Chapter 6 is omitted here. In practice, minimizing video buffer accesses by setting more than one pixel at a time in each byte of the buffer is not worthwhile. The overhead involved in keeping track of which bytes contain more than one updated pixel is greater than the time saved in reducing video buffer accesses. Besides, the code is complicated enough already.

Clipping

If you clip an ellipse within a rectangular window, the result is an arc (see Figure 7-8). The place to perform the clipping is in the `Set4Pixels()` routine. You can clip each pixel's (x,y) coordinates against the window boundary before you call `SetPixel()` to update the video buffer.

clipping window

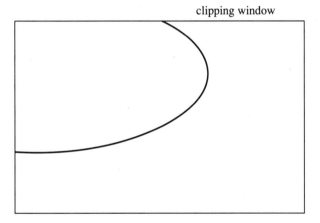

Figure 7-8. *Clipping an ellipse produces an arc.*

Implementing clipping in this way slows the ellipse-drawing routine somewhat. If your application rarely requires clipping, consider implementing two different versions of `Set4Pixels()`, one that performs clipping and one that omits it. Before calling `Ellipse()`, you can compare the maximum and minimum coordinate values of the pixels in the ellipse ($xc \pm a, yc \pm b$) with the clipping boundaries to determine whether it can be drawn without clipping. Only if clipping is required do you need to use the slower, clipping version of `Set4Pixels()`.

True Circles

After you implement the ellipse routine, you can draw true circles in all graphics modes on PC and PS/2 video subsystems. To display a circle, draw an ellipse with its major and minor axes scaled in proportion to your video display's horizontal and vertical resolutions. Listing 7-5 shows how you might do this in a 640-by-350 graphics mode on an EGA.

Because the scaling varies with the video mode, the same routine cannot draw circles in different video modes unless it accommodates the pixel coordinate scaling in each mode. Figure 4-9 in Chapter 4 is a table of pixel scaling factors for all graphics modes.

```
/* Listing 7-5 */

Circle10( xc, yc, xr, yr, n)              /* circles in 640x350 16-color mode */
int     xc,yc;          /* center of circle */
int     xr,yr;          /* point on circumference */
int     n;              /* pixel value */
{
        double  x,y;
        double  sqrt();
        double  Scale10 = 1.37;        /* pixel scaling factor */
        int     a,b;

        x = xr - xc;                   /* translate center of ellipse */
        y = (yr - yc) * Scale10;       /*  to origin */


        a = sqrt( x*x + y*y );         /* compute major and minor axes */
        b = a / Scale10;

        Ellipse10( xc, yc, a, b, n);   /* draw it */
}
```

Listing 7-5. *Using pixel coordinate scaling to display a circle in 640-by-350 16-color mode.*

8

Region Fill

What Is a Region?
Interior and Border Pixels ● Connectivity

Simple Fills with Horizontal Lines

Three Region Fill Algorithms
Simple Recursive Fill
Line-Adjacency Fill
Border Fill

Comparing the Algorithms

This chapter describes several methods for filling a region of the video buffer with a pattern of pixels. Region fill techniques are used in many areas of computer graphics programming, including color manipulation, shading, and representation of three-dimensional objects, as well as in applications such as image processing, image data transmission, and computer animation.

This chapter contains working source code for three region fill algorithms, but the discussion is by no means comprehensive. These algorithms and implementations are intended to be working models that you can experiment with, modify, and optimize for your own applications.

What Is a Region?

A region is a connected group of pixels in the video buffer that is delineated by some sort of boundary. You can think of a region in the video buffer as comprising an interior and a border. To understand how the algorithms in this chapter are implemented, however, it is worth considering how a region can be clearly defined in terms of pixel values and pixel geometry in the video buffer.

Interior and Border Pixels

In this chapter, a region is assumed to be surrounded by pixels whose values distinguish them from the pixels in the interior. You could assume, for instance, that all interior pixels have the same value, in which case a border pixel is simply any pixel whose value differs from the values of pixels in the interior (see Figure 8-1a). You could also assign a range of allowable pixel values to both interior and border pixels. The algorithms in this chapter adhere to the convention that all pixels in the border have one specified value and pixels in the interior can be of any other value (see Figure 8-1b).

In many applications, it is practical to use a range of pixel coordinates to define all or part of a region's border. The definition of a ''border pixel'' can thus be broadened to include pixels outside a predetermined range of (x,y) coordinates. In this way a region can be bounded by the limits of the screen buffer or by a software window, as well as by pixels of a predetermined value or range of values.

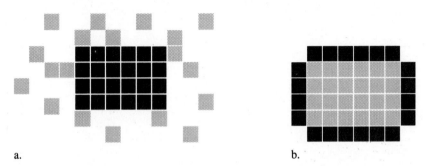

a.   b.

Figure 8-1. *In Figure 8-1a, a region is defined by interior pixels of a given value. In Figure 8-1b, a region is defined by border pixels of a given value.*

Connectivity

To distinguish border pixels from interior pixels, you must also specify the way the pixels are connected. If you allow interior pixels to be connected diagonally as well as orthogonally (horizontally and vertically), you must assume that the border pixels surrounding the region are always connected orthogonally (see Figure 8-2a). Conversely, if you allow border pixels to be diagonally connected, you must constrain interior pixels to orthogonal connections (see Figure 8-2b). Consider the reason for this constraint: If both border and interior pixels could be diagonally connected, then interior pixels could be connected to pixels outside the border at places where border pixels are diagonally connected.

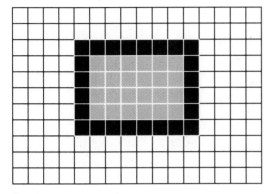

a.

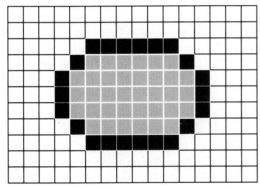

b.

Figure 8-2. *Connectivity of pixels. In Figure 8-2a, border pixels (black) are orthogonally connected, while interior pixels (gray) are both orthogonally and diagonally connected. In Figure 8-2b, border pixels are both orthogonally and diagonally connected, so interior pixels are only connected orthogonally.*

Simple Fills with Horizontal Lines

Before you become involved with the intricacies of region fill algorithms, remember that you can fill many regular geometric shapes without using a specialized algorithm. A common application of this technique is shown in Listing 8-1. This routine fills a rectangular region in the video buffer with pixels of a specified value. It is fast, because the subroutine that draws horizontal lines is fast.

```
/* Listing 8-1 */

FilledRectangle( x1, y1, x2, y2, n )
int     x1,y1;                    /* upper left corner */
int     x2,y2;                    /* lower right corner */
int     n;                        /* pixel value */
{
        int     y;

        for (y = y1; y< = y2; y++)      /* draw rectangle as a set of */
          Line( x1, y, x2, y, n );      /*  adjacent horizontal lines */
}
```

Listing 8-1. *Filling a rectangle with horizontal lines.*

Creating similar routines to draw filled triangles, hexagons, and circles is not difficult, because of these objects' regularity and symmetry. Writing a general-purpose routine that can fill convex or irregular polygons is more difficult; in this case, you must scan-convert each of the polygon's sides (using, for example, Bresenham's algorithm from Chapter 6) to create a list of the pixels that define the border of the polygon. This list contains pairs of pixels that can then be connected with horizontal lines to fill the interior of the polygon.

 Several good textbooks deal with the problem of scan-converting and filling arbitrary polygons. For example, see *Fundamentals of Interactive Computer Graphics* by J. D. Foley and A. VanDam (Addison–Wesley 1982).

Though polygon fill techniques have many uses, some applications require filling a region with completely arbitrary borders, such as a map or an irregular shape that was drawn interactively. In this case, your fill routine must define the region using only the pixel values in the video buffer. The remainder of this chapter presents algorithms and working source code for three such routines.

Three Region Fill Algorithms

The three algorithms described here are all designed with IBM video subsystems in mind. They use the pixel manipulation and line-drawing subroutines developed in Chapters 4, 5, and 6. Also, all three algorithms assume that border pixels can be diagonally connected and that interior pixels must be orthogonally connected (as in Figure 8-2b). You can thus fill regions with boundaries drawn using the line-drawing and ellipse-drawing routines in Chapters 6 and 7, since those line and ellipse routines draw diagonally connected figures.

Furthermore, all three algorithms can fill a region that contains a hole in its interior (see Figure 8-3). Such holes are collections of border pixels that are not contiguous with the pixels in the region's outer border. Each algorithm is designed to detect the presence of holes and to properly fill the interior pixels surrounding them.

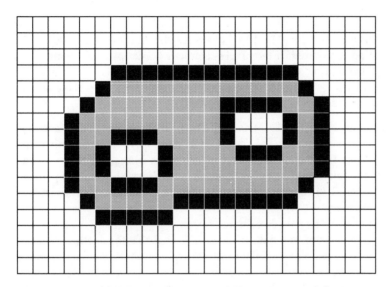

Figure 8-3. *A region whose interior (gray pixels) contains two holes.*

Simple Recursive Fill

One way to fill a region is to start by filling a given "seed" pixel in its interior, and then to fill each of the seed's immediate neighbors, each of the neighbors' neighbors, and so on until the entire region is filled. The C routine in Listing 8-2, `PixelFill()`, shows how to do this. In `PixelFill()`, as in the other algorithms in this chapter, pixels in the interior of the region are assumed to be connected horizontally and vertically, but not diagonally. (`PixelFill()` can be easily modified to fill diagonally connected regions if so desired.)

```
/* Listing 8-2 */

int     FillValue;      /* value of pixels in filled region */
int     BorderValue;    /* value of pixels in border */

PixelFill( x, y )
int     x,y;
{
        int     v;

        v = ReadPixel( x, y );
```

Listing 8-2. *A simple recursive region fill.*   *(continued)*

Listing 8-2. *Continued.*

```
            if ( (v!=FillValue) && (v!=BorderValue) )
            {
              SetPixel( x, y, FillValue );

              PixelFill( x-1, y );
              PixelFill( x+1, y );
              PixelFill( x, y-1 );
              PixelFill( x, y+1 );
            }
}
```

Before it fills a pixel, `PixelFill()` examines the pixel's value to determine whether filling is required. If the pixel is neither a border pixel nor a previously filled pixel, the routine updates the pixel value and calls itself recursively. Because `PixelFill()` does not fill previously filled pixels, the routine works properly even in regions with holes.

Although simple, `PixelFill()` is inefficient. One reason is that on average only one of the four recursive calls to `PixelFill()` ever does anything. (Each pixel can only be filled once, but each time a pixel is filled, four recursive calls are made to the function. The only exception is in the case of the seed pixel.) Thus, `PixelFill()` accomplishes nothing about 75 percent of the time, which is not very efficient.

Another problem with `PixelFill()` is that the depth of recursion can increase beyond the limits of available stack memory. For example, the default stack space for code generated with the Microsoft C compiler is 2 KB. You can easily exceed this limit by using `PixelFill()` to fill even relatively small regions.

Line-Adjacency Fill

A better approach is to regard the interior of the region as a group of adjacent line segments that are connected vertically instead of as a group of pixels connected both vertically and horizontally. An algorithm that fills adjacent line segments tends to be much more efficient than a pixel-by-pixel recursive fill, because it inspects and fills pixels more efficiently. Also, this conception of the region is closer to the physical representation of pixels in the video buffer, in which pixels are arranged in horizontal rows to be displayed during the raster scan.

The routine in Listing 8-3, `LineAdjFill()`, implements a line-adjacency algorithm for filling a region. Its general strategy is to locate each group of horizontally connected pixels in the interior of the region. Like the simple recursive fill, this algorithm also starts at a seed pixel known to be in the region's interior. It scans left and right to find the ends of the seed pixel's row, then fills the entire row.

```
/* Listing 8-3 */

#define UP        -1
#define DOWN       1


LineAdjFill( SeedX, SeedY, D, PrevXL, PrevXR )
int     SeedX,SeedY;            /* seed for current row of pixels */
int     D;                      /* direction searched to find current row */
int     PrevXL,PrevXR;          /* endpoints of previous row of pixels */
{
        int     x,y;
        int     xl,xr;
        int     v;

        y = SeedY;              /* initialize to seed coordinates */
        xl = SeedX;
        xr = SeedX;

        ScanLeft( &xl, &y );    /* determine endpoints of seed line segment */
        ScanRight( &xr, &y );

        Line( xl, y, xr, y, FillValue );        /* fill line with FillValue */

/* find and fill adjacent line segments in same direction */

        for (x = xl; x <= xr; x++)      /* inspect adjacent rows of pixels */
        {
          v = ReadPixel( x, y+D );
          if ( (v != BorderValue) && (v != FillValue) )
            x = LineAdjFill( x, y+D, D, xl, xr );
        }

/* find and fill adjacent line segments in opposite direction */

        for (x = xl; x < PrevXL; x++)
        {
          v = ReadPixel( x, y-D );
          if ( (v != BorderValue) && (v != FillValue) )
            x = LineAdjFill( x, y-D, -D, xl, xr );
        }

        for (x = PrevXR; x < xr; x++)
        {
          v = ReadPixel( x, y-D );
          if ( (v != BorderValue) && (v != FillValue) )
            x = LineAdjFill( x, y-D, -D, xl, xr );
        }

        return( xr );
}

ScanLeft( x, y )
int     *x,*y;
{
        int     v;
```

Listing 8-3. *A line-adjacency fill routine.*   *(continued)*

Listing 8-3. *Continued.*

```
        do
        {
          --(*x);                        /* move left one pixel */
          v = ReadPixel( *x, *y );       /* determine its value */
        }
        while ( (v != BorderValue) && (v != FillValue) );

        ++(*x);           /* x-coordinate of leftmost pixel in row */
}

ScanRight( x, y )
int     *x,*y;
{
        int     v;

        do
        {
          ++(*x);                        /* move right one pixel */
          v = ReadPixel( *x, *y );       /* determine its value */
        }
        while ( (v != BorderValue) && (v != FillValue) );

        --(*x);           /* x-coordinate of rightmost pixel in row */
}
```

The algorithm proceeds by locating all groups of horizontally connected pixels
that are vertically adjacent to the group it just scanned. Each time it finds an adjacent group of not-yet-filled pixels, LineAdjFill() is called recursively to fill
them. The algorithm terminates when all interior pixels have been filled.

Figure 8-4 illustrates the order in which LineAdjFill() fills a simple region
comprising seven line segments. The seed pixel is assumed to lie inside line segment 1, and the routine is initially called with an upward search direction. The
routine first searches the row of pixels above the seed (that is, line segment 2) for
unfilled pixels. Because the row has not yet been filled, the routine is called
recursively to fill it. Similarly, line segments 3 and 4 are filled by subsequent
recursive calls to LineAdjFill(). At this point, neither line segment 4 nor line

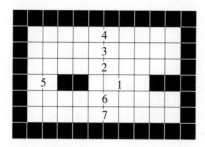

Figure 8-4. *Given a seed pixel in line segment 1, LineAdjFill() fills the adjacent line segments in this region in numerical order.*

segment 3 has any unfilled pixels adjacent to it, but when the pixels below line segment 2 are scanned, line segment 5 is discovered and filled. Finally, line segments 6 and 7 are filled recursively.

A line-adjacency graph (LAG) is essentially a diagram of the connections between the adjacent line segments in the interior of a region (see Figure 8-5). The problem of filling a region is equivalent to traversing its LAG in such a way that all nodes in the graph are visited. In practice, traversing the LAG is relatively easy (there are several textbook algorithms for graph traversal) compared to generating the graph given only the pixels in the video buffer (which is essentially what LineAdjFill() does). For more information see ''Filling Regions in Binary Raster Images: A Graph-Theoretic Approach'' by U. Shani (*SIGGRAPH Proceedings* 1980, pp. 321–327).

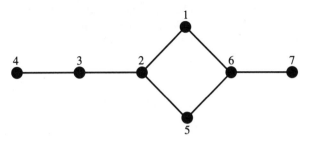

Figure 8-5. *A simple line-adjacency graph (LAG).*

LineAdjFill() is much more efficient than PixelFill(), because it rarely visits a pixel more than once to determine whether it needs to be filled. Each time the routine is called, it fills one line segment and then inspects the adjacent rows of pixels for unfilled pixels. The routine does not examine pixels that were inspected during the previous invocation of the routine (that is, pixels between PrevXL and PrevXR), nor does it inspect pixels to be filled by subsequent invocations (that is, pixels between the current value of *x* and the value returned from a call to LineAdjFill()). The recursive logic becomes clear when you trace the execution of the routine as it fills a region such as the one diagrammed in Figure 8-4.

If you implement a line-adjacency fill algorithm in assembly language, you can improve its efficiency by maintaining a push-down stack of parameters and executing the function iteratively rather than recursively. The skeleton of the algorithm then becomes

```
push ( .. initial parameters on stack .. );
while ( .. stack not empty .. )
  LineAdjFill();
```

The fill routine pops the topmost parameters off the stack and pushes new sets of parameters instead of calling itself recursively.

```
LineAdjFill
{
  pop ( .. current parameters off of stack .. )
  .
  .
  .
  if ( .. adjacent line needs to be filled .. )
    push ( .. new parameters .. )
}
```

In assembly language, a single machine instruction can perform each push and pop, so the algorithm's performance is greatly improved.

A line-adjacency algorithm can be adapted to fill a region with a pattern of pixels as well as with a single pixel value. For this reason, it is used commonly in commercial graphics packages. (IBM BASICA and Microsoft GW-BASIC are examples.) Modifying the algorithm to do patterned fills requires that the horizontal line-drawing routine be replaced with a pattern-drawing routine and that the test that determines whether a pixel has been filled take into account the pixel values in the fill pattern.

These modifications may seem innocuous, but they can significantly degrade the fill routine's performance. The logic required to detect the presence of previously filled pixels can be complicated, particularly if you allow the fill pattern to contain pixels with the same value as border pixels.

Border Fill

Because the border of a region defines the extent of its interior, it is possible to fill a region by following the connected border pixels at the ends of the adjacent line segments that make up the interior. (See "Contour Filling in Raster Graphics" by T. Pavlidis, *Computer Graphics,* August 1981, p. 29). As long as you fill the region at the same time that you trace the border, however, this kind of border-tracing fill algorithm offers no clear advantage over a line-adjacency algorithm.

However, if you separate the problem of tracing the border from that of filling the region's interior, the resulting algorithm becomes more flexible. The process of filling a region then breaks down into three discrete steps:

1) Create an ordered list of the border pixels (trace the border).

2) Scan the interior of the region for holes.

3) "Connect the dots" in the list from left to right with horizontal lines, thereby filling the region.

The routine `BorderFill()` in Listing 8-4 performs a region fill using this three-step method. The algorithm executes the three steps iteratively, once for the boundary of the region and once for each hole in the interior of the region.

```
/* Listing 8-4 */

#define BLOCKED      1
#define UNBLOCKED    2
#define TRUE         1
#define FALSE        0

struct  BPstruct                        /* table of border pixels */
{
        int     x,y;
        int     flag;
}
        BP[3000];                       /* (increase if necessary) */

int     BPstart;                        /* start of table */
int     BPend = 0;                      /* first empty cell in table */
int     FillValue;                      /* value of pixels in filled region */
int     BorderValue;                    /* value of pixels in border */


BorderFill( x, y )
int     x,y;
{
        do                              /* do until entire table is scanned */
        {
          TraceBorder( x, y );          /* trace border starting at x,y */
          SortBP( BP );                 /* sort the border pixel table */
          ScanRegion( &x, &y );         /* look for holes in the interior */
        }
        while (BPstart < BPend);

        FillRegion();                   /* use the table to fill the interior */
}

ScanRegion( x, y )
int     *x,*y;
{
        int     i = BPstart;
        int     xr;

        while (i < BPend)
        {
          if (BP[i].flag == BLOCKED)    /* skip pixel if blocked */
            ++i;

          else
          if (BP[i].y != BP[i+1].y)     /* skip pixel if last in line */
            ++i;

          else
          {                             /* if at least one pixel to fill ... */
            if (BP[i].x < BP[i+1].x-1)  /* scan the line */
            {
              xr = ScanRight( BP[i].x+1, BP[i].y );

              if (xr<BP[i+1].x)         /* if a border pixel is found ... */
              {
                *x = xr;                /* return its x,y coordinates */
                *y = BP[i].y;
```

Listing 8-4. *A region fill routine that traces a region's border.*   *(continued)*

Listing 8-4. *Continued.*

```
                    break;
                }
            }

        i += 2;                        /* advance past this pair of pixels */
        }
    }

    BPstart = i;
}

SortBP()                          /* uses Microsoft C library quicksort routine */
{
    int     CompareBP();

    qsort( BP+BPstart, BPend-BPstart, sizeof(struct BPstruct), CompareBP );
}

CompareBP( arg1, arg2 )           /* returns -1 if arg1<arg2, 1 if arg1>arg2 */
struct  BPstruct  *arg1,*arg2;
{
    int     i;

    i = arg1->y - arg2->y;        /* sort by y-coordinate */
    if (i != 0)
      return( (i < 0) ? -1 : 1 ); /* (return -1 if i<0, 1 if i>0) */

    i = arg1->x - arg2->x;        /* sort by x-coordinate */
    if (i != 0)
      return( (i < 0) ? -1 : 1 );

    i = arg1->flag - arg2->flag;  /* sort by flag */
      return( (i < 0) ? -1 : 1 );
}

FillRegion()
{
    int     i;


    for(i = 0; i < BPend;)
    {
      if (BP[i].flag == BLOCKED)    /* skip pixel if blocked */
        ++i;

      else
      if (BP[i].y != BP[i+1].y)     /* skip pixel if last in line */
        ++i;

      else
      {                             /* if at least one pixel to fill ... */
        if (BP[i].x < BP[i+1].x-1)  /* draw a line */
          Line( BP[i].x+1, BP[i].y, BP[i+1].x-1, BP[i+1].y, FillValue );

        i += 2;
      }
    }
}
```

(continued)

Listing 8-4. *Continued.*

```
/* border tracing routine */

struct  BPstruct CurrentPixel;
int     D;                              /* current search direction */
int     PrevD;                          /* previous search direction */
int     PrevV;                          /* previous vertical direction */

TraceBorder( StartX, StartY )
int     StartX,StartY;
{
        int     NextFound;              /* flags */
        int     Done;

/* initialize */

        CurrentPixel.x = StartX;
        CurrentPixel.y = StartY;

        D = 6;                          /* current search direction */
        PrevD = 8;                      /* previous search direction */
        PrevV = 2;                      /* most recent vertical direction */

/* loop around the border until returned to the starting pixel */

        do
        {
          NextFound = FindNextPixel();
          Done =
            (CurrentPixel.x == StartX) && (CurrentPixel.y == StartY);
        }
        while (NextFound && !Done);

/* if only one pixel in border, add it twice to the table */

        if (!NextFound)                         /* pixel has no neighbors */
        {
          AppendBPList( StartX, StartY, UNBLOCKED );
          AppendBPList( StartX, StartY, UNBLOCKED );
        }

/* if last search direction was upward, add the starting pixel to the table */

        else
        if ( (PrevD <= 3) && (PrevD >= 1) )
          AppendBPList( StartX, StartY, UNBLOCKED );
}

FindNextPixel()
{
        int     i;
        int     flag;


        for (i = -1; i <= 5; i++)
        {
          flag = FindBP( (D+i) & 7 );    /* search for next border pixel */
```

(continued)

Listing 8-4. *Continued.*

```
        if (flag)                        /* flag is TRUE if found */
         {
           D = (D+i) & 6;                /* (D+i) MOD 2 */
           break;                        /* exit from loop */
         }
       }

       return( flag );
}

FindBP( d )
int    d;                       /* direction to search for next border pixel */
{
       int     x,y;

       x = CurrentPixel.x;
       y = CurrentPixel.y;

       NextXY( &x, &y, d );             /* get x,y of pixel in direction d */

       if ( BorderValue == ReadPixel( x, y ) )
        {
          AddBPList( d );               /* add pixel at x,y to table */
          CurrentPixel.x = x;           /* pixel at x,y becomes current pixel */
          CurrentPixel.y = y;
          return( TRUE );
        }

       else
         return( FALSE );
}

NextXY( x, y, Direction )
int    *x,*y;
int    Direction;
{
       switch( Direction )              /*    3 2 1    */
        {                               /*    4   0    */
          case 1:                       /*    5 6 7    */
          case 2:
          case 3:
              *y -= 1;                  /* up */
              break;
          case 5:
          case 6:
          case 7:
              *y += 1;                  /* down */
              break;
        }

       switch(Direction)
        {
          case 3:
          case 4:
          case 5:
              *x -= 1;                  /* left */
              break;
```

(continued)

Listing 8-4. *Continued.*

```
        case 1:
        case 0:
        case 7:
                *x += 1;                /* right */
                break;
        }
}

AddBPList( d )
int     d;
{
        if (d == PrevD)
          SameDirection();

        else
        {
          DifferentDirection( d );
          PrevV = PrevD;                /* new previous vertical direction */
        }

        PrevD = d;                      /* new previous search direction */
}

SameDirection()
{
        if (PrevD == 0)                 /* moving right ... */
          BP[BPend-1].flag = BLOCKED;   /* block previous pixel */

        else
        if (PrevD != 4)                 /* if not moving horizontally */
          AppendBPList( CurrentPixel.x, CurrentPixel.y, UNBLOCKED );
}

DifferentDirection( d )
int     d;
{

/* previously moving left */

        if (PrevD == 4)
        {
          if (PrevV == 5)               /* if from above ... */
            BP[BPend-1].flag = BLOCKED; /* block rightmost in line */

          AppendBPList( CurrentPixel.x, CurrentPixel.y, BLOCKED );
        }

/* previously moving right */

        else
        if (PrevD == 0)                 /* previously moving right ... */
        {
          BP[BPend-1].flag = BLOCKED;   /* block rightmost in line */

          if (d == 7)                   /* if line started from above */
            AppendBPList( CurrentPixel.x, CurrentPixel.y, BLOCKED );
          else
            AppendBPList( CurrentPixel.x, CurrentPixel.y, UNBLOCKED );
        }
```

(continued)

Listing 8-4. *Continued.*

```
/* previously moving in some vertical direction */

        else
        {
          AppendBPList( CurrentPixel.x, CurrentPixel.y, UNBLOCKED );

/* add pixel twice if local vertical maximum or minimum */

          if ( ( (d>=1) && (d<=3) ) && ( (PrevD >= 5) && (PrevD <= 7) ) ||
               ( (d>=5) && (d<=7) ) && ( (PrevD >= 1) && (PrevD <= 3) ) )
            AppendBPList( CurrentPixel.x, CurrentPixel.y, UNBLOCKED );
        }
}

AppendBPList( p, q, f )
int     p,q;                    /* pixel x,y coordinates */
int     f;                      /* flag */
{
        BP[BPend].x = p;
        BP[BPend].y = q;
        BP[BPend].flag = f;

        ++BPend;                /* increment past last entry in table */
}

/* routine to scan a line for a border pixel */

int     Xmax;                   /* largest valid pixel x-coordinate */

ScanRight( x, y )
int     x,y;
{
        while ( ReadPixel( x, y ) != BorderValue )
        {
          ++x;                          /* increment x */
          if (x == Xmax)                /* if end of line in buffer ... */
            break;                      /* exit from the loop */
        }

        return( x );
}
```

The module `TraceBorder()` creates a table that contains the pixel address
of every pixel in the region's border. `SortBP()` then sorts the table of border
pixels by increasing *y*- and *x*-coordinates. The routine `ScanRegion()`
examines the interior line segment between each pair of border pixels in the
table. If it detects a border pixel within the line segment, `ScanRegion()`
assumes it has encountered a hole in the region; it then returns the border pixel's
(*x,y*) coordinates so that `TraceBorder()` and `SortBP()` can update the table
with the hole's border pixels. This process continues until the entire interior of
the region has been scanned. Then `FillRegion()` uses the sorted list of border
pixels to fill the region by drawing a horizontal line between each pair of pixels
in the list.

`TraceBorder()` starts with a seed pixel on the right-hand border of the region. It steps clockwise from pixel to pixel in the border. Because the search proceeds clockwise, the interior of the region is always to the right of the direction in which the search is moving. If a pixel is not adjacent to the interior, the algorithm does not identify it as a border pixel. The algorithm ensures that the border pixels it detects are indeed adjacent to the interior by always examining pixels to the right of the search direction first.

The algorithm identifies its search direction with one of the eight numeric codes shown in Figure 8-6. (This technique is taken from "Algorithms for Graphics and Image Processing" by T. Pavlidis [*Computer Science Press,* 1982].) Thus, in Figure 8-7, the algorithm moves from pixel *b* to pixel *c* in direction 6 (downward). To find the next pixel in the border, the algorithm starts by examining the pixel to the right of direction 6; that is, direction 4. This pixel is not a border pixel, but the pixel in direction 5 (pixel *d*) is, so *d* is added to the list. The algorithm continues to trace the border until it returns to the starting pixel. (The search terminates immediately in the case of a degenerate "border" consisting of only one pixel.)

`TraceBorder()` performs another task in addition to identifying the pixels in the border. It also indicates whether each border pixel defines the left or right endpoint of a horizontal interior line segment. (Because `FillRegion()` draws horizontal lines from left to right, `TraceBorder()` marks each border pixel with a flag indicating whether the pixel can be used as a left border.) Furthermore, if a pixel can serve as both a left and a right border (see Figure 8-8),

3	2	1
4 ←		→ 0
5	6	7

Figure 8-6. *Numeric codes for border pixel trace directions.*

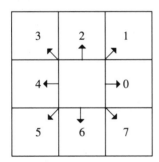

	Direction
a → b	6
b → c	6
c → d	5
d → e	5
e → f	4
f → g	4

Figure 8-7. *Border pixel identification in TraceBorder().*

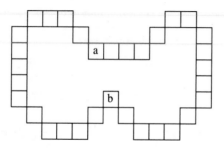

Figure 8-8. *Pixels may border the interior on the left, right, or both directions: Pixel* a *is a border pixel on the right of a row of interior pixels; it is blocked to its right by other border pixels. Pixel* b *serves as both a left and a right border.*

`TraceBorder()` adds it to the table twice. The logic in `SameDirection()` and `DifferentDirection()` accomplishes these tasks.

`TraceBorder()` may seem complex, but it is a relatively fast routine. The slowest steps in `BorderFill()` are actually `SortBP()`, which sorts the table of border pixels, and `ScanRegion()`, which searches for border pixels in the interior of the region. If `SortBP()` and `ScanRegion()` are slow, `BorderFill()` will be slow, because these routines are executed iteratively, once for each hole in the region.

You can significantly improve `BorderFill()`'s performance by modifying `TraceBorder()` so that it builds its list of border pixels in the proper order to begin with, avoiding the sort altogether. You can build the ordered list efficiently using any of several data structures, including a linked list, a heap, or a fixed-size table. This type of modification is particularly effective when the algorithm is used to fill regions that contain one or more holes. Instead of sorting the list each time it detects a hole, the modified algorithm simply inserts the hole's border pixels into the list.

Writing `ScanRegion()` in a high-level language is relatively easy, but because the routine examines all pixels in the interior of the region, you should write it in assembly language so it will execute rapidly. Furthermore, using assembly language on the EGA, the VGA, and the InColor Card offers a distinct advantage, because the graphics control hardware in these subsystems can examine eight pixels at a time and indicate which, if any, match the border pixel value. The assembly-language routine `ScanRight()` in Listing 8-5, which can be used in EGA and VGA 16-color graphics modes, runs 50 times faster than the C version in Listing 8-4.

```
            TITLE    'Listing 8-5'
            NAME     ScanRight10
            PAGE     55,132

;
; Name:       ScanRight10
;
```

Listing 8-5. *An assembly-language version of ScanRight().*   *(continued)*

Listing 8-5. *Continued.*

```
; Function:      Scan for a pixel of a given value in 16-color EGA/VGA graphics
;
; Caller:        Microsoft C:
;
;                    int ScanRight10(x,y);
;
;                    int x,y;                        /* starting pixel */
;
;                    extern  int BorderValue;        /* value of border pixel */
;
;                Returns the x-coordinate of the rightmost border pixel.
;

ARGx            EQU     word ptr [bp+4] ; stack frame addressing
ARGy            EQU     word ptr [bp+6]

ByteOffsetShift EQU     3                       ; used to convert pixels to byte offset
BytesPerLine    EQU     80                      ; 80 for most 16-color graphics modes
                                                ;   (40 for 320x200 16-color)


DGROUP          GROUP   _DATA

_TEXT           SEGMENT byte public 'CODE'
                ASSUME  cs:_TEXT,ds:DGROUP

                EXTRN   PixelAddr10:near

                PUBLIC  _ScanRight10
_ScanRight10    PROC    near

                push    bp                      ; preserve caller registers
                mov     bp,sp
                push    di
                push    si

; calculate pixel address of (0,y)

                mov     ax,ARGy         ; AX := y
                xor     bx,bx           ; BX := 0
                call    PixelAddr10     ; ES:BX -> buffer
                mov     di,bx           ; ES:DI -> buffer

; calculate offset of x in row

                mov     ax,ARGx
                mov     si,ax           ; SI,AX := x
                mov     cl,ByteOffsetShift
                shr     si,cl           ; SI := offset of x in row y
                add     di,si           ; DI := offset of x in buffer

; calculate a bit mask for the first byte to scan

                mov     cl,al
                and     cl,7            ; CL := x & 7
                mov     ch,0FFh
                shr     ch,cl           ; CH := bit mask for first scanned byte
```

(continued)

Listing 8-5. *Continued.*

```
; configure the Graphics Controller

                mov     dx,3CEh             ; DX := Graphics Controller port addr

                mov     ah,_BorderValue     ; AH := pixel value for Color Compare reg
                mov     al,2                ; AL := Color Compare Reg number
                out     dx,ax

                mov     ax,805h             ; AH := 00001000b (Read Mode 1)
                out     dx,ax               ; AL := Mode reg number

                mov     ax,0F07h            ; AH := 00001111b (Color Compare reg value)
                out     dx,ax               ; AL := Color Compare reg number

; inspect the first byte for border pixels

                mov     al,es:[di]          ; AL := nonzero bits corresponding to
                                            ;   border pixels
                inc     di                  ; ES:DI -> next byte to scan
                and     al,ch               ; apply bit mask
                jnz     L01                 ; jump if border pixel(s) found

; scan remainder of line for border pixels

                mov     cx,BytesPerLine
                sub     cx,si               ; CX := BytesPerLine - (byte offset of
                                            ;   starting pixel)
                dec     cx                  ; CX := # of bytes to scan

                repe    scasb               ; scan until nonzero byte read; i.e.,
                                            ;   border pixel(s) found

; compute x value of border pixel

                mov     al,es:[di-1]        ; AL := last byte compared
L01:            sub     di,bx               ; DI := offset of byte past the one which
                                            ;   contains a border pixel
                mov     cl,ByteOffsetShift
                shl     di,cl               ; DI := x-coordinate of 1st pixel in byte

                mov     cx,8                ; CX := loop limit
L02:            shl     al,1                ; isolate first border pixel
                jc      L03

                loop    L02

L03:            sub     di,cx               ; DI := x-coordinate of border pixel

; restore default Graphics Controller state and return to caller

                mov     ax,2                ; AH := 0 (default Color Compare value)
                out     dx,ax               ; restore Color Compare reg

                mov     al,5                ; AH := 0, AL := 5
                out     dx,ax               ; restore Mode reg
```

(continued)

Listing 8-5. *Continued.*

```
                mov     ax,di           ; AX := return value

                pop     si              ; restore caller registers and return
                pop     di
                mov     sp,bp

                pop     bp
                ret

_ScanRight10    ENDP

_TEXT           ENDS


_DATA           SEGMENT word public 'DATA'

                EXTRN    _BorderValue:byte

_DATA           ENDS

                END
```

The fastest step in BorderFill() is the fill itself, because horizontal lines can be drawn rapidly. Thus, if you need to fill the same region repeatedly or to copy the same filled region several times, you can preserve the list of border pixels generated the first time you execute BorderFill(). This greatly accelerates subsequent fills, because you can skip the border-tracing and sorting steps.

Comparing the Algorithms

Which region fill algorithm is best? Each algorithm described in this chapter has its pros and cons. You can compare them in several ways. A valid comparison considers the simplicity of the algorithm, the speed of the compiled code, and the suitability of each algorithm for particular types of region fills.

The recursive, pixel-by-pixel algorithm implemented as PixelFill() is about as simple as you can get. The source code is short and easy to implement in assembly language as well as in a high-level language. However, PixelFill() is too inefficient and too highly recursive to be generally useful.

The line-adjacency fill algorithm LineAdjFill() is more complicated than PixelFill(). Nevertheless, LineAdjFill() improves on the performance of PixelFill() because it examines pixel groups instead of individual pixels. LineAdjFill() also runs faster when it is written to access the video buffer in one-byte increments instead of one-pixel increments. LineAdjFill() is also much less recursive than PixelFill(), so its runtime memory requirements are smaller than those of PixelFill().

The three-step algorithm implemented in BorderFill() is more complicated and somewhat slower than the other two algorithms. The advantage of using

`BorderFill()` is its generality. Its modules can be readily adapted to alternate types of region fills, including pattern fills and fills of regions defined as numeric lists of (*x,y*) coordinates.

The performance of `BorderFill()` depends on the number of holes in the region. It is as fast as `LineAdjFill()` in filling a region without holes. However, when the region to be filled looks like Swiss cheese, `BorderFill()` slows down because it must update the sorted list of border pixels whenever it fills around a hole.

Nevertheless, `BorderFill()` can do several things that the other algorithms cannot. For example, it can reliably fill regions that contain previously filled pixels. Unlike `BorderFill()`, both `PixelFill()` and `LineAdjFill()` rely on the implicit assumption tht no interior pixels have the same value as the fill value. Thus, `BorderFill()` correctly fills the region shown in Figure 8-9, but both of the other routines fail.

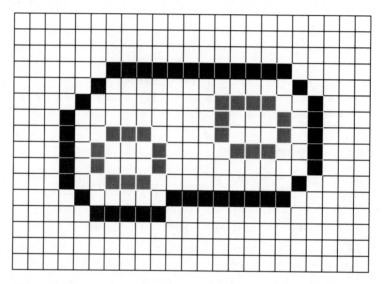

Figure 8-9. *A test case for fill algorithms. Neither PixelFill() nor LineAdjFill() can correctly fill this region with gray pixels, because the "holes" are treated as if they have been already filled.*

 You could modify a routine such as `LineAdjFill()` so that its detection of holes in the region does not depend on the presence of previously filled pixels. This means the algorithm must somehow keep track of pixels it has already filled. One way to do this is to keep track of points where the border reaches a local minimum or maximum (see Figure 8-10). These locations can identify the top and bottom of a hole in the region, enabling the fill algorithm to determine when to stop working its way around the hole.

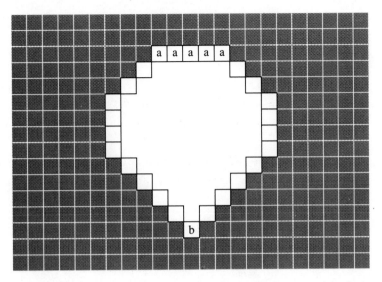

Figure 8-10. *An algorithm can detect the presence of a hole in a region by locating the border's local maximum and minimum. Pixels marked* a *identify a local maximum. Pixels marked* b *identify a local minimum.*

For some applications, BorderFill() has a strong advantage over the other algorithms, because its border-tracing and sorting steps generate a list of numeric pixel coordinates. This list completely defines a two-dimensional region of pixels. You can translate or change the scale of the region by applying the appropriate conversions to the list of border pixels. As long as you preserve the pixels' order in the list, you can use the FillRegion() routine in BorderFill() to fill the region the list defines. For this reason, the BorderFill() algorithm is best suited for applications that must copy arbitrary regions, change their scale or size, or draw them repeatedly into the video buffer.

Furthermore, by modifying the horizontal line routine in BorderFill() you can easily fill a region with an arbitrary pattern or allow pixel AND, OR, and XOR functions. Although you can augment PixelFill() or LineAdjFill() in this way, the source code can become complicated because these algorithms inspect pixels to determine whether they have been filled.

The trade-offs in complexity and performance in these algorithms leave a great deal to your programming judgment. No single region fill algorithm is best for all possible graphics applications. Your choice of implementation should depend on your performance demands, the requirements of the application itself, the capabilities of your video display hardware, and the effort you can afford to expend in integrating and optimizing the code.

9

Graphics Text

Character Definition Tables
Video BIOS Support
Creating a Character Definition Table

Software Character Generators
Video BIOS Support ● Pixel Handling

Designing a Software Character Generator
Horizontal Alignment
Variable Character Sizes ● Clipping
Character Orientation
Cooperating with the Video BIOS
More Power, More Complexity

Implementing a Software Character Generator
CGA ● HGC and HCG+ ● MCGA
EGA and VGA ● InColor Card

Few programs are complete without some sort of text display. Most graphics applications incorporate text with graphics images. In graphics modes, the software that draws characters requires the same thoughtful design and construction as do routines that draw geometric figures such as lines and ellipses.

In alphanumeric video modes, of course, displaying text is easy. You simply place a character code and attribute in the video buffer and let the hardware character generator put pixels on the screen. In graphics modes, however, your program must store every pixel of every character in the video buffer.

This chapter discusses how to translate character codes into the pixel patterns that form characters in graphics modes. The programming examples are hardware-specific, of course, but you can adapt the table-driven character generator described here for use with other computers and in other graphics applications.

Character Definition Tables

Every character that an IBM video subsystem displays is made up of a pattern of contiguous pixels. The pixels are arranged to appear as coherent, recognizable characters on the screen. The pixel pattern that represents a character is the same no matter where in the buffer or on the screen the character is located.

The most convenient way to describe the pixel patterns that represent the characters in a character set is to create a table in which bit patterns represent the pixel patterns. Such a character definition table contains a bit pattern for every displayable character (see Figure 9-1). Each character's bit pattern is defined within a rectangular matrix. When the character matrix is the same size for all characters in the table, and the definitions in the table are organized by character code, converting a character code to an offset into the table is easy.

You can use a character definition table formatted in this way in alphanumeric as well as graphics modes in video subsystems that support RAM-based alphanumeric character definitions. Chapter 10 covers this topic in detail.

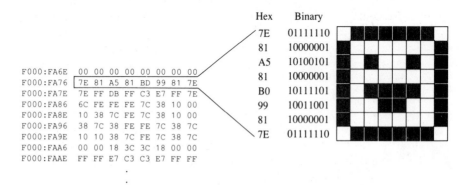

Figure 9-1. *The beginning of the bit patterns that define IBM's ROM BIOS 8-by-8 character definitions.*

Video BIOS Support

The PC and PS/2 ROM BIOS contains default character definition tables for use in graphics modes. The size of the characters in the table depends on the vertical resolution of the video mode. In 200-line, CGA-compatible video modes, the default character matrix is 8 pixels wide and 8 pixels high; in 350-line graphics modes, it is 8 wide by 14 high; in 400-line and 480-line modes, it is 8 by 16. In all graphics modes, the default characters are 8 pixels wide simply because there are 8 bits in a byte. Because each byte in a character definition table represents 8 horizontal pixels, defining characters as a multiple of 8 pixels in width makes the table easy to manipulate in software.

No equivalent constraint applies to the height of characters defined in a character definition table. In practice, however, the character matrix used with IBM video subsystems should rarely be smaller than 8 by 6 pixels or larger than 8 by 16 pixels. With a character matrix outside this range, the displayed height and width of the characters become disproportionate and the characters tend to appear too short or too elongated to be easily read.

Default CGA Characters

Figure 9-1 shows the beginning of the character definition table for the default character set in CGA graphics modes. The table contains an 8-byte definition for each of the first 128 ASCII characters (0 through 7FH). The first eight bytes of the table correspond to character code 0, the second eight bytes to character code 1, and so forth. The bit pattern in each group of eight bytes represents the pixel pattern displayed for the corresponding row of pixels in the character. The first of the eight bytes in each group corresponds to the topmost row of eight pixels.

This table of 8-by-8 character definitions is located at F000:FA6E in the motherboard ROM on all PCs and PS/2s. However, the table defines only the first 128 ASCII characters. Character definitions for the second group of 128 ASCII codes (80H through 0FFH) are found in a table whose address is stored in interrupt vector 1FH (0000:007C). Because the motherboard BIOS contains no definitions for these characters, the address is initialized to 0000:0000. If you use the ROM BIOS to display ASCII characters between 80H and 0FFH in CGA graphics modes without pointing this interrupt vector to a character definition table, the "characters" you see on the screen are whatever binary patterns happen to lie in the first 1024 bytes of RAM.

 The MS-DOS utility GRAFTABL leaves a table of definitions for characters 80H through 0FFH resident in RAM and updates the interrupt 1FH vector to point to it. The characters defined in GRAFTABL are the same as those the alphanumeric character generator displays for ASCII codes 80H through 0FFH.

Default EGA, VGA, and MCGA Characters

The ROM BIOS in the EGA, VGA, and MCGA subsystems contains definitions for all 256 ASCII codes for all graphics modes. (You can access these tables directly; their addresses may be obtained by calling INT 10H function 11H with AL = 30H.) When you select a graphics mode with INT 10H function 0, the video BIOS loads the address of the appropriate character definition table for the graphics mode into interrupt vector 43H (0000:010C). In CGA-compatible 200-line graphics modes, the BIOS also points the interrupt 1FH vector to the definitions for characters 80H through 0FFH.

Creating a Character Definition Table

The easiest way to obtain a character definition table is to use one of the default BIOS tables. If the staid, placid characters in those tables aren't to your liking, you can find many others commercially available or in the public domain.

Several standard character sets are defined and registered with the International Standards Organization (ISO). IBM refers to these character sets as *code pages* and has assigned arbitrary identification numbers to them. For example, the standard IBM PC ASCII character set is designated by code page 437; the Canadian French code page is 863; and code page 850 is the general-purpose "multilingual" character set devised by IBM for languages that use a Latin alphabet.

Both MS-DOS (starting in version 3.3) and OS/2 allow applications to switch between code pages on an EGA or VGA. When a program displays characters with operating system function calls, the operating system uses the character definitions in the currently selected code page. Applications that use foreign language character sets should, whenever possible, exploit the code pages supported by the operating system.

When you define your own character set, you can select among several alternative methods. The ugly alternative is to build your character definition table by specifying every byte in source code. Figure 9-2 shows the beginning of such a table. A more elegant alternative is to use a character-set editing program. With such editors, you use cursor-control keys or a pointing device such as a light pen or mouse to specify the bit patterns in the table. Character-set editors are also available both commercially and in the public domain. (You can even write your own, using the routines in this book.)

Another approach is to start with one of the BIOS character sets and transform the bit patterns in a regular way. For example, you could reverse the bit patterns in a table by converting 0s to 1s and 1s to 0s (that is, apply a bitwise logical NOT to each byte in the table), thus creating a "reverse" character set.

```
CharDefs        db      000h,000h,000h,000h,000h,000h,000h,000h ; character 0
                db      03Ch,066h,0C0h,0C0h,0C0h,066h,03Ch,000h ; character 1
                db      0FCh,066h,066h,07Ch,06Ch,066h,0E6h,000h ; character 2
                db      0FEh,062h,068h,078h,068h,062h,0FEh,000h ; character 3
                db      078h,0CCh,0CCh,078h,0CCh,0CCh,078h,000h ; character 4
                db      078h,030h,030h,030h,030h,030h,078h,000h ; character 5
                db      0CCh,0CCh,0CCh,0CCh,0CCh,078h,030h,000h ; character 6
                db      0FEh,062h,068h,078h,068h,062h,0FEh,000h ; character 7
                            .
                            .
                            .
```

Figure 9-2. *A hand-coded character definition table.*

Software Character Generators

A software routine that uses the bit patterns in a character definition table to draw
characters in the video buffer is called a software character generator. A software
character generator performs several functions. It locates the bit pattern for a
given character code, translates the bit pattern into a corresponding pattern of
pixels, and updates pixels at a specified location in the video buffer.

Video BIOS Support

The video BIOS provides a software character generator that is used whenever INT
10H functions 09H, 0AH, 0EH, and 13H are called in graphics modes. The software character generator in the IBM PC and AT uses only the 8-by-8 characters
defined at F000:FA6E and at the address indicated by interrupt vector 1FH. The
version in the EGA and PS/2 BIOS uses the table to which interrupt vector 43H
points; this version determines the height of displayed characters from the BIOS
variable POINTS at 0040:0085.

You can use the BIOS software character generator to display characters from any
character definition table by updating the appropriate interrupt vectors with the
address of the table. On the EGA and PS/2s, use INT 10H function 11H to do this.

The BIOS character generator is convenient to use, but it is somewhat limited in
its capabilities. In particular, it can only store byte-aligned characters in the video
buffer. If you are willing to sacrifice compatibility with the INT 10H interface,
you can write a faster software character generator that is more powerful than the
default video BIOS version.

Pixel Handling

You store characters in the video buffer by changing the values of the appropriate
pixel groups. You can update the video buffer simply by replacing old pixel
values with new ones. You can also perform bitwise logical operations (AND, OR,
or XOR) to update the pixels.

Your routine to display text in graphics modes can handle the background pixels in the character matrix in one of two ways. One is to preserve the contents of the video buffer as much as possible by updating only foreground pixels; that is, by updating only those pixels that represent the character itself (see Figure 9-3a). The other is to update all foreground and background pixels within the bounds of the rectangular character matrix (see Figure 9-3b).

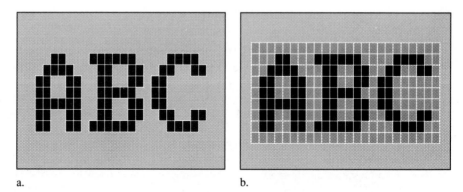

a.   b.

Figure 9-3. *Characters written without background pixels (a.) and with background pixels (b.).*

Updating only the character's foreground pixels preserves as many pixels in the video buffer as possible. This may be the best way to display text in front of a detailed or patterned graphics image. However, reading the displayed characters can be difficult if the graphics image in some way blends with the character. For example, text is invisible against a region filled with pixels having the same value as the character's foreground pixels.

To avoid such problems, you can update all foreground and background pixels in the character matrix each time you store a character in the buffer. This avoids a background pattern inadvertently masking the characters. The trade-off is that each time you store a character in the buffer you must replace the previous contents of the buffer with a rectangular blot.

The source code for the two types of graphics text routines is similar. The examples in this chapter demonstrate the second type, which makes them more complicated than routines that draw only foreground pixels. You can convert the routines to draw only the foreground pixels by eliminating the code for incorporating the background pixels.

Designing a Software Character Generator

Software character generators for IBM PC video subsystems have a number of design considerations in common. Because the performance of your character generator strongly influences the overall performance of many graphics applications, always consider the trade-offs between function and simplicity in your character generator routines.

Horizontal Alignment

In graphics modes, the left edge of a character is not necessarily byte-aligned. When a character is written so that its leftmost pixels fall somewhere in the middle of a byte in the video buffer (see Figure 9-4a), the character generator must shift and mask the character matrix so that only pixels that are part of the character are updated.

Usually, however, characters are written into the video buffer at byte-aligned pixel addresses (see Figure 9-4b). This is the case, for example, whenever the display is used in a "teletype mode"; that is, when each line of characters starts at the left edge of the display. Generating byte-aligned characters requires no rotation or masking of pixels, so using a separate routine for byte-aligned characters improves the character generator's performance.

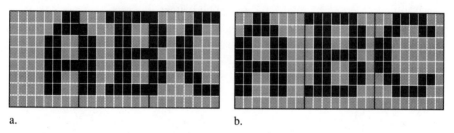

a.   b.

Figure 9-4. *Alignment of characters in the video buffer. In Figure 9-4a, characters are not aligned; in Figure 9-4b, characters are byte-aligned.*

Variable Character Sizes

Writing a character generator that accommodates characters of different heights is relatively easy. The height of a character corresponds to the number of bytes in its definition in the character definition table. You can thus use the height of your characters as a loop limit inside the character generator routine without significantly affecting the complexity of the routine.

Handling characters of different widths is more difficult. If the width of a character does not fit exactly into an integer number of bytes, you must mask each row of pixels in the character as you store it in the video buffer. Again, the extra overhead of forming the appropriate bit mask and masking pixels in the video buffer complicates and slows the character generator routine.

Clipping

You can clip characters in several ways. The simplest is to clip the entire character before you store it in the video buffer; if any portion of the character matrix would lie outside the clipping area, don't write the character.

Clipping a character so that only a portion of it is stored in the video buffer is more difficult. One way to do this is to modify the character generator so that any clipped portion of a character is not written to the buffer. Another approach is to write the entire character into an auxiliary buffer and then copy the clipped character into the video buffer with a pixel block copy routine (see Chapter 11).

Character Orientation

Usually, characters are displayed so that they can be read from left to right and from the top down. To change this orientation, apply the appropriate transformation to the bit patterns in the character definition table. For example, the subroutine in Listing 9-1 rotates the 8-byte bit pattern that represents an 8-by-8 character so that the displayed characters read upward. With this transformation, you can use the same character generator to display vertically or horizontally oriented characters. Only the bit patterns differ.

```
        mov     si,seg OldCharDef
        mov     ds,si
        mov     si,offset OldCharDef      ; DS:SI -> old character definition

        mov     di,seg NewCharDef
        mov     es,di
        mov     di,offset NewCharDef      ; ES:DI -> new character definition

        mov     bx,1                 ; BH := 0
                                     ; BL := bit mask

L01:    push    si                   ; preserve SI
        mov     cx,8                 ; CX := number of bits in each byte

L02:    lodsb                        ; AL := next byte in old
                                     ;   character definition
        and     al,bl                ; mask one bit
        cmp     bh,al                ; set carry flag if mask bit
                                     ;   is nonzero
```

(continued)

Listing 9-1. *A routine that rotates an 8-by-8 character definition by 90 degrees.*

Listing 9-1. *Continued.*

```
        rcl     ah,1            ; rotate bit into AH
        loop    L02             ; loop across old character definition

        mov     al,ah
        stosb                   ; store next byte in new
                                ;   character definition
        pop     si              ; DS:SI -> start of old
                                ;   character definition
        shl     bl,1            ; BL := new bit mask
        jnz     L01             ; loop until bit mask is
                                ;   shifted out of BL
```

Cooperating with the Video BIOS

Even if your character definition tables and character generator software avoid using video BIOS functions, you should nevertheless try to preserve compatibility by cooperating with the BIOS routines when possible. In 200-line graphics modes, you should update the address in interrupt vector 1FH whenever you use an 8-by-8 character definition table that includes the second 128 ASCII characters. On the EGA, VGA, and MCGA, you should generally use INT 10H function 11H to keep the BIOS interrupt vectors and Video Display Data Area variables up to date.

More Power, More Complexity

You can add functionality to a software character generator in several ways. You might, for example, write a character generator that refers to a table of relative character widths to display proportionally spaced characters. As your routine reads bit patterns from the character definition table, you might have it shift them to the right by a predetermined number of pixels to generate bold or italic character sets. You might apply a pattern of pixel values to the foreground pixels you update. You might allow a character definition table to extend beyond the usual range of 256 characters; the more characters you define, the wider range of characters you can display at one time. Any of these possibilities adds power and flexibility to your software character generator, but all of them complicate your source code and ultimately slow it down.

Implementing a Software Character Generator

All software character generator examples in this chapter require that you specify the *x*- and *y*-coordinates of the pixel in the upper left corner of the displayed character matrix. Each routine detects the special case where the character matrix is byte-aligned in the video buffer, but the routines do not validate pixel coordinates or perform any clipping. All the routines except `DisplayChar10()` update pixels in the video buffer by replacing their values. To perform a bitwise AND, OR, or XOR operation, you must modify the routines (see Chapter 5).

CGA

In 640-by-200 2-color mode on the CGA, the software character generator applies the bit patterns in the character definition table directly to the pixels in the video buffer (see Listing 9-2). When the character is byte-aligned in the video buffer, the routine copies pixel values directly from the character definition table. Otherwise, for each row of eight pixels in the character, a rotated 16-bit mask is used to zero the proper eight pixels in the buffer. Then the pixels from the character definition table are rotated into position and stored in the buffer using a bitwise OR operation.

```
                TITLE    'Listing 9-2'
                NAME     DisplayChar06
                PAGE     55,132

;
; Name:          DisplayChar06
;
; Function:      Display a character in 640x200 2-color mode
;
; Caller:        Microsoft C:
;
;                      void DisplayChar06(c,x,y,fgd,bkgd);
;
;                      int c;                /* character code */
;
;                      int x,y;              /* upper left pixel */
;
;                      int fgd,bkgd;         /* foreground and background
;                                               pixel values */
;
;

ARGc            EQU      word ptr [bp+4]  ; stack frame addressing
ARGx            EQU      word ptr [bp+6]
ARGy            EQU      word ptr [bp+8]
ARGfgd          EQU      byte ptr [bp+10]
ARGbkgd         EQU      byte ptr [bp+12]

VARmask         EQU               [bp-8]
VARtoggle       EQU               [bp-10]


_TEXT           SEGMENT byte public 'CODE'
                ASSUME  cs:_TEXT

                EXTRN    PixelAddr06:near

                PUBLIC  _DisplayChar06
_DisplayChar06  PROC     near

                push     bp                ; preserve caller registers
                mov      bp,sp
                sub      sp,4              ; stack space for local variables
                push     di
                push     si
                push     ds
```

Listing 9-2. *A software character generator for 640-by-200 2-color mode.*   *(continued)*

Listing 9-2. *Continued.*

```
; set up foreground pixel toggle mask

                mov     ah,ARGfgd       ; AH := 0 or 1 (foreground pixel value)
                ror     ah,1            ; high-order bit of AH := 0 or 1
                cwd                     ; propagate high-order bit through DX
                not     dx              ; DX :=      0 if foreground = 1
                                        ;     or FFFFh if foreground = 0
                mov     VARtoggle,dx

; calculate first pixel address

                mov     ax,ARGy         ; AX := y
                mov     bx,ARGx         ; BX := x
                call    PixelAddr06     ; ES:BX -> buffer
                                        ; CL := # bits to shift left

                xor     cl,7            ; CL := # bits to rotate right

                mov     ax,0FF00h
                ror     ax,cl           ; AX := bit mask in proper position
                mov     VARmask,ax

; set up video buffer addressing

                mov     dx,2000h        ; increment for video buffer interleave
                mov     di,80-2000h     ; increment from last to first interleave

                test    bx,2000h        ; set zero flag if BX in 1st interleave
                jz      L01

                xchg    di,dx           ; exchange increment values if 1st pixel
                                        ;   lies in 1st interleave

; set up character definition table addressing

L01:            push    bx              ; preserve buffer address

                mov     ax,40h
                mov     ds,ax           ; DS := segment of BIOS Video
                                        ;   Display Data area
                mov     ch,ds:[85h]     ; CH := POINTS (pixel rows in character)

                xor     ax,ax
                mov     ds,ax           ; DS := absolute zero

                mov     ax,ARGc         ; AL := character code
                cmp     al,80h
                jae     L02

                mov     bx,43h*4        ; DS:BX -> int 43h vector if char < 80h
                jmp     short L03

L02:            mov     bx,1Fh*4        ; DS:BX -> int 1Fh vector if char >= 80h
                sub     al,80h          ; put character code in range of table
```

(continued)

Listing 9-2. *Continued.*

```
L03:            lds     si,ds:[bx]      ; DS:SI -> start of character table
                mul     ch              ; AX := offset into char def table
                                        ;   (POINTS * char code)
                add     si,ax           ; SI := addr of char def

                pop     bx              ; restore buffer address

                test    cl,cl           ; test # bits to rotate
                jnz     L20             ; jump if character is not byte-aligned


; routine for byte-aligned characters

                mov     ah,VARtoggle    ; AH := foreground toggle mask
                xchg    ch,cl           ; CX := POINTS

L10:            lodsb                   ; AL := bit pattern for next pixel row
                xor     al,ah           ; toggle pixels if foreground = 0
                mov     es:[bx],al      ; store pixels in buffer

                add     bx,dx           ; BX := next row in buffer
                xchg    di,dx           ; swap buffer increments
                loop    L10
                jmp     short Lexit


; routine for non-byte-aligned characters

L20:            mov     ax,VARmask
                and     es:[bx],ax      ; mask character pixels in buffer

                xor     ah,ah
                lodsb                   ; AX := bit pattern for next pixel row
                xor     al,VARtoggle    ; toggle pixels if foreground = 0

                ror     ax,cl           ; rotate pixels into position
                or      es:[bx],ax      ; store pixels in buffer

                add     bx,dx           ; BX := next row in buffer
                xchg    di,dx           ; swap buffer increments
                dec     ch
                jnz     L20

Lexit:          pop     ds              ; restore caller registers and return
                pop     si
                pop     di
                mov     sp,bp
                pop     bp
                ret

_DisplayChar06  ENDP

_TEXT           ENDS

                END
```

The routine for 320-by-200 4-color mode in Listing 9-3 is more complicated because each bit in the character definition must be expanded into the appropriate 2-bit pixel value. A 0 bit in the character definition table becomes a 2-bit background pixel value; a 1 bit in the table is expanded into a 2-bit foreground pixel value. Thus, each byte in the table is transformed into a word of pixels.

```
                TITLE    'Listing 9-3'
                NAME     DisplayChar04
                PAGE     55,132

;
; Name:          DisplayChar04
;
; Function:      Display a character in 320x200 4-color graphics mode
;
; Caller:        Microsoft C:
;
;                       void DisplayChar04(c,x,y,fgd,bkgd);
;
;                       int c;                  /* character code */
;
;                       int x,y;                /* upper left pixel */
;
;                       int fgd,bkgd;           /* foreground and background
;                                                  pixel values */
;

ARGc            EQU     word ptr [bp+4] ; stack frame addressing
ARGx            EQU     word ptr [bp+6]
ARGy            EQU     word ptr [bp+8]
ARGfgd          EQU             [bp+10]
ARGbkgd         EQU             [bp+12]

VARshift        EQU     word ptr [bp-8]
VARincr         EQU     word ptr [bp-10]


DGROUP          GROUP   _DATA

_TEXT           SEGMENT byte public 'CODE'
                ASSUME  cs:_TEXT,ds:DGROUP

                EXTRN   PixelAddr04:near

                PUBLIC  _DisplayChar04
_DisplayChar04  PROC    near

                push    bp                      ; preserve caller registers
                mov     bp,sp
                sub     sp,4                    ; stack space for local variables
                push    di
                push    si
                push    ds
```

Listing 9-3. *A software character generator for 320-by-200 4-color mode.*   *(continued)*

Listing 9-3. *Continued.*

```
; propagate pixel values

                mov     bx,offset DGROUP:PropagatedPixel
                mov     al,ARGfgd
                xlat                    ; propagate foreground pixel value
                mov     ah,al
                mov     ARGfgd,ax
                mov     al,ARGbkgd
                xlat                    ; propagate background pixel value
                mov     ah,al
                mov     ARGbkgd,ax

; calculate first pixel address

                mov     ax,ARGy         ; AX := y
                mov     bx,ARGx         ; BX := x
                call    PixelAddr04     ; ES:BX -> buffer
                                        ; CL := # bits to shift left
                                        ;   to mask pixel
                mov     ch,0FCh
                shl     ch,cl           ; CH := bit mask for right side of char

                xor     cl,6            ; CL := 6 - CL (# bits to rotate char
                                        ;   into position)
                mov     VARshift,cx

; set up video buffer addressing

                mov     di,2000h        ; increment for video buffer interleave
                mov     VARincr,80-2000h ; increment from last to first interleave

                test    bx,2000h        ; set zero flag if BX in 1st interleave
                jz      L01
                xchg    VARincr,di      ; exchange increment values if 1st pixel
                                        ;   lies in 1st interleave

; set up character definition table addressing

L01:            push    bx              ; preserve buffer address

                mov     ax,40h
                mov     ds,ax           ; DS := segment of BIOS Video
                                        ;   Display Data area
                mov     ch,ds:[85h]     ; CH := POINTS (pixel rows in character)

                xor     ax,ax
                mov     ds,ax           ; DS := absolute zero

                mov     ax,ARGc         ; AL := character code
                cmp     al,80h
                jae     L02

                mov     bx,43h*4        ; DS:BX -> int 43h vector if char < 80h
                jmp     short L03

L02:            mov     bx,1Fh*4        ; DS:BX -> int 1Fh vector if char >= 80h
                sub     al,80h          ; put character code in range of table
```

(continued)

Listing 9-3. *Continued.*

```
L03:            lds     si,ds:[bx]      ; DS:SI -> start of character table
                mul     ch              ; AX := offset into char def table
                                        ;   (POINTS * char code)
                add     si,ax           ; SI := addr of char def

                pop     bx              ; restore buffer address

                xchg    ch,cl           ; CH := # bits to rotate
                                        ; CL := POINTS

                test    ch,ch           ; test # bits to rotate
                jnz     L20             ; jump if character is not byte-aligned


; routine for byte-aligned characters

L10:            lodsb                   ; AL := bit pattern for next pixel row
                xor     dx,dx           ; DX := initial value for doubled bits
                mov     ah,8            ; AH := # of bits in pattern

L11:            shr     al,1            ; cf := lo-order bit of AL
                rcr     dx,1            ; hi-order bit of CX := cf
                sar     dx,1            ; double hi-order bit of DX
                dec     ah              ; loop 8 times
                jnz     L11

                mov     ax,dx           ; AX,DX := doubled bit pattern
                and     ax,ARGfgd       ; AX := foreground pixels
                not     dx
                and     dx,ARGbkgd      ; DX := background pixels

                or      ax,dx           ; AX := eight pixels
                xchg    ah,al           ; put bytes in proper order
                mov     es:[bx],ax      ; update video buffer

                add     bx,di           ; BX := next row in buffer
                xchg    di,VARincr      ; swap buffer increments

                loop    L10
                jmp     short Lexit


; routine for non-byte-aligned characters

L20:            xor     ch,ch           ; CX := POINTS

L21:            push    cx              ; preserve CX

                mov     cx,VARshift     ; CH := mask for right side of char
                                        ; CL := # bits to rotate

                lodsb                   ; AL := bit pattern for next pixel row
                xor     dx,dx           ; DX := initial value for doubled bits
                mov     ah,8            ; AH := # of bits in pattern

L22:            shr     al,1            ; DX := double bits in AL
                rcr     dx,1            ;   (same as above)
```

(continued)

Listing 9-3. *Continued.*

```
                       sar      dx,1
                       dec      ah
                       jnz      L22

                       xchg     dh,dl          ; DH := bits for right half of char
                                               ; DL := bits for left half of char
                       mov      ax,dx
                       and      ax,ARGfgd      ; AX := foreground pixels
                       not      dx
                       and      dx,ARGbkgd     ; DX := background pixels

                       or       dx,ax          ; DX := eight pixels
                       ror      dx,cl          ; DH := left and right side pixels
                                               ; DL := middle pixels
                       mov      al,ch
                       xor      ah,ah          ; AX := mask for left and middle
                                               ;  bytes of char
                       and      es:[bx],ax     ; zero pixels in video buffer

                       not      ax
                       and      ax,dx
                       or       es:[bx],ax     ; update pixels in left and middle bytes

                       mov      al,ch          ; AL := mask for right-hand byte
                       not      al
                       and      es:[bx+2],al   ; mask pixels in right-hand byte in buffer
                       and      ch,dl
                       or       es:[bx+2],ch   ; update pixels in right-hand byte

                       add      bx,di          ; BX := next row in buffer
                       xchg     di,VARincr     ; swap buffer increments

                       pop      cx             ; restore CX
                       loop     L21

Lexit:                 pop      ds             ; restore caller registers and return
                       pop      si
                       pop      di
                       mov      sp,bp
                       pop      bp
                       ret

_DisplayChar04     ENDP

_TEXT              ENDS


_DATA              SEGMENT word public 'DATA'

PropagatedPixel DB          00000000b      ; 0
                DB          01010101b      ; 1
                DB          10101010b      ; 2
                DB          11111111b      ; 3

_DATA              ENDS

                   END
```

In Listing 9-3, when the character is byte-aligned in the video buffer, the routine moves the 16-bit word of pixels directly into the buffer. A character that is not byte-aligned spans three bytes in the buffer. In this case, the routine must rotate the eight pixels in each row of the character into position. Then the first two bytes of the character in the buffer are masked and updated, followed by the third (rightmost) byte of the character.

HGC and HGC+

A routine for the 720-by-348 monochrome graphics mode on the HGC and the HGC+ can use the same bit-masking technique that the CGA 640-by-200 2-color routine uses. You could convert DisplayChar06() into a Hercules-compatible routine by revising the call to PixelAddr06() and by changing video buffer addressing to accommodate the different buffer interleaves on the two adapters.

It is worthwhile, however, to exploit the HGC's 720-pixel horizontal resolution by displaying characters in a matrix that is 9 pixels wide, so that each row on the screen contains 80 evenly spaced characters. The routine in Listing 9-4 does this by appending a ninth bit to each 8-bit pattern it reads from the character definition table. The ninth bit is 0 except for box-drawing characters (ASCII 0C0–0DFH). For these characters, the ninth bit is a copy of the rightmost bit in the bit pattern. (This mimics the function of the hardware character generator in alphanumeric modes. See Chapter 10.)

```
                    TITLE    'Listing 9-4'
                    NAME     DisplayCharHGC
                    PAGE     55,132

;
; Name:          DisplayCharHGC
;
; Function:      Display a character in Hercules 720x348 monochrome graphics mode
;
; Caller:        Microsoft C:
;
;                       void DisplayCharHGC(c,x,y,fgd,bkgd);
;
;                       int c;                  /* character code */
;
;                       int x,y;                /* upper left pixel */
;
;                       int fgd,bkgd;           /* foreground and background
;                                                   pixel values */
;

ARGc            EQU     word ptr [bp+4] ; stack frame addressing
ARGx            EQU     word ptr [bp+6]
ARGy            EQU     word ptr [bp+8]
ARGfgd          EQU     byte ptr [bp+10]
ARGbkgd         EQU     byte ptr [bp+12]
```

(continued)

Listing 9-4. *A software character generator for Hercules monochrome graphics mode.*

Listing 9-4. *Continued.*

```
VARmask          EQU              [bp-8]
VARtoggle        EQU              [bp-10]
VAR9bits         EQU      byte ptr [bp-12]


_TEXT            SEGMENT byte public 'CODE'
                 ASSUME  cs:_TEXT

                 EXTRN    PixelAddrHGC:near

                 PUBLIC   _DisplayCharHGC
_DisplayCharHGC PROC     near

                 push    bp              ; preserve caller registers
                 mov     bp,sp
                 sub     sp,6            ; stack space for local variables
                 push    di
                 push    si
                 push    ds

; calculate first pixel address

                 mov     ax,ARGy         ; AX := y
                 mov     bx,ARGx         ; BX := x
                 call    PixelAddrHGC    ; ES:BX -> buffer
                                         ; CL := # bits to shift left

                 xor     cl,7            ; CL := # bits to rotate right

; set up 8- or 9-bit mask

                 mov     ax,40h
                 mov     ds,ax           ; DS := segment of BIOS Video
                                         ;   Display Data area

                 mov     ax,0FF00h       ; AX := 8-bit mask
                 mov     VAR9bits,0      ; zero this flag

                 cmp     byte ptr ds:[4Ah],90    ; does CRT_COLS = 90?
                 je      L01             ; jump if characters are 8 pixels wide

                 mov     ah,7Fh          ; AX := 9-bit mask
                 cmp     ARGc,0C0h
                 jb      L01             ; jump if character code ...

                 cmp     ARGc,0DFh
                 ja      L01             ; ... outside of range 0C0-0DFh

                 inc     VAR9bits        ; set flag to extend to 9 bits

L01:             ror     ax,cl           ; AX := bit mask in proper position
                 mov     VARmask,ax

; set up foreground pixel toggle mask

                 mov     ah,ARGfgd       ; AH := 0 or 1 (foreground pixel value)
                 ror     ah,1            ; high-order bit of AH := 0 or 1
```

(continued)

Listing 9-4. *Continued.*

```
                cwd                         ; propagate high-order bit through DX
                not     dx                  ; DX :=       0 if foreground = 1
                                            ;      or FFFFh if foreground = 0
                mov     ax,VARmask
                not     ax
                and     dx,ax               ; zero unused bits of toggle mask in DX
                mov     VARtoggle,dx

; set up character definition table addressing

                push    bx                  ; preserve buffer address

                mov     ch,ds:[85h]         ; CH := POINTS (pixel rows in character)

                xor     ax,ax
                mov     ds,ax               ; DS := absolute zero

                mov     ax,ARGc             ; AL := character code
                cmp     al,80h
                jae     L02

                mov     bx,43h*4            ; DS:BX -> int 43h vector if char < 80h
                jmp     short L03

L02:            mov     bx,1Fh*4            ; DS:BX -> int 1Fh vector if char >= 80h
                sub     al,80h              ; put character code in range of table

L03:            lds     si,ds:[bx]          ; DS:SI -> start of character table
                mul     ch                  ; AX := offset into char def table
                                            ;   (POINTS * char code)
                add     si,ax               ; SI := addr of char def

                pop     bx                  ; restore buffer address

; mask and set pixels in the video buffer

L20:            mov     ax,VARmask
                and     es:[bx],ax          ; mask character pixels in buffer

                xor     ah,ah
                lodsb                       ; AX := bit pattern for next pixel row
                cmp     VAR9bits,0
                je      L21                 ; jump if character is 8 pixels wide

                ror     ax,1                ; copy lo-order bit of AX into ...
                rcl     al,1                ;   hi-order bit

L21:            ror     ax,cl               ; rotate pixels into position
                xor     ax,VARtoggle        ; toggle pixels if foreground = 0
                or      es:[bx],ax          ; store pixels in buffer
                add     bx,2000h            ; increment to next portion of interleave
                jns     L22
                add     bx,90-8000h         ; increment to first portion of interleave

L22:            dec     ch
                jnz     L20
```

(continued)

Listing 9-4. *Continued.*

```
Lexit:          pop    ds              ; restore caller registers and return
                pop    si
                pop    di
                mov    sp,bp
                pop    bp
                ret

_DisplayCharHGC ENDP

_TEXT           ENDS

                END
```

 Note how the CGA and Hercules routines use interrupt vector 43H to point to the start of the current character definition table. This is the interrupt vector the EGA and VGA ROM BIOS uses for this purpose. Also, the routines determine the size of the displayed character matrix by inspecting the variables POINTS (0040:0085) and CRT_COLS (0040:004A) in the BIOS Video Display Data Area. If you are not using an EGA, MCGA, or VGA, the BIOS won't keep the interrupt vector and POINTS up to date; in this case, your program should either update these values explicitly or maintain equivalent values elsewhere.

MCGA

In 640-by-480 2-color mode on the MCGA, pixels are stored eight to a byte, so you can adapt the 640-by-200 2-color character generator for use in this mode by modifying its video buffer addressing. A character generator for 320-by-200 256-color mode is a little different, because each bit in the character definition table expands into a byte in the video buffer (see Listing 9-5).

```
                TITLE   'Listing 9-5'
                NAME    DisplayChar13
                PAGE    55,132

;
; Name:          DisplayChar13
;
; Function:      Display a character in MCGA/VGA 320x200 256-color mode
;
; Caller:        Microsoft C:
;
;                        void DisplayChar13(c,x,y,fgd,bkgd);
;
;                        int c;                  /* character code */
;
```

(continued)

Listing 9-5. *A character generator for MCGA and VGA 320-by-200 256-color mode.*

Listing 9-5. *Continued.*

```
;                        int x,y;                    /* upper left pixel */
;
;                        int fgd,bkgd;               /* foreground and background
;                                                        pixel values */
;

ARGc            EQU     word ptr [bp+4] ; stack frame addressing
ARGx            EQU     word ptr [bp+6]
ARGy            EQU     word ptr [bp+8]
ARGfgd          EQU     byte ptr [bp+10]
ARGbkgd         EQU     byte ptr [bp+12]

BytesPerLine    EQU     320

_TEXT           SEGMENT byte public 'CODE'
                ASSUME  cs:_TEXT

                EXTRN   PixelAddr13:near

                PUBLIC  _DisplayChar13
_DisplayChar13  PROC    near

                push    bp                  ; preserve caller registers
                mov     bp,sp
                push    di
                push    si
                push    ds

; calculate first pixel address

                mov     ax,ARGy         ; AX := y
                mov     bx,ARGx         ; BX := x
                call    PixelAddr13     ; ES:BX -> buffer
                mov     di,bx           ; ES:DI -> buffer

; set up character definition table addressing

                mov     ax,40h
                mov     ds,ax           ; DS := segment of BIOS Video
                                        ;   Display Data area
                mov     cx,ds:[85h]     ; CX := POINTS (pixel rows in character)

                xor     ax,ax
                mov     ds,ax           ; DS := absolute zero

                mov     ax,ARGc         ; AL := character code
                mov     bx,43h*4        ; DS:BX -> int 43h vector if char < 80h
                lds     si,ds:[bx]      ; DS:SI -> start of character table
                mul     cl              ; AX := offset into char def table
                                        ;   (POINTS * char code)
                add     si,ax           ; SI := addr of char def

; store the character in the video buffer

                mov     bl,ARGfgd       ; BL := foreground pixel value
                mov     bh,ARGbkgd      ; BH := background pixel value
```

(continued)

Listing 9-5. *Continued.*

```
L10:            push    cx              ; preserve CX across loop
                mov     cx,8            ; CX := character width in pixels
                lodsb
                mov     ah,al           ; AH := bit pattern for next pixel row

L11:            mov     al,bl           ; AL := foreground pixel value
                shl     ah,1            ; carry flag := high-order bit
                jc      L12             ; jump if bit pattern specifies a
                                        ;  foreground pixel (bit = 1)
                mov     al,bh           ; AL := background pixel value

L12:            stosb                   ; update one pixel in the buffer
                loop    L11

                add     di,BytesPerLine-8 ; increment buffer address to next
                                        ;  row of pixels
                pop     cx
                loop    L10             ; loop down character

                pop     ds              ; restore caller registers and return
                pop     si
                pop     di
                mov     sp,bp
                pop     bp
                ret


_DisplayChar13  ENDP

_TEXT           ENDS
                END
```

EGA and VGA

The routine for the EGA and VGA in Listing 9-6 uses the Graphics Controller to update pixels in the video buffer. The routine is similar in some ways to the routine for the CGA's 640-by-200 2-color mode, because each byte of the video buffer represents eight pixels. Of course, the code is complicated by the need to program the Graphics Controller to handle the foreground and background pixel values.

The routine writes each row of pixels in the character by latching the bit planes, updating the foreground pixels, updating the background pixels, and then writing the latches back to the bit planes. The Graphics Controller cannot conveniently update both foreground and background pixels at the same time, so the routine must perform these operations separately.

```
                TITLE   'Listing 9-6'
                NAME    DisplayChar10
                PAGE    55,132

;
; Name:          DisplayChar10
;
```

(continued)

Listing 9-6. *A software character generator for native EGA and VGA graphics modes.*

Listing 9-6. *Continued.*

```
; Function:      Display a character in native EGA and VGA graphics modes
;
; Caller:        Microsoft C:
;
;                       void DisplayChar10(c,x,y,fgd,bkgd);
;
;                       int c;                  /* character code */
;
;                       int x,y;                /* upper left pixel */
;
;                       int fgd,bkgd;           /* foreground and background
;                                                  pixel values */
;

ARGc            EQU     word ptr [bp+4] ; stack frame addressing
ARGx            EQU     word ptr [bp+6]
ARGy            EQU     word ptr [bp+8]
ARGfgd          EQU     byte ptr [bp+10]
ARGbkgd         EQU     byte ptr [bp+12]

VARshift        EQU                 [bp-8]

BytesPerLine    =       80          ; (or 40 in 320x200 16-color mode)
RMWbits         =       18h         ; Read-Modify-Write bits

_TEXT           SEGMENT byte public 'CODE'
                ASSUME  cs:_TEXT

                EXTRN   PixelAddr10:near

                PUBLIC  _DisplayChar10
_DisplayChar10  PROC    near

                push    bp                  ; preserve caller registers
                mov     bp,sp
                sub     sp,2                ; stack space for local variable
                push    di
                push    si
                push    ds

; calculate first pixel address

                mov     ax,ARGy             ; AX := y
                mov     bx,ARGx             ; BX := x
                call    PixelAddr10         ; ES:BX -> buffer
                                            ; CL := # bits to shift left to mask
                                            ;   pixel
                inc     cx
                and     cl,7                ; CL := # bits to shift to mask char

                mov     ch,0FFh
                shl     ch,cl               ; CH := bit mask for right side of char
                mov     VARshift,cx

                push    es                  ; preserve video buffer segment
                mov     si,bx               ; SI := video buffer offset
```

(continued)

Listing 9-6. *Continued.*

```
; set up character definition table addressing

                mov     ax,40h
                mov     ds,ax           ; DS := segment of BIOS Video
                                        ;   Display Data area
                mov     cx,ds:[85h]     ; CX := POINTS (pixel rows in character)

                xor     ax,ax
                mov     ds,ax           ; DS := absolute zero

                mov     ax,ARGc         ; AL := character code
                mov     bx,43h*4        ; DS:BX -> int 43h vector
                les     di,ds:[bx]      ; ES:DI -> start of character table
                mul     cl              ; AX := offset into char def table
                                        ;   (POINTS * char code)
                add     di,ax           ; DI := addr of char def

                pop     ds              ; DS:SI -> video buffer

; set up Graphics Controller registers

                mov     dx,3CEh         ; Graphics Controller address reg port

                mov     ax,0A05h        ; AL :=  Mode register number
                                        ; AH :=  Write Mode 2 (bits 0-1)
                                        ;        Read Mode 1 (bit 4)
                out     dx,ax

                mov     ah,RMWbits      ; AH := Read-Modify-Write bits
                mov     al,3            ; AL := Data Rotate/Function Select reg
                out     dx,ax

                mov     ax,0007         ; AH := Color Don't Care bits
                                        ; AL := Color Don't Care reg number
                out     dx,ax           ; "don't care" for all bit planes

; select output routine depending on whether character is byte-aligned

                mov     bl,ARGfgd       ; BL := foreground pixel value
                mov     bh,ARGbkgd      ; BH := background pixel value

                cmp     byte ptr VARshift,0   ; test # bits to shift
                jne     L20             ; jump if character is not byte-aligned


; routine for byte-aligned characters

                mov     al,8            ; AL := Bit Mask register number

L10:            mov     ah,es:[di]      ; AH := pattern for next row of pixels
                out     dx,ax           ; update Bit Mask register
                and     [si],bl         ; update foreground pixels

                not     ah
                out     dx,ax
                and     [si],bh         ; update background pixels
```

(continued)

Listing 9-6. *Continued.*

```
            inc     di              ; ES:DI -> next byte in char def table
            add     si,BytesPerLine ; increment to next line in video buffer
            loop    L10
            jmp     short Lexit


; routine for non-byte-aligned characters

L20:        push    cx              ; preserve loop counter
            mov     cx,VARshift     ; CH := mask for left side of character
                                    ; CL := # bits to shift left

; left side of character

            mov     al,es:[di]      ; AL := bits for next row of pixels
            xor     ah,ah
            shl     ax,cl           ; AH := bits for left side of char

                                    ; AL := bits for right side of char
            push    ax              ; save bits for right side on stack
            mov     al,8            ; AL := Bit Mask Register number
            out     dx,ax           ; set bit mask for foreground pixels

            and     [si],bl         ; update foreground pixels

            not     ch              ; CH := mask for left side of char
            xor     ah,ch           ; AH := bits for background pixels
            out     dx,ax           ; set bit mask

            and     [si],bh         ; update background pixels

; right side of character

            pop     ax
            mov     ah,al           ; AH := bits for right side of char
            mov     al,8
            out     dx,ax           ; set bit mask

            inc     si              ; DS:SI -> right side of char in buffer

            and     [si],bl         ; update foreground pixels

            not     ch              ; CH := mask for right side of char
            xor     ah,ch           ; AH := bits for background pixels
            out     dx,ax           ; set bit mask

            and     [si],bh         ; update background pixels

; increment to next row of pixels in character

            inc     di              ; ES:DI -> next byte in char def table
            dec     si
            add     si,BytesPerLine ; DS:SI -> next line in video buffer

            pop     cx
            loop    L20
```

(continued)

Listing 9-6. *Continued.*

```
; restore default Graphics Controller registers

Lexit:          mov     ax,0FF08h       ; default Bit Mask
                out     dx,ax

                mov     ax,0005         ; default Mode register
                out     dx,ax

                mov     ax,0003         ; default Data Rotate/Function Select
                out     dx,ax

                mov     ax,0F07h        ; default Color Don't Care
                out     dx,ax

                pop     ds              ; restore caller registers and return
                pop     si
                pop     di
                mov     sp,bp
                pop     bp
                ret

_DisplayChar10  ENDP

_TEXT           ENDS
                END
```

InColor Card

The technique for storing characters in the video buffer on the Hercules InColor Card, shown in Listing 9-7, is different from that on the EGA or VGA because you can use the InColor Card's Read/Write Color register (1AH) and write mode 0 to update both foreground and background pixel values in one operation. Thus, the actual process of updating the bit planes collapses into relatively few machine instructions.

However, the InColor Card cannot perform pixel AND, OR, or XOR operations in hardware. To do this, you must write additional subroutines that use the Plane Mask register to map logical operations onto the bit planes (see Chapter 5).

```
                TITLE   'Listing 9-7'
                NAME    DisplayCharInC
                PAGE    55,132

;
; Name:          DisplayCharInC
;
; Function:      Display a character in InColor 720x348 16-color mode
;
; Caller:        Microsoft C:
;
;                       void DisplayCharInC(c,x,y,fgd,bkgd);
;
```

(continued)

Listing 9-7. *A software character generator for Hercules InColor graphics modes.*

Listing 9-7. *Continued.*

```
;                      int c;                   /* character code */
;
;                      int x,y;                 /* upper left pixel */
;
;                      int fgd,bkgd;            /* foreground and background
;                                                    pixel values */
;

ARGc            EQU     word ptr [bp+4]  ; stack frame addressing
ARGx            EQU     word ptr [bp+6]
ARGy            EQU     word ptr [bp+8]
ARGfgd          EQU     byte ptr [bp+10]
ARGbkgd         EQU     byte ptr [bp+12]

VARmask         EQU     word ptr [bp-8]
VAR9bits        EQU     byte ptr [bp-10]

_TEXT           SEGMENT byte public 'CODE'
                ASSUME  cs:_TEXT

                EXTRN   PixelAddrHGC:near

                PUBLIC  _DisplayCharInC
_DisplayCharInC PROC    near

                push    bp               ; preserve caller registers
                mov     bp,sp
                sub     sp,4             ; stack space for local variables
                push    di
                push    si
                push    ds

; calculate first pixel address

                mov     ax,ARGy          ; AX := y
                mov     bx,ARGx          ; BX := x
                call    PixelAddrHGC     ; ES:BX -> buffer
                                         ; CL := # bits to shift left to mask
                                         ;   pixel
                xor     cl,7             ; CL := # bits to rotate right

                push    es               ; preserve video buffer segment
                mov     si,bx            ; DI := video buffer offset

; set up flag for 8-bit or 9-bit characters

                mov     ax,40h
                mov     ds,ax            ; DS := segment of BIOS Video
                                         ;   Display Data area

                mov     ax,0FF00h        ; AX := 8-bit mask
                mov     VAR9bits,0       ; zero this flag

                cmp     byte ptr ds:[4Ah],90    ; does CRT_COLS = 90?
                je      L01              ; jump if characters are 8 pixels wide
```

(continued)

Listing 9-7. *Continued.*

```
                  mov      ah,7Fh            ; AX := 9-bit mask
                  cmp      ARGc,0C0h
                  jb       L01               ; jump if character code ...

                  cmp      ARGc,0DFh
                  ja       L01               ; ... outside of range 0C0-0DFh

                  inc      VAR9bits          ; set flag to extend to 9 bits

L01:              ror      ax,cl             ; AX := bit mask in proper position
                  mov      VARmask,ax

; set up character definition table addressing

                  mov      ax,40h
                  mov      ds,ax             ; DS := segment of BIOS Video
                                             ;   Display Data area
                  mov      ch,ds:[85h]       ; CH := POINTS (pixel rows in character)

                  xor      ax,ax
                  mov      ds,ax             ; DS := absolute zero

                  mov      ax,ARGc           ; AL := character code
                  cmp      al,80h
                  jae      L02

                  mov      bx,43h*4          ; DS:BX -> int 43h vector if char < 80h
                  jmp      short L03

L02:              mov      bx,1Fh*4          ; DS:BX -> int 1Fh vector if char >= 80h
                  sub      al,80h            ; put character code in range of table

L03:              les      di,ds:[bx]        ; ES:DI -> start of character table
                  mul      ch                ; AX := offset into char def table
                                             ;   (POINTS * char code)
                  add      di,ax             ; DI := addr of char def

                  pop      ds                ; DS:SI -> video buffer

; set up control registers

                  mov      dx,3B4h           ; control register I/O port

                  push     cx                ; preserve CX
                  mov      ah,ARGbkgd        ; AH := background pixel value
                  mov      cl,4
                  shl      ah,cl             ; AH bits 4-7 := background pixel value
                  or       ah,ARGfgd         ; AH bits 0-3 := foreground pixel value
                  pop      cx                ; restore CX

                  mov      al,1Ah            ; AL := Read/Write Color reg number
                  out      dx,ax             ; set Read/Write Color value

; mask and set pixels in the video buffer

L20:              xor      bh,bh
                  mov      bl,es:[di]        ; BX := bit pattern for next pixel row
```

(continued)

Listing 9-7. *Continued.*

```
                inc     di              ; increment pointer to char def table
                cmp     VAR9bits,0

                je      L21             ; jump if character is 8 pixels wide

                ror     bx,1            ; copy lo-order bit of BX into ...
                rcl     bl,1            ;   hi-order bit

L21:            ror     bx,cl           ; rotate pixels into position

                mov     ax,5F19h        ; AH bit 6 := 1 (mask polarity)
                                        ; AH bits 4-5 := 01b (write mode 1)
                                        ; AH bits 0-3 := 1111b (don't care bits)
                                        ; AL := 19h (Read/Write Control reg)
                out     dx,ax           ; set up Read/Write Control reg

                or      [si],bl         ; update foreground pixels
                or      [si+1],bh

                mov     ah,6Fh          ; set up write mode 2
                out     dx,ax

                or      bx,VARmask      ; BX := background pixel bit pattern
                or      [si],bl         ; update background pixels
                or      [si+1],bh

                add     si,2000h        ; increment to next portion of interleave
                jns     L22

                add     si,90-8000h     ; increment to first portion of interleave

L22:            dec     ch
                jnz     L20

; restore default InColor register values

                mov     ax,4019h        ; default Read/Write Control reg
                out     dx,ax

                mov     ax,071Ah        ; default Read/Write Color reg
                out     dx,ax

                pop     ds              ; restore caller registers and return
                pop     si
                pop     di
                mov     sp,bp
                pop     bp
                ret

_DisplayCharInC ENDP

_TEXT           ENDS

                END
```

10

Alphanumeric Character Sets

Character Definition Tables
Alphanumeric Character Definitions in ROM
Alphanumeric Character Definitions in RAM

Updating Character Generator RAM
EGA and VGA ● HGC+ ● InColor Card ● MCGA

Using RAM-based Character Sets
ASCII Character Sets
Extended Character Sets
Compatibility Problems with Extended Character Codes

Changing the Displayed Character Matrix
EGA ● VGA ● MCGA ● HGC+ and InColor Card

Graphics Windows in Alphanumeric Modes
HGC+ and InColor Card ● EGA and VGA ● MCGA

One of the easiest ways to speed up a program's video interface is to use an alphanumeric video mode. To gain this speed advantage, however, you must accept the limitations of the video subsystem's alphanumeric character generator.

On the original MDA and CGA, the only characters you could display in alphanumeric mode were those defined in a table located in ROM on the adapter. The hardware character generator on these adapters was not designed to use a character definition table located in RAM. However, the EGA, the MCGA, the VGA, the HGC+, and the InColor Card can all display alphanumeric characters defined in RAM.

This chapter shows you how to exploit RAM-based alphanumeric character sets on these subsystems. It describes how to format character definition tables and where to place them in RAM to be used in alphanumeric modes. It discusses the pros and cons of using extended character sets that contain more than the usual 256 ASCII characters. The chapter concludes with techniques for displaying true graphics images in an alphanumeric video mode.

Character Definition Tables

Like the software graphics character generators described in Chapter 9, the hardware alphanumeric character generator in all IBM video subsystems references a memory-resident character definition table that contains bit-pattern representations of the pixels in each displayable character. Unlike the graphics-mode tables, whose location in memory may vary, the alphanumeric tables must lie in a predesignated portion of memory to allow the alphanumeric character generator to access them.

Alphanumeric Character Definitions in ROM

The MDA, the CGA, and the Hercules adapters have an alphanumeric character definition table located in ROM that is not within the CPU's address space. Only the character generator hardware can access it. The character set that these adapters display in alphanumeric modes is therefore not controlled by software.

On the EGA, the MCGA, and the VGA, the alphanumeric character generator uses a table of bit patterns stored in RAM rather than in dedicated ROM. The video ROM BIOS contains tables with which it initializes character generator RAM whenever it establishes an alphanumeric video mode. Because these video subsystems can set up alphanumeric modes with different vertical resolutions, the sizes of the default alphanumeric characters vary (see Figure 10-1).

200-Line Modes
The CGA's 200-line alphanumeric modes use an 8-by-8 character matrix. In 80-by-25 alphanumeric mode, the screen is thus 640 pixels wide; in 40-by-25 alphanumeric mode, the screen is 320 pixels wide. Although the CGA uses the same character set and font in its alphanumeric and graphics modes, the character definitions for alphanumeric modes reside in dedicated ROM, accessible only to

Adapter	Video Mode	Character Matrix (width by height in pixels)
MDA, HGC	Monochrome	9-by-14
CGA	40-by-25 16-color	8-by-8
	80-by-25 16-color	8-by-8
EGA	80-by-25 16-color	8-by-8 (200-line resolution)
		8-by-14 (350-line resolution)
	80-by-25 monochrome	9-by-14
MCGA	40-by-25 16-color	8-by-16
	80-by-25 16-color	8-by-16
VGA	40-by-25 16-color	8-by-8 (200-line resolution)
		8-by-14 (350-line resolution)
		9-by-16 (400-line resolution)
	80-by-25 16-color	8-by-8 (200-line resolution)
		8-by-14 (350-line resolution)
		9-by-16 (400-line resolution)
	80-by-25 monochrome	9-by-14 (350-line resolution)
		9-by-16 (400-line resolution)
HGC+	80-by-25 monochrome	9-by-14
InColor Card	80-by-25 16-color	9-by-14

Figure 10-1. *The default alphanumeric character matrix in various video modes.*

the hardware character generator. (As described in Chapter 9, the graphics-mode definitions are found in the ROM BIOS and in a table in RAM addressed by the vector for interrupt 1FH.)

The CGA comes with two tables of 8-by-8 characters in the alphanumeric character generator's ROM. A jumper on the adapter selects which table the alphanumeric character generator uses. By default, jumper P3 on the CGA is not connected, and the usual "double-dot" 8-by-8 characters are displayed. If you connect jumper P3, the CGA's alphanumeric character generator uses a "single-dot" font (see Figure 10-2). The "single-dot" characters appear sharper on some monitors because their vertical strokes are only one pixel wide.

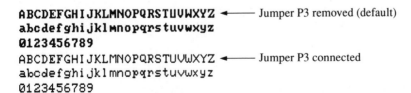

Figure 10-2. *Double-dot and single-dot alphanumeric character sets on the CGA.*

350-Line Modes

In 350-line alphanumeric modes on the MDA and the Hercules adapters, the characters are defined in an 8-by-14 matrix. Again, the character definition table resides in ROM outside the CPU address space that is dedicated to the hardware character generator. Because the horizontal resolution is 720 pixels on these adapters, each 8-by-14 character actually is displayed in a matrix 9 pixels wide. Thus, each row on the screen contains 720÷9, or 80, characters.

If characters are defined in ROM in an 8-by-14 matrix but displayed in a 9-by-14 matrix, where does the extra pixel come from? The hardware character generator in the MDA, the Hercules cards, the EGA, and the VGA (in monochrome mode) adds an extra pixel to the right of each row of eight pixels in each character. For the block graphics characters (ASCII 0C0H through 0DFH), the value of the right-most pixel is replicated in each row. For all remaining character codes, the extra pixel is displayed with the character's background attribute.

Since the ninth (rightmost) pixel in block graphics characters is a copy of the eighth, these characters abut and can be used to draw horizontal lines. All other displayable characters are separated from each other by that ninth pixel. The resulting display appears less crowded than it would be without the extra space.

 With the EGA and the VGA, you can control whether or not the alpha-numeric character generator replicates the eighth pixel of block graphics characters. When bit 2 of the Attribute Controller's Mode Control register (10H) is set to 1, the ninth pixel is the same as the eighth. When bit 2 is set to 0, the ninth pixel is a background pixel.

400-Line Modes

The default alphanumeric modes of both the MCGA and the VGA have 400-line vertical resolution. The characters used in these modes are defined in an 8-by-16 matrix. On the VGA, the 8-by-16 characters are displayed in a 9-by-16 matrix, just as on an MDA or an EGA with a monochrome display.

Alphanumeric Character Definitions in RAM

The EGA, the VGA, the MCGA, the HGC+, and the InColor Card all have alphanumeric character generators that use character definition tables located in predesignated areas of RAM. In all these subsystems, this RAM lies within the address space of the video buffer. If you know how character generator RAM is mapped, you can write programs that read or update the alphanumeric character definition tables and thereby change the displayed alphanumeric character set.

EGA and VGA

In alphanumeric modes on the EGA and the VGA, the video buffer is organized as four parallel memory maps, just as in graphics modes. In alphanumeric modes, however, only maps 0 and 1 contain displayable data (see Figure 10-3). Even-numbered bytes (character codes) in the CPU's address space are located in map 0, and odd-numbered bytes (attribute bytes) are located in map 1. This mapping is invisible to the CPU; the CRTC internally translates odd addresses to offsets into map 1 and even addresses into references to map 0.

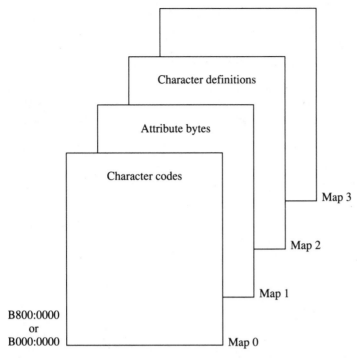

Figure 10-3. *Video RAM layout in EGA and VGA alphanumeric modes.*

The alphanumeric character generator uses a set of 256-character tables stored in map 2. The EGA supports four such tables (see Figure 10-4); the VGA supports eight (see Figure 10-5). Each table consists of 256 32-byte bit patterns, so the maximum height of the character matrix is 32 scan lines. When the displayed character matrix contains fewer than 32 lines, the character generator ignores the extra bytes in each character definition.

On the EGA, each of the four alphanumeric character definition tables starts at a 16 KB boundary. Since only 8 KB (256 characters × 32 bytes per character) are used, 8 KB of unused RAM follows each table. On the VGA, these unused areas in map 2 can contain additional character definitions. Of course, in writing an application that must run on both the EGA and the VGA, you should avoid using these extra tables because the EGA does not support them.

 On the IBM EGA, which may be equipped with less than 256 KB of video RAM, the number of character definition tables you can load into video RAM depends on the amount of RAM installed on the card. For example, without IBM's Graphics Memory Expansion Card, an IBM EGA has only 64 KB of video RAM, so each video memory map in alphanumeric modes contains only 16 KB, and only one character definition table will fit in map 2.

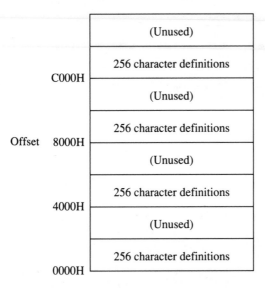

Figure 10-4. *Character generator RAM in EGA video memory map 2.*

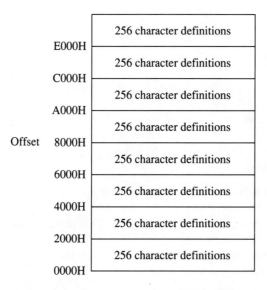

Figure 10-5. *Character generator RAM in VGA video memory map 2.*

HGC+

Character generator RAM on the HGC+ starts at B000:4000 and extends to the end of available video RAM at B000:FFFF (see Figure 10-6). You can fill this entire 48 KB area with character definitions. Each character definition is 16 bytes long, so a table that defines 256 characters occupies 4 KB. Thus, this RAM can hold 3072 character definitions.

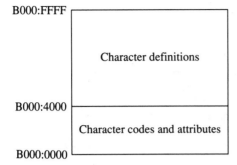

B000:FFFF

Character definitions

B000:4000

Character codes and attributes

B000:0000

Figure 10-6. *Video RAM layout in alphanumeric modes on the HGC+.*

If the HGC+ is configured so that video RAM above B000:8000 is masked out of the CPU address space (that is, bit 1 of the Configuration Switch at 3BFH is set to 0), then only the 16 KB of RAM between B000:4000 and B000:7FFF can be used for character definitions.

InColor Card

Character generator RAM occupies the same range of addresses on the InColor Card as on the HGC+, that is, B000:4000 through B000:FFFF. Also, each InColor character definition is 16 bytes long. Unlike the HGC+, however, the 16-color InColor Card uses all four bit planes in this range of addresses for character definitions (see Figure 10-7).

Because of this, you can control the value of each pixel in each character you define. You can also program the InColor Card so that different bit planes define different characters; when the characters are displayed, their attribute bytes select which bit plane is used. By loading each of the four bit planes with different character definitions, you can maintain as many as 12,288 (3072 × 4) character definitions in RAM. Or, to preserve compatibility with the HGC+, you can load all four bit planes with the same bit patterns.

In using both the EGA and the Hercules cards, be careful in changing from an alphanumeric mode that uses a RAM-based character definition table to a graphics mode. The same RAM that contains pixel data in graphics modes is used to store character definitions in alphanumeric modes. You can corrupt or erase your character definition tables by updating the video buffer in a graphics mode and then returning to an alphanumeric mode.

MCGA

Unlike the EGA and VGA, the MCGA has no parallel memory maps in which to store character definitions. Instead, alphanumeric character definitions are maintained in the 32 KB of video RAM between A000:0000 and A000:7FFF. You can store as many as four 8 KB character definition tables at A000:0000, A000:2000, A000:4000, and A000:6000 (see Figure 10-8).

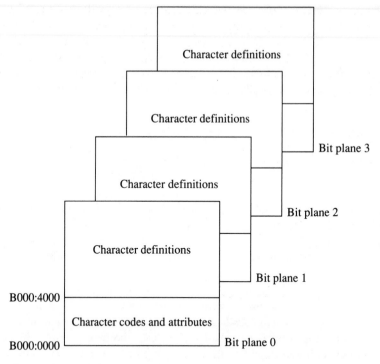

Figure 10-7. *Video RAM layout in alphanumeric modes on the Hercules InColor Card. Character definitions start at B000:4000 in all four bit planes.*

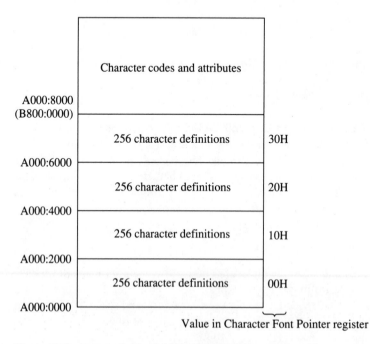

Figure 10-8. *Layout of video RAM in MCGA alphanumeric modes.*

The format of the MCGA's character definition tables is very different from that of any other tables discussed thus far. Each 8 KB table is divided into 16 512-byte lists of character codes and bit patterns (see Figure 10-9). Each list corresponds to one scan line of the characters being defined; the first list represents the bit patterns in the topmost scan line of each character, the second list corresponds to the second scan line, and so on (see Figure 10-10). Since there are 16 lists, the maximum height of a character is 16 lines.

```
           0  1  2  3  4  5  6  7  8  9  A  B  C  D  E  F   0123456789ABCDEF
A000:0400 00 00 01 7E 02 7E 03 00 04 00 05 00 06 00 07 00   ...¨.¯..........
A000:0410 08 FF 09 00 0A FF 0B 1E 0C 3C 0D 3F 0E 7F 0F 00   .........<.?....
A000:0420 10 C0 11 06 12 18 13 66 14 7F 15 C6 16 00 17 18   .......f........
A000:0430 18 18 19 18 1A 00 1B 00 1C 00 1D 00 1E 00 1F 00   ................
A000:0440 20 00 21 18 22 66 23 00 24 7C 25 00 26 38 27 30   .!."f#.$|%.&8'0
A000:0450 28 0C 29 30 2A 00 2B 00 2C 00 2D 00 2E 00 2F 00   (.)0*.+.,.-.../.
A000:0460 30 7C 31 18 32 7C 33 7C 34 0C 35 FE 36 38 37 FE   0|1.2|3|4.5.687.
A000:0470 38 7C 39 7C 3A 00 3B 00 3C 00 3D 00 3E 00 3F 7C   8|9|:.;.<.=.>.?|
A000:0480 40 00 41 10 42 FC 43 3C 44 F8 45 FE 46 FE 47 3C   @.A.B.C<D.E.F.G<
A000:0490 48 C6 49 3C 4A 1E 4B E6 4C F0 4D C6 4E C6 4F 38   H.I<J.K.L.M.N.O8
A000:04A0 50 FC 51 7C 52 FC 53 7C 54 7E 55 C6 56 C6 57 C6   P.Q|R.S|T¨U.V.W.
A000:04B0 58 C6 59 66 5A FE 5B 3C 5C 00 5D 3C 5E 6C 5F 00   X.YfZ.[<\.]<¨1_.
A000:04C0 60 18 61 00 62 E0 63 00 64 1C 65 00 66 38 67 00   `.a.b.c.d.e.f8g.
A000:04D0 68 E0 69 18 6A 06 6B E0 6C 38 6D 00 6E 00 6F 00   h.i.j.k.18m.n.o.
A000:04E0 70 00 71 00 72 00 73 00 74 10 75 00 76 00 77 00   p.q.r.s.t.u.v.w.
A000:04F0 78 00 79 00 7A 00 7B 0E 7C 18 7D 70 7E 76 7F 00   x.y.z.(.|.)p¨v..
A000:0500 80 3C 81 CC 82 18 83 38 84 CC 85 30 86 6C 87 00   .<.....8...0.1..
A000:0510 88 38 89 CC 8A 30 8B 66 8C 3C 8D 30 8E C6 8F 38   .8...0.f.<.0...8
A000:0520 90 60 91 00 92 3E 93 38 94 C6 95 30 96 78 97 30   .`...>.8...0.x.0
A000:0530 98 C6 99 C6 9A C6 9B 18 9C 6C 9D 66 9E CC 9F 1B   .........1.f...
A000:0540 A0 30 A1 18 A2 30 A3 30 A4 76 A5 00 A6 6C A7 6C   .0...0.0.v....1.1
A000:0550 A8 30 A9 00 AA 00 AB C0 AC C0 AD 18 AE 00 AF 00   .0.............
```

Figure 10-9. *One of 16 lists of character codes and bit patterns in MCGA character generator RAM. This table defines the bit patterns for the third scan line of each character. Character codes are in the even-numbered bytes. The odd-numbered bytes contain the corresponding bit patterns.*

```
           0  1  2  3  4  5  6  7  8  9  A  B  C  D  E  F   0123456789ABCDEF
A000:0000 00 00 01 00 02 00 03 00 04 00 05 00 06 00 07 00   ................
A000:0010 08 FF 09 00 0A FF 0B 00 0C 00 0D 00 0E 00 0F 00   ................

A000:0200 00 00 01 00 02 00 03 00 04 00 05 00 06 00 07 00   ................
A000:0210 08 FF 09 00 0A FF 0B 00 0C 00 0D 00 0E 00 0F 00   ................

A000:0400 00 00 01 7E 02 7E 03 00 04 00 05 00 06 00 07 00   ...¨.¯..........
A000:0410 08 FF 09 00 0A FF 0B 1E 0C 3C 0D 3F 0E 7F 0F 00   .........<.?....

A000:0600 00 00 01 81 02 FF 03 00 04 00 05 18 06 18 07 00   ................
A000:0610 08 FF 09 00 0A FF 0B 0E 0C 66 0D 33 0E 63 0F 18   .........f.3.c..

A000:0800 00 00 01 A5 02 DB 03 6C 04 10 05 3C 06 3C 07 00   .......1...<.<..
A000:0810 08 3F 09 00 0A FF 0B 1A 0C 66 0D 3C 0E 7F 0F 00   .......f.?....

A000:0A00 00 00 01 81 02 FF 03 FE 04 38 05 3C 06 7E 07 00   .........8.<.¨..
A000:0A10 08 FF 09 3C 0A C3 0B 32 0C 66 0D 30 0E 63 0F DB   ...<...2.f.0.c..

A000:0C00 00 00 01 81 02 FF 03 FE 04 7C 05 E7 06 FF 07 18   .........|......
A000:0C10 08 E7 09 66 0A 99 0B 78 0C 66 0D 30 0E 63 0F 3C   ...f...x.f.0.c.<

A000:0E00 00 00 01 BD 02 C3 03 FE 04 FE 05 E7 06 FF 07 3C   ...............<
A000:0E10 08 C3 09 42 0A BD 0B CC 0C 3C 0D 30 0E 63 0F E7   ...B.....<.0.c..

A000:1000 00 00 01 99 02 E7 03 FE 04 7C 05 E7 06 7E 07 3C   .........|...¨.<
A000:1010 08 C3 09 42 0A BD 0B CC 0C 18 0D 30 0E 63 0F 3C   ...B.......0.c.<

A000:1200 00 00 01 81 02 FF 03 7C 04 38 05 18 06 18 07 18   .......|.8......
A000:1210 08 E7 09 66 0A 99 0B CC 0C 7E 0D 70 0E 67 0F DB   ...f......¨.p.g..

A000:1400 00 00 01 81 02 FF 03 38 04 10 05 18 06 18 07 00   .......8........
A000:1410 08 FF 09 3C 0A C3 0B CC 0C 18 0D F0 0E E7 0F 18   ...<............

A000:1600 00 00 01 7E 02 7E 03 10 04 00 05 3C 06 3C 07 00   ...¨.¯.....<.<..
A000:1610 08 FF 09 00 0A FF 0B 78 0C 18 0D E0 0E E6 0F 18   .......x........
```

Figure 10-10. *MCGA character definitions for the first 12 scan lines of the first 16 characters. The top scan line for each character is defined starting at A000:0000, the second scan line starting at A000:0200, and so on. (Only the first 32 bytes of each 512-byte list are shown.)*

Updating Character Generator RAM

After you create a table of character definitions (discussed in Chapter 9), you must make the table accessible to the hardware character generator by properly locating it in the video buffer. One way to do this is to create the table in RAM (outside the video buffer) and then copy it to character generator RAM. You can also read the table directly from a disk file into character generator RAM. Either technique works on any of the video subsystems discussed here.

EGA and VGA

To copy a character definition table into video memory map 2, you must program both the Sequencer's Memory Mode register and its Map Mask register, as well as the Graphics Controller's Mode and Miscellaneous registers, to make memory map 2 directly addressable. You can then copy character definitions to any of the available table locations in map 2. After you update map 2, restore the Sequencer and Graphics Controller registers to values appropriate for the alphanumeric video mode you are using.

Listing 10-1a demonstrates how the Sequencer and Graphics Controller are programmed on both the EGA and the VGA to make character generator RAM in map 2 accessible. Listing 10-1b is the converse routine; it restores the Sequencer and Graphics Controller registers to their alphanumeric mode default values. You can use the routines in Listings 10-1a and 10-1b in a program that copies character definitions directly from a file into character generator RAM (as shown in Listings 10-2a and 10-2b).

```
                    TITLE   'Listing 10-1a'
                    NAME    CGenModeSet
                    PAGE    55,132

;
; Name:              CGenModeSet
;
;                    Direct access to EGA and VGA alpha character generator RAM
;
; Caller:            Microsoft C:
;
;                            void CGenModeSet ();
;

DGROUP              GROUP   _DATA

_TEXT               SEGMENT byte public 'CODE'
                    ASSUME  cs:_TEXT,ds:DGROUP

                    PUBLIC  _CGenModeSet
_CGenModeSet        PROC    near

                    push    bp                  ; preserve caller registers
                    mov     bp,sp
                    push    si
```

Listing 10-1a. *Using character generator RAM on the EGA and VGA.*   *(continued)*

Listing 10-1a. *Continued.*

```
; Program the Sequencer

                cli                     ; disable interrupts
                mov     dx,3C4h         ; Sequencer port address
                mov     si,offset DGROUP:SeqParms
                mov     cx,4

L01:            lodsw                   ; AH := value for Sequencer register
                                        ; AL := register number
                out     dx,ax           ; program the register
                loop    L01
                sti                     ; enable interrupts

; Program the Graphics Controller

                mov     dl,0CEh         ; DX := 3CEH (Graphics Controller port
                                        ;                   address)
                mov     si,offset DGROUP:GCParms
                mov     cx,3

L02:            lodsw                   ; program the Graphics Controller
                out     dx,ax
                loop    L02

                pop     si
                pop     bp
                ret

_CGenModeSet    ENDP

_TEXT           ENDS


_DATA           SEGMENT word public 'DATA'

; Format of the parameters is:  Lo-order byte:  Register number
;                               Hi-order byte:  Value for reg

SeqParms        DW      0100h           ; synchronous reset
                DW      0402h           ; CPU writes only to map 2
                DW      0704h           ; sequential addressing
                DW      0300h           ; clear synchronous reset

GCParms         DW      0204h           ; select map 2 for CPU reads
                DW      0005h           ; disable odd-even addressing
                DW      0006h           ; map starts at A000:0000

_DATA           ENDS

                END
```

```
                    TITLE    'Listing 10-1b'
                    NAME     CGenModeClear
                    PAGE     55,132
;
; Name:              CGenModeClear
;
;                    Restore EGA or VGA alphanumeric mode after accessing
;                     character generator RAM
;
; Caller:            Microsoft C:
;
;                            void CGenModeClear();
;

DGROUP             GROUP    _DATA

_TEXT              SEGMENT byte public 'CODE'
                   ASSUME  cs:_TEXT,ds:DGROUP

                   PUBLIC  _CGenModeClear
_CGenModeClear     PROC     near

                   push     bp              ; preserve caller registers
                   mov      bp,sp
                   push     si

; Program the Sequencer

                   cli                      ; disable interrupts
                   mov      dx,3C4h         ; Sequencer port address
                   mov      si,offset DGROUP:SeqParms
                   mov      cx,4

L01:               lodsw                    ; AH := value for Sequencer register
                                            ; AL := register number
                   out      dx,ax           ; program the register
                   loop     L01
                   sti                      ; enable interrupts

; Program the Graphics Controller

                   mov      dl,0CEh         ; DX := 3CEH (Graphics Controller port
                                            ;                       address)
                   mov      si,offset DGROUP:GCParms
                   mov      cx,3

L02:               lodsw                    ; program the Graphics Controller
                   out      dx,ax
                   loop     L02

                   mov      ah,0Fh          ; AH := INT 10H function number
                   int      10h             ; get video mode
                   cmp      al,7
                   jne      L03             ; jump if not monochrome mode

                   mov      ax,0806h        ; program Graphics Controller
                   out      dx,ax           ;  to start map at B000:0000
```

Listing 10-1b. *Restoring character generator RAM on the EGA and VGA.*   *(continued)*

Listing 10-1b. *Continued.*

```
L03:                pop     si
                    pop     bp
                    ret

_CGenModeClear      ENDP

_TEXT               ENDS

_DATA               SEGMENT word public 'DATA'

; Format of the parameters is:  Lo-order byte:  Register number
;                                Hi-order byte:  Value for reg

SeqParms            DW      0100h           ; synchronous reset
                    DW      0302h           ; CPU writes to maps 0 and 1
                    DW      0304h           ; odd-even addressing
                    DW      0300h           ; clear synchronous reset

GCParms             DW      0004h           ; select map 0 for CPU reads
                    DW      1005h           ; enable odd-even addressing
                    DW      0E06h           ; map starts at B800:0000

_DATA               ENDS

                    END
```

```
                    TITLE   'Listing 10-2a'
                    NAME    CGenRead1
                    PAGE    55,132

;
; Name:      CGenRead1
;
;            Read 256 character definitions into EGA or VGA character RAM
;
; Caller:    Microsoft C:
;
;                    void CGenRead1(f,p);
;
;                    int     f;      /* file handle */
;                    int     p;      /* bytes per character definition */
;

ARGf                EQU     [bp+4]
ARGp                EQU     [bp+6]

CGenRAMSeg          EQU     0A000h          ; start of character generator RAM
CGenRAMOffset       EQU     0
CGenDefSize         EQU     32              ; size in bytes of one character def

_TEXT               SEGMENT byte public 'CODE'
                    ASSUME  cs:_TEXT

                    PUBLIC  _CGenRead1
```

Listing 10-2a. *Loading character definitions on an EGA or VGA.*   *(continued)*

Listing 10-2a. *Continued.*

```
_CGenRead1      PROC    near

                push    bp                  ; preserve registers
                mov     bp,sp
                push    ds
                push    si
                push    di

; zero character definition RAM

                mov     di,CGenRAMSeg
                mov     es,di               ; ES := char gen RAM segment
                mov     di,CGenRAMOffset

                mov     cx,256*CGenDefSize/2    ; CX := number of words to zero
                xor     ax,ax
                rep     stosw

; load character definitions from file

                mov     cx,256              ; assume 256 character defs in the file

                mov     bx,ARGf             ; BX := file handle
                mov     si,ARGp             ; CX := bytes per character definition
                push    es
                pop     ds
                mov     dx,CGenRAMOffset    ; DS:DX -> start of character gen RAM

L01:            xchg    cx,si               ; CX := number of bytes to read
                                            ; SI := loop counter
                mov     ah,3Fh              ; AH := INT 21H function number
                int     21h
                add     dx,CGenDefSize      ; DS:DX -> next character def in RAM
                xchg    cx,si               ; CX := loop counter
                                            ; SI := number of bytes to read
                loop    L01

                pop     di                  ; restore registers and exit
                pop     si
                pop     ds
                pop     bp
                ret

_CGenRead1      ENDP

_TEXT           ENDS

                END
```

```
/* Listing 10-2b */

#include        <fcntl.h>
#include        <stdio.h>

main(argc,argv)
int     argc;
char    **argv;
{
        int     i;
        int     FileHandle;
        int     Points;                 /* bytes per character definition */
        long    lseek();
        long    FileSize;

        if (argc != 2)                  /* verify filename */
        {
          printf( "\nNo filename specified\n" );
          exit( 1 );
        }

        FileHandle = open( argv[1], O_RDONLY );         /* open the file */

        if ( FileHandle == -1 )
        {
          printf( "\nCan't open '%s'\n", argv[1] );
          exit( 2 );
        }

        CGenModeSet();          /* make character generator RAM addressable */

        FileSize = lseek( FileHandle, 0L, SEEK_END );   /* get file size */
        Points = FileSize / 256;                /* determine character size */

        lseek( FileHandle, 0L, SEEK_SET );      /* start of file */

        CGenRead1( FileHandle, Points );

        CGenModeClear();        /* restore previous alphanumeric mode */
}
```

Listing 10-2b. *Calling CGenRead1 from a C program.*

A faster and more portable way to load character definitions into RAM is to use
INT 10H function 11H with AL = 0 (see Listings 10-3a and 10-3b). When you use
the INT 10H function, you can selectively update any portion of a table in map 2
by choosing appropriate values for DX (the character offset into the table) and CX
(the number of character definitions to update). To use this video BIOS function,
you must first store the character definition table in an intermediate buffer. This
technique consumes more memory than reading character definitions directly
from disk, but it results in faster code.

```
                    TITLE    'Listing 10-3a'
                    NAME     CGenRead2
                    PAGE     55,132
;
; Name:             CGenRead2
;
;                   Use video BIOS to read 256 character definitions into EGA or VGA
;                    character RAM
;
; Caller:           Microsoft C:
;
;                            void CGenRead2(f);
;
;                            int     f;      /* file handle */
;


ARGf                EQU      [bp+4]

DGROUP              GROUP    _DATA

_TEXT               SEGMENT byte public 'CODE'
                    ASSUME  cs:_TEXT

                    PUBLIC   _CGenRead2
_CGenRead2          PROC     near

                    push     bp              ; preserve registers
                    mov      bp,sp

; load character definitions from file

                    mov      cx,256*32       ; assume 256 32-byte character defs
                                             ;  in the file
                    mov      bx,ARGf         ; BX := file handle
                    mov      dx,offset DGROUP:CharBuf ; DS:DX -> start of buffer

                    mov      ah,3Fh          ; AH := INT 21H function number
                    int      21h             ; read the file
                                             ; AX := number of bytes read

; call video BIOS to load character generator RAM

                    push     ds
                    pop      es
                    mov      bp,offset DGROUP:CharBuf   ; ES:BP -> character defs
                    mov      bl,0            ; BL := block of char gen RAM to load
                    mov      bh,ah           ; AH := bytes per character
                                             ;         (number of bytes read) / 256
                    mov      cx,256          ; number of character defs to store
                    xor      dx,dx           ; first character number
                    mov      ax,1100h        ; AH := 11H (INT 10H function number)
                                             ; AL := 0 (subfunction number)
                    int      10h

                    pop      bp              ; restore BP and exit
                    ret

_CGenRead2          ENDP
```

Listing 10-3a. *Using the BIOS to load character definitions.*   *(continued)*

Listing 10-3a. *Continued.*

```
_TEXT              ENDS

_DATA              SEGMENT word public 'DATA'

CharBuf            DB      256*32 dup(?)

_DATA              ENDS

                   END
```

```
/* Listing 10-3b */

#include           <fcntl.h>

main(argc,argv)
int     argc;
char    **argv;
{
        int     i;
        int     FileHandle;

        if (argc != 2)                                  /* verify filename */
        {
          printf( "\nNo filename specified\n" );
          exit( 1 );
        }

        FileHandle = open( argv[1], O_RDONLY );         /* open the file */

        if ( FileHandle == -1 )
        {
          printf( "\nCan't open '%s'\n", argv[1] );
          exit( 2 );
        }

        CGenRead2( FileHandle );        /* call video BIOS to load file into */
                                        /*  character generator RAM */
}
```

Listing 10-3b. *Calling CGenRead2 from a C program.*

The INT 10H function 11H services can also update character generator RAM from
the character tables in the ROM BIOS. To use one of the ROM BIOS character definition tables, call INT 10H function 11H with AL = 1 (for 8-by-14 character definitions) or AL = 2 (for 8-by-8 definitions). (See Listing 10-4.)

```
        mov    ax,1102h      ; AH := INT 10H function number
                             ; AL := 02h (load ROM BIOS 8x8 characters)
        mov    bl,0          ; BL := character generator RAM bank
        int    10h           ; load alphanumeric character set
```

Listing 10-4. *Using a ROM BIOS character definition table.*

HGC+

Moving a character definition table into RAM is easier on the HGC+, because memory addressing is simpler. Character generator RAM is mapped linearly, starting at B000:4000. Since each 256-character table occupies 4 KB (256×16), subsequent 256-character tables start at B000:5000, B000:6000, and so on.

Because HGC+ memory has no bit planes, you can access character generator RAM as easily as any other system RAM. You can, for example, use a single REP MOVSB instruction to move bit patterns into character generator RAM from elsewhere in system RAM, or you can read a character definition table directly into RAM from a disk file. For example, you can modify Listing 10-2a to read a file directly into HGC+ character generator RAM by changing the values of CGenRAMSeg to B000H, CGenStartOffset to 4000H, and CGenDefSize to 16.

InColor Card

Although the InColor Card uses all four bit planes to store character definitions, you can use virtually the same routine to copy bit patterns into its character generator RAM that you use on the HGC+. The only difference is that you can select which of the four bit planes to update. Do this by setting bits 4 through 7 of the Plane Mask register (18H) to write-protect one or more of the bit planes. For compatibility with the HGC+, set these four bits to 0 so that all four bit planes contain the same bit patterns.

MCGA

As on the Hercules adapters, character generator RAM on the MCGA is mapped linearly in the video buffer. Thus, you can update MCGA character definitions simply by writing the bit patterns in the appropriate format in the character definition tables.

If you update the MCGA character definition tables directly, however, your program must store bit patterns and character codes in the format expected by the MCGA character generator. It is usually better to use INT 10H function 11H to copy character definitions into MCGA character generator RAM. This video BIOS function translates character definition tables from the linear format used on the EGA and VGA into the formatted lists used on the MCGA.

The MCGA is different from the other video subsystems discussed here in that its alphanumeric character generator does not fetch bit patterns from the tables at A000:0000 as it generates characters. Instead, the character generator uses two internal character definition tables, called font pages. To display the characters from one of the four tables in video RAM, you must load the table into one of the character generator's font pages. Listing 10-5 shows how this is done.

```
                    TITLE     'Listing 10-5'
                    NAME      SetFontPages
                    PAGE      55,132


;
; Name:             SetFontPages
;
;                   Update MCGA Font Pages
;
; Caller:           Microsoft C:
;
;                           void SetFontPages(n0,n1);
;
;                           int    n0,n1;  /* font page values */
;

ARGn0               EQU       [bp+4]
ARGn1               EQU       [bp+6]


_TEXT               SEGMENT byte public 'CODE'
                    ASSUME  cs:_TEXT


                    PUBLIC  _SetFontPages
_SetFontPages       PROC    near

                    push    bp                  ; preserve caller registers
                    mov     bp,sp

                    mov     ax,1103h            ; AH := INT 10H function number
                                                ; AL := 3 (Set Block Specifier)
                    mov     bl,ARGn1            ; BL := value for bits 2-3
                    shl     bl,1
                    shl     bl,1                ; BL bits 2-3 := n1
                    or      bl,ARGn0            ; BL bits 0-1 := n0
                    int     10h                 ; load font pages

                    pop     bp
                    ret

_SetFontPages       ENDP

_TEXT               ENDS

                    END
```

Listing 10-5. *Loading font pages on an MCGA.*

Thus, displaying a new alphanumeric character set on the MCGA is a two-step
process. First, you store character definition tables in one or more of the four 8 KB
blocks of video RAM reserved for this purpose. Then you update the character
generator's font pages to display the characters.

Using RAM-based Character Sets

When you use characters defined in a RAM-based table, you must choose how the
alphanumeric character generator is to decode the character codes and attributes
stored in the displayed portion of the video buffer. Using the usual 256-character

ASCII set, with 8-bit character codes and 8-bit attributes, is simplest. However, to display more than 256 different characters at once or to switch rapidly between character sets, you must use a wider range of "extended" character codes and a different set of attributes.

ASCII Character Sets

The simplest way to customize alphanumeric characters is to use 8-bit ASCII character codes and attributes with a RAM-based character definition table. Because there are only 256 ASCII character codes, you can display only one 256-character set at a time. However, the character codes and attribute bytes stored in the displayed portion of the video buffer retain their usual format, so software that knows nothing about the RAM-based character definitions can run unchanged while displaying the RAM-based character set.

EGA, VGA, and MCGA

Whenever you select an alphanumeric video mode using the video BIOS, the alphanumeric character generator is configured to display the characters defined in the first table in character generator RAM. Thus, to display a different set of ASCII characters, all you need do is update the table. As described above, INT 10H function 11H provides a convenient mechanism for doing this. This same BIOS function also lets you display the 256 characters defined in any of the other character definition tables as described later in this chapter.

HGC+ and InColor Card

When you power up an HGC+ or an InColor Card, the alphanumeric character generator uses the ROM-based character definition table by default. To display a different ASCII character set, configure the alphanumeric character generator to use the RAM-based table (see Listing 10-6) and then load a character definition table into video RAM at B000:4000.

To do this, set bit 0 of the adapter's xMode register (14H) to 1. This causes the adapter to display the characters defined in the table in RAM at B000:4000. Also, set bit 0 of the Configuration Switch register (3BFH) to 1 to make character generator RAM addressable at B000:4000. (This configuration is called "4K Ram-Font mode" in Hercules documentation.) After you update character generator RAM, you can protect it from subsequent modification by resetting bit 0 of the Configuration Switch register.

```
        mov     dx,3B4h
        mov     ax,0114h        ; AH bit 0 := 1 (enable RAM character
                                ;                     generator)
                                ; AL := 14h (xMode register number)
        out     dx,ax
```

(continued)

Listing 10-6. *Configuring an HGC+ or InColor Card for updating character generator RAM.*

Listing 10-6. *Continued.*

```
        mov     dl,0BFh         ; DX := 3BFh (Config Switch register)
        mov     al,1            ; AL bit 0 := 1 (make RAM at B000:4000
                                ;   addressable)
        out     dx,al

        .
        .                       ; (update character generator RAM)
        .

        mov     dx,3BFh         ; DX := 3BFh (Config Switch register)
        mov     al,0            ; AL bit 0 := 0 (exclude RAM at
                                ;   B000:4000 from memory map)
        out     dx,al
```

Updating character generator RAM is more complicated on the InColor Card because all four bit planes are used for character definitions. The complexity lies in the way colors are displayed for characters defined in the bit planes. A character's color is determined not only by its foreground and background attributes, but also by the bit planes used to define its pixel pattern.

The InColor Card combines the pixel values in a character definition (in character generator RAM) with the character's foreground and background attributes (in the displayed portion of the video buffer) to produce a 4-bit attribute for every pixel in the character. The logic used is:

```
(pixel_value AND foreground_attribute) OR

(NOT pixel_value AND background_attribute)
```

In the example in Figure 10-11, one of the pixels in a character has a value of 2 (0010B) in the character definition table. The character's attribute byte in the video buffer specifies a foreground value of 0 and a background value of 7 (0111B). The InColor Card thus displays this pixel with an attribute of (2 AND 0) OR (NOT 2 AND 7), or 5.

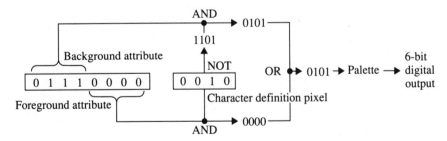

Figure 10-11. *InColor foreground color attribute decoding using RAM-based character definitions (8-bit character codes). The pixel value in the character definition and both attributes in the character's attribute byte all contribute to foreground attribute decoding.*

Using colors on the InColor Card is simpler if you load all four bit planes with identical bit patterns so that all pixels in the character definitions have the value

0FH (1111B). Then a character's foreground and background attributes depend solely on the values in its attribute byte. Alternatively, you can specify a foreground attribute of 0FH (1111B) and a background attribute of 0 for every character in the video buffer. In this case, the displayed colors depend solely on the pixel values in the character definitions.

A more practical use of the InColor Card's character definition RAM is to load each bit plane with a different character definition table. Then each bit in a character's foreground attribute acts as a mask to select a different character set. Of course, a 4-bit foreground attribute is still generated, as in Figure 10-11, so in effect each character set is associated with the color that corresponds to its bit plane. You can, of course, display the character sets in any colors you want by programming the palette registers.

To load the bit planes separately, use the high-order nibble in the Plane Mask register (18H) to write-protect the bit planes each time you load a different character set. This permits you to use different foreground attributes to display the different character sets. For example, if all four bit planes contain different character sets, you can select each of the four character sets by using the foreground attributes 1, 2, 4, and 8.

Extended Character Sets

All of the video subsystems discussed in this chapter have enough character generator RAM to store definitions for more than 256 characters, so they all provide a way for the character generator to recognize extended character codes larger than the usual eight bits.

EGA and VGA

On the EGA and the VGA, the usual range of 256 ASCII codes is doubled by using bit 3 of a character's attribute byte to designate one of the character definition tables in map 2 (see Figure 10-12). In this way, 512 different characters can be displayed in an alphanumeric mode.

Normally, the value of bit 3 of a character's attribute byte does not affect the character set displayed. This is why: The value of this bit selects one of two bit fields in the Sequencer Character Map Select register. In turn, the value in each of these two bit fields designates one of the available character definition tables in RAM. When the video BIOS establishes a video mode, it loads a default set of character definitions into the first character definition table in map 2 and clears both bit fields in the Character Map Select register. Thus, default alphanumeric characters are defined by the bit patterns in the first table in map 2, regardless of the value of bit 3 of the attribute bytes of the characters displayed.

Changing the value in the Character Map Select register, however, changes the character definition tables associated with bit 3 of each character's attribute byte. If two different values appear in the bit fields in the Character Map Select register, the value of bit 3 designates one of two different character definition tables.

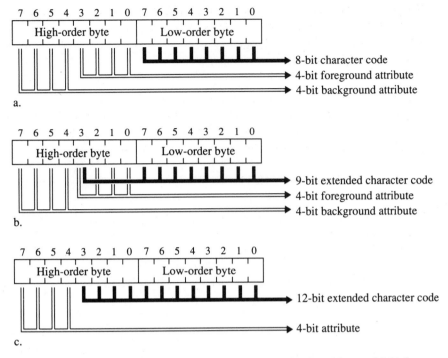

a.

b.

c.

Figure 10-12. *Character codes and attributes. Figure 10-12a shows the usual 8-bit format. Figure 10-12b shows the extended 9-bit format used on the EGA, VGA, and MCGA. Figure 10-12c shows the extended 12-bit format used on the HGC+ and InColor Card.*

For example, in Figure 10-13, bit 3 is set to 1, so bits 2, 3, and 5 of the Character Map Select register designate which character definition table to use. (This example pertains to the VGA; on the EGA, only bits 2 and 3 of the Character Map Select value would be meaningful.)

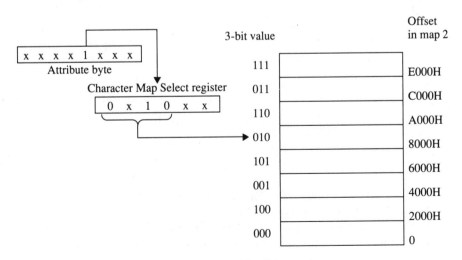

Figure 10-13. *Function of the VGA Character Map Select register.*

Listing 10-7 illustrates two methods of updating this register. Although the technique of using an INT 10H function call generally requires less code and is more portable, you might prefer to program the Sequencer directly in applications that require rapid switching between character sets.

```
; using the video BIOS

        mov     ax,1103h        ; AH := INT 10H function number
                                ; AL := 3
        mov     bl,CharMapValue ; BL := value for Character Map Select register
        int     10h


; programming the register directly

        mov     dx,3C4h         ; DX := Sequencer I/O port
        mov     ax,100h         ; AH bit 1 := 0 (synchronous reset)
                                ; AL := 0 (Sequencer Reset register number)
        cli                     ; disable interrupts
        out     dx,ax           ; reset Sequencer

        mov     ah,CharMapValue ; AH := value for Character Map Select register
        mov     al,3            ; AL := 3 (Char Map Select register number)
        out     dx,ax           ; update this register

        mov     ax,300h         ; AH bit 1 := 1 (clear synchronous reset)
                                ; AL := 0 (Reset register number)
        out     dx,ax           ; clear the reset
        sti                     ; enable interrupts
```

Listing 10-7. *Programming the Sequencer Character Map Select register on the EGA and VGA.*

If both bit fields in the Character Map Select register contain the same value, the value of bit 3 of a character's attribute byte does not affect which character set is used. If the bit fields designate different character definition tables, then the value of bit 3 of each character's attribute byte selects between two different character sets. Keep in mind, however, that bit 3 is also part of each character's 4-bit foreground attribute. When bit 3 of a character's foreground attribute is set to 0, the character's displayed color is taken from one of the first eight palette registers (0000B through 0111B). When bit 3 is set to 1, the color derives from one of the second eight palette registers (1000B through 1111B).

Thus, the two 256-character sets selected by bit 3 are displayed with two different sets of eight palette register values. This is handy if you want to associate a particular set of colors with a character set. Otherwise, you might prefer to load the second eight palette registers with the same set of values as the first eight so that the value of bit 3 of a character's attribute byte has no effect on its displayed color. Another technique is to mask bit 3 of the foreground attribute by zeroing bit 3 of the Attribute Controller's Color Plane Enable register, as in Listing 10-8. Because the value in the Color Plane Enable register masks the 4-bit attribute value, zeroing bit 3 in this register allows only the first eight palette registers to be referenced, regardless of the value of bit 3 in a character's attribute byte.

```
mov     ax,1000h           ; AH := 10H (INT 10H function number)
                           ; AL := 0 (set specified register)
mov     bx,0712h           ; BH := 0111b (Color Plane Enable value)
                           ; BL := 12H (Color Plane Enable reg number)
int     10h                ; update Color Plane Enable register
```

Listing 10-8. *Zeroing bit 3 of the Color Plane Enable register. This causes bit 3 of a character's attribute byte to have no effect on its displayed attribute.*

MCGA

The MCGA supports 8-bit and 9-bit character codes with the same BIOS interface as the EGA and VGA, although the hardware implementation is different. On the MCGA, the two character definition tables selected by bit 3 of a character's attribute byte are the ones in the MCGA's two internal font pages. Although you can load the font pages by programming the MCGA's Character Generator Interface register (12H), Character Font Pointer register (13H), and Number of Characters to Load register (14H), it is easier to use INT 10H function 11H with AL = 3.

As on the EGA and VGA, bit 3 of a character's attribute byte does double duty as part of the 9-bit character code as well as the high-order bit of the character's foreground attribute. If you want to use the same colors for both 256-character sets, you can call INT 10H function 10H to store the same set of color values in the second eight video DAC color registers as you do in the first eight. You can also call INT 10H function 10H to mask bit 3 out of alphanumeric attribute decoding (see Listing 10-8).

HGC+ and InColor Card

On the HGC+ and the InColor Cards, you can configure the character generator to regard the four low-order bits of each character's attribute byte as part of the character code. Do this by setting both bit 2 and bit 1 of the xMode register to 1. (Hercules calls this configuration "48K RamFont mode.")

By using 12-bit character codes, you can display all characters defined anywhere in the Hercules adapter's 48 KB of character generator RAM. In practice, you can regard all 48 KB of character generator RAM as one continuous character definition table. However, in some applications, you might find it more convenient to think of character generator RAM as a set of twelve 256-character tables, where the four high-order bits of the character code designate one of the tables, and the eight low-order bits designate a character definition within a table.

When 12 bits are used as an extended character code, only bits 4 through 7 of the high-order byte specify a character's attribute (see Figure 10-12c). The attributes that Hercules assigned to these bits differ somewhat from the usual monochrome display attributes (see Figure 10-14).

Attribute Bit	Enable Blink Bit = 1 (blink enabled)	Enable Blink Bit = 0 (blink disabled)
7	High-intensity	Boldface
6	Blink	Reverse
5	Overstrike	No overstrike
4	Underline	No underline

Figure 10-14. *Extended attribute set on the HGC+ and the InColor Card.*

When using 12-bit character codes on the HGC+ and the InColor Card, you can specify the scan line on which the overstrike and underscore attributes appear. Bits 0 through 3 of the Underscore register (15H) control the position of the underscore. Bits 0 through 3 of the Overstrike register (16H) control the position of the overstrike. On the InColor Card, you can also control the displayed color of the underscore and overstrike by storing a value between 1 and 0FH in bits 4 through 7 of the corresponding control register.

As on the HGC+, the 12-bit character codes on the InColor Card designate locations in the character definition tables. Attribute decoding is more complicated on the InColor Card, however (see Figure 10-15). The 4-bit foreground attribute generated for each pixel in a character is derived by combining the character's 4-bit attribute with the pixel's value in the character definition table.

MDA-compatible Attributes (Exception register bit 5 = 1)		
	Enable Blink On	Enable Blink Off
Foreground	(pixel value) OR (background)	(pixel value) XOR (background)
Background	0 if bit 7 of attribute = 0	0 if bit 6 of attribute = 0
	8 if bit 7 of attribute = 1	0FH if bit 6 of attribute = 1
Color Attributes (Exception register bit 5 = 0)		
Foreground	(pixel value) AND (NOT attribute)	
Background	0	

Figure 10-15. *InColor Card color attribute decoding using 12-bit character codes.*

As was the case when using 8-bit character codes, the peculiar interaction of character attributes with the pixel values in the character definition table makes controlling colors difficult. To simplify matters, you can store the same character definitions in all four bit planes when using color attribute decoding; this allows each character's 4-bit attribute to specify all 16 colors. When using MDA-compatible attributes, you can store the same bit patterns in bit planes 0 through 2 and zero bit plane 3. Again, this allows each character's 4-bit attribute to completely control the displayed attributes.

If you elect to store different character definition tables in each bit plane, each of a character's attribute bits can select one of the bit planes. Again, you should program the palette registers carefully so that characters from different bit planes are displayed with appropriate colors.

Compatibility Problems with Extended Character Codes

Most PC and PS/2 programs, including the BIOS, MS-DOS, and most commercially available applications, expect you to use 8-bit ASCII character codes. This means you can update character generator RAM with an 8-bit ASCII character set in a different font, but you cannot take advantage of the extended 9-bit or 12-bit character codes supported by IBM and Hercules.

If you use the INT 10H interface to display characters with extended character codes, you must be careful when you use certain ROM BIOS functions. For example, INT 10H function 0AH, which stores an 8-bit character code in the video buffer, is not very useful for writing characters with a 9-bit or a 12-bit extended character code. On the other hand, you can use INT 10H function 9, which handles a 16-bit character code and attribute combination, to process extended character codes and attributes.

When you run an application that uses extended character codes, you can encounter problems when your application interacts inadvertently with software that doesn't recognize the different character-attribute format. Consider what might happen if a RAM-resident utility program popped up in the middle of your application without being "aware" that you were using extended character codes. When the utility program placed 8-bit character codes and attributes in the buffer, the alphanumeric character generator would interpret them as extended character codes and attributes. The results would probably be unusable.

Changing the Displayed Character Matrix

There is another dimension to customizing a RAM-based character definition table: You can control the height of the character matrix in which characters are displayed. The height of the displayed character matrix determines how many rows of characters appear on the screen. For example, a 350-line display accommodates 43 rows of 8-by-8 characters but only 25 rows of 8-by-14 characters.

With all of the subsystems discussed in this chapter, you can vary the displayed height of alphanumeric characters by programming the CRT Controller to display characters the same size as the characters defined in character generator RAM. Thus, to display 8-by-8 characters on a 350-line display, you place 8-by-8 character definitions into character generator RAM and then program the CRTC to display characters that are 8 pixels high.

On the EGA and the VGA, you can perform both these tasks by calling INT 10H function 11H, although in some situations you may prefer to update the character definitions or program the CRTC explicitly. Hercules adapters, of course, have no ROM BIOS, so you must do the work yourself.

EGA

Consider how you would display 43 rows of 8-by-8 characters in an EGA alphanumeric mode with 350-line vertical resolution, as in Listing 10-9. In this example, the call to INT 10H function 11H with AL = 12H copies the ROM's 8-by-8 character set (normally used in 200-line video modes) into the first of the four tables in map 2 and then calculates the proper CRTC register values based on the values of POINTS and ROWS in the BIOS Video Display Data Area.

```
; establish 80x25 alphanumeric mode (350-line vertical resolution)

        mov     ax,3            ; AH := 0 (INT 10H function number)
        int     10h             ; AL := 3 (80x25 16-color mode)

; load video BIOS 8x8 characters into alphanumeric character generator

        mov     ax,1112h        ; AH := INT 10H function number
                                ; AL := 8x8 character set load
        mov     bl,0            ; BL := block to load
        int     10h             ; load 8x8 characters into RAM

; set cursor position in character matrix

        mov     ax,40h
        mov     es,ax           ; ES -> video BIOS data area
        mov     dx,es:[63h]     ; DX := CRTC address port from 0040:0063
                                ;   (3B4H or 3D4H)
        mov     ax,060Ah        ; AH := 6 (Cursor Start value)
                                ; AL := 0AH (Cursor Start reg number)
        out     dx,ax           ; update CRTC Cursor Start register

        mov     ax,000Bh        ; AH := 0 (Cursor End value)
                                ; AL := 0BH (Cursor End reg number)
        out     dx,ax           ; update CRTC Cursor End register

; use alternate video BIOS print screen routine

        mov     ah,12h          ; AH := INT 10H function number
        mov     bl,20h          ; BL := subfunction number
        int     10h             ; update INT 5 vector (print screen)
```

Listing 10-9. *Establishing an 80-by-43 alphanumeric mode on an EGA.*

INT 10H function 11H calls INT 10H function 1 to set the position of the alphanumeric cursor in the displayed character matrix. As described in Chapter 3, the EGA BIOS version of INT 10H function 1 computes this cursor position incorrectly, leading to an improperly displayed cursor. Therefore, the routine in Listing 10-9 updates the CRTC Cursor Start and Cursor End registers directly.

 If your program changes the number of displayed character rows, it should also call INT 10H function 12H to select the EGA BIOS's alternate print screen routine. This routine functions identically to the one in the motherboard BIOS except that it uses the Video Display Data Area value ROWS to determine how many lines to print. (The motherboard BIOS routine disregards ROWS and always prints 25 lines.)

VGA

You can also use INT 10H function 11H on the VGA to establish an alphanumeric mode with a nondefault character matrix (see Listing 10-10). On the VGA, you set the vertical resolution of the video mode using INT 10H function 12H (with BL = 30H) before calling function 11H. Also, the cursor emulation computations are performed properly in the VGA BIOS, so no extra code is required to avoid cursor emulation on the VGA.

```
; establish 80x25 alphanumeric mode with 400-line vertical resolution

        mov     ax,1202h        ; AH := 12h (INT 10H function number)
                                ; AL := 2 (select 400 scan lines)
        mov     bl,30h          ; subfunction number
        int     10h

        mov     ax,3            ; AH := 0 (INT 10H function number)
        int     10h             ; AL := 3 (80x25 16-color mode)

; load video BIOS 8x8 characters into alphanumeric character generator

        mov     ax,1112h        ; AH := INT 10H function number
                                ; AL := 8x8 character set load
        mov     bl,0            ; BL := block to load
        int     10h             ; load 8x8 characters into RAM
```

Listing 10-10. *Establishing an 80-by-50 alphanumeric mode on a VGA.*

MCGA

The MCGA can only display characters with 2, 4, 6, 8, 10, 12, 14, or 16 scan lines. (This is a limitation of the MCGA's Memory Controller.) To change the displayed character matrix, use INT 10H function 11H to load a new character set into the character generator. Then program the Scan Lines per Character register (09H) with a value from 0 through 7; if the value is n, the number of scan lines displayed in the character matrix is $(n + 1) \times 2$. Listing 10-11 shows how to set up an 8-by-10 character matrix using the MCGA's 400-line vertical resolution to produce 40 rows of 80 characters.

```
; establish 80x25 alphanumeric mode

        mov     ax,3            ; AH := 0 (INT 10H function number)
                                ; AL := 3 (80x25 16-color mode)
        int     10h

; zero the bit patterns in character generator RAM

        mov     di,0A000h
        mov     es,di
        xor     di,di           ; ES:DI -> character generator RAM
        xor     ax,ax           ; AH := 0 (bit pattern)
                                ; AL := 0 (initial character code)
        mov     cx,256*16       ; CX := number of words
```

Listing 10-11. *Establishing an 80-by-40 alphanumeric mode on an MCGA.*   *(continued)*

Listing 10-11. *Continued.*

```
L01:    stosw                   ; store character code and zero
        inc     al              ; AL := next character code
        loop    L01

; load video BIOS 8x8 characters into alphanumeric character generator

        mov     ax,1102h        ; AH := INT 10H function number
                                ; AL := 8x8 character set load
        mov     bl,0            ; BL := block to load
        int     10h             ; load 8x8 characters into RAM

        mov     ax,1103h        ; AH := INT 10H function number
                                ; AL := character generator load
        mov     bl,0            ; BL := blocks to load
        int     10h             ; load characters into character generator

; program CRT Controller to display 8x10 characters

        mov     dx,3D4h         ; DX := MCGA I/O port address
        mov     ax,409h         ; AL := 9 (register number)
                                ; AH := 4 (value for register)
        out     dx,ax           ; update Scan Lines register

        mov     al,0Ah          ; AL := 0AH (register number)
        out     dx,ax           ; update Cursor Start register

        mov     al,0Bh          ; AL := 0BH (register number)
        out     dx,ax           ; update Cursor End register

; update status variables in video BIOS data segment

        mov     ax,40h
        mov     ds,ax           ; DS -> video BIOS data segment

        mov     word ptr ds:[4Ch],80*40*2 ; update CRT_LEN in BIOS data area
        mov     byte ptr ds:[84h],40-1  ; update ROWS
        mov     word ptr ds:[85h],10    ; update POINTS
```

For some values in the Scan Lines per Character register, the MCGA incorrectly displays the bottommost scan line of the screen. Specifically, when the value in the Scan Lines per Character register is 1, 3, 5, or 6, the MCGA replicates part of the topmost scan line on the screen at the bottom of the screen. Thus, you should generally avoid using these values for the Scan Lines per Character register.

HGC+ and InColor Card

You must program the HGC+ CRTC explicitly to change the number of displayed lines in alphanumeric characters. The subroutine SetHercCRTC in Listing 10-14 illustrates a table-driven technique for setting up the CRTC's vertical timing parameters for a variety of character sizes. Figure 10-16 summarizes the CRTC timing parameters recommended by Hercules for any character matrix between 4 and 16 scan lines high as well as for characters that are either 8 or 9 pixels wide.

CRTC register	Width of Character Matrix	
	8 Pixels	9 Pixels
00H	6DH	61H
01H	5AH	50H
02H	5CH	52H
03H	0FH	0FH

CRTC register	Height of Character Matrix (in pixels)												
	4	5	6	7	8	9	10	11	12	13	14	15	16
04H	5CH	4Ah	3DH	34H	2DH	28H	24H	20H	1DH	1BH	19H	17H	16H
05H	02H	00H	04H	06H	02H	01H	00H	07H	0AH	06H	06H	0AH	02H
06H	58H	46H	3AH	32H	2BH	26H	23H	1FH	1DH	1AH	19H	17H	15H
07H	59H	46H	3BH	33H	2CH	27H	23H	20H	1DH	1BH	19H	17H	16H

Figure 10-16. *CRTC timing parameters for height and width of the alphanumeric character matrix (HGC+ and InColor Card).*

On the InColor Card, the techniques for changing the displayed character matrix parallel those used on the HGC+. The values you place in the CRTC registers for each possible character matrix are also the same.

Programming Examples

The routines on the following pages unify the programming techniques for changing the displayed character matrix on the EGA (see Listing 10-12), on the VGA (see Listing 10-13), and on the HGC+ and InColor Card (see Listing 10-14). In each case, the function AlphaModeSet () programs the alphanumeric character generator and the CRTC to accommodate the dimensions of the specified character matrix and character code size.

```
              TITLE    'Listing 10-12'
              NAME     AlphaModeSet
              PAGE     55,132

;
; Name:        AlphaModeSet
;
;              Program the CRTC in 80-column EGA alphanumeric modes
;
; Caller:      Microsoft C:
;
;                   void AlphaModeSet(w,h,c);
;
;                   int    w;     /* width of character matrix */
;                   int    h;     /* height of character matrix */
;                   int    c;     /* character code size */
;
```

Listing 10-12. *Programming the EGA alphanumeric character size.*   *(continued)*

Listing 10-12. *Continued.*

```
ARGw            EQU      byte ptr [bp+4]            ; must be 8 or 9 pixels wide
ARGh            EQU      byte ptr [bp+6]            ; must be 2-32 pixels high
ARGc            EQU      byte ptr [bp+8]            ; must be 8 or 9 bits

CRT_MODE        EQU      49h               ; addresses in video BIOS data area
CRT_COLS        EQU      4Ah
ADDR_6845       EQU      63h

DGROUP          GROUP    _DATA

_TEXT           SEGMENT byte public 'CODE'
                ASSUME  cs:_TEXT,ds:DGROUP

                PUBLIC   _AlphaModeSet
_AlphaModeSet   PROC     near

                push     bp                ; preserve caller registers
                mov      bp,sp
                push     si

; Program the CRTC

                mov      bx,40h
                mov      es,bx             ; ES := video BIOS data segment

                mov      bl,ARGw           ; BL := character width
                mov      bh,ARGh           ; BH := character height
                call     SetCRTC

; Program the Sequencer and Attribute Controller for 8 or 9 dots per character

                mov      dx,3C4h
                mov      ax,0100h          ; AH bit 1 := 0 (synchronous reset)
                                           ; AL := 0 (Reset register number)
                cli                        ; disable interrupts
                out      dx,ax             ; Sequencer synchronous reset

                mov      bx,1              ; BH,BL := values for 8-wide chars:
                                           ;  BH := 0 (value for Horiz Pel Pan)
                                           ;  BL := 1 (value for Clocking Mode)
                cmp      ARGw,8
                je       L01               ; jump if 8-wide characters
                mov      bx,0800h          ; BH,BL := values for 9-wide characters

L01:            mov      ah,bl             ; AH := value for Clocking Mode reg
                mov      al,1              ; AL := Clocking Mode reg number
                out      dx,ax             ; program the Sequencer

                mov      ax,0300h          ; AH := 3 (disable reset)
                                           ; AL := 0 (Sequencer register number)
                out      dx,ax             ; disable Sequencer reset
                sti                        ; enable interrupts

                mov      bl,13h            ; BL := Horizontal Pel Pan reg number
                mov      ax,1000h          ; AH := 10H (INT 10H function number)
                                           ; AL := 0 (set specified register)
                int      10h               ; program Attribute Controller
```

(continued)

Listing 10-12. *Continued.*

```
; Program the Attribute Controller for 8- or 9-bit character codes

                mov     ax,1000h        ; AH := 10H (INT 10H function number)
                                        ; AL := 0 (set specified register)
                mov     bx,0F12h        ; BH := 0FH (Color Plane Enable value)
                                        ; BL := 12H (Color Plane Enable reg #)
                cmp     ARGc,8
                je      L02             ; jump if 8-bit character codes

                mov     bh,7            ; BH bit 3 := 0 (ignore bit 3 of all
                                        ;  attributes)
L02:            int     10h             ; update Color Plane Enable register

; update video BIOS data area

                cmp     byte ptr es:[CRT_MODE],7
                jne     L03             ; jump if not monochrome mode

                mov     ax,720          ; AX := displayed pixels per row
                div     ARGw            ; AL := displayed character columns
                mov     es:[CRT_COLS],al

L03:            pop     si
                pop     bp
                ret

_AlphaModeSet   ENDP


SetCRTC         PROC    near            ; Caller:    BH = character height
                                        ;            BL = character width
                push    dx
                mov     dx,es:[ADDR_6845]   ; CRTC I/O port

; establish CRTC vertical timing and cursor position in character matrix

                push    bx              ; preserve height and width
                mov     ax,1110h        ; AH := 11H (INT 10H function number)
                                        ; AL := 0 (user alpha load)
                xor     cx,cx           ; CX := 0 (store no characters)
                int     10h             ; call BIOS to program CRTC for
                                        ;  height of characters

                pop     ax              ; AH := character height
                push    ax              ; preserve height and width
                sub     ah,2            ; AH := starting scan line for cursor
                mov     al,0Ah          ; AL := 0AH (Cursor Start reg number)
                out     dx,ax           ; update CRTC Cursor Start register

                mov     ax,000Bh        ; AH := 0 (Cursor End value)
                                        ; AL := 0BH (Cursor End reg number)
                out     dx,ax           ; update CRTC Cursor End register

; establish CRTC horizontal timing

                pop     bx              ; BX := character height and width
                cmp     byte ptr es:[CRT_MODE],7
```

(continued)

Listing 10-12. *Continued.*

```
                        jne     L10                     ; exit if not monochrome mode

                        xor     bh,bh                   ; BX := character width
                        sub     bl,8                    ; BX := 0 or 1
                        neg     bx                      ; BX := 0 or 0FFFFH
                        and     bx,14                   ; BX := 0 or 14 (offset into table)
                        mov     si,bx                   ; SI := offset into table

                        add     si,offset DGROUP:HorizParms      ; DS:SI -> parameters
                        call    UpdateCRTC

L10:                    pop     dx
                        ret

SetCRTC                 ENDP


UpdateCRTC              PROC    near                    ; Caller:      DX = CRTC address port
                                                        ;              DS:SI -> parameters
                                                        ; Destroys:    AX,CX

                        mov     cx,7                    ; CX := number of registers to update

L20:                    lodsw                           ; AH := data for CRTC register in AL
                        out     dx,ax                   ; update the register
                        loop    L20

                        ret

UpdateCRTC              ENDP

_TEXT                   ENDS


_DATA                   SEGMENT word public 'DATA'

HorizParms              DW      6C00h,5901h,6002h,2403h,5B04h,6A05h,2D13h   ; 8-wide
                        DW      6000h,4F01h,5602h,3A03h,5104h,6005h,2813h   ; 9-wide

_DATA                   ENDS
                        END
```

```
                        TITLE   'Listing 10-13'
                        NAME    AlphaModeSet
                        PAGE    55,132


;
; Name:          AlphaModeSet
;
;                Program the CRTC in 80-column VGA alphanumeric modes
;
; Caller:        Microsoft C:
```

Listing 10-13. *Programming the VGA alphanumeric character size.*   *(continued)*

Listing 10-13. *Continued.*

```
;
;                    void AlphaModeSet(w,h,c);
;
;              int       w;      /* width of character matrix */
;              int       h;      /* height of character matrix */
;              int       c;      /* character code size */
;

ARGw           EQU       byte ptr [bp+4]      ; must be 8 or 9 pixels wide
ARGh           EQU       byte ptr [bp+6]      ; must be 2-32 pixels high
ARGc           EQU       byte ptr [bp+8]      ; must be 8 or 9 bits

CRT_COLS       EQU       4Ah                  ; addresses in video BIOS data area
ADDR_6845      EQU       63h

DGROUP         GROUP     _DATA

_TEXT          SEGMENT byte public 'CODE'
               ASSUME  cs:_TEXT,ds:DGROUP

               PUBLIC    _AlphaModeSet
_AlphaModeSet  PROC      near

               push      bp                   ; preserve caller registers
               mov       bp,sp
               push      si

; Program the CRTC

               mov       bx,40h
               mov       es,bx                ; ES := video BIOS data segment

               mov       bl,ARGw              ; BL := character width
               mov       bh,ARGh              ; BH := character height
               call      SetCRTC

; Program the Sequencer and Attribute Controller for 8 or 9 dots per character

               mov       dx,3C4h
               mov       ax,0100h             ; AH bit 1 := 0 (synchronous reset)
                                              ; AL := 0 (Reset register number)
               cli                            ; disable interrupts
               out       dx,ax                ; Sequencer synchronous reset

               mov       bx,1                 ; BH,BL := values for 8-wide chars:
                                              ;   BH := 0 (value for Horiz Pel Pan)
                                              ;   BL := 1 (value for Clocking Mode)
               cmp       ARGw,8
               je        L01                  ; jump if 8-wide characters

               mov       bx,0800h             ; BH,BL := values for 9-wide characters

L01:           mov       ah,bl                ; AH := value for Clocking Mode reg
               mov       al,1                 ; AL := Clocking Mode reg number
               out       dx,ax                ; program the Sequencer
```

(continued)

Listing 10-13. *Continued.*

```
                mov     ax,0300h        ; AH := 3 (disable reset)
                                        ; AL := 0 (Sequencer register number)
                out     dx,ax           ; disable Sequencer reset
                sti                     ; enable interrupts

                mov     bl,13h          ; BL := Horizontal Pel Pan reg number
                mov     ax,1000h        ; AH := 10H (INT 10H function number)
                                        ; AL := 0 (set specified register)
                int     10h             ; program Attribute Controller

; Program the Attribute Controller for 8- or 9-bit character codes

                mov     ax,1000h        ; AH := 10H (INT 10H function number)
                                        ; AL := 0 (set specified register)
                mov     bx,0F12h        ; BH := 0FH (Color Plane Enable value)
                                        ; BL := 12H (Color Plane Enable reg #)
                cmp     ARGc,8
                je      L02             ; jump if 8-bit character codes

                mov     bh,7            ; BH bit 3 := 0 (ignore bit 3 of all
                                        ;   attributes)
L02:            int     10h             ; update Color Plane Enable register

; update video BIOS data area

                mov     ax,720          ; AX := displayed pixels per row
                div     ARGw            ; AL := displayed character columns
                mov     es:[CRT_COLS],al

                pop     si
                pop     bp
                ret

_AlphaModeSet   ENDP


SetCRTC         PROC    near            ; Caller:      BH = character height
                                        ;              BL = character width
                push    dx
                mov     dx,es:[ADDR_6845]  ; CRTC I/O port

; establish CRTC vertical timing and cursor position in character matrix

                push    bx              ; preserve char height and width
                mov     ax,1110h        ; AH := 11H (INT 10H function number)
                                        ; AL := 0 (user alpha load)
                xor     cx,cx           ; CX := 0 (store no characters)
                int     10h             ; call BIOS to program CRTC
                pop     bx

; enable I/O writes to CRTC registers

                mov     al,11h          ; AL := Vertical Retrace End reg number
                out     dx,al
                inc     dx
                in      al,dx           ; AL := current value of this register
                dec     dx
```

(continued)

Listing 10-13. *Continued.*

```
                mov     ah,al           ; AH := current value
                mov     al,11h          ; AL := register number
                push    ax              ; save on stack

                and     ah,01111111b    ; zero bit 7
                out     dx,ax           ; update this register

; establish CRTC horizontal timing

                xor     bh,bh           ; BX := character width
                sub     bl,8            ; BX := 0 or 1
                neg     bx              ; BX := 0 or 0FFFFH
                and     bx,14           ; BX := 0 or 14 (offset into table)
                mov     si,bx           ; SI := offset into table

                add     si,offset DGROUP:HorizParms    ; DS:SI -> parameters
                call    UpdateCRTC

; write-protect CRTC registers

                pop     ax              ; AX := previous VR End register data
                out     dx,ax           ; restore this register

                pop     dx
                ret

SetCRTC         ENDP


UpdateCRTC      PROC    near            ; Caller:     DX = CRTC address port
                                        ;             DS:SI -> parameters
                                        ; Destroys:   AX,CX

                mov     cx,7            ; CX := number of registers to update
L10:            lodsw                   ; AH := data for CRTC register in AL
                out     dx,ax           ; update the register
                loop    L10

                ret

UpdateCRTC      ENDP

_TEXT           ENDS


_DATA           SEGMENT word public 'DATA'

HorizParms      DW      6A00h,5901h,5A02h,8D03h,6304h,8805h,2D13h   ; 8-wide
                DW      5F00h,4F01h,5002h,8203h,5504h,8105h,2813h   ; 9-wide

_DATA           ENDS

                END
```

```
                    TITLE    'Listing 10-14'
                    NAME     AlphaModeSet
                    PAGE     55,132
;
; Name:        AlphaModeSet
;
; Function:    Program the CRTC in alphanumeric modes on HGC+ or InColor Card
;
; Caller:      Microsoft C:
;
;                      void AlphaModeSet(w,h,c);
;
;                      int    w;     /* width of character matrix */
;                      int    h;     /* height of character matrix */
;                      int    c;     /* character code size */
;

ARGw          EQU      byte ptr [bp+4]           ; must be 8 or 9 pixels wide
ARGh          EQU      byte ptr [bp+6]           ; must be 4-16 pixels high
ARGc          EQU      byte ptr [bp+8]           ; must be 8 or 12 bits

CRT_COLS      EQU      4Ah
CRT_LEN       EQU      4Ch
CRT_MODE_SET  EQU      65h
ROWS          EQU      84h

DGROUP        GROUP    _DATA

_TEXT         SEGMENT  byte public 'CODE'
              ASSUME   cs:_TEXT,ds:DGROUP

              PUBLIC   _AlphaModeSet
_AlphaModeSet PROC     near

              push     bp                   ; preserve caller registers
              mov      bp,sp
              push     ds
              push     si

; Set Configuration Switch to bring RAM starting at B000:4000 into memory map

              mov      dx,3BFh              ; DX := Configuration Switch port
              mov      al,1                 ; AL bit 1 := 0 (exclude 2nd 32K of
                                            ;                        video buffer)
                                            ; AL bit 0 := 1 (make RAM at B000:4000
              out      dx,ax                ;                        addressable)

; Blank the screen to avoid interference during CRTC programming

              mov      dx,3B8h              ; DX := CRTC Mode Control Register port
              xor      al,al                ; AL bit 3 := 0 (disable video signal)
              out      dx,al                ; blank the screen

; Program the CRTC

              mov      bh,ARGw              ; BH := character width
              mov      bl,ARGh              ; BL := character height
              call     SetHercCRTC
```

(continued)

Listing 10-14. *Programming the alphanumeric character size on the HGC+ and InColor Card.*

Listing 10-14. *Continued.*

```
; Set the xModeReg

                mov     dx,3B4h         ; DX := CRTC address port
                mov     ax,114h         ; AH bit 0 := 1 (enable RAM-based
                                        ;   character generator)
                                        ; AL := 14h (xModeReg number)
                cmp     ARGw,9
                je      L01             ; jump if 9-wide characters

                or      ah,2            ; AH bit 1 := 1 (8-wide characters)

L01:            cmp     ARGc,8
                je      L02             ; jump if 8-bit character codes

                or      ah,4            ; AH bit 2 := 1 (12-bit character codes)

L02:            out     dx,ax           ; update the register

; update video BIOS data area

                mov     ax,40h
                mov     ds,ax           ; DS := video BIOS data segment

                mov     ax,720          ; AX := displayed pixels per row
                div     ARGw            ; AL := displayed character columns
                mov     ds:[CRT_COLS],al

                mov     ax,350          ; AX := number of displayed scan lines
                div     ARGh            ; AL := displayed character rows
                dec     al              ; AL := (character rows) - 1
                mov     ds:[ROWS],al

                inc     al
                mul     byte ptr ds:[CRT_COLS]
                shl     ax,1            ; AX := rows * columns * 2
                mov     ds:[CRT_LEN],ax

; re-enable display and exit

                mov     dx,3B8h         ; DX := CRT Mode Control port
                mov     al,ds:[CRT_MODE_SET]    ; restore previous value
                out     dx,al

                pop     si
                pop     ds
                pop     bp
                ret

_AlphaModeSet   ENDP


SetHercCRTC     PROC    near            ; Caller:     BH = character width
                                        ;             BL = character height

                push    dx
                mov     dx,3B4h         ; DX := CRTC Address Reg port 3B4h
```

(continued)

Listing 10-14. *Continued.*

```
; establish cursor position in character matrix

            mov     ah,bl
            dec     ah                  ; AH := value for Max Scan Line reg
            mov     al,9                ; AL := Max Scan Line register number
            out     dx,ax

            mov     al,0Bh              ; AL := Cursor End reg number
            out     dx,ax               ; set cursor to end on last line of
                                        ;    character matrix

            sub     ax,101h             ; AH := second-to-last line
                                        ; AL := 0AH (Cursor Start reg number)
            out     dx,ax               ; set cursor to start on second-to-
                                        ;  last line

; compute offsets into parameter tables

            sub     bx,0804h            ; BH := 0 or 1
                                        ; BL := 0 through 12
            add     bx,bx
            add     bx,bx               ; BH := 0 or 4
                                        ; BL := 0 through 48
; establish CRTC horizontal timing

            push    bx                  ; preserve BX
            mov     bl,bh
            xor     bh,bh               ; BX := 0 or 4
            add     bx,offset DGROUP:HorizParms    ; DS:BX -> parameters

            mov     al,0                ; AL := first CRTC reg to update
            call    UpdateCRTC

; establish vertical timing

            pop     bx
            xor     bh,bh               ; BX := 0 through 48
            add     bx,offset DGROUP:VertParms     ; DS:BX -> parameters

            mov     al,4                ; AL := first CRTC reg to update
            call    UpdateCRTC

            pop     dx                  ; restore DX
            ret

SetHercCRTC     ENDP

UpdateCRTC      PROC    near            ; Caller:     AL = first reg number
                                        ;             DX = CRTC address port
                                        ;             DS:BX -> parameters
                                        ; Destroys:   AX,CX

            mov     cx,4                ; CX := number of registers to update

L10:        mov     ah,[bx]             ; AH := data for CRTC register in AL
            out     dx,ax               ; update the register
            inc     ax                  ; AL := next register number
```

(continued)

Listing 10-14. *Continued.*

```
                      inc     bx                ; DS:BX -> next value in table
                      loop    L10
                      ret

UpdateCRTC            ENDP

_TEXT                 ENDS


_DATA                 SEGMENT word public 'DATA'

HorizParms            DB      6Dh,5Ah,5Ch,0Fh      ; 8 pixels wide
                      DB      61h,50h,52h,0Fh      ; 9 pixels wide


VertParms             DB      5Ch,02h,58h,59h      ; 4 scan lines high
                      DB      4Ah,00h,46h,46h      ; 5
                      DB      3Dh,04h,3Ah,3Bh      ; 6
                      DB      34h,06h,32h,33h      ; 7
                      DB      2Dh,02h,2Bh,2Ch      ; 8
                      DB      28h,01h,26h,27h      ; 9
                      DB      24h,00h,23h,23h      ; 10
                      DB      20h,07h,1Fh,20h      ; 11
                      DB      1Dh,0Ah,1Dh,1Dh      ; 12
                      DB      1Bh,06h,1Ah,1Bh      ; 13
                      DB      19h,06h,19h,19h      ; 14
                      DB      17h,0Ah,17h,17h      ; 15
                      DB      16h,02h,15h,16h      ; 16

_DATA                 ENDS

                      END
```

Graphics Windows in Alphanumeric Modes

When you update a RAM-resident character definition table, you alter the appearance of any characters displayed using those definitions. The contents of the displayed portion of the video buffer need not be updated. You can exploit this characteristic of RAM-based character definitions to display pixel-addressable graphics images in an alphanumeric mode, thereby displaying text with maximum speed while including pixel-by-pixel graphics images on the same screen.

The technique is similar on both IBM and Hercules subsystems. Tile an area of the screen with a sequence of characters whose attribute selects a character definition table that contains the graphics image (see Figure 10-17). The graphics image is created and modified by updating the appropriate character definitions in the table. You can regard the character definition table as a sort of virtual graphics buffer and access individual pixels within it just as you do in the usual graphics modes.

On the InColor Card, you can specify the value of each individual pixel you store in the character definition table as though you were using 720-by-348 16-color graphics mode. On other subsystems, however, only one memory map is used for

These characters are from one character set

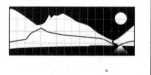

These characters are from a special character set. Each character is one "tile"; taken together, the tiled characters form a complete graphics image.

Figure 10-17. *A tiled graphics window in an alphanumeric mode.*

character definitions, so you do not have pixel-by-pixel attribute control. Instead, pixels in the character definition table have a value of 0 or 1; the attributes with which the character codes are stored in the video buffer determine the appearance of the pixels.

Listing 10-15 illustrates the technique for producing a tiled graphics window in 80-column alphanumeric mode on the EGA and VGA. The first part of the program creates the tiled window by storing the second 128 ASCII characters in four rows of 32 at the start of the video buffer (that is, in the upper left corner of the screen). Then the program clears the window by setting the second 128 character definitions to 0.

To update a pixel in the window, the subroutine `SetPixel()` computes a byte offset in the character definition table that corresponds to the pixel's location in the tiled window. As in graphics modes, the routine accesses each individual pixel with a bit mask.

```
/* Listing 10-15 */

#define Points          14      /* displayed scan lines per character */
#define StartCharCode   0x80    /* first character code in "window" */
#define CGenDefSize     32      /* (use 16 for Hercules) */


char far *CRT_MODE = 0x00400049;        /* BIOS video mode number */
int  far *CRT_COLS = 0x0040004A;        /* characters per row */

char far *VideoBuffer;                  /* pointer to video buffer */
char far *CharDefTable = 0xA0000000;    /* pointer to char def RAM */
                                        /* (use 0xB0004000 for Hercules) */
main()
{
        int     i;
        int     CharCode;
        int     CharOffset;
```

Listing 10-15. *Creating a tiled graphics window on the EGA or VGA.*   *(continued)*

Listing 10-15. *Continued.*

```
int     CharScanLine;
int     CharDefOffset;
int     Row,Column;

/* establish alphanumeric mode */

if (*CRT_MODE == 7)              /* set video buffer pointer */
  VideoBuffer = 0xB0000000;
else
  VideoBuffer = 0xB8000000;

AlphaModeSet( 8, Points, 8 );

/* establish a tiled graphics window in the upper left corner */

CharCode = StartCharCode;

for ( Row = 0; Row < 4; Row++ )
  for ( Column = 0; Column < 32; Column++ )
  {
    CharOffset = (Row*(*CRT_COLS) + Column) * 2;
    VideoBuffer[CharOffset] = CharCode++;
  }

/* clear the window */

CGenModeSet();          /* make character generator RAM addressable */

for (CharCode = StartCharCode; CharCode < 256; CharCode++ )
  for ( CharScanLine = 0; CharScanLine < Points; CharScanLine++ )
  {
    CharDefOffset = CharCode * CGenDefSize + CharScanLine;
    CharDefTable[CharDefOffset] = 0;
  }

/* draw a few lines */

for ( i = 0; i < 256; i++ )          /* horizontal lines */
{
  SetPixel( i, 0 );
  SetPixel( i, 4*Points-1 );
}

for ( i = 0; i < 4*Points-1; i++ )   /* vertical lines */
{
  SetPixel( 0, i );
  SetPixel( 255, i );
}

for( i = 0; i < Points*4; i++ )      /* diagonal lines */
{
  SetPixel( i, i );
  SetPixel( 255-i, i );
}

CGenModeClear();                     /* restore alphanumeric mode */
}
```

(continued)

Listing 10-15. *Continued.*

```
SetPixel( x, y )
int     x,y;              /* pixel coordinates */
{
        int     CharCode;
        int     CharScanLine;
        int     BitMask;
        int     CharDefOffset;

        CharCode = StartCharCode + (y/Points)*32 + x/8;
        CharScanLine = y % Points;              /* y MOD Points */
        BitMask = 0x80 >> (x % 8);              /* 10000000b SHR (x MOD 8) */

        CharDefOffset = CharCode*CGenDefSize + CharScanLine;
        CharDefTable[CharDefOffset] |= BitMask; /* OR the pixel */
}
```

HGC+ and InColor Card

Clearly, the size of a tiled graphics window is restricted if you use 8-bit character codes because the 8-bit ASCII character set contains only 256 characters. If you configure a Hercules adapter for 12-bit character codes, however, you can create much larger tiled windows without running out of character codes. Also, you can create larger windows by displaying taller characters (that is, by increasing the height of the displayed character matrix). Of course, if you use taller characters you decrease the number of rows of text that you can display at the same time; this can be a drawback in some applications.

You can use similar programming techniques for alphanumeric graphics on Hercules adapters and on IBM subsystems. For example, Listing 10-15 can be modified for use with the HGC+ and InColor Card by changing the values of `CGenDefSize` and `CharDefTable` and removing the calls to the functions `CGenModeSet()` and `CGenModeClear()`.

 In establishing a graphics window on a Hercules card, avoid using a character matrix that is 9 pixels wide. Because the ninth (rightmost) pixel in each character is actually a hardware-generated copy of the eighth dot, you cannot control it independently by updating the character definition table.

EGA and VGA

On the EGA and VGA, you can create larger tiled graphics windows if you use 9-bit extended character codes. For instance, you could dedicate one 256-character definition table to text characters and a second character definition table to graphics tiling characters. Nevertheless, the EGA and VGA are still limited to displaying no more than 512 different characters at a time, so the largest tiled graphics window is much smaller than it can be on a Hercules adapter.

When you update pixels in the tiled window, you should minimize the number of times your program resets the Sequencer (for example, in the routines `CGenModeSet()` and `CGenModeClear()`). If you reset the Sequencer each time you update a pixel, you might create screen interference. (Synchronizing Sequencer resets with the vertical retrace interval can eliminate this interference but can also greatly decrease the speed of a program.) If you draw a complicated graphics figure containing many pixels, draw the entire figure at one time as in Listing 10-15.

MCGA

Character definition tables in MCGA character generator RAM are formatted differently than those on the EGA and VGA, so a routine that manipulates pixels in character generator RAM must address the tables differently (see Listing 10-16). Also, remember that the screen does not reflect changes to the MCGA's character definition tables until you load the character generator's font pages (see Listing 10-5).

```
SetPixel( x, y )
int     x,y;            /* pixel coordinates */
{
        int     CharCode;
        int     CharScanLine;
        int     BitMask;
        int     CharDefOffset;

        /* the window is 32 characters across */
        CharCode = StartCharCode + (y/Points)*32 + x/8;

        CharScanLine = y % Points;              /* y MOD Points */
        BitMask = 0x80 >> (x % 8);              /* 10000000b SHR (x MOD 8) */

        CharDefOffset = CharCode*2 + CharScanLine*512 + 1;
        CharDefTable[CharDefOffset] |= BitMask; /* OR the pixel */
}
```

Listing 10-16. *A routine to set pixels in a tiled graphics window on the MCGA.*

11

Bit Blocks and Animation

Bit Block Move
CGA and MCGA ● EGA and VGA ● HGC ● InColor Card

Bitwise Pixel Operations
XOR ● NOT ● AND ● OR

Bit Block Tiling

Animation
XOR Animation
Overlapping Bit Block Moves

A Graphics-Mode Cursor
XOR ● Bit Block Move

This chapter is about moving things around in the video buffer and on the screen. Some of the most useful and entertaining graphics-mode programs create the appearance of on-screen motion. Objects as mundane as a cursor or as unusual as an alien spaceship can appear to move across the screen if you erase them and then immediately redraw them in successive locations. PC and PS/2 video subsystems are not particularly well equipped to support this kind of real-time animation, but the techniques in this chapter should help you fully exploit their capabilities.

You might think of video animation in the same context as video games, but animation has other uses in computer graphics. For instance, all interactive graphics programs require a moving cursor that allows the user to point to screen locations. Many drawing or design programs let the user move shapes and images around the screen. Robotic control programs indicate the status of a robot arm with an animated representation of its position. You can create such animation effects using the techniques in this chapter.

Bit Block Move

The basic software tool for many animation techniques is the bit block move—a routine that copies a rectangular block of pixels into, out of, or within the video buffer. The name "bit block move" describes this routine well. After all, a rectangle of pixels is in essence nothing more than a block of bits. Still, a bit block move routine can do more than simply copy pixel values. As can other video graphics drawing routines, a bit block move routine can update pixel values using the bitwise logical operations AND, OR, and XOR. These operations can create attractive effects when used as part of bit block moves.

To copy a bit block from one location to another within the video buffer in PC and PS/2 video subsystems, it is usually more efficient to use an intermediate buffer in system RAM. You first copy pixel values from the video buffer into the intermediate buffer, then copy the values from this buffer to the desired position in the video buffer.

Creating an intermediate copy of the pixels in a bit block might seem superfluous, but in most situations it is preferable to trying to move the bit block entirely within the video buffer. For example, neither the EGA nor the InColor Card supports direct logical operations (AND, OR, and XOR) between pixels in the bit planes. Also, CPU accesses to video RAM are slower than equivalent accesses to system RAM. Thus, when multiple copies of the same bit block are to be stored in the video buffer, making a single copy in system RAM and then making multiple copies from system RAM to video RAM is more efficient.

CGA and MCGA

Listing 11-1 is a bit block move routine for the CGA. The routine GetBitBlock() copies a block of pixels from the video buffer to a buffer in system RAM. The complementary routine StoreBitBlock(), in Listing 11-2, copies pixels from system RAM to the video buffer. `StoreBitBlock()` contains subroutines to perform AND, OR, or XOR operations on the pixels in system RAM using the previous contents of the video buffer.

```
                    TITLE    'Listing 11-1'
                    NAME     GetBitBlock06
                    PAGE     55,132


;
; Name:              GetBitBlock06
;
; Function:          Copy bit block from video buffer to system RAM
;                      in 640x200 2-color mode
;
; Caller:            Microsoft C:
;
;                          int GetBitBlock06(x0,y0,x1,y1,buf);
;
;                              int x0,y0;      /* upper left corner of bit block */
;                              int x1,y1;      /* lower right corner */
;                              char far *buf;  /* buffer */
;
; Notes:             Returns size of bit block in system RAM.

ARGx0             EQU     word ptr [bp+4]
ARGy0             EQU     word ptr [bp+6]
ARGx1             EQU     word ptr [bp+8]
ARGy1             EQU     word ptr [bp+10]
ADDRbuf           EQU             [bp+12]

VARPixelRows      EQU     word ptr [bp-2]
VARPixelRowLen    EQU     word ptr [bp-4]
VARincr           EQU     word ptr [bp-6]

ByteOffsetShift EQU     3                   ; reflects number of pixels per byte


_TEXT             SEGMENT byte public 'CODE'
                  ASSUME  cs:_TEXT

                  EXTRN    PixelAddr06:near

                  PUBLIC  _GetBitBlock06
_GetBitBlock06    PROC    near

                  push    bp                ; preserve caller registers
                  mov     bp,sp
                  sub     sp,6              ; establish stack frame
                  push    ds
                  push    si
                  push    di

; compute dimensions of bit block

                  mov     ax,ARGx1
                  sub     ax,ARGx0
```

(continued)

Listing 11-1. *A routine to copy a block of pixels from the CGA video buffer to system RAM.*

Listing 11-1. *Continued.*

```
                mov     cx,0FF07h          ; CH := unshifted bit mask
                                           ; CL := AND mask for AL
                and     cl,al              ; CL := number of pixels in last
                                           ;   byte of row
                xor     cl,7               ; CL := number of bits to shift
                shl     ch,cl              ; CH := bit mask for last byte of row
                mov     cl,ch
                push    cx                 ; save on stack

                mov     cl,ByteOffsetShift
                shr     ax,cl
                inc     ax                 ; AX := number of bytes per row
                push    ax                 ; save on stack

                mov     ax,ARGy1
                sub     ax,ARGy0
                inc     ax                 ; AX := number of pixel rows
                push    ax                 ; save on stack

; establish addressing

                mov     ax,ARGy0
                mov     bx,ARGx0
                call    PixelAddr06        ; ES:BX -> x0,y0 in video buffer
                xor     cl,7               ; CL := number of bits to shift left
                push    es
                pop     ds
                mov     si,bx              ; DS:SI -> video buffer

                mov     bx,2000h           ; BX := increment from 1st to 2nd
                                           ;   interleave in CGA video buffer
                test    si,2000h
                jz      L01                ; jump if x0,y0 is in 1st interleave

                mov     bx,80-2000h        ; increment from 2nd to 1st interleave

L01:            mov     VARincr,bx         ; initialize this variable

                les     di,ADDRbuf         ; ES:DI -> buffer in system RAM

; build 5-byte bit block header

                pop     ax
                mov     VARPixelRows,ax
                stosw                      ; byte 0-1 := number of pixel rows
                pop     ax
                mov     VARPixelRowLen,ax
                stosw                      ; byte 2-3 := bytes per pixel row
                pop     ax
                mov     ch,al              ; CH := bit mask for last byte
                stosb                      ; byte 4 := bit mask for last byte

; copy from video buffer to system RAM

L02:            mov     bx,VARPixelRowLen
                push    si                 ; preserve SI at start of pixel row
```

(continued)

Listing 11-1. *Continued.*

```
L03:            lodsw                       ; AL := next byte in video buffer
                                            ; AH := (next byte) + 1
                dec     si                  ; DS:SI -> (next byte) + 1
                rol     ax,cl               ; AL := next 4 pixels in row
                stosb                       ; copy to system RAM
                dec     bx                  ; loop across row
                jnz     L03

                and     es:[di-1],ch        ; mask last byte of row
                pop     si                  ; DS:SI -> start of row
                add     si,VARincr          ; DS:SI -> start of next row
                xor     VARincr,2000h XOR (80-2000H)   ; update increment

                dec     VARPixelRows
                jnz     L02                 ; loop down rows

                mov     ax,di
                sub     ax,ADDRbuf          ; AX := return value (size of bit block
                                            ;   in system RAM)

                pop     di                  ; restore registers and exit
                pop     si
                pop     ds
                mov     sp,bp
                pop     bp
                ret

_GetBitBlock06  ENDP

_TEXT           ENDS

                END
```

```
                TITLE   'Listing 11-2'
                NAME    StoreBitBlock06
                PAGE    55,132

;
; Name:         StoreBitBlock06
;
; Function:     Copy bit block from video buffer to system RAM
;                 in 640x200 2-color mode
;
; Caller:       Microsoft C:
;
;                       void StoreBitBlock06(buf,x,y);
;
;                           char far *buf;   /* buffer */
;                           int x,y;    /* upper left corner of bit block */
;
```

(continued)

Listing 11-2. *A routine to copy a block of pixels from system RAM to the CGA video buffer.*

Listing 11-2. *Continued.*

```
ADDRbuf          EQU      dword ptr [bp+4]
ARGx             EQU      word ptr [bp+8]
ARGy             EQU      word ptr [bp+10]

VARPixelRows     EQU      word ptr [bp-2]
VARPixelRowLen   EQU      word ptr [bp-4]
VARincr          EQU      word ptr [bp-6]


DGROUP           GROUP    _DATA


_TEXT            SEGMENT byte public 'CODE'
                 ASSUME   cs:_TEXT,ds:DGROUP

                 EXTRN    PixelAddr06:near

                 PUBLIC   _StoreBitBlock06
_StoreBitBlock06 PROC     near

                 push     bp                    ; preserve caller registers
                 mov      bp,sp
                 sub      sp,6                  ; establish stack frame
                 push     ds
                 push     si
                 push     di

; establish addressing

                 mov      ax,ARGy
                 mov      bx,ARGx
                 call     PixelAddr06           ; ES:BX -> byte offset of x,y
                 xor      cl,7                  ; CL := number of bits to shift right

                 mov      di,bx                 ; ES:DI -> x,y in video buffer
                 mov      bx,2000h              ; BX := increment from 1st to 2nd
                                                ;   interleave in CGA video buffer
                 test     di,2000h
                 jz       L01                   ; jump if x,y is in 1st interleave

                 mov      bx,80-2000h           ; increment from 2nd to 1st interleave

L01:             mov      VARincr,bx            ; initialize this variable

                 mov      bx,StoreBitBlockOp  ; BX := subroutine address

                 lds      si,ADDRbuf          ; ES:DI -> buffer in system RAM

; obtain dimensions of bit block from header

                 lodsw                          ; AX := number of pixel rows
                 mov      VARPixelRows,ax
                 lodsw                          ; AX := bytes per pixel row
                 mov      VARPixelRowLen,ax
                 lodsb                          ; AL := bit mask for last byte in row
                 mov      ch,al

                 jmp      bx                    ; jump to subroutine
```

(continued)

Listing 11-2. *Continued.*

```
ReplaceBitBlock:
                cmp     cx,0FF00h       ; if mask = 0FFH and bits to shift = 0
                jnz     L15             ;  jump if not byte-aligned

; routine for byte-aligned bit blocks

                mov     cx,VARPixelRowLen

L10:            push    di              ; preserve DI and CX
                push    cx
                rep     movsb           ; copy one pixel row into video buffer
                pop     cx              ; restore DI and CX
                pop     di
                add     di,VARincr      ; ES:DI -> next pixel row in buffer
                xor     VARincr,2000h XOR (80-2000h) ; update increment
                dec     VARPixelRows
                jnz     L10             ; loop down pixel rows

                jmp     Lexit

; routine for all other bit blocks

L15:            not     ch              ; CH := mask for end of row
                mov     dx,0FF00h
                ror     dx,cl           ; DX := rotated mask for each byte

                mov     bx,VARPixelRowLen
                dec     bx              ; BX := bytes per row - 1

L16:            push    di
                test    bx,bx
                jz      L18             ; jump if only one byte per row

                push    bx

L17:            and     es:[di],dx      ; mask next 8 pixels in video buffer
                lodsb                   ; AL := pixels in bit block
                xor     ah,ah
                ror     ax,cl           ; AX := pixels rotated into position
                or      es:[di],ax      ; set pixels in video buffer
                inc     di              ; ES:DI -> next byte in bit block
                dec     bx
                jnz     L17

                pop     bx

L18:            mov     al,ch
                mov     ah,0FFh         ; AX := mask for last pixels in row
                ror     ax,cl           ; AX := mask rotated into position
                and     es:[di],ax      ; mask last pixels in video buffer
                lodsb                   ; AL := last byte in row
                xor     ah,ah
                ror     ax,cl           ; AX := pixels rotated into position
                or      es:[di],ax      ; set pixels in video buffer
```

(continued)

Listing 11-2. *Continued.*

```
                  pop     di
                  add     di,VARincr       ; ES:DI -> next pixel row in buffer
                  xor     VARincr,2000h XOR (80-2000h)
                  dec     VARPixelRows
                  jnz     L16              ; loop down pixel rows

                  jmp     Lexit

XORBitBlock:
                  mov     bx,VARPixelRowLen

L20:              push    di
                  push    bx

L21:              lodsb                    ; AL := pixels in bit block
                  xor     ah,ah
                  ror     ax,cl            ; AX := pixels rotated into position
                  xor     es:[di],ax       ; XOR pixels into video buffer
                  inc     di               ; ES:DI -> next byte in bit block
                  dec     bx
                  jnz     L21

                  pop     bx
                  pop     di
                  add     di,VARincr       ; ES:DI -> next pixel row in buffer
                  xor     VARincr,2000h XOR (80-2000h)
                  dec     VARPixelRows
                  jnz     L20              ; loop down pixel rows

                  jmp     Lexit

ANDBitBlock:
                  not     ch               ; CH := mask for end of row

                  mov     bx,VARPixelRowLen
                  dec     bx               ; BX := bytes per row - 1

L30:              push    di
                  test    bx,bx
                  jz      L32              ; jump if only one byte per row

                  push    bx

L31:              lodsb                    ; AL := pixels in bit block
                  mov     ah,0FFh
                  ror     ax,cl            ; AX := pixels rotated into position
                  and     es:[di],ax       ; AND pixels into video buffer
                  inc     di               ; ES:DI -> next byte in bit block
                  dec     bx
                  jnz     L31

                  pop     bx

L32:              lodsb                    ; AL := last byte in row
                  or      al,ch            ; mask last pixels in row
                  mov     ah,0FFh
                  ror     ax,cl            ; AX := pixels rotated into position
                  and     es:[di],ax       ; AND pixels into video buffer
```

(continued)

Listing 11-2. *Continued.*

```
                   pop      di
                   add      di,VARincr        ; ES:DI -> next pixel row in buffer
                   xor      VARincr,2000h XOR (80-2000h)
                   dec      VARPixelRows
                   jnz      L30               ; loop down pixel rows

                   jmp      Lexit


ORBitBlock:
                   mov      bx,VARPixelRowLen

L40:               push     di
                   push     bx

L41:               lodsb                      ; AL := pixels in bit block
                   xor      ah,ah
                   ror      ax,cl             ; AX := pixels rotated into position
                   or       es:[di],ax        ; OR pixels into video buffer
                   inc      di                ; ES:DI -> next byte in bit block
                   dec      bx
                   jnz      L41

                   pop      bx
                   pop      di
                   add      di,VARincr        ; ES:DI -> next pixel row in buffer
                   xor      VARincr,2000h XOR (80-2000h)
                   dec      VARPixelRows
                   jnz      L40               ; loop down pixel rows


Lexit:             pop      di                ; restore registers and exit
                   pop      si
                   pop      ds
                   mov      sp,bp
                   pop      bp
                   ret

_StoreBitBlock06 ENDP

_TEXT              ENDS


_DATA              SEGMENT word public 'DATA'

StoreBitBlockOp DW    ReplaceBitBlock ; address of selected subroutine
                                      ;   (replace, XOR, AND, OR)

_DATA              ENDS

                   END
```

In the MCGA's 640-by-480 2-color and 320-by-200 256-color modes, pixel addressing is different than in the two CGA-compatible modes. Otherwise, versions of GetBitBlock() and StoreBitBlock() are similar in all MCGA modes.

EGA and VGA

In native EGA and VGA graphics modes, the bit block move routine must move the contents of all four bit planes to system RAM. The GetBitBlock() routine in Listing 11-3 extracts bytes from each bit plane using read mode 0 and selecting each bit plane in turn with the Graphics Controller's Read Map Mask register. StoreBitBlock(), in Listing 11-4, then uses write mode 0 to copy data into the bit planes. The bit planes are isolated in write mode 0 by programming the Sequencer's Map Mask register.

Do not use the routines in Listings 11-3 and 11-4 on an EGA with only 64 KB of video RAM. Because the memory maps are chained together to form the two bit planes used in 640-by-350 graphics modes, these routines will not work properly in this situation. (Chapter 4 discusses this in greater detail.)

```
                TITLE    'Listing 11-3'
                NAME     GetBitBlock10
                PAGE     55,132

;
; Name:          GetBitBlock10
;
; Function:      Copy bit block from video buffer to system RAM
;                   in native EGA and VGA graphics modes
;
; Caller:        Microsoft Ç:
;
;                        int GetBitBlock10(x0,y0,x1,y1,buf);
;
;                             int x0,y0;     /* upper left corner of bit block */
;                             int x1,y1;       /* lower right corner */
;                             char far *buf;   /* buffer */
;
; Notes:         Returns size of bit block in system RAM.
;


ARGx0           EQU      word ptr [bp+4]
ARGy0           EQU      word ptr [bp+6]
ARGx1           EQU      word ptr [bp+8]
ARGy1           EQU      word ptr [bp+10]
ADDRbuf         EQU               [bp+12]

VARPixelRows    EQU      word ptr [bp-2]
VARPixelRowLen  EQU      word ptr [bp-4]

BytesPerRow     EQU      80
ByteOffsetShift EQU      3                    ; reflects number of pixels per byte

_TEXT           SEGMENT byte public 'CODE'
                ASSUME  cs:_TEXT

                EXTRN    PixelAddr10:near
```

(continued)

Listing 11-3. *A routine to copy a block of pixels from the EGA or VGA video buffer to system RAM in native graphics modes.*

Listing 11-3. *Continued.*

```
                PUBLIC  _GetBitBlock10
_GetBitBlock10  PROC    near

                push    bp              ; preserve caller registers
                mov     bp,sp
                sub     sp,4            ; establish stack frame
                push    ds
                push    si
                push    di

; compute dimensions of bit block

                mov     ax,ARGx1
                sub     ax,ARGx0
                mov     cx,0FF07h       ; CH := unshifted bit mask
                                        ; CL := AND mask for AL
                and     cl,al           ; CL := number of pixels in last
                                        ;  byte of row
                xor     cl,7            ; CL := number of bits to shift
                shl     ch,cl           ; CH := bit mask for last byte of row
                mov     cl,ch
                push    cx              ; save on stack

                mov     cl,ByteOffsetShift
                shr     ax,cl
                inc     ax              ; AX := number of bytes per row
                push    ax              ; save on stack

                mov     ax,ARGy1
                sub     ax,ARGy0
                inc     ax              ; AX := number of pixel rows
                push    ax              ; save on stack

; establish addressing

                mov     ax,ARGy0
                mov     bx,ARGx0
                call    PixelAddr10     ; ES:BX -> x0,y0 in video buffer
                xor     cl,7            ; CL := number of bits to shift left
                push    es
                pop     ds
                mov     si,bx           ; DS:SI -> video buffer

                les     di,ADDRbuf      ; ES:DI -> buffer in system RAM

; build 5-byte bit block header

                pop     ax
                mov     VARPixelRows,ax
                stosw                   ; byte 0-1 := number of pixel rows
                pop     ax
                mov     VARPixelRowLen,ax
                stosw                   ; byte 2-3 := bytes per pixel row
                pop     ax
                mov     ch,al           ; CH := bit mask for last byte in row
                stosb                   ; byte 4 := bit mask for last byte
```

(continued)

Chapter 11: Bit Blocks and Animation **353**

Listing 11-3. *Continued.*

```
; set up Graphics Controller

                mov     dx,3CEh             ; DX := Graphics Controller address port

                mov     ax,0005             ; AH := 0 (read mode 0, write mode 0)
                                            ; AL := 5 (Mode register number)
                out     dx,ax               ; set up read mode 0

                mov     ax,0304h            ; AH := 3 (first bit plane to read)
                                            ; AL := 4 (Read Map Select reg number)

; copy from video buffer to system RAM

L01:            out     dx,ax               ; select next memory map to read
                push    ax                  ; preserve memory map number
                push    VARPixelRows        ; preserve number of pixel rows
                push    si                  ; preserve offset of x0,y0

L02:            mov     bx,VARPixelRowLen
                push    si                  ; preserve SI at start of pixel row

L03:            lodsw                       ; AL := next byte in video buffer
                                            ; AH := (next byte) + 1
                dec     si                  ; DS:SI -> (next byte) + 1
                rol     ax,cl               ; AL := next 4 pixels in row
                stosb                       ; copy to system RAM
                dec     bx                  ; loop across row
                jnz     L03

                and     es:[di-1],ch        ; mask last byte in row
                pop     si                  ; DS:SI -> start of row
                add     si,BytesPerRow      ; DS:SI -> start of next row

                dec     VARPixelRows
                jnz     L02                 ; loop down rows

                pop     si                  ; DS:SI -> start of bit block
                pop     VARPixelRows        ; restore number of pixel rows
                pop     ax                  ; AH := last map read
                                            ; AL := Read Map Select reg number
                dec     ah
                jns     L01                 ; loop across bit planes

                mov     ax,di
                sub     ax,ADDRbuf          ; AX := return value (size of bit block
                                            ;   in system RAM)

                pop     di                  ; restore registers and exit
                pop     si
                pop     ds
                mov     sp,bp
                pop     bp
                ret

_GetBitBlock10  ENDP

_TEXT           ENDS

                END
```

```
                TITLE     'Listing 11-4'
                NAME      StoreBitBlock10
                PAGE      55,132


;
; Name:         StoreBitBlock10
;
; Function:     Copy bit block from video buffer to system RAM
;                 in native EGA and VGA graphics modes
;
; Caller:       Microsoft C:
;
;                       void StoreBitBlock10(buf,x,y);
;
;                               char far *buf;   /* buffer */
;                               int x,y;    /* upper left corner of bit block */
;


ADDRbuf         EQU       dword ptr [bp+4]
ARGx            EQU       word ptr [bp+8]
ARGy            EQU       word ptr [bp+10]

VARPixelRows    EQU       word ptr [bp-2]
VARPixelRowLen  EQU       word ptr [bp-4]
VARRowCounter   EQU       word ptr [bp-6]
VARStartMask    EQU       word ptr [bp-8]
VAREndMaskL     EQU       word ptr [bp-10]
VAREndMaskR     EQU       word ptr [bp-12]

BytesPerRow     EQU       80              ; logical width of video buffer
ByteOffsetShift EQU       3               ; reflects number of pixels per byte
RMWbits         EQU       18h             ; selects replace, XOR, AND, or OR

_TEXT           SEGMENT byte public 'CODE'
                ASSUME  cs:_TEXT

                EXTRN   PixelAddr10:near

                PUBLIC  _StoreBitBlock10
_StoreBitBlock10 PROC    near

                push    bp              ; preserve caller registers
                mov     bp,sp
                sub     sp,12           ; establish stack frame
                push    ds
                push    si
                push    di

; establish addressing

                mov     ax,ARGy
                mov     bx,ARGx
                call    PixelAddr10     ; ES:BX -> byte offset of x,y
                inc     cl
                and     cl,7            ; CL := number of bits to shift left

                                                        (continued)
```

Listing 11-4. *A routine to copy a block of pixels from system RAM to the EGA or VGA video buffer in native graphics mode.*

Listing 11-4. *Continued.*

```
                mov     di,bx            ; ES:DI -> x,y in video buffer

                lds     si,ADDRbuf       ; ES:DI -> buffer in system RAM

; obtain dimensions of bit block from header

                lodsw                    ; AX := number of pixel rows
                mov     VARPixelRows,ax
                lodsw                    ; AX := bytes per pixel row
                mov     VARPixelRowLen,ax
                lodsb                    ; AL := bit mask for last byte in row
                mov     ch,al

; set up Graphics Controller

                mov     dx,3CEh          ; DX := Graphics Controller I/O port

                mov     ah,RMWbits       ; AH := value for Data Rotate/Function
                mov     al,3             ;  Select register
                out     dx,ax            ; update this register

                mov     ax,0805h         ; AH := 8 (read mode 1, write mode 0)
                                         ; AL := 5 (Mode register number)
                out     dx,ax            ; set up read mode 0

                mov     ax,0007          ; AH := 0 (don't care for all maps;
                                         ;  CPU reads always return 0FFH)
                                         ; AL := 7 (Color Don't Care reg number)
                out     dx,ax            ; set up Color Don't Care reg

                mov     ax,0FF08h        ; AH := 0FFH (value for Bit Mask reg)
                out     dx,ax            ; set up Bit Mask reg

                mov     dl,0C4h          ; DX := 3C4H (Sequencer I/O port)
                mov     ax,0802h         ; AH := 1000B (value for Map Mask reg)
                                         ; AL := 2 (Map Mask register number)

                cmp     cx,0FF00h        ; if mask <> 0FFH or bits to shift <> 0
                jne     L15              ;  jump if not byte-aligned

; routine for byte-aligned bit blocks

                mov     cx,VARPixelRowLen

L10:            out     dx,ax            ; enable one bit plane for writes
                push    ax               ; preserve Map Mask value
                push    di               ; preserve video buffer offset of x,y
                mov     bx,VARPixelRows

L11:            push    di               ; preserve DI and CX
                push    cx

L12:            lodsb                    ; AL := next byte of pixels
                and     es:[di],al       ; update bit plane
                inc     di
                loop    L12
```

(continued)

Listing 11-4. *Continued.*

```
                pop     cx                  ; restore DI and CX
                pop     di
                add     di,BytesPerRow      ; ES:DI -> next pixel row in buffer
                dec     bx
                jnz     L11                 ; loop down pixel rows

                pop     di                  ; ES:DI -> video buffer offset of x,y
                pop     ax                  ; AH := current Map Mask reg value
                shr     ah,1                ; AH := new Map Mask value
                jnz     L10                 ; loop across all bit planes

                jmp     Lexit

; routine for non-aligned bit blocks

L15:            push    ax                  ; preserve Map Mask reg values

                mov     bx,0FFh             ; BH := 0 (mask for first byte in row)
                                            ; BL := 0FFh
                mov     al,ch               ; AL := mask for last byte in pixel row
                cbw                         ; AH := 0FFh (mask for last-1 byte)

                cmp     VARPixelRowLen,1
                jne     L16                 ; jump if more than one byte per row

                mov     bl,ch
                mov     ah,ch               ; AH := mask for last-1 byte
                xor     al,al               ; AL := 0 (mask for last byte)

L16:            shl     ax,cl               ; shift masks into position
                shl     bx,cl

                mov     bl,al               ; save masks along with ...
                mov     al,8                ; Bit Mask register number
                mov     VAREndMaskL,ax
                mov     ah,bl
                mov     VAREndMaskR,ax
                mov     ah,bh
                mov     VARStartMask,ax

                mov     bx,VARPixelRowLen
                pop     ax                  ; restore Map Mask reg values

; set pixels row by row in the bit planes

L17:            out     dx,ax               ; enable one bit plane for writes
                push    ax                  ; preserve Map Mask value
                push    di                  ; preserve video buffer offset of x,y
                mov     dl,0CEh             ; DX := 3CEH (Graphics Controller port)

                mov     ax,VARPixelRows
                mov     VARRowCounter,ax    ; initialize loop counter
```

(continued)

Listing 11-4. *Continued.*

```
; set pixels at start of row in currently enabled bit plane

L18:            push    di              ; preserve offset of start of pixel row
                push    si              ; preserve offset of row in bit block
                push    bx              ; preserve bytes per pixel row

                mov     ax,VARStartMask
                out     dx,ax           ; set Bit Mask reg for first byte of row

                lodsw                   ; AH := 2nd byte of pixels
                                        ; AL := 1st byte of pixels
                dec     si              ; DS:SI -> 2nd byte of pixels
                test    cl,cl
                jnz     L19             ; jump if not left-aligned

                dec     bx              ; BX := bytes per row - 1
                jnz     L20             ; jump if at least 2 bytes per row
                jmp     short L22       ; jump if only one byte per row

L19:            rol     ax,cl           ; AH := left part of 1st byte,
                                        ;        right part of 2nd byte
                                        ; AL := right part of 1st byte,
                                        ;        left part of 2nd byte
                and     es:[di],ah      ; set pixels for left part of first byte
                inc     di
                dec     bx              ; BX := bytes per row - 2

L20:            push    ax              ; preserve pixels
                mov     ax,0FF08h
                out     dx,ax           ; set Bit Mask reg for succeeding bytes
                pop     ax

                dec     bx
                jng     L22             ; jump if only 1 or 2 bytes in pixel row

; set pixels in middle of row

L21:            and     es:[di],al      ; set pixels in right part of current
                inc     di              ;  byte and left part of next byte

                lodsw                   ; AH := next+1 byte of pixels
                dec     si              ; AL := next byte of pixels
                rol     ax,cl           ; AH := left part of next byte, right
                                        ;        part of next+1 byte
                                        ; AL := right part of next byte, left
                                        ;        part of next+1 byte
                dec     bx
                jnz     L21             ; loop across pixel row

; set pixels at end of row

L22:            mov     bx,ax           ; BH := right part of last byte, left
                                        ;        part of last-1 byte
                                        ; BL := left part of last byte, right
                                        ;        part of last-1 byte
                mov     ax,VAREndMaskL  ; AH := mask for last-1 byte
                                        ; AL := Bit Mask reg number
```

(continued)

Listing 11-4. *Continued.*

```
                out     dx,ax             ; set Bit Mask register
                and     es:[di],bl        ; set pixels for last-1 byte

                mov     ax,VAREndMaskR    ; mask for last byte in pixel row
                out     dx,ax             ; last byte in pixel row
                and     es:[di+1],bh      ; set pixels for last byte

                pop     bx                ; BX := bytes per pixel row
                pop     si
                add     si,bx             ; DS:SI -> next row in bit block
                pop     di
                add     di,BytesPerRow    ; ES:DI -> next pixel row in buffer
                dec     VARRowCounter
                jnz     L18               ; loop down pixel rows

                pop     di                ; ES:DI -> video buffer offset of x,y
                pop     ax                ; AX := current Map Mask value
                mov     dl,0C4h           ; DX := 3C4H
                shr     ah,1              ; AH := next Map Mask value
                jnz     L17               ; loop across bit planes

; restore Graphics Controller and Sequencer to their default states

Lexit:          mov     ax,0F02h          ; default Map Mask value
                out     dx,ax

                mov     dl,0CEh           ; DX := 3CEh
                mov     ax,0003           ; default Data Rotate/Function Select
                out     dx,ax

                mov     ax,0005           ; default Mode value
                out     dx,ax

                mov     ax,0F07h          ; default Color Compare value
                out     dx,ax

                mov     ax,0FF08h         ; default Bit Mask value
                out     dx,ax

                pop     di                ; restore registers and exit
                pop     si
                pop     ds
                mov     sp,bp
                pop     bp
                ret

_StoreBitBlock10 ENDP

_TEXT           ENDS

                END
```

HGC

Bit block move routines for HGC and HGC+ 720-by-348 monochrome graphics mode are similar to routines for CGA 640-by-200 2-color mode. The differences are in how they calculate pixel addresses and in the way the video buffer is interleaved.

InColor Card

The routines for the InColor Card's 720-by-348 16-color mode resemble the EGA routines in Listings 11-3 and 11-4, because both adapters' video buffers are mapped in parallel bit planes. Differences between the routines lie in the way pixel addresses are computed, in how the video buffer is interleaved, and in how individual bit planes are accessed. On the InColor Card, you can use the same technique as ReadPixelInC() (discussed in Chapter 5) to program the Read/Write Control and Color registers and isolate the contents of each bit plane. Similarly, a bit block store routine for the InColor Card follows StorePixelInC() in its use of the Plane Mask register and the Read/Write Control and Color registers.

Bitwise Pixel Operations

If you experimented with the pixel-programming and line-drawing examples in previous chapters, you probably know why the bitwise logical operations—XOR, AND, and OR—are useful in video graphics programming. In this case, you can skip the next few paragraphs. Otherwise, read on to see how video graphics programs can exploit the ability to perform XOR, AND, and OR on pixel values.

XOR

The XOR operation is useful because it is reversible. When you change a pixel's value in the video buffer using the XOR function, you can restore its original value by repeating the operation. For example, if a pixel in the video buffer has the value 9, setting its value by XORing it with a value of 5 results in a pixel value of 0CH. XORing the resulting pixel value (0CH) with a value of 5 restores the original pixel value of 9.

This implies that you can XOR objects into the video buffer and onto the screen, and then erase them, without worrying about saving and restoring the contents of the video buffer. The use of XOR has limitations, however. One is that an image containing zero-value pixels cannot be XORed into the video buffer. Because XORing a pixel with 0 leaves the pixel's value unchanged, only nonzero pixels in the image affect the video buffer.

Another more serious limitation is that a patterned background can obscure the image you are trying to XOR into the video buffer. Consider Figure 11-1, in which a text string is XORed against progressively distracting backgrounds. The text is perfectly readable against a solid background, but a striped background significantly obscures the letters. In the worst case, XORing a single-color image into a pattern of random pixels results only in another pattern of random pixels.

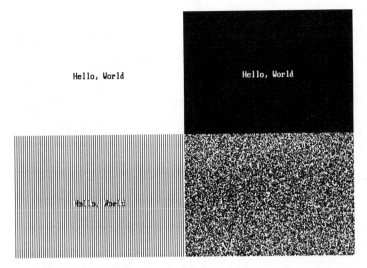

Figure 11-1. *Effects of XORing a text string against various backgrounds.*

NOT

A bitwise NOT operation on a pixel value toggles all 1 bits to 0 and all 0 bits to 1. Obviously, two sequential NOT operations will leave the pixel value unchanged. A common programming practice in monochrome graphics modes is to use NOT to toggle a reverse video state. For instance, a black-on-white character can be reversed to white-on-black by performing NOT operations on its pixels.

The effect of NOT on multibit pixel values is less clear. In this situation, the NOT operation converts one pixel value into some other pixel value, but the colors corresponding to these two values may be unrelated. Thus, in a color graphics mode, performing a NOT operation on all pixels in a character matrix changes both the foreground and background values, but the resulting color combination may not be particularly attractive or even readable. In manipulating pixels in color graphics, use NOT with caution.

 A bitwise NOT is equivalent to performing a bitwise XOR using a binary value of all 1 bits. This means you can use any of the pixel XOR routines developed in this book to perform NOT operations as well. Thus, little can be gained by writing special-purpose NOT routines for pixel manipulation.

AND

The bitwise logical operation AND is also useful in manipulating graphics images. Consider, for instance, how you might go about drawing the striped circle in Figure 11-2b. You could do it the hard way, by intersecting a set of parallel lines with the circle. This procedure would be laborious, however, because of the extra programming and increased computational overhead involved in determining the intersection points.

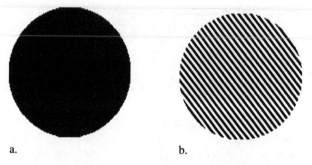

a.   b.

Figure 11-2. *Using AND to draw a striped circle. The circle in Figure 11-2a consists of pixels of the maximum possible value. The lines are drawn across the circle using a pixel AND operation to produce the striped circle in Figure 11-2b.*

It is much easier to draw a filled circle (see Figure 11-2a) with pixels of the maximum possible value (that is, all bits set to 1) against a background of zero-value pixels. This circle is used as a mask against which you AND the pixels in the parallel lines. When pixels in each line are ANDed with pixels inside the circle, their original values are stored intact in the video buffer. Outside the circle, the result of ANDing the line pixels with the zero background always results in zero-value pixels being stored in the buffer. The result: a striped circle.

You can apply this technique to any graphics form, but it is particularly attractive in conjunction with a bit block move routine. You can superimpose patterned images with a short sequence of bit block moves using pixel AND and OR operations. In Figure 11-3, a circular chunk of pattern B is superimposed on pattern A by using a mask to isolate a "hole" in pattern A. The inverse of the same mask

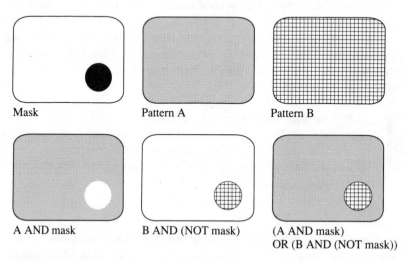

Mask   Pattern A   Pattern B

A AND mask   B AND (NOT mask)   (A AND mask)
                                               OR (B AND (NOT mask))

Figure 11-3. *Masking patterned images with pixel AND operations.*

extracts the congruent piece of pattern B. The two masked patterns are then superimposed by a third bit block move that uses OR (or XOR) to update pixels.

OR

The bitwise OR operator is less frequently used than XOR for manipulating pixel values. The OR operation, unlike XOR or NOT, is not reversible. The result of ORing pixels always depends on their previous values in the video buffer.

One typical use of the pixel OR operation is to accentuate intersections of forms in the video buffer. Consider what happens when you OR two different-colored areas into a 16-color video buffer (see Figure 11-4). If one rectangle is filled with pixels of value 3 and the other rectangle with pixels of value 5, the pixels at the intersection points have the value 7 (3 OR 5). With the usual default color palette, the upper rectangle appears cyan, the lower rectangle is violet, and the intersection is white.

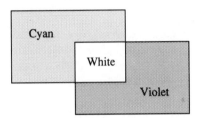

Figure 11-4. *ORing two colored areas into a 16-bit video buffer.*

Bit Block Tiling

You can use bit block move routines to fill an area of the video buffer with any arbitrary pattern. Do this by tiling the buffer through bit block moves to adjoining rectangular areas of the buffer (see Figure 11-5). Using the AND mask technique, you can tile any arbitrary form, such as the circle in Figure 11-6, with a pattern contained in a bit block.

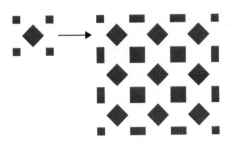

Figure 11-5. *Bit block tiling.*

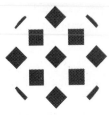

Figure 11-6. *Tiling with AND mask.*

 You can use a variation of bit block tiling as a sort of software character generator. If you define a group of bit blocks, each of which represents a character in a character set, you can tile the screen with characters. This is one technique for displaying proportionally spaced characters.

Animation

PC and PS/2 video subsystems have no built-in hardware to support animation. Consequently, moving images across the screen is a task relegated to software. (This is a good reason to make your video graphics routines as efficient as possible.) Several software techniques can produce real-time video animation. Each technique is best suited to a particular type of animation.

XOR Animation

You can take advantage of the reversibility of the logical XOR operation to make any pixel or set of pixels appear to move across the display. To make an object appear to move, XOR it into the video buffer twice. The object flickers onto the screen the first time it is drawn. It immediately disappears the second time it is drawn. If you repeatedly redraw the object in a slightly different position, it appears to move across the screen.

Outlining

Consider the C fragment in Listing 11-5. This bit of code makes a circle appear to grow outward from its center by repeatedly XORing it into the video buffer with a gradually increasing radius.

```
/* Listing 11-5 */

main()
{
        int     xc      = 400;          /* center of circle */
        int     yc      = 125;
        int     a,b;                    /* semimajor and semiminor axes */
        int     n = 12;                 /* pixel value */
        int     i;
        float   ScaleFactor = 1.37;     /* for 640x350 16-color mode */
```

Listing 11-5. *XORing a circle into the video buffer.*   *(continued)*

Listing 11-5. *Continued.*

```
        for( i=0; i<10; i++ )
          for( a=0; a<100; a++ )
          {
            b = (float) a / ScaleFactor;    /* scale semiminor axis */
            Ellipse( xc, yc, a, b, n );     /* draw a circle */
            Ellipse( xc, yc, a, b, n );     /* draw it again */
          }
}
```

This technique is frequently used interactively to outline a rectangular area of the display. The outline is rapidly XORed into and out of the video buffer as the user moves a pointing device such as a mouse. Just as the circle created by the routine in Listing 11-5 appears to grow, a rectangular outline can appear to move, grow, or shrink in response to the user's actions.

The routine in Listing 11-6 slides a rectangle across the screen. At each iteration, the rectangle is drawn and then erased using lines that are XORed into the video buffer. In this example, the rectangle's onscreen location is changed within an iterative loop. In practice, however, the rectangle's size and location could be changed in response to input from the keyboard or from a pointing device. In this case, the rectangle would be erased and redrawn whenever the input indicated a change in position.

```
/* Listing 11-6 */

#define Xmax      640

main()
{
        int     x0      = 0;            /* corners of box at 0,0 and 150,100 */
        int     y0      = 0;
        int     x1      = 150;
        int     y1      = 100;
        int     n = 12;                 /* pixel value */


        while( x1 < Xmax )                      /* slide box right */
          XORBox( x0++, y0, x1++, y1, n );

        while( x0 > 0 )                         /* slide box left */
          XORBox( --x0, y0, --x1, y1, n );
}


XORBox ( x0, y0, x1, y1, n )
int     x0,y0,x1,y1;            /* pixel coordinates of opposite corners */
int     n;                     /* pixel value */
{
        Rectangle( x0, y0, x1, y1, n );        /* draw the box */
        Rectangle( x0, y0, x1, y1, n );        /* erase the box */
}
```

Listing 11-6. *XORing a rectangle into the video buffer.*   *(continued)*

Listing 11-6. *Continued.*

```
Rectangle( x0, y0, x1, y1, n )
int     x0,y0,x1,y1;
int     n;
{
        Line( x0, y0, x0, y1, n );
        Line( x0, y0, x1, y0, n );
        Line( x1, y1, x0, y1, n );
        Line( x1, y1, x1, y0, n );
}
```

Rubberbanding

A related technique based on the XOR operation is rubberbanding, in which a
moving object remains attached to a stationary object by a straight line. The technique is called rubberbanding because the line that connects the two objects appears to stretch as it moves. Listing 11-7 is similar to Listing 11-6, but moves a
rubberbanded line around the point at (150,100).

```
/* Listing 11-7 */

#define Xmax    640                         /* screen dimensions in 640x350 mode *
#define Ymax    350

main()
{
        int     x0      = 150;      /* fixed endpoint at 150,100 */
        int     y0      = 100;
        int     x       = 0;        /* moving endpoint at 0,0 */
        int     y       = 0;
        int     n       = 12;       /* pixel value */


        for( ; x<Xmax; x++ )                      /* move right */
          XORLine( x0, y0, x, y, n );

        for( --x; y<Ymax; y++ )                   /* move down */
          XORLine( x0, y0, x, y, n );

        for( --y; x>=0; --x )                     /* move left */
          XORLine( x0, y0, x, y, n );

        for( x++; y>=0; --y )                     /* move up */
          XORLine( x0, y0, x, y, n );
}


XORLine ( x0, y0, x1, y1, n )
int     x0,y0,x1,y1;             /* endpoints */
int     n;                       /* pixel value */
{
        Line( x0, y0, x1, y1, n );           /* the line is onscreen */
        Line( x0, y0, x1, y1, n );           /* the line is erased */
}
```

Listing 11-7. *XORing a line into the video buffer.*

Bit Block Moves

You can use XOR with a bit block move to animate any arbitrary group of pixels. But use this technique only with a relatively small bit block, since generally a bit block contains many more pixels to be drawn and redrawn than does a line or a rectangle. The longer it takes to maneuver the bit block around the screen, the slower your video routine performs.

Problems with XOR Animation

Objects that are animated by XOR operations always flicker. The reason is obvious: An object is visible only after you first XOR it into the buffer. The second XOR makes it disappear. The resulting flicker draws attention to the animated object, and may be desirable, particularly if the object is repeatedly XORed even when you aren't moving it. On the other hand, the flickering can be distracting, particularly on color displays where the XORed object alternates between two garish colors.

You can sometimes alleviate flickering during XOR animation by inserting a software ''pause'' between the first and second XOR operations. This pause can be an empty loop, a call to some short subroutine, or perhaps a wait for the next vertical blanking interval. In any case, because the XORed object remains on the screen slightly longer, it may flicker less.

The animated image can disappear if the loop that performs the XOR operations inadvertently becomes synchronized with the display refresh cycle. In this situation, the animated object is never visible if both XOR operations occur outside the relatively brief time interval when the raster is displaying the relevant portion of the video buffer. Solving this sort of problem is tricky because it involves both the speed of your program and the size of the animated image.

Overlapping Bit Block Moves

In some applications, you can avoid XOR animation problems by rapidly redrawing a block of pixels in overlapping locations in the video buffer (see Figure 11-7 and Listing 11-8). The bit block in Figure 11-7 has a margin of background pixels along its left edge. Each time you store the bit block in the video buffer, this margin overlaps the foreground pixels in the previously drawn block. Without this margin, unexpected streaks of foreground pixels trail the bit block as it moves to the right across the screen.

Although they are fast enough for most purposes, the bit block move routines in this chapter are too slow for such performance-intensive applications as arcade-style video games. You can tailor the code in several ways to increase the animation speed if you're willing to sacrifice their general-purpose approach.

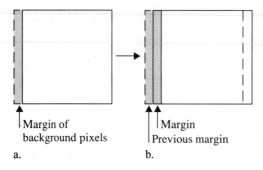

Margin of
background pixels

a.

Margin
Previous margin

b.

Figure 11-7. *Overlapping bit block moves. The bit block is drawn (Figure 11-7a), then drawn again slightly to the right (Figure 11-7b). The margin of background pixels restores the background as the bit block is "moved" to the right.*

```
char far buf[(32/4)*21+5];        /* bit block buffer large enough */
                                  /*  to contain a 32- by 21-pixel block */

Line( 1, 10, 21, 10, Fgd );       /* a right-pointing arrowhead */
Line( 21,  0, 31, 10, Fgd );      /*  in a 32- by 21-pixel bit block */
Line( 21, 20, 31, 10, Fgd );
Line( 21,  0, 21, 20, Fgd );

GetBitBlock( 0, 0, 31, 20, buf );      /* copy the bit block to */
                                       /*  system RAM */
for ( i = 0; i < 300; i++ )
  StoreBitBlock( buf, i, 0 );          /* slide rightward */
```

Listing 11-8. *A program to move a block of pixels using the overlapping technique.*

One technique is to limit the bit block routines to byte-aligned (or, on the CGA and the HGC, word-aligned) blocks of pixels. This eliminates much of the bit-mask logic and lets you make full use of the 80x86 MOVS instruction. Another approach is to write routines that handle bit blocks of a fixed, predetermined size. This lets you replace some iterative loops in the routines with repetitive sequences of in-line code. Unfortunately, even highly optimized CGA and EGA animation routines rarely come close to the speed you can expect from arcade-style video display hardware.

A Graphics-Mode Cursor

In alphanumeric modes, the on-screen cursor indicates the location where your program expects the user's next input. Most alphanumeric-mode programs rely on the hardware-generated blinking cursor to indicate the current input location. In graphics modes, on the other hand, hardware does not support a cursor; your software must generate one.

Implementing a cursor in a graphics mode is somewhat complicated, because you must draw the form that represents the cursor directly into the video buffer, while preserving the pixels that the operation overwrites. You can do this in two ways: by using XOR to display the cursor, or by saving and restoring the bit block that is overlaid by the cursor.

XOR

The simplest way to display a graphics cursor is to XOR it into and then out of the video buffer. This technique is the same one used to animate graphics images, and the same pros and cons apply.

Probably the worst side effect of XORing a graphics cursor into the video buffer is that the color displayed for the XORed cursor can change with the background. The cursor can all but disappear on a patterned background or on a background with a displayed color near that of the XORed cursor.

Palette programming can prevent this problem. For example, the EGA palette in Figure 11-8 is set up assuming that all pixels in the cursor shape have the value 8 (1000B) and that all preexisting pixels in the video buffer have a value from 0 through 7. With this arrangement, XORing the cursor into the video buffer causes it always to be displayed with color value 3FH (high-intensity white). The obvious drawback is that this technique halves the number of colors you can display.

Palette Register	Color Value
00H	0
01H	1
02H	2
03H	3
04H	4
05H	5
06H	6
07H	7
08H	3FH
09H	3FH
0AH	3FH
0BH	3FH
0CH	3FH
0DH	3FH
0EH	3FH
0FH	3FH

Figure 11-8. *EGA palette values for a high-intensity white XOR graphics cursor.*

Bit Block Move

Another approach is to make a copy of the bit block of pixels that the cursor replaces. You can then erase the cursor by restoring the pixels in the video buffer from the copy. This technique is attractive because it lets you use any means you choose to draw the cursor.

A good way to draw the cursor, once you have made a copy of the underlying pixels in the video buffer, is to copy the cursor shape into the buffer with a bit block move. Obviously, this technique works best with a rectangular cursor. To draw a cursor of any arbitrary shape, use a two-step process (see Figure 11-9). First, zero a group of pixels in the shape of the cursor in the video buffer with a bit block AND operation. Then draw the cursor with a bit block OR or XOR operation.

 Whenever you use a graphics-mode cursor, you must ensure that the cursor is erased before updating the video buffer. If you do not, your program may inadvertently update the portion of the video buffer that contains the cursor image. The next cursor move will restore the contents of the buffer to what they were before the cursor was drawn, leaving a "hole" where the cursor was (see Figure 11-10).

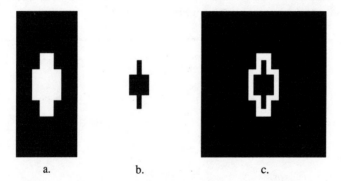

a.   b.   c.

Figure 11-9. *Drawing a graphics cursor with a 2-step mask-and-replace technique: First, a mask (Figure 11-9a) is ANDed into the video buffer. Then the cursor shape (Figure 11-9b) is ORed into the buffer to give the result in Figure 11-9c.*

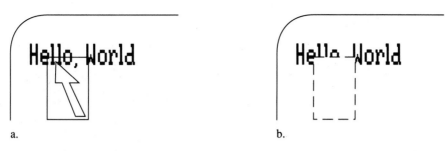

a.   b.

Figure 11-10. *If a graphics cursor is accidentally overwritten (Figure 11-10a), a "hole" appears when the cursor is erased (Figure 11-10b).*

12

Some Advanced Video Programming Techniques

A Vertical Interrupt Handler
EGA and VGA ● MCGA

Panning on the EGA and VGA
Positioning the Screen Window ● Panning
Resizing the Video Buffer

Bit-Plane Layering

EGA and VGA Split Screen

The Light Pen Interface
Light Pen Position ● Light Pen Switch
Determining Hercules Video Modes

This chapter deals with some of the less frequently exploited capabilities of PC and PS/2 video subsystems. Most programmers do not concern themselves with these hardware features, because they are infrequently used in most video software. Still, each of these hardware features lends itself to programming techniques that can be used in certain applications where nothing else is as effective.

Nothing in this chapter requires "gonzo programming" or any magical knowledge of the hardware. You should nevertheless be comfortable with 80x86 assembly-language programming before tackling the details of this material. Most of the chapter describes programming techniques for the EGA and the VGA, but the discussions of the light pen interface and bit-plane layering are pertinent to Hercules adapters as well.

A Vertical Interrupt Handler

It's neither the interrupt nor the handler that's vertical—it's the fact that the CRTC on the EGA, the VGA, and the MCGA can generate a hardware interrupt at the start of the vertical blanking interval, that is, at the start of the scan line after the bottom line of displayed video buffer data. An interrupt handler for this Vertical Interrupt can thus update the video buffer or program the video hardware without interfering with the display.

The interrupt is generated on interrupt request line 2 (IRQ2). The computer's programmable interrupt controller (PIC) is set up during the ROM BIOS coldstart to map IRQ2 to interrupt vector 0AH, so a Vertical Interrupt handler should be designed to handle interrupt 0AH.

The programmable interrupt controller used in the IBM PC, PC/AT, and PS/2 Models 50, 60, and 80 is the Intel 8259A; in the PS/2 Model 30, the same functions are supported in a proprietary VLSI chip, the I/O Support Gate Array. In all cases, however, the programming interface to the PIC for managing Vertical Interrupts is the same.

EGA and VGA

The scan line number at which the interrupt is issued is 1 greater than the value in the CRTC's Vertical Display Enable End register (12H). The value in this register specifies the number of scan lines of video buffer data that are displayed, so the CRTC generates Vertical Interrupts at the start of the vertical blanking interval.

Bits 4 and 5 of CRTC's Vertical Retrace End register (11H) control whether and when the CRTC signals a Vertical Interrupt. You set bit 5 to 1 to enable the CRTC to generate the interrupt. Bit 4 controls a 1-bit latch whose status appears in bit 7 of Input Status Register Zero (3C2H). You must zero bit 4 to clear the status latch. When you set bit 4 to 1, the latch status bit changes from 0 to 1 when the next vertical interrupt occurs, and remains set to 1 until you again clear the latch.

To use the Vertical Interrupt feature, you must perform the following actions:

- Point the interrupt 0AH vector to a Vertical Interrupt handler.

- Enable IRQ2.

- Enable the Vertical Interrupt.

The routine in Listing 12-1 shows how to do this. Note how this routine is coordinated with the interrupt handler itself. The routine preserves the interrupt 0AH vector so the interrupt handler can chain to the previous handler if necessary, and so the routine can eventually restore the previous interrupt vector when the interrupt handler is no longer needed.

```
                TITLE    'Listing 12-1'
                NAME     VREGA
                PAGE     55,132

;
; Name:         VREGA
;
; Function:     Vertical Interrupt Service routine for EGA and VGA
;
; Caller:       Microsoft C:
;
;                       int EnableISR0A();      /* returns 0 if installed ok */
;
;                       void DisableISR0A();
;

CRT_MODE        EQU      49h                    ; addresses in video BIOS data area
ADDR_6845       EQU      63h

DGROUP          GROUP    _DATA

_TEXT           SEGMENT byte public 'CODE'
                ASSUME  cs:_TEXT,ds:DGROUP

ISR0A           PROC     far                    ; Interrupt handler for INT 0Ah

                push     ax                     ; preserve registers
                push     dx
                push     ds

                mov      ax,seg DGROUP
                mov      ds,ax                   ; DS -> DGROUP

; determine whether a Vertical Interrupt has occurred

                mov      dx,3C2h                 ; DX := I/O port for
                                                 ;    Input Status Register Zero
                in       al,dx
                test     al,80h                  ; test bit 7 of the Status Reg value
                jnz      L10                     ; jump if vertical interrupt
```

Listing 12-1. *Handling Vertical Interrupts on the EGA and VGA.*   *(continued)*

Listing 12-1. *Continued.*

```
; not a Vertical Interrupt so chain to previous interrupt handler

                pushf                   ; simulate an INT
                call    ds:PrevISR0A    ;   to the previous INT 0Ah handler
                jmp     short Lexit

; handle a Vertical Interrupt

L10:            mov     dx,Port3x4      ; DX := 3B4h or 3D4h

                in      al,dx           ; AL := value of CRTC address reg
                push    ax              ; preserve this value

                mov     ax,DefaultVREnd ; AH := default value for VR End reg
                                        ; AL := 11h (register number)
                and     ah,11101111b    ; AH bit 4 := 0 (clear interrupt latch)
                out     dx,ax           ; update VR End register
                jmp     $+2             ; wait for CRTC to respond

; send End of Interrupt to Intel 8259A Programmable Interrupt Controller
;   to allow subsequent IRQ2 interrupts to occur

                mov     al,20h          ; 8259A I/O port
                out     20h,al          ; send nonspecific EOI to 8259A
                jmp     $+2             ; wait for PIC to respond
                sti                     ; enable interrupts

; do something useful ...

                inc     word ptr _VRcount       ; increment a counter

; enable CRTC to generate another interrupt

                cli                     ; disable interrupts
                mov     ax,DefaultVREnd ; AH := default value for VR End reg
                                        ; AL := 11h (register number)
                and     ah,11011111b    ; AH bit 5 := 0 (enable vertical int)
                or      ah,00010000b    ; AH bit 4 := 1 (enable int latch)
                out     dx,ax
                jmp     $+2

                pop     ax
                out     dx,al           ; restore previous Address reg value

Lexit:          pop     ds              ; restore registers and exit
                pop     dx
                pop     ax
                iret


ISR0A           ENDP

;
; EnableISR0A — enable Vertical Interrupt Handler
;
                PUBLIC  _EnableISR0A
_EnableISR0A    PROC    near
```

(continued)

Listing 12-1. *Continued.*

```
                push    bp                 ; preserve caller registers
                mov     bp,sp
                push    si
                push    di

                mov     ax,40h
                mov     es,ax              ; ES -> video BIOS data area

; save default CRTC register values

                mov     dx,es:[ADDR_6845]  ; DX := CRTC Address port
                mov     Port3x4,dx         ; save port address

                mov     ax,1A00h           ; AH := 1AH (INT 10H function number)
                                           ; AL := 0 (read Display Combination)
                int     10h                ; AL := 1AH if function 1AH supported
                                           ; BL := active video subsystem
                cmp     al,1Ah
                jne     L20                ; jump if not a VGA

                cmp     bl,7
                je      L21                ; jump if VGA

                cmp     bl,8
                je      L21                ; jump if VGA

                mov     ax,0FFFFh          ; return 0FFFFh if neither EGA nor VGA
                jmp     short L23

; get default value for EGA Vertical Retrace End register

L20:            mov     al,es:[CRT_MODE]   ; AL := video BIOS mode number
                mov     bx,offset DGROUP:EGADefaultVals
                xlat                       ; AL := default value for VR End reg
                jmp     short L22

; get default value for VGA Vertical Retrace End register

L21:            mov     al,VREndReg        ; AL := VR End register number
                out     dx,al
                inc     dx                 ; DX := 3B5H or 3D5H
                in      al,dx              ; AL := current value for register

L22:            mov     VREndValue,al      ; save this value

; save old interrupt 0Ah vector

                mov     ax,350Ah           ; AH := 35H (INT 21h function number)
                                           ; AL := 0AH (interrupt number)
                int     21h                ; ES:BX := previous INT 0AH vector

                mov     word ptr PrevISR0A,bx
                mov     word ptr PrevISR0A+2,es ; save previous vector
```

(continued)

Listing 12-1. *Continued.*

```
; update interrupt 0AH vector with address of this handler

                push    ds              ; preserve DS
                mov     dx,offset ISR0A
                push    cs
                pop     ds              ; DS:DX -> ISR0A
                mov     ax,250Ah        ; AH := 25H (INT 21H function number)
                                        ; AL := 0AH (interrupt number)
                int     21h             ; update INT 0AH vector
                pop     ds              ; restore DS

; enable IRQ2 by zeroing bit 2 of the 8259A's mask register

                cli                     ; clear interrupts
                mov     dx,21h          ; DX := 8259A mask register
                in      al,dx           ; AL := mask register value
                and     al,11111011b    ; reset bit 2
                out     dx,al

; enable vertical interrupts

                mov     dx,Port3x4      ; DX := 3B4H or 3D4H
                mov     ax,DefaultVREnd

                and     ah,11001111b
                out     dx,ax           ; clear bits 4 and 5 of VR End reg
                jmp     $+2             ; wait for CRTC to respond
                or      ah,00010000b
                out     dx,ax           ; set bit 4
                jmp     $+2
                sti                     ; enable interrupts

                xor     ax,ax           ; AX := 0 (return value)

L23:            pop     di              ; restore registers and exit
                pop     si
                mov     sp,bp
                pop     bp
                ret

_EnableISR0A    ENDP


;
; DisableISR0A - disable Vertical Interrupt Handler
;
                PUBLIC  _DisableISR0A
_DisableISR0A   PROC    near


                push    bp
                mov     bp,sp
                push    si
                push    di
                push    ds
```

(continued)

Listing 12-1. *Continued.*

```
; disable vertical interrupts

                cli                     ; disable interrupts
                mov     dx,Port3x4
                mov     ax,DefaultVREnd
                out     dx,ax           ; restore Vertical Retrace End reg
                jmp     $+2
                sti                     ; enable interrupts

; restore previous interrupt 0Ah handler

                lds     dx,PrevISR0A    ; DS:DX := previous INT 0AH vector
                mov     ax,250Ah        ; AH := 25H (INT 21H function number)
                                        ; AL := 0AH (interrupt number)
                int     21h


                pop     ds              ; restore registers and exit
                pop     di
                pop     si
                mov     sp,bp
                pop     bp
                ret

_DisableISR0A   ENDP


_TEXT           ENDS

_DATA           SEGMENT word public 'DATA'

                EXTRN   _VRcount:word   ; declared in C caller

PrevISR0A       DD      ?               ; save area for old int 0Ah vector
Port3x4         DW      ?               ; 3B4h or 3D4h

DefaultVREnd    LABEL   word
VREndReg        DB      11h             ; Vertical Retrace End register number
VREndValue      DB      ?               ; default value for VR End register

EGADefaultVals  DB      2Bh,2Bh,2Bh,2Bh,24h,24h,23h,2Eh ; default values for
                DB      00h,00h,00h,00h,00h,24h,23h,2Eh ;  EGA VR End reg
                DB      2Bh

_DATA           ENDS

                END
```

The handler itself, in procedure ISR0A, gains control whenever interrupt 0AH occurs. To distinguish between the hardware Vertical Interrupt on IRQ2 and a possible software interrupt 0AH, the handler examines bit 7 of Input Status Register Zero. If this bit is 1, a Vertical Interrupt has occurred, and the handler continues about its business. If the bit is 0, no Vertical Interrupt has occurred, so the handler chains to the previous interrupt 0AH handler.

T I P

A drawback to using the Vertical Interrupt is that any hardware interrupt on IRQ2 causes the status bit in Input Status Register Zero to be set. Thus, although the status bit can be used to detect software interrupt 0AH, an interrupt handler cannot distinguish between EGA Vertical Interrupts and IRQ2 interrupts generated by other hardware unless the other hardware can be reliably interrogated. Since some other IBM PC adapters can use IRQ2 (for example, the bus version of the Microsoft Mouse), you can reliably use the Vertical Interrupt only when certain about the exact hardware configuration of the PC on which your program is running.

Once the handler detects a Vertical Interrupt (that is, bit 7 of Input Status Register Zero is 1), it issues a nonspecific end-of-interrupt (EOI) instruction to the interrupt controller so that subsequent IRQ2 interrupts can be processed. Reentrance is not a problem, because additional Vertical Interrupts will not be signalled until the handler itself clears and reenables the status latch. Once the EOI has been issued, the handler is free to perform some useful action. In this example, it simply increments a counter. Just before exiting, the handler reprograms the Vertical Retrace End register to enable the next Vertical Interrupt.

The example in Listing 12-2 shows how you can integrate a Vertical Interrupt handler into a high-level program. The example is intentionally simple. It does nothing but count a designated number of Vertical Interrupts and display a message. Of course, your own Vertical Interrupt handler might perform more complicated actions than simply updating a variable. For instance, you could perform animation by updating the video buffer each time the interrupt occurs. You might also update the CRT and Attribute controllers to produce a panning effect using techniques described later in this chapter.

```
/* Listing 12-2 */

int     VRcount = 0;              /* vertical interrupt counter */

main()
{
        if ( EnableISR0A() )
        {
          printf( "\nCan't enable vertical interrupt handler\n" );
          exit( 1 );
        }

        while (VRcount < 600)
          printf( "\015Number of vertical interrupts:  %d", VRcount );

        DisableISR0A();
}
```

Listing 12-2. *Using a Vertical Interrupt handler in a C program.*

T I P Hardware support for the Vertical Interrupt feature can vary. IBM's VGA adapter, for example, does not support Vertical Interrupts at all. On some EGA clones, the polarity of bit 7 in Input Status Register Zero is opposite to that of the equivalent EGA bit; that is, a Vertical Interrupt has occurred when bit 7 is 0. (Second-source manufacturers of EGA-compatible adapters do not always emulate every detail of the EGA's occasionally inscrutable hardware design.) To ensure that your Vertical Interrupt handler works correctly on EGA clones, determine the status bit's polarity when the bit is in a known state and devise your test for the Vertical Interrupt accordingly.

MCGA

A Vertical Interrupt handler for the MCGA, such as the one in Listing 12-3, is similar to the handler for the EGA and the VGA. On the MCGA, the Interrupt Control register (11H) contains the control and status bits used to set up and detect a Vertical Interrupt. Zeroing bit 5 of the Interrupt Control register enables the MCGA to generate a Vertical Interrupt. Zeroing bit 4 clears the interrupt status latch. Setting bit 4 to 1 allows the MCGA to detect subsequent interrupts. Bit 6 is the interrupt status bit. The MCGA sets this bit to 1 to indicate that a Vertical Interrupt has occurred.

```
                TITLE    'Listing 12-3'
                NAME     VRMCGA
                PAGE     55,132

;
; Name:         VRMCGA
;
; Function:     Vertical Interrupt Service routine for MCGA
;
; Caller:       Microsoft C:
;
;                     int EnableISR0A();        /* returns 0 if installed ok */
;
;                     void DisableISR0A();
;

ADDR_6845       EQU      63h

DGROUP          GROUP    _DATA

_TEXT           SEGMENT byte public 'CODE'
                ASSUME   cs:_TEXT,ds:DGROUP

ISR0A           PROC     far            ; Interrupt handler for INT 0Ah

                push     ax             ; preserve registers
                push     dx
                push     ds

                mov      ax,seg DGROUP
                mov      ds,ax          ; DS -> DGROUP
```

Listing 12-3. *Handling Vertical Interrupts on the MCGA.*   *(continued)*

Listing 12-3. *Continued.*

```
                mov     dx,Port3x4      ; DX := CRTC Address reg number
                in      al,dx
                push    ax              ; preserve CRTC Address reg value

; determine whether a Vertical Interrupt has occurred

                mov     al,IContReg     ; AL := register number
                out     dx,al
                jmp     $+2             ; wait for MCGA to respond
                inc     dx              ; DX := 3D5H
                in      al,dx           ; AL := current Interrupt Control
                                        ;  register value
                dec     dx
                test    al,40h          ; test bit 6
                jnz     L10             ; jump if Vertical Interrupt

; not a Vertical Interrupt so chain to previous interrupt handler

                pushf                   ; simulate an INT to the
                call    ds:PrevISR0A    ;  previous INT 0Ah handler
                jmp     short Lexit

; handle a Vertical Interrupt

L10:            mov     ax,DefaultICont ; AH := default value for
                                        ;  Interrupt Control register
                                        ; AL := 11h (register number)
                and     ah,11101111b    ; AH bit 4 := 0 (clear interrupt latch)
                out     dx,ax           ; update Interrupt Control reg
                jmp     $+2             ; wait for MCGA to respond

; send End of Interrupt to Programmable Interrupt Controller
;   to allow subsequent IRQ2 interrupts to occur

                mov     al,20h          ; PIC I/O port
                out     20h,al          ; send nonspecific EOI to PIC
                jmp     $+2             ; wait for PIC to respond
                sti                     ; enable interrupts

; do something useful ...

                inc     word ptr _VRcount      ; increment a counter

; enable CRTC to generate another interrupt

                cli                     ; disable interrupts
                mov     ax,DefaultICont ; AH := default value for
                                        ;  Interrupt Control register
                                        ; AL := 11h (register number)
                and     ah,11011111b    ; AH bit 5 := 0 (enable Vert Int)
                or      ah,00010000b    ; AH bit 4 := 1 (enable int latch)
                out     dx,ax
                jmp     $+2

Lexit:          pop     ax
                out     dx,al           ; restore previous 3D4H value
```

(continued)

Listing 12-3. *Continued.*

```
                pop     ds              ; restore registers and exit
                pop     dx
                pop     ax
                iret

ISR0A           ENDP

;
; EnableISR0A — enable Vertical Interrupt Handler
;
                PUBLIC  _EnableISR0A
_EnableISR0A    PROC    near

                push    bp              ; preserve caller registers
                mov     bp,sp
                push    si
                push    di


                mov     ax,40h
                mov     es,ax           ; ES -> video BIOS data area


; save default CRTC register values

                mov     dx,es:[ADDR_6845]  ; DX := CRTC Address port
                mov     Port3x4,dx      ; save port address

                mov     ax,1A00h        ; AH := 1AH (INT 10H function number)
                                        ; AL := 0 (read Display Combination)
                int     10h             ; AL := 1AH if function 1AH supported
                                        ; BL := active video subsystem
                cmp     al,1Ah
                jne     L20             ; jump if not an MCGA

                cmp     bl,0Bh
                je      L21             ; jump if MCGA

                cmp     bl,0Ch
                je      L21             ; jump if MCGA

L20:            mov     ax,0FFFFh       ; return 0FFFFh if not an MCGA
                jmp     short L23

; get default value for MCGA Interrupt Control register

L21:            mov     al,IContReg     ; AL := Interrupt Control reg number
                cli
                out     dx,al
                jmp     $+2
                inc     dx              ; DX := 3D5H
                in      al,dx           ; AL := current value for register
                sti

                mov     IContValue,al   ; save this value
```

(continued)

Listing 12-3. *Continued.*

```
; save old interrupt 0Ah vector

                mov     ax,350Ah        ; AH := 35H (INT 21h function number)
                                        ; AL := 0AH (interrupt number)
                int     21h             ; ES:BX := previous INT 0AH vector

                mov     word ptr PrevISR0A,bx
                mov     word ptr PrevISR0A+2,es ; save previous vector

; update interrupt 0AH vector with address of this handler

                push    ds              ; preserve DS
                mov     dx,offset ISR0A
                push    cs
                pop     ds              ; DS:DX -> ISR0A
                mov     ax,250Ah        ; AH := 25H (INT 21H function number)
                                        ; AL := 0AH (interrupt number)
                int     21h             ; update INT 0AH vector
                pop     ds              ; restore DS

; enable IRQ2 by zeroing bit 2 of the PIC's mask register

                cli                     ; clear interrupts
                mov     dx,21h          ; DX := PIC mask register
                in      al,dx           ; AL := mask register value
                and     al,11111011b    ; reset bit 2
                out     dx,al

; enable Vertical Interrupts

                mov     dx,Port3x4      ; DX := CRTC Address port
                mov     ax,DefaultICont


                and     ah,11001111b
                out     dx,ax           ; clear bits 4 and 5 of Int Control reg
                jmp     $+2             ; wait for MCGA to respond
                or      ah,00010000b
                out     dx,ax           ; set bit 4
                jmp     $+2
                sti                     ; enable interrupts

                xor     ax,ax           ; AX := 0 (return value)

L23:            pop     di              ; restore registers and exit
                pop     si
                mov     sp,bp
                pop     bp
                ret

_EnableISR0A    ENDP


;
; DisableISR0A — disable Vertical Interrupt handler
;
                PUBLIC  _DisableISR0A
_DisableISR0A   PROC    near
```

(continued)

Listing 12-3. *Continued.*

```
                push    bp
                mov     bp,sp
                push    si
                push    di
                push    ds

; disable Vertical Interrupts

                cli                     ; disable interrupts
                mov     dx,Port3x4
                mov     ax,DefaultICont
                out     dx,ax           ; restore Interrupt Control register
                jmp     $+2
                sti                     ; enable interrupts

; restore previous interrupt 0Ah handler

                lds     dx,PrevISR0A    ; DS:DX := previous INT 0AH vector
                mov     ax,250Ah        ; AH := 25H (INT 21H function number)
                                        ; AL := 0AH (interrupt number)
                int     21h

                pop     ds              ; restore registers and exit
                pop     di
                pop     si
                mov     sp,bp
                pop     bp
                ret

_DisableISR0A   ENDP

_TEXT           ENDS

_DATA           SEGMENT word public 'DATA'

                EXTRN   _VRcount:word   ; declared in C caller

PrevISR0A       DD      ?               ; save area for old int 0Ah vector
Port3x4         DW      ?               ; 3B4h or 3D4h

DefaultICont    LABEL   word
IContReg        DB      11h             ; Interrupt Control register number
IContValue      DB      ?               ; default value for Int Control reg

_DATA           ENDS

                END
```

 On the EGA and MCGA, if a Vertical Interrupt handler gains control while a video BIOS (INT 10H) function is executing, the interrupt handler may inadvertently disrupt BIOS CRTC programming. The reason can be traced to a subroutine buried in the IBM BIOS in these video subsystems. This subroutine is called by several video BIOS routines to perform I/O port output to video hardware registers, including CRT Controller, Sequencer, Graphics Controller, and Attribute Controller registers.

Unfortunately, this subroutine is not impervious to interrupts. It contains a sequence of two 8-bit port writes (OUT DX, AL). The first OUT loads the designated address register. The second OUT writes a data byte to the corresponding data register. If an interrupt occurs between the two port writes, and if the interrupt handler itself writes to the same port, the BIOS subroutine's second port write may be invalid.

To avoid this situation on the EGA and MCGA, the Vertical Interrupt handlers in Listings 12-1 and 12-3 read the value of the CRTC Address register at port 3D4H (3B4H on an EGA with a monochrome display). On the EGA, this value is only readable for about 15 milliseconds after the port has been written, but this is enough time for the Vertical Interrupt handler to read and preserve the value of the CRTC Address register. The handler can thus restore the value before it returns from the interrupt.

Panning on the EGA and VGA

The 256 KB video buffer of the EGA and the VGA can store several screens of data. Thus, in a sense, what is displayed represents a "screen window," a sort of hardware window into the contents of the video buffer.

Positioning the Screen Window

On an adapter such as the MDA or the CGA, the CRT Controller's Start Address registers control which portion of the video buffer is displayed. Because these registers contain a byte offset into the video buffer, you can control the position of the screen window only to the nearest byte. On the other hand, the CRT Controller on the EGA and the VGA can position the start of the screen window at any given pixel position.

In graphics modes, the contents of the CRTC's Start Address High and Start Address Low registers (0CH and 0DH) locate the screen window to the nearest byte offset in the video buffer. The contents of the CRTC's Preset Row Scan register (08H) and the Attribute Controller's Horizontal Pel Pan register (13H) "fine-tune" the screen window's position pixel by pixel (see Figure 12-1).

When you change the screen window's position smoothly, pixel by pixel, the displayed image appears to pan across the screen. A convenient way to do this is to write a routine that locates the screen window at a specified pixel position and then call the routine iteratively from within a loop. This routine, as demonstrated in Listing 12-4, must distinguish between alphanumeric and graphics modes. It must also handle a 9-pixel-wide character matrix in VGA and EGA monochrome alphanumeric modes.

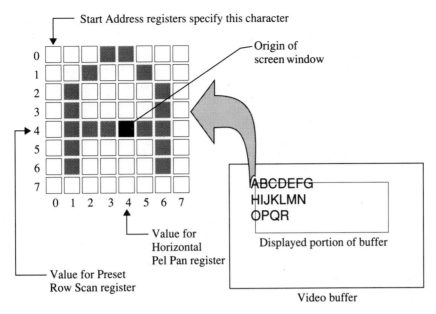

Start Address registers specify this character

Origin of
screen window

0
1
2
3
4
5
6
7

0 1 2 3 4 5 6 7

Value for
Horizontal
Pel Pan register

Value for Preset
Row Scan register

ABCDEFG
HIJKLMN
OPQR

Displayed portion of buffer

Video buffer

Figure 12-1. *Control of the displayed portion of the video buffer in alphanumeric modes.*

```
                        TITLE    'Listing 12-4'
                        NAME     ScreenOrigin
                        PAGE     55,132


;
; Name:          ScreenOrigin
;
; Function:      Set screen origin on EGA and VGA
;
; Caller:        Microsoft C:
;
;                        void ScreenOrigin(x,y);
;
;                                int   x,y;    /* pixel x,y coordinates */
;

ARGx            EQU      [bp+4]
ARGy            EQU      [bp+6]


CRT_MODE        EQU      49h               ; addresses in video BIOS data area
ADDR_6845       EQU      63h
POINTS          EQU      85h
BIOS_FLAGS      EQU      89h

DGROUP          GROUP    _DATA

_TEXT           SEGMENT byte public 'CODE'
                ASSUME   cs:_TEXT,ds:DGROUP

                PUBLIC  _ScreenOrigin
```

Listing 12-4. *Setting the screen origin on the EGA and VGA.* *(continued)*

Listing 12-4. *Continued.*

```
_ScreenOrigin    PROC      near

                 push      bp                    ; preserve caller registers
                 mov       bp,sp
                 push      si
                 push      di

                 mov       ax,40h
                 mov       es,ax                 ; ES -> video BIOS data area
                 mov       cl,es:[CRT_MODE]

                 mov       ax,ARGx               ; AX := pixel x-coordinate
                 mov       bx,ARGy               ; BX := pixel y-coordinate

                 cmp       cl,7
                 ja        L01                   ; jump if graphics mode

                 je        L02                   ; jump if monochrome alpha
                 test      byte ptr es:[BIOS_FLAGS],1
                 jnz       L02                   ; jump if VGA
                 jmp       short L03

; setup for graphics modes (8 pixels per byte)

L01:             mov       cx,8                  ; CL := 8 (displayed pixels per byte)
                                                 ; CH := 0
                 div       cl                    ; AH := bit offset in byte
                                                 ; AL := byte offset in pixel row
                 mov       cl,ah                 ; CL := bit offset (for Horiz Pel Pan)
                 xor       ah,ah
                 xchg      ax,bx                 ; AX := y
                                                 ; BX := byte offset in pixel row

                 mul       word ptr _BytesPerRow
                                                 ; AX := byte offset of start of row
                 jmp       short L05

; setup for VGA alphanumeric modes and EGA monochrome alphanumeric mode
;   (9 pixels per byte)

L02:                                             ; routine for alpha modes
                 mov       cx,9                  ; CL := 9 (displayed pixels per byte)
                                                 ; CH := 0
                 div       cl                    ; AH := bit offset in byte
                                                 ; AL := byte offset in pixel row
                 dec       ah                    ; AH := -1, 0-7
                 jns       L04                   ; jump if bit offset 0-7
                 mov       ah,8                  ; AH := 8
                 jmp       short L04
; setup for EGA color alphanumeric modes (8 pixels per byte)

L03:             mov       cx,8                  ; CL := 8 (displayed pixels per byte)
                                                 ; CH := 0
                 div       cl                    ; AH := bit offset in byte
                                                 ; AL := byte offset in pixel row
```

(continued)

Listing 12-4. *Continued.*

```
L04:            mov     cl,ah               ; CL := value for Horiz Pel Pan reg
                xor     ah,ah
                xchg    ax,bx               ; AX := y
                                            ; BX := byte offset in row
                div     byte ptr es:[POINTS]  ; AL := character row
                                            ; AH := scan line in char matrix
                xchg    ah,ch               ; AX := character row
                                            ; CH := scan line (value for Preset
                                            ;           Row Scan register)
                mul     word ptr _BytesPerRow   ; AX := byte offset of char row
                shr     ax,1                ; AX := word offset of character row


L05:            call    SetOrigin

                pop     di                  ; restore registers and exit
                pop     si
                mov     sp,bp
                pop     bp
                ret

_ScreenOrigin   ENDP


SetOrigin       PROC    near                ; Caller:  AX = offset of character row
                                            ;          BX = byte offset within row
                                            ;          CH = Preset Row Scan value
                                            ;          CL = Horizontal Pel Pan value

                add     bx,ax               ; BX := buffer offset

                mov     dx,es:[ADDR_6845]   ; CRTC I/O port (3B4H or 3D4H)
                add     dl,6                ; video status port (3BAH or 3DAH)

; update Start Address High and Low registers

L20:            in      al,dx               ; wait for start of vertical retrace
                test    al,8
                jz      L20

L21:            in      al,dx               ; wait for end of vertical retrace
                test    al,8
                jnz     L21

                cli                         ; disable interrupts
                sub     dl,6                ; DX := 3B4H or 3D4H

                mov     ah,bh               ; AH := value for Start Address High
                mov     al,0Ch              ; AL := Start Address High reg number
                out     dx,ax               ; update this register

                mov     ah,bl               ; AH := value for Start Address Low
                inc     al                  ; AL := Start Address Low reg number
                out     dx,ax               ; update this register
                sti                         ; enable interrupts

                add     dl,6                ; DX := video status port
```

(continued)

Listing 12-4. *Continued.*

```
L22:            in      al,dx               ; wait for start of vertical retrace
                test    al,8
                jz      L22

                cli                         ; disable interrupts

                sub     dl,6                ; DX := 3B4H or 3D4H
                mov     ah,ch               ; AH := value for Preset Row Scan reg
                mov     al,8                ; AL := Preset Row Scan reg number
                out     dx,ax               ; update this register

                mov     dl,0C0h             ; DX := 3C0h (Attribute Controller port)
                mov     al,13h OR 20h       ; AL bit 0-4 := Horiz Pel Pan reg number
                                            ; AL bit 5 := 1
                out     dx,al               ; write Attribute Controller Address reg
                                            ;    (The Attribute Controller address
                                            ;     flip-flop has been reset by the
                                            ;     IN at L22.)
                mov     al,cl               ; AL := value for Horiz Pel Pan reg
                out     dx,al               ; update this register

                sti                         ; reenable interrupts
                ret

SetOrigin       ENDP

_TEXT           ENDS


_DATA           SEGMENT word public 'DATA'

                EXTRN   _BytesPerRow:word           ; bytes per pixel row

_DATA           ENDS

                END
```

ScreenOrigin() accepts as input the *x*- and *y*-coordinates of the pixel that
identifies the origin (the upper left corner) of the screen. The routine first updates
the CRTC's Start Address registers. In effect, this positions the screen at the upper
left pixel of the character that contains the origin in alphanumeric modes, or at
the leftmost pixel in the byte that contains the origin in graphics modes. Then
ScreenOrigin() positions the screen exactly by updating the Horizontal Pel
Panning and Preset Row Scan registers.

The content of the Attribute Controller Horizontal Pel Panning register corresponds to the bit offset of the pixel in the screen's upper left corner. The value to
store in this register is thus

```
x MOD 8
```

In the case of 9-pixel characters in VGA alphanumeric modes and in 80-by-25
monochrome mode on the EGA, the value is

```
(x + 8) MOD 9
```

The Horizontal Pel Panning register is programmed the same way in both alphanumeric and graphics modes. This is not the case, however, for the CRTC's Preset Row Scan register, which controls the vertical position of the start of the screen.

In alphanumeric modes, the number of rows of pixels displayed for each row of characters in the video buffer depends on the height of the displayed character matrix. This is the value stored as POINTS in the ROM BIOS Video Display Data Area. The Start Address registers position the screen to a particular character in the video buffer, and the Preset Row Scan register indicates which line in the character matrix contains the origin of the screen. The Preset Row Scan register thus contains a value between 0 (the top line of the character) and POINTS-1 (the bottom line). In graphics modes, the pixels in each byte in the video buffer correspond one-to-one with pixels on the screen, so the Preset Row Scan register always contains 0.

To avoid interference with the display, updates to the Horizontal Pel Panning, Preset Row Scan, and Start Address registers should be synchronized with the display refresh cycle. The Horizontal Pel Panning register must be updated during the vertical blanking interval. On the other hand, the CRTC samples the values in the Start Address and Preset Row Scan registers at the beginning of vertical retrace, so these registers should be updated when vertical retrace is not active.

Panning

The routine in Listing 12-5 shows how you can call ScreenOrigin() to pan the screen up and down or across the video buffer. Because the position of the virtual screen always changes during a vertical blanking interval, the panning effect is smooth, with no interference on the screen.

```
Pan( x0, y0, x1, y1 )
int     x0,y0;          /* starting pixel coordinates */
int     x1,y1;          /* ending pixel coordinates */
{
        int     i = x0;
        int     j = y0;
        int     Xinc,Yinc;      /* horizontal and vertical increments */


        if ( x0 < x1 )          /* compute signs of increments */
          Xinc = 1;
        else
          Xinc = -1;

        if ( y0 < y1 )
          Yinc = 1;
        else
          Yinc = -1;
```

(continued)

Listing 12-5. *A routine to perform smooth pixel-by-pixel panning on an EGA or VGA.*

Listing 12-5. *Continued.*

```
        while ( (i != x1) || (j != y1) )
        {
          if (i != x1)                    /* compute next screen origin */
            i += Xinc;
          if (j != y1)
            j += Yinc;

          ScreenOrigin( i, j );           /* move screen origin */
        }
}
```

Resizing the Video Buffer

Horizontal panning introduces a problem. The way the video buffer is normally mapped, the first byte of each line of data in the buffer immediately follows the last byte of the previous line. If you try to pan horizontally with this map, each line appears to wrap around the screen as the screen window moves across the video buffer. To perform horizontal panning usefully, you should resize the video buffer so each line of data in it is wider than the screen window.

The value in the CRT Controller's Offset register (13H) controls the way the CRTC maps lines in the video buffer. As it scans the raster, the CRTC uses the value in this register to locate the start of each line in the video buffer map. Normally, lines in the video buffer are the same width as displayed lines. Increasing the value in the Offset register widens the lines in the video buffer map so only part of each line can be displayed at one time. This lets you pan horizontally without wraparound.

For example, consider how you could double the logical width of the video buffer in 80-by-25 alphanumeric mode. By default, the video BIOS stores the value 28H in the CRTC's Offset register, so the CRTC regards each line in the buffer as being 40 words (80 bytes) wide. Although each logical line in the buffer contains 160 bytes of data (80 character codes and 80 attribute bytes), character codes and attributes are stored in different video memory maps (see Figure 10-3 in Chapter 10). Thus, to double the logical line width, store 50H (80 decimal) in the CRTC's Offset register. The CRTC will still display 80 characters in each row on the screen, but it skips 160 characters of data between rows of characters in the video buffer.

When you resize the video buffer by programming the CRTC's Offset register, be careful not to exceed the bounds of the 256 KB video buffer. For example, in 640-by-350 16-color graphics mode, one screen's worth of pixels occupies 28,000 bytes (80 bytes per line × 350 lines) in each of the 64 KB video memory maps. If you resize the video buffer by increasing the value stored in the CRTC Offset register, you cannot go beyond 187 bytes per line in this video mode without exceeding the 64 KB limit.

The routine BufferDims () in Listing 12-6a can be called to redimension the video buffer in either graphics or alphanumeric modes. It accepts as parameters the desired horizontal and vertical dimensions of the buffer in pixels. The routine updates the relevant variables in the video BIOS data area and then programs the CRTC Offset register with the appropriate value. The example in Listing 12-6b shows how BufferDims() could be called to transform a default 80-by-25 alphanumeric mode into a 160-by-102 mode in which the Pan() routine in Listing 12-5 can be used.

```
                    TITLE    'Listing 12-6a'
                    NAME     BufferDims
                    PAGE     55,132


;
; Name:              BufferDims
;
; Function:          Set video buffer dimensions on EGA
;
; Caller:            Microsoft C:
;
;                          void BufferDims(x,y);
;
;                                  int     x,y;    /* horizontal and vertical */
;                                                  /*  dimensions in pixels */
;

ARGx                EQU      word ptr [bp+4]
ARGy                EQU      word ptr [bp+6]


CRT_MODE            EQU      49h               ; addresses in video BIOS data area
CRT_COLS            EQU      4Ah
CRT_LEN             EQU      4Ch
ADDR_6845           EQU      63h
ROWS                EQU      84h
POINTS              EQU      85h

_TEXT               SEGMENT byte public 'CODE'
                    ASSUME   cs:_TEXT

                    PUBLIC   _BufferDims
_BufferDims         PROC     near

                    push     bp                ; preserve BP
                    mov      bp,sp

                    mov      ax,40h
                    mov      es,ax             ; ES -> video BIOS data area

; determine width of displayed character matrix (8 or 9 pixels)

                    mov      bx,8              ; BX := 8 pixels wide
                    cmp      byte ptr es:[CRT_MODE],7 ; check BIOS mode number
                    jne      L01               ; jump if not monochrome

                    inc      bx                ; BX := 9 pixels wide

; update video BIOS data area
```

Listing 12-6a. *Redimensioning the video buffer.*   *(continued)*

Listing 12-6a. *Continued.*

```
L01:            mov     ax,ARGx          ; AX := number of pixels per row
                div     bl               ; AL := number of character columns
                mov     es:[CRT_COLS],al
                mov     bh,al            ; BH := number of character columns

                mov     ax,ARGy          ; DX:AX := number of pixel rows
                div     byte ptr es:[POINTS]  ; AL := number of character rows
                dec     al
                mov     es:[ROWS],al

                inc     al
                mul     bh               ; AX := character rows * character cols
                mov     es:[CRT_LEN],ax  ; update video BIOS data area

; update CRTC Offset register

                mov     ah,bh
                shr     ah,1             ; AH := number of words per row
                mov     al,13h           ; AL := CRTC Offset register number
                mov     dx,es:[ADDR_6845] ; DX := 3B4H or 3D4H
                out     dx,ax

                pop     bp               ; restore BP and exit
                ret

_BufferDims     ENDP

_TEXT           ENDS

                END
```

```c
/* Listing 12-6b */

#define CharColumns     160                 /* desired character dimensions */
#define CharRows        102

#define CharacterWidth  8                   /* 8 for EGA color modes */
                                            /* 9 for EGA monochrome or VGA */

int     BytesPerRow = CharColumns * 2;   /* for 80-column alphanumeric modes */

main()
{
        int     i;
        int far *POINTS = 0x00400085;    /* (in video display data area) */

        BufferDims( CharColumns * CharacterWidth, CharRows * (*POINTS) );

        for( i = 0; i < CharColumns / 10; i++ ) /* display a long line */
          printf("0123456789");

        Pan( 0, 0, 80 * CharacterWidth, 0 );    /* pan right */
        Pan( 80 * CharacterWidth, 0, 0, 0 );    /* pan left */
        Pan( 0, 0, 0, 50 * (*POINTS) );         /* pan down */
        Pan( 0, 50 * (*POINTS), 0, 0);          /* pan up */
}
```

Listing 12-6b. *Creating a 160-by-102 alphanumeric mode.*

Bit-Plane Layering

In EGA and VGA 16-color graphics modes and in the InColor Card's 720-by-348 16-color mode, you can display any combination of the four bit planes. On the EGA and VGA, the four low-order bits of the Attribute Controller's Color Plane Enable register (12H) control which bit planes are displayed. Similarly, on the In-Color Card, the four low-order bits of the Plane Mask register (18H) determine which bit planes are displayed. In all three subsystems, all four bits are set to 1 to enable the display of all four bit planes. You can zero any combination of these bits to prevent display of the corresponding bit planes.

When you disable a bit plane in this way, pixel values are interpreted as though the corresponding bit in each pixel were set to 0. The contents of a disabled bit plane are unaffected. This means you can draw different images into different bit planes and display them selectively. When bit planes containing different images are displayed together, the images appear to overlap, as if the bit planes were transparent and layered one above the other.

Consider the example in Figure 12-2. The grid is drawn in bit plane 3 and the cylinder in bit planes 0 through 2. (A quick way to draw both figures into the bit planes is to OR the appropriate pixel values into the video buffer.) If you use a default 16-color palette, the grid appears gray, and the cylinder can have any of the usual eight unintensified colors.

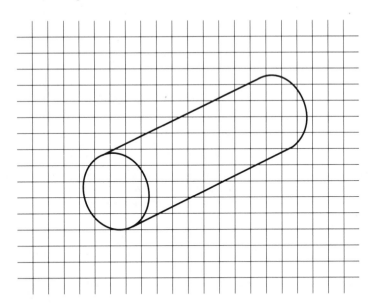

Figure 12-2. *Bit-plane layering. The cylinder's pixels have values between 0 and 7 (bit planes 0 through 2); the grid's pixels have the value 8 (bit plane 3 only). Selectively enabling or disabling bit planes 0 through 2 and bit plane 3 displays the cylinder, the grid, or both.*

If all four bit planes are displayed, both grid and cylinder appear on the screen. If you disable bit plane 3, the grid disappears. If you disable bit planes 0 through 2, displaying only bit plane 3, the cylinder disappears and only the grid is visible. In all three cases, the contents of the bit planes remain intact.

In using the default palette register values with the grid and cylinder, you'll find the pixels at which the grid and cylinder intersect are displayed with intensified colors. You can avoid this by updating the palette so that the colors displayed for the intersection points (pixel values 9 through 0FH) are the same as the corresponding unintensified colors (1 through 7). Then, when both grid and cylinder are displayed, the cylinder appears in front of the grid.

EGA and VGA Split Screen

You can configure the CRT Controller on the EGA and the VGA to display two different portions of the video buffer on the same screen (see Figure 12-3). To do this, program the CRTC's Line Compare register (18H) with the raster line at which you want to split the screen, as shown in Listing 12-7a and Listing 12-7b.

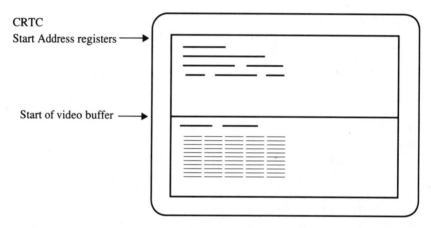

Figure 12-3. *Appearance of an EGA or VGA split screen. The top part of the screen displays data from the location in the video buffer specified by the CRTC Start Address registers. The bottom part of the screen displays data from the start of the video buffer.*

The contents of the CRTC Start Address registers determine which portion of the video buffer is displayed in the top part of the screen. As the raster is drawn during each display refresh cycle, the CRTC compares the current scan line with the value in the Line Compare register. When the values are equal, the CRTC resets its internal address counter so that the remaining scan lines in the raster are drawn using data from the start of the video buffer. Thus, the top of the video buffer is always displayed in the bottom part of the split screen.

Both the EGA and the VGA accommodate Line Compare values larger than eight bits (0FFH or 255 scan lines) by using other CRTC registers to contain additional high-order bits. Thus, bit 8 of the Line Compare value is represented in bit 4 of the CRTC Overflow register (07H). On the VGA, a ninth bit must also be specified for the Line Compare value; this bit is represented in bit 6 of the the Maximum Scan Line register (09H). Programming the CRTC with a Line Compare value thus requires you to update two different registers on the EGA and three different registers on the VGA.

```
                TITLE    'Listing 12-7a'
                NAME     SplitScreen
                PAGE     55,132


;
; Name:         SplitScreen
;
; Function:     Horizontal split screen on EGA
;
; Caller:       Microsoft C:
;
;                       void SplitScreen(n);
;
;                               int     n;      /* scan line at which */
;                                               /*  to split screen */
;


ARGn            EQU     word ptr [bp+4]


ADDR_6845       EQU     63h

_TEXT           SEGMENT byte public 'CODE'
                ASSUME  cs:_TEXT

                PUBLIC  _SplitScreen
_SplitScreen    PROC    near

                push    bp              ; preserve BP
                mov     bp,sp

                mov     ax,40h
                mov     es,ax           ; ES -> video BIOS data area
                mov     dx,es:[ADDR_6845] ; DX := CRTC address port

; wait for vertical retrace

                add     dl,6            ; DX := 3BAH or 3DAH (CRT status port)
L01:            in      al,dx           ; wait for end of vertical retrace
                test    al,8
                jnz     L01

L02:            in      al,dx           ; wait for start of vertical retrace
                test    al,8
                jz      L02
                sub     dl,6            ; DX := CRTC address port

; isolate bits 0-7 and bit 8 of the Line Compare value
```

Listing 12-7a. *Splitting the screen on the EGA.*   *(continued)*

Listing 12-7a. *Continued.*

```
                mov     ax,ARGn        ; AX := scan line value
                mov     bh,ah
                and     bh,1           ; BH bit 0 := Line Compare bit 8
                mov     cl,4
                shl     bh,cl          ; BH bit 4 := Line Compare bit 8

; program the CRTC registers

                mov     ah,al          ; AH := low-order 8 bits of value
                mov     al,18h         ; AL := Line Compare register number
                out     dx,ax          ; update Line Compare register

                mov     ah,1Fh         ; default value for EGA 350-line modes
                                       ;   (use 11h in EGA 200-line modes)
                and     ah,11101111b   ; AH bit 4 := 0
                or      ah,bh          ; AH bit 4 := Line Compare bit 8
                mov     al,7           ; AL := Overflow register number
                out     dx,ax          ; update Overflow register

                pop     bp             ; restore BP and exit
                ret

_SplitScreen    ENDP

_TEXT           ENDS

                END
```

```
                TITLE   'Listing 12-7b'
                NAME    SplitScreen
                PAGE    55,132

;
; Name:         SplitScreen
;
; Function:     Horizontal split screen on VGA
;
; Caller:       Microsoft C:
;
;                       void SplitScreen(n);
;
;                               int     n;      /* scan line at which */
;                                               /*  to split screen */
;

ARGn            EQU     word ptr [bp+4]


ADDR_6845       EQU     63h

_TEXT           SEGMENT byte public 'CODE'
                ASSUME  cs:_TEXT

                PUBLIC  _SplitScreen
```

Listing 12-7b. *Splitting the screen on the VGA.*   *(continued)*

Listing 12-7b. *Continued.*

```
_SplitScreen    PROC    near

                push    bp              ; preserve BP
                mov     bp,sp

                mov     ax,40h
                mov     es,ax           ; ES -> video BIOS data area
                mov     dx,es:[ADDR_6845]   ; DX := CRTC address port

; wait for vertical retrace

                add     dl,6            ; DX := 3BAH or 3DAH (CRT status port)
L01:            in      al,dx           ; wait for end of vertical retrace
                test    al,8
                jnz     L01

L02:            in      al,dx           ; wait for start of vertical retrace
                test    al,8
                jz      L02
                sub     dl,6            ; DX := CRTC address port

; isolate bits 0-7, bit 8, and bit 9 of the Line Compare value

                mov     ax,ARGn         ; AX := scan line value
                mov     bh,ah           ; BH bits 0-1 := bits 8-9 of
                                        ;   Line Compare value

                mov     bl,bh
                and     bx,0201h        ; BH bit 1 := Line Compare bit 9
                                        ; BL bit 0 := Line Compare bit 0

                mov     cl,4
                shl     bx,cl           ; BH bit 5 := Line Compare bit 9
                                        ; BL bit 4 := Line Compare bit 8
                shl     bh,1            ; BH bit 6 := Line Compare bit 9

; update the CRTC registers

                mov     ah,al           ; AH := low-order 8 bits of value
                mov     al,18h          ; AL := Line Compare register number
                out     dx,ax           ; update Line Compare register

                mov     al,7            ; AL := Overflow register number
                out     dx,al
                inc     dx
                in      al,dx           ; AL := current Overflow reg value
                dec     dx

                mov     ah,al
                and     ah,11101111b    ; AH bit 4 := 0
                or      ah,bl           ; AH bit 4 := Line Compare bit 8
                mov     al,7            ; AL := Overflow register number
                out     dx,ax           ; update Overflow register

                mov     al,9            ; AL := Max Scan Line register number
                out     dx,al
                inc     dx
                in      al,dx           ; AL := current Max Scan Line reg value
                dec     dx
```

(continued)

Listing 12-7b. *Continued.*

```
              mov      ah,al
              and      ah,10111111b      ; AH bit 6 := 0
              or       ah,bh             ; AH bit 6 := Line Compare bit 9
              mov      al,9              ; AL := Max Scan Line reg number
              out      dx,ax             ; update Max Scan Line register

              pop      bp                ; restore BP and exit
              ret

_SplitScreen  ENDP

_TEXT         ENDS
              END
```

 Because the CRTC uses the Line Compare value while it is actively updating the raster, the best time to change this value is during a vertical retrace interval as in Listings 12-7a and 12-7b.

The video BIOS default Line Compare value is the maximum possible value (1FFH on the EGA, 3FFH on the VGA). Use this default value to "unsplit" the screen. There are also certain values that the CRTC does not handle in a useful manner. On both the EGA and VGA, do not specify a Line Compare value that is between the Vertical Retrace Start and Vertical Total values. Also, in 200-line modes on the VGA, the Line Compare register value should be an even number.

In native graphics modes in the IBM EGA, the CRTC duplicates the scan line at which the screen is split. This anomaly is also found in some EGA clones.

You might find it convenient to regard the bottom portion of the split screen as a sort of window superimposed on the top portion. Use the first portion of the video buffer for the window foreground (the lower part of the split screen) and some other portion of the buffer for the background.

One attractive way to use the split-screen feature is to scroll the split smoothly up or down the screen. Do this by incrementing or decrementing the value in the Line Compare register within a loop, as is done by the routine in Listing 12-8.

```
#define MaxScanLine      349              /* (depends on video mode) */

for ( i = MaxScanLine; i >= 0; --i )      /* scroll up */
  SplitScreen( i );

for ( i = 0; i < MaxScanLine; i++ )       /* scroll down */
  SplitScreen( i );

SplitScreen( 0x3FF );                     /* restore default value */
```

Listing 12-8. *Smooth vertical scrolling of a split screen on the EGA or VGA.*

The Light Pen Interface

On most video subsystems covered in this book, the CRT Controller can return the position of a light pen. When you trigger a light pen, it sends a signal to the CRTC at the moment the video display's electron beam sweeps past the pen's light sensor. The CRTC responds by storing the current value of its internal address counter into its Light Pen High and Light Pen Low registers. This value corresponds to the offset in the video buffer of the data displayed in the raster at the point where the light pen was triggered. Thus, the value in the Light Pen High and Low registers can be translated into row and column coordinates for screen locations.

 You can't attach a light pen to IBM's MDA, but Hercules monochrome adapters can support one. However, a light pen used with a monochrome display must be capable of operating with the high-persistence P39 phosphor used in green monochrome displays.

Light Pen Position

The light pen position that the CRTC returns is not an exact pixel location. One reason is simply that the value returned in the CRTC's Light Pen registers is a byte offset into the video buffer, so the light pen's horizontal position can be determined only to the nearest byte of pixels. Another source of inaccuracy is that the CRTC chip itself introduces a small amount of delay between the time it receives a signal from the light pen and the time it stores a value in its Light Pen registers. The value returned in the Light Pen registers thus can be as much as 5 bytes too large; the actual amount of error must be determined empirically.

The light pen programming interface, shown in Figure 12-4, is similar on all IBM and Hercules adapters. To determine a light pen's position, your program must first reset the CRTC's light pen latch by writing a 0 to I/O port 3DBH (3BBH on an MDA, a Hercules adapter, or an EGA with a monochrome display). Then it must poll the Status Port at 3DAH (3BAH in monochrome modes). When bit 1 of the Status Port value changes from 0 to 1, the light pen has been triggered and the routine can obtain its location from the CRTC (see Listing 12-9a).

After reading the light pen location from the Light Pen registers, you must apply an empirical correction for the intrinsic delay in the CRTC. The routine in Listing 12-9b, for the EGA's 80-by-25 alphanumeric mode, subtracts 7 from the value that the CRTC returns. To convert the result into a pixel location, subtract the value in the Start Address High and Start Address Low registers from the corrected CRTC value. (You can get the Start Address value by dividing the value in CRT_START in the Video Display Data Area by 2. You can also read it from the Start Address High and Start Address Low registers on the EGA, the HGC+, and the InColor Card.) Then divide the difference by the number of characters in each row of the video buffer. (This value is represented in the CRTC's Horizontal Displayed register, or in CRT_COLS on the EGA.) The quotient is the *y*-coordinate of the light pen location. The remainder is the character column corresponding to the position of the light pen.

MDA, HGC, HGC+, and InColor Card

I/O Port	Function
3B9H	Set light pen latch
3BAH bit 1	Light pen trigger
3BAH bit 2	Light pen switch (IBM adapters only)
3BBH	Reset light pen latch

CGA, EGA

I/O Port	Function
3DAH bit 1	Light pen trigger
3DAH bit 2	Light pen switch (IBM adapters only)
3DBH	Reset light pen latch
3DCH	Set light pen latch

Figure 12-4. *Light pen programming interface. Note: In EGA monochrome modes, read light pen trigger and switch status from 3BAH instead of 3DAH.*

```
                TITLE    'Listing 12-9a'
                NAME     GetLightPen
                PAGE     55,132

;
; Name:         GetLightPen
;
; Function:     Get light pen position
;
; Caller:       Microsoft C:
;
;                        int GetLightPen();      /* returns buffer offset */
;

ADDR_6845       EQU      63h

_TEXT           SEGMENT byte public 'CODE'
                ASSUME  cs:_TEXT

                PUBLIC  _GetLightPen
_GetLightPen    PROC    near

                push    bp
                mov     bp,sp

                mov     ax,40h
                mov     es,ax           ; ES -> video BIOS data area

                mov     dx,es:[ADDR_6845]  ; DX := 3B4H or 3D4H

                add     dl,7            ; DX := 3BBH or 3DBH
                xor     al,al           ; AL := 0
                out     dx,al           ; reset CRTC light pen latch
                jmp     $+2             ; ensure that CRTC has time to respond

                dec     dx              ; DX := 3BAH or 3DAH
```

Listing 12-9a. *Getting the light pen's location from the CRTC.*   *(continued)*

Listing 12-9a. *Continued.*

```
L01:            in      al,dx           ; wait for light pen to be triggered
                test    al,2
                jz      L01

                cli                     ; disable interrupts
                sub     dl,6            ; DX := 3B4H or 3D4H
                mov     al,10h          ; AL := Light Pen High register number
                out     dx,al
                inc     dx
                in      al,dx
                mov     ah,al           ; AH := Light Pen High value
                dec     dx

                mov     al,11h          ; AL := Light Pen Low register number
                out     dx,al
                inc     dx
                in      al,dx           ; AX := offset at which light pen
                                        ;  was triggered
                sti                     ; reenable interrupts

                pop     bp
                ret

_GetLightPen    ENDP

_TEXT           ENDS

                END
```

```
/* Listing 12-9b */

main()
{
        int     BufferOffset,Row,Column;
        int far *CRT_START = 0x0040004E;
        char far *CRT_COLS = 0x0040004A;

        printf( "\nCRT_COLS = %d", (int) (*CRT_COLS) );

        for( ; ; )
        {
          BufferOffset = GetLightPen();

          printf( "\nLight pen offset:  %4xh", BufferOffset );

          BufferOffset = BufferOffset - 7;          /* empirical correction */

          BufferOffset = BufferOffset - (*CRT_START)/2; /* offset relative to */
                                                        /*  start of screen   */

          Row = BufferOffset / (int)(*CRT_COLS);        /* character row */
          Column = BufferOffset % (int)(*CRT_COLS);     /* character column */

          printf( "  Column = %d  Row = %d", Column, Row );
        }
}
```

Listing 12-9b. *Using GetLightPen in a C program.*

If this seems like more trouble than it's worth, you're probably right. On IBM video adapters, you can call INT 10H function 4 to return the light pen location. If you plan to use a light pen with a Hercules adapter, however, you're on your own.

Light Pen Switch

On IBM adapters, you can determine whether the light pen switch is depressed by examining bit 2 of the Status Port value returned from port 3DAH (3BAH in monochrome modes). This bit is set to 1 while the switch is closed. It returns to 0 when the switch is opened. You should usually test the status of the light pen switch before attempting to read the CRTC's Light Pen registers.

Determining Hercules Video Modes

The Light Pen registers can also be used to determine video modes on Hercules adapters. In most applications, determining the current video mode is not a problem, because the application itself establishes the mode. Sometimes, however, a program may not know the video mode *a priori*. For example, a screen dump program (see Appendix B) may need to determine the video mode to correctly interpret the contents of the video buffer. Similarly, a RAM-resident "pop up" program should save and then restore the video mode into which it "pops."

You can easily determine the current ROM BIOS video mode by calling INT 10H function 0FH. The task is more difficult for the Hercules adapters, because the BIOS does not keep track of the video mode. You can sometimes infer the video mode from the Video Display Data Area variables CRT_COLS, CRT_LEN, and POINTS, but not everybody who writes programs for Hercules adapters keeps these variables updated.

Moreover, there is no direct way to interrogate the hardware to determine the video mode. For example, the Mode Control register (3B8H), used to select the video mode, is unfortunately a write-only register. Nevertheless, you can infer a Hercules adapter's video mode by latching the 6845's Light Pen High and Low registers (10H and 11H) at the start of vertical retrace, as shown in Listing 12-10.

```
                    TITLE   'Listing 12-10'
                    NAME    GetHercMode
                    PAGE    55,132

; Name:          GetHercMode
;
; Function:      Determine video mode on Hercules adapters by estimating the size
;                of the displayed portion of the video buffer.
;
; Caller:        Microsoft C:
;
;                        int GetHercMode(n);     /* returns approximate size */
;                                                /*  of displayed portion of */
;                                                /*  video buffer in words   */
```

Listing 12-10. *Identifying the current video mode on a Hercules adapter.*   *(continued)*

Listing 12-10. *Continued.*

```
_TEXT              SEGMENT byte public 'CODE'
                   ASSUME  cs:_TEXT

                   PUBLIC  _GetHercMode
_GetHercMode       PROC    near

                   push    bp                ; preserve BP
                   mov     bp,sp

; reset CRTC light pen latch

                   mov     dx,3BBh           ; DX := light pen reset port
                   out     dx,al             ; OUT to this port clears the latch
                                             ;   (the value in AL doesn't matter)

; wait for start of next vertical retrace

                   dec     dx                ; DX := 3BAH (CRT status port)
L01:               in      al,dx             ; wait for start of vertical retrace
                   test    al,80h
                   jnz     L01

L02:               in      al,dx             ; wait for end of vertical retrace
                   test    al,80h
                   jz      L02

                   cli                       ; disable interrupts
L03:               in      al,dx             ; wait for start of vertical retrace
                   test    al,80h
                   jnz     L03

; latch the current CRTC address counter in the Light Pen registers

                   dec     dx                ; DX := 3B9H
                   out     dx,al             ; OUT to this port loads the latch
                   sti                       ; reenable interrupts

; return the value in the Light Pen registers

                   mov     dl,0B4h           ; DX := 3B4H (CRTC address port)
                   mov     al,10h            ; AL := Light Pen High register number
                   out     dx,al
                   inc     dx
                   in      al,dx             ; read this register
                   dec     dx
                   mov     ah,al             ; AH := current Light Pen High value

                   mov     al,11h            ; AL := Light Pen Low register number
                   out     dx,al
                   inc     dx
                   in      al,dx             ; AX := current light pen latch value
                                             ;   (i.e., value of CRTC address counter
                                             ;    at start of vertical retrace)
                   pop     bp
                   ret
```

(continued)

Listing 12-10. *Continued.*

```
_GetHercMode      ENDP

_TEXT             ENDS

                  END
```

The routine in Listing 12-10 waits for the start of vertical retrace and triggers the light pen at this point with an OUT instruction to port 3B9H. The Light Pen registers reflect the value of the CRTC's internal address counter at the point where vertical retrace begins. (This value is the product of the values in the CRTC Horizontal Displayed and Vertical Sync registers.) You can expect the Light Pen registers to contain at least 7D0H (80 words per character row × 25 rows) in 80-by-25 alphanumeric mode and 0F4BH (45 words per character row × 87 rows) in 720-by-348 graphics mode. Inspecting the Light Pen value thus reveals whether the HGC is in alphanumeric or graphics mode.

In practice, the Light Pen value returned is somewhat larger than these expected values because of the delay in the CRTC timing. This imprecision makes the technique somewhat less useful on the HGC+ and InColor cards, where you must distinguish among all the different character sizes that can be displayed by the CRTC in alphanumeric mode. For example, the value returned by GetHercMode() when 9-by-8 characters are displayed is near 0DC0H (80 × 44) and near 0DB6H (90 × 39) when 8-by-9 characters are displayed. Because the Light Pen value is inexact, you may not be able to distinguish these two different CRTC configurations.

13

Graphics Subroutines in High-Level Languages

Linking Graphics Subroutines
Subroutine Calls
Interrupts to a Memory-Resident Driver
Inline Code

Global Data Areas

Layered Graphics Interfaces
Direct Hardware Programming
Extended BIOS Interface
High-Level Interface

Most programming examples in this book are written in assembly language, the language of choice for programs that need to control hardware precisely and to run as fast as possible. Nevertheless, most IBM PC programmers prefer not to write large applications entirely in assembly language because they can write, debug, and maintain a program in a high-level language much more effectively.

As you write the code for a program that produces video output, you must balance the convenience and conceptual clarity a high-level language provides against the speed and exact control provided by assembly language. A good rule of thumb is to use assembly language whenever you directly access the video buffer or the video subsystem's control registers. The rest of the time, you can generally obtain satisfactory performance using any compiled high-level language.

This chapter focuses on the interface between programs written in high-level languages and the low-level, assembly-language drivers that actually access the video hardware. You can implement the interface in several ways. The method you select should depend on the language you are using, your familiarity with the memory models and parameter-passing techniques that your compiler uses, and (as always) your own good judgment in evaluating the alternatives.

The last part of the chapter introduces several different high-level video programming interfaces. The focus is on the reasons why high-level programming interfaces are used and the programming approach involved in using them.

Linking Graphics Subroutines

You can tie low-level graphics subroutines to high-level applications in several ways. The three techniques discussed here—subroutine calls, calling a set of memory-resident routines, and using inline code in a high-level-language program—have all been proved in various graphics applications. As usual, the "best" method to use in any given application is a matter of judgment.

Subroutine Calls

This book contains numerous subroutines that are designed to be called from within a high-level-language program. Most are to be linked to programs compiled with the Microsoft C compiler. However, you can link these subroutines to any high-level-language program if you know the proper protocol for structuring executable code, and for passing parameters to a subroutine and returning values from it. The routines in Listings 13-1 through 13-4 show how to call the same assembly-language subroutine from Microsoft C, Microsoft FORTRAN, Turbo Pascal, and interpreted BASIC.

```
TITLE    'Listing 13-1a'
NAME     SetPixel
PAGE     55,132
```

(continued)

Listing 13-1a. *The SetPixel subroutine (Microsoft C small-model calling conventions).*

Listing 13-1a. *Continued.*

```
;
; Name:          SetPixel
;
; Function:      Set the value of a pixel in native EGA graphics modes.
;
; Caller:        Microsoft C (small memory model):
;
;                       void SetPixel(x,y,n);
;
;                       int x,y;                /* pixel coordinates */
;                       int n;                  /* pixel value */
;
; Notes:         This is the same routine as in Chapter 5.
;

ARGx            EQU     word ptr [bp+4] ; stack frame addressing
ARGy            EQU     word ptr [bp+6]
ARGn            EQU     byte ptr [bp+8]

RMWbits         EQU     0               ; read-modify-write bits


_TEXT           SEGMENT byte public 'CODE'
                ASSUME  cs:_TEXT

                EXTRN   PixelAddr:near

                PUBLIC  _SetPixel
_SetPixel       PROC    near

                push    bp              ; preserve caller registers
                mov     bp,sp

                mov     ax,ARGy         ; AX := y
                mov     bx,ARGx         ; BX := x
                call    PixelAddr       ; AH := bit mask
                                        ; ES:BX -> buffer
                                        ; CL := # bits to shift left

; set Graphics Controller Bit Mask register

                shl     ah,cl           ; AH := bit mask in proper position
                mov     dx,3CEh         ; GC address register port
                mov     al,8            ; AL := Bit Mask register number
                out     dx,ax

; set Graphics Controller Mode register

                mov     ax,0005h        ; AL := Mode register number
                                        ; AH := Write Mode 0 (bits 0,1)
                                        ;       Read Mode 0 (bit 3)
                out     dx,ax

; set Data Rotate/Function Select register

                mov     ah,RMWbits      ; AH := Read-Modify-Write bits
                mov     al,3            ; AL := Data Rotate/Function Select reg
                out     dx,ax
```

(continued)

Listing 13-1a. *Continued.*

```
; set Set/Reset and Enable Set/Reset registers

                mov     ah,ARGn         ; AH := pixel value
                mov     al,0            ; AL := Set/Reset reg number
                out     dx,ax

                mov     ax,0F01h        ; AH := value for Enable Set/Reset (all
                                        ;   bit planes enabled)
                                        ; AL := Enable Set/Reset reg number
                out     dx,ax

; set the pixel value

                or      es:[bx],al      ; load latches during CPU read
                                        ; update latches and bit planes during
                                        ;   CPU write

; restore default Graphics Controller registers

                mov     ax,0FF08h       ; default Bit Mask
                out     dx,ax

                mov     ax,0005         ; default Mode register
                out     dx,ax

                mov     ax,0003         ; default Function Select
                out     dx,ax

                mov     ax,0001         ; default Enable Set/Reset
                out     dx,ax

                mov     sp,bp           ; restore caller registers and return
                pop     bp
                ret

_SetPixel       ENDP

_TEXT           ENDS

                END
```

```
/* Listing 13-1b */

/* draws an n-leaved rose of the form   rho = a * cos(n * theta) */

#define Leaves          (double)11      /* n must be an odd number */

#define Xmax            640
#define Ymax            350
#define PixelValue      14
#define ScaleFactor     (double) 1.37

main()
{
        int     x,y;                    /* pixel coordinates */
        double  a;                      /* length of the semi-axis */
```

Listing 13-1b. *Calling SetPixel() from a C program.*   *(continued)*

Listing 13-1b. *Continued.*

```
        double  rho,theta;              /* polar coordinates */
        double  pi = 3.14159265358979;
        double  sin(),cos();

        void SetPixel();


        a = (Ymax/2) - 1;               /* a reasonable choice for a */

        for (theta=0.0; theta < pi; theta+=0.001)
        {
          rho = a * cos( Leaves * theta );        /* apply the formula */

          x = rho * cos( theta );       /* convert to rectangular coords */
          y = rho * sin( theta ) / ScaleFactor;

                                        /* plot the point */
          SetPixel( x + Xmax/2, y + Ymax/2, PixelValue );
        }
}
```

```
                TITLE    'Listing 13-2a'
                NAME     SETPEL
                PAGE     55,132


;
; Name:          SETPEL
;
; Function:      Set the value of a pixel in native EGA graphics modes.
;
; Caller:        Microsoft Fortran
;
;                     integer*2      x,y,n
;                     call SETPEL(x,y,n)
;
;

ADDRx           EQU     dword ptr [bp+14]      ; x, y, and n are referenced
ADDRy           EQU     dword ptr [bp+10]      ;   by 32-bit addresses
ADDRn           EQU     dword ptr [bp+6]

RMWbits         EQU     0


SETPEL_TEXT     SEGMENT byte public 'CODE'
                ASSUME  cs:SETPEL_TEXT

                EXTRN   PixelAddr:far

                PUBLIC  SETPEL
SETPEL          PROC    far

                push    bp
                mov     bp,sp
```

(continued)

Listing 13-2a. *The SETPEL subroutine (Microsoft FORTRAN calling conventions).*

Listing 13-2a. *Continued.*

```
; get parameters via 32-bit addresses on stack

            les     bx,ADDRn                ; ES:BX -> n
            push    es:[bx]                 ; preserve n on stack

            les     bx,ADDRy
            mov     ax,es:[bx]              ; AX := y

            les     bx,ADDRx
            mov     bx,es:[bx]              ; BX := x

            call    PixelAddr               ; compute pixel address

            shl     ah,cl

; program the Graphics Controller

            mov     dx,3CEh
            mov     al,8
            out     dx,ax

            mov     ax,0005h
            out     dx,ax

            mov     ah,RMWbits
            mov     al,3
            out     dx,ax

            pop     ax                      ; AX := n
            mov     ah,al                   ; AH := n
            mov     al,0
            out     dx,ax

            mov     ax,0F01h
            out     dx,ax

; update the pixel, restore the default Graphics Controller state, and return

            or      es:[bx],al              ; update the pixel

            mov     ax,0FF08h               ; restore default Graphics
            out     dx,ax                   ;   Controller values

            mov     ax,0005
            out     dx,ax

            mov     ax,0003
            out     dx,ax

            mov     ax,0001
            out     dx,ax

            mov     sp,bp                   ; restore registers and exit
            pop     bp
            ret     12                      ; discard caller's parms

SETPEL      ENDP

SETPEL_TEXT ENDS
            END
```

```
c Listing 13-2b
c
c draws an n-leaved rose of the form  rho = a * cos(n*theta)

        real*8          Leaves /11/
        real*8          ScaleFactor /1.37/

        integer*2       Xmax /640/, Ymax /350/, PixelValue /14/

        integer*2       x,y
        real*8          a
        real*8          rho,theta
        real*8          pi /3.14159265358979/
        real*8          sin,cos

        a = (Ymax/2) - 1

        do 100 theta = 0.0, pi, 0.001

        rho = a * cos( Leaves * theta )

        x = rho * cos( theta )
        y = rho * sin( theta ) / ScaleFactor

100     call SETPEL( x + Xmax/2, y + Ymax/2, PixelValue )

        stop
        end
```

Listing 13-2b. *Calling SETPEL() from a FORTRAN program.*

```
                TITLE   'Listing 13-3a'
                NAME    SETPEL
                PAGE    55,132

;
; Name:          SETPEL
;
; Function:      Set the value of a pixel in 320x200 4-color mode
;
; Caller:        Turbo Pascal
;
;                 PROCEDURE SETPEL(VAR x,y:INTEGER; PixelValue:INTEGER);
;                  EXTERNAL 'setpel.bin';
;
; Notes:         The code segment is named _TEXT so that PixelAddr may be linked
;                in the same segment.
;

ADDRx           EQU     dword ptr [bp+10]       ; x and y are VAR so their
ADDRy           EQU     dword ptr [bp+6]        ;   addresses are passed
ARGn            EQU     byte ptr [bp+4]         ; n's value is passed on
                                                ;   the stack

_TEXT           SEGMENT byte public 'CODE'
                ASSUME  cs:_TEXT
```

(continued)

Listing 13-3a. *The SETPEL subroutine (Turbo Pascal calling conventions).*

Listing 13-3a. *Continued.*

```
                 EXTRN    PixelAddr:near

SETPEL           PROC     near

                 push     bp                  ; preserve caller registers
                 mov      bp,sp
                 push     ds

; make this routine addressable through SI

                 call     L01                 ; push offset of L01

L01:             pop      si                  ; CS:SI -> L01
                 sub      si,offset L01

; get parameters via 32-bit addresses on stack

                 lds      di,ADDRy            ; DS:DI -> y
                 mov      ax,[di]             ; AX := y

                 lds      di,ADDRx            ; DS:DI -> x
                 mov      bx,[di]             ; BX := x

                 call     PixelAddr           ; AH := bit mask
                                              ; ES:BX -> buffer
                                              ; CL := # bits to shift left

                 mov      al,ARGn             ; AL := pixel value
                 shl      ax,cl               ; AH := bit mask in proper position
                                              ; AL := pixel value in proper position

; jump through the variable SetPixelOp to the appropriate routine

                 mov      di,cs:SetPixelOp[si]    ; DI := address
                 add      di,si               ; DI := relocated address
                 jmp      di
                                              ; routine to replace pixel value

ReplacePixel:    not      ah                  ; AH := inverse bit mask
                 and      es:[bx],ah          ; zero the pixel value
                 or       es:[bx],al          ; set the pixel value
                 jmp      short L02

                                              ; routine to AND pixel value

ANDPixel:        not      ah                  ; AH := inverse bit mask
                 or       al,ah               ; AL := all 1's except pixel value
                 and      es:[bx],al
                 jmp      short L02


ORPixel:         or       es:[bx],al          ; routine to OR pixel value
                 jmp      short L02


XORPixel:        xor      es:[bx],al          ; routine to XOR pixel value
```

(continued)

Listing 13-3a. *Continued.*

```
L02:            pop     ds              ; restore regs and exit
                mov     sp,bp
                pop     bp
                ret     10              ; discard parameters and return

SETPEL          ENDP


SetPixelOp      DW      ReplacePixel    ; contains addr of pixel operation


_TEXT           ENDS

                END
```

```
{ Listing 13-3b }

PROGRAM rose;    { draws an n-leaved rose of the form  rho = a * cos(n*theta) }

CONST
    Leaves          = 11.0;                      { must be an odd number }

    Xmax            = 320;
    Ymax            = 200;
    PixelValue      = 3;
    ScaleFactor     = 1.20;
    Pi              = 3.14159265358979;

VAR
    x,y:            INTEGER;                  { pixel coordinates }
    a:              REAL;               { length of the semi-axis }
    rho,theta:      REAL;                     { polar coordinates }

PROCEDURE SETPEL(VAR x,y:INTEGER; PixelValue:INTEGER); EXTERNAL 'setpel.bin';

BEGIN
    GraphColorMode;                          { set 320x200 4-color mode }
    a := (Ymax/2) - 1;                       { a reasonable choice for a }

    theta := 0.0;
    WHILE theta < Pi DO
    BEGIN
        rho := a * Cos(Leaves * theta);              { apply the formula }

        x := Trunc(rho * Cos(theta));     { convert to rectangular coords }
        y := Trunc(rho * Sin(theta) / ScaleFactor);

        x := x + Trunc(Xmax/2);                      { center on screen }
        y := y + Trunc(Ymax/2);

        SETPEL(x,y,PixelValue);                      { plot the point }

        theta := theta + 0.001;
    END
END.
```

Listing 13-3b. *Calling SETPEL() from a Turbo Pascal program.*

```
                    TITLE    'Listing 13-4a'
                    NAME     SETPEL
                    PAGE     55,132
          ;
          ; Name:          SETPEL
          ;
          ; Function:      Set the value of a pixel in 320x200 4-color mode
          ;
          ; Caller:        IBM BASICA or Microsoft GWBASIC
          ;
          ; Notes:         The code segment is named _TEXT so that PixelAddr may be linked
          ;                in the same segment.
          ;
          ADDRx          EQU      word ptr [bp+10]
          ADDRy          EQU      word ptr [bp+8]
          ADDRn          EQU      word ptr [bp+6]

          CGROUP         GROUP    _TEXT,END_TEXT

          _TEXT          SEGMENT byte public 'CODE'
                         ASSUME  cs:CGROUP,ds:CGROUP
                         EXTRN   PixelAddr:near

          ; header for BASIC BLOAD
                         DB       0FDh
                         DW       2 dup(0)
                         DW       (offset CGROUP:BLEnd)-7 ; size of subroutine

          ; start of subroutine
          SETPEL         PROC     far
                         push     bp                 ; preserve caller registers
                         mov      bp,sp
                         push     es

          ; make this routine addressable through SI
                         call     L01                ; push offset of L01
          L01:           pop      si                 ; CS:SI -> L01
                         sub      si,offset L01

          ; get parameters via 16-bit addresses on stack
                         mov      di,ADDRy           ; DS:DI -> y
                         mov      ax,[di]            ; AX := y
                         mov      di,ADDRx
                         mov      bx,[di]            ; BX := x
                         call     PixelAddr          ; AH := bit mask
                                                     ; ES:BX -> buffer
                                                     ; CL := # bits to shift left
                         mov      di,ADDRn
                         mov      al,[di]            ; AL := pixel value
                         shl      ax,cl              ; AH := bit mask in proper position
                                                     ; AL := pixel value in proper position
          ; jump through the variable SetPixelOp to the appropriate routine
                         mov      di,SetPixelOp[si]       ; DI := address
                         add      di,si              ; DI := relocated address
                         jmp      di
                                                     ; routine to replace pixel value
          ReplacePixel:  not      ah                 ; AH := inverse bit mask
                         and      es:[bx],ah         ; zero the pixel value
                         or       es:[bx],al         ; set the pixel value
                         jmp      short L02
```

Listing 13-4a. *The SETPEL subroutine (BASICA calling convention).*   *(continued)*

Listing 13-4a. *Continued.*

```
                                        ; routine to AND pixel value
ANDPixel:       not     ah              ; AH := inverse bit mask
                or      al,ah           ; AL := all 1s except pixel value
                and     es:[bx],al
                jmp     short L02

ORPixel:        or      es:[bx],al      ; routine to OR pixel value
                jmp     short L02
XORPixel:       xor     es:[bx],al      ; routine to XOR pixel value
L02:            pop     es              ; restore registers
                mov     sp,bp
                pop     bp
                ret     6               ; discard parameters and return
SETPEL          ENDP

SetPixelOp      DW      ReplacePixel    ; contains addr of pixel operation
_TEXT           ENDS

END_TEXT        SEGMENT byte public 'CODE'
BLEnd           LABEL   BYTE            ; this segment is linked after _TEXT,
                                        ;  so this label can be used to compute
                                        ;  the size of the _TEXT segment
END_TEXT        ENDS
                END
```

```
100 ' Listing 13-4b
110 ' Draws an n-leaved rose of the form  rho = a * cos(n*theta)
120 DEFINT A-Z
130 LEAVES = 11
140 XMAX = 320 : YMAX = 200
150 PIXELVALUE = 2
160 SCALEFACTOR# = 1.2
170 PI# = 3.14159265358979#
180 X = 0 : Y = 0                       ' pixel coordinates
190 A# = 0                              ' length of the semi-axis
200 RHO# = 0 : THETA# = 0               ' polar coordinates
210 '
220 SETPEL = 0
230 DIM SPAREA(256)                     ' reserve RAM for the subroutine
240 SETPEL = VARPTR(SPAREA(1))          ' address of subroutine
250 BLOAD "setpel.bin",SETPEL           ' load subroutine into RAM
260 '
270 SCREEN 1 : COLOR 0,0 : CLS          ' set 320x200 4-color mode
280 A# = (YMAX / 2) - 1                 ' a reasonable choice for A
290 THETA# = 0
300 WHILE (THETA# < PI#)
310  RHO# = A# * COS(LEAVES * THETA#)   ' apply the formula
320  X = RHO# * COS(THETA#)             ' convert to rectangular coords
330  Y = RHO# * SIN(THETA#) / SCALEFACTOR#
340  X = X + XMAX/2                      ' center on screen
350  Y = Y + YMAX/2
360  CALL SETPEL(X,Y,PIXELVALUE)        ' plot the point
370  THETA# = THETA# + .001
380 WEND
390 END
```

Listing 13-4b. *Calling SETPEL from a BASICA program.*

One of the ways these assembly-language subroutines differ is that they use different memory models. A memory model describes the segment organization of a program—whether executable code is separated from program data, and whether segments are accessed with 16-bit (near) or 32-bit (far) addresses. For example, a small-model program has one near code and one near data segment; a large-model program can have multiple far code and far data segments. The subroutines in Listings 13-1 through 13-4 conform to the default memory models used by the different language translators.

The protocol for passing parameters also varies among compilers and programming languages. In Pascal, for example, parameters are pushed on the stack in the order they appear in the PROCEDURE statement, while in C, parameters are pushed in reverse order. Also, either the actual value of a parameter or its address may be passed; this depends on the programming language you use as well as on the type of data involved. Each compiler's reference manual contains details on its parameter-passing protocol.

Microsoft C

Source code examples in previous chapters that can be called from a C program are all designed to be linked with small- or compact-model programs. To call them from a medium- or large-model program, you must make three modifications to the source code to make it conform to these memory models' subroutine-calling conventions.

- Change the name of the executable code segment.

- Use the far keyword in assembler PROC directives.

- Modify the stack frame addressing to accommodate the calling routine's 32-bit return address.

For example, to call SetPixel10() within a medium-model C program, change the name of the _TEXT segment in SetPixel10()'s source code to a name of the form module_TEXT and use the far keyword in the routine's PROC directive. Also, adjust the stack frame addresses by two bytes to account for the 32-bit return address.

Microsoft FORTRAN

Microsoft's FORTRAN compiler does not generate small- or compact-model programs, so the far addressing conventions applicable to medium- and large-model programs apply to FORTRAN-callable assembly-language graphics subroutines. The C-callable version in Listing 13-1a and the FORTRAN equivalent in Listing 13-2a differ in several ways. These differences relate to the way parameters are passed on the stack to the subroutine.

The C compiler passes the current values of each subroutine argument in reverse order, so the first argument is on top of the stack. The FORTRAN compiler passes the 32-bit address of each argument's value in the order in which the arguments appear in the subroutine's argument list. The C subroutine obtains the argument values directly from the stack; the FORTRAN routine must obtain the arguments' addresses from the stack, then use the addresses to obtain the values. Also, in C, the routine that called the subroutine discards the arguments on the stack. In contrast, in FORTRAN the called subroutine cleans up the stack when it exits.

 The Microsoft C, FORTRAN, and Pascal compilers let you specify the parameter-passing protocol used to call a particular subroutine. For example, you can write a C-callable subroutine and then access it using the appropriate compiler directive in your FORTRAN or Pascal program. This interlanguage linking capability became available in MS C version 3.00, MS Pascal version 3.3, and MS FORTRAN version 3.3.

Including a compiler directive in your high-level source code can be more convenient than modifying an assembly-language subroutine. For example, a C subroutine can be called from a FORTRAN program by declaring the subroutine in a FORTRAN INTERFACE unit:

```
interface to subroutine SP10[C](x,y,n)
integer*2 x,y,n
end
```

This INTERFACE unit instructs the FORTRAN compiler to generate code that calls the subroutine _sp10() using C's parameter-passing protocol. However, this technique does not affect the memory model used; the C-callable routine is called with a far call, because it lies in a different segment from the FORTRAN caller. Thus, _sp10() must still be declared with the far keyword, and the stack frame must be addressed with the assumption that a 32-bit far return address lies on top of the stack when the procedure is called.

If you intend to write graphics routines that can be called from either Microsoft C, Pascal, or FORTRAN, you should use a medium or large memory model, so the routine can be called as a far procedure. You can use any parameter-passing protocol; the Microsoft language translators can generate code for all of them.

Turbo Pascal

Turbo Pascal links EXTERNAL assembly-language subroutines dynamically. However, Turbo Pascal's dynamic linker does not perform address relocation or resolve symbolic references between the main program and the subroutine. Thus, the assembly-language subroutine has a very simple structure. Listing 13-3a is an example of this type of subroutine. Note how the subroutine performs "self-relocation" by initializing a register with the starting offset of the subroutine (using a CALL L01 followed by a POP), then adding this value to all references to labels within the subroutine.

BASIC

IBM BASICA and Microsoft GWBASIC have their own intrinsic video output routines. However, you can use assembly-language subroutines to customize your BASIC programs for video modes or hardware not supported by these BASIC interpreters. Listings 13-4a and 13-4b show how to do this.

Like Turbo Pascal, BASICA requires you to link your subroutine dynamically. In Listing 13-4a, the subroutine is assembled in the form of a binary file that can be loaded with the BASIC BLOAD command, as in lines 220–250 of Listing 13-4b. In BASICA, as in Pascal, parameters are passed to the subroutine in the order they are specified in the high-level source code. Unlike the Turbo Pascal subroutine, however, the BASIC subroutine is a far procedure. Also, in BASIC the addresses of parameters are passed instead of the values of the parameters themselves.

Interrupts to a Memory-Resident Driver

Another way to implement the interface between high-level-language programs and machine-language graphics routines is to make the graphics routines resident in memory. When they are, programs can access the graphics routines by executing a software interrupt. This is the design of the interface used by all video BIOS routines in the PC and PS/2 families. The routines reside at a fixed address in ROM. Interrupt vector 10H is initialized at bootup to point to a service routine that calls the BIOS routines.

Your own video output routines can be accessed in a similar manner if you make them resident in RAM and set an interrupt vector to point to them. (On the PC and PS/2s, interrupt numbers 60H through 67H are reserved for such user-defined interrupts.) Listing 13-5 is an example of a simple RAM-resident routine that stores pixels in the EGA's 640-by-350 16-color mode. The source for this routine assembles to a .EXE file that installs the routine in RAM and sets interrupt vector 60H to point to the code that sets the pixel value. After the interrupt vector is initialized, any program can access the routine by loading the CPU registers with the pixel location and value and then executing interrupt 60H.

```
                TITLE    'Listing 13-5'
                NAME     SetPixel
                PAGE     55,132
;
; Name:         SetPixel
;
; Function:     Set the value of a pixel in native EGA graphics modes.
;
; Caller:       Memory-resident routine invoked via interrupt 60H:
;
;                       mov ax,PixelX       ; pixel x-coordinate
;                       mov bx,PixelY       ; pixel y-coordinate
;                       mov cx,PixelValue   ; pixel value
```

(continued)

Listing 13-5. *A RAM-resident routine to write pixels in 640-by-350 graphics mode.*

Listing 13-5. *Continued.*

```
; Notes:                - Assemble and link to create SETPIXEL.EXE.
;                       - Execute once to make SetPixel resident in memory and to point
;                           the INT 60H vector to the RAM-resident code.
;                       - Requires MS-DOS version 2.0 or later.
;

RMWbits        EQU     0

_TEXT          SEGMENT byte public 'CODE'
               ASSUME  cs:_TEXT

               EXTRN   PixelAddr:near

               PUBLIC  SetPixel
SetPixel       PROC    near                    ; RAM-resident interrupt 60H handler

               sti                             ; enable interrupts
               push    ax                      ; preserve caller registers on
               push    bx                      ;   caller's stack
               push    cx
               push    dx

               push    cx                      ; preserve pixel value on stack

               call    PixelAddr               ; compute pixel address
               shl     ah,cl

               mov     dx,3CEh                 ; program the Graphics Controller
               mov     al,8                    ; AL := Bit Mask register number
               out     dx,ax
               mov     ax,0005h
               out     dx,ax

               mov     ah,RMWbits              ; AH := Read-Modify-Write bits
               mov     al,3                    ; AL := Data Rotate/Function Select reg
               out     dx,ax
               pop     ax
               mov     ah,al                   ; AH := pixel value
               mov     al,0
               out     dx,ax

               mov     ax,0F01h
               out     dx,ax

               or      es:[bx],al              ; set the pixel value

               mov     ax,0FF08h               ; restore default Graphics Controller
               out     dx,ax                   ;   values

               mov     ax,0005
               out     dx,ax

               mov     ax,0003
               out     dx,ax

               mov     ax,0001
               out     dx,ax
```

(continued)

Listing 13-5. *Continued.*

```
                    pop     dx              ; restore caller registers and return
                    pop     cx
                    pop     bx
                    pop     ax
                    iret

SetPixel            ENDP

_TEXT               ENDS


TRANSIENT_TEXT      SEGMENT para
                    ASSUME  cs:TRANSIENT_TEXT,ss:STACK

Install             PROC    near

                    mov     ax,2560h        ; AH := 25H (INT 21H function number)
                                            ; AL := 60H (interrupt number)
                    mov     dx,seg _TEXT
                    mov     ds,dx
                    mov     dx,offset _TEXT:SetPixel   ; DS:DX -> interrupt handler

                    int     21h             ; point INT 60H vector to
                                            ;  SetPixel routine

                    mov     dx,cs           ; DX := segment of start of transient
                                            ;  (discardable) portion of program
                    mov     ax,es           ; ES := Program Segment Prefix
                    sub     dx,ax           ; DX := size of RAM-resident portion
                    mov     ax,3100h        ; AH := 31H (INT 21H function number)
                                            ; AL := 0 (return code)
                    int     21h             ; Terminate but Stay Resident

Install             ENDP

TRANSIENT_TEXT      ENDS

STACK               SEGMENT para stack 'STACK'

                    DB      80h dup(?)      ; stack space for transient portion
                                            ;  of program
STACK               ENDS

                    END     Install
```

Inline Code

A technique familiar to many C, Modula-2, and Turbo Pascal programmers is to
implement low-level subroutines as inline machine instructions in high-level
source code. Doing so can simplify the problem of using consistent memory-
model and parameter-passing protocols, because the high-level-language compiler
handles these implicitly. However, inline code is rarely portable and can be difficult to adapt for use with other languages.

Global Data Areas

When you link video output subroutines to a high-level program, you face the problem of transferring information about the current state of the video hardware between the high-level program and the subroutines. Although you can pass such information to subroutines using argument lists, a better approach is to use a global data structure that both the high-level program and the low-level subroutines can access. Information contained in a global data area can include:

- Hardware identification (''EGA with 350-line color display'')

- Hardware coordinate system (orientation of x- and y-axes, maximum x- and y-coordinates)

- Video buffer status, including video mode, buffer dimensions (maximum x- and y-coordinates), and currently displayed portion of the buffer

- Foreground and background pixel values for text and graphics output

- Color values for palette registers

- Current pixel operation (replace, XOR, AND, OR, or NOT)

- Current region fill pattern

- Current line-drawing style (thick or thin line, dashed or broken line)

In many applications it is better to maintain several global areas instead of just one. Because almost all PC and PS/2 video hardware supports more than one display mode, you can create a separate global data block for each mode and make an entire block ''current'' when you select a video mode. In a windowing environment, a block of global data can apply to each displayable window. In addition to the above information, such a block can also describe the way graphics images and text are mapped into a window. This can include clipping boundaries, vertical and horizontal scaling, or window visibility (whether a window is on or off the screen, overlapping another window, and so on).

Using a global data area has several advantages. Because both high-level and low-level routines can determine output hardware status, you can write hardware-independent programs that examine the descriptive information in the global data area to determine how to format their output. This information is relatively static, so maintaining it in a global area helps minimize redundant parameter passing between graphics routines. Moreover, global data areas can be used contextually: the contents of a global data area can be saved, modified transiently, and restored.

 Of course, the information in a global data area can pertain to output devices other than video adapters and displays. A graphics interface that accommodates printers or plotters can also incorporate information about their status in a global data area.

Layered Graphics Interfaces

After implementing an interface between your low-level video output routines and your high-level program, you may still find that a certain amount of high-level source code is concerned with low-level hardware-dependent manipulations such as pixel coordinate scaling and clipping. You can insulate high-level application code from considerations about hardware capabilities by creating one or more intermediate layers of functionality between the high-level application and the hardware drivers.

A simple layered graphics interface is depicted schematically in Figure 13-1. The bottom layer comprises a set of hardware driver routines like the ones in this book. The top layer provides a set of subroutines that can be called by a high-level application. The routines in the top layer may call the hardware drivers in the bottom layer directly, or there may be one or more intermediate binding layers interposed between the high-level routines and the hardware drivers. In any case, the top-level subroutines present a consistent, hardware-independent software interface to the programmer who uses a high-level language, and thereby insulate high-level programs from the vagaries of video hardware programming.

The ROM video BIOS provides an example of this sort of layering. The set of routines that you invoke by issuing INT 10H serves as an intermediate layer between assembly-language applications and the low-level routines that actually program the hardware. From the application's point of view, the INT 10H interface is relatively hardware-independent; the video BIOS programs the graphics controller, updates the video buffer, and performs many other hardware-dependent programming tasks. Because the video BIOS routines contain the hardware-dependent code, a program that uses the BIOS is to some extent portable to different types of video hardware.

You can, of course, build many more functions into a layered interface than the video BIOS provides. For example, commercially available video graphics interfaces can produce sophisticated graphics and perform video control functions, including geometric transformations (scaling, translation, rotation of graphics images), three-dimensional graphics (hidden-line removal, three-dimensional surface representation), or sophisticated color mixing and shading. Such graphics

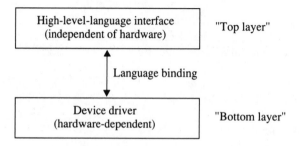

Figure 13-1. *A simple layered graphics interface.*

packages can support output to printers or plotters, as well as to video displays. In this case, the layered interface provides a set of routines and data structures that allow a high-level program to determine the status of an output device and to select appropriate output attributes (line style, drawing color, and so on) on each device.

In an operating environment that relies heavily on a graphics-oriented video interface, access to operating system functions can be combined with video output routines in a high-level application program interface (API). This is the approach taken in Apple's Macintosh and in Microsoft Windows. In both these environments, support for system functions like windows, pull-down menus, and icons is integrated into a unified, graphics-oriented API.

Most layered graphics interfaces comprise more than one intermediate layer. Furthermore, each layer can be broken into several independent modules. The desire to preserve software portability, particularly as existing software is adapted to new video hardware, is the main reason for this. Many PC graphics programs are designed so that the end-user can customize the hardware-dependent layer(s) to a particular hardware configuration. This is a great convenience for the user, since adapting a program with a layered video interface to a newly acquired piece of hardware is no more difficult than installing a new device driver or relinking the program with a new subroutine library.

The price you pay for this flexibility is a certain amount of extra code needed to support the layered interface, so programs run somewhat slower. You must consider this trade-off whenever you write an application that relies on video display output. Although the benefits of using a layered graphics interface are great, many applications are simpler to develop and run faster when you dispense with the formal graphics interface and use only the necessary low-level drivers.

To get an idea of the type of programming required when you use a layered graphics interface, consider how you might draw a filled rectangle in a video graphics mode. The following examples show how you could do this using one of the routines developed earlier in this book and using two different layered graphics interfaces. As you compare the source code and the programming technique in each of the following examples, you will see where the advantages and disadvantages of each graphics interface might lie.

Direct Hardware Programming

The routine in Listing 13-6 draws a filled rectangle directly, by computing the endpoints of the set of adjacent line segments that make up the rectangle and using a horizontal line-drawing routine to update the video buffer. Strictly speaking, this routine could be written entirely in assembly language by adapting one of the line-drawing routines from Chapter 6. The high-level routine in Listing 13-6 runs nearly as fast, however, since most of the time is spent drawing the lines, not computing their endpoints.

```
/* Listing 13-6 */

FilledRectangle( x1, y1, x2, y2, n )
int     x1,y1;                  /* upper left corner */
int     x2,y2;                  /* lower right corner */
int     n;                      /* pixel value */
{
        int     y;

        for (y = y1; y <= y2; y++)      /* draw rectangle as a set of */
          Line( x1, y, x2, y, n );      /*  adjacent horizontal lines */
}
```

Listing 13-6. *Using C to draw a filled rectangle.*

If raw speed is the major constraint on your program, this is the best way to draw a rectangle. The code, however, is relatively nonportable, because it makes implicit assumptions about such hardware-dependent constraints as the (x,y) coordinate system and color capabilities of the video subsystem. You could not use a routine such as the one in Listing 13-6 in a multitasking or windowing operating environment, because it programs the video hardware directly and could therefore inadvertently corrupt video output from a concurrently executing program.

Extended BIOS Interface

As mentioned previously, the video ROM BIOS provides a certain amount of hardware independence and portability through the interrupt 10H interface. The trade-off, of course, is speed and a certain amount of flexibility. Apart from inefficient implementations, the INT 10H routines are relatively unstructured and limited in their capabilities. As IBM video subsystems have become more complex, additional functionality has been grafted onto the INT 10H interface, making it more powerful but increasingly difficult to master.

Direct Graphics Interface Standard (DGIS) is a firmware interface developed by Graphics Software Systems that extends the capabilities of the INT 10H interface in a structured manner. DGIS was designed to provide a uniform low-level interface to video hardware based on graphics coprocessors such as the Intel 82786 or the Texas Instruments TMS34010. Programming with DGIS is reminiscent of programming with IBM's video BIOS, but many elements of a high-level graphics interface have also been incorporated into DGIS.

DGIS implements a hardware-independent interface by describing actual video subsystems, or *devices*, in terms of their possible display modes, or *configurations*. An application can interrogate DGIS to determine what devices are supported in the computer. It then selects a subsequent video output configuration, based on the configuration's resolution, number of colors, graphics and/or alphanumeric text support, and so on.

For example, Listing 13-7 calls DGIS to draw the same filled rectangle as before. This time, however, instead of programming the hardware, the source code is concerned primarily with programming the interface. The routine first establishes the presence of a suitable graphics output device in the computer by calling the DGIS Inquire Available Devices function. This function returns a list of available DGIS devices; in a system with an EGA, for example, the configurations associated with the "EGA" device correspond to the EGA's video modes.

```
                TITLE    'Listing 13-7'
                NAME     dgisrect
;
; Name:          dgisrect
; Function:      draw a filled rectangle using DGIS
;
; Notes:         assemble and link to create DGISRECT.EXE
;
CR              EQU      0Dh
LF              EQU      0Ah

_TEXT           SEGMENT byte public 'CODE'
                ASSUME  cs:_TEXT,ds:_DATA,ss:STACK
EntryPoint      PROC     far
                mov      ax,seg _DATA
                mov      ds,ax                    ; DS -> _DATA
                push     ss
                pop      es                       ; ES -> stack segment

; look for installed DGIS devices
                xor      dx,dx                    ; DX = 0 (buffer length)
                xor      cx,cx                    ; CX = 0
                xor      bx,bx                    ; BX = 0
                mov      ax,6A00h                 ; AX = DGIS opcode (Inquire
                                                  ;       Available Devices)

                int      10h
                or       cx,cx
                jnz      L01                      ; jump if device(s) installed
                mov      dx,offset _DATA:Msg0
                jmp      ErrorExit

; find a graphics output device in the list of installed DGIS devices
L01:            inc      cx                       ; CX = (# of bytes in list) + 1
                and      cx,0FFFEh                ; CX = even number of bytes
                mov      bp,sp
                sub      sp,cx                    ; establish stack frame
                                                  ;   (SS:BP -> end of frame)
                mov      di,sp                    ; ES:DI -> start of stack frame
                push     di                       ; save for later
                mov      dx,cx                    ; DX = size of buffer
                xor      cx,cx
                xor      bx,bx
                mov      ax,6A00h                 ; AX = DGIS opcode (Inquire
                                                  ;       Available Devices)
                int      10h                      ; get device list at ES:DI
                pop      di                       ; ES:DI -> device list

L02:            cmp      word ptr es:[di+2],0     ; is this a graphics device?
                je       L04                      ; jump if so
                sub      bx,es:[di]               ; BX = bytes remaining in list
                jnz      L03                      ; jump if more devices in list
                mov      dx,offset _DATA:Msg1
                jmp      ErrorExit
```

Listing 13-7. *Using DGIS to draw a filled rectangle.*   *(continued)*

Listing 13-7. *Continued.*

```
L03:            add     di,es:[di]              ; ES:DI -> next device in list
                jmp     L02

; establish a logical connection to the graphics device
;   using the first available configuration on the device
L04:            les     di,es:[di+6]            ; ES:DI -> device entry point
                mov     word ptr GrDevEntry,di
                mov     word ptr GrDevEntry+2,es ; save entry point
                mov     cx,0                    ; CX = first configuration index
                mov     ax,0027h                ; AX = DGIS opcode (Connect)
                call    dword ptr GrDevEntry    ; connect to graphics device
                cmp     bx,-1                   ; test returned handle
                jne     L05                     ; jump if connected
                mov     dx,offset _DATA:Msg2
                jmp     ErrorExit

L05:            mov     ChannelHandle,bx        ; save the handle for later
                mov     ax,001Bh                ; AX = DGIS opcode (Init DGI)
                call    dword ptr GrDevEntry    ; initialize the device with
                                                ;   default attributes
; draw a filled rectangle using default attributes
                mov     di,100                  ; DI = lower right corner y
                mov     si,100                  ; SI = lower right corner x
                mov     dx,0                    ; DX = upper left corner y
                mov     cx,0                    ; CX = upper left corner x
                mov     bx,ChannelHandle        ; BX = handle
                mov     ax,003Fh                ; AX = DGIS opcode (Output
                call    dword ptr GrDevEntry    ;      Filled Rectangle)

; disconnect and exit
                mov     bx,ChannelHandle        ; BX = handle
                mov     ax,002Bh                ; AX = DGIS opcode (Disconnect)
                call    dword ptr GrDevEntry

Lexit:          mov     ax,4C00h
                int     21h                     ; return to DOS

ErrorExit:      mov     ah,9
                int     21h                     ; display error message
                mov     ax,4C01h
                int     21h                     ; return to DOS

EntryPoint      ENDP

_TEXT           ENDS
_DATA           SEGMENT para public 'DATA'

GrDevEntry      DD      ?                       ; graphics device entry point
ChannelHandle   DW      ?                       ; handle to connected device
                                                ;   configuration

Msg0            DB      CR,LF,'No DGIS devices installed',CR,LF,'$'
Msg1            DB      CR,LF,'No graphics devices installed',CR,LF,'$'
Msg2            DB      CR,LF,'Can''t connect to graphics device',CR,LF,'$'
_DATA           ENDS

STACK           SEGMENT stack 'STACK'
                DB      400h dup(?)
STACK           ENDS
                END     EntryPoint
```

The application program "connects" to an appropriate configuration, which DGIS identifies with a handle. The application can then associate an *attribute context* with the handle; the attribute context is a data structure that defines drawing colors, line styles, clipping boundaries, and so on. Subsequent calls to DGIS graphics output functions like `OutputFilledRectangle` refer to the attribute context associated with a specified handle.

This general sequence of operations is inherently flexible. One reason is that it lets an application program access hardware features without actually programming the hardware. For example, an application can use DGIS functions to change a color palette or update pixels without writing directly to hardware control registers or to the video buffer.

However, an application that performs video output through a DGIS interface runs slower than an equivalent application that programs the video hardware directly. As always, when you interpose a layer of functionality between your application and the hardware, you gain increased functionality and portability at the price of a decrease in speed. You must decide whether this trade-off is worthwhile in your own applications.

High-Level Interface

There are several high-level graphics interface implementations available for IBM video subsystems. These high-level interfaces differ from DGIS and the IBM video BIOS in that they are implemented as software libraries or RAM-loadable device drivers instead of firmware routines. All of them relieve you of the need to program the hardware directly, and all provide a structured programming interface that can be used in a program written in a high-level language.

The differences between the high-level graphics interfaces lie in the amount and type of functionality built into them. For example, the Virtual Device Interface (VDI) is a proposed ANSI standard designed to promote hardware independence in programs written in high-level languages. VDI presents a consistent programming interface to all graphics output hardware, including video subsystems, printers, and plotters. (The Graphics Development Toolkit sold by Graphics Software Systems and IBM support VDI.)

Another well-known interface is the Graphical Kernel System (GKS), an internationally recognized ANSI standard. GKS offers a highly structured interface with powerful graphics data manipulation features. GKS deals not with individual hardware devices but with *workstations* that can include several related input and output devices (such as a display, a keyboard, and a mouse). A GKS implementation can be layered above a lower-level interface like VDI; an application can then use either interface without sacrificing functionality or portability.

Still another type of high-level interface integrates graphics output with the computer's operating environment, as does the Graphics Device Interface (GDI) in Microsoft Windows. In contrast to DGIS, which is designed to be a low-level interface to display hardware, GDI serves as a high-level interface to Windows' graphics-oriented operating environment. In a layered graphics interface, GDI would be closer to the topmost layer while an interface like DGIS would be near the bottom. In fact, you can install Windows to run on top of DGIS; a Windows application can then use GDI functions which in turn call DGIS functions to access the hardware (Figure 13-2).

The C source code fragment in Listing 13-8 merely scratches the surface of GDI programming in Windows, but it should give you an idea of how the video interface is structured. Most of the code in the example establishes a *device context* for the `Rectangle()` function to use. In GDI, a device context is a global data structure that contains information on the colors with which text and graphics are drawn, as well as scaling factors for pixel (*x,y*) coordinates, clipping boundaries, and other information. Windows maintains a device context for each window on the screen. Each device context is identified by a 16-bit handle. When an application calls a GDI output function like `Rectangle()` or `Ellipse()`, it passes the handle of a device context to the function; the function then refers to the information in the device context to produce output in a window.

To produce graphics output in a window, a Windows application starts by calling the Windows function `CreateWindow()`, which returns a handle (hWnd) that identifies the window. The application then monitors Windows' applicaiton message queue to determine when to update the window.

To generate output to the window, the application can use another Windows function, `BeginPaint()`, to associate a device context (identified with the handle hDC) with the window. The application then uses GDI functions to establish drawing attributes and pixel coordinate mapping in the device context. In the example in Listing 13-8, the attributes of the rectangle's border (line style and color) are specified by creating a data structure that becomes part of the device context.

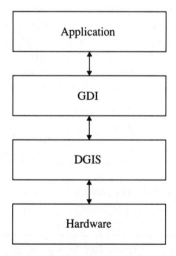

Figure 13-2. *Microsoft Windows GDI installed on DGIS.*

```
HDC         hDC;                    /* device context handle */
HPEN        hpen;
HBRUSH      hbrush;
PAINTSTRUCT ps;
.
.
.

/* initialize device context for window */

hDC = BeginPaint( hWnd, &ps );
.
.
.

/* associate attributes with device context */

hpen = CreatePen( PS_SOLID, 0, GetSysColor(COLOR_WINDOWTEXT) );
SelectObject( hDC, (HANDLE)hpen );

hbr = CreateSolidBrush( GetNearestColor(hDC,RectFillColor) );
SelectObject( hDC, (HANDLE)hbr );
.
.
.

/* draw a filled rectangle */

Rectangle( hDC, 0, 0, 100, 100 );
.
.
.

EndPaint( hWnd, &ps );
```

Listing 13-8. *Using Microsoft Windows GDI (version 1.03) to draw a filled rectangle.*

The function CreatePen() creates the data structure and returns an identifying handle that is assigned to the variable hpen. The function SelectObject() then updates the device context with this information. Similarly, calls to CreateSolidBrush() and SelectObject() establish the color and pattern used to fill the rectangle.

When Rectangle() executes, it uses the "pen" and "brush" attributes in the device context to draw the rectangle's border and interior. The (x,y) coordinates specified in the call to Rectangle() indicate the rectangle's upper left and lower right corners. The coordinates do not indicate absolute pixel locations in the video buffer; they specify points in the coordinate system that relates to the window in which the rectangle is displayed.

GDI's general design is similar to that of other high-level graphics interfaces — the hardware-dependent, machine-language routines are isolated in the lowest layer of the interface, and portable, hardware-independent functions are implemented in the interface's upper layers. The differences among GDI, VDI, and other high-level graphics interfaces lie not so much in implementation details as in the types and complexity of the graphics functions they can perform.

Appendix A

Video BIOS Summary

All computers in the IBM PC and PS/2 family have a BIOS (Basic Input/Output System) in ROM. The ROM BIOS contains a set of assembly-language routines that provide a low-level programming interface for accessing various hardware features, including disk drives, the system timer, serial I/O ports, a parallel printer, and, of course, the video hardware. By building a video BIOS in ROM into every machine, IBM has attempted to provide a common software interface for the various machines, despite substantial hardware differences among the IBM PC, the PC/XT, the PC/AT, and the PS/2s.

To a large extent, this endeavor succeeded. Transporting programs between IBM PCs with different hardware tends to be easier when the programs access the hardware only by calling ROM BIOS routines. This is particularly true of programs that manipulate the video display. When you consider the many video display configurations available, you might regard the BIOS as a sort of "lowest common denominator" for the software developer.

Still, you might not always choose to use ROM BIOS routines for video output for several reasons. For one, ROM BIOS video support routines are not very fast. When performance is critical, you probably will not use them. The speed of the routines is rarely important for tasks performed infrequently, such as loading a character set into RAM or changing a video display mode. On the other hand, in displaying graphics images or producing animation effects, using the BIOS can substantially decrease performance.

Many other tasks are better performed by your operating system rather than the BIOS. For example, when you call the BIOS to write characters to the screen, you bypass any operating system processing of those characters. The BIOS routines know nothing about input/output redirection, windowing, or other functions the operating system provides.

Clearly, the video ROM BIOS is essential to IBM PC video programming, but the extent to which your programs use it is a matter for your judgment.

Hardware Supported by ROM Video BIOS

MDA and CGA

The ROM BIOS on the motherboard of every IBM/PC, PC/XT, and PC/AT supports both the MDA and the CGA. Also, the PS/2 Model 30's video BIOS supports an MDA, in addition to its integrated MCGA. When you power a PC on, the vector for interrupt 10H is initialized to point to the video service routine in ROM.

IBM's technical documentation frequently refers to the motherboard ROM BIOS in the PCs and PS/2s as the "planar" BIOS. The planar BIOS routines start at F000:E000 in the CPU's address space.

EGA

IBM's EGA contains its own set of video drivers in ROM, located at C000:0000. The EGA's cold boot routines initialize interrupt 10H to point to its service routine in the EGA ROM BIOS. The EGA BIOS uses the interrupt 42H vector to point to the motherboard video service routine. Because the EGA's interrupt 10H routines access the motherboard BIOS routines whenever necessary through INT 42H, you rarely need to execute this interrupt explicitly.

MCGA

The video ROM BIOS in the PS/2 Models 25 and 30 supports the integrated MCGA subsystem in these computers. The Model 30's ROM BIOS supports the concurrent use of an MDA, but a CGA cannot be used in the same machine because its I/O port assignments and video memory usage conflict with those of the MCGA.

VGA

Video ROM routines in the PS/2 Models 50, 60, and 80, starting at E000:0000, support the VGA exclusively. The other video adapters described in this book cannot be installed in these computers because they are incompatible with the PS/2 MicroChannel bus.

VGA Adapter

The VGA Adapter's video ROM BIOS routines start at C000:0000. The BIOS routines on the VGA Adapter are the same as those in the PS/2 Model 50, 60, and 80 video BIOS, except for minor differences related to the different hardware implementations of the adapter and the integrated VGA subsystem.

Interrupt 10H

The BIOS video routines are written in assembly language and accessed by performing 80x86 interrupt 10H. The INT 10H interface is designed for assembly-language programs, but you can call the BIOS routines directly from programs written in languages such as C or Pascal if your language compiler provides a way to execute the interrupt.

You select a BIOS video support routine by loading a function number into register AH. To pass parameters to the BIOS routine, place their values in the 80x86 registers before executing INT 10H. Values that the BIOS routines return to your program are left in registers as well.

The IBM PC motherboard BIOS routines explicitly preserve the contents of registers DS, ES, BX, CX, DX, SI, and DI (unless they are used for parameter passing). The EGA, MCGA, and VGA BIOS routines also preserve register BP.

If you are using the IBM PC or PC/XT planar BIOS, preserve register BP across INT 10H calls to the BIOS. For example:

```
push bp             ; preserve BP
int  10h            ; call the BIOS
pop  bp             ; restore BP
```

As a rule, BIOS video input/output routines do not validate data, nor do they return status codes or error flags. Thus, your programs should never attempt to access an invalid video buffer address, select a video page in a video mode that does not support them, or access hardware not installed in your system. The BIOS routines do not reliably detect any of these errors.

Video BIOS Data Areas

Video Display Data Area

The BIOS routines maintain several dynamic variables in an area of memory called the Video Display Data Area. Figure A-1 contains a summary of these variables' addresses, their symbolic names, and their contents.

Address	Name	Type	Description
0040:0049	CRT_MODE	Byte	Current BIOS video mode number
0040:004A	CRT_COLS	Word	Number of displayed character columns
0040:004C	CRT_LEN	Word	Size of video buffer in bytes
0040:004E	CRT_START	Word	Offset of start of video buffer
0040:0050	CURSOR_POSN	Word	Array of eight words containing the cursor position for each of eight possible video pages. The high-order byte of each word contains the character row, the low-order byte the character column.
0040:0060	CURSOR_MODE	Word	Starting and ending lines for alphanumeric cursor. The high-order byte contains the starting (top) line; the low-order byte contains the ending (bottom) line.
0040:0062	ACTIVE_PAGE	Byte	Currently displayed video page number
0040:0063	ADDR_6845	Word	I/O port address of CRT Controller's Address register (3B4H for monochrome, 3D4H for color).
0040:0065	CRT_MODE_SET	Byte	Current value for Mode Control register (3B8H on MDA, 3D8H on CGA). On the EGA and VGA, the value emulates those used on the MDA and CGA.
0040:0066	CRT_PALETTE	Byte	Current value for the CGA Color Select register (3D9H). On the EGA and VGA, the value emulates those used on the MDA and CGA.
0040:0084	ROWS	Byte	Number of displayed character rows − 1

Figure A-1. *BIOS Video Display Data Area.*   *(continued)*

Figure A-1. *Continued.*

Address	Name	Type	Description
0040:0085	POINTS	Word	Height of character matrix
0040:0087	INFO	Byte	(See Figure A-1a)
0040:0088	INFO_3	Byte	(See Figure A-1b)
0040:0089	Flags	Byte	Miscellaneous flags (see Figure A-1c)
0040:008A	DCC	Byte	Display Combination Code table index
0040:00A8	SAVE_PTR	Dword	Pointer to BIOS Save Area (see Figure A-3)

Bit	Description
7	Reflects bit 7 of video mode number passed to INT 10H function 0
6–5	Amount of video RAM: 00b - 64K 01b - 128K 10b - 192K 11b - 256K
4	(reserved)
3	1 - video subsystem is inactive
2	(reserved)
1	1 - video subsystem is attached to monochrome display
0	1 - alphanumeric cursor emulation is enabled

Figure A-1a. *Mapping of INFO byte at 0040:0087 in the EGA and VGA Video Display Data Area.*

Bit	Description
7	Input from feature connector on FEAT1 (bit 6 of Input Status register 0) in response to output on FC1 (bit 1 of Feature Control register)
6	Input from feature connector on FEAT0 (bit 5 of Input Status register 0) in response to output on FC1 (bit 1 of Feature Control register)
5	Input from feature connector on FEAT1 (bit 6 of Input Status register 0) in response to output on FC0 (bit 0 of Feature Control register)
4	Input from feature connector on FEAT0 (bit 5 of Input Status register 0) in response to output on FC0 (bit 0 of Feature Control register)
3	Configuration switch 4 (1 - off, 0 - on)
2	Configuration switch 3 (1 - off, 0 - on)
1	Configuration switch 2 (1 - off, 0 - on)
0	Configuration switch 1 (1 - off, 0 - on)

Figure A-1b. *Mapping of INFO_3 byte at 0040:0088 in the EGA and VGA Video Display Data Area. Bits 4 through 7 reflect the power-on status of the EGA feature connector. Bits 0 through 3 reflect the settings of the four EGA configuration switches. (The switch values are emulated by the VGA BIOS, depending on the type of display attached.)*

Bit	Description
7	Alphanumeric scan lines (with bit 4):

bit 7	bit 4	
0	0	350-line mode
0	1	400-line mode
1	0	200-line mode
1	1	(reserved)

Bit	Description
6	1 - display switching is enabled
	0 - display switching is disabled
5	(reserved)
4	(see bit 7)
3	1 - default palette loading is disabled
	0 - default palette loading is enabled
2	1 - using monochrome monitor
	0 - using color monitor
1	1 - gray scale summing is enabled
	0 - gray scale summing is disabled
0	1 - VGA active
	0 - VGA not active

Figure A-1c. *Mapping of Flags byte at 0040:0089 in MCGA and VGA Video Display Data Area.*

Video BIOS routines update the values in the Video Display Data Area to reflect the status of the video subsystem. If you alter the video environment without invoking an INT 10H routine, be sure you update the relevant variables in the Video Display Data Area. Failing to do so can cause the BIOS video routines to malfunction.

Save Areas

The ROM BIOS routines on the EGA, the MCGA, and the VGA support a set of save areas, which are dynamic tables of video hardware and BIOS information. The video BIOS can use these save areas to supplement the Video Display Data Area. You can also use them to override the usual video BIOS defaults for character sets, palette programming, and other configuration functions.

The video BIOS save areas are linked by a set of doubleword (segment:offset) pointers (see Figure A-2). Use the variable SAVE_PTR (at 0040:00A8 in the Video Display Data Area) to locate the save areas. SAVE_PTR contains the address of the SAVE POINTER table (see Figure A-3). This table contains addresses of as many as seven data structures, each with a different format and a different set of data pertaining to operation of the video hardware or of the video BIOS routines.

The fifth address in the SAVE POINTER table is that of the SECONDARY SAVE POINTER table (see Figure A-4), which only the VGA's BIOS uses. This table also contains the addresses of several data structures with contents relating to the functioning of the video hardware and the BIOS.

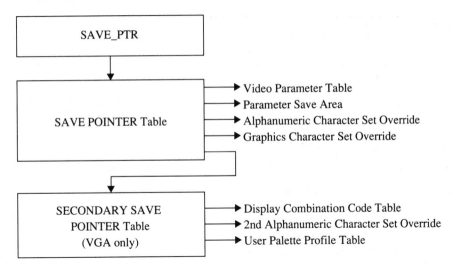

Figure A-2. *Video BIOS Save Areas.*

Offset	Type	Description
0	Dword	Address of Video Parameter table
4	Dword	Address of Parameter Save Area (EGA, VGA only)
8	Dword	Address of Alphanumeric Character Set Override
0CH	Dword	Address of Graphics Character Set Override
10H	Dword	Address of SECONDARY SAVE POINTER table (VGA only)
14H	Dword	(reserved)
18H	Dword	(reserved)

Figure A-3. *SAVE POINTER table (EGA, MCGA, VGA).*

Offset	Type	Description
0	Word	Length of SECONDARY SAVE POINTER table in bytes
2	Dword	Address of Display Combination Code table
6	Dword	Address of second Alphanumeric Character Set Override
0AH	Dword	Address of User Palette Profile table
0EH	Dword	(reserved)
12H	Dword	(reserved)
16H	Dword	(reserved)

Figure A-4. *SECONDARY SAVE POINTER table (VGA only).*

Apart from the SAVE POINTER and SECONDARY SAVE POINTER tables, the only data structures provided in the ROM BIOS are the Video Parameter table and, on the VGA, the Display Combination Code table. Thus, the only initialized addresses in the SAVE POINTER table are those of the Video Parameter table and of the SECONDARY SAVE POINTER table. The only initialized address in the SECONDARY SAVE POINTER table belongs to the Display Combination Code table. Remaining addresses are initialized to 0.

Video Parameter Table

This data structure contains configuration parameters used by the BIOS video mode set routines. The table contains entries for each available video mode. Its structure and format differ on the EGA, the MCGA, and the VGA. Figure A-5 is a typical entry in the VGA Video Parameter table. Formats for table entries in the EGA and MCGA BIOS are similar.

Offset	Type	Description
0	Byte	Value for CRT_COLS
1	Byte	Value for ROWS
2	Byte	Value for POINTS
3	Word	Value for CRT_LEN
5	4-byte array	Values for Sequencer registers 1–4
9	Byte	Value for Miscellaneous Output register
0AH	25-byte array	Values for CRTC registers 0–18H
23H	20-byte array	Values for Attribute Controller registers 0–13H
37H	9-byte array	Values for Graphics Controller registers 0–8

Figure A-5. *Format of a VGA Video Parameter table entry. The VGA Video Parameter table comprises 29 such entries.*

Parameter Save Area

When present, this table contains the values of the EGA or the VGA Graphics Controller palette registers (00H through 0FH) and the Overscan register (11H), as shown in Figure A-6. The video BIOS updates the Parameter Save Area whenever it updates the corresponding Attribute Controller registers.

Offset	Type	Description
0	16-byte array	Current contents of Graphics Controller Palette registers
10H	Byte	Current contents of Graphics Controller Overscan register
11H–0FFH	(reserved)	

Figure A-6. *Parameter Save Area. This area is 256 bytes in size.*

When a User Palette Profile (see Figure A-10 later in this discussion) overrides the default palette register values, the Parameter Save Area is updated with default values, not those in the User Palette Profile.

Alphanumeric Character Set Override

This data structure (see Figure A-7) indicates an alphanumeric character set to be used instead of the BIOS default character set. The character set is loaded whenever the video BIOS is called to select one of the video modes that the data structure specifies.

Offset	Type	Description
0	Byte	Length in bytes of each character definition
1	Byte	Character generator RAM bank
2	Word	Number of characters defined
4	Word	First character code in table
6	Dword	Address of character definition table
0AH	Byte	Number of displayed character rows
0BH	Byte array	Applicable video modes
	Byte	0FFH (end of list of video modes)

Figure A-7. *Alphanumeric Character Set Override.*

On the VGA, you can specify a second 256-character set by creating a second Alphanumeric Character Set Override data structure and storing its address in the SECONDARY SAVE POINTER table.

Graphics Character Set Override

This data structure (see Figure A-8) overrides the default BIOS character set selection whenever the video BIOS sets up one of the specified video modes.

Offset	Type	Description
0	Byte	Number of displayed character rows
1	Word	Length in bytes of each character definition
3	Dword	Address of character definition table
7	Byte array	Applicable video modes
	Byte	0FFH (end of list of video modes)

Figure A-8. *Graphics Character Set Override.*

Display Combination Code Table

Figure A-9 lists all combinations of video subsystems that the video BIOS supports. The description of INT 10H function 1AH in this appendix explains how this table is used.

The MCGA video BIOS contains a Display Combination Code table in ROM to support INT 10H function 1AH. However, the MCGA BIOS does not support a SECONDARY SAVE POINTER table, so you can't modify its DCC table.

Offset	Type	Description
0	Byte	Number of entries in table
1	Byte	DCC table version number
2	Byte	Maximum display type code
3	Byte	(reserved)
4	Word array	Each pair of bytes in the array describes a valid display combination (see INT 10H function 1AH)

Figure A-9. *Display Combination Code table.*

User Palette Profile Table

This data structure contains user-specified overrides for the default Attribute Controller Palette and Overscan register values, for the default values in the 256 video DAC color registers, and for the default value in the CRTC Underline Location register (see Figure A-10). Only the VGA video BIOS supports this table.

Offset	Type	Description
0	Byte	Underlining: 1 - Enable in all alphanumeric modes 0 - Enable in monochrome alphanumeric mode −1 - Disable in all alphanumeric modes
1	Byte	(reserved)
2	Word	(reserved)
4	Word	Number of Attribute Controller registers in table
6	Word	First Attribute Controller register number
8	Dword	Address of Attribute Controller register table
0CH	Word	Number of video DAC Color registers in table
0EH	Word	First video DAC Color register number
10H	Dword	Address of video DAC Color register table
14H	Byte array	Applicable video modes
	Byte	0FFH (end of list of video modes)

Figure A-10. *User Palette Profile table.*

Video BIOS Save Area Programming

To use a data structure supported in the SAVE POINTER and SECONDARY SAVE POINTER tables, place the data structure in RAM and update the appropriate SAVE POINTER or SECONDARY SAVE POINTER addresses to point to it. Because the default SAVE POINTER and SECONDARY SAVE POINTER tables are located in ROM, you must copy these tables to RAM and update SAVE_PTR (0040:00A8) appropriately before you can modify them.

Listings A-1 and A-2 demonstrate two uses of the video BIOS save areas. The routine in Listing A-1 provides a parameter save area for the EGA or VGA BIOS. Once the parameter save area is established, its first 17 bytes are updated with the contents of the Attribute Controller's 16 palette registers and its Overscan register each time the video BIOS writes to them.

```
              TITLE    'Listing A-1'
              NAME     EstablishPSA
              PAGE     55,132

;
; Name:        EstablishPSA
;
; Function:    Establish a Parameter Save Area for the EGA or VGA video BIOS.
;              This save area will reflect the current values of the Attribute
;              Controller's Palette and Overscan registers.
;
; Caller:      Microsoft C:
;
;                       void EstablishPSA();
;

SAVE_PTR       EQU      0A8h

DGROUP         GROUP    _DATA

_TEXT          SEGMENT byte public 'CODE'
               ASSUME  cs:_TEXT,ds:DGROUP,es:DGROUP

               PUBLIC  _EstablishPSA
_EstablishPSA  PROC    near

               push    bp
               mov     bp,sp
               push    si
               push    di

; preserve previous SAVE_PTR

               push    ds
               pop     es              ; ES -> DGROUP
               mov     di,offset DGROUP:Old_SAVE_PTR

               mov     ax,40h
               mov     ds,ax           ; DS -> video BIOS data area
               mov     si,SAVE_PTR     ; DS:SI -> SAVE_PTR

               mov     cx,4
               rep     movsb

; copy SAVE POINTER table to RAM

               lds     si,es:Old_SAVE_PTR ; DS:SI -> SAVE POINTER table
               mov     di,offset DGROUP:SP_TABLE1
               mov     cx,7*4          ; number of bytes to move
               rep     movsb

; update SAVE_PTR with the address of the new SAVE POINTER table

               mov     ds,ax           ; DS -> video BIOS data area
               mov     si,SAVE_PTR
               mov     word ptr [si],offset DGROUP:SP_TABLE1
               mov     [si+2],es
```

(continued)

Listing A-1. *Using a Parameter Save Area to keep track of EGA or VGA palette registers.*

```
; update SAVE POINTER table with address of Parameter Save Area

                push    es
                pop     ds        ; DS -> DGROUP

                mov     word ptr SP_TABLE1[4],offset DGROUP:PSA
                mov     word ptr SP_TABLE1[6],ds

; restore registers and exit

                pop     di
                pop     si
                mov     sp,bp
                pop     bp
                ret

_EstablishPSA   ENDP

_TEXT           ENDS


_DATA           SEGMENT word public 'DATA'

Old_SAVE_PTR    DD      ?                  ; previous value of SAVE_PTR
SP_TABLE1       DD      7 dup(?)           ; RAM copy of SAVE POINTER table
PSA             DB      256 dup(0)         ; Parameter Save Area

_DATA           ENDS

                END
```

Listing A-2 shows how to specify the palette values to be used when the video BIOS routines are invoked to establish a new video mode. First, place the values in a table whose address is stored in a User Palette Profile data structure. Then place the address of this data structure in the SECONDARY SAVE POINTER table. (Since this example uses the SECONDARY SAVE POINTER table, you can run it only on the VGA.)

```
                TITLE   'Listing A-2'
                NAME    EstablishUPP
                PAGE    55,132


;
; Name:          EstablishUPP
;
; Function:      Establish a User Palette Profile Save Area for the VGA
;                video BIOS.  This save area overrides the usual default
;                palette values for a specified list of video modes.
;
; Caller:        Microsoft C:
;
;                        void EstablishUPP();
```

(continued)

Listing A-2. *Using a User Palette Profile to override the default VGA palette.*

Listing A-2. *Continued.*

```
SAVE_PTR          EQU       0A8h

DGROUP            GROUP     _DATA

_TEXT             SEGMENT byte public 'CODE'
                  ASSUME    cs:_TEXT,ds:DGROUP,es:DGROUP

                  PUBLIC    _EstablishUPP
_EstablishUPP     PROC      near

                  push      bp
                  mov       bp,sp
                  push      si
                  push      di

; preserve previous SAVE_PTR

                  push      ds
                  pop       es              ; ES -> DGROUP
                  mov       di,offset DGROUP:Old_SAVE_PTR

                  mov       ax,40h
                  mov       ds,ax           ; DS -> video BIOS data area
                  mov       si,SAVE_PTR     ; DS:SI -> SAVE_PTR

                  mov       cx,4
                  rep       movsb

; copy SAVE POINTER table to RAM

                  lds       si,es:Old_SAVE_PTR ; DS:SI -> SAVE POINTER table
                  mov       di,offset DGROUP:SP_TABLE1
                  mov       cx,7*4          ; number of bytes to move
                  rep       movsb

; update SAVE_PTR with the address of the new SAVE POINTER table

                  mov       ds,ax           ; DS -> video BIOS data area
                  mov       si,SAVE_PTR
                  mov       word ptr [si],offset DGROUP:SP_TABLE1
                  mov       [si+2],es

; copy SECONDARY SAVE POINTER table to RAM

                  lds       si,es:SP_TABLE1[16] ; DS:SI -> SEC SAVE POINTER table
                  mov       di,offset DGROUP:SP_TABLE2
                  mov       cx,[si]
                  rep       movsb

; update new SAVE POINTER table with address of new SECONDARY SAVE POINTER table

                  push      es
                  pop       ds        ; DS -> DGROUP
```

(continued)

```
                    mov        word ptr SP_TABLE1[16],offset DGROUP:SP_TABLE2
                    mov        word ptr SP_TABLE1[18],ds

; update SECONDARY SAVE POINTER with address of User Palette Profile

                    mov        word ptr SP_TABLE2[10],offset DGROUP:UPP
                    mov        word ptr SP_TABLE2[12],ds

; restore registers and exit

                    pop        di
                    pop        si
                    mov        sp,bp
                    pop        bp
                    ret

_EstablishUPP       ENDP

_TEXT               ENDS


_DATA               SEGMENT word public 'DATA'

Old_SAVE_PTR        DD         ?                    ; previous value of SAVE_PTR

SP_TABLE1           DD         7 dup(?)             ; copy of SAVE POINTER table

SP_TABLE2           DW         ?                    ; copy of SECONDARY SAVE POINTER table
                    DD         6 dup(?)

UPP                 DB         0                    ; underlining flag
                    DB         0                    ; (reserved)
                    DW         0                    ; (reserved)
                    DW         17                   ; # of palette & overscan registers
                    DW         0                    ; first register specified in table
                    DW         DGROUP:PalTable ; pointer to palette table
                    DW         seg DGROUP
                    DW         0                    ; number of video DAC color regs
                    DW         0                    ; first video DAC register
                    DD         0                    ; pointer to video DAC color table
                    DB         3,0FFh               ; list of applicable video modes

PalTable            DB         30h,31h,32h,33h,34h,35h,36h,37h ; a custom palette
                    DB         00h,01h,02h,03h,04h,05h,14h,07h
                    DB         01h                         ; overscan reg

_DATA               ENDS

                    END
```

 Generally, your application should restore SAVE_PTR to its original value when the SAVE POINTER tables and save areas are no longer needed. If you want to preserve these tables in RAM for use by subsequent applications, use the MS-DOS "Terminate-but-Stay-Resident" function (INT 21H function 31H) so that the RAM containing the tables is not freed when the program that creates them terminates.

Interrupt 1DH Vector

This interrupt vector contains the address of a table of video initialization values (see Figure A-11). These values are useful only for the MDA and the CGA; however, the table is maintained for compatibility among all PCs and PS/2s.

Offset	Type	Description
0	16-byte array	CRTC registers for 40-by-25 alphanumeric mode (CGA)
10H	16-byte array	CRTC registers for 80-by-25 alphanumeric mode (CGA)
20H	16-byte array	CRTC registers for 320-by-200 4-color or 640-by-200 2-color graphics modes (CGA)
30H	16-byte array	CRTC registers for 80-by-25 monochrome (MDA)
40H	Word	Video buffer length (40-by-25 alphanumeric mode)
42H	Word	Video buffer length (80-by-25 alphanumeric mode)
44H	Word	Video buffer length (CGA graphics modes)
46H	Word	Video buffer length (CGA graphics modes)
48H	8-byte array	Number of displayed character columns for video BIOS modes 0 through 7
50H	8-byte array	Values for CRT Mode Control register 3x8H for video BIOS modes 0 through 7

Figure A-11. *MDA and CGA Video Initialization table. This table's address is stored in the vector for INT 1DH.*

IBM PC and PS/2 Video BIOS Functions (INT 10H Interface)

The following pages provide detailed descriptions of each BIOS function available through software interrupt 10H. The descriptions are intended to complement the function summaries and assembly-language source code listings in IBM's technical literature. The accompanying source code fragments represent typical programming examples that you can modify for your own purposes.

This summary includes information on the ROM BIOS routines found on the motherboard, the EGA, the MCGA, and the VGA. However, not all the routines are available or function identically on all computers in the IBM PC and PS/2 family.

All information in this chapter is based on IBM technical specifications and on the following dated versions of the video ROM:

- IBM PC motherboard ROM: 10/27/82

- IBM PC/AT motherboard ROM: 6/10/85

- IBM EGA ROM: 9/13/84

- IBM PS/2 Model 30 (MCGA) ROM: 9/2/86

- IBM PS/2 Model 60 (VGA) ROM: 2/13/87

- IBM PS/2 (VGA) Display Adapter ROM: 10/27/86

Function 0: Select Video Mode

Caller registers:

AH = 0
AL = video mode number:

0	40-by-25 16-color alphanumeric, color burst disabled
1	40-by-25 16-color alphanumeric, color burst enabled
2	80-by-25 16-color alphanumeric, color burst disabled
3	80-by-25 16-color alphanumeric, color burst enabled
4	320-by-200 4-color graphics, color burst enabled
5	320-by-200 4-color graphics, color burst disabled
6	640-by-200 2-color graphics, color burst enabled
7	80-by-25 monochrome alphanumeric (MDA, Hercules, EGA, and VGA only)
8	160-by-200 16-color graphics (PCjr only)
9	320-by-200 16-color graphics (PCjr only)
0AH	640-by-200 4-color graphics (PCjr only)
0BH	Reserved (used by EGA BIOS function 11H)
0CH	Reserved (used by EGA BIOS function 11H)
0DH	320-by-200 16-color graphics (EGA and VGA only)
0EH	640-by-200 16-color graphics (EGA and VGA only)
0FH	640-by-350 monochrome graphics (EGA and VGA only)
10H	640-by-350 16-color graphics (VGA, EGA with at least 128 KB)
	640-by-350 4-color graphics (64 KB EGA)
11H	640-by-480 2-color graphics (MCGA, VGA only)
12H	640-by-480 16-color graphics (VGA only)
13H	320-by-200 256-color graphics (MCGA and VGA only)

Returned values:

(none)

Video Display Data Area updates:

0040:0049	CRT_MODE
0040:004A	CRT_COLS
0040:004C	CRT_LEN
0040:004E	CRT_START
0040:0050	CURSOR_POSN
0040:0060	CURSOR_MODE
0040:0062	ACTIVE_PAGE
0040:0063	ADDR_6845
0040:0065	CRT_MODE_SET
0040:0066	CRT_PALETTE
0040:0084	ROWS

```
0040:0085   POINTS
0040:0087   INFO
0040:0088   INFO_3
```

INT 10H function 0 puts the video subsystem in the video mode you specify with the value in register AL. Function 0 programs the CRT Controller, selects a default color palette, and optionally clears the video buffer. You can modify several default tasks that function 0 performs by setting flags in the Video Display Data Area (see INT 10H function 12H) or by providing character set or palette attribute overrides in BIOS save areas.

Video mode numbers 0BH and 0CH are reserved for the EGA BIOS support routine for RAM-loadable character sets, in which video memory map 2 is selectively enabled so a table of character definitions can be loaded.

On the EGA, the MCGA, and the VGA, composite video displays are not supported, and there is no color burst signal to control. Thus, mode 0 is the same as mode 1, mode 2 = mode 3, and mode 4 = mode 5.

If you use this BIOS routine to request a video mode your system hardware does not support, the results are unreliable. In particular, if you select mode 7 (monochrome alphanumeric) with a CGA, the motherboard BIOS programs the CGA's CRT Controller with parameters appropriate for an MDA, which results in incomprehensible noise on the CGA screen. The third example below shows how to solve this problem by setting bits 4 and 5 of EQUIP_FLAG (0040:0010) to indicate which subsystem the BIOS is to use.

On the EGA, the MCGA, and the VGA, if bit 7 of the requested video mode number in AL is set to 1, the video buffer is not cleared when the new video mode is selected. Thus, a program can alternate between two video subsystems without losing the contents of their video buffers.

The following example selects 320-by-200 4-color graphics mode.

```
        mov  ax,0004      ; AH := 0 (INT 10H function number)
                          ; AL := 4 (video mode number)
        int  10h
```

This routine shows how to change modes on the EGA without clearing the video buffer.

```
        mov  ax,000EH     ; select a video mode (in this case,
                          ;   640x200 16-color mode)
        or   al,10000000b ; set bit 7
        int  10h
```

To select video modes in a system containing both a CGA and an MDA, use a routine such as the following.

```
        mov   ax,40h
        mov   es,ax
        and   byte ptr es:[10h],11001111b      ; zero bits 4 and 5 of EQUIP_FLAG
        or    byte ptr es:[10h],00110000b      ; set bits 4 and 5:
                                               ;   11b - monochrome
                                               ;   10b - color (80x25)
                                               ;   01b - color (40x25)
                                               ;   00b - (unused)
        mov   ax,0007
        int   10h                              ; select monochrome mode 7

        and   byte ptr es:[10],11001111b       ; zero those bits
        or    byte ptr es:[10],00100000b       ; bits for 80x25 16-color
        mov   ax,0003
        int   10h                              ; select 80x25 16-color mode 3
```

Function 1: Set Alphanumeric Cursor Size

Caller registers:

> AH = 1
> CH = top line of cursor
> CL = bottom line of cursor

Returned values:

> (none)

Video Display Data Area update:

0040:0060   CURSOR_MODE

INT 10H function 1 programs the CRT Controller to display the specified alphanumeric cursor. It programs the CRT Controller's Cursor Start and Cursor End
registers so that the alphanumeric cursor appears between the specified lines in
the character matrix. The contents of register CX are copied into
CURSOR_MODE.

If the value in CH is 20H the alphanumeric cursor is disabled.

On the EGA and the VGA, if bit 0 of the INFO byte (0040:0087) is set to 0, the BIOS
processes the top and bottom line values passed in CH and CL relative to an eight-
line character matrix. Chapter 3 discusses this "cursor emulation" in detail.

Use INT 10H function 1 only in alphanumeric video modes.

To select a full-height cursor in video mode 3 (80-by-25 16-color alphanumeric
mode) on a CGA:

```
        mov   cx,0007h      ; CH := 0 (top line)
                            ; CL := 7 (bottom line of the 8x8 character matrix)
        mov   ah,1          ; AH := 1 (INT 10H function number)
        int   10h
```

On an EGA with a 350-line monitor, video mode 3 is a 350-line alphanumeric mode with an 8-by-14 character matrix. Nevertheless, the above code normally runs unchanged in this situation, because the BIOS "emulates" the corresponding 200-line CGA mode and programs the Cursor Start and End registers accordingly.

Function 2: Set Cursor Location

Caller registers:

AH = 2
BH = video page
DH = character row
DL = character column

Returned values:

(none)

Video Display Data Area update:

0040:0050   CURSOR_POSN

INT 10H function 2 updates the BIOS Video Display Data Area with a new cursor position. If the value in BH references the currently displayed video page, this routine also programs the CRT Controller to update the displayed cursor position.

To set the cursor position to column 10, row 5, in 80-by-25 16-color mode:

```
mov   ah,2        ; AH := 2 (INT 10H function number)
mov   bh,1        ; BH := video page
mov   dh,5        ; DH := row
mov   dl,10       ; DL := column
int   10h
```

Function 3: Return Cursor Status

Caller registers:

AH = 3
BH = video page number

Returned values:

CH = top line of cursor
CL = bottom line of cursor
DH = character row
DL = character column

Video Display Data Area updates:

(none)

INT 10H function 3 returns the character cursor location for the specified video page. The character row and column values are copied from CURSOR_POSN in the Video Display Data Area.

The values returned in CH and CL are copied from CURSOR_MODE, also in the Video Display Data Area. They are meaningful only in alphanumeric modes.

To determine the current cursor location (and size in an alphanumeric mode) in video page 0:

```
mov  ah,3        ; AH := 3 (INT 10H function number)
mov  bh,0        ; BH := 0 (video page)
int  10h
```

Function 4: Return Light Pen Position

Caller registers:

AH = 4

Returned values:

AH = 1 if valid light pen position returned
    = 0 if no light pen position returned
BX = pixel *x*-coordinate
CH = pixel *y*-coordinate (CGA and EGA video modes 4, 5, and 6)
CX = pixel *y*-coordinate (EGA except modes 4, 5, and 6)
DH = character row
DL = character column

Video Display Data Area updates:

(none)

INT 10H function 4 gets the current position of the light pen from the CRT Controller's Light Pen High and Light Pen Low registers.

If the light pen switch is not set, or if the light pen latch has not been triggered (that is, if the CRTC's Light Pen High and Light Pen Low registers do not contain a valid light pen address), function 4 returns 0 in register AH. Otherwise, function 4 sets AH to 1, leaves the light pen position in registers BX, CX, and DX, and resets the light pen trigger.

When function 4 returns, BX contains the calculated pixel *x*-coordinate at which the light pen was triggered. Since the CRTC returns the light pen position as a byte address, the value in BX is only as accurate as the number of pixels in each byte of the video buffer. (In 640-by-200 2-color mode, for example, each byte of the video buffer represents eight pixels; function 4 therefore returns the pixel x-coordinates of every eighth pixel.) The light pen position is calculated relative to the start of the displayed portion of the video buffer (CRT_START).

INT 10H function 4 returns the pixel y-coordinate in either CH (in the motherboard BIOS) or CX (in all video modes in the EGA BIOS except modes 4, 5, and 6). For example, in 320-by-200 4-color graphics mode, the pixel y-coordinate is always returned in CH, but in 80-by-25 16-color alphanumeric mode, the value is returned in CH on a CGA but in CX on an EGA.

The values that function 4 returns in DH and DL represent the character row and column at which the light pen was triggered.

INT 10H function 4 always returns AH = 0 on the MCGA and the VGA, which do not support light pens.

To determine the light pen status in any video mode, call INT 10H function 4:

```
mov  ah,4          ; AH := 4 (INT 10H function number)
int  10h
```

For example, if you trigger the light pen near the center of the display in 640-by-350 16-color mode, the values returned by this function might be:

AH =   1 (valid light pen results were returned)
BX = 320 (x-coordinate of first pixel at the byte address where the pen was
                triggered)
CX = 175 (pixel y-coordinate)
DH =   12 (character row)
DL =   40 (character column)

Function 5: Select Video Page

Caller registers:

AH = 5
AL = video page number

Returned values:

(none)

Video Display Data Area updates:

0040:004E CRT_START
0040:0062 ACTIVE_PAGE

INT 10H function 5 selects which portion of the video buffer is displayed on the CGA, the EGA, the MCGA, and the VGA. It works by programming the CRTC Start Address registers. You can use the function in 40-by-25 or 80-by-25 alphanumeric video modes (BIOS modes 0, 1, 2, and 3) in any of these subsystems.

On the CGA, the entire 16 KB video buffer is used in both 320-by-200 and 640-by-200 graphics modes, so no video paging is possible. Calls to function 5 are ignored in these modes.

On the MCGA, the EGA, and the VGA, video pages are available in both alphanumeric and graphics modes up to the limits of video RAM. However, the BIOS routine does not check whether video RAM is sufficient to support a requested video page; if the requested video page lies outside the video buffer, the resulting display is unusable.

The BIOS maintains a current cursor location for as many as eight video pages in CURSOR_POSN. When you invoke Function 5, the BIOS moves the cursor to where it was located the last time the requested video page was displayed.

The following routine sets the displayed portion of the CGA's video buffer to start at B800:1000 (video page 1) in 80-by-25 alphanumeric mode:

```
mov   ax,0501h        ; AH := 5 (INT 10H function number)
                      ; AL := 1 (video page number)
int   10h
```

Function 6: Scroll Up

Caller registers:

AH = 6
AL = number of lines to scroll
BH = attribute
CH = upper left corner row
CL = upper left corner column
DH = lower right corner row
DL = lower right corner column

Returned values:

(none)

Video Display Data Area updates:

(none)

INT 10H function 6 performs a row-by-row upward scroll of characters in a designated area of the active video page. You specify the number of rows of characters to scroll in AL. The rectangular area in which the scroll is to be performed is defined by its upper left corner, specified in CH and CL, and its lower right corner, specified in DH and DL.

The attribute you specify in BH is used for all blank lines inserted in the bottom of the scrolled area. In alphanumeric modes, this attribute is formatted in the usual manner, with the background attribute in the high nibble and the foreground attribute in the low nibble. In graphics modes, the format of the attribute in BH depends on the mode.

In 640-by-200 2-color and 320-by-200 4-color modes, and in 640-by-480 2-color mode on the MCGA, the value in BH represents a 1-byte pixel pattern. The byte represents eight 1-bit pixels in 2-color modes or four 2-bit pixels in 320-by-200 4-color mode. The pixel pattern is replicated throughout all lines that function 6 blanks in the scroll area. In all other EGA, MCGA, and VGA graphics modes, the value in BH determines the value of all pixels in the blanked lines.

In 320-by-200 4-color mode on the EGA, the MCGA, and the VGA, function 6 always scrolls video page 0, regardless of which video page is currently displayed.

Specifying 0 as the number of rows to scroll in AL causes the entire scroll area to be blanked.

In 80-by-25 16-color alphanumeric mode, you can scroll the entire screen up one line with the following sequence:

```
mov   ax,601h      ; AH := 6 (INT 10H function number)
                   ; AL := 1 (number of lines to scroll up)
mov   bh,7         ; BH := 7 (attribute)
mov   cx,0         ; CH := upper left corner:  row 0
                   ; CL := upper left corner:  column 0
mov   dx,184Fh     ; DH := lower right corner:  row 24 (18H)
                   ; DL := lower right corner:  column 79 (4FH)
int   10h
```

In the same video mode, you could clear only the top three lines of the display with a background attribute of 1 (blue on a CGA) and a foreground attribute of 7 (white) using this routine:

```
mov   ax,600h      ; AH := INT 10H function number
                   ; AL := 0 (clear the scroll area)
mov   bh,17h       ; BH := attribute (background 1, foreground 7)
mov   cx,0         ; CH,CL := upper left corner at (0,0)
mov   dx,024Fh     ; DH,DL := lower right corner at (79,2)
int   10h
```

To get the same result in 640-by-350 16-color graphics mode on the EGA, you set the value in BH to indicate a pixel value instead of an alphanumeric attribute:

```
mov   ax,600h
mov   bh,1         ; BH := pixel value
mov   cx,0
mov   dx,024Fh
int   10h
```

In 640-by-200 2-color mode, the following call to INT 10H function 6 fills the display with vertical stripes of alternating pixel values:

```
mov   ax,600h
mov   bh,10101010b    ; BH := pixel pattern
mov   cx,0
mov   dx,184Fh
int   10h
```

Function 7: Scroll Down

Caller registers:

AH = 7
AL = number of lines to scroll
BH = attribute
CH = upper left corner row
CL = upper left corner column
DH = lower right corner row
DL = lower right corner column

Returned values:

(none)

Video Display Data Area updates:

(none)

INT 10H function 7 performs a row-by-row downward scroll of characters in a designated area of the active video page. Except for the direction of the scroll, this BIOS function is identical to function 6.

Function 8: Return Character Code and Attribute at Cursor

Caller registers:

AH = 8
BH = video page

Returned values:

AH = attribute (alphanumeric modes only)
AL = ASCII code

Video Display Data Area updates:

(none)

INT 10H function 8 returns the ASCII code of the character at the current cursor position in the video page that BH specifies. In alphanumeric modes, this is done by reading a single word from the video buffer. In graphics modes, the routine compares the character matrix at the cursor position to the bit patterns in the current graphics character definition table.

In graphics modes, the PC/XT and PC/AT BIOS uses the ROM character definitions at F000:FA6E; the EGA, MCGA, and VGA BIOS uses the definitions designated by the interrupt 43H vector. For ASCII codes 80–0FFH in CGA-compatible graphics modes 4, 5, and 6, the BIOS uses the characters defined in the table indicated by the interrupt 1FH vector.

To determine the character code for a character in a graphics mode, the BIOS routine regards nonzero pixels as foreground pixels. It is the pattern of foreground (nonzero) and background (zero) pixels that is compared to the bit patterns in the table. If the pixel pattern in the video buffer matches a bit pattern in the character definition table, the BIOS determines the character's ASCII code from the bit pattern's location in the table. If the pixel pattern in the video buffer does not match any bit pattern in the table, the BIOS routine returns 0 in AL.

In 320-by-200 4-color mode on the EGA, the MCGA, and the VGA, this function works properly only in video page 0.

The following code fragment reads the character in the screen's upper left corner:

```
mov   ah,0Fh          ; AH := 0FH (INT 10H function number)
int   10h             ; leaves BH = active video page
mov   ah,2            ; AH := 2 (INT 10H function number)
mov   dx,0            ; DH,DL := row 0, column 0
int   10h             ; sets cursor position to (0,0)
mov   ah,8            ; AH := 8 (INT 10H function number)
int   10h             ; leaves AL = ASCII code
```

Function 9: Write Character and Attribute at Cursor

Caller registers:

AH = 9
AL = ASCII code
BH = background pixel value (320-by-200 256-color mode) or video page (all other modes)
BL = foreground pixel value (graphics modes) or attribute value (alphanumeric modes)
CX = repetition factor

Returned values:

(none)

Video Display Data Area updates:

(none)

INT 10H function 9 writes a character one or more times into the video buffer without moving the cursor. You must specify a repetition factor of 1 or greater in CX. The BIOS writes a string composed of the character in AL into the buffer. The length of the string is determined by the repetition factor in CX.

In alphanumeric modes, both the ASCII code and the corresponding attribute byte are updated for each character written into the video buffer. In graphics modes, each character is written into the buffer in a rectangular area the size of the character matrix. The value in BL is used for the character's foreground pixels. In 320-by-200 256-color graphics mode, the value in BH specifies the character's background pixel value; in all other graphics modes, BH designates a video page, so the character's background pixels are 0. In all graphics modes except 320-by-200 256-color mode, the character is XORed into the buffer if bit 7 of BL is set to 1.

INT 10H function 9 does not compare the repetition factor with the number of displayed character columns. In alphanumeric modes, this may not matter; the video buffer map is such that a string too long to be displayed in one row of characters wraps to the next row. In graphics modes, however, a string should be no longer than the remainder of the current character row.

You must specify a video page in register BH in alphanumeric modes as well as in native EGA graphics modes, but the value in BH is ignored by the EGA, the MCGA, and the VGA BIOS in 320-by-200 4-color graphics mode.

The following routine writes a string of 20 asterisks to the upper left corner of the display in 80-by-25 16-color mode. The foreground value in each character's attribute byte is set to 7, and the background value is set to 1. The cursor is positioned with a call to INT 10H function 2 before the string is written with function 9.

```
        mov   ah,2         ; AH := 2 (INT 10H function number)
        mov   bh,0         ; BH := video page
        mov   dx,0         ; DH := cursor row
                           ; DL := cursor column
        int   10h          ; set cursor position to (0,0)
        mov   ah,9         ; AH := 9 (INT 10H function number)
        mov   al,'*'       ; AL := ASCII code
        mov   bl,17h       ; BL := attribute byte
        mov   cx,20        ; CX := repetition factor
        int   10h
```

Function 0AH: Write Character(s) at Cursor Position

Caller registers:

AH = 0AH
AL = ASCII code

BH = background pixel value (320-by-200 256-color mode) or video page (all other modes)

BL = foreground pixel value (graphics modes only)

CX = repetition factor

Returned values:

(none)

Video Display Data Area updates:

(none)

INT 10H function 0AH is the same as INT 10H function 9, with this exception: In alphanumeric video modes, only the character code is written into the video buffer. The character's attribute remains unchanged in the buffer.

This example clears one character row from the cursor position to its end. Before calling function 0AH, the example determines the active video page and the number of displayed character columns with a call to INT 10H function 0FH, and the cursor position using INT 10H function 3.

```
        mov   ah,0Fh           ; AH := 0FH (INT 10H function number)
        int   10h              ; leaves AH = number of columns,
                               ;          BH = active video page
        mov   al,ah
        xor   ah,ah            ; AX := number of columns
        push  ax
        mov   ah,3             ; AH := 3 (INT 10H function number)
        int   10h              ; leaves DH,DL = cursor position
        pop   cx               ; CX := displayed character columns
        sub   cl,dl            ; CX := number of remaining chars in line
        xor   bl,bl            ; BL := foreground pixel value
        mov   ax,0A20h         ; AH := 0AH (INT 10H function number)
                               ; AL := 20H (ASCII blank character)
        int   10h
```

Function 0BH: Set Overscan Color, Select 4-Color Palette

Caller registers:

AH = 0BH

BH = 0 to set border or background color

= 1 to select 4-color palette

BL = color value (if BH = 0)

palette value (if BH = 1)

Returned values:

(none)

Video Display Data Area update:

0040:0066   CRT_PALETTE

INT 10H function 0BH comprises two subfunctions selected according to the value
in BH. Function 0BH is intended for use only in 320-by-200 4-color mode and in
CGA alphanumeric modes, but you can use it with caution in other video modes.

BH = 0

When BH = 0 on the CGA and the MCGA, the BIOS loads the low-order five bits of
the value in BL into the Color Select register (3D9H). In 320-by-200 4-color
graphics mode, bits 0–3 determine the background color (the color displayed for
pixels of value 0) as well as the border color. In 640-by-200 and 640-by-480 2-color
modes, bits 0–3 specify the color of foreground (nonzero) pixels. On the CGA,
these same four bits also determine the border color in alphanumeric modes.

Bit 4 of the Color Select register selects between normal and high-intensity colors
in CGA and MCGA graphics modes (see Chapter 4). For compatibility, the BIOS
for the EGA and the VGA emulates this effect by using a palette of high-intensity
colors when bit 4 of BL is set.

In 200-line modes on the EGA and VGA, the value in BL is placed in the Attribute
Controller's Overscan Color register (11H). This sets the border color. If either
subsystem is in a graphics mode, the same value is also stored in palette register
0. This establishes the same color for all pixels of value 0.

Don't use function 0BH with BL = 0 in other EGA and VGA video modes. In some
modes, the BIOS routine stores incorrect color values in the Palette and Overscan
registers, while in others it does nothing at all. You should use INT 10H function
10H to program the Attribute Controller on the EGA and VGA.

Once the color register or Attribute Controller has been programmed, the BIOS
routine copies bit 5 of CRT_PALETTE in the Video Display Area to bit 0 of register BL, and transfers control to the routine for BH = 1.

BH = 1

When BH = 1, the low-order bit of the value in BL determines which of two
4-color palettes is used for 320-by-200 4-color mode (see Figure A-12). On the
CGA and the MCGA, this bit is copied into bit 5 of the Color Select register
(3D9H). On the EGA and the VGA, the bit determines which set of color values is
loaded into the Attribute Controller's Palette registers. The colors correspond to
the CGA's 320-by-200 4-color palettes. (See Chapter 4 for more details.)

Pixel Value (bit 0 of BL = 0)	Color Displayed
1	Green
2	Red
3	Yellow

Pixel Value (bit 0 of BL = 1)	Color Displayed
1	Cyan
2	Violet
3	White

Figure A-12. *Function 0BH 4-color palettes.*

Function 0BH with BH = 1 has no effect in alphanumeric modes. In graphics modes other than 320-by-200 4-color mode, however, the Color Select register (on the CGA and the MCGA) is loaded or the palette registers (on the EGA and the VGA) are updated as if 320-by-200 4-color mode were in effect. For this reason, you should use this subfunction cautiously in graphics modes other than 320-by-200 4-color mode.

The following example has three different effects, depending on the current video mode. In 200-line alphanumeric modes, it sets the border color; in 320-by-200 4-color mode it sets both border and background colors; and in CGA or MCGA 2-color graphics modes, it sets the foreground color.

```
mov  ah,0BH          ; AH := 0BH (INT 10H function number)
mov  bh,0            ; BH := subfunction number
mov  bl,BorderColor  ; BL := color value
int  10h
```

To select a 4-color palette in 320-by-200 4-color mode, call function 0BH with BH = 1:

```
mov  ah,0Bh
mov  bh,1            ; BH := subfunction number
mov  bl,0            ; bit 0 of BL := 0 (red-green-yellow palette)
int  10h
```

In 320-by-200 4-color mode, select a high-intensity set of colors by calling function 0BH with BH = 0 and with bit 4 of BL set to 1:

```
mov  ah,0Bh
mov  bh,0
mov  bl,10h          ; bit 4 selects high-intensity palette
                     ; bits 3-0 select border/background color
int  10h
```

Function 0CH: Store Pixel Value

Caller registers:

> AH = 0CH
> AL = pixel value
> BH = video page
> CX = *x*-coordinate
> DX = *y*-coordinate

Returned values:

> (none)

Video Display Data Area updates:

> (none)

INT 10H function 0CH updates the value of a pixel at a specified location in the video buffer. In all graphics modes except 320-by-200 256-color mode, if the high-order bit of the value in AL is set to 1, the value in AL is XORed into the video buffer. Otherwise, the value in AL becomes the pixel's new value.

On the EGA, the MCGA, and the VGA, the value in BH is used to select among available video pages in the current video mode. However, the value in BH is ignored in 320-by-200 4-color mode.

To set the value of a pixel in a 350-line graphics mode on an EGA with only 64 KB of video RAM, you must account for the chaining of memory maps to bit planes (as discussed in Chapter 4). In this situation, the BIOS routine expects you to specify the pixel value in AL using only its odd-numbered bits. Thus, the four possible pixel values should be specified as 0 (0000B), 1 (0001B), 4 (0100B), and 5 (0101B) instead of 0, 1, 2, and 3.

The following routine shows how you would set the value of the pixel at (200,100) to 1 in any graphics mode:

```
mov   ah,0Ch          ; AH := 0CH (INT 10H function number)
mov   al,1            ; AL := pixel value
mov   cx,200          ; CX := x-coordinate
mov   dx,100          ; DX := y-coordinate
int   10h
```

To XOR a pixel value into the video buffer, set bit 7 of AL to 1 before executing interrupt 10H, as in the following procedure:

```
mov   ah,0Ch
mov   al,1
mov   cx,200
mov   dx,100
or    al,10000000b    ; set bit 7 to indicate XOR
int   10h
```

This code fragment illustrates the special situation that arises in a 350-line video mode on an IBM EGA with only 64 KB of video RAM. The code sets the value of the pixel at (75,50) to 3.

```
mov   ah,0Ch
mov   al,0101b      ; AL := pixel value of 3 (11B)
                    ; represented in odd bits only
mov   cx,75
mov   dx,50
int   10h
```

Function 0DH: Return Pixel Value

Caller registers:

AH = 0DH
BH = video page
CX = x-coordinate
DX = y-coordinate

Returned values:

AL = pixel value

Video Display Data Area updates:

(none)

INT 10H function 0DH returns the value of a pixel at a specified location in the video buffer.

On an EGA in 320-by-200 4-color mode, the function ignores the video page value specified in BH.

IBM's EGA BIOS (9/13/84 version) contains a bug in INT 10H function 0DH. In 350-line graphics modes on an IBM EGA with only 64 KB of video RAM, the value returned in AL is incorrect. Apparently, the BIOS routine calculates the pixel's byte offset in the video buffer without properly accounting for the mapping of even addresses to even bit planes and odd addresses to odd bit planes.

To determine the value of the pixel at (100,100), you could execute the following sequence of instructions:

```
mov   ah,0Dh        ; AH := 0DH (INT 10H function number)
mov   bh,0          ; BH := video page (0 in this example)
mov   cx,100        ; CX := x-coordinate
mov   dx,100        ; DX := y-coordinate
int   10h           ; leaves AL = pixel value
```

Function 0EH: Display Character in Teletype Mode

Caller registers:

AH = 0EH
AL = ASCII code
BH = video page (PC BIOS versions dated 10/19/81 and earlier)
BL = foreground pixel value (graphics modes only)

Returned values:

(none)

Video Display Data Area update:

0040:0050   CURSOR_POSN

INT 10H function 0EH calls INT 10H function 0AH to display the character you pass in register AL. Unlike function 0AH, however, function 0EH moves the cursor, and ASCII codes 7 (bell), 8 (backspace), 0DH (carriage return), and 0AH (linefeed) are treated as cursor control commands instead of displayable characters. Function 0EH always updates the active (currently displayed) video page except as noted above.

If the character is displayed in the rightmost character column, function 0EH advances the cursor to the start of the next character row. If necessary, function 0EH calls INT 10H function 06H to scroll the screen. In alphanumeric modes, the attribute of the displayed character is used for the scroll. In graphics modes, the scroll attribute is always 0.

In alphanumeric modes, the attribute byte at the position where the character is written determines the character's foreground and background attributes. For this reason, you should probably fill the video buffer with the desired alphanumeric attributes before using function 0EH.

In graphics modes, the character is written into the video buffer in a rectangular area the size of the character matrix. The character's pixels have the value BL specifies, and the remaining background pixels have a value of 0. Because the value in BL is passed through to INT 10H function 0AH, you can set bit 7 so that the character is XORed into the video buffer.

NOTE: Unfortunately, function 0EH does not expand tab characters (ASCII code 9) into blanks.

The following routine shows how you might use function 0EH to display a string of characters.

```
            mov   cx,StringLength         ; CX := number of bytes in string
            jcxz  L02                      ; do nothing if null string
            mov   si,StringAddr            ; DS:SI := address of string
            mov   bl,GraphicsAttribute     ; BL := attribute (graphics modes only)
L01:        lodsb                          ; AL := next character in string
            mov   ah,0Eh                    ; AH := 0EH (INT 10H function number)
            int   10h
            loop  L01
L02:        .
            .
            .
```

Function 0FH: Return Current Video Status

Caller register:

AH = 0FH

Returned values:

AH = number of displayed character columns
AL = video mode number
BH = active video page

Video Display Data Area updates:

(none)

INT 10H function 0FH returns information about the current video mode and the width of the displayed portion of the video buffer. The number of character columns (returned in AH) and the number of the current video page (returned in BH) are copied from CRT_COLS and ACTIVE_PAGE in the Video Display Data Area.

The value returned in AL is copied from CRT_MODE in the Video Display Data Area. It corresponds to the video display modes tabulated for function 0. On the EGA and the VGA, bit 7 of the value in AL is derived from bit 7 of the INFO byte. (INT 10H function 0 sets bit 7 of the INFO byte whenever you use function 0 to select a video mode without clearing the video buffer.)

This example shows how to determine the current position of the displayed cursor. Before calling INT 10H function 3 to find out the cursor position, the example uses function 0FH to determine the currently displayed video page.

```
            mov   ah,0Fh         ; AH := 0FH (INT 10H function number)
            int   10h            ; leaves BH = active video page
            mov   ah,3           ; AH := 3 (INT 10H function number)
            int   10h            ; leaves DH,DL = cursor position
```

Function 10H: Set Palette Registers, Set Intensity/Blink Attribute

Caller registers:

    AH   = 10H

Update a specified palette register:

    AL   = 0
    BH   = color value
    BL   = palette register number

Specify the overscan (border) color:

    AL   = 1
    BH   = color value

Update all 16 palette registers plus the Overscan register:

    AL   = 2
    ES:DX = address of 17-byte table

Select Background Intensity or Blink attribute:

    AL   = 3
    BL   = 0 for background intensity (blink disabled)
           = 1 for blink

Read a specified palette register:

    AL   = 7
    BL   = palette register number

Returned value:
    BH   = contents of specified palette register

Read the contents of the Overscan register:

    AL   = 8

Returned value:
    BH   = contents of Overscan register

Read all 16 palette registers plus the Overscan register:

    AL   = 9
    ES:DX = address of 17-byte table

Returned values:
Bytes 00H through 0FH of table contain palette register values.
Byte 10H of table contains Overscan register value.

Update the specified video DAC Color register:

AL   = 10H
BX   = color register number
CH   = green value
CL   = blue value
DH   = red value

Update a block of video DAC color registers:

AL   = 12H
BX   = first register to update
CX   = number of registers to update
ES:DX = address of table of red-green-blue values

Set Attribute Controller Color Select State:

AL   = 13H
BL   = 0 to set Mode Control register bit 7, 1 to set Color Select register
BH   = value for bit 7 (if BL = 0) or value for Color Select register
        (if BL = 1)

Read specified video DAC Color register:

AL   = 15H
BX   = color register number

Returned values:
CH   = green
CL   = blue
DH   = red

Read a block of video DAC color registers:

AL   = 17H
BX   = first register to read
CX   = number of registers to read
ES:DX = address of table of red-green-blue values

Returned values:
Bytes 0 through $3n - 1$ (where n is the number of registers passed in CX) contain the red-green-blue values read from the specified block of color registers.

Update video DAC Mask register:

AL   = 18H
BL   = new mask value

Read video DAC Mask register:

AL   = 19H

Returned value:
BL   = value read from video DAC Mask register

Read Attribute Controller Color Select register:

AL   = 1AH

Returned values:
BL   = bit 7 of Mode Control register
BH   = bits 2 through 3 of Color Select register (if BL = 0)
          bits 0 through 3 of Color Select register (if BL = 1)

Perform gray-scaling on a block of video DAC color registers:

AL   = 1BH
BX   = first color register in block
CX   = number of color registers

Video Display Data Area updates:

0040:0065   CRT_MODE_SET
0040:0066   CRT_PALETTE

INT 10H function 10H exists only in the EGA, MCGA, and VGA BIOS. The function comprises 16 subfunctions that are selected according to the value in AL. Figure A-13 shows the support that the various subsystems provide for these subfunctions. All subfunctions work in both alphanumeric and graphics modes.

Subfunctions 0 through 9 support attribute and palette programming. Subfunctions 10H through 1BH support the video DAC on the MCGA and the VGA.

AL = 0
When AL = 0 on the EGA and the VGA, function 10H updates the value in one of the palette registers in the Attribute Controller. The routine loads the value in BH into the register that BL specifies.

Although this subfunction's intended purpose is to load a color value into a palette register, the BIOS routine does not validate the register number in BL. Thus, you can also use it to update the Attribute Controller's Mode Control, Overscan, Color Plane Enable, and Horizontal Pel Panning registers.

On the MCGA, when BH = 7 and BL = 12H, the BIOS routine sets bit 3 of the Video DAC Mask register (3C6H) to 0. This causes the BIOS to regard bit 3 of all 4-bit pixel values or alphanumeric attributes as a "don't care" bit in reference to the Video DAC color registers, so only the first eight registers can be referenced. This is useful in displaying two 256-character sets in an alphanumeric mode (see Chapter 10). The MCGA BIOS ignores all other values in BH or BL.

Subfunction	EGA	MCGA	VGA
0	x	x	x
1	x		x
2	x		x
3	x	x	x
4 (reserved)			
5 (reserved)			
6 (reserved)			
7			x
8			x
9			x
10H		x	x
11H (reserved)			
12H		x	x
13H			x
14H (reserved)			
15H		x	x
16H (reserved)			
17H		x	x
18H		x	x
19H		x	x
1AH			x
1BH		x	x

Figure A-13. *INT 10H Function 10H support in EGA, MCGA, and VGA BIOS.*

AL = 1

When AL = 1 on the EGA and the VGA, the BIOS copies the value in BH into the Attribute Controller's Overscan register (11H).

AL = 2

When AL = 2 on the EGA and the VGA, the BIOS expects ES:DX to contain the address of a 17-byte table of values for the 16 Palette registers (bytes 0 through 15) and for the Overscan register (byte 16). The routine copies these values into the corresponding registers in the Attribute Controller.

AL = 3

When AL = 3 on the EGA and the VGA, the value in BL determines the value of bit 3 of the Attribute Controller's Mode Control register (10H). If BL = 0, bit 3 of the Mode Control register value is set to 0, disabling the blinking attribute. If BL is 1, bit 3 is set to 1 to enable blinking.

When AL = 3 on the MCGA, bit 5 of the Color Control register (3D8H) is set to reflect the value in BL. If BL = 0, bit 5 is set to 0 to disable blinking. If BL is 1, bit 5 is set to 1.

AL = 7

When AL = 7 on the VGA, the value in the Attribute Controller Palette register that BL specified is returned in BH. Because the BIOS does not check the specified register number, this subfunction may be used to return the contents of any VGA Attribute Controller register.

AL = 8

When AL = 8 on the VGA, the contents of the Attribute Controller's Overscan register are returned in BH.

AL = 9

When AL = 9 on the VGA, the contents of all 16 palette registers and the Overscan register are returned to a 17-byte table whose address was passed to the BIOS in the register pair ES:DX.

AL = 10H

When AL = 10H on the MCGA and the VGA, the video DAC color register that BX specifies is updated with the red, green, and blue values specified in DH, CH, and CL. Only the low-order six bits of each of the three color values are significant.

If gray-scale summing is enabled, the value stored in the color register is the gray-scale value that corresponds to the specified color values (see INT 10H function 12H with BL = 33H).

AL = 12H

When AL = 12H on the MCGA and the VGA, a block of consecutive video DAC color registers is updated from the table whose address is passed in ES:DX. The value in BX (00H through 0FFH) indicates the first color register to update, and CX contains the number of registers affected. The BIOS routine performs no error checking; if the sum of the values in BX and CX is greater than 256 (100H), the routine wraps around and updates the first color register(s) in the video DAC.

If gray-scale summing is enabled, the values stored in the color registers are the gray-scale values that correspond to the color values in the table (see INT 10H function 12H with BL = 33H).

You must format the table in three-byte groups. Each group must contain a red color value in the first byte, a green value in the second byte, and a blue value in the third byte. Only the low-order six bits of each color value are significant.

AL = 13H

On the VGA, when AL = 13H, the ROM BIOS updates the Attribute Controller's Mode Control register (10H) and the Color Select register (14H) to enable grouping of the 256 video DAC color registers into blocks of 16 or 64 registers each, as discussed in Chapter 3.

When BL = 0, the BIOS uses the value passed in BH to update bit 7 of the Mode Control register. When BH = 1, bit 7 is set to 1. This causes the BIOS to use bits 0 and 1 of the Color Select register in place of bits 4 and 5 of the palette register values. When BH = 0, bit 7 is set to 0, and all six low-order bits of the values in the palette registers are significant.

When BL = 1, the value in BH is stored in the appropriate bit field in the Color Select register. If bit 7 of the Mode Control register is 1, bits 0 through 3 of the value in BH are copied into bits 0 through 3 of the Color Select register. If bit 7 of the Mode Control register is 0, bits 0 through 1 of BH are copied into bits 2 through 3 of the Color Select register.

AL = 15H
When AL = 15H on the MCGA and the VGA, the contents of the video DAC color register specified in BX are returned in registers DH (red), CH (green), and CL (blue). Only the low-order six bits of each of the color values are significant.

AL = 17H
When AL = 17H on the MCGA and the VGA, the values from a block of adjacent video DAC color registers are copied to the table whose address is passed in ES:DX. The value in BX (00H through 0FFH) indicates the first color register to be read, and CX contains the number of registers affected. The BIOS routine performs no error checking; the sum of the values in BX and CX should not exceed 256 (100H).

The table must contain three bytes for every color register read. Color values for each register are stored sequentially in the table in three-byte groups. The first byte of each group contains the color register's red value, the second its green value, and the third its blue value.

AL = 18H
On the MCGA and the VGA, when AL = 18H, the value in BL is copied into the video DAC Mask register (3C6H).

AL = 19H
On the MCGA and the VGA, when AL = 19H, the value in the video DAC Mask register (3C6H) is returned in BL.

NOTE: The BIOS on the VGA Adapter does not support subfunctions 18H and 19H. Also, IBM's BIOS Interface Technical Reference does not document these subfunctions, so they might not be supported in future BIOS releases.

AL = 1AH
On the VGA, when AL = 1AH, the current values of bit 7 of the Attribute Controller's Mode Control register (10H) and bits 0 through 3 of the Color Select register (14H) are returned in BL and BH respectively. If bit 7 of the Mode Control register is 1, the value in BH represents bits 0 through 3 of the Color Select register. If bit 7 of the Mode Control register is 0, only bits 2 through 3 are returned as bits 0 through 1 of BH.

AL = 1BH

On the MCGA and the VGA, when AL = 1BH, gray-scale summing is performed on a block of consecutive video DAC color registers. BX indicates the first color register affected. CX specifies the number of registers to update.

The following example uses INT 10H function 10H to update the color value in a single palette register:

```
        mov   ax,1000h        ; AH := 10H (INT 10H function number)
                              ; AL := 0
        mov   bh,6            ; BH := new color value (yellow)
        mov   bl,7            ; BL := palette register number
        int   10h
```

To update the Overscan register and change the displayed border color, call function 10H with AL = 1:

```
        mov   ax,1001h        ; AH := 10H
                              ; AL := 1
        mov   bh,1            ; BH := color value for overscan
        int   10h
```

To load all 16 palette registers and the Overscan register from a table, call function 10H with AL = 2:

```
        mov   ax,1002h               ; AH := 10H
                                     ; AL := 2
        mov   dx,seg PaletteTable
        mov   es,dx
        mov   dx,offset PaletteTable ; ES:DX -> table of palette register values
        int   10h
        .
        .
        .
PaletteTable db     00h,01h,02h,03h,04h,05h,06h,07h ; palette registers 0-7
             db     38h,39h,3Ah,3Bh,3Ch,3Dh,3Eh,3Fh ; palette regs 8-0FH
             db     00h                             ; Overscan reg
```

To disable the blinking attribute, call function 10H with AL = 3 and BL = 0:

```
        mov   ax,1003h        ; AH := 10H
                              ; AL := 3
        mov   bl,0            ; BL := 0 (disable blinking)
        int   10h
```

The following fragment performs gray-scale summing on the first 16 video DAC color registers. The remaining 240 registers are unaffected.

```
        mov   ax,101Bh        ; AH := 10H
                              ; AL := 1BH
        mov   bx,0            ; BX := first color register affected
        mov   cx,16           ; CX := number of color registers
        int   10h
```

Function 11H: Character Generator Interface

Caller registers:

AH   = 11H

Load alphanumeric character definitions.

User-specified character definition table:
AL   = 0
BH   = points (bytes per character definition)
BL   = table in character generator RAM
CX   = number of characters defined in table
DX   = ASCII code of first character defined
ES:BP = address of user-specified table

ROM BIOS 8-by-14 character definitions:
AL   = 1
BL   = table in character generator RAM

ROM BIOS 8-by-8 character definitions:
AL   = 2
BL   = table in character generator RAM

ROM BIOS 8-by-16 character definitions:
AL   = 4
BL   = table in character generator RAM

Select displayed character definition tables.

AL   = 3
BL   = value for Character Map Select register (EGA, VGA)
       = character generator RAM table numbers (MCGA)

Load alphanumeric character definitions and program the CRT Controller.

User-specified character definition table:
AL   = 10H
BH   = points
BL   = table in character generator RAM
CX   = number of characters defined in table
DX   = ASCII code of first character defined
ES:BP = address of user-specified table

ROM BIOS 8-by-14 character definitions:
AL   = 11H
BL   = table in character generator RAM

ROM BIOS 8-by-8 character definitions:
AL   = 12H
BL   = table in character generator RAM

ROM BIOS 8-by-16 character definitions:
AL   = 14H
BL   = table in character generator RAM

Load graphics character definitions.

User-specified 8-by-8 character definition table for interrupt 1FH vector:
AL   = 20H
ES:BP = address of user-specified character definition table

User-specified character definition table:
AL   = 21H
BL   = 0 (character rows per screen specified in DL)
       = 1 14 character rows per screen
       = 2 25 character rows per screen
       = 3 43 character rows per screen
CX   = points (bytes per character definition)
DL   = character rows per screen (when BL = 0)
ES:BP = address of user-specified character definition table

ROM BIOS 8-by-14 character definitions:
AL   = 22H
BL   = character rows per screen (as above)
DL   = (as above)

ROM BIOS 8-by-8 character definitions:
AL   = 23H
BL   = character rows per screen (as above)
DL   = (as above)

ROM BIOS 8-by-16 character definitions:
AL   = 24H
BL   = character rows per screen (as above)
DL   = (as above)

Get current character generator information.

AL   = 30H
BH   = 0 Contents of interrupt 1FH vector
       = 1 Contents of interrupt 43H vector
       = 2 Address of ROM 8-by-14 character table
       = 3 Address of ROM 8-by-8 character table
       = 4 Address of second half of ROM 8-by-8 character table
       = 5 Address of ROM 9-by-14 alternate character table
       = 6 Address of ROM 8-by-16 character table
       = 7 Address of ROM 9-by-16 alternate character table

Returned values:

CX   = POINTS (height of character matrix)
DL   = ROWS (displayed character rows − 1)
ES:BP = address of character definition table

Video Display Data Area updates:

0040:004C   CRT_LEN
0040:0060   CURSOR_MODE
0040:0084   ROWS
0040:0085   POINTS

INT 10H function 11H comprises a gamut of subfunctions that support both the alphanumeric and the graphics character generators on the EGA, the MCGA, and the VGA. You choose a subfunction with the value you specify in AL. The contents of the other registers depend on the subfunction.

AL = 0, 1, 2, or 4

You can use subfunctions 0, 1, 2, and 4 to load a table of character definitions into video RAM for use by the character generator. (Chapter 10 describes this in detail.) All four subfunctions are available on the VGA. On the EGA, the BIOS ignores subfunction 4. The MCGA BIOS does not contain an 8-by-14 character definition table, so calls with AL = 1 are treated as calls with AL = 4.

On the MCGA, character definitions in character generator RAM are not displayed until they are loaded into the character generator's internal font pages (see Chapter 10). To accomplish this through the video BIOS, follow each call to function 11H performed with AL = 0, 1, 2, or 4 with a call to function 11H with AL = 3.

The MCGA's CRTC can only display characters that are 2, 4, 6, 8, 10, 12, 14, or 16 lines high. Thus, BH should specify one of these values. Also, for compatibility with the VGA BIOS, the MCGA BIOS routine extends character definitions for 14-line characters into definitions for 16-line characters by duplicating the 14th line of each character definition.

AL = 3

On the EGA and the VGA, when AL = 3, function 11H loads the value passed in BL into the Sequencer's Character Map Select register. On the EGA and the MCGA, bits 0 and 1 of BL indicate which of four 256-character tables is used when bit 3 of a character's attribute byte is 0. Bits 2 and 3 of BL indicate which table is used when bit 3 of a character's attribute is 1. On the VGA, bits 0, 1, and 4 specify one of eight tables to be used when a character's attribute bit 3 is 0, and bits 2, 3, and 5 specify the table used when attribute bit 3 is 1.

If both bit fields in BL specify the same character definition table, only that table is loaded and displayed.

AL = 10H, 11H, 12H, or 14H

Subfunctions 10H, 11H, 12H, and 14H are analogous to subfunctions 0, 1, 2, and 4 in that they load an alphanumeric character definition table into video RAM. The difference is that, for these subfunctions on the EGA and the VGA, the BIOS reprograms the CRT Controller to accommodate the height of the character matrix. On the MCGA, calls to function 11H with AL = 10H, 11H, 12H, and 14H are treated as calls to functions 0, 1, 2, and 4 respectively.

NOTE: Disable alphanumeric cursor emulation before using these subfunctions on the EGA. The EGA BIOS cursor emulation routine does not always produce a satisfactory alphanumeric cursor. (Chapter 3 discusses this in detail.)

AL = 20H

If AL = 20H, the address in ES:BP is copied into the interrupt 1FH vector at 0000:007C. This vector points to a table of 8-by-8 character definitions for ASCII codes 80H through FFH. This character definition table is used by the BIOS in CGA-compatible 320-by-200 4-color and 640-by-200 2-color graphics modes.

AL = 21H, 22H, 23H, or 24H

Subfunctions 21H, 22H, 23H, and 24H make a character definition table accessible to the BIOS graphics-mode character generator. They are analogous to subfunctions 0, 1, 2, and 4 respectively. The BIOS updates the interrupt 43H vector and the Video Display Data Area variables POINTS and ROWS with values that describe the specified graphics character definitions.

The BIOS does not reprogram the CRT Controller when it loads graphics-mode character definition tables.

AL = 30H

If AL = 30H, INT 10H function 11H returns information about the BIOS character generator's current status. The value in POINTS in the Video Display Data Area is copied into register CX, the value of ROWS is returned in DL, and the address of one of eight character definition tables is returned in ES:BP. The value in BH indicates which table's address is returned.

NOTE: If you call this subfunction on the EGA with BH equal to 6 or 7, or on the MCGA with BH equal to 5 or 7, the address returned in ES:BP is undefined.

To select an 80-by-43 alphanumeric mode on a 350-line display, invoke INT 10H function 11H to load the ROM 8-by-8 character set and reprogram the CRTC to display 43 character rows. (Dividing 350 lines by 8 lines per character gives 43 character rows.) The following example assumes that the EGA is already in an 80-by-25 alphanumeric mode (BIOS mode number 3 or 7).

```
mov   ax,40h
mov   es,ax
```

```
        push es:[87h]              ; preserve INFO
        or   byte ptr es:[87h],1   ; disable cursor emulation
        mov  ax,1112h              ; AH := 11H (INT 10H function number)
                                   ; AL := 12H (subfunction:  load 8x8
                                   ;   alphanumeric characters, reprogram CRTC)
        mov  bl,0                  ; BL := table 0 in character generator RAM
        int  10h
        pop  es:[87h]              ; restore INFO
```

Function 12H: Video Subsystem Configuration (Alternate Select)

Caller registers:

>   AH   = 12H

Return video configuration information:

>   BL   = 10H

>   *Returned values:*
>   BH   = default BIOS video mode
>   0   Color
>   1   Monochrome
>   BL   = amount of EGA video RAM
>   0   64 KB
>   1   128 KB
>   2   192 KB
>   3   256 KB
>   CH   = feature bits
>   CL   = configuration switch setting

Select alternate Print Screen routine:

>   BL   = 20H

Select scan lines for alphanumeric modes:

>   BL   = 30H
>   AL   = 0   200 scan lines
>   1   350 scan lines
>   2   400 scan lines

>   *Returned value:*
>   AL   = 12H

Select default palette loading:

>   BL   = 31H
>   AL   = 0   Enable default palette loading
>   = 1   Disable default palette loading

Returned value:
AL   = 12H

CPU access to video RAM:

BL   = 32H
AL   = 0   Enable CPU access to video RAM and I/O ports
       = 1   Disable CPU access to video RAM and I/O ports

Returned value:
AL   = 12H

Gray-scale summing:

BL   = 33H
AL   = 0   Enable gray-scale summing
       = 1   Disable gray-scale summing

Returned value:
AL   = 12H

Cursor emulation:

BL   = 34H
AL   = 0   Enable cursor emulation
       = 1   Disable cursor emulation

Returned value:
AL   = 12H

PS/2 video display switching:

BL   = 35H
AL   = 0   Initial adapter video off
          1   Initial planar video on
          2   Switch active video off
          3   Switch inactive video on
ES:DX = address of 128-byte save area (for AL = 0, 2, or 3)

Returned value:
AL   = 12H

Video refresh control:

BL   = 36H
AL   = 0   Enable refresh
          1   Disable refresh

Returned value:
AL   = 12H

Video Display Data Area updates:

(see below)

INT 10H function 12H comprises nine subfunctions selected using the value in BL.

BL = 10H

When BL = 10H on the EGA and the VGA, this BIOS routine returns information about the configuration of the video subsystem. This information is copied from INFO and INFO_3 in the Video Display Data Area. These variables are initialized in the BIOS power-on startup code.

The value returned in BH reflects whether the video subsystem is configured for a color (BH = 0) or monochrome (BH = 1) video mode. Bits 0 and 1 in BL indicate how much video RAM is present. The values returned in CH and CL are derived from the INFO_3 byte. Bits 4 through 7 of INFO_3 (input from the EGA feature connector) are copied to bits 0 through 3 of CH. Bits 0 through 3 of INFO_3 (configuration switch settings) are copied to bits 0 through 3 of CL.

BL = 20H

When BL = 20H on the MCGA, the EGA, and the VGA, the BIOS points the interrupt 5 vector at 0000:0014 to an alternate Print Screen routine contained in the video ROM BIOS. The difference between this routine and the default planar BIOS routine is that the video ROM version uses the Video Display Data Area variable ROWS to determine the number of character rows to print. The PC/XT and PC/AT planar BIOS versions always print 25 rows.

BL = 30H

When BL = 30 on the VGA, the BIOS routine updates bits 0–3 of the INFO_3 byte (0040:0088) and bits 7 and 4 of the Flags byte at 0040:0089. INT 10H function 0 refers to INFO_3 and the Flags byte to determine whether to configure the video subsystem for a 200-line, 350-line, or 400-line mode when it establishes an alphanumeric video mode. You can thus select among 200-line, 350-line, and 400-line alphanumeric modes by first executing INT 10H function 12H with BL = 30H and AL = 0, 1, or 2, and then calling INT 10H function 0 to set the video mode.

This function normally returns the value 12H in AL. If the VGA is inactive (bit 3 of INFO is set to 1), the function returns with AL = 0.

BL = 31H

When BL = 31H on the MCGA or VGA, the BIOS routine updates bit 3 of the Flags byte at 0040:0089 to indicate whether ROM BIOS default palette values should be loaded when a video mode is selected using INT 10H function 0. If the value 0 is passed in AL, bit 3 of the Flags byte is set to 0 to enable default palette setting. If AL = 1, bit 3 is set to 1 to disable default palette setting.

When a valid value is passed in AL, the function returns with AL = 12H.

BL = 32H

When BL = 32H on the MCGA or the VGA, the value in AL specifies whether CPU access to the video buffer and I/O ports is enabled (AL = 0) or disabled (AL = 1). Although the hardware interface for control of video addressing differs on the MCGA, the VGA, and the VGA Adapter, this BIOS function is the same in all three subsystems (see Chapter 2).

When a valid value is passed in AL, the function returns with AL = 12H.

NOTE: Although the EGA video BIOS does not support this function, you can control CPU addressing of video RAM on the EGA by updating bit 1 of the Miscellaneous Output register (3C2H).

BL = 33H

When BL = 33H on the MCGA or the VGA, the BIOS routine updates bit 1 of the Flags byte at 0040:0089 to indicate whether red-green-blue color values should be averaged to gray-scale values when INT 10H functions 0 and 10H update the video DAC color registers. If the value 0 is passed in AL, bit 1 of the Flags byte is set to 1 to enable gray-scale summing. If AL = 1, bit 1 is set to 0 to disable gray-scale summing.

When a valid value is passed in AL, the function returns with AL = 12H.

BL = 34H

When BL = 34H on the VGA, the BIOS routine updates bit 0 of INFO (0040:0087) to indicate whether BIOS cursor emulation is in effect. If the value 0 is passed in AL, bit 0 of INFO is set to 0 to enable cursor emulation. If AL = 1, bit 0 is set to 1 to disable cursor emulation.

When a valid value is passed in AL, the function returns with AL = 12H.

BL = 35H

INT 10H function 1AH with BL = 35H provides a set of routines that support switching between two PS/2 video subsystems in the same computer. In a computer that contains two different PS/2-compatible video subsystems, calls to this function let a program separately access the video BIOS on a video adapter and the video BIOS on a PS/2 motherboard.

When you boot a PS/2 that contains a PS/2-compatible video adapter, the adapter subsystem is always the active subsystem by default. To use the PS/2's planar (motherboard) subsystem, you must use the display switch interface to disable the adapter subsystem and enable the planar subsystem.

You can specify four related subfunctions for function 12H with BL = 35H, using the value passed in register AL. The four subfunctions are designed to be called in pairs. Subfunctions 0 and 1 should be called once each to initialize the BIOS display switch interface and to establish a default video mode for the planar video subsystem. Subsequent calls to subfunctions 2 and 3 then let you switch between the two video subsystems.

When AL = 0, the adapter BIOS initializes the display switch interface. First, the adapter BIOS calls the motherboard BIOS to set bit 6 of the Flags byte at 0040:0089 to 1 to indicate that the interface is supported. Next, the current Video Display Data Area and video interrupt vectors are preserved in the 128-byte buffer whose address is passed in ES:DX, and the video interrupt vectors are redirected to the motherboard BIOS. Finally, the adapter's video buffer and control port addressing are disabled (see INT 10H function 12H, BL = 32H).

When AL = 1, the motherboard BIOS establishes a default 80-by-25 alphanumeric mode on the planar video subsystem.

When AL = 2 and bit 6 of the Flags byte is 1, the contents of the Video Display Data Area and video interrupt vectors are copied to the 128-byte buffer whose address is passed in ES:DX, and the video interrupt vectors are redirected to the currently inactive BIOS. Then video buffer and control port addressing are disabled for the currently active subsystem. A call to this subfunction should normally be followed by a call with AL = 3.

When AL = 3 and bit 6 of the Flags byte is 1, the contents of the Video Display Data Area and interrupt vectors are restored from the buffer whose address is in ES:DX. (This buffer should contain information previously saved by a call with AL = 0 or AL = 2.) Then video buffer and control port addressing are enabled, using the restored video information.

When a valid value is passed in AL, and when both the adapter BIOS and the planar BIOS support the display switch interface, each of the four subfunctions returns with AL = 12H.

NOTE: The PS/2 Model 30 BIOS (dated 12/12/86 and earlier) and the PS/2 Model 25 BIOS (dated 6/26/87) contain a bug that makes the display switch interface unusable. The problem should be corrected in later BIOS versions.

BL = 36H
When BL = 36H on the VGA, the value in AL specifies whether the BIOS routine enables (AL = 0) or disables (AL = 1) video refresh. (Temporarily disabling video refresh can speed software that performs repeated video memory accesses.) Bit 5 of the VGA's Sequencer Clocking Mode register (01H) controls whether video refresh is enabled or disabled. When the value 0 is passed in AL, bit 5 is set to 0 to enable video refresh; when AL is 1, bit 5 is set to 1 to disable video refresh.

The function always returns with AL = 12H.

To obtain EGA configuration information, call INT 10H function 12H with BL = 10H:

```
mov   ah,12h
mov   bl,10h
int   10h
```

To vector the EGA BIOS alternate Print Screen routine, call INT 10H function 12H with BL = 20H:

```
mov   ah,12h
mov   bl,20h
int   10h
```

To implement display switching between a VGA Adapter and the MCGA in a PS/2 Model 30:

```
; save areas for video BIOS display switch interface

VGAsave    db    128 dup(?)      ; save area for VGA
MCGAsave   db    128 dup(?)      ; save area for MCGA

; initialize display switching (execute this code only once)

    mov   ax,1200h              ; AH := 12H (INT 10H function number)
                               ; AL := 0
    mov   bl,35h               ; BL := 35H (display switch interface)
    mov   dx,seg VGAsave
    mov   es,dx
    mov   dx,offset VGAsave     ; ES:DX -> save area for VGA BIOS info
    int   10h
    cmp   al,12h
    jne   Error                ; exit if display switching not supported

    mov   ax,1201h
    mov   bl,35h
    int   10h                  ; disable adapter, enable planar video

; switch from planar (MCGA) to adapter (VGA) subsystem

    mov   ax,1202h             ; AL := 2 (switch active
                               ;   video off)
    mov   bl,35h
    mov   dx,seg VGAsave
    mov   es,dx
    mov   dx,offset VGAsave     ; ES:DX -> save area for
                               ;   currently active subsystem
    int   10h

    mov   ax,1203h             ; AL := 3 (switch inactive
                               ;   video on)
    mov   bl,35h
    mov   dx,offset MCGAsave    ; ES:DX -> save area for
                               ;   subsystem to be made active
    int   10h

; (to switch from adapter to planar, interchange VGAsave and
;  MCGAsave in the calls with AL = 2 and AL = 3)
```

Function 13H: Display Character String

Caller registers:

AH = 13H

AL = 0   BL contains attribute for string. Cursor position not updated.
      = 1   BL contains attribute for string. Cursor position updated.
      = 2   String contains embedded attribute bytes. Cursor position not updated.
      = 3   String contains embedded attribute bytes. Cursor position updated.

BH = video page
BL = attribute
CX = string length
DH = character row
DL = character column
ES:BP = address of start of string

Returned values:

(none)

Video Display Data Area updates:

0040:0050   CURSOR_POSN

INT 10H function 13H writes a character string into the video buffer. Bell, backspace, linefeed, and carriage-return characters embedded in the string are treated as commands rather than displayable characters. If the string cannot be displayed in one row of characters, function 13H wraps the string around to the start of the next line. Function 13H also scrolls the screen upward as necessary.

The string is copied from the address you specify in ES:BP to the location in the video buffer indicated by registers DH and DL (character row and column) and register BH (video page). You must also specify the number of characters in the string in register CX.

Function 13H comprises four subfunctions that are selected according to the value in AL. These four subfunctions allow you to select the method of specifying display attributes for characters in the string and to control the cursor's final position after the string is displayed.

You can specify the attribute used for each character either in BL (AL = 0 or 1) or by pairing each character code with its attribute in the string itself (AL = 2 or 3). Also, you can indicate whether the cursor will stay in place after the string is written (AL = 0 or 2) or will move to the character position just past the end of the string (AL = 1 or 3).

In all graphics modes except 320-by-200 256-color mode, setting bit 7 of the attribute value in BL to 1 causes the BIOS to XOR the string into the video buffer.

The video page specified in BH must be 0 in 320-by-200 4-color mode.

NOTE: On the PC/AT, the EGA, and the MCGA, linefeed and carriage-return characters are always written to the currently displayed video page, regardless of the value you specify in BH. If you write a string containing any of these control characters to a video page not currently displayed, function 13H writes them to the wrong video page.

The following routine writes the string ''Hello, World'' into the video buffer in video page 0 at row 12, column 34. An attribute value of 7 is used for all characters in the string.

```
        mov   ax,1300h            ; AH := 13H (INT 10H function number)
                                  ; AL := 0 (attribute specified in BL,
                                  ;   don't move the cursor)
        mov   bh,0                ; BH := video page
        mov   bl,7                ; BL := attribute
        mov   cx,12               ; CX := number of characters to display
        mov   dh,12               ; DH := row 12
        mov   dl,34               ; DL := column 34
        mov   bp,seg HelloString
        mov   es,bp
        mov   bp,offset HelloString  ; ES:BP := string address
        int   10h
        .
        .
        .
HelloString db    'Hello, World'
```

This example displays the digits 1 through 7 in the upper left corner of video page 0. The attribute used for each digit corresponds to the digit:

```
        mov   ax,1303h            ; AH := 13H (INT 10H function number)
                                  ; AL := 3 (string contains embedded
                                  ;   attribute bytes, move cursor to end
                                  ;   of string)
        mov   bh,0                ; BH := video page
        mov   cx,7                ; CX := number of characters to display
        mov   dx,0                ; DH := row 0
                                  ; DL := column 0
        mov   bp,seg StringData
        mov   es,bp
        mov   bp,offset StringData  ; ES:BP := address of string
        int   10h
        .
        .
        .
StringData db    '1',1,'2',2,'3',3,'4',4,'5',5,'6',6,'7',7
```

Function 14H: (PC Convertible only)

Function 15H: (PC Convertible only)

Function 16H: (reserved)

Function 17H: (reserved)

Function 18H: (reserved)

Function 19H: (reserved)

Function 1AH: Video Display Combination

Caller registers:

AH   = 1AH

Return video display combination:

AL   = 0

Returned values:
AL   = 1AH
BL   = active display
BH   = inactive display

Set video display combination:

AL   = 1
BL   = active display
BH   = inactive display

Returned value:
AL   = 1AH

Video Display Data Area update:

0040:008A   DCC byte

INT 10H function 1AH returns or updates the video BIOS video display combination status. This status is represented in the DCC byte at 0040:008A in the Video Display Data Area. This byte contains an index into the ROM BIOS Display Combination Code table, which contains a list of byte pairs that specify valid combinations of one or two video subsystems. Video subsystems are designated by the following values.

FFH	Unrecognized video subsystem
0	No display
1	MDA with monochrome display
2	CGA with color display
3	(reserved)
4	EGA with color display
5	EGA with monochrome display
6	Professional Graphics Controller
7	VGA with analog monochrome display
8	VGA with analog color display
9	(reserved)
0AH	MCGA with digital color display
0BH	MCGA with analog monochrome display
0CH	MCGA with analog color display

AL = 0

When AL = 0 on the MCGA or the VGA, the video BIOS routine uses the value in the DCC byte as an index into its Display Combination Code table and copies the 2-byte table entry into BH and BL. If two video subsystems are present, one subsystem must be monochrome and the other color; the BIOS routine determines which is active by examining bits 4 through 5 of EQUIP_FLAG (0040:0010).

AL = 1

When AL = 1 on the MCGA or the VGA, the BIOS routine scans the Display Combination Code table for the combination specified in BH and BL. If the specified combination is found in the table, the DCC byte is updated with the appropriate index into the table. If the specified combination is not found, 0FFH is stored in the DCC byte.

When a valid value (0 or 1) is passed in AL, INT 10H function 1AH returns with AL = 1AH.

The following sequence returns the display combination in registers BH and BL.

```
        mov  ax,1A00h              ; AH := 1AH (INT 10H function number)
                                   ; AL := 0
        int  10h
        cmp  al,1AH
        jne  ErrorExit             ; jump if function not supported
                                   ; at this point BL = active display
                                   ; BH = inactive display
```

If this sequence is executed on a PS/2 Model 30 with an analog monochrome display attached to the MCGA and a monochrome display attached to an MDA, the values returned are:

AL = 1AH
BL = 0BH (active display = MCGA with analog monochrome)
BH =   1 (inactive display = MDA with digital monochrome)

Function 1BH: Video BIOS Functionality/State Information

Caller registers:

AH   = 1BH
BX   = implementation type (must be 0)
ES:DI = address of 64-byte buffer

Returned values:

ES:DI = buffer updated with function and state information
AL   = 1BH

Video Display Data Area updates:

(none)

INT 10H function 1BH returns a table of video BIOS state information on the MCGA and the VGA. The table contains dynamic information (shown in Figure A-14) that is determined when function 1BH is invoked, as well as static information (shown in Figure A-15) describing the capabilities of the video BIOS itself.

The dynamic information is copied into the 64-byte buffer whose address is passed to the BIOS routine in ES:DI. The 32-bit address of the static information table is returned as bytes 0 through 3 of the dynamic information table.

When called with BX = 0, INT 10H function 1BH always returns with AL = 1BH.

Offset	Data Type	Description
0	Dword	Address of static functionality table
4	Byte	Video mode
5	Word	Number of displayed character columns
7	Word	Length of displayed portion of video buffer in bytes
9	Word	Start address of upper left corner of video buffer
0BH	16-byte array	Table of cursor locations (column, row) for eight video pages
1BH	Byte	Cursor end line
1CH	Byte	Cursor start line
1DH	Byte	Active video page
1EH	Word	I/O port for CRTC Address register
20H	Byte	CRT_MODE_SET (current value of 3x8H register)
21H	Byte	CRT_PALETTE (current value of 3x9H register)
22H	Byte	Number of displayed character rows
23H	Word	POINTS (height of displayed character matrix)
25H	Byte	Active display combination code
26H	Byte	Inactive display combination code

(continued)

Figure A-14. *Dynamic video state table returned by INT 10H function 1BH.*

Offset	Data Type	Description
27H	Word	Number of displayed colors (0 for monochrome)
29H	Byte	Number of video pages supported
2AH	Byte	Raster scan lines:
		0: 200 lines
		1: 350 lines
		2: 400 lines
		3: 480 lines
2BH	Byte	Alphanumeric character table used when attribute bit 3 is 0 (VGA only)
2CH	Byte	Alphanumeric character table used when attribute bit 3 is 1 (VGA only)
2DH	Byte	Miscellaneous state information (bits are set to 1 if state is true)
		Bit 0: all modes active on all video subsystems (always 0 on MCGA)
		Bit 1: gray-scale summing enabled
		Bit 2: monochrome display attached
		Bit 3: default palette loading disabled
		Bit 4: cursor emulation enabled
		Bit 5: blinking attribute enabled
		(bits 6-7 reserved)
2EH	Byte	(reserved)
2FH	Byte	(reserved)
30H	Byte	(reserved)
31H	Byte	Video RAM available
		0: 64K
		1: 128K
		2: 192K
		3: 256K
32H	Byte	Save area status (bits are set to 1 if state is true)
		Bit 0: two alphanumeric character sets are active (VGA only)
		Bit 1: dynamic save area is active
		Bit 2: alphanumeric character set override is active
		Bit 3: graphics character set override is active
		Bit 4: palette override is active
		Bit 5: display combination code extension is active
		(bits 6-7 reserved)
33H through 3FH		(reserved)

Offset	Data Type	Description
0	Byte	Video modes supported (bits = 1 if a mode is supported) Bit 0: mode 0 Bit 1: mode 1 Bit 2: mode 2 Bit 3: mode 3 Bit 4: mode 4 Bit 5: mode 5 Bit 6: mode 6 Bit 7: mode 7
1	Byte	Video modes supported (bits = 1 if a mode is supported) Bit 0: mode 8 Bit 1: mode 9 Bit 2: mode 0AH Bit 3: mode 0BH Bit 4: mode 0CH Bit 5: mode 0DH Bit 6: mode 0EH Bit 7: mode 0FH
2	Byte	Video modes supported (bits = 1 if a mode is supported) Bit 0: mode 10H Bit 1: mode 11H Bit 2: mode 12H Bit 3: mode 13H Bit 4: (reserved) Bit 5: (reserved) Bit 6: (reserved) Bit 7: (reserved)
3	Byte	(reserved)
4	Byte	(reserved)
5	Byte	(reserved)
6	Byte	(reserved)
7	Byte	Scan lines available in alphanumeric modes (bits = 1 if supported) Bit 0: 200 lines Bit 1: 350 lines Bit 2: 400 lines
8	Byte	Maximum number of displayable alphanumeric character sets
9	Byte	Number of available alphanumeric character definition tables in character generator RAM
0AH	Byte	Miscellaneous video BIOS capabilities (bits = 1 if available) Bit 0: all modes on all monitors (INT 10H function 0) (Note: This bit is always 0 on MCGA) Bit 1: gray-scale summing (INT 10H function 10H and 12H) Bit 2: character set loading (INT 10H function 11H) Bit 3: default palette loading (INT 10H function 0)

(continued)

Figure A-15. *Static functionality table. This table's address is returned by INT 10H function 1BH. The table describes the capabilities of the ROM BIOS in the video subsystem.*

Figure A-15. *Continued.*

Offset	Data Type	Description
		Bit 4: cursor emulation (INT 10H function 1)
		Bit 5: 64-color palette (INT 10H function 10H)
		Bit 6: video DAC loading (INT 10H function 10H)
		Bit 7: control of video DAC via Attribute Controller Color Select (INT 10H function 10H)
0BH	Byte	Miscellaneous video BIOS capabilities (bits = 1 if available)
		Bit 0: light pen support (INT 10H function 4)
		Bit 1: save/restore video state (INT 10H function 1CH)
		Bit 2: blinking/background intensity (INT 10H function 10H)
		Bit 3: Display Combination Code (INT 10H function 1AH)
		(bits 4-7 reserved)
0CH	Byte	(reserved)
0DH	Byte	(reserved)
0EH	Byte	Save area capabilities
		Bit 0: multiple alphanumeric character sets
		Bit 1: dynamic save area
		Bit 2: alphanumeric character set override
		Bit 3: graphics character set override
		Bit 4: palette override
		Bit 5: Display Combination Code extension
		(bits 6-7 reserved)
0FH	Byte	(reserved)

The following sequence returns video BIOS state information in the buffer whose address is passed in ES:DI.

```
        mov     ax,1B00h            ; AH := 1BH (INT 10H function number)
                                    ; AL := 0
        mov     bx,0                ; BX := 0 (Implementation type)
        mov     di,seg StateTable
        mov     es,di
        mov     di,offset StateTable ; ES:DI -> buffer
        int     10h
        cmp     al,1BH
        jne     ErrorExit           ; jump if function not supported
        .
        .                           ; at this point StateTable contains
        .                           ;  the dynamic information table
StateTable db 64 dup(?)
```

Function 1CH: Save or Restore Video State

Caller registers:

AH   =   1CH

Return save/restore buffer size:

AL   = 0
CX   = requested states
      Bit 0:   video hardware state
      Bit 1:   video BIOS data areas
      Bit 2:   video DAC state
      Bits 3–0FH: reserved

Returned values:
AL   = 1CH
BX   = buffer size in 64-byte blocks

Save requested state(s):

AL   = 1
CX   = requested states (as above)
ES:BX = buffer address

Restore requested state(s):

AL   = 2
CX   = requested states (as above)
ES:BX = buffer address

Video Display Data Area updates:

(see below)

INT 10H function 1CH, supported only on the VGA, lets you save and restore the state of the video hardware and video ROM BIOS. INT 10H function 1CH comprises three subfunctions selected by the value passed in AL. For each subfunction, you must set the low-order three bits in CX to indicate the combination of video subsystem states you wish to save or restore. You must also pass the address of a save/restore buffer in ES:BX whenever you use function 1CH to save or restore the video state.

AL = 0
When AL = 0, function 1CH returns the size of the buffer required to store the state information for states requested in CX. The value returned in BX is in 64-byte blocks.

Function 1CH returns AL = 1CH when called with AL = 0 and at least one of the low-order three bits in CX set to 1.

AL = 1
When AL = 1, function 1CH copies the state information requested in CX into the buffer whose address is passed in ES:BX.

AL = 2
When AL = 2, function 1CH restores the video hardware state, the BIOS state, or both using information saved in the buffer whose address is passed in ES:BX.

NOTE: The BIOS routine may modify the current video state as it executes function 1CH. If you plan not to change the video state after saving it with function 1CH, restore the video state immediately afterward (using function 1CH with AL = 2) to ensure that it isn't inadvertently modified.

The following sequence runs under MS-DOS version 2.0 or later. It calls MS-DOS INT 21H function 48H to allocate RAM for a save/restore buffer. It then calls INT 10H function 1CH to save the current video state.

```
        mov     ax,1C00h            ; AH := 1CH (INT 10H function number)
                                    ; AL := 0
        mov     cx,111b             ; CX := 111b (all three video states)
        int     10h
        cmp     al,1Ch
        jne     ErrorExit           ; jump if function not supported
        shl     bx,1                ; convert number of 64-byte blocks
        shl     bx,1                ;   to number of 16-byte blocks
        mov     ah,48h              ; AH := 48H (MS-DOS INT 21H function number)
        int     21h                 ; AX := segment of allocated buffer
        jc      ErrorExit           ; jump if error
        mov     es,ax
        xor     bx,bx               ; ES:BX -> buffer
        mov     cx,111b             ; CX := 111b (all three video states)
        mov     ax,1C01h            ; AH := INT 10H function number
                                    ; AL := 1
        int     10h                 ; save video state in buffer
```

Appendix B

Printing the Screen

Many computer users find it convenient to "snapshot" the current contents of the video display. Although all members of the IBM PC and PS/2 series come with a short ROM BIOS routine that dumps the contents of the video buffer to a printer, you may need to write your own video snapshot program to supplement the ROM routine. This appendix discusses how to use the BIOS screen dump utility, as well as why and how to write your own.

Alphanumeric Modes

You invoke the motherboard ROM's alphanumeric screen dump routine by executing software interrupt 5. (The ROM BIOS keyboard handler issues this interrupt when you press Shift-PrtSc.) This routine copies the contents of the currently displayed video page to the printer in 80-by-25 or 40-by-25 alphanumeric mode. The routine prints only the ASCII character codes, ignoring the attribute bytes in the video buffer.

EGA, MCGA, VGA

The EGA, the MCGA, and the VGA ROM BIOS contain a more flexible version of the INT 5 screen dump routine. That version uses the Video Display Data Area value ROWS (0040:0084) to determine how many rows of characters to print. (The motherboard ROM version always prints 25 rows.) An IBM PC/XT or PC/AT uses the motherboard version by default. To make the EGA or VGA ROM BIOS routine accessible through interrupt 5, call INT 10H function 12H with BL = 20H. This points the interrupt 5 vector to the more flexible routine.

Block Graphics Characters

Because most printers are designed to work with many different computers, not just IBM PCs, manufacturers do not always design their printers to print the same 256 ASCII characters that the video hardware displays in alphanumeric modes. In particular, the characters used for block graphics are not always available on PC-compatible printers. These characters may print differently than they are displayed or they may not print at all.

Graphics Modes

The ROM BIOS does not support screen dumps in graphics modes, so in these modes you must use some other program to print the video buffer's contents.

GRAPHICS

GRAPHICS is a RAM-resident graphics-mode screen dump program that Microsoft supplies as part of MS-DOS under the name GRAPHICS.COM or GRAPHICS.EXE. This program establishes a memory-resident screen dump program for CGA graphics modes (320-by-200 4-color and 640-by-200 2-color) when executed. The program uses an IBM- or Epson-compatible dot-matrix printer for output.

The RAM-resident portion of GRAPHICS traps interrupt 5 and tests the current video mode. If a graphics mode is active, it performs the screen dump. Otherwise, the BIOS interrupt 5 routine gets control and performs the alphanumeric-mode screen dump. Thus, once GRAPHICS.COM or GRAPHICS.EXE has been executed, you can obtain a graphics-mode screen dump by pressing Shift-PrtSc, just as you would in alphanumeric video modes.

Writing a Screen Dump Routine

If you want screen snapshots in native EGA, VGA, or MCGA graphics modes or on a Hercules adapter, or if GRAPHICS produces unsatisfactory output on your printer, you can write your own screen dump routine. Listing B-1 is an example of a simple routine for CGA graphics modes. ScreenDumpCGA can be incorporated into an assembly-language program or a high-level-language program by calling it with the appropriate register values and memory model. (See Chapter 13 for more on this topic.) You might also build ScreenDumpCGA into a Terminate-but-Stay-Resident program that, like GRAPHICS, chains into the interrupt 5 vector and executes whenever Shift-PrtSc is pressed.

```
                TITLE   'Listing B-1'
                NAME    ScreenDumpCGA
                PAGE    55,132

;
; Name:         ScreenDumpCGA
;
; Function:     Screen Dump for CGA 640x200 2-color and 320x200 4-color modes
;
; Caller:       (undefined)
;
; Notes:        The main procedure of this program, ScreenDumpCGA, may be
;               called from an application program or as part of a TSR
;               (Terminate-but-Stay-Resident) handler for interrupt 5.
;

STDPRN          =       4                 ; MS-DOS standard printer handle


DGROUP          GROUP   _DATA

_TEXT           SEGMENT byte public 'CODE'
                ASSUME  cs:_TEXT,ds:DGROUP


;
; PrintLine
;
;       Writes one line of characters to the standard printer device.   Ignores
;       errors.
;

PrintLine       PROC    near              ; Caller:      DS:DX -> data
                                          ;              CX = # of bytes
```

Listing B-1. *A simple screen dump routine for the CGA.*   *(continued)*

```
                        mov     bx,STDPRN
                        mov     ah,40h           ; INT 21h function 40h:  write
                        int     21h
                        ret

PrintLine       ENDP

;
; PrinterGraphics
;
;       Puts the printer in its "graphics mode."  This routine must be
;       customized for different printers.
;

PrinterGraphics PROC    near                    ; Configures Epson MX-80 printer
                                                ;   for 480 dots/line

                        mov     dx,offset DGROUP:EpsonGraphics
                        mov     cx,3
                        call    PrintLine
                        ret

PrinterGraphics ENDP

;
; PrinterDefault
;
;       Puts the printer in its default (non-graphics) mode.  Again, this
;       routine must be customized for different printers.
;

PrinterDefault  PROC    near                    ; Configures Epson MX-80 for default
                                                ;   alphanumeric output

                        mov     dx,offset DGROUP:EpsonReset
                        mov     cx,2
                        call    PrintLine
                        ret

PrinterDefault  ENDP

;
; ChopZeros
;
;       Chops trailing zeros from the printer output buffer.
;

ChopZeros       PROC    near            ; Caller:     ES:DI -> buffer
                                        ;             CX = buffer length
                                        ; Returns:    CX = adjusted length

                        jcxz    L01             ; exit if buffer is empty

                        add     di,cx
                        dec     di              ; ES:DI -> last byte in buffer

                        xor     al,al           ; AL := 0 (byte to scan for)
```

(continued)

```
                    std                     ; scan backwards
                    repe    scasb
                    cld                     ; restore direction flag
                    je      L01             ; jump if buffer filled with zeros

                    inc     cx              ; adjust length past last nonzero byte

L01:                ret

ChopZeros           ENDP


;
; PrintPixels
;
;       Prints one row of pixels on an Epson MX-80.
;

PrintPixels         PROC    near            ; Caller:       DI = offset of buffer
                                            ;               CX = buffer length

                    push    ds
                    pop     es              ; ES := DS

                    push    di              ; preserve buffer offset
                    call    ChopZeros
                    push    cx              ; preserve length

                    mov     word ptr DataHeader+2,cx  ; store buffer length
                                                      ;  in output data header
                    mov     dx,offset DGROUP:DataHeader
                    mov     cx,4
                    call    PrintLine       ; print data header

                    pop     cx              ; CX := buffer length
                    pop     dx              ; DX := buffer offset
                    call    PrintLine       ; print the pixels

                    mov     dx,offset DGROUP:CRLF
                    mov     cx,2
                    call    PrintLine

                    ret

PrintPixels         ENDP


;
; TranslatePixels
;
;       Copies one printable row of pixels from the video buffer to the
;       print buffer.  This routine can be modified at will to change the
;       scaling or orientation of the printed image, to interpolate gray-
;       scale values for color pixels, etc.
;
;       This routine formats the printer buffer for output to an Epson
;       MX-80.  The page is printed sideways, with two horizontal printed pixels
;       for each vertical pixel in the video buffer.  Since the CGA screen
;       is 200 pixels high, the printed output is 400 pixels wide.
;
```

(continued)

```
TranslatePixels PROC      near              ; Caller:        SI = video buffer offset
                                            ;                ES:DI -> print buffer

                push      ds                ; preserve DS
                mov       ds,VideoBufSeg    ; DS:SI -> video buffer

                add       di,398            ; ES:DI -> 2 bytes before end of buffer

                mov       cx,200            ; CX := # of vertical pixels
                mov       bx,2000h+1        ; BX := 1st video buffer increment
                mov       dx,81-2000h       ; DX := 2nd video buffer increment

                std                         ; fill the print buffer backwards

L11:            lodsb                       ; AL := 8 pixels from video buffer
                mov       ah,al             ; AX := 8 doubled pixels
                stosw                       ; write them to print buffer

                add       si,bx             ; increment to next interleave of
                xchg      bx,dx             ;  video buffer

                loop      L11

                cld                         ; clear direction flag
                pop       ds                ; restore DS
                ret

TranslatePixels ENDP

;
; ScreenDumpCGA
;

ScreenDumpCGA   PROC      near              ; Caller:        DS = DGROUP

                call      PrinterGraphics   ; configure the printer for graphics

                push      ds
                pop       es                ; DS,ES := DGROUP
                xor       si,si             ; SI := offset of start of video buffer
L21:            push      si
                mov       di,offset DGROUP:PrintBuf
                call      TranslatePixels   ; copy one printable row of pixels

                mov       cx,400
                mov       di,offset DGROUP:PrintBuf
                call      PrintPixels       ; print them

                pop       si
                inc       si
                cmp       si,80             ; loop across all 80 columns in
                jb        L21               ;  the video buffer

                call      PrinterDefault    ; restore the printer to its default
                                            ;  state
                ret
```

(continued)

Listing B-1. *Continued.*

```
ScreenDumpCGA     ENDP

_TEXT             ENDS

_DATA             SEGMENT word public 'DATA'

PrintBuf          DB      400 dup(?)        ; print output buffer

VideoBufSeg       DW      0B800h

EpsonGraphics     DB      1Bh,33h,18h
EpsonReset        DB      1Bh,40h
DataHeader        DB      1Bh,4Bh,00h,00h
CRLF              DB      0Dh,0Ah

_DATA             ENDS
                  END
```

ScreenDumpCGA copies pixels from the video buffer into an intermediate print buffer. It formats the print buffer so that its contents can be sent directly to the printer (an Epson MX-80 in this example). Since the video buffer can be accessed randomly, ScreenDumpCGA reads pixels from it in an order that is conveniently transmitted to the printer.

The heart of ScreenDumpCGA is the subroutine TranslatePixels. This routine maps pixels from the video buffer into the print buffer. In this example, the routine is short and fast, because it uses a simple transformation to convert video buffer pixels to printer pixels. Because the Epson MX-80 prints vertically oriented groups of pixels (see Figure B-1), the easiest way to print an image from the horizontally mapped video buffer is to rotate it by 90 degrees.

To customize ScreenDumpCGA, concentrate on how best to map pixels from the video buffer to your printer. Change the TranslatePixels routine to scale or rotate the pixels differently, or modify ScreenDumpCGA to change the order in which the contents of the video buffer are copied to the printer.

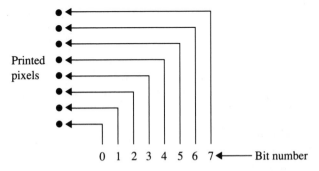

Figure B-1. *Pixel mapping for a typical dot-matrix graphics printer. As the print head moves across the page, it prints eight rows of pixels at a time. Each byte of data transmitted to the printer controls 8 vertical pixels as shown.*

For example, you could modify ScreenDumpCGA and TranslatePixels
to dump the contents of the EGA or VGA video buffer in 640-by-350 16-color mode
as in Listing B-2. The modified routine prints all nonzero pixels in the video
buffer as black dots. Note how the Graphics Controller's read mode 1 simplifies
this task in TranslatePixels.

```
                     TITLE    'Listing B-2'
                     NAME     ScreenDumpEGA
                     PAGE     55,132

; Name:              ScreenDumpEGA
;
; Function:          Screen Dump for EGA 640x350 16-color mode
;
; Caller:            (undefined)
;
; Notes:             The main procedure of this program, ScreenDumpEGA, may be
;                    called from an application program or as part of a TSR
;                    (Terminate-but-Stay-Resident) handler for interrupt 5.

STDPRN          =        4                  ; MS-DOS standard printer handle

DGROUP          GROUP    _DATA

_TEXT           SEGMENT byte public 'CODE'
                ASSUME   cs:_TEXT,ds:DGROUP

; PrintLine
;
;        Writes one line of characters to the standard printer device.  Ignores
;        errors.
;

PrintLine       PROC     near               ; Caller:        DS:DX -> data
                                             ;                CX = # of bytes
                mov      bx,STDPRN
                mov      ah,40h              ; INT 21h function 40h:  Write
                int      21h
                ret

PrintLine       ENDP

; PrinterGraphics
;
;        Puts the printer in its "graphics mode."  This routine must be
;        customized for different printers.
;

PrinterGraphics PROC     near               ; Configures Epson MX-80 printer
                                             ;   for 480 dots/line

                mov      dx,offset DGROUP:EpsonGraphics
                mov      cx,3
                call     PrintLine
                ret
PrinterGraphics ENDP
```

Listing B-2. *An EGA screen printing routine.*   *(continued)*

Listing B-2. *Continued.*

```
;
; PrinterDefault
;
;          Puts the printer in its default (non-graphics) mode.  Again, this
;          routine must be customized for different printers.
;

PrinterDefault  PROC    near                ; Configures Epson MX-80 for default
                                            ;   alphanumeric output

                mov     dx,offset DGROUP:EpsonReset
                mov     cx,2
                call    PrintLine
                ret

PrinterDefault  ENDP


;
; ChopZeros
;
;          Chops trailing zeros from the printer output buffer.
;

ChopZeros       PROC    near                ; Caller:     ES:DI -> buffer
                                            ;             CX = buffer length
                                            ; Returns:    CX = adjusted length

                jcxz    L01                 ; exit if buffer is empty

                add     di,cx
                dec     di                  ; ES:DI -> last byte in buffer

                xor     al,al               ; AL := 0 (byte to scan for)

                std                         ; scan backwards
                repe    scasb
                cld                         ; restore direction flag
                je      L01                 ; jump if buffer filled with zeros

                inc     cx                  ; adjust length past last nonzero byte

L01:            ret

ChopZeros       ENDP


;
; PrintPixels
;
;          Prints one row of pixels on an Epson MX-80.
;

PrintPixels     PROC    near                ; Caller:    DI = offset of buffer
                                            ;            CX = buffer length

                push    ds
                pop     es                  ; ES := DS
```

(continued)

```
                    push    di                      ; preserve buffer offset
                    call    ChopZeros
                    push    cx                      ; preserve length

                    mov     word ptr DataHeader+2,cx  ; store buffer length
                                                    ;   in output data header
                    mov     dx,offset DGROUP:DataHeader
                    mov     cx,4
                    call    PrintLine               ; print data header

                    pop     cx                      ; CX := buffer length
                    pop     dx                      ; DX := buffer offset
                    call    PrintLine               ; print the pixels

                    mov     dx,offset DGROUP:CRLF
                    mov     cx,2
                    call    PrintLine

                    ret

PrintPixels     ENDP


;
; TranslatePixels
;
;       Copies one printable row of pixels from the video buffer to the
;       print buffer.  This routine can be modified at will to change the
;       scaling or orientation of the printed image, to interpolate gray-
;       scale values for color pixels, etc.
;
;       This routine formats the printer buffer for output to an Epson
;       MX-80.  The page is printed sideways, so the printed output is
;       350 pixels wide.
;

TranslatePixels PROC    near                    ; Caller:      SI = video buffer offset
                                                ;              ES:DI -> print buffer

                    push    ds                  ; preserve DS
                    mov     ds,VideoBufSeg      ; DS:SI -> video buffer

                    add     di,349              ; ES:DI -> last byte in print buffer

                    mov     cx,350              ; CX := # of vertical pixels

; set up the Graphics Controller for read mode 1

                    mov     dx,3CEh             ; Graphics Controller I/O port
                    mov     ax,805h             ; AH := 00001000b (read mode 1)
                                                ; AL := Mode register number
                    out     dx,ax

                    mov     ax,002              ; AH := 0 (color compare value)
                    out     dx,ax               ; AL := Color Compare register number

                    mov     ax,0F07h            ; AH := 00001111b (color don't care mask)
                    out     dx,ax               ; AL := Color Don't Care register number
```

(continued)

Listing B-2. *Continued.*

```
; fill the print buffer; all nonzero pixels in the video buffer are printed

            std                     ; fill the print buffer backwards
L11:        lodsb                   ; AL := 8-pixel color compare value
                                    ;   (bits = 0 if pixel <> 0)
            not     al              ; AL := 8 printable pixels
            stosb                   ; store in print buffer

            add     si,81           ; increment to next row in video buffer
            loop    L11

            cld                     ; clear direction flag

; restore Graphics Controller default state

            mov     ax,5            ; AH := read mode 0, write mode 0
            out     dx,ax           ; AL := Mode register number

            mov     ax,7            ; AH := 0 (color don't care mask)
            out     dx,ax           ; AL := Color Don't Care register number

            pop     ds              ; restore DS
            ret

TranslatePixels ENDP


;
; ScreenDumpEGA
;

ScreenDumpEGA   PROC    near        ; Caller:      DS = DGROUP

            call    PrinterGraphics ; configure the printer for graphics

            push    ds
            pop     es              ; DS,ES := DGROUP

            xor     si,si           ; SI := offset of start of video buffer

L21:        push    si
            mov     di,offset DGROUP:PrintBuf
            call    TranslatePixels ; copy one printable row of pixels

            mov     cx,350
            mov     di,offset DGROUP:PrintBuf
            call    PrintPixels     ; print them

            pop     si
            inc     si
            cmp     si,80           ; loop across all 80 columns in
            jb      L21             ;   the video buffer

            call    PrinterDefault  ; restore the printer to its default
                                    ;   state
            ret

ScreenDumpEGA   ENDP
```

(continued)

```
_TEXT           ENDS

_DATA           SEGMENT word public 'DATA'

PrintBuf        DB       350 dup(?)        ; print output buffer

VideoBufSeg     DW       0A000h

EpsonGraphics   DB       1Bh,33h,18h
EpsonReset      DB       1Bh,40h
DataHeader      DB       1Bh,4Bh,00h,00h
CRLF            DB       0Dh,0Ah

_DATA           ENDS
                END
```

RAM-Based Alphanumeric Character Definitions

You can also modify the graphics-mode screen dump routine to print RAM-based characters used in alphanumeric modes on the EGA, MCGA, VGA, HGC+, and InColor Card. The technique is to use the character codes stored in the displayed portion of the video buffer to index the bit patterns in character definition RAM. The bit pattern that defines each character can then be used as a dot pattern for the printer.

As an example, Listing B-3 shows how this can be done for the characters defined in the default character definition table in memory map 2 on the EGA or VGA. The routine prints each column of characters in the video buffer by filling the buffer (PrintBuf) with the bit patterns that define each of the characters. Memory map 0 (containing the character codes) and map 2 (containing the character definitions) are addressed separately in the subroutine TranslatePixels by programming the Sequencer and Graphics Controller as discussed in Chapter 10.

```
                TITLE    'Listing B-3'
                NAME     ScreenDumpAlpha
                PAGE     55,132

;
; Name:         ScreenDumpAlpha
;
; Function:     Screen Dump for EGA alphanumeric modes with 350-line resolution
;
; Caller:       (undefined)
;
; Notes:        The main procedure of this program, ScreenDumpAlpha, may be
;               called from an application program or as part of a TSR
;               (Terminate-but-Stay-Resident) handler for interrupt 5.
;


STDPRN          =        4                 ; MS-DOS standard printer handle

DGROUP          GROUP    _DATA
```

(continued)

Listing B-3. *Using RAM-based character definition tables to print the character set.*

Listing B-3. *Continued.*

```
_TEXT           SEGMENT byte public 'CODE'
                ASSUME  cs:_TEXT,ds:DGROUP,es:DGROUP


;
; PrintLine
;
;       Writes one line of characters to the standard printer device.  Ignores
;       errors.
;

PrintLine       PROC    near            ; Caller:      DS:DX -> data
                                        ;              CX = # of bytes
                mov     bx,STDPRN
                mov     ah,40h          ; INT 21h function 40h:  Write
                int     21h
                ret

PrintLine       ENDP


;
; PrinterGraphics
;
;       Puts the printer in its "graphics mode."  This routine must be
;       customized for different printers.
;

PrinterGraphics PROC    near            ; Configures Epson MX-80 printer
                                        ;   for 480 dots/line

                mov     dx,offset DGROUP:EpsonGraphics
                mov     cx,3
                call    PrintLine
                ret

PrinterGraphics ENDP


;
; PrinterDefault
;
;       Puts the printer in its default (non-graphics) mode.  Again, this
;       routine must be customized for different printers.
;

PrinterDefault  PROC    near            ; Configures Epson MX-80 for default
                                        ;   alphanumeric output

                mov     dx,offset DGROUP:EpsonReset
                mov     cx,2
                call    PrintLine
                ret

PrinterDefault  ENDP


;
; ChopZeros
;
;       Chops trailing zeros from the printer output buffer.
```

(continued)

```
ChopZeros       PROC    near            ; Caller:      ES:DI -> buffer
                                        ;              CX = buffer length
                                        ; Returns:     CX = adjusted length

                jcxz    L01             ; exit if buffer is empty

                add     di,cx
                dec     di              ; ES:DI -> last byte in buffer

                xor     al,al           ; AL := 0 (byte to scan for)

                std                     ; scan backwards
                repe    scasb
                cld                     ; restore direction flag
                je      L01             ; jump if buffer filled with zeros

                inc     cx              ; adjust length past last nonzero byte

L01:            ret

ChopZeros       ENDP


;
; PrintPixels
;
;       Prints one row of pixels on an Epson MX-80.
;

PrintPixels     PROC    near            ; Caller:      DI = offset of buffer
                                        ;              CX = buffer length

                push    ds
                pop     es              ; ES := DS

                push    di              ; preserve buffer offset
                call    ChopZeros
                push    cx              ; preserve length

                mov     word ptr DataHeader+2,cx  ; store buffer length
                                        ;      in output data header
                mov     dx,offset DGROUP:DataHeader
                mov     cx,4
                call    PrintLine       ; print data header

                pop     cx              ; CX := buffer length
                pop     dx              ; DX := buffer offset
                call    PrintLine       ; print the pixels

                mov     dx,offset DGROUP:CRLF
                mov     cx,2
                call    PrintLine

                ret

PrintPixels     ENDP
```

(continued)

Listing B-3. *Continued.*

```
;
; TranslatePixels
;
;       Copies one printable row of pixels from the first character definition
;       table in map 2 to the print buffer.
;
;       This routine formats the printer buffer for output to an Epson
;       MX-80.  The page is printed sideways, so the printed output is
;       350 pixels wide.
;

TranslatePixels PROC    near            ; Caller:        SI = video buffer offset
                                        ;                ES:DI -> print buffer

                push    ds              ; preserve DS
                mov     ds,VideoBufSeg  ; DS:SI -> video buffer

                add     di,es:PrintBufSize
                dec     di              ; ES:DI -> last byte in print buffer

                mov     dx,3CEh         ; Graphics Controller I/O port

; fill the print buffer

                mov     cx,es:Rows      ; CX := number of character rows

L11:            push    cx              ; preserve CX and SI
                push    si

                mov     ax,0004h        ; AH := value for Read Map Select reg
                                        ; AL := Read Map Select reg number
                out     dx,ax           ; select map 0 (character codes)

                lodsb                   ; AX := next char code in video buffer
                mov     cl,5
                shl     ax,cl           ; AX := AX * 32
                mov     si,ax           ; SI := offset of character definition
                                        ;   in map 2
                mov     ax,0204h
                out     dx,ax           ; select map 2 (bit patterns)

                mov     cx,es:Points    ; CX := size of character definition

L12:            cld
                lodsb                   ; AL := 8-bit pattern from character
                                        ;   definition table
                                        ; SI := SI + 1
                std
                stosb                   ; store bit pattern in print buffer
                                        ; DI := DI - 1
                loop    L12             ; loop down character definition

                pop     si              ; restore SI and CX
                pop     cx

                add     si,es:Columns   ; DS:SI -> next row of characters
                loop    L11             ; loop down character rows
```

(continued)

Listing B-3. *Continued.*

```
                    cld                         ; clear direction flag
                    pop     ds                  ; restore DS
                    ret

TranslatePixels ENDP

;
; ScreenDumpAlpha
;

ScreenDumpAlpha PROC     near                ; Caller:        DS = DGROUP

                    call    PrinterGraphics ; configure the printer for graphics

                    call    CGenModeSet     ; address EGA memory maps in parallel:
                                            ;   map 0 contains character codes
                                            ;   map 2 contains character definitions

; copy screen dimensions from Video Display Data Area

                    mov     ax,40h
                    mov     es,ax               ; ES -> video BIOS data area
                    mov     al,es:[84h]         ; AX := ROWS
                    inc     ax
                    mov     Rows,ax
                    mov     ax,es:[4Ah]         ; AX := CRT_COLS
                    add     ax,ax               ; * 2 for proper buffer addressing
                    mov     Columns,ax
                    mov     ax,es:[85h]         ; AX := POINTS
                    mov     Points,ax
                    mul     Rows                ; AX := ROWS * POINTS
                    mov     PrintBufSize,ax

; print the screen

                    push    ds
                    pop     es                  ; DS,ES := DGROUP
                    xor     si,si               ; SI := offset of start of video buffer

L21:                push    si
                    mov     di,offset DGROUP:PrintBuf
                    call    TranslatePixels ; copy one printable row of pixels

                    mov     cx,PrintBufSize
                    mov     di,offset DGROUP:PrintBuf
                    call    PrintPixels     ; print them
                    pop     si
                    add     si,2            ; increment to next character column
                    cmp     si,Columns      ; loop across all character columns
                    jb      L21

                    call    CGenModeClear   ; restore previous alphanumeric mode
                    call    PrinterDefault  ; restore the printer to its default
                                            ;   state
                    ret
ScreenDumpAlpha ENDP
```

(continued)

Listing B-3. *Continued.*

```
;
; CGenModeSet  (from Chapter 10)
;

CGenModeSet     PROC    near

                push    si              ; preserve these registers
                push    cx

                cli                     ; disable interrupts
                mov     dx,3C4h         ; Sequencer port address
                mov     si,offset DGROUP:SetSeqParms
                mov     cx,4

L31:            lodsw                   ; AH := value for Sequencer register
                                        ; AL := register number
                out     dx,ax           ; program the register
                loop    L31
                sti                     ; enable interrupts

                mov     dl,0CEh         ; DX := 3CEH (Graphics Controller port
                                        ;                     address)
                mov     si,offset DGROUP:SetGCParms
                mov     cx,3

L32:            lodsw                   ; program the Graphics Controller
                out     dx,ax
                loop    L32

                pop     cx              ; restore registers and return
                pop     si
                ret

CGenModeSet     ENDP


;
; CGenModeClear  (from Chapter 10)
;

CGenModeClear   PROC    near

                push    si              ; preserve these registers
                push    cx

                cli                     ; disable interrupts
                mov     dx,3C4h         ; Sequencer port address
                mov     si,offset DGROUP:ClearSeqParms
                mov     cx,4

L41:            lodsw                   ; AH := value for Sequencer register
                                        ; AL := register number
                out     dx,ax           ; program the register
                loop    L41
                sti                     ; enable interrupts

                mov     dl,0CEh         ; DX := 3CEH (Graphics Controller port
                                        ;                     address)
```

(continued)

Listing B-3. *Continued.*

```
                    mov     si,offset DGROUP:ClearGCParms
                    mov     cx,3

L42:                lodsw                       ; program the Graphics Controller
                    out     dx,ax
                    loop    L42

                    mov     ah,0Fh              ; AH := INT 10H function number
                    int     10h                 ; get video mode

                    cmp     al,7
                    jne     L43                 ; jump if not monochrome mode

                    mov     ax,0806h            ; program Graphics Controller
                    out     dx,ax               ;  to start map at B000:0000

L43:                pop     cx                  ; restore registers and return
                    pop     si
                    ret

CGenModeClear       ENDP

_TEXT               ENDS

_DATA               SEGMENT word public 'DATA'

PrintBuf            DB      400 dup(?)          ; print output buffer

VideoBufSeg         DW      0A000h

EpsonGraphics       DB      1Bh,33h,18h
EpsonReset          DB      1Bh,40h
DataHeader          DB      1Bh,4Bh,00h,00h
CRLF                DB      0Dh,0Ah
Columns             DW      ?                   ; number of displayed character columns
Rows                DW      ?                   ; number of displayed character rows
Points              DW      ?                   ; vertical size of character matrix
PrintBufSize        DW      ?                   ; Rows * Points

SetSeqParms         DW      0100h               ; parameters for CGenModeSet
                    DW      0402h
                    DW      0704h
                    DW      0300h

SetGCParms          DW      0204h
                    DW      0005h
                    DW      0006h

ClearSeqParms       DW      0100h               ; parameters for CGenModeClear
                    DW      0302h
                    DW      0304h
                    DW      0300h

ClearGCParms        DW      0004h
                    DW      1005h
                    DW      0E06h

_DATA               ENDS
                    END
```

Appendix C

Identifying Video Subsystems

Programs need to determine the configuration of the video hardware on which they are run for two reasons. One is to maintain portability. A program that recognizes the video subsystems in the computer in which it runs can adapt itself to specific hardware configurations. Imagine, for example, a program that displays both text and graphics images. This program could display text and graphics on a single screen in a computer with only one video subsystem, but it could also take full advantage of a dual-display configuration by placing text on one screen and graphics on the other.

Another reason to enable a program to examine its video hardware environment is to allow use of the fastest possible video output routines. For example, if your program runs in an alphanumeric mode on a CGA, you may need to avoid snow by synchronizing with the CRT Controller's timing signals. However, this overhead can be avoided if the program is running on some other video subsystem. If your program "knows" that it's not running on a CGA, it can use faster video output routines that omit the overhead of avoiding snow.

CGA and Clones

Unfortunately, for Color Graphics Adapters and clones, no reliable way exists to determine whether the hardware manages conflicts over video buffer memory access without display interference (see Chapter 3). If your program must run on a CGA, you might wish to ask the user to configure your alphanumeric output routines by testing whether or not they produce snow.

You can also detect whether your program is running on a CGA work-alike that does not have the alphanumeric snow problem. If you know that your program may run on a CGA work-alike such as the video hardware built into a COMPAQ or an AT&T 6300, you can search the ROM BIOS for a string indicating the name of the computer, for example, "COMPAQ". You might also inspect the ROM BIOS ID byte at F000:FFFE to determine whether your program is running on a member of the IBM PC family that does not have the snow problem (such as the PCjr).

Other Video Adapters

Although determining whether a particular CGA or clone has a problem with alphanumeric snow can be hard, distinguishing among the various common IBM video adapters is relatively easy. Some of the techniques described in this appendix rely on serendipitous peculiarities of different adapters' firmware or hardware, but all are based on IBM and Hercules recommendations.

PS/2s

On the PS/2s, INT 10H function 1AH lets you determine which video subsystems are present and active in the computer (see Appendix A). Of course, the PS/2 video BIOS does not recognize non-IBM video adapters. For example, if you use a

Hercules adapter in a PS/2 Model 30, a call to INT 10H function 1AH returns only the information that an MDA-compatible adapter is present in the system. Identifying the adapter is then up to you.

VideoID, the routine in Listing C-1, detects the presence of either one or two adapters. If two adapters are present, VideoID indicates which is active (that is, which one the BIOS is currently using for output). The techniques used to identify each adapter are described in the listing.

```
                    TITLE    'Listing C-1 — VideoID'
                    NAME     VideoID
                    PAGE     55,132


;
; Name:         VideoID
;
; Function:     Detects the presence of various video subsystems and associated
;               monitors.
;
; Caller:       Microsoft C:
;
;                       void VideoID(VIDstruct);
;
;                       struct
;                       {
;                         char VideoSubsystem;
;                         char Display;
;                       }
;                               *VIDstruct[2];
;
;               Subsystem ID values:
;                               0  = (none)
;                               1  = MDA
;                               2  = CGA
;                               3  = EGA
;                               4  = MCGA
;                               5  = VGA
;                             80h = HGC
;                             81h = HGC+
;                             82h = Hercules InColor
;
;               Display types:  0  = (none)
;                               1  = MDA-compatible monochrome
;                               2  = CGA-compatible color
;                               3  = EGA-compatible color
;                               4  = PS/2-compatible monochrome
;                               5  = PS/2-compatible color
;
;
;       The values returned in VIDstruct[0].VideoSubsystem and
;       VIDstruct[0].Display indicate the currently active subsystem.
;

ARGpVID         EQU     word ptr [bp+4] ; stack frame addressing


VIDstruct       STRUC                   ; corresponds to C data structure
```

Listing C-1. *A routine to identify PC and PS/2 video subsystems.*   *(continued)*

Listing C-1. *Continued.*

```
Video0Type      DB      ?               ; first subsystem type
Display0Type    DB      ?               ; display attached to first subsystem
Video1Type      DB      ?               ; second subsystem type
Display1Type    DB      ?               ; display attached to second subsystem


VIDstruct       ENDS


Device0         EQU     word ptr Video0Type[di]
Device1         EQU     word ptr Video1Type[di]


MDA             EQU     1               ; subsystem types
CGA             EQU     2
EGA             EQU     3
MCGA            EQU     4
VGA             EQU     5
HGC             EQU     80h
HGCPlus         EQU     81h
InColor         EQU     82h


MDADisplay      EQU     1               ; display types
CGADisplay      EQU     2
EGAColorDisplay EQU     3
PS2MonoDisplay  EQU     4
PS2ColorDisplay EQU     5


TRUE            EQU     1
FALSE           EQU     0



DGROUP          GROUP   _DATA

_TEXT           SEGMENT byte public 'CODE'
                ASSUME  cs:_TEXT,ds:DGROUP

                PUBLIC  _VideoID
_VideoID        PROC    near

                push    bp              ; preserve caller registers
                mov     bp,sp
                push    si
                push    di

; initialize the data structure that will contain the results

                mov     di,ARGpVID      ; DS:DI -> start of data structure

                mov     Device0,0       ; zero these variables
                mov     Device1,0

; look for the various subsystems using the subroutines whose addresses are
;   tabulated in TestSequence; each subroutine sets flags in TestSequence
;   to indicate whether subsequent subroutines need to be called

                mov     byte ptr CGAflag,TRUE
                mov     byte ptr EGAflag,TRUE
                mov     byte ptr Monoflag,TRUE
```

(continued)

Listing C-1. *Continued.*

```
                    mov     cx,NumberOfTests
                    mov     si,offset DGROUP:TestSequence

L01:                lodsb                   ; AL := flag
                    test    al,al
                    lodsw                   ; AX := subroutine address
                    jz      L02             ; skip subroutine if flag is false

                    push    si
                    push    cx
                    call    ax              ; call subroutine to detect subsystem
                    pop     cx
                    pop     si

L02:                loop    L01

; determine which subsystem is active

                    call    FindActive
                    pop     di              ; restore caller registers and return
                    pop     si
                    mov     sp,bp
                    pop     bp
                    ret

_VideoID            ENDP

;
; FindPS2
;
;       This subroutine uses INT 10H function 1Ah to determine the video BIOS
;         Display Combination Code (DCC) for each video subsystem present.
;

FindPS2             PROC    near

                    mov     ax,1A00h
                    int     10h             ; call video BIOS for info

                    cmp     al,1Ah
                    jne     L13             ; exit if function not supported (i.e.,
                                            ;   no MCGA or VGA in system)

; convert BIOS DCCs into specific subsystems & displays

                    mov     cx,bx
                    xor     bh,bh           ; BX := DCC for active subsystem
                    or      ch,ch
                    jz      L11             ; jump if only one subsystem present

                    mov     bl,ch           ; BX := inactive DCC
                    add     bx,bx
                    mov     ax,[bx+offset DGROUP:DCCtable]

                    mov     Device1,ax

                    mov     bl,cl
                    xor     bh,bh           ; BX := active DCC
```

(continued)

Listing C-1. *Continued.*

```
L11:            add     bx,bx
                mov     ax,[bx+offset DGROUP:DCCtable]

                mov     Device0,ax

; reset flags for subsystems that have been ruled out

                mov     byte ptr CGAflag,FALSE
                mov     byte ptr EGAflag,FALSE
                mov     byte ptr Monoflag,FALSE

                lea     bx,Video0Type[di]   ; if the BIOS reported an MDA ...
                cmp     byte ptr [bx],MDA
                je      L12

                lea     bx,Video1Type[di]
                cmp     byte ptr [bx],MDA
                jne     L13

L12:            mov     word ptr [bx],0     ; ... Hercules can't be ruled out
                mov     byte ptr Monoflag,TRUE

L13:            ret

FindPS2         ENDP


;
; FindEGA
;
; Look for an EGA.  This is done by making a call to an EGA BIOS function
;   which doesn't exist in the default (MDA, CGA) BIOS.

FindEGA         PROC    near            ; Caller:      AH = flags
                                        ; Returns:     AH = flags
                                        ;              Video0Type and
                                        ;                Display0Type updated

                mov     bl,10h          ; BL := 10h (return EGA info)
                mov     ah,12h          ; AH := INT 10H function number
                int     10h             ; call EGA BIOS for info
                                        ; if EGA BIOS is present,
                                        ;   BL <> 10H
                                        ;   CL = switch setting
                cmp     bl,10h
                je      L22             ; jump if EGA BIOS not present

                mov     al,cl
                shr     al,1            ; AL := switches/2
                mov     bx,offset DGROUP:EGADisplays
                xlat                    ; determine display type from switches
                mov     ah,al           ; AH := display type
                mov     al,EGA          ; AL := subsystem type
                call    FoundDevice

                cmp     ah,MDADisplay
                je      L21             ; jump if EGA has a monochrome display
```

(continued)

Listing C-1. *Continued.*

```
                  mov     CGAflag,FALSE   ; no CGA if EGA has color display
                  jmp     short L22

L21:              mov     Monoflag,FALSE  ; EGA has a mono display, so MDA and
                                          ;   Hercules are ruled out
L22:              ret

FindEGA           ENDP


;
; FindCGA
;
;       This is done by looking for the CGA's 6845 CRTC at I/O port 3D4H.
;

FindCGA           PROC    near            ; Returns:      VIDstruct updated

                  mov     dx,3D4h         ; DX := CRTC address port
                  call    Find6845
                  jc      L31             ; jump if not present

                  mov     al,CGA
                  mov     ah,CGADisplay
                  call    FoundDevice

L31:              ret

FindCGA           ENDP


;
; FindMono
;
;       This is done by looking for the MDA's 6845 CRTC at I/O port 3B4H. If
;       a 6845 is found, the subroutine distinguishes between an MDA
;       and a Hercules adapter by monitoring bit 7 of the CRT Status byte.
;       This bit changes on Hercules adapters but does not change on an MDA.
;       The various Hercules adapters are identified by bits 4 through 6 of
;       the CRT Status value:
;
;             001b = HGC+
;             101b = InColor card

FindMono          PROC    near            ; Returns:      VIDstruct updated

                  mov     dx,3B4h         ; DX := CRTC address port
                  call    Find6845
                  jc      L44             ; jump if not present

                  mov     dl,0BAh         ; DX := 3BAh (status port)
                  in      al,dx
                  and     al,80h
                  mov     ah,al           ; AH := bit 7 (vertical sync on HGC)
```

(continued)

Listing C-1. *Continued.*

```
                 mov     cx,8000h        ; do this 32768 times
L41:             in      al,dx
                 and     al,80h          ; isolate bit 7
                 cmp     ah,al
                 loope   L41             ; wait for bit 7 to change

                 jne     L42             ; if bit 7 changed, it's a Hercules

                 mov     al,MDA          ; if bit 7 didn't change, it's an MDA
                 mov     ah,MDADisplay
                 call    FoundDevice
                 jmp     short L44

L42:             in      al,dx
                 mov     dl,al           ; DL := value from status port
                 and     dl,01110000b    ; mask off bits 4 thru 6

                 mov     ah,MDADisplay   ; assume it's a monochrome display

                 mov     al,HGCPlus      ; look for an HGC+
                 cmp     dl,00010000b
                 je      L43             ; jump if it's an HGC+

                 mov     al,HGC          ; look for an HGC
                 cmp     dl,01010000b
                 jne     L43

                 mov     al,InColor      ; it's an InColor card
                 mov     ah,EGAColorDisplay

L43:             call    FoundDevice

L44:             ret

FindMono         ENDP


;
; Find6845
;
;       This routine detects the presence of the CRTC on an MDA, CGA, or HGC.
;       The technique is to write and read register 0Fh of the chip (Cursor
;       Location Low).  If the same value is read as written, assume the chip
;       is present at the specified port address.
;

Find6845         PROC    near            ; Caller:      DX = port addr
                                         ; Returns:     cf set if not present
                 mov     al,0Fh
                 out     dx,al           ; select 6845 reg 0Fh (Cursor Low)
                 inc     dx

                 in      al,dx           ; AL := current Cursor Low value
                 mov     ah,al           ; preserve in AH
                 mov     al,66h          ; AL := arbitrary value
                 out     dx,al           ; try to write to 6845

                 mov     cx,100h
```

(continued)

Listing C-1. *Continued.*

```
L51:            loop    L51             ; wait for 6845 to respond

                in      al,dx
                xchg    ah,al           ; AH := returned value
                                        ; AL := original value
                out     dx,al           ; restore original value

                cmp     ah,66h          ; test whether 6845 responded
                je      L52             ; jump if it did (cf is reset)

                stc                     ; set carry flag if no 6845 present

L52:            ret

Find6845        ENDP



;
; FindActive
;
;       This subroutine stores the currently active device as Device0.   The
;       current video mode determines which subsystem is active.
;

FindActive      PROC    near

                cmp     word ptr Device1,0
                je      L63             ; exit if only one subsystem

                cmp     Video0Type[di],4    ; exit if MCGA or VGA present
                jge     L63                 ;   (INT 10H function 1AH
                cmp     Video1Type[di],4    ;    already did the work)
                jge     L63

                mov     ah,0Fh
                int     10h             ; AL := current BIOS video mode

                and     al,7
                cmp     al,7            ; jump if monochrome
                je      L61             ;   (mode 7 or 0Fh)

                cmp     Display0Type[di],MDADisplay
                jne     L63             ; exit if Display0 is color
                jmp     short L62

L61:            cmp     Display0Type[di],MDADisplay
                je      L63             ; exit if Display0 is monochrome

L62:            mov     ax,Device0      ; make Device0 currently active
                xchg    ax,Device1
                mov     Device0,ax

L63:            `ret

FindActive      ENDP
```

(continued)

Listing C-1. *Continued.*

```
;
; FoundDevice
;
;       This routine updates the list of subsystems.
;

FoundDevice     PROC    near                    ; Caller:   AH = display #
                                                ;           AL = subsystem #
                                                ; Destroys: BX
                lea     bx,Video0Type[di]
                cmp     byte ptr [bx],0
                je      L71                     ; jump if 1st subsystem

                lea     bx,Video1Type[di]       ; must be 2nd subsystem

L71:            mov     [bx],ax                 ; update list entry
                ret

FoundDevice     ENDP

_TEXT           ENDS


_DATA           SEGMENT word public 'DATA'

EGADisplays     DB      CGADisplay       ; 0000b, 0001b  (EGA switch values)
                DB      EGAColorDisplay  ; 0010b, 0011b
                DB      MDADisplay       ; 0100b, 0101b
                DB      CGADisplay       ; 0110b, 0111b
                DB      EGAColorDisplay  ; 1000b, 1001b
                DB      MDADisplay       ; 1010b, 1011b

DCCtable        DB      0,0                     ; translate table for INT 10h func 1Ah
                DB      MDA,MDADisplay
                DB      CGA,CGADisplay
                DB      0,0
                DB      EGA,EGAColorDisplay
                DB      EGA,MDADisplay
                DB      0,0
                DB      VGA,PS2MonoDisplay
                DB      VGA,PS2ColorDisplay
                DB      0,0
                DB      MCGA,EGAColorDisplay
                DB      MCGA,PS2MonoDisplay
                DB      MCGA,PS2ColorDisplay

TestSequence    DB      ?                       ; this list of flags and addresses
                DW      FindPS2                 ; determines the order in which this
                                                ; program looks for the various
EGAflag         DB      ?                       ; subsystems
                DW      FindEGA

CGAflag         DB      ?
                DW      FindCGA

Monoflag        DB      ?
                DW      FindMono
```

(continued)

Listing C-1. *Continued.*

```
NumberOfTests      EQU        ($-TestSequence)/3

_DATA              ENDS

                   END
```

The `VideoID` routine checks for adapters by a process of elimination. For example, if the routine is run on a PS/2, the INT 10H call returns the desired information. On PC/XTs and PC/ATs, if an EGA with a monochrome display is detected, there is no reason to look for an MDA or a Hercules card in the same system. If a monochrome adapter is present, the routine differentiates between the MDA and the various Hercules adapters.

 INT 10H function 1AH on the VGA adapter fails to report the presence of the MCGA when the adapter is installed in a PS/2 Model 30. Also, function 1AH in the MCGA ignores the presence of an EGA if one is installed in a Model 30. If you are concerned about these combinations, you must test for them explicitly after you call INT 10H function 1AH. (In the first situation, inspect the motherboard BIOS identfication byte at F000:FFFE to detect the presence of a Model 30. In the second situation, execute INT 10H function 12H with BL = 10H to detect the presence of an EGA.)

The C program in Listing C-2 demonstrates how you might use `VideoID`.

```
/* Listing C-2 */

main()
{
        char      *SubsystemName();
        char      *DisplayName();

        static struct
        {
          char   Subsystem;
          char   Display;
        }
        VIDstruct[2];


        /* detect video subsystems */

        VideoID( VIDstruct );


        /* show results */

        printf( "Video subsystems in this computer:" );
```

Listing C-2. *Calling VideoID from a C program.*   *(continued)*

Listing C-2. *Continued.*

```
        printf( "\n  %s (%s)", SubsystemName(VIDstruct[0].Subsystem),
          DisplayName(VIDstruct[0].Display) );

        if ( VIDstruct[1].Subsystem )
          printf( "\n  %s (%s)", SubsystemName(VIDstruct[1].Subsystem),
            DisplayName(VIDstruct[1].Display) );
}


char *SubsystemName( a )
char    a;
{
        static char *IBMname[] =
        {
          "(none)",
          "MDA",
          "CGA",
          "EGA",
          "MCGA",
          "VGA"
        };

        static char *Hercname[] =
        {
          "HGC",
          "HGC+",
          "InColor"
        };

        if ( a & 0x80 )
          return ( Hercname[a & 0x7F] );
        else
          return( IBMname[a] );
}


char *DisplayName( d )
char    d;
{
        static char *name[] =
        {
          "(none)",
          "MDA-compatible monochrome display",
          "CGA-compatible color display",
          "EGA-compatible color display",
          "PS/2-compatible monochrome display",
          "PS/2-compatible color display"
        };

        return( name[d] );
}
```

Glossary

This glossary includes some of the acronyms, abbreviations, buzzwords, engineering terms, and programming jargon that appear frequently throughout this book.

80x86: Refers to all the processors in the Intel 8086 family. The IBM PCs and PS/2s all use one of these processors: 8086, 8088, 80286, or 80386.

active display: In a computer that contains two video subsystems and displays, the display to which a program sends its output.

adapter: A modular, plug-in circuit that performs a specialized task such as generating video output. Well-known IBM PC video adapters include the MDA, CGA, HGC, EGA, and VGA Adapter.

ANSI: American National Standards Institute. One of ANSI's many activities is to certify the standardization of programming tools, including languages (such as C and FORTRAN) and software interfaces (such as GKS).

APA: All Points Addressable; describes graphics modes on the CGA, EGA, and Hercules graphics cards.

API: Application Program Interface; a set of system-level routines that can be used in an application program for basic input and output, file management, and so on. In a graphics-oriented operating environment like Microsoft Windows, high-level support for video graphics output is part of the API.

ASCII: American Standard Code for Information Interchange. The ASCII standard specifies the basic character set used in IBM PCs and PS/2s.

aspect ratio: The ratio of a video screen's width to its height. A typical IBM PC display has an aspect ratio of about 4:3. This term is also frequently used to describe pixels: If you think of a pixel as being rectangular, its aspect ratio would be the ratio of its width to height.

attributes: Color, intensity, blinking, and other displayed characteristics of characters or pixels.

BIOS: Basic Input/Output System; a low-level programming interface to the system's major I/O devices.

bit plane: Video RAM containing formatted graphics data. In IBM video subsystems up to four bit planes can be addressed in parallel, with pixel values represented by the bits at corresponding locations in the bit planes.

CGA: IBM's Color Graphics Adapter.

character code: A numeric code associated with a character. The default ASCII character set used in all PCs and PS/2s comprises 256 8-bit character codes.

character matrix: The rectangular array of pixels in which characters are displayed on the screen. On IBM's Monochrome Display Adapter, each character is displayed in a character matrix that is 9 dots wide and 14 dots high. On the Color Graphics Adapter, the character matrix is 8 by 8.

character set: A set of alphabetic and numeric characters and symbols.

clipping: The process of determining which portions of a graphics image lie within a specified boundary.

code page: A character set designed for use with computers. Each character in a code page is associated with a numeric code (such as an ASCII or EBCDIC code).

CPU: Central Processing Unit, or the main processor in a computer. For example, the CPU is an Intel 8088 in PCs and an 80286 in PC/ATs.

CRT: Cathode Ray Tube, or the picture tube you see when you look at your computer monitor. Some people refer to the entire monitor (the tube and its associated circuitry) as a CRT.

CRTC: CRT Controller; a chip that controls a video display's timing signals.

DGIS: Direct Graphics Interface Specification; a firmware graphics interface designed for video subsystems based on hardware graphics coprocessors.

display: A video monitor.

driver: Software or firmware that directly programs a specific hardware unit such as a video adapter or a printer.

EBCDIC: Extended Binary Coded Decimal Interchange Code; the character-set implementation used on IBM mainframe computers.

EGA: Enhanced Graphics Adapter.

font: A description of the style and shapes of the characters in a character set.

gate array: An integrated circuit that is partly prefabricated in its manufacture. An application-specific integrated circuit based on gate array technology can be less expensive and manufactured more rapidly than a custom integrated circuit.

GKS: Graphical Kernel System; a standard high-level graphics interface.

HGC: Hercules monochrome Graphics Card.

HGC+ (HGC Plus): Hercules Graphics Card Plus; a monochrome video adapter like the HGC, but with a hardware character generator that can use RAM-based character sets.

InColor: Hercules InColor Card; a 16-color version of the HGC+.

latch: A hardware register external to the CPU and used for transient storage of data. For example, the EGA Graphics Controller uses four internal 8-bit latches to mediate data transfers between the bit planes and the CPU.

LSI: Large Scale Integration.

MCGA: Multi-Color Graphics Array; the video subsystem integrated into the PS/2 Model 30. Also, Memory Controller Gate Array, one of the components of the Model 30's video subsystem.

MDA: IBM's Monochrome Display Adapter.

MDPA: Monochrome Display and Printer Adapter; same as an MDA.

monitor: The hardware that displays your computer's video output; comprises a CRT (cathode ray tube) and associated circuitry.

MPA: Monochrome/Printer Adapter; same as an MDA.

palette: A range of colors that can be displayed by a video subsystem.

pel: A pixel.

PGA: Professional Graphics Adapter; another name for IBM's PGC.

PGC: IBM's Professional Graphics Controller.

pixel: One dot or point in an image that is composed of a matrix of dots or points. The image on the video screen or on a page printed by a dot-matrix printer is composed of a large number of pixels. (The word "pixel" is a rough acronym for "picture element.")

planar BIOS: BIOS routines found in ROM on the IBM PC or PS/2 motherboard.

PS/2: Personal System/2.

PS/2 Display Adapter: A VGA-compatible IBM video adapter that may be used in a PC/XT, PC/AT, or PS/2 Model 30; commonly called "VGA Adapter."

raster: The group of closely spaced horizontal scan lines that makes up a displayed video image.

RGB: Red, Green, Blue; the three primary colors displayed by the monitors used in PC and PS/2 video subsystems. All other colors are blends of these three primaries. Video displays that are driven by separate red, green, and blue signals are often called RGB displays.

scan line: One horizontal line traced across the screen by a CRT's electron beam.

VDI: Computer Graphics Virtual Device Interface; a proposed ANSI standard high-level graphics interface. The Graphics Development Toolkit (GDT) sold by IBM and Graphics Software Systems is a commercial implementation of VDI.

VGA: Video Graphics Array. People refer to the video subsystem integrated into the PS/2 Models 50, 60, and 80, as well as the IBM PS/2 Display Adapter, as the "VGA." Strictly speaking, however, the VGA is the circuitry in the video subsystem that performs the tasks of the CRT Controller, the Sequencer, the Graphics Controller, and the Attribute Controller. Most of this circuitry is contained in a single VLSI chip.

VGA Adapter: The IBM PS/2 Display Adapter.

video buffer: A buffer that contains the data that appears on the video display; variously known as a "display buffer," "frame buffer," "refresh buffer," or "regenerative buffer."

Video Control Data Area: Part of the Video Display Data Area. The block of RAM from 0040:0049 through 0040:0066 is Video Control Data Area 1; the block between 0040:0084 and 0040:008A is Video Control Data Area 2.

Video Display Data Area: A global data area maintained by the ROM BIOS for storage of parameters related to its INT 10H video I/O routines.

VLSI: Very Large Scale Integration.

Index

*References to source code listings
and illustrative figures are in
italics.*

A

Adapter. *See* Video adapter
Algorithm. *See* Circle; Ellipse;
　　Line; Region fill
All Points Addressable (APA)
　　modes 86
Alphanumeric mode. *See* Video
　　modes, alphanumeric
Alternate select. *See* Interrupt 10H,
　　function 12H
Analog video signals 5–6. *See also*
　　Video DAC
Animation 364–68
Application Program Interface
　　(API) 425
Aspect ratio 100
Assembly language 7–9, 168, 408
Attribute Controller (EGA and
　　VGA)
　　programming 35–36, 53–56,
　　　60–62, 466–72
　　registers 35–36
Attributes
　　alphanumeric mode
　　　CGA 51–53
　　　EGA 53–56, 320–21
　　　HGC 51
　　　HGC+ 51, 321–22
　　　InColor Card 56–58, 321–23
　　　MCGA 58–60, 63–64, 321
　　　MDA 49–51
　　　VGA 60–64, 320–21
　　graphics mode
　　　CGA 100–103
　　　EGA 103–7
　　　HGC 103
　　　InColor Card 107
　　　MCGA 107–10
　　　VGA 110

B

BASIC 416–17, 420
BIOS (Basic Input/Output System).
　　See also Interrupt 10H
　　about 6–11, 420, 424
　　anomalies 82, 385–86, 481,
　　　484, 521
　　data area
　　　about 438–39, 442–46
　　　Alphanumeric Character Set
　　　　Override 441
　　　Display Combination Code
　　　　table 441–42, 485–86
　　　Graphics Character Set
　　　　Override 441

BIOS *(continued)*
　　　Parameter Save Area 440
　　　SAVE POINTER table
　　　　438–40
　　　SECONDARY SAVE
　　　　POINTER table
　　　　438–40
　　　User Palette Profile table 442
　　　Video Parameter table 440
　　hardware supported by 434–35
　　planar 434
　　programming interface 7–11,
　　　435–36
　　status 8–11, 437–38, 465,
　　　485–86, 487–90
　　video modes
　　　determining 465, 487–88
　　　establishing 448–50
Bit block. *See also* CGA; EGA;
　　HGC; MCGA; VGA
　　about 344
　　animation 367–68
　　tiling 363–64
Bit planes
　　about 112–14
　　layering 395–96
　　programming
　　　EGA 114–21
　　　InColor Card 121–25
　　　VGA 114–21
　　write-protecting
　　　EGA 121
　　　InColor Card 124
Blanking
　　horizontal 17, *27–28*
　　vertical 18
Blinking. *See also* Interrupt 10H,
　　function 10H
　　alphanumeric mode
　　　CGA 52–53
　　　EGA 54–55
　　　InColor 57
　　　MDA 50
　　graphics mode 106–7
Border (region fill). *See* Region fill
Border (video display). *See*
　　Overscan
Bresenham, J.E. 164

C

C language 10–11, 408–9, 418–19
Cathode ray tube. *See* CRT
　　Controller
CGA (Color Graphics Adapter)
　　about 2–4

CGA *(continued)*
　　alphanumeric mode
　　　attributes 51–53
　　　character generator 47–49,
　　　　298–99
　　　data representation 47–49
　　　snow 66–74
　　BIOS 434
　　graphics I/O
　　　bit block 344–51
　　　circle 242
　　　ellipse 230–33
　　　line 170–84
　　　pixel 125–27, 137–40,
　　　　462–63
　　　text 269, 276–83, 458–59,
　　　　464–65, 483–84
　　graphics mode
　　　attributes 100–103
　　　character generator 276–83
　　　data representation 87–88
Character definition tables
　　alphanumeric mode
　　　address map 300–305
　　　BIOS 298, 313, 324–26, 441,
　　　　473–77
　　　dedicated ROM 298–99
　　　format 300–305
　　graphics mode
　　　BIOS 269–70, 441, 457,
　　　　473–77
　　　format 268–71
Character generator. *See also*
　　Character definition tables
　　alphanumeric mode 48,
　　　298–305, 473–77
　　graphics mode 271–75, 364,
　　　458–59, 464–65,
　　　473–77, 483–84
Character string. *See* Text
Circle. *See also* Ellipse
　　algorithm 222–23, 242
　　clipping 241
Code page 270
Cohen, D. 217
Color Select register (VGA)
　　60–62, 467, 468, 470–71
Compaq 51, 512
Composite video 2, 15
Configuration Switch (Hercules)
　　33, 42, 303, 316
CRT Controller (CRTC)
　　about 16
　　programming 18–26

CRT Controller *(continued)*
  registers
    CGA *19*, 20
    EGA 21–22
    Hercules 20–21
    MCGA 22–23
    MDA 18–20
    VGA 23
  status *(see* CRT Status register)
  timing
    computations 24–26
    horizontal 17–18, 25, 27–28
    vertical 18, 26
    write-protecting 31–32
CRT Status register 26–29, *67–72*
Cursor
  alphanumeric
    emulation by BIOS 82,
      450–51, 478, 480
    invisible 83, 450
    location 76–78, 451–52
    size 76–83, 450–51, 451–52
  graphics 368–71

D

DAC. *See* Video DAC
Decoder gate array (InColor Card)
  121–22
DGIS (Direct Graphics Interface
  Standard) 426–29, 430
Digital video signals 5–6
Display
  active
  interference *(see* Snow)
  refresh 15–18, 478, 481
  switching
    BIOS support for 40, 450,
      478, 480–82
    configurations *(see*
      Dual-display
      configurations)
  video 2–6, 15
Display Combination Code
  441–42, 485–86
Display Enable 18–19, *27–28,*
  67–72
DOS. *See* MS-DOS
Dot clock 24
Dual-display configurations 40–43

E

EGA (Enhanced Graphics
  Adapter)
  about 5
  alphanumeric mode
    attributes 53–56, 320–21
    character generator 47–49,
      298–302, 306–13, 441,
      473–77, 504–10

EGA, alphanumeric mode
  (continued)
    data representation 47–49,
      316, 318–20
  BIOS 435
  graphics I/O
    bit block 352–59
    circle 242
    ellipse 230–41
    line 191–98
    pixel 127–31, 141–50,
      409–17, 462–63
    region fill 260–63
    text 270, 288–92, 458–59,
      464–65, 483–84
  graphics mode
    attributes 103–7
    character generator 288–92,
      441, 473–77
    data representation 89–91
Ellipse
  algorithm
    derivation 224–33
    optimization 233–41
    scan-conversion 223–24, 232
  clipping 241
  implementation 230–41
Enable Blink bit 57
Encoder gate array (InColor Card)
  121–22
EQUIP_FLAG *7–8*, 9–10, 40, 449,
  486
Exception register (InColor Card)
  56–57, 107

F

Fill. *See* Region fill; Video buffer,
  fill
Font pages (MCGA) 314–15,
  341, 475
FORTRAN 411–13, 418–19

G

GDI (Graphics Device Interface)
  429–31
GKS (Graphical Kernel
  System) 429
Global data area 423
GRAFTABL 269
GRAPHICS 494–95
Graphics Controller (EGA
  and VGA)
  about 114–15
  programming 115–21
  read/write modes
    read mode 0 116, *142*, 352
    read mode 1 *115*, 116–17, *262,*
      290, 502
    write mode 0 117–19,
      141–45, 352

Graphics Controller, read/write
  modes *(continued)*
    write mode 1 119–20
    write mode 2 120, 145–47,
      290
    write mode 3 120, *121*
  registers 34–35, *116*
Graphics Memory Expansion Card
  (EGA) 89
Graphics mode. *See* Video mode,
  graphics
Graphics window (alphanumeric
  mode) 337–41
Gray-scale
  palette 60, 62–63
  summing 63–64, 468, 470, 472,
    478, 480
GWBASIC. *See* BASIC

H

Hercules Color Card 5
Hercules InColor Card. *See*
  InColor Card
HGC (Hercules Graphics Card)
  about 4
  alphanumeric mode
    attributes 51
    character generator 47–49
    data representation 47–49
    determining 404–6
  graphics I/O
    bit block 359
    circle 242
    ellipse 230–33
    line 184–91
    pixel 127, 140
    text 283–86
  graphics mode
    attributes 103
    character generator 283–86
    data representation 88–89
    determining 404–6
    establishing 36, 38–40
HGC+ (Hercules Graphics
  Card Plus)
  about 4–5
  alphanumeric mode
    attributes 51, 321–22
    character generator 47–49,
      298, 302–3
    data representation 47–49,
      321–22
    determining 404–6
    establishing 326–27, 334–37
  graphics I/O *(see also* HGC)
    pixel 127, 140
  graphics mode *(see* HGC)
Horizontal sync. *See* Retrace,
  horizontal

I

IBM PS/2. *See* PS/2
InColor Card
  about 5
  alphanumeric mode
    attributes 56–58, 321–23
    character generator 47–49,
      298, 303
    data representation 47–49,
      321–23
    determining 404–6
    establishing 326–27, 334–37
  compared with EGA 122
  graphics I/O
    bit block 360
    circle 242
    ellipse 230–33
    line 209–14
    pixel 132–34, 147–51
    text 292–95
  graphics mode
    attributes 107
    character generator 292–95
    data representation 91
    determining 404–6
    establishing 36, 38–40
Inline code 422
Intel 8259A 374
Intel 82786 426
Intensity 15. *See also* Attributes
Interface. *See* Layered interface;
      Subroutines
Interrupt 5. *See* Print screen
Interrupt 0AH. *See* Vertical
      interrupt
Interrupt 10H
  about 7–11, 434, 435–36, 447
  functions
    00H (Select Video Mode)
      7–8, 64, *102*, 103, 106, 270,
      448–50, 479
    01H (Set Alphanumeric
      Cursor Size) 76–77, 82–83,
      450–51
    02H (Set Cursor Location)
      78, 451
    03H (Return Cursor Status)
      451–52
    04H (Return Light Pen
      Position) 452–53
    05H (Select Video Page) *75*,
      453–54
    06H (Scroll Up) 454–56
    07H (Scroll Down) 456
    08H (Return Character Code
      and Attribute at Cursor)
      456–57
    09H (Write Character and
      Attribute at Cursor) 271,
      323, 457–58

Interrupt 10H, functions
    (continued)
    0AH (Write Character(s) at
      Cursor Position) 271, 323,
      458–59
    0BH (Set Overscan Color,
      Select 4-Color Palette) 64,
      100, 459–61
    0CH (Store Pixel Value) 143,
      462–63
    0DH (Return Pixel
      Value) 463
    0EH (Display Character in
      Teletype Mode) 271,
      464–65
    0FH (Return Current Video
      Status) *9*, *11*, 465
    10H (Set Palette Registers,
      Set Intensity/Blink
      Attribute) *36*, 55, *60*,
      62–63, *321*, 466–72
    11H (Character Generator
      Interface) 270, 271, 311–13,
      320, 321, 324–26, 473–77
    12H (Video Subsystem
      Configuration) 42–43,
      324–25, 477–82
    13H (Display Character
      String) 271, 483–84
    1AH (Video Display
      Combination)
      485–86, 512–13, *515*
    1BH (Video BIOS
      Functionality/State
      Information) 487–90
    1CH (Save or Restore Video
      State) 490–92
Interrupt 1DH 447
Interrupt 1FH 269–71, 275, *277*,
      457, 474, 476
Interrupt 43H 270–71, *277*,
      286, 474
I/O Support Gate Array
      (MCGA) 374

K

Kappel, M.R. 225, 232

L

Language. *See* Assembly language;
      BASIC; C language;
      FORTRAN; Pascal
Latch
  graphics mode
    EGA and VGA 112–20
    InColor Card 122–25
  vertical interrupt 374
Latch Protect register (InColor
      Card) 122, 124

Layered interface
  about 424–25
  BIOS 424, 426
  DGIS 426–28
  GDI 429–31
  GKS 429
  VDI 429
Light pen
  about 401
  programming 401–6, 452–53
Line
  algorithm
    derivation 163–66
    optimization 166–69
    scan-conversion 162–63
  clipping 215–20
  implementation
    CGA 170–84
    EGA 191–98
    HGC 184–91
    InColor Card 209–14
    MCGA 198–208
    VGA 208
Line-adjacency graph (LAG) 251
Linking 11, 408, 418–20

M

Macintosh 425
MCGA (Multi-Color
      Graphics Array)
  about 5–6
  alphanumeric mode
    attributes 58–60, 63–64, 321
    character generator 47–49,
      300, 303–5, 473–77
    data representation 47–49,
      321
  BIOS 435
  graphics I/O
    bit block 344–51
    circle 242
    ellipse 230–33
    line 198–208
    pixel 134–36, 151–54,
      462–63
    text 270, 286–88, 458–59,
      464–65, 483–84
  graphics mode
    attributes 107–10
    character generator 286–88,
      473–77
    data representation 91
MDA (Monochrome Display
      Adapter)
  about 2–4
  attributes 49–51
  BIOS 434
  character generator 47–49, 298
  data representation 47–49

Memory Controller Gate Array
(MCGA) 22–23
Memory-resident program 420–22
Microsoft Windows 425, 430–31
Miscellaneous Output register
(EGA) 42, 480
Mode Control register
CGA 31–32
Hercules 33, 38–40
MCGA 31–32
MDA 30
Monitor. See Display, video
Motorola 6845 16
MS-DOS 46, 270, 323, 494

N
Novak, M. 232

O
Optimization
alphanumeric mode 46–47, 512
graphics mode
ellipse 233–41
line 166–69, 170, 184,
198, 216
region fill 260, 263–65
text 271, 273
techniques 20–21, 23, 46–47,
97, 167–68
Overscan
color 64–66, 442–46, 459–61,
466, 469–70
EGA 65–66
horizontal 17–18, 26
vertical 18

P
Palette. See also Attributes
colors 54, 101, 104, 107–9, 461
programming
BIOS 440, 442–46, 459–61,
466–72, 477, 479
CGA 101–3
EGA and VGA 53–56, 103–7,
440, 442–46
InColor Card 56–58, 107
MCGA 58–60, 107–8
Panning (EGA and VGA) 386–92
Pascal 413–15, 419
Pavlidis, T. 252, 259
Personal System/2. See PS/2
Pixel
attributes
CGA 100–103
EGA 103–7
HGC 103
InColor Card 107
MCGA 107–10
VGA 110
connectivity 245

Pixel (continued)
coordinates
computation of 92–98
scaling 98–100, 222–23, 242
logical operations
about 136–37
AND 361–62
NOT 361
OR 363
XOR 360, 462
representation
in video buffer 87–92
on screen 15
value (see also individual names
of adapters)
reading 125–36, 463
setting 136–54, 338–41,
462–63
Plane Mask register (InColor Card)
122, 124, 314, 318, 395
Print screen
alphanumeric mode 494, 504–10
BIOS 324, 494–95, 477, 479
graphics mode 494–504
Programmable interrupt controller
(PIC) 374
Programming language. See
Assembly language;
BASIC; C language;
FORTRAN; Pascal
PS/2
Display Adapter. See VGA;
VGA Adapter
Model 25 2, 5–6, 435, 481. See
also MCGA
Model 30 2, 5–6, 435, 481, 482.
See also MCGA
Models 50, 60, and 80 2, 5–6,
435. See also VGA

R
Raster 15–18
Read mode. See Pixel, value,
reading
Read/Write Color register
(InColor Card) 122, 124,
292, 360
Read/Write Control register
(InColor Card) 122–25,
360
Refresh. See Display, refresh
Regeneration buffer. See Video
buffer
Region fill
about 244–45
algorithms
border trace 252–63
line adjacency 248–52
recursive 247–48
using horizontal lines 246
optimization 251–52, 260–63
scan-conversion 246

Retrace
horizontal 17, 25–26, 29
vertical 18, 26, 29
Reverse video 49. See also
Attributes
RGB (Red, Green, Blue) 2
ROM BIOS. See BIOS
Rubberbanding 366

S
Save area
BIOS (see BIOS, data area)
display switch 478, 480–81
video state 490–92
SAVE POINTER table. See BIOS,
data area
Scaling factors 99
Scan-conversion
about 162–63
ellipse 223–24, 232
line 162–64
region 246
Screen dump. See Print screen
Scrolling 454–56
SECONDARY SAVE POINTER
table. See BIOS, data area
Sequencer (EGA and VGA)
programming 34, 306–9,
318–20, 341
registers 34
Shani, U. 251
Shift-PrtSc 494–95
Snapshot. See Print screen
Snow 66–74
Split screen (EGA and VGA)
396–400
Sproull, R.F. 217
Status
BIOS (see BIOS, status)
CRT Controller 26–29, 404–6
register (see CRT Status
register)
video subsystem 477, 479,
485–86, 487–88
Subroutines
linking 11, 408, 418–20
memory models 418–19
parameter passing 418–20
structure
BASIC 416–17, 420
C 408–9, 418–19
FORTRAN 411–13, 418–19
Pascal 413–15, 419
Sutherland, I.E. 217

T
Text. See also Attributes
alphanumeric mode 66–74,
456–59, 464–65,
483–84

Text *(continued)*
  graphics mode *(see* names of
    individual adapters)
Tiling. *See* Bit block, tiling
TMS34010 426

U

Underline attribute 49–51, 56, 442.
  See also Attributes,
    alphanumeric mode

V

Van Aken, J.R. 225, 232
Van Dam, A. 246
VDI (Virtual Device Interface)
  429
Vertical interrupt
  EGA 374–81, 385–86
  MCGA 374, 381–86
  VGA 374–81, 385–86
Vertical sync. *See* Retrace, vertical
VGA (Video Graphics Array)
  about 6
  alphanumeric mode
    attributes 60–64, 320–21
    character generator 47–49,
      306–13, 441, 473–77,
      504–10
    data representation 47–49,
      316, 318–20
  BIOS 435
  graphics I/O
    bit block 352–59
    circle 242
    ellipse 230–41
    line 208
    pixel 136, 154, 462–63
    text 270, 288–92, 458–59,
      464–65, 483–84
  graphics mode
    attributes 110
    character generator 288–92,
      441, 473–77
    data representation 91–92
VGA Adapter 43, 381, 435. *See
    also* VGA
Video adapter 2, *3*. *See also* names
    of individual adapters
Video bandwidth. *See* Dot clock
Video BIOS. *See* BIOS
Video buffer
  about 15–16
  address map 41–43
  CPU access 41–43, 478, 480
  data representation
    alphanumeric mode 47–49,
      300–305
    graphics mode 87–92

Video buffer *(continued)*
  fill
    about 154
    CGA 155–56
    EGA 157–59
    HGC 156
    InColor Card 159–60
    MCGA 160
    VGA 157–59
  paging 74–76, 453–54
  panning 386–92
  resizing 392–94
  scrolling 454–56
  split screen 396–400
Video Control Data Area. *See*
    Video Display Data Area
Video DAC (Digital-to-Analog
    Converter)
  about 6, 58–59
  programming 59–63, 442,
    467–68, 470–72
Video display
  about 2–6, 15
  resolution 4–6
Video Display Data Area (VDDA)
  about 9–10
  format 436–38
  variables
    ACTIVE_PAGE *40*, 448,
      453, 465
    ADDR_6845 20, *40*, *50*, *75*,
      329, *377*, *389*, *394*, *397*, 448
    CRT_COLS 20, *40*, *284*, *286*,
      329, *339*, 401, 404, 448, 465
    CRT_LEN *40*, *326*, *394*, 404,
      448, 475
    CRT_MODE *40*, *329*, *339*,
      377, *388*, *394*, 448, 465
    CRT_MODE_SET *40*, *50*,
      102, *335*, 448, 468
    CRT_PALETTE *40*, 64, 100,
      102, 448, 460, 468
    CRT_START 20, *40*, *75*, 401,
      448, 453
    CURSOR_MODE *40*, 77,
      448, 450–51, 452, 475
    CURSOR_POSN *40*, 448,
      451–52, 454, 464, 483
    INFO *437*, 449, 450, 465,
      479–80
    INFO_3 *437*, 449, 479
    POINTS 271, *277–78*, 286,
      324, *326*, *389*, 391, *394*, 404,
      449, 475–76
    ROWS 324, *326*, *394*, 448,
      475–76, 494
    SAVE_PTR 438–40,
      443–46

Video Formatter (MCGA) 58–59
Video modes
  about 28–29
  alphanumeric
    about 46–47
    attributes 49–63
    data representation 47–49
  BIOS interface 7–9, 36–38
  determining
    BIOS 9, 465
    Hercules 404–6
  establishing 7–8, 38–40,
    323–27, 448–50
  graphics
    about 86
    attributes 100–110
    data representation 87–92
  hardware control 30–40
Video monitor. *See* Video display
Video page. *See* Video buffer,
    paging

W

Window
  alphanumeric mode 337–41
  Microsoft Windows 429–31
Write mode. *See* Pixel, value,
    setting

X

xMode register 34, 316, 321

Richard Wilton

Richard Wilton has been programming computers since the late 1960s. He has written systems software and graphics applications in FORTRAN, Pascal, C, Forth, and assembly language. His articles and reviews have appeared in several computer publications, including *BYTE*, *Computer Language*, and *The Seybold Outlook on Professional Computing*. Wilton lives in Los Angeles, California.

The manuscript for this book was prepared and submitted to Microsoft Press in electronic form. Text files were processed and formatted using Microsoft Word.

Cover design by Becker Design Associates
Interior text design by Darcie S. Furlan
Illustrations created on Adobe Illustrator™ by Nick Gregoric and Rick Bourgoin
Chapter opener artwork by Chuck Solway
Principal typographer: Ruth Pettis
Principal production artist: Peggy Herman

Text and display composition by Microsoft Press in Times Roman, using the Magna composition system and the Linotronic 300 laser imagesetter.